HOOVER INSTITUTION BIBLIOGRAPHICAL SERIES: XLI

INTERNATIONAL ORGANIZATION

An Interdisciplinary Bibliography

Compiled by
Michael Haas

HOOVER INSTITUTION PRESS
STANFORD UNIVERSITY · STANFORD, CALIFORNIA

The Hoover Institution on War, Revolution and Peace, founded at Stanford University in 1919 by the late President Herbert Hoover, is a center for advanced study and research on public and international affairs in the twentieth century. The views expressed in its publications are entirely those of the authors and do not necessarily reflect the views of the Hoover Institution.

© 1971 by Michael Haas
All rights reserved
Library of Congress Catalog Card Number: 68-28099
Standard Book Number: 8179-2411-6
Printed in West Germany
by Fremdsprachendruckerei Dr. Peter Belej, München 13

To the memory of
William Henry Vatcher, Jr.

CONTENTS

Foreword by J. David Singer xvii
Acknowledgments xxi
Introduction xxiii

PART A. INTERNATIONAL ORGANIZATIONS

1. LIBRARIES 3

2. PERIODICALS 4

3. BIBLIOGRAPHIES 10
   3.1 General Scope 10
   3.2 League of Nations System 15
   3.3 United Nations System 16
   3.4 Regional International Organizations 18
      3.4.1 General Scope 18
      3.4.2 Africa 18
      3.4.3 Asia and the Pacific 18
      3.4.4 Western Hemisphere 19
      3.4.5 Western Europe and the North Atlantic 20

4. TEXTBOOK TREATMENTS 21
   4.1 General Works 21
   4.2 League of Nations System 30
   4.3 United Nations System 33
   4.4 Regional International Organizations 37

5. DOCUMENTARY SOURCES 37
   5.1 General Sources 37
   5.2 League of Nations System 38
   5.3 United Nations System 41
   5.4 Regional International Organizations 45

6. BEHAVIORALIST APPROACHES 46
   6.1 Theoretical Approaches 46
      6.1.1 Integration Theory 46
      6.1.2 System Theory 46

   6.2 Empirical Research 60
      6.2.1 Roll Call Analysis and Bloc Voting 60
      6.2.2 Statistical and Systematic Case Studies 62
      6.2.3 Survey Research and Observational Techniques . . . 64

PART B. EARLY INTERNATIONAL ORGANIZATIONS

1. EARLY INTERNATIONAL STRUCTURES 69
   1.1 Classical Civilizations: Persia, Greece, Rome, etc. 69
   1.2 Ancient China 74
   1.3 Catholic Church and the Middle Ages 74
   1.4 Commercial Leagues: The Hansa and Other Efforts . . . 76

2. PHILOSOPHICAL PROPOSALS FOR INTERNATIONAL ORGANIZATION 78
   2.1 General Discussions 78
   2.2 Particular Thinkers 82
      2.2.1 Alberoni (1664—1752) 82
      2.2.2 Aquinas (1225—1274) 82
      2.2.3 Aristotle (384—322 B. C.) 82
      2.2.4 Augustine (354—430) 82
      2.2.5 Bellers (1654—1725) 83
      2.2.6 Bentham (1748—1832) 83
      2.2.7 Crucé (1590—1648) 83
      2.2.8 Dante (1265—1321) 83
      2.2.9 Dubois (1250—1312) 84
      2.2.10 Gargaz (fl. 1780) 84
      2.2.11 Grotius (1583—1645) 84
      2.2.12 K'ang Yu-wei (1858—1927) 85
      2.2.13 Kant (1724—1804) 85
      2.2.14 Locke (1623—1704) 86
      2.2.15 Penn (1644—1718) 87
      2.2.16 Podebrad (1440—1471) 87
      2.2.17 Richelieu (1585—1642) 87
      2.2.18 Rousseau (1712—1778) 88
      2.2.19 Saint-Pierre (1658—1743) 88
      2.2.20 Sully (1559—1641) 89

3. NINETEENTH CENTURY INTERNATIONAL ORGANIZATIONS 90
   3.1 Congress of Vienna (1814—1815) 90
   3.2 Holy Alliance 92
   3.3 The "European System" 93

4. PEACE MOVEMENT 100
   4.1 Proposals for International Organization 100
   4.2 Organization of the Peace Movement 105

5. INTERNATIONAL UNIONS 109
   5.1 Private Unions 109
   5.2 Public Unions 110

6. HAGUE SYSTEM 113
   6.1 History of International Arbitration 113
   6.2 Hague Conferences (1899 and 1907) 115
   6.3 Aftermath 119

PART C. LEAGUE OF NATIONS SYSTEM

1. DOCUMENTS AND BIBLIOGRAPHY 127

2. WORLD WAR I EFFORTS 127
   2.1 Proposals for Postwar International Organization . . . 127
   2.2 Organized Cooperation Among the Allies 137

3. VERSAILLES SYSTEM 140
   3.1 Versailles Conference (1919) 140
   3.2 Conference of Ambassadors (Paris) 147
   3.3 Reparations 147

4. GENERAL COMMENTARIS AND EVALUATIONS . . . 150

5. COVENANT 168
   5.1 Meaning and Interpretations 168
   5.2 Revisions and Proposed Amendments 173

6. CONSTITUTIONAL QUESTIONS 176
   6.1 General Problems 176
   6.2 Domestic Jurisdiction 177
   6.3 Financing 179
   6.4 Membership 180
   6.5 Voting 182

7. MAIN ORGANS 182
   7.1 Assembly 182
   7.2 Council 185
   7.3 Secretariat 187
       7.3.1 General Observations 187
       7.3.2 International Civil Service 188

8. ECONOMIC AND SOCIAL ACTIVITIES 191
   8.1 General Discussions 191
   8.2 Economic Functions 193
      8.2.1 General Observations 193
      8.2.2 European Reconstruction 195
      8.2.3 Problems Connected with the World Depression of the 1930s 197
      8.2.4 Raw Materials and Commodities 199
      8.2.5 Bank for International Settlements (Basel) . . . 200
   8.3 Communications and Transportation 200
      8.3.1 General Observations 200
      8.3.2 Communications 201
      8.3.3 Transportation 202
   8.4 International Labor Organization (Geneva) 204
      8.4.1 General Observations 204
      8.4.2 Role of the United States 213
   8.5 Social Questions 215
      8.5.1 General Observations 215
      8.5.2 Health and Nutrition 216
      8.5.3 Narcotic Drugs 218
      8.5.4 Minorities 220
      8.5.5 Refugees 224
      8.5.6 Slavery and Traffic in Women and Children . . . 226
   8.6 International Intellectual Cooperation 227

9. MANDATES SYSTEM AND DEPENDENT PEOPLES . . . 230
   9.1 Structure of the Mandates System 230
   9.2 Particular Mandates 237
      9.2.1 African Mandates 237
      9.2.2 Middle Eastern Mandates 238
         9.2.2.1 General Observations 238
         9.2.2.2 Iraq, Lebanon, Syria 238
         9.2.2.3 Palestine 239
      9.2.3 Pacific Mandates 244
   9.3 Role of the United States 246
   9.4 Administration of "Special Areas" 247
      9.4.1 General Observations 247
      9.4.2 Danzig 248
      9.4.3 Saar 249
      9.4.4 Shanghai Court 250
      9.4.5 Silesia 251
      9.4.6 Suez Canal 251
      9.4.7 Tangier 252

10. PERMANENT COURT OF INTERNATIONAL JUSTICE (Hague) 253
   10.1 General Observations 253
   10.2 Jurisdictional Problems 264
   10.3 Role of the United States 266
   10.4 Permanent Court of Arbitration (Hague) 268

11. POLITICAL ACTIVITIES: GENERAL ISSUES 269
   11.1 Collective Security and Sanctions 269
   11.2 Disarmament 276
   11.3 Legal Attempts to "Outlaw" War 286
      11.3.1 General Observations 286
      11.3.2 Geneva Protocol (1924) 288
      11.3.3 Locarno Agreements (1925) 290
      11.3.4 Kellog-Briand Pact (1928) 292
   11.4 Peaceful Change and Pacific Settlement 295

12. POLITICAL ACTIVITIES: PARTICULAR DISPUTES . . . 299
   12.1 Sino-Japanese Conflict (1931—1945) 299
   12.2 Chaco Conflict (1932—1935) 304
   12.3 Italo-Ethiopian Conflict (1934—1936) 305
   12.4 Other Questions 309

13. NATIONAL ACTORS AND THE LEAGUE SYSTEM . . . 310
   13.1 General Discussions 310
   13.2 Particular Countries 312
      13.2.1 British Commonwealth Countries . . . 312
      13.2.2 European Countries 314
      13.2.3 Far Eastern Coutries 316
      13.2.4 Latin American Countries 317
      13.2.5 Liberia 318
      13.2.6 Soviet Union 319
      13.2.7 United States 319

14. FINAL YEARS OF THE LEAGUE OF NATIONS 327

PART D. UNITED NATIONS SYSTEM

1. BIBLIOGRAPHIES AND DOCUMENTS 331

2. WORLD WAR II EFFORTS 331
   2.1 Pleas for Postwar International Organization . . . 331
   2.2 Negotiations Leading Up to the United Nations . . 343
   2.3 Wartime Collaborative Machinery 347
   2.4 San Francisco Conference (1945) 348
   2.5 Institutions to Execute the Peace 350

3. GENERAL COMMENTARIES AND EVALUATIONS . . . 355

4. CHARTER 376
   4.1 Meaning and Interpretations 376
   4.2 Revisions: Proposed, Adopted and by Evolution . . 382

5. CONSTITUTIONAL QUESTIONS 389
   5.1 General Discussions 389
   5.2 Domestic Jurisdiction 394
   5.3 Financing 399
   5.4 Membership 403

5.4.1 General Observations		403
5.4.2 Representation of China		405
5.5 Regionalism		407
5.6 Voting		407
5.6.1 General Observations		407
5.6.2 General Assembly Voting Procedure		409
5.6.3 Veto in the Security Council		409

6. MAIN ORGANS 411
   6.1 General Assembly 411
   6.2 Security Council 418
   6.3 Secretariat 421
      6.3.1 General Observations 421
      6.3.2 Secretary General 424
      6.3.3 International Civil Service 428

7. ECONOMIC AND SOCIAL ACTIVITIES 435
   7.1 General Discussions 435
   7.2 Economic Efforts 440
      7.2.1 General Observations 440
      7.2.2 Communications and Transportation 442
         7.2.2.1 General Observations 442
         7.2.2.2 Communications 442
         7.2.2.3 Transportation 443
      7.2.3 Economic Development and Technical Assistance . . 445
      7.2.4 Monetary and Lending Agencies 453
         7.2.4.1 General Observations 453
         7.2.4.2 International Bank for Reconstruction and Development (Washington) 456
         7.2.4.3 International Monetary Fund 457
            (Washington) 457
         7.2.4.4 Other Agencies 459
      7.2.5 Regional Economic Commissions 460
         7.2.5.1 General Observations 460
         7.2.5.2 Economic Commission for Africa (Addis Ababa) 460
         7.2.5.3 Economic Commission for Asia and the Far East (Bangkok) 461
         7.2.5.4 Economic Commission for Europe (Brussels) . 462
         7.2.5.5 Economic Commission for Latin America (Santiago) 463
      7.2.6 Trade Organizations 463
         7.2.6.1 General Observations 463
         7.2.6.2 Proposed International Trade Organization . . 464
         7.2.6.3 General Agreement on Tariffs and Trade (Geneva) 466
   7.3 Social Questions 468
      7.3.1 General Discussions 468
      7.3.2 Health Organizations 469
         7.3.2.1 General Observations 469
         7.3.2.2 Commission on Narcotic Drugs (Geneva) . 469
         7.3.2.3 Food and Agriculture Organization (Rome) . 470
         7.3.2.4 World Health Organization (Geneva) . . 472
         7.3.2.5 United Nations Children's Fund 474

7.3.3	Human Rights and Minorities	475
7.3.4	Intellectual Cooperation	481
	7.3.4.1 United Nations Educational, Scientific and Cultural Organization (Paris)	481
	7.3.4.2 Scientific Cooperation	488
	7.3.4.3 Information Policies	492
7.3.5	International Labor Organization (Geneva)	493
7.3.6	Refugees and Migration	497
	7.3.6.1 General Observations	497
	7.3.6.2 Palestine Refugee Problem	500
7.3.7	Relief and Rehabilitation	501

8. TRUSTEESHIP SYSTEM AND NON-SELF-COVERNING TERRITORIES 505
   8.1 General Discussions 505
   8.2 Particular Territories 513
       8.2.1 African Trusteeships 513
       8.2.2 Southwest African "Mandate" 515
       8.2.3 Pacific Trusteeships 517
   8.3 Administration of Special Areas 518

9. INTERNATIONAL COURT OF JUSTICE (Hague) . . . 519
   9.1 General Discussions 519
   9.2 Jurisdictional Problems 526
   9.3 Role of the Underdeveloped Countries 527
   9.4 Role of the United States 528
   9.5 Permanent Court of Arbitration (Hague) 528

10. POLITICAL ACTIVITIES: GENERAL ISSUES 529
    10.1 Collective Security and Sanctions 529
    10.2 Colonialism 536
    10.3 Disarmament 536
    10.4 Pacific Settlement 546
    10.5 Peacekeeping with International Forces 550
    10.6 Preventive Diplomacy 557

11. POLITICAL ACTIVITIES: PARTICULAR DISPUTES . . . 558
    11.1 Indo-Pakistan Conflict (1946—) 558
    11.2 Arab-Israeli Conflict (1947—) 561
    11.3 Korean War (1950—1953) 567
    11.4 Hungarian Revolution (1956) 571
    11.5 Suez Conflict (1956) 572
    11.6 Congo Conflict (1960—1964) 573
    11.7 Minor Disputes Involving India 576
    11.8 Disputes Involving Indonesia 577

11.9	Minor Disputes in the Levant and North Africa	578
11.10	Disputes in Southern Africa	579
11.11	Other Disputes	580

12. NATIONAL ACTORS AND THE UNITED NATIONS SYSTEM — 581
12.1	General Discussions	581
12.2	Particular Countries	585
	12.2.1 African Countries	585
	12.2.2 Asian Countries	587
	12.2.3 English-Speaking Commonwealth Countries	591
	12.2.4 Latin American Countries	594
	12.2.5 Middle Eastern Countries	596
	12.2.6 Soviet Bloc Countries	598
	12.2.7 United States	603
	12.2.8 Western European Countries	612

PART E. REGIONAL INTERNATIONAL ORGANIZATION

1. GENERAL BIBLIOGRAPHIES AND DOCUMENTS — 617

2. GENERAL DISCUSSIONS — 617

3. REGIONALISM IN RELATION TO THE UNITED NATIONS SYSTEM — 627

4. AFRICA — 630
4.1	Bibliographies	630
4.2	General Discussions on Pan Africanism	630
4.3	Attempts at Federation	633
	4.3.1 Central Africa	633
	4.3.2 East Africa	634
	4.3.3 West Africa	635
4.4	Attempts to Form Inter-African Organization Before the Organization of African Unity	636
4.5	Organization of African Unity (Addis Ababa)	637
4.6	Arab Africa	638

5. ASIA AND THE PACIFIC — 639
5.1	Bibliographies	639
5.2	General Discussions	639
5.3	Far Eastern Commission (Tokyo)	641
5.4	Anzus	642
5.5	Southeast Asian Treaty Organization (Bangkok)	642
5.6	South Pacific Commission (Noumea)	645

6. MIDDLE EAST AND THE ISLAMIC WORLD 647
   6.1 General Discussions 647
   6.2 League of Arab States (Cairo) 654
   6.3 Cento (Ankara) 657
   6.4 Maghreb 658

7. WESTERN HEMISPHERE 659
   7.1 Bibliographies 659
   7.2 General Discussions 659
   7.3 Pan American Conferences and the Pan American Union (Washington) Before 1948 665
   7.4 Organization of American States (Washington) . . . 675
      7.4.1 General Observations 675
      7.4.2 Relation to Other International Organizations . . 682
      7.4.3 Role of Canada 683
   7.5 Caribbean Regionalism 684
      7.5.1 Caribbean Commission (Hato Rey) 684
      7.5.2 West Indies Federation Efforts 686
   7.6 Central American Regionalism 687
   7.7 South American Regionalism and the Latin American Free Trade Association (Montevideo) 689
   7.8 Inter-American Development Bank (Washington) . . 691

8. WESTERN EUROPE AND THE NORTH ATLANTIC . . 692
   8.1 Bibliography 692
   8.2 General Discussions 692
      8.2.1 Europe Versus Atlantica as Integrating Communities . 692
      8.2.2 Relation to Other International Organizations . . 705
   8.3 Economic Organizations 708
      8.3.1 General Observations 708
      8.3.2 Benelux and Italo-French Customs Unions . . 712
      8.3.3 European Payments Union 713
      8.3.4 Marshall Plan, OEEC, and OECD (Paris) . . . 714
      8.3.5 The Communities 717
          8.3.5.1 General Observations 717
          8.3.5.2 European Coal and Steel Community (Luxembourg) 722
          8.3.5.3 European Economic Community (Luxembourg) 727
          8.3.5.4 European Free Trade Association (Geneva) . 731
          8.3.5.5 European Atomic Energy Community (Brussels) 732
          8.3.5.6 Courts of the Communities (Luxembourg) . 734
      8.3.6 European Investment Bank (Brussels) 735
      8.3.7 Bank for International Settlements (Basel) . . . 735

   8.4 Political Organizations 735
      8.4.1 European Union: Pro and Con 735
      8.4.2 European Assemblies 748
      8.4.3 Council of Europe (Strasbourg) 749
      8.4.4 Convention on Human Rights 752

8.5   Military Organizations 754
        8.5.1 Abortive European Defense Community 754
        8.5.2 North Atlantic Treaty Organization (Brussels) . . 755
  8.6   Intellectual and Cultural Organizations 773
  8.7   Scandinavian Regionalism 774
  8.8   National Actors and the Regional System of Western Europe
        and the North Atlantic 775
        8.8.1 African Countries 775
        8.8.2 British Commonwealth Countries 776
        8.8.3 France 784
        8.8.4 Germany 786
        8.8.5 Mediterranean Countries 787
        8.8.6 Scandinavian Countries 788
        8.8.7 Soviet Bloc Countries 789
        8.8.8 United States 790
        8.8.9 Other Countries 793

9. EASTERN AND CENTRAL EUROPE 796
  9.1   General Observations 796
  9.2   Balkan Regionalism 798
  9.3   Danubian Regionalism 801
  9.4   Communist Eastern European Regionalism 803
        9.4.1 General Observations 803
        9.4.2 COMECON (Moscow) 803
        9.4.3 Warsaw Pact (Moscow) 805

10. TRANSCONTINENTAL NONUNIVERSAL INTERNATIONAL
    ORGANIZATIONS 806
  10.1 British Commonwealth of Nations 806
        10.1.1 British Imperial Organization 806
        10.1.2 Development of the Commonwealth Idea . . . 808
        10.1.3 Contemporary Commonwealth 812
        10.1.4 Relation to Other International Organizations . . 820
        10.1.5 Colombo Plan (Colombo) 821
        10.1.6 National Actors and the Commonwealth System . 822
                10.1.6.1 General Observations on Members . . . 822
                10.1.6.2 African Countries 823
                10.1.6.3 Asian Countries 823
                10.1.6.4 Australia and New Zealand 824
                10.1.6.5 Canada 824
                10.1.6.6 European Countries 825
                10.1.6.7 South Africa 826
                10.1.6.8 United States 827
  10.2 Communist World and Socialist Internationals . . . 828
  10.3 French Community 831
  10.4 The "Third World" 832
        10.4.1 General Discussions 832
        10.4.2 African-Asian Conferences 833

PART F. NONGOVERNMENTAL ORGANIZATIONS

1. GENERAL DISCUSSIONS 837
2. NINETEENTH CENTURY EFFORTS 840
3. BUSINESS AND COMMERCIAL ORGANIZATIONS . . . 840
4. INTELLECTUAL ORGANIZATIONS 841
5. RELIGIOUS ORGANIZATIONS 842
6. RED CROSS 843
7. TRADE UNIONS 845
8. OTHER NONGOVERNMENTAL ORGANIZATIONS . . . 847

PART G. PROPOSALS FOR WORLD GOVERNMENT

1. GENERAL DISCUSSIONS 851
2. WORLD FEDERALISM 859
3. FUNCTIONALISM 869
4. CRITICAL DISCUSSIONS 870

Author Index 873
Subject Index 933

FOREWORD
by J. David Singer

Whenever a given social space is populated by a number of relatively autonomous human groups, there is bound to be some interdependence and interaction among those groups. That interdependence is likely, in turn, to be a mix of the cooperative and the competitive. While the separate groups are likely to be fairly competitive with one another in their pursuit of the more scarce material and and psychic "goods" (including security), they will also find themselves in a range of symbiotic relationships. Often such relationships will be part of an effort to coalesce against other groups, but occasionally all will find it desirable to combine in a struggle against nature.

Managing this mix of cooperative and competitive relationships usually turns out to be a difficult job, even when there is an obvious superordinate goal or a relatively dominant group in the system. Generally speaking, the efficacy with which inter-group relationships are managed will be a function of three conditions. One is the utilitarian factor — the extent to which there is a shared understanding that cooperative behavior is mutually (and more or less equally) advantageous. The efficacy of the utilitarian element usually depends partly, in turn, on the strength of the second condition: some normative consensus as to which ends are most desirable and which means toward them are most legitimate. The third essential condition — by no means independent of the first two — is the availability of accepted coercive institutions. When the "invisible hand" of the several group interests is inadequate (and it is difficult to think of a setting in which it is *not*), the system may fall back on a combination of shared norms and coercive institutions in order to effect a modicum of harmony.

These three elements, it would seem, are as essential to the governance of a group of cottage-dwelling families or trade unions as they are to a group of Mediterranean city-states or modern nation-states. It is unfortunate that many scholars, as well as practitioners and polemicists, fail to comprehend this complex and fragile basis of inter-group coordination. Thus the observer (not to mention the inhabitant) of any given social system is constantly exposed to all sorts of nostrums for reform, particularly for reform as it affects the contemporary global system. From one side, he is told to put morality aside and pursue merely national interests, whatever they may be. From another, the message calls for a spiritual rebirth: a shared belief in this or that metaphysical design will assure both inter-personal and inter-national harmony. Still others, often (paradoxically enough) the more chauvinistic among us, urge one form or another of a world police force. No student of world politics will have any difficulty recognizing these diverse schools of thought and citing the more ardent adherents of each.

One difficulty in the present day is that the research, as well as the polemics, of international organization is often characterized by this same monomania. For some, the dominant (or only) function of a given international organization is to further the interests of those governments which are able to control it. For others, an organization whose major focus is not on the building of a one-world (or one-region, or one-culture) outlook is not worth supporting. And for the "realist," unless such an organization can effectively coerce its component nations it is dismissed as ineffectual and irrelevant.

If this is indeed where we now find ourselves, it is essential that we better understand the inter-governmental and non-governmental organizations and their role in world politics. To do so, it is not enough to examine the United Nations or its immediate predecessor of the interwar period, and their related agencies. What is needed is more *general* knowledge about these organizations, their genesis and decline or demise, their structure, membership, and missions, and their impact on world politics. Such knowledge should, I submit, be based on an empirical domain which is large in both time and space; it should embrace not only the more than 200 inter-governmental and 1,700 non-governmental organizations in existence today, but the hundreds which have come and gone over the centuries which lie behind us.

A body of knowledge embracing so broad a spatial and temporal domain will, of course, elude us until we apply rigorous methods of description and analysis to the great variety and number of organizations and settings which comprise it. In recent years, as the scientific mode gradually find its way into the study of international organization, *part* of the problem shows signs of being ameliorated. But scientific method applied to a narrow empirical domain will not suffice; it must be brought to bear on the entire range of organizations. This, then, is one of the major values of the volume at hand. Picking up the enterprise so conscientiously begun by Professor Vatcher but abruptly terminated by his untimely death, Professor Haas has gone on to give us an extremely valuable instrument. In this bibliography, we have the most comprehensive and well-organized listing of scholarly work to yet become available in the international organization field.

Others might have used a different classification scheme or employed somewhat different criteria of inclusion and exclusion, but it would be gratuitous to criticize in the face of so massive an undertaking. The fact is that Haas saw the need for such a bibliography, undertook it with vigor, and brought it to fruition at great expense of time and energy. It is not only the best such volume available in English (or, to my knowledge, any other language); it is the only one of such scope and ambition.

Among its other virtues, this bibliography reflects its compiler's sensitivity to the multiple functions of international organizations. In assembling and arranging the several thousand items cited here, Haas has been careful neither to ignore nor to overstress the interest-maximization, norm-setting, or adjudicative-enforcement roles of international organizations. At the same time he has attended to a variety of other desiderata. Whereas some treatments of the subject suffer from confinement to a single disciplinary outlook, our compiler has taken care to embrace works representing law, religion, psychology, sociology, and anthropology, as well as history and political science. And whereas all too many of us still think of the national state as the sole and natural form of human association and hence concentrate only on inter-governmental organizations, Haas provides us with a rather full listing of works dealing with non-governmental organizations. As scholarly and political interest in multi-national corporations and extra-national professional groups (for example) grows in the next few years, this bibliography will provide an excellent point of departure.

Finally, and to reiterate my earlier point, this compilation has an historical depth which cannot help but improve the quality of scholarship in the field. Until we take a developmental view, we tend to think of the League and the United Nations as the total theory and substance of international organization. By carrying us back to earlier epochs, Haas invites us to take the longitudinal or developmental view, and to search for trends and recurring themes which may well be hidden in history's welter of facts and maze of impressions. For all we know, the global system of the late twentieth century may be in more ways akin to that of ancient Persia or medieval Europe than to the post-Napoleonic or pre-Hitlerian epochs, to name just a few of the contending models. If so, there may be some valuable lessons in the many historical works cited in this volume. And if we can view the past in the light of the most modern social science research methods, so much the better.

In sum, Haas brings us in this volume a major incentive to revitalize the study of international organization. I suspect that such a revitalization may already be under way, and that this bibliography can serve as an important amplifier of a nascent trend. To the extent that knowledge leads to intelligent policies, the compilation at hand may not only be a boon to scholarship; it also may even eventually make a difference in the probability of human survival. The global society needs—desperately, in my view—to be more adaptively organized, and any research concerned with such organization cannot help but be aided by this massive effort. Thus the community of scholars owes a great debt to the compiler and his predecessor. If those of us engaged in research on the problems of global organization use this study in a creative and diligent fashion, we may yet begin to develop the knowledge we so lack today in our search for the way from near-anarchy to a just and peaceful world order.

Ann Arbor
May 1970

ACKNOWLEDGMENTS

Most of the extant studies and bibliographies on the subject of international organization focus on the United Nations and on particular issues or crises in which the UN has been involved. This bibliography aims to break free from a parochial and topical orientation in order to provide historical depth along with contributions from all the social sciences. The major use of the bibliography, accordingly, will be to facilitate cross-historical comparative analysis and an accumulation of evidence in the tradition of historical sociology.

The present bibliography is an expansion in scope and magnitude of a card file that the late Professor William Henry Vatcher, Jr., was preparing for publication at the time of his death in 1965. Starting with the Vatcher collection, which was kindly provided by the executrix of his estate, a more elaborate system of classification was designed, and a systematic search for many new categories began. The resulting compilation contains four or five times the original number of references, for it was felt that previous bibliographies on the subject would be significantly augmented only by a much more comprehensive effort, one covering all historical periods and theoretical approaches.

The bibliography was compiled at the Hoover Institution on War, Revolution and Peace at Stanford University, one of the few research institutes in the world housing all of the official publications of the League of Nations. The detailed and ingenious system of subject, author, and title entries in the Hoover Library card catalog proved invaluable in assembling the collection. Special thanks are extended to the staff of the Hoover Institution for their unusually solicitous assistance during the compiling of references. The patient and helpful efforts of Mrs. Arline Paul deserve particular mention.

Mr. Daniel Burke, who is now a graduate student in political science at the University of Oregon, helped to shape the bibliography by persistently raising questions concerning the criteria of inclusion during the assembling of references. The burden of indexing the entries was ably, smoothly, and indefatigably assumed by Mrs. Virginia Winters. The bibliography cards were typed by Miss Marcia Madsen and Miss Jeanette Tomono, and the entire collection was prepared for publication under the direction of the Hoover Institution Publications Department.

Honolulu MICHAEL HAAS
March 1968

INTRODUCTION

Ordinarily it is the responsibility of a bibliographer to acquaint the student of a particular field with sources of written information that are reliable, balanced, useful, and at the same time to some extent exhaustive. Such a task inevitably leads the compiler to a sense of incompleteness, of not knowing exactly when or where to conclude the list, and perhaps even to a fear of collegial criticism for the omission of some significant work or subject. So it should be made clear that although this work includes nearly 8,000 references classified into about 300 divisions, it cannot be claimed to be comprehensive or complete because of of the broad scope of writings on the subject. Criteria to delimit the coverage had to be applied, and it is the purpose of this introduction to specify the rules of selection.

The major structure of the field of international organization is set forth in the table of contents, with the more specific strata and substrata outlined in the detailed listing of institutions, topics, and events contained within each category of the six main parts of the book. After an introductory section (part A), the major divisions (part B-E) start with the earlier periods of international history and proceed up to modern times. Subheadings are arranged either functionally, alphabetically, or chronologically. Sub-subheadings provide more refined inventories of the contents. The final two parts (F-G) deal with matters of more topical interest. Throughout, selections have been made in an attempt to locate writings pertaining to nearly every effort to institutionalize interactions between actors in the international arena.

Some of the more specific criteria for inclusion and exclusion within each heading are arbitrary and practical in nature. Because the bibliography is *about* international organization, most of the sources listed are secondary sources, and only some of the most important documentary series and other primary sources *from* international institutions are listed. A reference is selected only if international organization constitutes a main, rather than an incidental, focus. The coverage of books is wider than that of articles, which have been extracted principally from some fifty scholarly periodicals. Unpublished dissertations, polemical tracts, popularizations in pamphlet form, working papers, and newspaper and magazine articles are not included, though guides to some of these sources are noted in part A. The list of references has been restricted largely to English-language publications. Works published after December 1965 are not included.

Two indexes are appended. The *author index* gives reference numbers to persons named in a variety of capacities — as subject, author, editor, translator, or commentator; there is also a listing of agencies that serve as authors of individual publications. The *subject index* subdivides the scheme of categories used as the table of contents and brings together similar items appearing at different locations. Individual chapters in books are considered to be the equivalent of articles, so a given book might be cited in many locations, in accordance with each category under which its chapters are filed.

Even though the bibliography is self-consciously interdisciplinary, the reader will notice that history and political science writings are somewhat overrepresented in relation to those of the other social sciences. Such an imbalance is inescapable, given the present imbalance in sources of literature on the subject. It is hoped that this bibligraphy will so present the subject of international organization as to stimulate the interest of readers in other disciplines; the few cross-historical analyses and quantitative studies of international organization noted in the section on Behavioral Approaches in part A doubtless will multiply in the years ahead. The present volume establishes standarized sets of categories for research and provides a broad perspective on functional equivalents of international organization from the era of the Persian and Roman empires to the present. The volume is designed, in content and organization, to encourage future thought and inquiry into the problems of channeling contacts between nations and peoples.

Part A.
INTERNATIONAL ORGANIZATIONS

Part A. — General References

Inasmuch as the bibliography is devoted mainly to secondary source material, it seems appropriate to preface the compilation with a guide to primary documents and a listing of the most general types of secondary writings with which the researcher or interested layman will want to become acquainted.

1. LIBRARIES

United Nations depository libraries are likely to be the most satisfactory locations for research on international organization, and among these libraries three are devoted almost entirely to the subject.

1 **Library of the Palace of Peace (Hague).** Contains the most complete holdings on international legal organization, with an extensive set of secondary materials pertaining to the League of Nations and United Nations. Current holdings are recorded regularly in the *Dutch Journal of International Law* (in Dutch).

2 **United Nations, Library (Geneva).** The most complete set of primary and secondary holdings on international organization. A re-cataloging of League of Nations documents is now under way.

3 **United Nations, Library (New York).** Primarily a set of complete documents for the United Nations period, but has received recently the Woodrow Wilson Collection of secondary sources from Princeton University.

4 United Nations, Library (New York). **Consolidated Lists of Depository Libraries and Sales Agents and Offices of the United Nations and the Specialized Agencies.** 5th ed. New York, 1958. 44 p.

Part A. — General References

2. PERIODICALS

Each of the following journals is a major source in which one will encounter scholarly articles on international organization in nearly every issue. (Many of the issuing agencies and the frequencies with which the periodicals are published change during the life of a journal, so with a view to the reader's future consultation of these sources only current information is provided in each reference.)

5 **Academy of Political Science Proceedings.** New York, Academy of Political Science, Semiannually, 1910–.

6 **American Behavioral Scientist** (originally **Prod**).Beverly Hills, Sage Publications, Monthly except July and August, 1957–.

7 **American Historical Review.** New York, American Historical Association, Quarterly, 1895–.

8 **American Journal of International Law.** Washington, American Society of International Law, Quarterly, 1907–.

9 **American Political Science Review.** Washington, American Political Science Association, Quarterly, 1906–.

10 **American Society of International Law Proceedings.** Washington, American Society of International Law, Annually, 1907–.

11 **Annals of the American Academy of Political and Social Science.** Philadelphia, American Academy of Political and Social Science, Bimonthly, 1890–.

Part A. — General References

12 **Atlantic Community Quarterly.** Baltimore, Atlantic Council of the United States, Quarterly, 1963—.

13 **British Yearbook of International Law.** London, Royal Institute of International Affairs, Annually, 1920—.

14 **Canadian Yearbook of International Law.** Vancouver, International Law Association, Canadian Branch, Annually, 1963—.

15 **Current History.** Philadelphia, Events Publishing Company, Monthly, 1914—.

16 **Cooperation and Conflict. Nordic Studies in International Conflict.** Stockholm, Nordic Committee for the Study of International Politics, Semiannually, 1965—.

17 **Disarmament and Arms Control: An International Journal.** Oxford, Pergamon, Semiannually, 1963—.

18 **Foreign Affairs: An American Quarterly Review.** New York, Council on Foreign Relations, Quarterly, 1922—.

19 **Foreign Policy Reports** (originally **Foreign Policy Association Information Service**). New York, Council on Foreign Relations, Fortnightly, 1925—51.

20 **Geneva Studies** (originally **Geneva Special Studies**). Geneva, Geneva Research Center, Monthly, 1930—42.

21 **India Quarterly: A Journal of International Affairs.** New Delhi, Indian Council of International Affairs, Quarterly, 1945—.

22 **Indian Journal of International Law.** New Delhi, Indian Society of International Law, Quarterly, 1960—.

Part A. — General References

23 **Indian Year Book of International Affairs.** Madras, Indian Study Group of International Affairs, Annually, 1952—.

24 **Institute of World Affairs Proceedings** (originally **Institute of International Relations Proceedings**). Pasadena, Institute of World Affairs, Annually, 1926—.

25 **International Affairs** (originally **Journal of the Royal Institute of International Affairs**). London, Royal Institute of International Affairs, Quarterly, 1922—.

25a **International Associations.** Brussels, Union of International Associations, Monthly, 1949—.

26 **International and Comparative Law Quarterly.** London, British Institute of International and Comparative Law, Quarterly, 1952—.

27 **International Journal.** Toronto, Canadian Institute of International Affairs, Quarterly, 1946—.

28 **International Law Quarterly** (later merged with the **Journal of Comparative Legislation** to become the **International and Comparative Law Quarterly**). London, Stevens, Quarterly, 1945—49.

29 **International Conciliation.** New York, Carnegie Endowment for International Peace, Quarterly with a special issue entitled "Issues Before the General Assembly," 1907—.

30 **International Relations.** London, David Davies Institute of International Studies, Semiannually, 1954—.

31 **International Social Science Journal** (originally **International Social Science Bulletin**). Paris, UNESCO, Quarterly, 1949—.

Part A. — *General References*

32 **International Studies: Quarterly Journal of the Indian School of International Studies.** Bombay, Asia Publishing House, Quarterly, 1959—.

33 **International Studies Quarterly** (originally **San Francisco International Studies** and **Background**). Detroit, International Studies Association, Quarterly, 1957—.

34 **Japanese Annual of International Law.** Tokyo, Japan Branch of the International Law Association, Annually, 1957—.

35 **Journal of Common Market Studies.** Oxford, Blackwell, Quarterly, 1962—.

36 **Journal of Commonwealth Political Studies.** London, Institute of Commonwealth Studies, Triennially, 1961—.

37 **Journal of Conflict Resolution: A Quarterly for Research Related to War and Peace.** Ann Arbor, Center for Research on Conflict Resolution, University of Michigan, Quarterly, 1957—.

38 **Journal of International Affairs** (originally **Columbia Journal of International Affairs**). New York, School of International Affairs, Columbia University, Semiannually, 1947—.

39 **Journal of Peace Research.** Oslo, Peace Research Institute, Quarterly, 1964—.

40 **Journal of Politics.** Gainesville, Southern Political Science Association, University of Florida, Quarterly, 1939—.

41 **Orbis: A Quarterly Journal of World Affairs.** Phillladelphia, Foreign Policy Research Institute, University of Pennsylvania, Quarterly, 1957—.

Part A. — General References

42 **Pakistan Horizon.** Karachi, Pakistan Institute of International Affairs, Quarterly, 1948–.

43 **Political Quarterly.** London, Stevens, Quarterly, 1930–.

44 **Political Science Quarterly.** New York, Academy of Political Science, Columbia University, Quarterly, 1886–.

45 **Problems of Peace.** Geneva, Institute of International Relations, Annually, 1926–37.

46 **Recueil des Cours.** Leyde, Académie de Droit International, Triennially, 1923–.

47 **Transactions** (originally **Problems of the War**). London, Grotius Society, Annually, 1915–58.

48 **Western Political Quarterly.** Salt Lake City, Institute of Government, University of Utah, Quarterly, 1948–.

49 **World Affairs: The Quarterly Journal of the London Institute of World Affairs** (originally **New Commonwealth Quarterly** later **London Quarterly of World Affairs**). London, New Commonwealth Institute, Quarterly, 1935–46; New Series, London, Stevens, Quarterly, 1947–51.

50 **World Affairs Quarterly** (originally **World Affairs Interpreter**). Los Angeles, University of Southern California, Quarterly, 1930–59.

51 **World Justice.** Louvain, Research Center for International Social Justice, Quarterly, 1959–.

Part A. — *General References*

52 **World Peace Foundation Pamphlets** (originally **A League of Nations**). Boston, World Peace Foundation, Bimonthly, 1917–30.

53 **World Politics: A Quarterly Journal of International Relations.** Princeton, Princeton University Press, Quarterly, 1948–.

54 **World Polity: A Yearbook of Studies in International Law and Organization.** Washington, Institute of World Polity, Georgetown University, 1957–.

55 **World Today: Chatham House Review.** London, Royal Institute of International Affairs, Monthly, 1945–.

56 **Yearbook of International Associations.** Brussels, Union of International Associations, Annually, 1948–.

57 **Year Book of World Affairs.** London, Institute of World Affairs, Annually, 1947–.

Part A. — *General References*

3. BIBLIOGRAPHIES

3.1 GENERAL SCOPE

58 **American Journal of International Law.** Washington, American Society of International Law, Quarterly, 1907–.

Each issue contains a bibliography on international law and international relations, public documents, and digests of judicial decisions relating to international law; in earlier years the section entitled "Editorial Comments" presents summaries of international legal activities. Yearly volumes include texts of treaties, conventions, reports and other legal documents.

59 **American Political Science Review.** Washington, American Political Science Association, Quarterly, 1906–.

Each issue up to 1966 contains a section on bibliography; international organization coverage was most extensive after 1951. A section on doctoral dissertations appeared in each September issue since 1911, and now is a regular feature of *P. S.: Newsletter of the American Political Science Association.*

60 Association of Research Libraries. **Doctoral Dissertations Accepted by American Universities.** New York, Wilson, Annually, 1934–55.

61 Aufricht, Hans. **General Bibliography on International Organization and Post-War Reconstruction.** New York, Commission to Study the Organization of Peace, 1942. 28 p.

62 Bureau International du Travail, Bibliothèque. **Bibliographie de l'Organisation Internationale du Travail de 1929 à 1953.** Geneva, 1954. 68 p.

63 — —. **Catalogue des publications en langue française du Bureau International du Travail, 1919–1950.** Geneva, 1951. 411 p.

Part A. — General References

64 Conover, Helen F. (comp.). **Non-Self-Governing Areas with Special Emphasis on Mandates and Trusteeships: A Selected List of References.** Washington, Library of Congress, 1947. 2 vols.

65 **The Cumulative Book Index: World List of Books In the English Language.** New York, Wilson, Monthly except August, 1898—.

66 **Current Thought on Peace and War: A Semiannual Digest of Literature and Research in Progress on the Problems of World Order and Conflict.** White Plains, N. Y. Semiannually, 1960—.

67 **Dissertation Abstracts: Abstracts of Dissertations and Monographs in Microfilm.** Ann Arbor, University Microfilms, Monthly, 1938—.

Up to 1951 entitled *Microfilm Abstracts.*

68 Dore, Robert. **Essai d'une bibliographie des congrès internationaux.** Paris, Champion, 1923. 56 p.

69 **Foreign Affairs.** New York, Council on Foreign Relations, Quarterly, 1923—.

Each issue contains an annotated bibliography of secondary sources and a list of pertinent documents. Many articles are official statements by public figures.

70 Grazia, Alfred de. **The Universal Reference System.** Volume I, *International Affairs,* New York, Metron, 1965. xxxii + 1205 p.

71 Harley, J. Eugene. **Selected Bibliography on the Limitation of Armament,** *Institute of World Affairs Proceedings,* I (1926), 31—33.

72 Harmon, Robert B. **Political Science: A Bibliographical Guide to the Literature.** New York, Scarecrow, 1965. viii + 388 p.

73 Hewitt, A. R. **Guide to Resources for Commonwealth Studies in London, Oxford, and Cambridge; with Bibliographical and other Information.** London, Athlone, 1957. xiii + 219 p.

Part A. — *General References*

74 Hicks, Frederick C. **International Organization: An Annotated Reading List,** *International Conciliation*, CXXIV (January 1919), 67–115.

75 — —. **Internationalism: A Selected List of Books, Pamphlets and Periodicals,** *International Conciliation*, LXIV (March 1913), 5–30.

76 **Historical Abstracts, 1775–1945: Bibliography of the World's Periodical Literature.** Santa Barbara, Clio, Quarterly, 1955–.

77 **Intercom.** New York, Council on Foreign Relations, Bimonthly, 1959–.

78 **International Conciliation.** New York, Carnegie Endowment for International Peace, Quarterly, 1907–.

Many issues reprint public documents, especially during the two world wars. Since 1947 an extra issue each year is devoted to a summary of issues before the United Nations General Assembly.

79 **International Organization.** Boston, World Peace Foundation, Quarterly, 1947–.

Each issue contains a summary of activities of international organizations and a selected bibliography of secondary sources. The section on documentary sources, which began in November 1950, superseded *Documents of International Organizations: A Selected Bibliography*, which had been published concurrently with *International Organization*.

80 **International Political Science Abstracts.** Oxford, Blackwell, Quarterly, 1951–.

81 International Political Science Association. **International Bibliography of Political Science.** Paris, UNESCO, Annually, 1954–.

82 Kuehl, Warren F. **Dissertations in History: An Index to Dissertations Completed in History Departments of United States and Canada Universities, 1873–1960.** Lexington, University of Kentucky Press, 1965. xi + 249 p.

Part A. — General References

83   Monaco, Riccardo and Casadio, Franco Alberto. **International Organization: A Review of Some Western European Literature,** *International Organization,* XIII (Autumn, 1959), 550—55.

84   Moon, Parker T. **Syllabus on International Relations.** New York, Macmillan, 1925. 276 p.

Part X.

85   Roberts, Henry L., assisted by Gunther, Jean, Kreslins, Janis A., Ryan, Marul, and Giller, Nancy L. **Foreign Affairs Bibliography: A Selected and Annotated List of Books on International Relations 1952—1962.** New York, Bowker, 1964. xxi + 750 p.

Earlier editions were published for the years 1919—32, 1932—42, 1942—52, compiled respectively by William L. Langer and Hamilton Fish Armstrong; Robert Gale Woolbert; Henry L. Roberts, assisted by Jean Gunther and Janis A. Kreslins.

86   Rogers, William C. **International Administration: A Bibliography.** Foreword by Quincy Wright. Chicago, Public Administration Service, 1945. vi + 32 p.

87   Royal Institute of International Affairs. **Index to Periodical Articles 1950—1964 in the Library of the Royal Institute of International Affairs.** Boston, Hall, 1964. 2 vols.

Index code G deals with international organization.

88   Rudzinski, A. **Selected Bibliography on International Organization.** New York, Carnegie, 1953. 36 p.

89   Scanlon, Helen L. (comp.). **Current Research in International Affairs: A Selected Bibliography of Work in Progress by Private Research Agencies in the United States, United Kingdom, and Canada,** *International Conciliation,* CDXXXVII (January 1948), 7—59.

90   — —. **Current Research in International Affairs: A Selected Bibliography of Work in Progress by Private Research Agencies in the United States, United Kingdom, Canada, Australia. South Africa, India, and Pakistan,** *International Conciliation,* CDLVI (December 1949), 883—978.

Part A. — General References

91 **Social Science and Humanities Index** (originally **International Index**). New York, Wilson, Quarterly, 1907–.

92 Speeckaert, G. P. **International Institutions and International Organizations: A Select Bibliography.** Brussels, Union of International Associations, 1956. 116 p.

93 — —. **Select Bibliography on International Organization, 1885–1964.** Brussels, Union of International Associations, 1965. 150 p.

94 Stanton, Ruth E. (comp.). **Current Research in International Affairs: A Selected Bibliography of Work in Progress by Private Research Agencies in the United States, United Kingdom, Canada, Australia, South Africa and India,** *International Conciliation,* CDLXVI (December 1950), 591–698.

95 Stanton, Ruth E. and Nelms, Agnes (comps.). **Current Research in International Affairs: A Selected Bibliography of Work in Progress by Private Agencies in the United States, United Kingdom, Canada, Australia, South Africa, India, and Pakistan,** *International Conciliation,* CDXLVI (December 1948), 686–764.

96 Union of International Associations. **Directory of Periodicals Published by International Organizations.** 2d ed. Brussels, Union of International Associations, 1959. x + 241 p.

97 United Nations, Library (Geneva). **Monthly List of Selected Articles.** Geneva, Monthly, 1928.

The list was originally issued by the League of Nations. It has been issued by the United Nations since 1946.

98 United Nations, Library (New York). **New Publications in the Dag Hammarskjöld Library.** New York, Monthly 1949–.

99 United States, Library of Congress. **A List of American Doctoral Dissertations.** Washington, Annually, 1912–38.

Part A. — *General References*

100 Van Wagenen, Richard W. **Research in the International Organization Field.** Princeton, Princeton University Press, 1952. 78 p.

101 Williams, Stillman P. **Toward a Genuine World Security System: An Annotated Bibliography for Layman and Scholar.** Washington, United World Federalists, 1964. v + 65 p.

102 Zagayko, Florence F. **International Organization: A List of Basic Source Materials,** *Columbia Journal of Transnational Law,* I (Spring, 1962), 1—42.

3.2 LEAGUE OF NATIONS SYSTEM

103 Aufricht, Hans. **Guide to League of Nations Publications: A Bibliographical Survey of the Work of the League, 1920—1947.** New York, Columbia University Press, 1951. xix + 682 p.

104 Bouglé, C. **Le guide de l'étudiant en matière du Société des Nations.** Paris, Rivière, 1933. 131 p.

105 Doumia, J. (comp.). **Bibliographical List of Official and Unofficial Publications Concerning the Court of International Justice.** 2d ed. Hague, Permanent Court of International Justice, 1926. 159 p.

Supplements were issued yearly from 1927 to 1940/45.

106 League of Nations, Health Organisation. **Bibliography of the Technical Work of the Health Organisation of the League of Nations, 1920—1945.** Geneva, 1945. 235 p.

107 Metz, John. **Peace Literature of the War,** *International Conciliation,* XCVIII, Special Bulletin (January 1916), 31—51.

Part A. — *General References*

3.3 UNITED NATIONS SYSTEM

108 American Association for the United Nations. **Read your Way to World Understanding: A Selected Annotated Reading Guide of Books About the United Nations and the World in Which it Works for Peace and Human Welfare.** New York, Scarecrow, 1963. xv + 321 p.

109 Barnett, Sidney N. **Doctoral Dissertations in American Universities Concerning the United Nations,** *International Organization,* XVI (Summer, 1962), 668—75.

110 — —. **The United Nations: How to Teach the United Nations; Selected Bibliography.** New York, High School of Music and Art, 1954. 24 p.

111 Bates, Margaret L. and Turner, Robert K. **International Documentation: An Introduction,** *International Organization,* I (November 1947), 607—18.

112 Chamberlin, Waldo and Clark, Hartley. **Materials for Undergraduate Study of the United Nations,** *American Political Science Review,* XLIX (March 1954), 204—11.

113 Collart, Yves. **Disarmament: A Study Guide and Bibliography on the Efforts of the United Nations.** Hague, Nijhoff, 1958. 110 p.

114 General Agreement on Tariffs and Trade. **Gatt Bibliography.** Geneva, Palais des Nations, 1954. 40 p.

Supplements have appeared simce 1954.

115 Higham, J. **The U.N. International Law Commission: A Guide to the Documents, 1949—59,** *British Yearbook of International Law,* XXXVI (1960), 384—97.

116 International Labour Office, Library. **Bibliography on the International Labour Organization.** Geneva, 1954. 68 p.

Brings the *Bibliography of the International Labour Organization,* published in 1929, up to date.

Part A. — General References

117 Reid, H.D. **A Selected Bibliography for Teaching About the United Nations.** Rev. ed. Washington, United States Office of Education, 1951. 17 p.

118 Rubinstein, Alvin Z. **Selected Bibliography of Soviet Works on the United Nations, 1946–1959,** *American Political Science Review,* LIV (December 1960), 985–91.

119 Shepard, M. **International Administration: The United Nations and the Specialized Agencies; A Suggested List of References Dating from 1945.** Washington, Library of Congress, Legislative Reference Service, 1952. 28 p.

120 Taylor, Philip H. and Braibanti, Ralph J. D. **Administration of Occupied Areas: A Study Guide.** Syracuse, Syracuse University Press, 1948. iv + 111 p.

121 Thompson, Elizabeth M. **Resources for Teaching About the United Nations, With Annotated Bibliographies.** Washington, National Education Association, 1962. 90 p.

122 United Nations, International Court of Justice (Hague). **Bibliography of the International Court of Justice.** Hague, Annually, 1946–.

123 United Nations, Library (New York). **A Bibliography of the Charter of the United Nations.** New York, 1955. 128 p.

124 — —. **Selected Bibliography of Specialized Agencies Related to the United Nations.** New York, 1949. 28 p.

125 United States, Office of Education. **The United Nations and Related Organizations: A Bibliography.** Washington, 1960. 17 p.

17

Part A. — General References

3.4 REGIONAL INTERNATIONAL ORGANIZATIONS

3.4.1 GENERAL SCOPE

126 Carnell, Francis (comp.). **The Politics of the New States: A Select Annotated Bibliography with Special Reference to the Commonwealth.** London, Oxford University Press, 1961. xvi + 171 p.

127 Deutsch, Karl W. **An Interdisciplinary Bibliography on Nationalism, 1935—1953.** Cambridge, M.I.T. Press, 1956. 165 p.

An updated version is forthcoming.

128 Hamori, Laszlo. **Bibliography on Federalism.** Geneva, League of Nations, Library, 1940—42. 5 vols.

Available at the UN Library in New York.

129 Padelford, Norman J. **A Selected Bibliography of Regionalism and Regional Arrangements,** *International Organization,* X (November 1956), 575—603.

3.4.2 AFRICA

130 Johnson, Carol A. and Russell, Sara A. **Selected Bibliography: Africa and International Organization,** *International Organization,* XVI (Spring, 1962), 449—64.

3.4.3 ASIA AND THE PACIFIC

131 Research Centre on the Social Implications of Industrialization in South Asia. **South Asia Social Science Bibliography,** (originally **Social Science Bibliography**). Delhi, UNESCO, Annually, 1952—58.

132 South Pacific Commission. **Index of Social Science Research Theses on the South Pacific.** Noumea, New Caledonia, 1957. x + 79 p.

Part A. — *General References*

133 Stucki, Curtis W. **American Doctoral Dissertations on Asia, 1933—1962: Including Appendix of Master's Theses at Cornell University.** Ithaca, Southeast Asia Program, 1963. 204 p.

3.4.4 WESTERN HEMISPHERE

134 Barnes, Robert. **Bibliografía Preliminar obre la Integración Económica Centroamericana.** Unpublished manuscript. Washington, Pan American Union, 1961. 5 p.

135 **Handbook of Latin American Studies.** Gainesville, University of Florida Press, Annually, 1935—.
Annotated bibliography with a section on international relations.

136 Kantor, Harry. **A Bibliography of Unpublished Doctoral Dissertations and Master's Theses Dealing with the Governments, Politics, and International Relations of Latin America.** Gainesville, University of Florida Libraries, 1953. 85p.

137 Kidder, Frederick E. and Bushong, Allen D. **Theses on Pan American Topics Prepared by Candidates for Doctoral Degrees in Universities and Colleges in the United States and Canada.** Washington, Pan American Union, 1962. vi + 124 p.
Three earlier editions were compiled by the Union under the title *Theses on Pan American Topics Prepared by Candidates for Degrees in Colleges and Universities in the United States.*

138 Masters, Ruth D. **Handbook of International Organizations in the Americas.** Washington, Carnegie, 1945. 453 p.

139 Organization of American States, Pan American Union, Columbus Library. **Bibliografía de las Conferencias Interamericanas.** Washington, Unión Panamericano, 1954. 277 p.

Part A. — *General References*

3.4.5 WESTERN EUROPE AND THE NORTH ATLANTIC

140 **Atlantic Community Quarterly.** Baltimore, Atlantic Council of the United States, Quarterly, 1963—.

Each issue contains a section of decuments entitled "Source Material."

141 **Atlantic Studies.** Boulogne-sur-Seine, L'Institut Atlantique, Biannually, 1964—.

A bibliography of prospective and current but unpublished work on the Atlantic Community.

142 Conference on Atlantic Community (Bruges). **The Atlantic Community: An Introductory Bibliography.** Leyden, Sythoff, 1962. 2 vols.

Detailed annotations and index.

143 Conseil de l'Europe, Direction des Études. **Documentation sur l'idée européenne en général.** Strasbourg, 1951. 50 p.

144 Council of Europe. **Handbook of European Organizations.** Strasbourg, 1956. viii + 172 p.

145 **European Year Book,** Hague, Nijhoff, Annually, 1955—.

146 Institut für Europäische Politik und Wirtschaft. **Bibliographie zum Schumanplan.** Frankfurt, Institut für Europäische Politik und Wirtschaft, 1953. 151 p.

147 Kaiser, Karl. **L'Europe des Savants: European Integration and the Social Sciences,** *Journal of Common Market Studies*, IV (October 1965), 36—46.

148 North Atlantic Treaty Organization. **Bibliography.** Paris, Place Maréchal de Lattre de Tassigny, 1964. 205 p.

Part A. — General References

149 Organisation Européenne de Coopération Économique. **Aide Américaine à l'Europe 1947–1953: bibliographie sélectionnée.** Paris, Bibliothèque de l'OECE, 1954. 54 p.

150 Paklons, Leons L. **European Bibliography.** Bruges, Tempel, 1964. 217 p.

151 Pehrsson, Hjalmar and Wulf, Hanna (eds.). **The European Bibliography.** Leyden, Sijthoff, 1965. viii + 472 p.

152 Wild, J. E. **The European Common Market and The European Free Trade Association.** London, Library Association, 1962. 64 p.

4. TEXTBOOK TREATMENTS

4.1 GENERAL WORKS

153 Bailey, S. H. **The Framework of International Society.** London, Longmans, Green, 1932. v + 92 p.

154 Ball, M. Margaret, and Killough, Hugh B. **International Relations.** New York, Ronald, 1956.

Chapter XIV.

155 Burton, J. W. **International Relations: A General Theory.** Cambridge, Cambridge University Press, 1965. viii + 288 p.

Chapter V.

156 Carnegie Endowment for International Peace, Division of International Law. **International Organization and Administration: Definition and Use of Certain Terms.** Washington, Carnegie, 1943. xiii + 90 p.

157 Cheever, Daniel S. and Haviland, H. Field, Jr. **Organizing for Peace: International Organization in World Affairs.** Boston, Mifflin, 1954. x + 917 p.

Part A. — General References

158 Claude, Inis L., Jr. **Swords Into Plowshares: The Problems and Progress of International Organization.** 3d ed. New York, Random House, 1964. xvi + 497 p.

159 Colliard, Claude-Albert. **Institutions internationales.** Paris, Dalloz, 1956. 526 p.

160 Corbett, Percy E. **Law and Society in the Relations of States.** New York, Harcourt, Brace, 1951.

Chapters XII–XIII.

161 Dessauer, F. E. **Stability.** New York, Macmillan, 1949. 273 p.

162 Eagleton, Clyde. **International Government.** 3d ed. New York, Ronald, 1957. xxi + 665 p.

163 Frankel, Joseph. **International Relations.** New York, Oxford University Press, 1964.

Chapter VII.

164 Gerbet, Pierre. **Les organisations internationales.** Paris, Presses Universitaires de France, 1959. 128 p.

165 Goodspeed, Stephen S. **The Nature and Function of International Organization.** New York, Oxford University Press, 1963. xi + 676 p.

166 Greene, Fred. **Dynamics of International Relations.** New York, Holt, Rinehart and Winston, 1964.

Chapters XX–XXII.

167 Haas, Ernst B. and Whiting, Allen S. **Dynamics of International Relations.** New York, McGraw-Hill, 1956.

Chapter XIX.

Part A. — General References

168 Hartmann, Frederick H. **The Relations of Nations.** 3d ed. New York, Macmillan, 1967.

Chapters IX—X, XII.

169 Hayes, Carlton H. **The Historical Background of the League of Nations,** *The League of Nations*, Stephen Pierce Duggan (ed.). Boston, Atlantic Monthly Press, 1919, pp. 18—49.

170 Hedges, Robert Yorke. **International Organization.** Foreword by Paul Mantoux. New York, Putman, 1935. x + 212 p.

171 Hershey, Amos Shartle. **The Essentials of International Public Law and Organization.** Rev. ed. New York, Macmillan, 1927. xii + 784 p.

172 Herz, John H. **International Politics in the Atomic Age.** New York, Columbia University Press, 1959. viii + 360 p.

173 Hicks, Frederick C. **The New World Order: International Organization, International Law, International Cooperation.** Garden City, Doubleday, Page, 1920. viii + 496 p.

174 Hill, David J. **World Organization as Affected by the Nature of the Modern State.** New York, Columbia University Press, 1911. ix + 214 p.

175 Hill, Norman L. **International Administration.** New York, McGraw-Hill, 1931. 292 p.

176 — —. **International Politics.** New York, Harper and Row, 1963.

Chapters XVIII—XIX.

177 — —. **The Public International Conference.** London, Oxford University Press, 1929. 267 p.

Part A. — General References

178 Hinsley, Francis H. **Power and the Pursuit of Peace: Theory and Practice in the History of Relations Between States.** Cambridge, Cambridge University Press, 1963. 416 p.

179 Hodges, Charles. **The Background of International Relations.** New York, Wiley, 1931.

Chapter XVI.

180 Hughan, Jessie W. **A Study of International Government.** New York, Crowell, 1923. 401 p.

181 Jacob, Philip E. and Atherton, Alexine L. **Dynamics of International Organization: The Making of World Order.** Homewood, Dorsey, 1964. xvii + 723 p.

182 Joyce, James A. **The Story of International Cooperation.** Foreword by U Thant. New York, Watts, 1964. xi + 258 p.

183 — —. **World in the Making. The Story of International Cooperation.** New York, Schuman, 1953. 159 p.

184 Kellor, Frances A. and Hatvany, Antonia. **Security Against War.** New York, Macmillan, 1924. 2 vols.

185 Kulski, Wladyslaw Wszebor. **International Politics in a Revolutionary Age.** Philadelphia, Lippincott, 1964.

Chapter IX.

186 Leonard, L. Larry. **International Organization.** New York, McGraw-Hill, 1951. xv + 630 p.

187 Levi, Werner. **Documents Relating to International Organization.** Minneapolis, Burgess, 1946. 88 p.

Part A. — General References

188 — —. **Fundamentals of World Organization.** Minneapolis, University of Minnesota Press, 1950. ix + 233 p.

189 L'Huillier, Fernand. **Les institutions internationales et transnationales.** Preface by Marcel Prelot. Paris, Presses Universitaires, 1961. xiii + 295 p.

190 Mander, Linden A. **Foundations of Modern World Society.** 2d ed. Stanford, Stanford University Press, 1947. 948 p.

191 Mangone, Gerard J. **A Short History of International Organization.** New York, McGraw-Hill, 1954. ix + 326 p.
Each chapter concludes with a short set of documents.

192 Manning, Charles A. W. **The Nature of International Society.** New York, Wiley, 1962. xi + 220 p.

193 Maxwell, Bertram W. **International Relations.** New York, Crowell, 1939.
Chapter III.

194 Middlebush, Frederick A. and Hill, Chesney. **Elements of International Relations.** New York, McGraw-Hill, 1940.
Chapters VIII–IX, XXIV.

195 Mills, Lennox A. and McLaughlin, Charles H. **World Politics in Transition.** New York, Holt, 1957.
Chapter XV.

196 Mitrany, David. **The Progress of International Government.** New Haven, Yale University Press, 1933. 176 p.

197 Monaco, Riccardo. **Lezioni di organizzazione internazionale.** Torino, Giappichelli, 1961–65. 2 vols.

Part A. — General References

198 Morgenthau, Hans J. **Politics Among Nations.** 4th ed. New York, Knopf, 1967.

Chapter XXVII.

199 Morrow, Dwight W. **The Society of Free States.** New York, Harper, 1919. 224 p.

200 Mowat, Robert B. **International Relations.** New York, Macmillan, 1931.

Chapters XII–XIII.

201 Mower, Edmund, **International Government.** Boston, Heath, 1931. 736 p.

202 Muir, Ramsay. **Nationalism and Internationalism: The Culmination of Modern History.** Boston, Houghton, Mifflin, 1916. 229 p.

203 Newfang, Oscar. **World Federation,** P. Gault (trans.). New York, Barnes and Noble, 1939. xii + 121 p.; xi + 117 p.

204 Padelford, Norman J. and Lincoln, George A. **The Dynamics of International Politics.** New York, Macmillan, 1962.

Chapters XVIII–XIX.

205 — —. **International Politics.** New York, Macmillan, 1954.

Chapter XX.

206 Palmer, Norman D. and Perkins, Howard C. **International Relations.** 2d ed. Boston, Houghton, Mifflin, 1957.

Chapters XII–XIV.

207 Peaslee, Amos Jenkins. **International Governmental Organizations: Constitutional Documents.** 2d ed. Hague, Nijhoff, 1961. 2 vols.

Part A. — *General References*

208 Perris, G. H. **A Short History of War and Peace.** New York, Holt, 1911. vi + 256 p.

209 Possony, Stefan T. **Peace Enforcement.** *Yale Law Journal*, LV (August 1946), 910–49.

210 Potter, Pitman B. **The Classification of International Organizations,** *American Political Science Review*, XXIX (April 1935), 212–24; (June 1935), 403–17.

211 — —.**An Introduction to the Study of International Organization.** 4th ed. New York, Appleton-Century, 1935. xviii + 645 p.

212 — —. **Origin of the Term International Organization,** *American Journal of International Law*, XXXIX (October 1945), 803–806.

213 — —. **Political Science in the International Field: International Orgazation,** *Geneva Studies*, XI (June 1940), 21–35.

214 — —. **This World of Nations: Foundations, Institutions, Practices.** New York, Macmillan, 1929. xix + 366 p.

215 Rahman, Hafiz H. **International Law, Politics and Organisation.** Dacca, Ideal Publications, 1962. iv + 148 p.

216 Read, Elizabeth. **International Law and International Relations.** N. p., American Foundation, 1925.

Chapter XVII.

217 Reuter, Paul. **International Institutions,** J. M. Chapman (trans.). London, Allen and Unwin, 1958. 316 p.

218 Riddell, Walter A. **World Security by Conference.** Toronto, Ryerson, 1947. 216 p.

219 Russell, Frank M. **Theories of International Relations.** New York, Appleton-Century, 1936. viii + 651 p.

220 Schleicher, Charles P. **International Relations.** Englewood Cliffs, Prentice Hall, 1962.

Chapter VIII.

221 Schuman, Frederick L. **International Politics.** 6th ed. New. York, McGraw-Hill, 1969.

Chapter VII.

222 Schwarzenberger, Georg. **Power Politics.** 3d ed. London, Stevens, 1964.

Chapter XV.

223 Sereni, Angelo Piero. **Le organizzazioni internazionali.** Milan, Guiffre, 1959. xxviii + 326 p.

224 Sharp, Walter and Kirk, Grayson. **Contemporary International Politics.** New York, Farrar and Rinehart, 1941. 840 p.

225 Sprout, Harold H. and Sprout, Margaret. **Foundations of International Politics.** Princeton, Van Nostrand, 1962.

Chapter XVIII.

226 Steiner, H. Arthur. **Principles and Problems of International Relations.** New York, Harper, 1940.

Chapters XIII–XV.

Part A. — General References

227 Stoessinger, John. **The Might of Nations.** New York, Random House, 1962.

Chapters IX–X, XII.

228 Strausz-Hupé, R. and Possony, Stefan T. **International Relations in the Age of Conflict Between Democracy and Dictatorship.** New York, McGraw-Hill, 1954.

Chapters XXVI–XXVIII.

229 Talbott, E. Guy. **The Need for World Organization,** *World Affairs Quarterly*, XI (October 1940), 287–95.

Contains a listing of historical precedents beginning with the Achaean Letgue through the British Commonwealth, as well as a listing of historic proposals for world organization.

230 Trinker, Frederick W. **The Anatomy of World Order,** *OR* **A Glimpse at a Multifold World Organization.** Mexico City, Costa-Amic, 1946. 132 p.

231 Vandenbosch, Amry and Hogan, Willard N. **Toward World Order.** New York, McGraw-Hill, 1963. viii + 389 p.

232 Van Dyke, Vernon. **International Politics.** 2d ed. New York, Appleton-Century-Crofts, 1966.

Chapter XX.

233 Van Wagenen, Richard W. **Recent Contributions to the Field,** *International Organization*, X (August 1956), 402–20.

234 Varghese, Payappilly Itty. **International Law and Organization.** Lucknow, Eastern Book Company, 1952. xxii + 706 p.

235 Vinacke, Harold M. **International Organization.** New York, Crofts, 1934. x + 483 p.

236 Walsh, Edmund A. (ed.). **The History and Nature of International Relations.** New York, Macmillan, 1922. 299 p.

237 Wright, Quincy. **The Study of International Relations.** New York, Appleton-Century — Crofts, 1955.

Chapter XVIII.

4.2 LEAGUE OF NATIONS SYSTEM

238 Bassett, John S. **The League of Nations: A Chapter in World Politics.** New York, Longmans, Green, 1938. 415 p.

239 Butler, Geoffrey. **A Handbook to the League of Nations.** London, Longmans, Green, 1925. XVI + 239 p.

240 Eppstein, John (comp.). **Ten Years of the League of Nations: A History of the Origins of the League and Its Development from A. D. 1919 to 1929.** Introduction by Viscount Cecil of Chelwood; epilogue by Gilbert Murray. London, Fair Press, 1929. 175 p.

241 Erzberger, Matthias. **The League of Nations: The Way to The World's Peace,** Bernard Miall (trans.). New York, Holt, 1919. 331 p.

242 Fosdick, Raymond B., Rublee, George, Shotwell, J. T., Bourgeois, Léon, Weiss, André, Requin, Lt.-Col., Ormsby-Gore, W. Eza, el Vizoconde de, Butler, H. B., Strong, Richard P., Salter, J. A., Claveille, A., La Fontaine, Henri, Otlet, Paul. **The League of Nations Starts: An Outline by Its Organisers.** London, Macmillan, 1920. 282 p.

243 Göppert, Otto. **Der Völkerbund: Organisation und Tätigkeit des Völkerbundes.** Stuttgart, Kohlhammer, 1938. 734 p.

244 Guggenheim, Paul. **Der Völkerbund.** Leipzig, Teubner, 1932. 281 p.

Part A. — General References

245 Harley, John E. **The League of Nations and the New International Law.** Introduction by Theodore Marburg. New York, Oxford University Press, 1921. vii + 127 p.

246 Harris, H. Wilson. **What the League of Nations Is.** London, Allen and Unwin, 1925. 128 p.

247 Howard-Ellis, C. **The Origin, Structure and Working of the League of Nations.** Boston, Houghton, Mifflin, 1928. 528 p.

248 Hudson, Manley O. **Progress in International Organization.** Oxford, Oxford University Press, 1932. 162 p.

249 Juntke, Fritz and Sreistrup, Hans. **Das Deutsche Schriftum über den Völkerbund, 1917–1925.** Berlin, Struppe und Winckler, 1927. 71 p.

250 Knudson, John I. **A History of the League of Nations.** Atlanta, Smith, 1938. vi + 445 p.

251 League of Nations, Secretariat. **The Aims and Organisation of the League of Nations.** Geneva, 1929. 91 p.

252 — —. **The Aims, Methods and Activity of the League of Nations.** Geneva, 1935. 220 p.

253 — —. **Ten Years of World Co-operation.** Foreword by Eric Drummond. Geneva, 1930. 467 p.
Comprehensive bibliography, pp. 430–60.

254 League of Nations, Secretariat, Information Section. **Essential Facts About the League of Nations.** 10th ed. Geneva, 1939. 359 p.

255 — —. **The League of Nations: A Survey (January 1920 — December 1926).** Geneva, 1926. 117 p.

256 — —. **Politicial Activities.** Rev. ed. Geneva, 1925—27. 2 vols.

257 Myers, Denys. **Handbook of the League of Nations.** Boston, World Peace Foundation, 1935. 411 p.

258 — —. **Handbook of the League of Nations since 1920.** Boston, World Peace Foundation, 1930. 320 p.

259 Pollock, Frederick. **The League of Nations.** 2d ed. London, Stevens, 1922. 266 p.

260 Potter, Pitman B. and West, Roscoe. **International Civics.** New York, Macmillan, 1927.

Chapters XII—XIV.

261 Schücking, Walther M. A. and Wehberg, Hans. **Die Satzung des Völkerbundes.** 3d ed. Berlin, Vahlen, 1931. XXVII + 794 p.

262 Shotwell, James T. **On the Rim of the Abyss.** New York, Macmillan, 1936. 400 p.

263 Waldecker, Burkhart. **Die Stellung der Menschlichen Gesellschaft zum Völkerbund.** Berlin, Heymann, 1931. 374 p.

264 Walters, Francis Paul. **A History of the League of Nations.** London, Oxford University Press, 1960. xv + 833 p.

The most comprehensive volume on the League.

Part A. — General References

265   Webster, C. K., with Herbert, Sydney. **The League of Nations in Theory and Practice.** Boston, Houghton, Mifflin, 1933. 320 p.

266   Williams, Bruce S. **State Security and the League of Nations.** Baltimore, Johns Hopkins Press, 1927. x + 346 p.

267   Zimmern, Alfred E. **The League of Nations and the Rule of Law, 1918—1935.** 2d ed. London, Macmillan, 1939.
Part III.

4.3 UNITED NATIONS SYSTEM

268   Arne, Sigrid. **United Nations Primer.** Rev. ed. New York, Rinehart, 1948. 226 p.

269   Bailey, Sydney D. **The United Nations: A Short Political Guide.** New York, Praeger, 1963. 141 p.

270   Boyd, Andrew K. H. **The United Nations Organisation Handbook.** London, Pilot 1946. 210 p.

271   Carr, William G. **One World in the Making: The United Nations.** Boston, Ginn, 1946. 100 p.

272   Chase, Eugene P. **The United Nations in Action.** New York, McGraw-Hill, 1950. xii + 464 p.

273   Courlander, Harold. **Shaping our Times: What the United Nations Is and Does.** New York, Oceana, 1960. 242 p.

274   Coyle, David Cushman. **The United Nations and How it Works.** New York, Columbia University Press, 1966. xii + 256 p.

Part A. — *General References*

275 Dean, Vera Micheles. **The U. N. Today.** New York, Holt, Rinehart and Winston, 1965. 112 p.

276 Dolivet, Louis. **The United Nations: A Handbook on the New World Organization.** Preface by Trygve Lie. New York, Farrar and Straus, 1946. 152 p.

277 Eichelberger, Clark M. **U.N.: The First Twenty Years.** New York, Harper, 1965. XII + 176 p.

278 Falk, Richard A. and Mendlovitz, Saul H. **The Strategy of World Order** (Vol. 3: The United Nations). Foreword by Oscar Schachter. New York, World Law Fund, 1966. xv + 848 p.

279 Fried, John H. E. **Worldmark Encyclopedia of the Nations,** ed. Bernard Reines (Vol. 3: The United Nations). New York, Harper, 1965. xxvi + 286 p.

280 Galt, T. F. **How the United Nations Works.** New York, Crowell, 1947. 218 p.

281 Gardner, Richard N. **In Pursuit of World Order: U. S. Foreign Policy and International Organizations.** Foreword by Harlan Cleveland. New York, Praeger, 1964. xviii + 263 p.

282 Gerber, Norman. (ed.). **Primer for Peace: World Government for the Atomic Age.** Oak Ridge, Association of Oak Ridge Engineers and Scientists, 1947. 62 p.

283 Goodrich, Leland M. **The United Nations.** New York, Crowell, 1963. 419 p.

284 Goodrich, Leland M. and Simons, Anne P. **The United Nations and the Maintenance of International Peace and Security.** Washington, Brookings, 1955. xiii + 709 p.

Part A. — General References

285 Gross, Ernest A. **The United Nations: Structure for Peace.** New York, Harper, 1962. ix + 132 p.

286 Harley, J. Eugene. **Documentary Textbook on the United Nations: Humanity's March Towards Peace; A Volume Emphasizing Official Co-Operation for World Peace, Especially the United Nations and Related Specialized Agencies.** Foreword by Elbert D. Thomas. Los Angeles, Center for International Understanding, 1947. xx + 952 p.
Extensive bibliography.

287 Hill, Norman L. **International Organization.** New York, Harper, 1952. 627 p.

288 Krylov, Sergei Borisovich. **Materialy K Istorii Organizatsii Obyedinennykh Natsii. (Materials on the History of the Organization of the United Nations.)** Moscow, Academy of Sciences of the U. S. S. R., Institute of Law, 1949. 343 p.

The author (1887–1958) was a member of the International Court of Justice and was the Soviet delegate at Dumbarton Oaks and San Francisco. The object of this study, the author writes in the preface, is to show that the U. S. S. R. actively supported the principle embodied in the charter as drafted, and was fully prepared to support these principles. However, "the imperialist camp, headed by the United States, hypocritically taking cover behind allegations of international cooperation, but in reality striving to subordinate the United Nations to its imperialist interests, is retreating before our eyes from the principles laid down in the United Nations Charter and by this means undermining the very foundations of the organization."

289 Larus, Joel (ed.). **From Collective Security to Preventive Diplomacy: Readings in International Organization and the Maintenance of Peace.** New York, Wiley, 1965. xi + 556 p.

290 Leyden University. **United Nations Textbook.** 2d ed. Leyden, Groen, 1954. 424 p.

291 McClelland, Charles A. (ed.). **The United Nations: The Continuing Debate.** San Francisco, Chandler, 1960. xii + 198 p.

292 Maclaurin, John (pseud.). **The United Nations and Power Politics.** New York, Harper, 1951. xiii + 468 p.

Part A. — General References

293 Moore, Bernard (comp.).**ABC of the United Nations and International Organisations.** London, United Nations Association, 1949. 96 p.

Glossary of terms.

294 New Zealand, Department of External Affairs. **The United Nations and Specialized Agencies Handbook.** Wellington, 1962. 115 p.

295 Nicholas, Herbert George. **The United Nations as a Political Institution.** 2d ed. London, Oxford University Press, 1962. 232 p.

296 Szapiro, Jerzy. **The Newspaperman's United Nations: A Guide for Journalists About the United Nations and Specialized Agencies.** New York International Documents Service, 1961. 229 p.

297 United Nations, Department of Public Information. **Everyman's United Nations: The Structure, Functions, and Work of the Organization and Its Related Agencies During The Years 1945–1964.** Foreword by H. T. de Sá. 7th ed. New York, United Nations, 1964. x + 638 p.

298 — —. **Basic Facts About the United Nations.** 19th ed. New York, 1964. 60 p.

299 — —. **United Nations: What It Is, What It Does, How It Works.** New York, 1965. 31 p.

300 Vandenbosch, Amry and Hogan, Willard N. **The United Nations: Background, Organization, Functions, Activities.** New York, McGraw-Hill, 1952. xiii + 456 p.

301 Zocca, Marie and Zocca, Louis. **The United Nations: Action for Peace — A Layman's Guide.** New Brunswick, Rutgers University Press, 1955. 60 p.

4.4. REGIONAL INTERNATIONAL ORGANIZATIONS

302 Lawson, Ruth C. (ed.). **International Regional Organizations: Constitutional Foundations.** New York, Praeger, 1962. xviii + 387 p.

A collection of documents

303 Pinto, Roger. **Les organisations européennes.** 2d ed. Paris, Payot, 1965. 501 p.

304 Political and Economic Planning (London). **European Organizations.** London, Allen and Unwin, 1954. xvi + 372 p.

5. DOCUMENTARY SOURCES

A listing of all documentary sources would be endless, so the following references are limited to guides to documents, and to the most important regularly published materials providing information on political affairs.

5.1 GENERAL SOURCES

305 Haensch, Günther. **Internationale Terminologie: Diplomatie, Verträge, Internationale Organisationen, Konferenzen.** Stuttgart, Müller, 1954. 180 p.

306 International Labour Office. **The I. L. O. Yearbook.** Geneva, Annually, 1930–.

307 **International Labour Review.** Geneva, International Labour Office, Monthly, 1921–.

Part A. — General References

308 League of Nations. **Handbook of International Organizations.** Geneva, 1939. 491 p.

309 Union des Associations Internationales. **Les congrès internationaux de 1681 à 1899: list complète.** Brussels, Union des Associations Internationales, 1960. 76 p.

Chronological list of 2,000 selected congresses.

310 United States, Department of State. **International Organization and Conference Series.** Washington, Annually, 1946—.

Superseded *Conference Series* 1—105 (1929—47) in 1948, and *United States-United Nations Information Series*, 1—28 (1945—47). Series I deals with general aspects of participation in the United Nations and other general problems, containing *inter alia* the annual report by the President to Congress, *The United States and the United Nations*. Series II is devoted to conferences with American republics, Europe and the British Commonwealth, and the Far East. Series III contains documents pertaining to particular conferences of the main organs of the UN. Series IV reports on activities of the UN's specialized agencies.

311 Watkins, James T., IV and Robinson, J. William (eds.). **General International Organization: A Source Book.** Princeton, Van Nostrand, 1956. 248 p.

A collection of documents.

312 World Peace Foundation. **Documents of International Organizations: A Selected Bibliography.** Boston, World Peace Foundation, Quarterly, 1947—50. 3 vols.

Superseded by sections in *International Organization*, a journal published quarterly by the World Peace Foundation.

5.2 LEAGUE OF NATIONS SYSTEM

313 Breycha-Vauthier, A. C. von. **Sources of Information: A Handbook on the Publications of the League of Nations.** Preface by James Shotwell. New York, Columbia University Press, 1939. 118 p.

314 Carroll, Marie J. **Key to the League of Nations Documents Placed on Public Sale 1920—1929.** Boston, World Peace Foundation, 1930. 340 p.

Four supplements were issued, covering the years 1930, 1931, 1932—33, 1934—36.

Part A. — General References

315 Jackson, Judith and King-Hall, Stephen (eds.). **The League Year-Book.** New York, Macmillan, Annually, 1932—33.

Part I covers administrative and legal matters; Part II summarizes proceedings. Bibliography included.

316 Kluyver, Mrs. C. A. (ed.). **Documents on the League of Nations.** Leyden, Sijhoff, 1920. 367 p.

317 League of Nations. **Catalogue of Publications,** 1920—1935. Geneva, 1935.

Also, there are four supplements covering the years 1936, 1937, 1938, and 1939, respectively, and one supplement covering the years 1940—45.

318 League of Nations, Library. **Brief Guide to The League of Nations Publications.** Rev. ed. Geneva, 1930. 32 p.

319 League of Nations. **Official Journal.** Geneva, Monthly, 1920—46.

The official journal contains verbatim records of Council meetings, together with the texts of the reports and resolutions adopted by the Council, and the principal official documents received or sent by the Secretariat.

320 — —. **Records.** Geneva, Annually, 1920—46.

Verbatim records of the Assembly.

321 League of Nations, Secretariat, Information Section. **The League from Year to Year.** Geneva, Annually, 1927/28—38.

Similar to the *Yearbook of the United Nations.*

322 — —. **Monthly Summary of the League of Nations.** Geneva, Monthly, 1921—40.

323 Ottlik, George (ed.). **Annuaire de la Société des Nations.** Geneva, Payot, Annually, 1927—31, 1936—38.

Part A. — General References

324 Permanent Court of International Justice (Hague). **Annual Report of the Permanent Court of Justice.** Hague, Annually, 1922–45.

325 — —. **Permanent Court of International Justice: Statutes and Rules.** Leyden, Sythoff, 1922–39. 88 vols.

Acts and documents relating to the judgments and advisory opinions given by the Court.

326 — —. **World Court Reports: A Collection of the Judgments, Orders and Opinions of the Permanent Court of International Justice,** Manley O. Hudson (ed.). Washington, Carnegie, 1934–43. 4 vols.

327 Schiffer, Walter (comp.). **Repertoire of Questions of General International Law Before the League of Nations 1920–1940.** Geneva, Geneva Research Centre, 1942. 390 p.

328 United States, Senate, Committee on Foreign Relations. **Treaty of Peace with Germany. (Hearings Before the Committee on Foreign Relations, United States Senate, Sixty-Sixth Congress, First Session, on the Treaty of Peace with Germany signed at Versailles on June 28, 1919, and submitted to the Senate on July 20, 1919, by the President of the United States.)** Washington, United States Government Printing Office, 1919. 2 vols.

329 World Peace Foundation. **Handbook of the League of Nations,** *World Peace Foundation Pamphlets*, V, 4 (1922), 225–332.

Revised versions appear in volumes VII–XII, the latter authored by Denys P. Myers.

330 **Yearbook of the League of Nations.** Brooklyn, Brooklyn Daily Eagle, Annually, 1921–29.

Issues 1–4 are by Charles H. Levermore, published by *Brooklyn Daily Eagle;* 5–9 published by the World Peace Foundation. The last issue is by D. P. Myers and is entitled "Nine Years of the League of Nations, 1920–28."

5.3 UNITED NATIONS SYSTEM

331 **Annual Review of United Nations Affairs.** New York, New York University Graduate Program of International Studies, Annually, 1949–.

   Contains the proceedings of the Institute for Annual Review of United Nations Affairs, New York University.

332 Brimmer, Brenda, Chamberlin, Waldo, Hovet, Thomas, Jr., and Wall, Linwood R. **A Guide to the Use of United Nations Documents, Including Reference to the Specialized Agencies and Special U. N. Bodies.** Dobbs Ferry, Oceana, 1962. xv + 272 p.

333 Chamberlin, Waldo and Hovet, Thomas A., Jr. **Chronology and Fact Book of the United Nations, 1941–1961.** New York, Oceana, 1961. 64 p.

334 **The Chronicle of United Nations Activities: Weekly Report.** New York, Hasid, Weekly, 1956–61.

335 Davis, Edward P. **Periodicals of International Organizations.** Washington, Pan American Union, 1950.

   Part I: The United Nations and Specialized Agencies.

336 Hambro, Edvard I. **The Case Law of the International Court: A Repertoire of the Judgments, Advisory Opinions and Orders of the Permanent Justice.** Bibliography by J. Doumia; index by Audrey Welsby. Leyden, Sythoff, 1952. 3 vols.

337 **Issues Before the General Assembly,** *International Conciliation.* New York, Carnegie Endowment for International Peace, Annually in the September issue, 1947–.

338 Moor, Carol Carter and Chamberlain, Waldo. **How to Use United Nations Documents.** New York, New York University Press, 1952. iii + 26 p.

Part A. — General References

339 Patch, William H. **The Use of United Nations Documents.** Urbana, University of Illinois Graduate School of Library Service, Occasional Paper 64, March 1962. 27 p.

340 Royal Institute of International Affairs. **United Nations Documents, 1941–1945.** London, Royal Institute of International Affairs, 1946. 271 p.

341 Schapper, Morris B. (ed.). **United Nations Agreements.** Washington, American Council on Public Affairs, 1944. 376 p.

342 Sohn, Louis B. (ed.). **Basic Documents of the United Nations.** Brooklyn, Foundation Press, 1956. 307 p.

343 — —. **Cases and Other Materials on World Law.** Brooklyn, Foundation Press, 1950. xxii + 1,363 p.

344 — —. **Cases on United Nations Law.** New York, Foundation Press, 1956. xxv + 1,048 p.

345 Syatauw, J. J. G. **Decisions of the International Court of Justice: A Digest.** Leyden, Sythoff, 1963. 237 p.

Periodic supplements are issued.

346 United Nations, Department of Public Information. **United Nations Publications, 1945–1963: A Reference Catalogue.** New York, 1964. v + 72 p.

Since 1950 published annually as *United Nations Publications*. The Specialized Agencies related to the United Nations issue their own publications. Overlaps with the *United Nations Documents Index*.

347 United Nations. **Documents of the United Nations Conference on International Organization.** New York, United Nations Information Organizations, 1945–46. 22 vols.

Part A. — General References

348 United Nations, Economic and Social Council. **Catalogue of Economic and Social Projects of the United Nations and the Specialized Agencies.** New York, Monthly, 1949–.

349 United Nations, General Assembly. **Official Records.** New York, Annually, 1946–.

   Verbatim proceedings. Supplement 1 is the "Report of the Secretary General on the Work of the Organization"; Supplement 2, "Report of the Security Council to the General Assembly"; Supplement 3, "Report of the Economic and Social Council to the General Assembly"; Supplement 4, "Report of the Trusteeship Council to the General Assembly."

350 United Nations, International Court of Justice (Hague). **Yearbook.** Hague, Annually, 1947–.

351 United Nations, Library. **Index to Proceedings of the General Assembly.** New York, Annually, 1950–.

352 United Nations, Library (New York). **United Nations Documents Index.** New York, Monthly, 1950–.

   Earlier series published by the World Peace Foundation under the title *Documents of International Organization.*

353 United Nations, Office of Public Information. **United Nations Publications.** New York, Annually, 1948–.

354 — —. **UN Monthly Chronicle.** New York, Monthly except August, 1954–.

   Supersedes *United Nations Review.*

355 United Nations, Secretariat, Department of Public Information. **Yearbook of the United Nations.** Annually, 1947–.

   A survey of activities of the various organs.

Part A. — General References

356 United Nations, Secretariat, Protocol and Liaison Section. **Delegations to the United Nations.** New York, Annually, 1946—.

Before March/April 1952, issued as *Delegations to the United Nations:* from 1952 to August 1954, known as *Permanent Missions and Delegations to the United Nations.*

357 United Nations, Secretary General. **Repertory of Practice of United Nations Organs.** New York, 1955. 5 vols.

358 **United Nations News.** New York, Woodrow Wilson Foundation, Bi-monthly, 1946—49.

359 United States, Department of State. **Charter of the United Nations: Report to the President on the Results of the San Francisco Conference by the Chairman of the United States Delegation, the Secretary of State, June 26, 1945.** Department of State Publication 2349, Conference Series 71. Washington, United States Government Printing Office, 1945. 266 p.

360 — —. **Post-War Foreign Policy Preparation, 1939—1945.** Publication 3580, General Foreign Policy Series 15. Washington, United States Government Printing Office, 1950. ix + 726 p.

361 — —. **The United Nations Conference on International Organization: San Francisco, California, April 25 to June 26, 1945; Selected Documents.** Department of State Publication 2490, Conference Series 83. Washington, United States Government Printing Office, 1946. viii + 992 p.

362 — —. **United States-United Nations Information Series.** Washington, Government Printing Office, 1945—47.

There were 28 issues.

363 — —. **United States and the United Nations.** Report by the President ... to the Congress. Washington, United States Government Printing Office, Annually, 1947—.

Part A. — *General References*

364 United States, 81st Congress, 2d Session, Senate, Committee on Foreign Relations. **Revision of the United Nations Charter.** Washington, United States Government Printing Office, 1950. 808 p.

   Hearings before a subcommittee of the Committee on Foreign Relations on Resolutions Relative to the Revision of the United Nations Charter, Atlantic Union, World Federation, etc.

365 United States, Senate, Committee on Foreign Relations. **Review of the United Nations Charter: A Collection of Documents.** Washington, United States Government Printing Office, 1955. 895 p.

366 United States, 79th Congress, 1st Session, Senate, Committee on Foreign Relations. **The Charter of the United Nations.** Rev. ed. Washington, United States Government Printing Office, 1945. 723 p.

   Hearings before the Committee on the Charter of the United Nations for the Maintenance of International Peace and Security, submitted by the President of the United States on July 2, 1945.

367 **Who's Who in the United Nations.** Yonkers-on-Hudson, Burckel, 1951. 580 p.

368 Zeydel, Walter H. and Chamberlin, Waldo. **Enabling Instrument of Members of the United Nations; Part I: The United States of America.** New York, Carnegie, 1951. 126 p.

5.4 REGIONAL INTERNATIONAL ORGANIZATIONS

369 Davis, Edward P. **Periodicals of International Organizations.** Washington, Pan American Union, 1950.

   Part II: Inter-American Organizations.

370 Organization of American States, Pan American Union. **Annals.** Washington, Quarterly, 1949–.

371 — —. **Bulletin.** Washington, Monthly, 1873–.

   The series began originally as a United States Government document.

372 Roussier, Michel, with Stephan, Mary Vonne. **Les publications officielles des institutions européennes.** New York, Carnegie, 1954. 73 p.

373 Royal Institute of International Affairs. **Documents on Regional Organizations Outside Western Europe 1940—1949.** London, Royal Institute of International Affairs, 1950. 85 p.

6. BEHAVIORALIST APPROACHES

In contrast with traditional writing on practical problems or case studies, behavioralist approaches treat elements of international organization as units of analysis in testing general theories of human behavior. Integration theorists view the establishment of structure as an effort to facilitate coordination among political actors that already have many transactions with one another; research on international integration tends to focus on preconditions to an increase in structural linkage between international actors. System theory, on the other hand, emphasizes the total configuration and power structure, which establish certain boundaries to effective action by international institutions. Both theories, in turn, have been studied by researchers using a variety of research techniques.

6.1 THEORETICAL DISCUSSIONS

6.1.1 INTEGRATION THEORY

374 Angell, Robert C. **An Analysis of Trends in International Organizations,** *Peace Research Society, Papers,* III (1965), 185—96.

375 — —. **Discovering Paths to Peace,** *The Nature of Conflict: Studies on the Sociological Aspects of International Tensions,* International Sociological Association (ed.). Paris, UNESCO, 1957, pp. 204—23.

Part A. — General References

376 — —. **International Communication and the World Society,** *The World Community*, Quincy Wright (ed.). Chicago, University of Chicago Press, 1948, pp. 145—60.

Followed by discussion of Warner, Mead, Wright, Potter, Bruner, Rippy, Parsons, Gottschalk, Benedict, Morris, Morgenthau, McKeon, Likert, Emmerich, Young, Hart, Stoddard, Taft, Bloch, Boulding, Rogers, Marschak, Guérard, Herring.

377 Aron, R. **A Suggested Scheme for a Study of Federalism,** *International Social Science Journal*, IV (Spring, 1952), 45—54.

378 Balassa, Bela. **Toward a Theory of Economic Integration.** *Kyklos*, XIV 1 (1961), 1—17.

379 Bloomfield, Lincoln P. **The United States, the United Nations, and the Creation of Community,** *International Organization*, XIV (Autumn, 1960), 503—13.

380 Boulding, Kenneth E. **World Economic Contacts and National Policies,** *The World Community*, Quincy Wright (ed.). Chicago, University of Chicago Press, 1948, pp. 95—100.

Followed by discussion of Wright, Rippy, Metzler, Bloch, Potter, Werner, Marschak, Mead, Taft, Hardin, Morgenthau, Herring, Gottschalk, Guérard, Parsons, Riesman, McKeon, Wirth, Schultz, Emmerich, Whittlesey, Leiserson, Riefler, Polanyi.

381 Brinton, Crane. **From Many One: The Process of Political Integration, The Problem of World Government.** Cambridge, Harvard University Press, 1948. 126 p.

382 Brzezinski, Zbigniew. **Deviation Control: A Study in the Dynamics of Doctrinal Conflict,** *American Political Science Review*, LVI (March 1962), 5—22.

383 Callis, Melmut G. **The Sociology of International Relations,** *American Sociological Review*, XII (June 1947), 323—34.

Part A. — General References

384 Deutsch, Karl W. **The Growth of Nations: Some Recurrent Patterns of Political and Social Integration,** *World Politics,* V (January 1953), 168–95.

385 — —. **Nationalism and Social Communication: An Inquiry into the Foundations of Nationality.** New York, Wiley, 1953. x + 292 p.

386 — —. **Nationalism, Communication, and Community: An Interim Report,** *Perspectives on a Troubled Decade,* Lyman Bryson, Louis Finkelstein and R. M. MacIver (eds.). New York, Harper, 1950, pp. 339–64.
Comments by Quincy Wright.

387 — —. **Political Community at the International Level: Problems of Definition and Measurement.** Garden City, Doubleday, 1954 x + 70 p.

388 — —. **Supranational Organizations in the 1960's,** *Journal of Common Market Studies,* I (May 1963), 212–18.

389 — —. **The Trend of European Nationalism — The Language Aspect,** *American Political Science Review,* XXXVI (June 1942), 533–41.

390 Deutsch, Karl W., Burrell, Sidney A., Kann, Robert A., Lee, Maurice, Jr., Lichterman, Martin, Lindgren, Raymond E., Loewenheim, Francis L., and Van Wagenen, Richard W. **Political Community and the North Atlantic Area: International Organization in the Light of Historical Experience.** Princeton, Princeton University Press, 1957. xiii + 228 p.

391 Dicks, Henry V. **National Loyalty, Identity, and the International Soldier,** *International Organization,* XVII (Spring, 1963), 425–43.

392 Dunn, Frederick S. **War and the Minds of Men.** New York, Harper, 1950. xvi + 115 p.

393 Efimenco, N. Marbury. **Categories of International Integration,** *India Quarterly* XVI (July-September 1961), 259–69.

Part A. — *General References*

394 Etzioni, Amitai. **Atlantic Union, the Southern Continents, and the United Nations,** *International Conflict and Behavioral Science: The Craigville Papers,* Roger Fisher (ed.). New York, Basic Books, 1964, pp. 179–207.

395 — —. **The Dialectics of Supranational Unification,** *American Political Science Review,* LVI (December 1962), 927–35.

396 — —. **The Epigenesis of Political Communities at the International Level,** *American Journal of Sociology,* LXVIII (January 1963), 407–21.

397 — —. **European Unification: A Strategy of Change,** *World Politics,* XVI (October 1963), 32–51.

398 — —. **A Paradigm for the Study of Political Unification,** *World Politics,* XV (October 1962), 44–74.

399 — —.**Political Unification: A Comparative Study of Leaders and Forces.** New York, Holt, Rinehart and Winston, 1965. xx + 346 p.

400 Fertig, Norman R. **Centripetal Forces in World Order: The Sense of Community,** *Institute of World Affairs Proceedings,* XXXVI (1960), 27–41.

401 Finkelstein, Lawrence S. **New Trends in International Affairs,** *World Politics,* XVIII (October 1965), 117–26.

402 Friedrich, C. J. **New Dimensions of Federalism,** *American Society of International Law Proceedings,* LVII (1963), 238–40.

403 Griffin, Keith and Ffrench-Davis, Ricardo. **Customs Unions and Latin American Integration,** *Journal of Common Market Studies,* IV (October 1965), 1–21.

Part A. — General References

404 Guetzkow, Harold. **Isolation and Collaboration: A Partial Theory of Inter-Nation Relations,** *Journal of Conflict Resolution,* I (March 1957), 48–68.

405 — —. **Multiple Loyalties.** Princeton, Center of International Studies, 1955. 62 p.

406 Haas, Ernst B. **The Challenge of Regionalism,** *International Organization,* XII (Autumn, 1958), 440–58.

407 — —. **International Integration: The European and Universal Process,** *International Organization,* XV (Summer, 1961), 366–92.

408 Haas, Ernst B., and Schmitter, Phillipe C. **Economics and Differential Patterns of Political Integration: Projections About Unity in Latin America,** *International Organization,* XVIII (Autumn, 1964), 705–37.

409 Haviland, H. Field, Jr. **Building a Political Community,** *International Organization,* XVII (Summer, 1963), 733–52.

410 Hoffmann, Stanley. **Discord in Community: The North Atlantic Area As a Partial International System,** *International Organization,* XVII (Summer, 1963), 521–49.

411 Jacob, Philip E., and Toscano, James V. **The Integration of Political Communities.** New York, Lippincott, 1964. x + 314 p.

412 Landecker, Werner S. **The Dynamics of Political Integration in Federal Systems,** *International Social Science Journal,* IV (Spring, 1952), 55–70.

413 — —. **Integration and Group Structure: An Area for Research,** *Social Forces,* XXX (May 1952), 394–400.

414 — —. **The Scope of a Sociology of International Relations,** *Social Forces*, XVII (December 1938), 175—83.

415 — —. **S. Smend's Theory of Integration,** *Social Forces*, XXIX (October 1950), 39—48.

416 — —. **Types of Integration and Their Measurement,** *American Journal of Sociology*, LVI (January 1951), 332—40.

417 Lasswell, Harold D. **World Loyalty,** *The World Community*, Quincy Wright (ed.). Chicago, University of Chicago Press, 1948, pp. 200—25.

Followed by discussion of Q. Wright, C. Hart, K. Young, P. Potter, H. C. Bloch, A. Leiserson, H. Morgenthau, J. Bruner, R. Likert, T. Parsons, M. Mead, C. Hardin, R. McKeon.

418 Linnenberg, Clem C., Jr. **Twixt Chaos and Conformism,** *Perspectives on a Troubled Decade*, Lyman Bryson, Louis Finkelstein and R. M. MacIver (eds.). New York, Harper, 1950, pp. 833—61.

419 Mead, Margaret. **World Culture,** *The World Community*, Quincy Wright (ed.). Chicago, University of Chicago Press, 1948, pp. 47—56.

Followed by discussion of Q. Wright, H. MacNair, K. Polanyi, J. L. Adams, O. Whittlesey, J. Marschak, T. W. Schultz, R. Likert, H. S. Bloch, R. Angell, T. Parsons, W. Riefler, P. Potter, R. McKeon, P. Herring, C. Morris, D. Riesman, L. Gottschalk, K. Young, W. L. Warner, R. Benedict, K. G. Boulding, S. Hughes, J. F. Rippy, L. Wirth, H. Morgenthau.

420 Myrdal, Gunnar. **An International Economy.** New York, Harper, 1956. xi + 381 p.

421 **Organization in the Light of Historical Experience.** Princeton, Princeton University Press, 1957. xiii + 228 p.

422 Rivero, J. **Introduction to a Study of the Development of Federal Societies,** *International Social Science Journal*, IV (Spring, 1952), 5—42.

423 Rohn, Peter N. **Testing Deutsch's Indices of Community,** *American Behavioral Scientist,* III (September 1959), 7—9.

424 Rustow, Dankwart A. **On Deutsch's Indices of Community,** *American Behavioral Scientist,* III (March 1960), 31—32.

425 Scott, James Brown. **The United States of America: A Study in International Organization.** New York, Oxford University Press, 1920. 605 p.

426 Singer, J. David. **Consensus and International Political Integration,** *American Behavioral Scientist,* I (January 1958), 30—33.

427 Stark, W. **Ideologies Around the Problem of World Organisation,** *World Justice,* II (June 1961), 435—44.

428 Van Wagenen, Richard W. **The Concept of Community and the Future of the United Nations,** *International Organization,* XIX (Summer, 1965), 812—27.

429 — —. **International Integration: A Review,** *Journal of Conflict Resolution,* IX (December 1965), 526—31.

430 Wirth, Louis. **World Community, World Society, and World Government: An Attempt at a Clarification of Terms,** *The World Community,* Quincy Wright (ed.). Chicago, University of Chicago Press, 1948, pp. 1—8.

Followed by discussion of K. Young, A. Gérard, R. Angell, Q. Wright, M. Mead, R. Benedict, W. L. Warner, T. Parsons, H. S. Bloch, J. Marschak, R. McKeon, T. W. Schultz, P. Herring, C. Morris, H. Morgenthau, K. Polanyi, D. Riesman.

431 Wright, Quincy. **The Mode of Financing Unions of States as a Measure of Their Degree of Integration,** *International Organization,* XI (Winter, 1957), 30—40.

Size of the budget of a central government as an indicator of the degree of integration among the parts.

432 Wright, Quincy (ed.). **The World Community.** Chicago, University of Chicago Press, 1948. x + 323 p.

A collection of essays followed by a discussion among various scholars.

Part A. — General References

6.1.2 SYSTEM THEORY

See also G4.

433 Alger, Chadwick F. **Comparison of Intranational and International Politics,** *American Political Science Review,* LVII (June 1963), 406–19.

434 — —. **Hypotheses on Relationships Between the Organization of International Society and International Order,** *American Society of International Law Proceedings,* LVII (1963), 36–46.

Comments by D. R. Deener.

435 — —. **The Impact of International Organizations on the Practice of Diplomacy: A Review,** *Journal of Conflict Resolution,* VIII (March 1964), 79–82.

436 — —. **Non-Resolution Consequences of the United Nations and Their Effect on International Conflict,** *Journal of Conflict Resolution,* V (June 1961), 128–45.

437 Aron, Raymond. **Limits to the Powers of the United Nations,** *Annals of the American Academy of Political and Social Science,* CCXCVI (November 1954), 20–6.

438 Barnard, Chester I. **On Planning for World Government,** *Approaches to World Peace,* Lyman Bryson, Louis Finkelstein and Robert W. MacIver (eds.). New York, Harper, 1944, pp. 825–58.

439 Beloff, Max. **National Government and International Government,** *International Organization,* XIII (Autumn, 1959), 538–49.

440 Bloomfield, Lincoln P. **International Force in a Disarming — But Revolutionary — World,** *International Organization,* XVII (Spring, 1963), 444–64.

441 — —. **Law, Politics and International Disputes,** *International Conciliation,* DXVI (January 1958), 257–316.

442 Briggs, Herbert W. **Power Politics and International Organization,** *American Journal of International Law,* XXXIX (October 1945), 664–79.

A historical survey of the influence of state power on interstate arrangement since the Congress of Vienna, with a detailed analysis of UN Charter provisions.

443 Bryce, James. **International Relations.** New York, Macmillan, 1922.

Chapter IX.

444 Buehrig, Edward H. **The International Pattern of Authority,** *World Politics,* XVII (April 1965), 369–85.

445 Burns, C. Delisle. **Authority and Force in the State System,** *Problems of Peace,* Series 8 (1933), 262–82.

446 Carlston, Kenneth S. **Law and Organization in World Society.** Urbana, University of Illinois Press, 1962. 356 p.

447 Claude, Inis L., Jr. **Law and Politics in International Relations: Reflections of a Politics-Oriented Reader on a Law-Oriented Book; A Review,** *Journal of Conflict Resolution,* IV (June 1960), 225–28.

448 — —. **The Management of Power in the Changing United Nations,** *International Organization,* XV (Spring, 1961), 219–35.

449 — —. **Multilateralism — Diplomatic and Otherwise,** *International Organization,* XII (Winter, 1958), 43–52.

450 — —. **United Nations Use of Military Force,** *Journal of Conflict Resolution,* VII (June 1963), 117–29.

Part A. — *General References*

451 Cleveland, Harlan. **Crisis Diplomacy,** *Foreign Affairs*, XLI (July 1963), 638–49.

452 Coplin, William D. **International Law and Assumptions About the State System,** *World Politics*, XVII (July 1965), 615–34.

453 Dorsey, Gray L. **A Porch from Which to View World Organization,** *Foundations of World Organization*, Lyman Bryson, Louis Finkelstein, Harold D. Lasswell, and R. M. MacIver (eds.). New York, Harper, 1950, pp. 259–75.

454 Falk, Richard A. **Law As a Contributor to the Maintenance of a Peaceful World: A Review,** *Journal of Conflict Resolution*, IX (March 1965), 127–38.

455 Fisher, Roger. **Fractionating Conflict,** *International Conflict and Behavioral Science: The Craigville Papers*, Roger Fisher (ed.). New York, Basic Books, 1964, pp. 91–109.

456 Fox, William T. R. **The Management of Power: A Review,** *Journal of Conflict Resolution*, VIII (September 1964), 297–300.

457 Freeman, Harrop A. **Coercion of States in International Organizations.** Philadelphia, Pacifist Research Bureau, 1947. 57 p.

458 Goodrich, Leland M. **The Amount of World Organization Necessary and Possible,** *Yale Law Journal*, LV (August 1946), 950–65.

459 Haas, Ernst B. **Toward Controlling International Change,** *World Politics*, XVII (October 1964), 1–12.

460 Haas, Michael. **A Functional Approach to International Organization,** *Journal of Politics*, XXVII (August 1965), 498–517.

461 Hitchner, Dell G. **The Essentials of International Stability,** *Social Science,* XVIII (April 1943), 72—77.

462 Hoffmann, Stanley. **Erewhon or Lilliput? A Critical View of the Problem,** *International Organization,* XVII (Spring, 1963), 404—25.

463 — —. **The Role of International Organization: Limits and Probabilities,** *International Organization,* X (August 1956), 357—72.

464 — —. **Sisyphus, and the Avalanche: The United Nations, Egypt, and Hungary,** *International Organization,* XI (Summer, 1957), 446—69.

465 Kaplan, Morton A. **Balance of Power, Bipolarity and Other Models of International Systems,** *American Political Science Review,* LI (September 1957), 684—95.

466 — —. **System and Process in International Politics.** New York, Wiley, 1957. xxiv + 283 p.

467 Kaplan, Morton A. and Katzenbach, Nicholas. **The Patterns of International Politics and of International Law,** *American Political Science Review,* LIII (September 1953), 693—712.

468 — —. **The Political Foundations of International Law.** New York, Wiley, 1961. xi + 372 p.

469 Kelsen, Hans. **International Peace — By Court or Government?** *American Journal of Sociology,* XLVI (January 1941), 571—81.

470 Laves, Walter H. C. (ed.). **The Foundations of a More Stable World Order: Symposium.** Chicago, University of Chicago Press, 1941. 193 p.

471 Levi, Werner. **Fundamentals of World Organization.** Minneapolis, University of Minnesota Press, 1950. ix + 233 p.

472 Liska, George. **Continuity and Change in International Systems,** *World Politics,* XVI (October 1963), 118—36.

473 — —. **International Equilibrium: A Theoretical Essay on the Politics and Organization of Security.** Cambridge, Harvard University Press, 1957. 223 p.

474 Luard, David E. T. **Nationality and Wealth: A Study in World Government.** New York, Oxford University Press, 1964. 370 p.

475 — —. **The Growth of World Community,** *Annals of the American Academy of Political and Social Science,* CCCLI (January 1964), 170—79.

476 McKeon, Richard P. **World Community and the Relations of Cultures,** *Perspectives on a Troubled Decade,* Lyman Bryson, Louis Finkelstein and R. M. MacIver (eds.). New York, Harper, 1950, pp. 801—15.

477 Masters, Roger D. **A Multi-Bloc Model of the International System,** *American Political Science Review,* LV (December 1961), 780—98.

478 Morgenthau, Hans J. **International Organization and Foreign Policy,** *Foundations of World Organization,* Lyman Bryson, Louis Finkelstein, Harold D. Lasswell, and R. M. MacIver (eds.). New York, Harper, 1950, pp. 377—81.
Comments by S. Akhilananda, G. L. Dorsey, K. W. Thompson.

479 — —.**The Political Conditions for an International Police Force,** *International Organization,* XVII (Spring, 1963), 393—403.

480 Mowrer, Edgar A. **Profane Thoughts on a Sacred Subject,** *Iowa Law Review,* XXX (May 1945), 521—29.

Part A. — General References

481 Myers, Denys P. **The Bases of International Relations,** *American Journal of International Law,* XXXI (July 1937), 431—48.

Advocates "balance of Interest" over "balance of power."

482 Myrdal, Gunnar. **Realties and Illusions in Regard to Inter-Governmental Organisations.** London, Oxford University Press, 1955. 28 p.

483 Niemeyer, Gerhart. **Law Without Force: The Function of Politics in International Law.** Princeton, Princeton University Press, 1941. 408 p.

484 — —. **A Query About Assumptions on International Organization,** *World Politics,* VII (January 1955), 337—47.

485 — —. **Relevant and Irrelevant Doctrines Concerning International Relations,** *World Politics,* IV (January 1952), 282—92.

486 Parsons, Talcott. **Order and Community in the International Social System,** *International Politics and Foreign Policy,* James N. Rosenau (ed.). New York, Free Press, 1961, pp. 120—29.

487 — —. **Polarization of the World and International Order,** *Preventing World War III: Some Proposals,* Quincy Wright, William M. Evan, and Morton Deutsch (eds.). New York, Simon and Schuster, 1962, pp. 310—32.

488 — —. **The Power Bank: Notes on the Problem of World Order,** *Disarmament and Arms Control,* II (Summer, 1964), 317—30.

489 Pilotti, Massimo. **Les unions d'états,** *Recueil des Cours,* XXIV (1928) 445—545.

Classifies types of unions or associations between states and the distinguishing causal factors that determine types of unions.

490 Potter, Pitman B. **An Introduction to the Study of International Organization.** 4th ed. New York, Appleton-Century, 1935.

Chapters XII—XIV.

Part A. — General References

491 — —. **The Logic of International Relations and Organization,** *American Political Science Review*, XLIV (September 1950), 661–69.

492 — —. **World Institutions,** *The World Community*, Quincy Wright (ed.). Chicago, University of Chicago Press, 1948, pp. 259–66.

Comments by Q. Wright, H. Morgenthau, L. Gottschalk, J. Marschak, R. McKeon, H. Bloch, M. Mead, R. Likert, K. Polanyi, J. F. Rippy, T. Parsons, D. Riesman, R. Angell, H. Lasswell, H. Emmerich, H. S. Hughes, J. Bruner, J. L. Adams.

493 Riggs, Fred W. **International Relations As Prismatic System,** *The International System: Theoretical Essays*, Klaus Knorr and Sidney Verba (eds.). Princeton, Princeton University Press, 1961, pp. 144–81.

494 Rosecrance, Richard N. **Action and Reaction in World Politics: International Systems in Perspective.** Boston, Little, Brown, 1963. xxi + 314 p.

495 Rothwell, Charles Easton. **International Organization and World Politics,** *International Organization*, III (November 1949), 605–19.

496 Russell, Frank M. **Theories of International Relations.** New York, Appleton-Century, 1936.

Chapter XXIII.

497 Russell, Ruth B. **The Management of Power and Political Organization: Some Observations on Inis L. Claude's Conceptual Approach,** *International Organization*, XV (Autumn, 1961), 630–36.

498 Russett, Bruce M. **Toward a Model of Competitive International Politics,** *Journal of Politics*, XXV (February 1963), 226–47.

499 — —. **Trends in World Politics.** New York, Macmillan, 1965. 156 p.

500 Schelling, Thomas C. **Strategic Problems of an International Armed Force,** *International Organization*, XVII (Spring, 1963), 465–85.

Part A. — *General References*

501 Spencer, Arthur W. **The Organization of International Force,** *American Journal of International Law*, IX (January 1915), 45—71.

502 Thompson, Kenneth W. **Theory-Making in International Politics: A Review of George Liska, International Equilibrium; A Theoretical Essay on the Politics and Organization of Security,** *Journal of Conflict Resolution*, II (June 1958), 188—93.

503 Timm, Charles A. and Myers, S. D., Jr. **Basic Processes of International Government.** Dallas, Arnold Foundation, Southern Methodist University, 1937. 42 p.

504 Tucker, Robert W. **A Review of Morton A. Kaplan and Nicholas de B. Katzenbach, The Political Foundations of International Law,** *Journal of Conflict Resolution*, VII (March 1963), 69—75.

505 Waltz, Kenneth N. **Contention and Management in International Relations,** *World Politics*, XVII (July 1965), 720—44.

506 Wright, Quincy. **International Conflict and the United Nations,** *World Politics*, X (October 1957), 24—48.

507 — —. **A Review of Victor H. Wallace, Paths to Peace: A Study of War, Its Causes and Prevention,** *Journal of Conflict Resolution*, II (December 1958), 348—54.

6.2 EMPIRICAL RESEARCH

6.2.1 ROLL CALL ANALYSIS AND BLOC VOTING

508 Alker, Hayward R., Jr. **Dimensions of Conflict in the General Assembly,** *American Political Science Review*, LVIII (September 1964), 642—57.

509 — —. **Supranationalism in the United Nations,** *Peace Research Society, Papers*, III (1965), 197—212.

Part A. — General References

510 Alker, Hayward R., Jr. and Russett, Bruce M. **World Politics in the General Assembly.** New Haven, Yale University Press, 1965. xxvi + 326 p.

511 Anabtawi, Samir N. **The Afro-Asian States and the Hungarian Question,** *International Organization,* XVII (Autumn, 1963), 872—900.

512 Appleton, Sheldon. **The Eternal Triangle? Communist China, the United States and the United Nations.** East Lansing, Michigan State University Press, 1961. 264 p.

513 Ball, M. Margaret. **Bloc Voting in the General Assembly,** *International Organization,* V (February 1951), 3—31.

514 Goodwin, Geoffrey. **The Expanding United Nations: Voting Patterns,** *International Affairs,* XXXVI (April 1960), 174—87.

Caucusing groups.

515 Gregg, Robert W. **The Latin American Bloc in United Nations Elections,** *Southwestern Social Science Quarterly,* XLVI (September 1965), 146—54.

516 Haas, Ernst B. and Merkl, Peter H. **Parliamentarians Against Ministers: The Case of Western European Union,** *International Organization,* XIV (Winter, 1960), 37—59.

517 Hovet, Thomas, Jr. **Africa in the United Nations.** Evanston, Northwestern University Press, 1963. 336 p.

518 — —. **Bloc Politics in the United Nations.** Cambridge, Harvard University Press, 1960. 197 p.

519 Jack, Homer A. **Nonalignment and a Test Ban Agreement: The Role of the Nonaligned States,** *Journal of Conflict Resolution,* VII (September 1963), 542—52.

520 Lijphart, Arend. **The Analysis of Bloc Voting in the General Assembly: A Critique and a Proposal,** *American Political Science Review*, LVII (December 1963), 902—17.

521 Merkl, Peter H. **European Assembly Parties and National Delegations,** *Journal of Conflict Resolution*, VIII (March 1964), 50—64.

522 Padelford, Norman J. **Elections in the United Nations General Assembly: A Study in Political Behavior.** Cambridge, Massachusetts Institute of Technology, Center for International Studies, 1959. 72 p.

523 Rieselbach, Leroy N. **Quantitative Techniques for Studying Voting Behavior in the United Nations General Assembly,** *International Organization*, XVI (Spring, 1960), 291—306.

524 Rowe, Edward T. **The Emerging Anti-Colonial Consensus in the United Nations,** *Journal of Conflict Resolution*, VIII (September 1964), 209—30.

525 Triska, Jan and Koch, Howard E., Jr. **The Asian-African Nations and International Organization: Third Force or Collective Impotence?** *Review of Politics*, XXI (April 1959), 416—55.

6.2.2 STATISTICAL AND SYSTEMATIC CASE STUDIES

526 Deutsch, Karl W. **Nationalism and Social Communication: An Inquiry into the Foundations of Nationality.** New York, Wiley, 1953. x + 292 p.

527 Dravis, Irving B. and Davenport, W. S. **The Political Arithmetic of International Burden-Sharing,** *Journal of Political Economy*, LXXI (August 1963), 309—30.

A consideration of whether the United States finances international projects disproportionately.

528 Ellis, William W. and Salzberg, John. **Africa and the United Nations: A Statistical Note,** *American Behavioral Scientist*, VIII (April 1965), 30—32.

529 Goodrich, Leland M. **The UN Security Council,** *International Organization,* XII (Summer, 1958), 273–87.

530 Haas, Ernst B. **System and Process in the International Labor Organization: A Statistical Afterthought,** *World Politics,* XIV (January 1962), 322–52.

531 Hogan, Warren P. **Economic Relationships and the SEATO Powers,** *SEATO: Six Studies,* George Modelski (ed.). Melbourne, Cheshire, 1962, pp. 253–88.

532 Mayne, Richard. **Economic Integration in the New Europe: A Statistical Approach,** *Daedalus,* XCIII (Winter, 1964), 109–33.

533 Peterson, Keith S. **The Agendas of the United Nations General Assembly: A Content Analysis,** *Southwestern Social Science Quarterly,* XXXIX (December 1958), 232–41.

534 Rohn, Peter N. **Testing Deutsch's Indices of Community,** *American Behavioral Scientist,* III (September 1959), 7–9.

535 Rosenne, Shabtai. **The International Court and United Nations: Reflections on the Period 1946–1954,** *International Organization,* IX (May 1955), 244–56.

536 Russett, Bruce M. **Trends in World Politics.** New York, Macmillan, 1965. 156 p.

537 Singer, Marshall R. and Sensenig, Barton, III. **Elections Within the United Nations: An Experimental Study Utilizing Statistical Analysis,** *International Organization,* XVII (Autumn, 1963), 901–25.

538 Stratton, George M. **Is World Peace an Attainable Deal?** *Problems of War and Peace in the Society of Nations,* University of California International Relations Committee (ed.). Berkeley, University of California Press, 1937, pp. 129—55.

539 Teune, Henry and Synnestvedt, Sig. **Measuring International Alignments,** Philadelphia, University of Pennsylvania Foreign Policy Research Institute, 1965. 31 p.

540 Watkins, James T., IV. **Democracy and International Organization: The Experience of the League of Nations,** *American Political Science Review,* XXXVI (December 1942), 1136—41.

6.2.3 SURVEY RESEARCH AND OBSERVATIONAL TECHNIQUES

541 Abrams, Mark. **British Elite Attitudes and the European Common Market,** *Public Opinion Quarterly,* XXIX (Summer, 1965) 236—46.

542 Alger, Chadwick F. **Personal Contact in Intergovernmental Organizations,** *International Behavior,* Herbert C. Kelman (ed.). New York, Holt, Rinehart and Winston, 1965, pp. 523—47.

543 — —. **United Nations Participation As a Learning Experience,** *Public Opinion Quarterly,* XXVII (Fall, 1963), 411—26.

544 Appleton, Sheldon. **The Eternal Triangle? Communist China, the United States and the United Nations.** East Lansing, Michigan State University Press, 1961. 264 p.

545 Bie, Pierre de. **Certain Psychological Aspects of Benelux,** *International Social Science Journal,* III (Autumn, 1951), 540—52.

546 Buchanan, William, Krugman, Herbert E., and Van Wagenen, R. W. **An International Police Force and Public Opinion: Polled Opinion in the United States, 1939—1953.** Princeton, Center for Research on World Political Institutions, n. d. 39 p.

547 Congalton, A. A. and Kitton, M. J. **Public Opinion and the United Nations.** Wellington, Victoria University College, Department of Psychology, 1965. 84 p.

548 Gallup International. **Public Opinion and the European Community,** *Journal of Common Market Studies,* II (December 1963), 101–26.

549 Guetzkow, Harold. **Multiple Loyalties: Theoretical Approach to a Problem in International Organization.** Princeton, Center of International Studies, 1955. 62 p.

550 Herberichs, Gerard. **Is There No European Opinion?** *American Behavioral Scientist,* III (December 1959), 3–9.

Reprinted from *Internationale Spectator,* July 8, 1959.

551 Klineberg, Otto. **Some Experiences with International Organizations and International Conferences,** *Foundations of World Organization,* Lyman Bryson, Louis Finkelstein, Harold D. Lasswell, and R. M. MacIver (eds.). New York, Harper, 1950, pp. 281–88.

552 Kriesberg, L. **German Businessmen and Union Leaders and the Schuman Plan,** *Social Science,* XXXV (April 1960), 114–21.

553 — —. **German Public Opinion and the European Coal and Steel Community,** *Public Opinion Quarterly,* XXIII (Spring, 1959), 28–42.

554 Lentz, Theodore F. **Public Opinion Research for Peace: A Review and Discussion,** *Journal of Conflict Resolution,* IV (June 1960), 234–42.

555 Lerner, Daniel. **Britain Faces the Continent,** *Virginia Quarterly Review,* XXXIX (Winter, 1963), 12–25.

556 — —. **French Business Leaders Look at EDC: A Preliminary Report,** Public Opinion Quarterly, XX (Spring, 1956), 212–20.

557 Lerner, Daniel and Kramer, Marguerite N. **French Elite Perspective on the United Nations,** *International Organization,* XVII (Winter, 1963), 54–75.

558 Leslie, G. and Berry, B. **Note on Attitudes Toward the United Nations: An Experiment in Social Change,** *Social Forces,* XXXI (October 1953), 87—90.

559 McClintock, Charles G. and Hekhuis, Dale J. **European Community Deterrence: Its Organization, Utility, and Political Feasibility,** *Journal of Conflict Resolution,* V (September 1961), 230—53.

560 Roper, Elmo. **American Attitudes on World Organization,** *Public Opinion Quarterly,* XVII (Fall, 1953), 405—20.

Introduction by Thomas K. Finletter and comments by F. W. Abrams, N. Cousins, P. G. Hoffmann, R. M. Hutchins, O. B. Lord, R. Niebuhr, O. S. Roberts.

561 — —.**How Isolationist Is America Today?** *Atlantic Community Quarterly,* I (Winter, 1963—64), 486—94.

562 Schwarzenberger, Georg. **An Analysis of the Replies to Our Questionnaire on the** *de facto* **Revision of the Covenant,** *World Affairs,* IV (June 1938), 60—74.

563 Scott, William A. **Correlates of International Attitudes,** *Public Opinion Quarterly,* XXII (Winter, 1958), 464—72.

564 Scott, William A. and Withey, Stephen B. **The United States and the United Nations: The Public View.** New York, Manhattan, 1958. 314 p.

565 Star, S. and Hughes, H. **Report on an Educational Campaign: The Cincinnati Plan for the United Nations,** *American Journal of Sociology,* LX (January 1950), 389—400.

566 Torre, Mottram. **Psychiatric Observations of International Conferences,** *International Journal of Social Psychiatry,* I (1955), 48—50.

Part B.

EARLY INTERNATIONAL ORGANIZATIONS

Part B. — *Early International Organizations*

Ordinarily one thinks of international organization as flowering only with the establishment of the League of Nations after World War I. Nevertheless, the long history of institutionalized cooperation among states and peoples probably began as the ancient empires of the Near East grew to the point where their borders touched, trade flowed, and wars were on occasion waged. Whenever international aggression became unusually destructive or was perceived as irrational, plans for a different way of organizing the world arose.

1. EARLY INTERNATIONAL STRUCTURES

Unlike national political systems, which ordinarily have exhibited increasing levels of political control over their domain up to modern times, international systems have retrogressed from the well organized empires of early civilizations to the present era of fragmentation into a large number of sovereign states. A survey of organizational efforts in the earliest period of international history may, therefore, be instructive insofar as conditions for the success of inter-nation structures must have been present.

I.I CLASSICAL CIVILIZATIONS: PERSIA, GREECE, ROME, ETC.

567   Aymard, André. **Les assemblées de la Confédération Achaienne: étude critique d'institutions et d'histoire.** Bordeaux, Féret, 1938. 450 p.

568   Boak, A. E. R. **Greek Interstate Associations and the League of Nations,** *American Journal of International Law,* XV (July 1921), 375–83.

569   Bozeman, Adda B. **Politics and Culture in International History,** Princeton, Princeton University Press, 1960. xiii + 560 p.

570   Brinton, Crane. **From Many One.** Cambridge, Harvard University Press, 1948.
Chapter I.

571 Burnett, Edmund Cody. **The Government of Federal Territories in Europe,** *American Historical Association Annual Report,* I (1896), 393–454.

A description and analysis of the federations of ancient Greece, Switzerland, and the Netherlands.

572 Caldwell, Wallace E. **Hellenic Conceptions of Peace.** New York, Columbia University Press, 1919. 140 p.

573 Ferguson, W. S. **The Delian Amphictyony,** *Classical Review,* XVI (February 1901), 38–40.

574 Fling, Fred Morrow. **A Source Book of Greek History.** Boston, Heath, 1907. xiii + 370 p.

See especially chapters III, VI, and XIII, which contain material on the various leagues.

575 Freeman, Edward A. **History of Federal Government in Greece and Italy.** 2d ed. New York, Macmillan, 1893. 692 p.

The first and only volume of Mr. Freeman's *History of Federal Government* appeared in 1863 under the title *History of Federal Government from the Foundation of the Achaian League to the Disruption of the United States.* The above title is merely a reprint of the older volume, with the addition of a new chapter on Italy, and a new fragment on Germany.

576 Grady, Eleanor H. **Epigraphic Sources of the Delphic Amphictyony.** Walton, N. Y., Reporter, 1931, 127 p.

577 Hadas, Moses. **Federalism in Antiquity,** *Approaches to World Peace,* Lyman Bryson, Louis Finkelstein and Robert W. MacIver (eds.). New York, Harper, 1944, pp. 27–40.

Followed by comments of S. J. Case, C. N. Cochrane, W. S. Ferguson, A. D. Nock.

578 Hamilton, Alexander, Madison, James, and Jay, John. **The Federalist Papers.** New York, Anchor, 1961. xxvii + 328 p.

Paper XII, by Hamilton, discusses the Amphyctionic, Achaean, and other institutions analogous to the confederacy in the United States.

Part B. — Early International Organizations

579 Hart, Albert B. **Introduction to the Study of Federal Government.** Boston, Ginn, 1891.

Chapter II.

580 Jones, H. Stuart. **Administration,** *The Legacy of Rome*, Cyril Bailey (ed.). Oxford, Clarendon, 1923, pp. 91–139.

581 Joyce, James Avery. **The Story of International Cooperation.** New York, Watts, 1964.

Chapter II.

582 — —. **World in the Making.** New York, Schuman, 1953.

Chapter II.

583 Laidlaw, William Allison. **A History of Delos.** Oxford, Blackwell, 1933. 308 p.

584 Lange, Christian L. **Histoire de l'internationalisme.** New York, Putnam, 1919.

Chapter I.

585 Lewis, V. J. **The Peloponnesian League,** *New Commonwealth*, I (March 1953), 10.

586 Maine, Henry Sumner. **Lectures on the Early History of Institutions (A Sequel to "Ancient Law").** New York, Holt, 1888. viii + 412 p.

587 Niccolini, Giovanni. **La Confederazione Achaea.** Pavia, Mattei, 1914. 348 p.

588 Olmstead, A. T. **Assyrian Government of Dependencies,** *American Political Science Review*, XII (February 1917), 63–77.

589 Perris, G. H. **A Short History of War and Peace.** New York, Holt, 1911.
Chapter IV.

590 Polybius. **The Histories,** W. R. Patton (trans.). London, Heinemann, 1922–27. 6 vols.

591 Potter, Pitman B. **This World of Nations.** York, Macmillan, 1929.
Chapter I.

592 Rostovtseff, Michael I. **The Hellenistic World and Its Economic Development,** *American Historical Review,* XLI (January 1936), 231–52.

593 — —. **International Relations in the Ancient World,** *The History and Nature of International Relations,* Edmund A. Walsh. (ed.). New York, Macmillan, 1922, pp. 31–65.

594 Russell, Frank M. **Theories of International Relations.** New York, Appleton-Century, 1936.
Chapters IV–V.

595 Schuman, Frederick L. **International Politics.** 6th ed. New York, McGraw-Hill, 1958.
Chapter I.

596 Sidgwick, Henry. **The Development of European Polity.** London, Macmillan, 1903.
Chapter IX.

597 Tarn, William W. **Alexander the Great and the Unity of Mankind,** *Proceedings* (British Academy), XIX (1933), 123–66.

598 Ténékidès, George. **International Law and Federal Communities in the Greece of the Cities,** *Recueil des Cours,* XC (1956), 469–649.

Part B. — Early International Organizations

599 Thucydides. **The History of the Peloponnesian War,** David Green (ed.), Thomas Hobbes (tr.); introduction by Bertrand de Jouvenel. Ann Arbor, University of Michigan Press, 1959. 2 vols.

600 Tod, Marcus N. **International Arbitration Amongst the Greeks.** Oxford, Clarendon, 1913. xii + 196 p.

601 Toynbee, A. J. and Marston, F. S. **Alexander and Hellenism,** *The Evolution of World-Peace*, Francis S. Marvin (ed.). London, Oxford University Press, 1921, pp. 15—24.

602 Vinogradoff, Paul. **The Work of Rome,** *The Evolution of World-Peace*. Francis S. Marvin (ed.). London, Oxford University Press, 1921, pp. 25—42.

603 Wallbank, Frank Williams. **Aratos of Sicyon.** Cambridge, Cambridge University Press, 1933. 222 p.

604 West, Allen B. **The Tribute Lists of the Delian League,** *American Historical Review*, XXXV (January 1930), 267—75.

605 Williams, Marie V. **Internationalism in Ancient Greece,** *London Quarterly Review*, CLVI (July 1931), 12—18.

606 York, Elizabeth. **Leagues of Nations: Ancient, Mediaeval, and Modern.** London, Swarthmore, 1919. 337 p.

607 Zimmern, Alfred. **The Greek Commonwealth: Politics and Economics in Fifth-Century Athens.** New York, Modern Library, 1956. 487 p.

Part B. — *Early International Organizations*

1.2 ANCIENT CHINA

608   Dubs, Homer H. **The Concept of Unity in China** *The Quest for Political Unity in World History*, Stanley Pargellis (ed.). Washington, Government Printing Office, 1944, pp. 3—19.

609   Russell, Frank M. **Theories of International Relations.** New York, Appleton-Century, 1936.

   Chapters II—III.

610   Walker, Richard L. **The Multi-State System of Ancient China.** Hamden, Shoe-String, 1954. xii + 135 p.

1.3 CATHOLIC CHURCH AND THE MIDDLE AGES

611   Berber, F. J. **International Aspects of the Holy Roman Empire,** *Indian Year Book of International Affairs*, XIII, 2 (1964), 174—83.

612   Brinton, Crane. **From Many One.** Cambridge, Harvard University Press, 1948.

   Chapter II.

613   Davis, H. W. E. **Innocent the Third and the Mediaeval Church,** *The Evolution of World-Peace*, ed. Francis S. Marvin. London, Oxford University Press, 1921, pp. 43—63.

614   Gruber, John. **The Peace Negotiations of the Avignon Popes,** *Catholic Historical Review*, XIX (July 1933), 190—99.

615   Hart, Albert B. **Introduction to the Study of Federal Government.** Boston, Ginn, 1891.

   Chapter III.

Part B. — Early International Organizations

616 Hayes, Carlton J. H. **Medieval Diplomacy,** *The History and Nature of International Relations,* Edmund A. Walsh (ed.). New York, Macmillan, 1922, pp. 69—89.

617 Hudson, Cyril E. **The Church and International Affairs,** *International Affairs,* XXIII (January 1947), 1—10.

618 Joyce, James A. **The Story of International Cooperation.** New York, Watts, 1964.

Chapter III.

619 — —. **World in the Making.** New York, Schuman, 1953.

Chapter III.

620 Kantorowicz, Ernst H. **The Problem of Medieval World Unity,** *The Quest for Political Unity in World History,* Stanley Pargellis (ed.). Washington, Government Printing Office, 1944, pp. 31—37.

621 Krey, August C. **The International State of the Middle Ages: Some Reasons for Its Failure,** *American Historical Review,* XXVIII (October 1928), 1—12.

622 Lange, Christian L. **Histoire de l'internationalisme.** New York, Putnam, 1919.

Chapters II—III.

623 Latourette, Kenneth S. **Anno Domini: Jesus, History, and God.** 3d ed. New York, Harper, 1940. 248 p.

624 MacKinney, Loren C. **The People and Public Opinion in the Eleventh-Century Peace Movement,** *Speculum,* V (April 1930), 181—206.

625 Odescalchi, Edmond P. **The First Supranational World Government,** *Midwest Quarterly,* V (April 1964), 213—22.

626 Paradisi, Bruno. **International Law and Social Structure of the Middle Ages,** *Indian Year Book of International Affairs,* XIII, 2 (1964), 148 –73.

627 Roemer, William F. and Ellis, John Tracy. **The Catholic Church and Peace Efforts.** New York, Paulist Press, 1934. 63 p.

Peace efforts of the Church in the Middle Ages, history of papal arbitration.

628 Russell, Frank M. **Theories of International Relations.** New York, Appleton-Century, 1936.

Chapter VI.

629 Strayer, Joseph R. **Western Europe in the Middle Ages.** New York, Appleton-Century-Crofts, 1955. 245 p.

630 Wright, Robert F. **Medieval Internationalism: The Contribution of the Medieval Church to International Law and Peace.** London, Williams and Norgate, 1930. 240 p.

631 Wulf, Maurice de. **The Society of Nations in the Thirteenth Century,** *International Journal of Ethics,* XXIX (January 1919), 210–29.

632 Zimmermann, Michel. **La crise de l'organisation internationale à la fin du moyen-age,** *Recueil des Cours,* XLIV (1933), 319–437.

1.4 COMMERCIAL LEAGUES: THE HANSA AND OTHER EFFORTS

633 Cramer, Frederick H. **The Hanseatic League,** *Current History,* New Series, XVII (August 1949), 84–89.

634 Daenell, Ernst. **The Policy of the German Hanseatic League Respecting the Mercantile Marine,** *American Historical Review,* XV (October 1909), 47–53.

Part B. — Early International Organizations

635 Hart, Albert B. **Introduction to the Study of Federal Government.** Boston, Ginn, 1891.

   Chapter III.

636 Nash, E. Gee. **The Hansa: Its History and Romance.** New York, Dodd, Mead, 1929. 279 p.

637 Palais, Hyman. **England's First Attempt to Break the Commercial Monopoly of the Hanseatic League, 1377—1380,** *American Historical Review*, LXIV (July 1959), 852—65.

638 Robertson, J. M. **The Evolution of States.** New York, Putnam, 1913.

   Part V — Chapter III.

639 Walford, Cornelius. **An Outline History of the Hanseatic League, More Particularly in Its Bearing upon English Commerce,** *Transactions* (Royal Historical Society), Series 2, VII (1881), 82—136.

640 Westergaard, Waldemar. **The Hansa Towns and Scandinavia on the Eve of Swedish Independence,** *Journal of Modern History*, IV (September 1932), 349—60.

641 Winter, William L. **Netherland Regionalism and the Decline of the Hansa,** *American Historical Review*, LIII (January 1948), 279—87.

642 Zimmern, Helen. **The Hansa Towns.** London, Unwin, 1902. xvii + 289 p.

Part B. — Early International Organizations

2. PHILOSOPHIC PROPOSALS FOR INTERNATIONAL ORGANIZATION

With the rise of the nation state system, and the decline in influence of the papacy and the Holy Roman Empire, war ravaged Europe. Many thinkers offered the remedy of international organization, and their proposals did much to inspire later generations.

2.1 GENERAL DISCUSSIONS

643 Beales, A.C.F. **The History of Peace.** New York, Dial, 1931. viii + 355 p.

644 Cartwright, John K. **Contributions of the Papacy to International Peace,** *Catholic Historical Review*, VIII (April 1928), 157—68.

645 Darby, William Evans. **Some European Leagues of Peace,** *Transactions* (Grotius Society), IV (1918), 169—95.

646 Dupuis, Charles. **Les antecedents de la Société des Nations,** *Recueil des Cours*, LX (1937), 5—108.

647 Guerry, Emile M. **Popes and World Government,** Gregory J. Roettger (tr.), Foreword by Paul Émile Léger. Baltimore, Helicon, 1964. xvi + 254 p.

648 Harley, John Eugene. **From Achaean League to United Nations: Summary of Proposals and Efforts for International Cooperation and Peace,** *World Affairs Quarterly*, XIII (October 1942), 336—56.

649 Hemleben, Sylvester J. **Plans for World Peace Through Six Centuries.** Chicago, University of Chicago Press, 1943. xiv + 227 p.

Part B. — Early International Organizations

650 Hicks, Frederick C. **The Literature of Abortive Schemes of World Organization,** *American Library Institute: Papers and Proceedings,* 1919, pp. 160—78.

651 Hinsley, Francis H. **Power and the Pursuit of Peace.** Cambridge, Cambridge University Press, 1963.

Chapters I—II.

652 Hode, Jacques. **L'idée de fédération internationale dans l'historie.** Paris, Editions de la Vie Universitaire, 1921. 292 p.

653 Jaszi, Oscar. **World Organization for Durable Peace,** *Foundations of World Organization,* Lyman Bryson, Louis Finkelstein, Harold D. Lasswell, and R. M. MacIver (eds.). New York, Harper, 1950, pp. 21—52.

654 Joyce, James Avery. **The Story of International Cooperation.** New York, Watts, 1964.

Chapter VI.

655 — —. **World in the Making.** New York, Schuman, 1953.

Chapter VI.

656 Knowles, G. W. **Quakers and Peace.** London, Sweet and Maxwell, 1927. 52 p.

Introduction, bibliography on the Quaker movement, with selections from the writings of Fox, Pennington, Barclay, Penn, Gordon, Dymond, Grubb, Neatby.

657 Lange, Christian L. **Histoire de l'internationalisme.** New York, Putnam, 1919. 506 p.

658 Ledermann, Laslo. **Les précurseurs de l'organisation internationale,** Neuchâtel, Editions de la Baconnière, 1945. 177 p.

659 Levermore, Charles H. **Synopsis of Plans for International Organization,** *Advocate of Peace,* LXXXI (July 1919), 216—25; (August 1919), 252—66.

Part B. — Early International Organizations

660 Marriott, John A. **Commonwealth or Anarchy? A Survey of Projects of Peace from the Sixteenth to the Twentieth Century.** New York, Columbia University Press, 1939. 227 p.

661 Mathieu, Marie Henry Jean. **Evolution de l'idée de Société des Nations.** Nancy, Lorraine, Rigot, 1923. 268 p.

662 Matthews, Mary Alice. **Peace Projects: Select List of References on Plans for the Preservation of Peace from Medieval Times to the Present Day.** Washington, Carnegie, 1936. 60 p.

663 Meulen, Jacob ter. **Der Gedanke der Internationalen Organisation in Seiner Entwicklung.** Vol. I. Hague, Nijhoff, 1917. xi + 397 p.

664 Morrow, Dwight W. **The Society of Free States.** New York, Harper, 1919.
Chapter II.

665 Paullin, Theodore. **Comparative Peace Plans.** Philadelphia, Pacifist Research Bureau, 1943. 87 p.

666 Russell, Frank M. **The Growth of the Idea of International Organization,** *Contemporary World Politics*, Francis J. Brown, Charles Hodges and Joseph S. Roucek (eds.). New York, Wiley, 1939, pp. 377—91.

667 — —. **Theories of International Relations.** New York, Appleton-Century, 1936.
Chapters IX—X.

668 Sacks, Benjamin. **Peace Plans of the Seventeenth and Eighteenth Centuries.** Sandoval, N. M., Coronado Press, 1962. 108 p.

669 Schrader, Charles S. **The Concept of World Unity in Patristic Literature During the First Five Centuries,** *The Quest for Political Unity in World History*, Stanley Pargellis (ed.). Washington, Government Printing Office, 1944, pp. 21—29.

Part B. — Early International Organizations

670 Schuman, Frederick L. **The Commonwealth of Man: An Inquiry Into Power Politics and World Government.** New York, Knopf, 1952. 494 p.

671 Souleyman, Elizabeth V. **The Vision of World Peace in Seventeenth and Eighteenth Century France.** New York, Putnam, 1941. 232 p.

672 Stawell, Florence M. **Growth of International Thought.** London, Butterworth, 1929. 251 p.

673 Talbott, E. Guy. **The Need for World Organization,** *World Affairs Quarterly,* XI (October 1940), 287—95.

Contains a listing of historic precedents beginning with the Achaean League through the British Commonwealth, as well as a listing of historic proposals for world organization.

674 Tansill, Charles C. **Early Plans for World Peace,** *Historical Outlook,* XX (November 1929), 321—24.

675 Telfer, Vera. **Catholic Projects for a League of Nations,** *Catholic World,* CXX (October 1924), 73—80.

676 Trueblood, Benjamin F. **The Development of the Peace Idea, and Other Essays.** Introduction by Edwin D. Mead. Boston, Plimpton, 1932. xxviii + 243 p.

677 Wagar, W. Warren. **The City of Man: Prophecies of a World Civilization in Twentieth Century Thought.** Boston, Houghton, Mifflin, 1963. 310 p.

678 Waltz, Kenneth N. **Man, the State and War: A Theoretical Analysis.** New York, Columbia University Press, 1959. viii + 263 p.

679 Wright, Quincy. **Empires and World Governments Before 1918,** *Current History,* New Series, XXXIX (August 1960), 65—74.

680 Wynner, Edith, and Lloyd, Georgia. **Searchlight on Peace Plans.** New York, Dutton, 1944. 532 p.

2.2 PARTICULAR THINKERS

2.2.1 ALBERONI (1664–1752)

681 Alberoni, Giulio. **Cardinal Alberoni's Scheme for Reducing the Turkish Empire to Obedience of Christian Princes; and for a Partition of the Conquest Together with a Scheme of Perpetual Dyet for Establishing the Publick Tranquility,** *American Journal of International Law,* VII (January 1913), 83–107.

682 Darby, William E. **Cardinal Alberoni's Proposed European Alliance for the Subjugation and Settlement of the Turkish Empire, 1735,** *Transactions* (Grotius Society), V (1919), 71–81.

683 Vesnitch, M. R. **Cardinal Alberoni: An Italian Precursor of Pacifism and International Arbitration,** *American Journal of International Law,* VII (January 1913), 51–82.

2.2.2 AQUINAS (1225–1274)

684 Hutchins, Robert M. **St. Thomas and the World State.** Milwaukee, Marquette University Press, 1945. 53 p.

2.2.3 ARISTOTLE (384–322 B. C.)

685 Lyon, Peter. **Aristotle and the Commonwealth of Nations,** *Australian Outlook,* XVII (April 1963), 74–84.

2.2.4 AUGUSTINE (354–430)

686 Wright, Herbert F. **St. Augustine on World Peace,** *Catholic World,* CV (September 1917), 744–53.

2.2.5 BELLERS (1654—1725)

687   Fry, A. Ruth. **John Bellers, 1654—1725: Quaker, Economist and Social Reformer.** London, Cassell, 1935. xi + 174 p.

2.2.6 BENTHAM (1748—1832)

688   Bentham, Jeremy. **Plan for an Universal and Perpetual Peace.** Introduction by C. John Colombos. London, Sweet and Maxwell, 1927. 44 p.

689   Hinsley, Francis H. **Power and the Pursuit of Peace.** Cambridge, Cambridge University Press, 1963.
      Chapter V.

690   Wallas, Graham. **Jeremy Bentham,** *Political Science Quarterly,* XXXVIII (March 1923), 45—56.

2.2.7 CRUCÉ (1590—1648)

691   Crucé, Emeric. **The New Cyneas of Emeric Crucé,** T. W. Balch (ed. and trans.). Philadelphia, Allen, Lane, and Scott, 1909. 363 p.

2.2.8 DANTE (1265—1321)

692   Dante, Alighieri. **De Monarchia.** Edited with an introduction by W. A. V. Reade. Oxford, Clarendon, 1916. 376 p.

693   — —. **On World Government,** H. W. Schneider (trans.). 2d. rev. ed. New York, Liberal Arts, 1957. 80 p.

694   Ragg, Lonsdale, **Dante and a League of Nations,** *Anglo-Italian Review,* II (December 1918), 327—35.

2.2.9 DUBOIS (1250–1312)

695 Brandt, Walther I. **Pierre Dubois: Modern or Medieval?** *American Historical Review*, XXXV (April 1930), 507–21.

696 Dubois, Pierre. **The Recovery of the Holy Land,** Walter Brandt (trans.). New York, Columbia University Press, 1956. 281 p.

697 Knight, William S. M. **A Mediaeval Pacifist — Pierre Du Bois,** *Transactions* (Grotius Society) IX (1923), 1–15.
Comments by Sir Alfred Hopkinson, A. J. Jacobs, Manfred Nathan, H. H. Bellot.

2.2.10 GARGAZ (ca. 1780)

698 Gargaz, Pierre A. **A Project of Universal and Perpetual Peace, Written by Pierre André Gargaz, a Former Galley-Slave, and Printed by Benjamin Franklin at Passy in the Year 1782.** G. S. Eddy (trans.). New York, Eddy, 1922. 173 p.

2.2.11 GROTIUS (1583–1645)

699 Clark, G. N. **Grotius and International Law,** *The Evolution of World-Peace.* Francis S. Marvin (ed.). London, Oxford University Press, 1921, pp. 64–90.

700 Grotius, Hugo. **De jure belli ac pacis.** Trans., with an introduction by W. S. M. Knight. London, Sweet and Maxwell, 1922. 84 p.

701 Mandere, Henri C. G. J. van der. **Grotius and International Society of To-day,** *American Political Science Review*, XIX (November 1925), 800–808.

702 — —. **Hugo Grotius — Founder of International Law,** *Current History*, XXII (June 1925), 439–46.

703 Scott, James B. **Grotius' De Jure Belli ac Pacis: The Work of a Lawyer, Statesman and Theologian,** *American Journal of International Law,* XIX (July 1925), 461—69.

704 Wilson, George G. **Grotius: Law of War and Peace,** *American Journal of International Law,* XXXV (April 1941), 205—26.

2.2.12 K'ANG YU-WEI (1858—1927)

705 K'ang Yu-wei. **The One-World Philosophy of K'ang Yu-Wei.** Trans. with introduction and notes by L. G. Thompson. London, Allen and Unwin, 1958. 300 p.

2.2.13 KANT (1724—1804)

706 Delbos, B. Victor. **Les idées de Kant sur la paix perpétuelle,** *Nouvelle Revue,* CXIX (August 1899), 410—29.

707 Friedrich, Carl J. **The Ideology of the United Nations Charter and the Philosophy of Immanuel Kant 1795—1945,** *Journal of Politics,* IX (February 1947), 10—30.

708 — —. **Inevitable Peace.** Cambridge, Harvard University Press, 1948. xii + 281 p.

Contains Kant's essay, "Eternal Peace," as an appendix.

709 — —. (ed.). **The Philosophy of Kant: Immanuel Kant's Moral and Political Writings.** New York, Random House, 1959. 476 p.

710 Harrison, Austin. **Kant on the League of Nations,** *English Review,* XXIX (November 1919), 454—62.

Part B. — Early International Organizations

711 Hinsley, Francis H. **Power and the Pursuit of Peace.** Cambridge, Cambridge University Press, 1963.

Chapter IV.

712 Kant, Immanuel. **Perpetual Peace: A Philosophical Proposal,** Helen O'Brien (tr.). Introduction by Jesse H. Buckland. London, Sweet and Maxwell, 1927. 59 p.

713 — —. **Perpetual Peace.** Introduction by N. M. Butler. New York, Columbia University Press, 1939. 67 p.

714 Mead, Edwin D. **Immanuel Kant's Internationalism,** *Contemporary Review*, CVII (February 1915), 226–32.

715 Orzábal Quintana, Arturo. **Kant y la paz perpetua,** *Nosotros* (Buenos Aires), XLVI (April 1924), 441–57.

716 Paulsen, Friedrich. **Immanuel Kant: His Life and Doctrine,** J. E. Creighton and Albert Lefevre (trans.). New York, Scribner's, 1902. 419 p

717 Pullias, E. V. **William Penn and Immanuel Kant Speak Today,** *World Affairs Quarterly*, XVI (April 1945), 40–53.

718 Waltz, Kenneth. **Kant, Liberalism, and War,** *American Political Science Review*, LVI (June 1962), 331–40.

2.2.14 LOCKE (1632–1704)

719 Cox, Richard H. **Locke on War and Peace.** Oxford, Clarendon, 1960. 220 p.

Part B. — *Early International Organizations*

2.2.15 PENN (1644—1718)

720 Dobrée, Bonamy. **Wiliam Penn: Quaker and Pioneer.** Boston, Houghton, Mifflin, 1932. 346 p.

721 Hull, William Isaac. **William Penn and the Dutch Quaker Migration to Pennsylvania.** Swarthmore, Swarthmore College Press, 1935. 445 p.

722 Marriott, John A. **Commonwealth or Anarchy?** New York, Columbia University Press, 1939.

Chapter V.

723 Penn, William. **The Peace of Europe: The Fruits of Solitude and Other Writings.** New York, Dutton, n. d. xliv + 292 p.

724 Pullias, E. V. **William Penn and Immanuel Kant Speak Today,** *World Affairs Quarterly*, XVI (April 1945), 40—53.

725 Trueblood, Benjamin F. **The Development of the Peace Idea, and Other Essays.** Boston, Plimpton, 1932.

Chapters II, XII.

2.2.16 PODEBRAD (1420—1471)

726 Lewis, V. J. **The Bohemian Project of 1464,** *New Commonwealth*, II (December 1933), 10.

2.2.17 RICHELIEU (1585—1642)

727 Najam, E. W. **Europe: Richelieu's Blueprint for Unity and Peace,** *Studies In Philology*, LIII (January 1956), 25—34.

Europe is a five-act *comédie héroïque* in verse, performed only once, November 18, 1642, shortly before Cardinal Richelieu's death. It appeared under the authorship of Desmarets, but the ideas are clealy Richelieu's. It is a political allegory, the purpose of which was to defend the Cardinal's foreign policy.

2.2.18 ROUSSEAU (1712–1778)

728 Green, Frederick C. **Jean-Jacques Rousseau: A Critical Study of His Life and Writings.** Cambridge, Cambridge University Press, 1955. 376 p.

729 Hinsley, Francis H. **Power and the Pursuit of Peace.** Cambridge, Cambridge University Press, 1963.
Chapter III.

730 Hoffmann, Stanley. **Rousseau on War and Peace,** *American Political Science Review,* LVII (June 1963), 317–33.

731 Morley, John. **Rousseau.** London, Chapman and Hall, 1873. 2 vols.

732 Mowat, Robert B. **Jean-Jacques Rousseau.** Bristol, Arrowsmith, 1938. 368 p.

733 Rousseau, Jean Jacques. **Project of Perpetual Peace,** Edith M. Nuttall (tr.); introduction by G. Lowes Dickinson. London, Cobden-Sanderson, 1927. xxv + 141 p.

734 Winwar, Frances. **Jean-Jacques Rousseau: Conscience of an Era.** New York, Random House, 1961. 367 p.

2.2.19 SAINT-PIERRE (1658–1743)

735 Derocque, Gilberte. **Le projet de paix perpétuelle de l'Abbé de Saint-Pierre comparé au pacte de la Société des Nations.** Paris, Rousseau, 1929. 203 p.

736 Perkins, Merle L. **The Moral and Political Philosophy of the Abbé de Saint-Pierre.** Geneva, Droz, 1959. 157 p.

Part B. — Early International Organizations

737 Saint-Pierre, C. I. Castel de. **Selections from the Second Edition of the Abrégé du Projet de Paix Perpétuelle,** H. Hale Bellot (trans.); introduction by Paul Collinet. London, Sweet and Maxwell, 1927. 61 p.

738 Sarolea, Charles. **The Abbé de St. Pierre (1658—1743),** *Contemporary Review,* CXLVI (August 1934), 179—185.

2.2.20 SULLY (1559—1641)

739 Hemleben, Sylvester John. **Henry the Fourth's Plan for a League of Nations,** *Alumnae News of the College of New Rochelle,* IX (April 1932), 7—10.

740 Marriott, John A. **Commonwealth or Anarchy?** New York, Columbia University Press, 1939.

Chapter III.

741 Pfister, Christian. **Les "Economies Royales" de Sully et le Grand Dessein de Henry IV,** *Revue Historique,* LIV (January-April 1894), 300—24; LV (May-August 1894), 66—82ff; LVI (September-December 1894), 39—48ff.

742 Sully, Maximilien de Bethune, duc de. **Grand Design of Henry IV.** Introduction by David Ogg. London, Sweet and Maxwell, 1921. 56 p.

743 — —. **The Great Design of Henry IV, From the Memoirs of the Duke of Sully, and the United States of Europe,** Edward Everett Hale (tr.); introduction by Edwin D. Mead. Boston, Ginn, 1909. xxi + 91 p.

744 — —. **Memoires of the Duke of Sully, Prime Minister to Henry the Great.** London, Bohn, 1856. 4 vols.

Translated from the French. A new edition, revised and corrected, with additional notes and a historical introduction, attributed to Walter Scott.

Part B. — *Early International Organizations*

3. NINETEENTH CENTURY INTERNATIONAL ORGANIZATIONS

The Congress of Vienna, which met to conclude a treaty of peace following the Napoleonic wars, in many ways set an example for contemporary international organization. Negotiations among the "great powers,"a self-appointed steering committee which deliberated on a draft to present to the plenary session of the Congress, were unusually prolonged. Motivated in accordance with Tsar Alexander I's notion of a Holy Alliance, the major powers established themselves as a directorate capable of dictating policy to the small powers. The "European system" was an informal arrangement to keep peace, and was predicated on the hope that harmony would prevail among the stronger countries. But when disunity among these arose, the formal appearance of great power consultation proved empty, and a return to power politics and the balance-of-power device of pre-Napoleonic times was associated once more with an increase in warfare among states.

3.1 CONGRESS OF VIENNA

745   Beazley, C. R. **The Congress of Vienna,** *The Evolution of World-Peace,* Francis S. Marvin (ed.). London, Oxford University Press, 1921, pp. 119–31.

746   Cramer, Frederick H. **The Beginning of the End: Five Profiles from the Congress of Vienna,** *Current History,* New Series, XIV (January 1948), 6–13; (March 1948), 133–40; (April 1948), 197–204; (May 1948), 261–69; (June 1948), 325–31.

747   Dziewanowski, M. K. **Appeasement at Vienna,** *Current History,* New Series, XVI (January 1949), 16–21; (February 1949), 83–85.

748   Gooch, G. P. **The French Revolution As a World Force,** *The Evolution of World-Peace,* Francis S. Marvin (ed.). London, Oxford University Press, 1921, pp. 91–118.

749   Hazen, Charles D., Thayer, William R. and Lord, Robert H. **Three Peace Congresses of the Nineteenth Century.** Cambridge, Harvard University Press, 1917. 93 p.

750 Kissinger, Henry A. **The Congress of Vienna: A Reappraisal,** *World Politics,* VIII (January 1956), 264—80.

751 — —. **The Congress of Vienna,** *Power and Order: Six Cases in World Politics,* John G. Stoessinger and Alan F. Westin (eds.). New York, Harcourt, Brace and World, 1964, pp. 1—32.

752 La Garde, August. **Fêtes et souvenirs du Congrès de Vienne: Tableaux des salons, scenes, anecdotiques et portraits, 1814—1815.** Paris, Appert, 1843. 2 vols.

753 Lockhart, John G. **The Peace Makers, 1814—1815.** New York, Putnam, 1934. 376 p.

754 Meulen, Jacob ter. **Der Gedanke der internationalen Organisation in seiner Entwicklung.** Vol. II. Hague, Nijhoff, 1929. Chapters 1—2.

755 Nicolson, Harold G. **The Congress of Vienna: A Study in Allied Unity, 1812—1822.** New York, Viking, 1963. 312 p.

756 Peterson, Genevieve. **The Equality of States as Dogma and Reality: II, Political Inequality at the Congress of Vienna,** *Political Science Quarterly,* LX (December 1945), 532—54.

757 Rie, Robert. **The Origins of Public Law and the Congress of Vienna,** *Transactions* (Grotius Society), XXXVI (1950), 209—27.

758 Strakosch, Henry. **The Place of the Congress of Vienna in the Growth of International Law and Organisation,** *Indian Yearbook of International Affairs,* XIII (Part 2, 1964), 184—206.

759 Webster, Charles K. **The Congress of Vienna, 1814—1815.** London, Bell, 1934. xii+189 p.

> Prepared under the direction of the Historical Section of the British Foreign Office in 1920. The author states that this "monograph was written at the request of the Librarian of the Foreign Office in eleven weeks.... It is purely a *pièce de circonstance,* and will be followed, I hope, by a larger work on the same subject...." The work subsequently was reissued on various occasions, most recently by Thames and Hudson, London, in 1963.

760 — —. **England and the Polish Saxon Problem at the Congress of Vienna,** *Transactions* (Royal Historical Society), Series 3, VII (1913), 49–66.

761 — —. **Patterns of Peace-making,** *Foreign Affairs,* XXV (July 1947), 596–611.

762 Webster, Charles K., and Temperley, Harold W. V. **The Congress of Vienna, 1814–1815, and the Conference of Paris, 1919.** London, H. M. Stationery Office, 1923. 28 p.

Contains two parts: (1) a comparison of the organization and results of the two conferences by Webster; and (2) discussion by Temperley of attempts at international government in Europe during the period of the Congress of Vienna (1814–1825), and the period since the Treaty of Versailles (1919–1922).

763 Westcott, Allan. **A Historic Peace Conference: The Congress of Vienna and Its Workings Viewed As a Precedent of Timely Interest,** *Current History,* III (December 1917), 538–41.

3.2 HOLY ALLIANCE

764 Bourquin, Maurice. **Histoire de la Sainte Alliance.** Geneva, Georg, 1954. 507 p.

765 — —. **The Holy Alliance, an Attempt at a European Organisation,** *Recueil des Cours,* LXXXIII (1953), 377–461.

766 Cresson, William P. **The Holy Alliance: The European Background of the Monroe Doctrine.** New York, Oxford University Press, 1922. 147 p.

767 Dupuis, Charles. **Les antecedents de la Société des Nations,** *Recueil des Cours,* LX (1937), 5–108.

768 — —. **La Sainte-Alliance et le Directoire Européen de 1815 à 1818,** *Revue d'Histoire Diplomatique,* XLVIII (October–December 1934), 265–92.

Part B. — Early International Organizations

769 Ferrero, Guglielmo. **Problems of Peace, from the Holy Alliance to the League of Nations: A Message from a European Writer to Americans.** New York, Putnam, 1919. 281 p.

A survey of the political history of Europe from the Holy Alliance to the League of Nations. The writer makes a strong appeal for a League of Nations as an alliance of peoples, as opposed to the Holy Alliance as an alliance of the courts of Europe.

770 Fischer-Galati, Stephen A. **The Nature and Immediate Origins of the Treaty of Holy Alliance,** *History,* XXXVIII (February 1953), 26–39.

771 Grant, Arthur James. **The "Holy Alliance" and the League of Nations.** Foreword by Robert Cecil. London, League of Nations Union, 1923. 14 p.

772 Hodé, Jacques. **L'Idée de Fédération Internationale dans l'Historie.** Paris, Editions de la Vie Universitaire, 1921.

Chapter XVII.

773 Knapton, Ernest J. **The Lady of the Holy Alliance: The Life of Julie de Krudener.** New York, Columbia University Press, 1939. 262 p.

774 Nicolson, Harold G. **The Congress of Vienna.** New York, Viking, 1963.

Chapter XV.

775 M., J. O. **Alexander I and the Holy Alliance,** *New Commonwealth,* V (January 1937), 58–59.

776 York, Elizabeth. **League of Nations.** London, Swarthmore, 1919.

Chapter X.

3.3 THE "EUROPEAN SYSTEM"

777 Baldwin, Simeon E. **The International Congresses and Conferences of the Last Century As Forces Working Toward the Solidarity of the World,** *American Journal of International Law,* I (July 1907), 565–78.

778 Bassett, John S. **The Lost Fruits of Waterloo: Views of a League of Nations.** 2d ed. New York, Macmillan, 1919. 289 p.

Stated purpose of book: "The idea of a permanent peace through federated action, to show how that idea came up in connection with the war against Napoleon, how it was rejected for a concerted and balanced international system... and finally in what way the old system is responsible for the present war."

779 Boyce, Myrna M. **The Diplomatic Relations of England with the Quadruple Alliance, 1815–1830.** Iowa City, University of Iowa Press, 1918. 76 p.

780 Carpenter, William S. **The United States and the League of Neutrals of 1780,** *American Journal of International Law*, XV (October 1921), 511–22.

"The idea of a League of Nations in one with which the U. S. has been familiar since the beginning of its history. The form in which it first appeared to this country was in the Armed Neutrality of 1780."

781 Dunn, Frederick Sherwood. **International Legislation,** *Political Science Quarterly*, XLII (December 1927), 571–88.

782 — —. **The Practice and Procedure of International Conferences.** Baltimore, Johns Hopkins Press, 1929. 232 p.

783 Dupuis, Charles. **Le principe de l'equilibré et le concert européen de la Paix de Westphalie à l'Acte d'Algesiras.** Paris, Perrin, 1909. 525 p.

784 Dziewanowski, M. K. **Czartoryski: European Federalist,** *Current History*, New Series, XIX (July 1950), 21–28.

785 Erzberger, Matthias. **The League of Nations.** New York, Holt, 1919.

Chapter II.

786 Fisher, Hilda. **Europe After Napoleon,** *Current History*, New Series, VIII (June 1945), 522–27.

787 Gentz, Friedrich von. **The Dangers and Advantages of the Present State of Europe, Impartially Considered.** London, Stockdale, 1806. 30 p.

788 Goriainov, Serge. **The End of the Alliance of the Emperors,** *American Historical Review,* XXIII (January 1918), 324–49.

789 Greene, Fred. **Dynamics of International Relations.** New York, Holt, Rinehart and Winston, 1964.

Chapter IV.

790 Gregory, Winifred (ed.). **International Congresses and Conferences, 1840–1937: A Union List of Their Publications Available in Libraries of the United States and Canada.** New York, Wilson, 1938. 229 p.

791 Grey, Edward. **Twenty-five Years; 1892–1925.** New York, Stokes, 1925. 2 vols.

The last meeting of the Concert is described in Volume I, pp. 255-67.

792 Gruber, Richard G. **Internationale Staaten-Kongresse und Konferenzen, ihre Vorbereitung und Organisation: Eine völkerrechts-diplomatische Untersuchung auf Grund der Staatenkrisis vom Wiener Kongress 1814 bis zur Gegenwart.** Berlin, Puttkammer and Mühlbrecht, 1919. 348 p.

793 Hazen, Charles D., Thayer, William R. and Lord, Robert H. **Three Peace Congresses of The Nineteenth Century.** Cambridge, Harvard University Press, 1917. 93 p.

Congresses of Vienna, Paris, and Berlin.

794 Hearnshaw, Fossey J. C. **European Coalitions, Alliances, and Ententes Since 1792.** London, H. M. Stationery Office, 1920. 40 p.

795 Henderson, Gavin B. **The Diplomatic Revolution of 1854.** *American Historical Review,* XLIII (October 1937), 22–50.

796 Hershey, Amos Shartle. **The Public International Conference.** Stanford University Press, 1929. 267 p.

797 Hill, Norman L. **The Conference in International Relations,** *Southwestern Social Science Quarterly*, VIII (December 1927), 272—88.

798 Hinsley, Francis H. **Power and the Pursuit of Peace.** Cambridge, Cambridge University Press, 1963.

Chapters VIII—XI.

799 Hodé, Jacques. **L'Idée de Fédération Internationale dans l'Historie.** Paris, Edition de la Vie Universitaire, 1921.

Chapters XVIII-XX.

800 Hodges, Charles. **The Background of International Relations.** New York, Wiley, 1931.

Chapter XIV.

801 Holland, Thomas E. **The European Concert and the Eastern Question.** New York, Clarendon, 1885. 366 p.

802 Kissinger, Henry A. **A World Restored: Metternich, Castlereagh, and the Problems of Peace, 1812—1822.** London, Weidenfeld and Nicolson, 1957. 354 p.

803 Langer, William L. **European Alliances and Alignments, 1871—1890.** New York, Knopf, 1931. 608 p.

Comprehensive account of the major international issues and forces that produced the balance-of-power alliance system between 1871 and 1890.

804 Mangone, Gerard J. **A Short History of International Organization.** New York, McGraw-Hill, 1954.

Chapter II.

Part B. — Early International Organizations

805 Mann, Golo. **Secretary of Europe: The Life of Friedrich Gentz, Enemy of Napoleon,** W. W. Woglom (trans.). London, Oxford University Press, 1946. 323 p.

806 Marvin, F. S. **The Nineteenth Century,** *The Evolution of World-Peace,* Francis S. Marvin (ed.). London, Oxford University Press, 1921, pp. 132—45.

807 Medlicott, William N. **Bismarck, Gladstone, and the Concert of Europe.** London, Athlone, 1956. 353 p.

808 Morrow, Dwight W. **The Society of Free States.** New York, Harper, 1919.

  Chapter III.

809 Mowat, Robert B. **The Concert of Europe.** London, Macmillan, 1930. 386 p.

  This work deals with international relations, chiefly European, from January 1871 to August 1914.

810 — —. **The European States System.** London, Oxford, 1929. 96 p.

811 Nicolson, Harold G. **The Congress of Vienna.** New York, Viking, 1963.

  Chapter XVI.

812 Perris, G. H. **A Short History of War and Peace.** New York, Holt, 1911.

  Chapters V, X.

813 Phillimore, Walter G. F. **Three Centuries of Treaties of Peace and their Teaching.** London, Murray, 1919. xx + 227 p.

Part B. — Early International Organizations

814 Phillips, Walter Alison. **The Confederation of Europe: A Study of the European Alliance, 1813—1823, As an Experiment in the International Organization of Peace.** 2d. ed. London, Longmans, Green, 1920. xviii + 320 p.

815 Pollock, Frederick. **The League of Nations.** 2d ed. London, Stevens, 1922.

Chapter I.

816 Potter, Pitman B. **Développement de l'organisation internationale (1815—1914),** *Recueil des Cours,* LXIV (1938), 75—155.

817 Rosecrance, Richard N. **Action and Reaction in World Politics.** Boston, Little, Brown, 1963.

Chapters IV—VIII.

818 Satow, Ernest M. **International Congresses.** London, H. M. Stationery Office, 1920. 168 p.

819 Schenk, Hans G. A. V. **The Aftermath of the Napoleonic Wars: The Concert of Europe, an Experiment.** New York, Oxford University Press, 1947. x + 228 p.

820 Sharp, Walter, and Kirk, Grayson. **Contemporary International Politics.** New York, Farrar and Rinehart. 1941.

Chapter XX.

821 Spender, Harold. **The Peace of 1814—15,** *Current History,* XI (October 1919), 147—48.

822 Temperley, Harold W. V. **Canning and the Conference of the Four Allied Governments at Paris, 1823—1826,** *American Historical Review,* XXX (October 1924), 16—43.

Part B. — Early International Organizations

823 — —. **The Foreign Policy of Canning, 1822–1827: England, the Neo-Holy Alliance, and the New World.** London, Bell, 1925. 636 p.

824 Truyol y Serra, Antonio. **Origins and Structure of International Society,** *Recueil des Cours,* XCVI (1959), 557–641.

825 Webster, Charles Kingsley. **The Foreign Policy of Castlereagh, 1815–1822: Britain and the European Alliance.** London, Bell, 1958. 618 p.

826 — —. **Palmerston, Metternich, and the European System 1830–1841,** *Proceedings* British Academy), xx (June, 1934), 125–58.

827 Webster, Charles Kingsley and Herbert, Sydney. **The League of Nations in Theory and Practice.** London, Allen and Unwin, 1933.

Chapter I.

828 Woodward, Ernest L. **The Congress of Berlin, 1878.** London, H. M. Stationery Office, 1920. 48 p.

829 Woolf, L. S. **International Government.** New York, Brentano's, 1916.

Part I, Chapter V.

830 Zimmern, Alfred E. **The League of Nations and the Rule of Law,** 1918–1935. 2d ed. London, Macmillan, 1939.

Part I – Chapters III, VI.

4. PEACE MOVEMENT

With international aggression a problem once again in the nineteenth century, proposals for international organization were put forth in increasing number, but these plans differed in two respects from the earlier schemes. One difference was that the model of the Congress of Vienna, where small powers had lacked a voice, now stimulated much more detailed blueprints for specific peace-keeping institutions. The second feature was the appearance of a number of peace societies, which held international conferences to publicize and to plan for an eventual world parliament.

4.1 PROPOSALS FOR INTERNATIONAL ORGANIZATION

831   Atkinson, Henry A. **Theodore Marburg: The Man and his Work.** New York, Littman, 1951. 221 p.

832   Bliokh, Ivan S. **The Future of War, in Its Technical, Economic and Political Relations.** R. C. Long (trans.), with conversation with the author by W. T. Stead, and an introduction by Edwin D. Mead. Boston, Ginn, 1899. xxix + 380 p.

This work apparently influenced the decision of Tsar Nicholas to summon a peace conference in 1898.

833   Bluntschli, Johann Kaspar. **Die Organisation des Europäischen Staatenvereines.** Darmstadt, Wissenschaftliche Buchgesellschaft, 1962. 40 p.

This is the outline of Bluntschli's peace project, which bears a close relationship to that of Henry IV. It was first published in the popular journal *Gegenwart* in 1878, subsuquently as Vol. I, chapter XII, of Bluntschli's **Gesammelte Kleine Schriften,** published in 1879. Bluntschli was a professor at the University of Heidelberg.

834   Bridgman, Raymond L. **World Organization.** Boston, Ginn, 1905. vi + 172 p.

835   Carnegie, Andrew. **A League of Peace: A Rectorial Address Delivered to the Students in the University of St. Andrews, 17th October 1905.** Boston, 1906. 47 p.

Part B. — Early International Organizations

836 — —. **A League of Peace,** *International Conciliation,* III (November 1907), 3—43.

837 Channing, William Ellery. **Discourses on War.** Introduction by E. D. Mead. Boston, Ginn, 1903. 229 p.

838 Curti, Merle Eugene. **Bryan and World Peace,** *Smith College Studies in History,* XVI (April—July 1931), 113—262.

839 Davis, George B. **Doctor Francis Lieber's Instructions for the Government of Armies in the Field,** *American Journal of International Law,* I (January 1907), 13—25.

840 Duplissix, E. **L'organisation internationale.** Paris, Larose and Tenin, 1909. 151 p.

841 Earle, Edward Mead. **H. G. Wells, British Patriot in Search of a World State,** *Nationalism and Internationalism,* Edward Mead Earle (ed.). New York, Columbia University Press, 1950, pp. 79—121.

842 — —. **H. G. Wells, British Patriot in Search of a World State,** *World Politics,* II (January 1950), 181—208.

843 Halasz, Nicholas. **Nobel: A Biography of Nobel.** New York, Orion, 1959. 281 p.

844 Hendrick, Burton J. **The Life of Andrew Carnegie.** Garden City, Doubleday, Doran, 1932. 2 vols.

845 Higgins, A. Pearce. **James Lorimer,** *Juridical Review,* XLV (September 1933), 239—56.

Part B. — Early International Organizations

846 Hinsley, Francis H. **Power and the Pursuit of Peace.** Cambridge, Cambridge University Press, 1963.
Chapters VI—VII.

847 Hirst, Margaret E. **The Quakers in Peace and War: An Account of Their Peace Principles and Practice.** Introduction by Rufus M. Jones. London, Swarthmore, 1923. 560 p.

848 Holcombe, Arthur N. **Edwin Ginn's Vision of World Peace,** *International Organization,* XIX (Winter, 1965), 1—19.

849 Irvine, William. **Shaw, War and Peace, 1894—1919,** *Foreign Affairs,* XXV (January 1947), 314—27.

850 James, William. **The Moral Equivalent of War,** *International Conciliation,* XXVII (February 1910), 3—20.

851 Johnson, Joseph E. and Bush, Bernard. **Andrew Carnegie: Apostle of Peace,** *Perspectives on Peace,* Carnegie Endowment for International Peace (ed.). New York, Praeger, 1960, pp. 1—14.

852 Kamarguski, L. Alekseivitch. **Le tribunal international.** Paris, Pedone-Lauriel, 1887. 528 p.

853 Ladd, William. **An Essay on A Congress of Nations for the Adjustment of International Disputes Without Resort to Arms.** Introduction by James Brown Scott. New York, Oxford University Press, 1916. 162 p.
Reprint from the original edition of 1840. The introduction reviews the significant earlier writings.

854 Lange, Christian L. **Histoire de l'internationalisme.** New York, Putnam, 1919. 506 p.

855 Lieber, Francis. **Miscellaneous Writings.** Philadelphia, Lippincott, 1881. 2 vols.

856 Lorimer, James. **The Institutes of the Law of Nations: A Treatise of the Jural Relations of Separate Political Communities.** Edinburgh, Blackwood, 1883—84. 2 vols.

Lorimer's plan for world peace appears in Volume II, Chapter XIV, pp. 279—87.

857 — —. **On the Application of the Principle of Relative, or Proportional, Equality to International Organization,** *Transactions* (Royal Society of Edinburgh), 1867, pp. 557—71.

858 Marburg, Theodore. **Development of the League of Nations Idea: Documents and Correspondence of Theodore Marburg,** John H. Latané (ed.). New York, Macmillan, 1932. 2 vols.

859 Mead, Edwin Doak. **The Literature of the Peace Movement.** Boston, International School of Peace, 1910. 14 p.

860 — —. **Washington, Jefferson and Franklin on War.** Boston, World Peace Foundation, 1913. 15 p.

861 Mead, Lucia T. A. **Swords and Ploughshares: Or the Supplanting of the System of War by the System of Law.** New York, Putnam, 1912. xiv + 249 p.

862 Meulen, Jacob ter. **Der Gedanke der internationalen Organisation in seiner Entwicklung.** Vol. III, Part I. Hague, Nijhoff, 1929.

Chapters III, IV.

863 — —. **Der Gedanke der internationalen Organisation in seiner Entwicklung 1300—1800.** Vol. II, Part II. Hague, Nijhoff, 1940. xv + 373 p.

864 Nobelstiftelsen (Stockholm). **Nobel: The Man and His Prizes.** By H. Schück, R. Sohlman, A. Österling, G. Liljestrand, A. Westgren, M. Siegbahn, A. Schou and N. K. Ståhle. Norman, Okla., University of Oklahoma Press, 1951. 620 p.

865 Nys, Ernest. **Francis Lieber, His Life and Work,** *American Journal of International Law,* V (January 1911), 84–117; (April 1911), 355–93.

   It was upon Lieber's **Instructions for the Government and Armies in the Field,** General Order No. 100, Adjutant General's Office, 1863, that the Brussels Convention of 1874 was based.

866 Phillimore, Lord. **Schemes for Maintaining General Peace.** London, H. M. Stationery Office, 1920. 71 p.

867 Root, Elihu. **Francis Lieber,** *American Society of International Law Proceedings,* VII (1913), 8–24.

   Published concurrently in *American Journal of International Law.* Comments by George B. Davis.

868 Schwarzenberger, Georg. **William Ladd: An Examination of an American Proposal for an International Equity Tribunal.** 2d ed. Preface by James Brown Scott. London, Constable, 1936. xviii + 78 p.

869 Silberner, Edmund. **The Problem of War in Nineteenth Century Economic Thought.** A. H. Krappe (trans.). Princeton, Princeton University Press, 1946. xiv + 332 p.

870 Society of Friends. **Benjamin F. Trueblood: Prophet of Peace, 1847–1916.** New York, Mosher, 1916. 20 p.

871 Stead, William Thomas. **The United States of Europe on the Eve of the Parliament of Peace.** New York, Doubleday and McClure, 1899. 468 p.

872 Suttner, Berta F. S. von. **Ground Arms!** Alice A. Abbott (trans.). Chicago, McClurg, 1892. 286 p.

   From the German edition, **Die Waffen Nieder.**

873 — —. **Lay Down Your Arms: The Autobiography of Martha von Tilling.** 2d ed. New York, Longmans, Green, 1906. xii + 435 p.

   The Nobel prize-winning book arguing for disarmament.

Part B. — Early International Organizations

874 — —. **Memoirs.** Boston, Ginn, 1910. 2 vols.

875 Trueblood, Benjamin F. **The Development of the Peace Idea and Other Essays.** Boston, Plimpton, 1932.
Chapters IX–X.

876 — —. **The Federation of the World.** 3d ed. Boston, Houghton, Mifflin, 1899. x + 227 p.

877 Wishart, Andrew. **A Scottish Jurish and the League Idea,** *Juridical Review,* XXXIV (December 1922), 331–37.

878 Whyte, Frederic. **The Life of W. T. Stead.** New York, Houghton, Mifflin, 1925. 2 vols.

4.2 ORGANIZATION OF THE PEACE MOVEMENT

See also E 10.2.

879 Abrams, Irwin. **Emergence of the International Law Societies,** *Review of Politics,* XIX (July 1957), 361–80.

880 Allen, Devere. **The Fight for Peace.** New York, Macmillan, 1930. 740 p.
History of the American peace movement.

881 Brinton, Howard Haines. **Friends for 300 Years: The History and Beliefs of the Society of Friends Since George Fox Started the Quaker Movement.** New York, Harper, 1952. 232 p.

882 Butler, Nicholas Murray. **The Carnegie Endowment for International Peace,** *International Conciliation,* LXXVI (February 1914), 3–14.

883 Carr, E. H. **The League of Peace and Freedom, an Episode in the Quest for Collective Security,** *International Affairs,* XIV (November 1935), 837—44.

884 Curti, Merle Eugene. **The American Peace Crusade.** Durham, N. C., Duke University Press, 1929. 229 p.

885 — —. **The Learned Blacksmith: Letters and Journals of Elihu Burritt.** New York, Wilson-Erickson, 1937. 241 p.

886 — —. **Peace or War: The American Struggle, 1636—1936.** New York, Norton, 1936. 374 p.

887 England, G. A. **Fiat Pax: The Influence of the International Socialist Movement As a Factor in World-Peace,** *International Conciliation,* LXXXI (August 1914), 3—14.

888 Faries, John C. **The Rise of Internationalism.** New York, Gray, 1915. 207 p.

889 Ginn, Edwin. **Organizing the Peace Work.** Boston, World Peace Foundation, 1913. 10 p.

Address delivered at the Mohonk Conference, May 14, 1914, by the founder of the World Peace Foundation.

890 — —. **World Peace Foundation.** Boston, World Peace Foundation, 1911. 12 p.

891 Hill, Norman L. **The Public International Conference.** London, Oxford University Press, 1929.

Chapter V.

892 Hull, William Isaac. **The New Peace Movement: A Series of Adresses Delivered in 1908—1909.** Swarthmore, Pa. Swarthmore College Press, 1909. 76 p.

Part B. — Early International Organizations

893 Jones, Amy Heninway (comp.). **Carnegie Endowment for International Peace,** *International Conciliation*, CC (July 1924), 5–143.

An explanation of the Endowment, its founders, structure, bylaws, divisions, publications.

894 Kuehl, Warren F. **The World Federation League: A Neglected Chapter in the History of a Movement,** *World Affairs Quarterly*, XXX (January 1960), 349–64.

895 Lange, Christian L. **Histoire de la doctrine pacifique et de son influence sur le développement du droit international,** *Recueil des Cours*, XIII (1927), 171–426.

Survey of the history of pacifist ideas and of the peace movement, with special reference to international law.

896 Lochner, Louis P. **The Cosmopolitan Club Movement,** *International Conciliation*, LXI (December 1912), 3–14.

897 Lyons, Francis S. L. **Internationalism in Europe, 1815–1914.** Leyden, Sythoff, 1963.

Chapter V.

898 Marburg, Theodore. **Philosophy of the Third American Peace Congress,** *International Conciliation*, LIV (May 1912), 5–30.

899 Mead, Edwin Doak. **The American Peace Party and Its Present Aims and Duties.** Boston, World Peace Foundation, 1913. 10 p.

E. D. Mead (1849–1937) was author, lecturer, and Director of the World Peace Foundation, Boston, and attended as a delegate of the American Peace Foundation the international peace congresses of Glasgow, Rouen, Lucerne, Munich, and London. He was chairman of the Executive Committee, Thirteenth International Congress, Boston, 1904.

900 Moritzen, Julius. **The Peace Movement of America.** Introduction by James L. Tryon. New York, Putnam, 1912. 419 p.

901 Morley, Felix. **The Society of Nations: Its Organization and Constitutional Development.** Washington, D. C., Brookings, 1932. 678 p.

902 Neill, Charles P. **The Interest of the Wage-Earner in the Present Status of the Peace Movement,** *International Conciliation,* LVII (August 1912), 5—14.

Address at the Lake Mohonk Conference, May 17, 1912.

903 Passy, Frederic. **Peace Movement in Europe,** *American Journal of Sociology,* II (July 1896), 1—12.

904 Redlich, Marcellus D. A. R. von. **Résumé of the Movement for World Peace,** *Transactions* (Grotius Society), XXII (1936), 137—49.

905 Russell, Frank M. **Theories of International Relations.** New York, Appleton-Century, 1936.

Chapter XIV.

906 Sait, Edward M. **The Peace Movement: Ideals and Actualities,** *Institute of World Affairs Proceedings,* VIII (1931), 223—32.

907 Trueblood, Benjamin F. **The Historic Development of the Peace Idea.** Boston, American Peace Society, 1906. 24 p.

908 Universal Peace Congress. **Bulletin officiel du XXme Congrès Universel de la Paix.** Berne, Bureau International de la Paix, 1914. 407 p.

This series of peace congresses, composed of delegates of national societies and organizations, commenced in Paris in 1889 with Frederic Passy presiding. The twentieth and last congress before World War I was held at the Hague, August 18—23, 1913.

909 Weardale, Lord. **The First Universal Races Congress,** *International Conciliation,* XLII (May 1911), 3—9.

910 Whitney, Edson L. **The American Peace Society: A Centennial History.** Washington, D. C., American Peace Society, 1928. 360 p.

Part B. — Early International Organizations

5. INTERNATIONAL UNIONS

The new systems of transportation and communication resulting from the invention of the railway steam locomotive, the steamship, and the telegraph created a need for technical cooperation among nations. Though the intergovernmental and private organizations which arose from this need were non-political in character, important precedents for worldwide collaboration among nations were established by them. (Many of these agencies have continued as autonomous bodies up to the present. Public unions tended to be absorbed within the League or the UN, so they are filed by function in Parts C and D; private unions have been referred to as "nongovernmental organizations," the subject of Part F of the bibliography.)

5.1 PRIVATE UNIONS

911 Barton, Clara. **The Red Cross.** Washington, American National Red Cross, 1898. 684 p.

912 Bewes, Wyndham A. **Transactions of the International Law Association, 1873—1924.** London, Sweet and Maxwell, 1925. viii + 257 p.

913 British and Foreign Anti-Slavery Society. **A Chronological Summary of the Work of the British and Foreign Anti-Slavery Society During the Nineteenth Century (1839—1900).** London, British and Foreign Anti-Slavery Society, 1901. 107 p.

914 Burns, C. Delisle. **International Politics.** London, Methuen, 1920.

Chapters VII—VIII.

915 Dunant, Jean Henri. **Un Souvenir de Solferino.** Geneva, Cherbuliez, 1862. 95 p.

Translated and published in 1939 by the organization which Dunant's plea begot, the Red Cross, under the title **A Memory of Solferino.**

916 Lange, Christian L. **The Interparliamentary Union,** *International Conciliation*, LXV (April 1913), 3—14.

917 Lyons, Francis S. L. **Internationalism in Europe, 1815—1914.** Leyden, Sythoff, 1963. 412 p.

918 Nuñez Brian, Joaquin. **Pan American Railway Congress Association: Brief Historical Review, 1906—1954.** Buenos Aires, Pan American Railway Congress Association, 1955. 18 p.

919 Potter, Pitman B. **An Introduction to the Study of International Organization.** 4th ed. New York, Appleton-Century, 1935.

Chapter X.

920 Pratt, Sereno S. **Contribution of Commercial Bodies to International Unity,** *International Conciliation*, L (January 1912), 5—18.

On the international activities of Chambers of Commerce. Issue contains essays on the relation of finance and commerce to "international good will."

921 Union Interparlementaire. **L'union Interparlementaire de 1889 à 1939: ouvrage publié par les soins du Bureau Interparlementaire à l'occasion du cinquantenaire de l'Union.** Geneva, Payot, 1939. 386 p.

922 Union of International Associations. **The 1,978 International Organizations Founded Since the Congress of Vienna: Chronological List.** Introduction by G. P. Speeckaert. Brussels, Union of International Associations, 1957. xxviii + 204 p.

5.2 PUBLIC UNIONS

923 Abt, G. **Vingt-cinq ans d'activité de l'Office International d'Hygiène Publique, 1900—1933.** Paris, Office International d'Hygiène Publique, 1933. 140 p.

924 Allen, Stephen H. **International Relations.** Princeton, Princeton University Press, 1920.

Chapter IV.

Part B. — Early International Organizations

925 Erzberger, Matthias. **The League of Nations.** New York, Holt, 1919.

Chapter V.

926 Kaeckenbeeck, Georges. **International Rivers.** London, H. M. Stationery Office, 1920. 68 p.

927 Krehbiel, Edward. **The European Commission of the Danube: An Experiment in International Administration,** *Political Science Quarterly,* XXXIII (March 1918), 38—55.

928 La Fontaine, Henri and Otlet, Paul. **International Associations of Various Types,** *The League of Nations Starts,* Raymond B. Fosdick, George Rublee, J. T. Shotwell, Léon Bourgeois, André Weiss, Lt.-Col. Requin, W. Ormsby-Gore, el Vizconde de Eza, H. B. Butler, Richard P. Strong, J. A. Salter, A. Claveille, Henri La Fontaine, Paul Otlet. London, Macmillan, 1920, pp. 201—209.

929 Lyons, Francis S. L. **Internationalism in Europe 1815—1914.** Leyden, Sythoff, 1963. 412 p.

930 Morrow, Dwight W. **The Society of Free States.** New York, Harper, 1919.

Chapter V.

931 Moynier, G. **Les Bureaux internationaux des unions universelles.** Paris, Cherbuliez, 1892. 174 p.

932 Myers, Denys P. **Representation in Public International Organs,** *American Journal of International Law,* VIII (January 1914), 81—108.

933 Otlet, Paul and La Fontaine, Henri. **International Associations of Various Types,** *The League of Nations Starts,* Raymond B. Fosdick, George Rublee, J. T. Shotwell, Léon Bourgeois, André Weiss, Lt.-Col. Requin, W. Ormsby-Gore, el Vizconde de Eza, H. B. Butler, Richard P. Strong, J. A. Salter, A. Claveille, Henri La Fontaine, Paul Otlet. London, Macmillan, 1920, pp. 201—209.

Part B. — Early International Organizations

934 Potter, Pitman B. **An Introduction to the Study of International Organization.** 4th. ed. New York, Appleton-Century, 1935.
Chapter X.

935 — —. **This World of Nations.** New York, Macmillan, 1929.
Chapter XI.

936 Read, Elizabeth. **International Law and International Relations.** N. p., American Foundation, 1925.
Chapter XVI.

937 Reiff, Henry. **The United States and International Administrative Unions: Some Historical Aspects,** *International Conciliation,* CCCXXXII (September 1937), 627—57.

938 Reinsch, Paul S. **International Unions and Their Administration,** *American Journal of International Law,* I (July 1907), 579—623.

939 — —. **Public International Unions: Their Work and Organization; A Study in International Administrative Law.** Boston, Ginn, 1911. viii + 189 p.

940 Sayre, Francis B. **Experiments in International Administration.** New York, Harper, 1919. 200 p.

941 Sly, John F. **The Genesis of the Universal Postal Union: A Study in the Beginnings of International Organization,** *International Conciliation,* CCXXXIII (October 1927), 9—57.

942 Universal Postal Union. **L'Union Postale Universelle: sa fondation et son développement, 1874—1949.** Berne, Universal Postal Union, 1949. 311 p.

945 Woolf, L. S. **International Government.** New York, Brentano's, 1916.
Part II – Chapter III.

944 Zimmern, Alfred E. **The League of Nations and the Rule of Law, 1918—1935.** 2d ed. London, Macmillan, 1939.
Part I – Chapter IV.

Part B. — *Early International Organizations*

6. HAGUE SYSTEM

Starting with the first Hague Conference in 1899 a system of arrangements pointed toward the eventual establishment of a league of nations. The periodic conference, the humanization of warfare, and the use of arbitration and other devices for the pacific settlement of disputes comprised what could be designated as the "Hague system." Had a third Hague conference been held after another eight-year interval, it would have met in 1915. By that time the cataclysm of World War I had revealed the inadequacy of the piecemeal efforts during the nineteenth century to establish international organizations.

6.1 HISTORY OF INTERNATIONAL ARBITRATION

945 Darby, William Evans. **International Arbitration: International Tribunals.** London, Dent, 1904. viii + 516 p.

  A collection of the various schemes which have been propounded, and of instances in nineteenth-century international settlements involving the application of international arbitration.

946 Evans, Howard. **Sir Randal Cremer: His Life and Work.** Boston, Ginn, 1910. 356 p.

  Cremer, founder in 1870 of the International Arbitration League, was awarded the Nobel Peace Price in 1903. He was also organizer and founder of the International Working Men's Association in Great Britain, to which he donated his Prize money, on condition that two-thirds of its council should always be chosen from the industrialized classes, "the future rulers of the world." He was a prominent member of Parliament, campaigning for complete parliamentary control over foreign and imperial policy.

947 Fraser, Henry L. **A Sketch of the History of International Arbitration,** *Cornell Law Quarterly*, XI (February 1926), 179—208.

948 Hill, Norman L. **British Arbitration Policies,** *International Conciliation*, CCLII (February 1930), 9—68.

  A history of British efforts with respect to arbitration and their origin in the peace movement. Documents in appendices.

949 **Lake Mohonk Conference on International Arbitration.** Lake Mohonk, N. Y., annually, 1885—1916.

Reports of annual conferences, first organized in June 1885 by Albert K. Smiley.

950 Lange, Christian L. **Histoire de l'internationalisme.** New York, Putnam, 1919. 506 p.

951 Lord, Eleanor L. **International Arbitration,** *Annals of the American Academy of Political and Social Science,* II (January 1892), 471—87.

952 Matthael, Louise E. **The Place of Arbitration and Mediation in Ancient Systems of International Ethics,** *Classical Quarterly,* II (October 1908), 241—64.

953 Moch, Gaston. **Histoire sommaire de l'arbitrage permanent.** Monaco, Institut International de la Paix, 1910. 215 p.

954 Moore, John Bassett. **Application of the Principle of International Arbitration on the American Continents,** *Annals of the American Academy of Political and Social Science,* XXII (July 1903), 35—44.

955 — —. **The United States and International Arbitration,** *American Historical Association Annual Report,* 1891, pp. 65—85.

956 Morris, Robert C. **International Arbitration and Procedure.** New Haven, Conn., Yale University Press, 1911. xii + 238 p.

957 Myers, Denys P. **The Origin of the Hague Arbitral Courts,** *American Journal of International Law,* VIII (October 1914), 769—801; X (April 1916), 270—311.

958 Penfield, William L. **International Arbitration,** *American Journal of International Law,* I (April 1907), 330—41.

959 Ralston, Jackson H. **International Arbitration, from Athens to Locarno.** Stanford, Calif., Stanford University Press, 1929. 417 p.

960 Scott, James Brown. **Development of Diplomacy in Modern Times,** *The History and Nature of International Relations*, Edmund A. Walsh (ed.). New York, Macmillan, 1922, pp. 93—129.

961 Simpson, John L. and Fox, Hazel. **International Arbitration.** London, Stevens, 1959. 330 p.

Chapter I deals with the history of arbitration from 1794.

962 Trueblood, Benjamin F. **The Development of the Peace Idea, and Other Essays.** Boston, Plimpton, 1932.

Chapter V.

963 — —. **International Arbitration at the Opening of the Twentieth Century.** Boston, American Peace Society, 1906. 20 p.

964 Westermann, W. L. **Interstate Arbitration in Antiquity,** *Classical Journal*, II (March 1907), 197—211.

6.2 HAGUE CONFERENCES (1899 and 1907)

965 Addams, Jane, Baich, Emily G. and Hamilton, Alice. **Women at The Hague.** New York, Macmillan, 1915. 171 p.

966 Allen, Stephen H. **International Relations.** Princeton, N. J., Princeton University Press, 1920.

Chapter VII.

967 Baldwin, Simeon E. **Eleventh Convention of the Hague Conference, 1907,** *American Journal of International Law*, II (April 1908), 307—12.

Part B. — Early International Organizations

968   Carnegie Endowment for International Peace. **The Proceedings of the Hague Peace Conferences.** New Yokr, Oxford University Press, 1920 —21. 5 vols.

969   Choate, Joseph H. **The Two Hague Conferences.** Princeton, Princeton University Press, 1913. 109 p.

970   Clarke, R. Floyd. **A Permanent Court of International Arbitration: Its Necessity and Value,** *American Journal of International Law*, I (April 1907), 342—408.

971   Davis, Calvin De Armond. **The United States and the First Hague Peace Conference.** Ithaca, Cornell University Press, 1962. xii + 236 p.

972   d'Estournelles de Constant, Baron. **The Results of the Second Hague Conference,** *International Conciliation*, IV (December 1907), 10—15.

973   Ford, Thomas King. **The Genesis of the First Hague Conference,** *Political Science Quarterly*, LI (September 1936), 355—82.

974   Hicks, Frederick Charles. **The Equality of States and the Hague Conferences,** *American Journal of International Law*, II (July 1908), 530—61.
Author traces and discusses the theory of equality of states in international law.

975   Higgins, Alexander P. **The Hague Peace Conferences Concerning the Laws and Usages of War: Texts and Conventions with Commentaries.** Cambridge, Eng., Cambridge University Press, 1909. xiv + 632 p.
Implications of the Hague conferences to laws of warfare.

976   Hill, David Jayne. **The Net Result an The Hague,** *Review of Reviews*, XXXVI (December 1907), 727—30.

977   — —. **The Second Peace Conference at The Hague,** *American Journal of International Law*, I (July 1907), 671—91.

Part B. — Early International Organizations

978 Holls, Frederick William. **The Peace Conference at The Hague, and Its Bearings on International Law and Policy.** New York, Macmillan, 1900. xxvi + 572 p.

979 Hull, William Isaac. **Obligatory Arbitration and the Hague Conferences,** *American Journal of International Law,* II (October 1908), 731—42.

980 — —. **The Two Hague Conferences and Their Contributions to International Law.** Boston, Ginn, 1908. xiv + 516 p.

981 — —. **The United States and Latin America at The Hague,** *International Conciliation,* XLIV (July 1911), 3—13.

982 Lammasch, Heinrich. **Compulsory Arbitration at the Second Hague Conference,** *American Journal of International Law,* IV (January 1910), 83—94.

983 Lawrence, Thomas J. **International Problems and Hague Conferences.** London, Dent, 1908. x + 210 p.

A popular account of the Hague conferences, considered not as isolated phenomena but as points in the evolution of international society.

984 Mangone, Gerard J. **A Short History of International Organization.** New York, McGraw-Hill, 1954.

Chapter IV.

985 Mead, Lucia Ames. **The Hague and Peace Conferences,** *A League of Nations,* Edith M. Phelps (ed.). New York, Wilson, 1919, pp. 28—41.

986 Miller, David Hunter. **Nationality and Other Problems Discussed at The Hague,** *Foreign Affairs,* VIII (July 1930), 632—40.

987 Morrow, Dwight W. **The Society of Free States.** New York, Harper, 1919.

Chapter IV.

988 Myers, Denys P. **The Origin of the Hague Arbitral Courts. II: The Proposed Court of Arbitral Justice,** *American Journal of International Law,* X (April 1916), 270–327.

989 Pollock, Frederick. **The League of Nations.** 2d ed. London, Stevens, 1922.

Chapter III.

990 Potter, Pitman B. and West, Roscoe. **International Civics.** New York, Macmillan, 1927.

Chapter VIII.

991 Reinsch, Paul S. **Failures and Successes at the Second Hague Conference,** *American Political Science Review,* II (February 1908), 204–20.

992 Schücking, Walter M. A. **The International Union of the Hague Conferences.** Charles Fenwick (tr.). Oxford, Clarendon, 1918. 342 p.

993 Scott, James Brown. **The Hague Peace Conferences of 1899 and 1907.** Baltimore, Johns Hopkins Press, 1909. 2 vols.

994 — —. (ed.). **The Proceedings of the Hague Peace Conference.** New York, Oxford University Press, 1920–21. 5 vols.

995 — —. **The Proposed Court of Arbitral Justice,** *American Journal of International Law,* II (October 1908), 772–810.

996 — —. **The Work of the Second Hague Peace Conference,** *American Journal of International Law,* II (January 1908), 1—28.

997 Trueblood, Benjamin F. **The Development of the Peace Idea, and Other Essays.** Boston, Plimpton, 1932.

Chapter VI.

998 — —. **The Success and Failures of the Second Hague Conference.** Boston, American Peace Society, n.d. 7 p.

999 White, Andrew D. **The First Hague Conference.** Boston, World Peace Foundation, 1912. 123 p.

1000 Zimmern, Alfred E. **The League of Nations and the Rule of Law, 1918—1935.** 2d ed. London, Macmillan, 1939.

Part I — Chapter X.

6.3 AFTERMATH

1001 **Arbitration Journal.** Quarterly, 1946—.

1002 Baff, William E. **The Evolution of Peace by Arbitration,** *American Law Review,* LIII (March—April 1919), 229—68.

1003 Balch, Thomas. **International Courts of Arbitration,** *Law Magazine and Review* (London), Series 3, III (November 1874), 1026—46.

1004 Boer, C. H. de. **The Peace Palace.** Rotterdam, Nijgh and van Ditmar, 1948. 35 p.

1005 Bourne, Randolph S. **Arbitration and International Politics,** *International Conciliation,* LXX (September 1913), 3–14.

1006 Carlston, Kenneth S. **The Process of International Arbitration.** New York, Columbia University Press, 1946. 318 p.

1007 Clark, John B. **An Economic View of War and Arbitration,** *International Conciliation,* XXXII (July 1910), 3–10.
An address before the 16th annual Lake Mohonk Conference.

1008 Darby, W. Evans. **The Enforcement of the Hague Conventions,** *Transactions* (Grotius Society), II (1916), 135–55.

1009 Duchosal, J. M. E. **The Revision of the Geneva Conventions,** *Political Quarterly,* XIX (January–March 1948), 32–40.

1010 Erzberger, Matthias. **The League of Nations.** New York, Holt, 1919.
Chapter VII.

1011 Foreign Policy Association. **International Arbitration and Plans for an American Locarno,** *Foreign Policy Reports,* III (June 8, 1927), 87–97.

1012 Foster, John W. **Arbitration and the Hague Court.** Boston, Houghton, Mifflin, 1904. 147 p.

1013 François, J. P. A. **The Permament Court of Arbitration,** *Recueil des Cours,* LXXXVII (1955), 460–551.

1014 Hudson, Manley O. **The Permanent Court of Arbitration,** *American Journal of International Law,* XXVII (July 1933), 440–60.

Part B. — Early International Organizations

1015 Hull, William Isaac. **The Third Hague Conference: Reasons Why It Should Be Held Now.** New York, Church Peace Union and the World Alliance for International Friendship Through the Churches, 1938. 15 p.

1016 Jenks, C. Wilfred. **The Prospects of International Adjudication.** London, Stevens, 1963. 900 p.

In this volume the author argues that the progress of international adjudication lags seriously behind current advances in other sectors of international organization, and urges that a thorough review of the jurisdiction and procedures of international courts and tribunals, and of the principles on which they develop the law, is overdue.

1017 Kellor, Frances A. and Hatvany, Antonia. **Security Against War.** New York, Macmillan, 1924.

Chapter XXVI.

1018 La Fontaine, H. **The Existing Elements of a Constitution of the United States of the World,** *International Conciliation,* XL (October 1911), 3—13.

1019 **Lake Mohonk Conference on International Arbitration.** Lake Mohonk, N. Y., annually, 1885—1916.

1020 Lammasch, Heinrich. **The Anglo-American Arbitration Treaty,** *International Conciliation,* XLIX (December 1911), 3—13.

1021 Lansing, Robert. **The Need of Revision of Procedure Before International Courts of Arbitration,** *American Society of International Law Proceedings,* VI (1912), 158—67.

Comments by B. Trueblood.

1022 Marburg, Theodore. **The Washington Meeting of the American Society for the Judicial Settlement of International Disputes,** *American Political Science Review,* V (May 1911), 181—93.

Part B. — Early International Organizations

1023 Mead, Edwin D. **The Results of the Two Hague Conferences and the Demands Upon the Third Conference.** Boston, World Peace Foundation, 1911. 14 p.

1024 Moore, John Bassett. **Comment on the Treaties,** *International Conciliation,* XLVIII (November 1911), 27—32.

   Reprinted from *The Independent,* August 17, 1911. The issue contains texts of American arbitration treaties with Great Britain and France; majority and minority reports from the Committee on Foreign Relations; comments by Simeon Baldwin and President Taft.

1025 — —. **International Cooperation,** *International Conciliation,* C (March 1916), 3—14.

1026 Narayan, C. V. L. **The United Nations' Convention on International Commercial Arbitration, 1958,** *Indian Journal of International Law,* I (1960—61), 33—37.

1027 Permanent Court of Arbitration. **The Hague Court Reports** (Hague). Edited and with an introduction by James Brown Scott. 2 vols. New York, Oxford University Press. Vol. I, 1916; Vol. II, 1932.

1028 Ralston, Jackson H. **Forces Making for International Conciliation and Peace,** *International Conciliation,* XLIX (December 1911), 14—21.

1029 — —. **International Arbitral Law and Procedure, Being a Résumé of the Procedure and Practice of International Commissions, and Including the Views of Arbitrators upon Questions Arising Under the Law of Nations.** Boston, Ginn, 1910. xx + 352 p.

1030 — —. **Some Suggestions As to the Permanent Court of Arbitration,** *American Journal of International Law,* I (April 1907), 321—29.

1031 Scott, James Brown. **The Evolution of a Permanent International Judiciary,** *American Journal of International Law,* VI (April 1912), 316—58.

1032 — —. **The Project Relative to a Court of Arbitral Justice.** Washington, Carnegie, 1920. 106 p.

1033 — —. **Recommendation for a Third Peace Conference at The Hague,** *American Journal of International Law,* II (October 1908), 815—22.

1034 Sillac, M. Jarousse de. **Periodical Peace Conferences,** *American Journal of International Law,* V (October 1911), 968—86.

1035 Smith, Herbert A. **International Law-Making,** *Transactions* (Grotius Society), XVI (1930), 93—103.
Comments by W. Bewes, A. Jaffe, H. M. Pratt, Cmdr. Palliccia, R. W. Lee.

1036 Tryon, James L. **A Permanent Court of International Justice,** *American Society of International Law Proceedings,* VI (1912), 144—57.

1037 van der Mandere, H. Ch. G. J. **Work of the Hague Tribunals,** *Current History,* XXI (December 1924), 383—90.

1038 Vinacke, Harold M. **International Organization.** New York, Crofts, 1934.
Chapter IX.

1039 White, Henry. **The Organization and Procedure of the Third Hague Conference,** *American Society of International Law Proceedings,* VI (1912), 178—87.
Comments by W. M. Collier, T. P. Ion, and D. P. Myers.

1040 Wright, Hamilton. **The International Opium Commission,** *American Journal of International Law*, III (July 1909), 648—73.

"It was the first step towards the solution of the opium problem by international action. It was the second Commission of its kind to meet since the formulation of the Hague rules of 1899 as to the functions of such Commissions. Its organization, its rules of procedure, the spirit in which it attacked its problem avoided a majority and minority report and declared unanimously, establish a precedent for the guidance of all future Commissions of Inquiry."

1041 Zimmern, Alfred E. **The League of Nations and the Rule of Law,** 1918—1935. 2d ed. London, Macmillan, 1939.

Part I — Chapter XI.

Part C.

LEAGUE OF NATIONS SYSTEM

Part C. — League of Nations System

The "League of Nations system" refers to the institutions, activities and practices associated with the League of Nations, and with related agencies that operated semiautonomously or autonomously during the interwar period. The latter are included in Part C because coordination with the League of intergovernmental global organizations was inevitable and widespread among organs formally outside the League of Nations structure.

1. DOCUMENTS AND BIBLIOGRAPHY

See A 3.2 and A 5.2.

2. WORLD WAR I EFFORTS

2.1 PROPOSALS FOR POSTWAR INTERNATIONAL ORGANIZATION

1042 Adler, Felix. **A Parliament of Parliaments,** *Academy of Political Science Proceedings,* VII (2, 1917), 246–50.

1043 Andrews, Fannie Fern. **The Central Organization for a Durable Peace,** *Annals of the American Academy of Political and Social Science,* LXVI (July 1916), 16–21.

1044 Angell, Norman. **America and the New World State: A Plea for American Leadership in International Organization.** New York, Putnam, 1915. 305 p.

1045 — —. **War Aims: The Need for a Parliament for the Allies.** London, Headley, 1917. 127 p.

1046 Ashbee, Charles Robert. **The American League to Enforce Peace: An English Interpretation.** Introduction by G. Lowes Dickinson. London, Allen and Unwin, 1917. 92 p.

1047 Balch, Thomas W. **A World Court in the Light of the United States Supreme Court.** Philadelphia, Allen, Lane and Scott, 1918. 163 p.

1048 Baldwin, Simeon E. **The Membership of a World Tribunal for Promoting Permanent Peace,** *American Journal of International Law,* XII (July 1918), 453–61.

1049 — —. **Suspension from the Society of Nations, a Sufficient Sanction for a World-Court Judgment,** *American Law Review,* LII (September–October 1918), 695–700.

1050 Barker, Ernest. **A Confederation of the Nations, Its Powers and Constitution.** Oxford, Clarendon, 1918. 54 p.

1051 Bartlett, Ruhl Jacob. **The League to Enforce Peace.** Chapel Hill, University of North Carolina Press, 1944. 252 p.

1052 Bisschop, W. R. **International Leagues,** *Transactions* (Grotius Society), II (1916), 117–34.

1053 Bourgeois, Léon, V. A. **Le pacte de 1919 et la Société des Nations.** Paris, Fasquelle, 1919. 279 p.

> A collection of the author's speeches and articles on the League, 1916–1919. Bourgeois urges the establishment of an international military organization.

1054 — —. **Pour La Société des Nations.** Paris, Fasquelle, 1910, xii + 467 p.

1055 Bourne, Randolph S. (ed.). **Towards an Enduring Peace: A Symposium of Peace Proposals and Programs, 1914–1916.** New York, American Association for International Conciliation, 1916. xv + 336 p.

1056 Brailsford, Henry Noel. **A League of Nations.** London, Headley, 1917. 332 p.

Part C. — League of Nations System

1057 Bryan, William Jennings. **The Proposal for a League to Enforce Peace—Negative,** *International Conciliation,* CVI (September 1916), 21—35.
Taft argued the affirmative.

1058 Bryce, James. **Essays and Addresses in War Time.** New York, Macmillan, 1918. 208 p.
See especially the section, "Scheme Drafted by a British Group, 1915," pp. 206—208, which was the "Bryce group" Proposal for the Avoidance of War, February 24, 1915.

1059 Buehrig, Edward H. **Woodrow Wilson and Collective Security,** *Wilson's Foreign Policy in Perspective,* Edward H. Buehrig (ed.). Bloomington, Indiana University Press, 1957, pp. 34—60.

1060 — —. **Woodrow Wilson and the Balance of Power.** Bloomington, Indiana University Press, 1955.
Chapters VI—IX.

1061 Butler, Nicholas Murray. **The International Mind: An Argument for the Judicial Settlement of International Disputes.** New York, Scribner, 1912. xii + 121 p.

1062 — —. **A League of Nations,** *International Conciliation,* CXXXI (October 1918), 526—30.
Reprinted from *London Daily Chronicle,* July 27, 1918.

1063 Buxton, Charles R. (ed.). **Towards a Lasting Settlement.** London, Allen and Unwin, 1916. 216 p.

1064 Carnegie Endowment for International Peace, Division of International Law. **Official Communications and Speeches Relating to Peace Proposals, 1916—1917.** Washington, Carnegie, 1917. 96 p.

1065 Central Organization for a Durable Peace (Hague). **A Durable Peace: Official Commentary on the Minimum Program.** Hague, 1915. 46 p.
This is the international association founded at The Hague in 1915 to study and advocate a settlement at the conclusion of the war that would guarantee a stable peace.

Part C. — League of Nations System

1066 Crosby, Oscar T. **An Armed International Tribunal, the Sole Peace-Keeping Mechanism,** *Annals of the American Academy of Political and Social Science,* LXVI (July 1916), 32–34.

1067 Dennis, William C. **International Organization: Executive and Administrative,** *American Society of International Law Proceedings,* XI (1917), 91–101.

1068 Dickinson, Goldsworthy Lowes. **The Basis of a Permanent Peace,** *Towards a Lasting Settlement,* Charles R. Buxton (ed.). New York, Macmillan, 1916, pp. 11–36.

1069 — —. **Choice Before Us.** London, Allen and Unwin, 1918. 274 p.

1070 — —. **The Foundations of a League of Peace.** Boston, World Peace Foundation, 1915. 20 p.

1071 Dutton, Samuel T., Wald, Lillian D., and Storey, Moorefield. **Discussion of World Organization,** *Academy of Political Science Proceedings,* VII, 2 (1917), 251–56.

1072 Eliot, Charles William. **The Road Toward Peace: A Contribution to the Study of the Causes of the European War and of the Means of Preventing War in the Future.** Boston, Houghton, Mifflin, 1915, 286 p.
Comprises addresses, correspondence, and letters to the editor.

1073 Erzberger, Matthias. **The League of Nations.** New York, Holt, 1919.
Chapter I.

1074 Fenwick, Charles G. **International Organization: Judicial,** *American Society of International Law Proceedings,* XI (April 1917), 64–75.
Comments by La Fontaine, Ion, Myers, Hill, Hays, Russell, Eliot, Scott.

1075 Filene, Edward A. **The Road to a Durable Peace,** *Annals of the American Academy of Political and Social Science,* LXVI (July 1916), 44–49.

Part C. — League of Nations System

1076 Fuller, Dale C. **Lenin's Attitude Toward an International Organization for the Maintenance of Peace, 1914—1917,** *Political Science Quarterly*, LXIV (June 1949), 245—61.

1077 Goldsmith, Robert. **A League to Enforce Peace.** New York, Macmillan, 1917. 331 p.

1078 Grey, Edward. **The League of Nations.** London, Oxford University Press, 1918. 15 p.

1079 Hobson, John A. **Towards International Government.** New York, Macmillan, 1915. 216 p.

1080 Holt, Hamilton. **The League to Enforce Peace,** *Academy of Political Science Proceedings*, VII, 2 (1917), 257—61.

1081 — —. **The Way to Disarm: A Practical Proposal,** *General International Organization*, James T. Watkins IV and J. William Robinson (eds.). Princeton, N.J., Van Nostrand, 1956, pp. 47—51.

Reprinted from *The Independent*, September 28, 1914. Holt was a leading figure in the New York Peace Society. This article inspired the meetings out of which emerged the League to Enforce Peace.

1082 Hull, William I. **Three Plans for a Durable Peace,** *Annals of the American Academy of Political and Social Science*, LXVI (July 1916), 12—15.

1083 — —. **A World Court,** *Academy of Political Science Proceedings*, VII, 2 (1917), 221—27.

1084 Joy, William. **War and Peace: The Evils of the First and a Plan for Preserving the Last.** New York, Oxford University Press, 1919. 69 p.

Reprinted from the original edition of 1842, with an introductory note by James Brown Scott.

1085 Joyce, James Avery. **World in the Making.** New York, Schuman, 1953.

Chapter VIII.

1086 Kallen, Horace M. **The Structure of Lasting Peace: An Inquiry into the Motives of War and Peace.** Boston, Jones, 1918. 187 p.

1087 Knudson, John I. **A History of the League of Nations.** Atlanta, Smith, 1938.
Chapter I.

1088 Kocourek, Albert. **Some Reflections on the Problem of a Society of Nations,** *American Journal of International Law*, XII (July 1918), 498–518.

1089 La Fontaine, Henri. **The Great Solution: Magnissima Charta.** Boston, World Peace Foundation, 1916. 177 p.

1090 Lape, Esther Everett (ed.). **Ways to Peace: Twenty Plans Selected from the Most Representative of Those Submitted to the American Peace Award for the Best Practicable Plan by Which the United States May Cooperate with Other Nations To Achieve and Preserve the Peace of the World.** Preface by Edward W. Bok. New York, Scribner, 1924. xvi + 465 p.
Essays by E. Borchard, C. A. Herter, W. S. Culbertson, G. Borglum, S. P. Wilson, M. C. Thomas, S. Strunsky, C. W. Eliot, E. Buncken, J. McA. Palmer, D. S. Jordan, M. D. Hudson, J. W. Stinson, D. Atkins, I. Stanfield, E. J. Howe, C. H. Brent, N. Isaacs, P. H. Arthur.

1091 Latané, John H. (ed.). **Development of the League of Nations Idea: Documents and Correspondence of Theodore Marburg.** New York, Macmillan, 1932. 2 vols.

1092 Lawrence, Thomas J. **The Society of Nations: Its Past, Present, and Possible Future.** New York, Oxford University Press, 1919. 194 p.

1093 League to Enforce Peace, American Branch. **Enforced Peace: Proceedings of the First Annual National Assemblage of the League to Enforce Peace, May 26–27, 1916.** With introductory chapter and appendices giving the proposals of the League, its officers and committees. New York, League to Enforce Peace, 1916. 204 p.

1094 — —. **Historical Light on the League to Enforce Peace.** Boston, World Peace Foundation, 1916. 21 p.

1095 — —. **Independence Hall Conference Held in the City of Philadelphia, Bunker Hill Day (June 17th), 1915, Together with Speeches Made at a Public Banquet in the Bellevue-Stratford Hotel on the Preceding Evening.** New York, League to Enforce Peace, 1915. 65 p.

1096 — —. **Win the War for Permanent Peace: Addresses Made at the National Convention of the League to Enforce Peace in the City of Philadelphia, May 16 th and 17th, 1918; Convention Platform and Governors' Declaration.** New York, League to Enforce Peace, 1918. 253 p.

1097 Lodge, Henry Cabot. **Force and Peace,** *Annals of the American Academy of Political and Social Science,* LX (July 1915), 197–212.

1098 Lyons, F. S. L. **Internationalism in Europe 1815–1914.** Leyden, Sythoff, 1963.

Part V.

1099 MacCracken, John H. **The Basis of a Durable Peace,** *Annals of the American Academy of Political and Social Science,* LXVI (July 1916), 35–43.

1100 Marburg, Theodore. **The League to Enforce Peace—A Reply to Critics,** *Annals of the American Academy of Political and Social Science,* LXVI (July 1916), 50–59.

1101 — —. **World Court and League of Peace,** *Annals of the American Academy of Political and Social Science,* LXI (September 1915), 276–83.

1102 Metz, John. **Peace Literature of the War,** *International Conciliation,* XCVIII, special bulletin (January 1916), 31–51.

Part C. — League of Nations System

1103 Minor, Raleigh Colston. **International Organization: Constitution of a Legislative Body,** *American Society of International Law Proceedings,* XI (1917), 56—64.

1104 — —. **A Republic of Nations: A Study of the Organization of a Federal League of Nations.** New York, Oxford University Press, 1918. xxxiii + 316 p.

1105 Morrow, Dwight W. **The Society of Free States.** New York, Harper, 1929. 223 p.

1106 Myers, Denys P. **The Commission of Inquiry: The Wilson-Bryan Peace Plan, Its Origin and Development.** Boston, World Peace Foundation, 1913. 27 p.

1107 — —. **The Conciliation Plan of the League to Enforce Peace, with American Treaties in Force.** Boston, World Peace Foundation, 1916. 35 p.

1108 Nijhoff, Martinus (ed.). **War Obviated by an International Police: A Series of Essays Written in Various Countries.** Hague, Nijhoff, 1915. iv + 233 p.

Excerpts from writings of van Vollenhoven, van Asbeck, den beer Poortugael, van Hoven, Dunlop, Erich, Roosevelt, Kinkaid, Goodrich, Butler, Carnegie, Fried, Bourgeois, Schuecking, Lawrence, Angell and Grey.

1109 Olson, William Clinton. **Theodore Roosevelt's Conception of an International League,** *World Affairs Quarterly,* XXIX (January 1959), 329—53.

1110 Overstreet, Harry Allen. **What a League of Nations Shall Be,** *A League of Nations,* Edith M. Phelps (ed.). New York, Wilson, 1919, pp. 123—33.

1111 Petersson, Hans F. **Power and International Order: An Analytical Study of Four Schools of Thought and Their Approaches to the War, the Peace and a Post-War System, 1914—1919.** Hans F. Petersson and John Spencer (trans.). Lund, Sweden, Gleerup, 1964. xv + 374 p.

Part C. — League of Nations System

1112 Pollard, Albert F. **The League of Nations: An Historical Argument.** Oxford, Clarendon, 1918. 68 p.

1113 Reeves, Jesse S. **The Justiciability of International Disputes,** *American Political Science Review*, X (February 1916), 70—79.

1114 Schvan, August. **Six Essentials to Permanent Peace,** *Annals of the American Academy of Political and Social Science*, LX (July 1915), 222—29.

1115 Scott, James Brown. **International Organization: Executive and Administrative,** *American Society of International Law Proceedings*, XI (1917), 101—107.

1116 — —. (ed.). **Official Statements of War Aims and Peace Proposals, December 1916 to November 1918.** Washington, Carnegie, 1921. 315 p.

1117 Smuts, Jan. **The League of Nations: A Practical Suggestion.** London: Hodder and Stoughton, 1918. 71 p.

1118 Stallybrass, William T. S. **A Society of States: Sovereignty, Independence, and Equality in a League of Victors.** New York, Dutton, 1919. xvii + 242 p.

1119 Taft, William Howard. **The Proposal for a League to Enforce Peace— Affirmative,** *International Conciliation*, CVI (September 1916), 3—20.

Bryan argued the negative.

1120 — —. **Taft Papers on League of Nations.** Theodore Marburg and Horace E. Flack (eds.). New York, Macmillan, 1920. 340 p.

1121 Tenney, A. A. **Theories of Social Organization and the Problem of International Peace,** *Political Science Quarterly*, XXX (March 1915), 1—14.

Part C. — League of Nations System

1122 Trueblood, Benjamin F. **The Development of the Peace Idea, and Other Essays.** Boston, Plimpton, 1932.

  Chapter VIII.

1123 — —. **A Periodic Congress of the Nations.** Rev. ed. Boston, American Peace Society, 1907. 12 p.

1124 Turner, Frederick Jackson. **American Sectionalism and World Organization,** *American Historical Review,* XLVII (April 1952), 547—51.

  Preface by William Diamond to Turner's document of November 1918, "International Political Parties in a Durable League of Nations."

1125 Walters, Francis Paul. **A History of the League of Nations.** London, Oxford University Press, 1960.

  Chapter III.

1126 Webster, Charles Kingsley and Herbert, Sydney. **The League of Nations in Theory and Practice.** London, Allen and Unwin, 1933.

  Chapter II.

1127 Wells, Herbert George. **The Idea of a League of Nations: In the Fourth Year; Anticipations of a World Peace.** New York, Macmillan, 1918. 154 p.

1128 Wheeler, Everett P. **A Permanent Court of International Justice,** *American Society of International Law Proceedings,* VI (1912), 171—76.

  Comments by C. L. Lange.

1129 Williams, Talcott. **An International Court, an International Sheriff and World Peace,** *Annals of the American Academy of Political and Social Science,* LXI (September 1915), 274—75.

1130 Winkler, Henry R. **The League of Nations Movement in Great Britain, 1914—1919.** New Brunswick, Rutgers University Press, 1952. xiii + 288 p.

Part C. — League of Nations System

1131   Woolf, Leonard S. (ed.). **The Framework of a Lasting Peace.** London, Allen and Unwin, 1917. 154 p.

1132   — —. **International Government: Together With a Project by a Fabian Committee for a Supernational Authority That Will Prevent War.** Introduction by Bernard Shaw. New York, Brentano's, 1916. xxiii + 412 p.

1133   — —. **International Government: Two Reports.** London, Allen and Unwin, 1923. 388 p.

1134   Zimmern, Alfred E. **The League of Nations and the Rule of Law, 1918—1935.** 2d ed. London, Macmillan, 1939.

   Part II — Chapters III—IX.

2.2 ORGANIZED COOPERATION AMONG THE ALLIES

1135   Beveridge, William H. **British Food Control.** London, Oxford University Press, 1928. 447 p.

1136   Bliss, Tasker H. **The Evolution of the Unified Command,** *Foreign Affairs*, I (December 1922), 1—30.

1137   Cotton, Joseph P., and Morrow, Dwight W. **The Making of International Cooperation During the Great War,** *The League of Nations*, Stephen Pierce Duggan (ed.). Boston, Atlantic Monthly Press, 1919, pp. 50—63.

1138   Dawes, Charles G. **A Journal of the Great War.** Boston, Houghton, Mifflin, 1921. 2 vols.

1139   Eliot, George Fielding. **Unified Command: Lessons from the Past,** *Foreign Affairs*, XXI (October 1942), 11—20.

1140   Fayle, Charles Ernest. **Seaborne Trade and Merchant Shipping in the War.** London, Murray, 1920—24. 3 vols.

Part C. — *League of Nations System*

1141 Grant, Ulysses S. **America's Part in the Supreme War Council During the War,** *Records* (Columbia Historical Society), XXIX—XXX (1927), 295—340.

1142 Hankey, Maurice P. A. **Diplomacy by Conference,** *Proceedings of the British Institute of International Affairs,* I (1920), 4—27.

1143 — —. **The Supreme Command, 1914—1918.** London, Allen and Unwin, 1961. 2 vols.

1144 Hoover, Herbert. **The Economic Administration During the Armistice,** *What Really Happened at Paris,* Edward M. House and Charles Seymour (eds.). New York, Scribner, 1921, pp. 336—47.

1145 Kuhl, Hermann von. **Unity of Command Among the Central Powers,** *Foreign Affairs,* II (September 15, 1923), 130—46.

1146 Lloyd, Edward M. H. **Experiments in State Control at the War Office and the Ministry of Food.** Oxford, Clarendon, 1924. 460 p.

1147 Marston, Frank Swain. **The Peace Conference of 1919: Organization and Procedure.** London, Oxford University Press, 1944.

Chapter I.

1148 Maurice, Frederick B. **Lessons of Allied Cooperation: Naval, Military and Air, 1914—1918.** London, Oxford University Press, 1942. vii + 195 p.

1149 — —. **Unity of Policy Among Allies,** *Foreign Affairs,* XXI (January 1943), 322—30.

1150 Money, Leo George Chiozza. **The Triumph of Nationalisation.** London, Cassell, 1920. 275 p.

Written from the point of view indicated in the title, but includes much firsthand information not otherwise available on wartime organization.

1151 Morrow, Dwight W. **The Society of Free States.** New York, Harper, 1919.
Chapter VI.

1152 Palmer, Frederick. **Bliss, Peacemaker: The Life and Letters of General Tasker Howard Bliss.** New York, Dodd, Mead, 1934. 477 p.

1153 Ritchie, Hugh. **The "Navicert" System During the World War.** Washington, Carnegie, 1938. 83 p.

1154 Rublee, George. **Inter-Allied Machinery in War-Time,** *The League of Nations Starts*, Raymond B. Fosdick, George Rublee, J. T. Shotwell, Léon Bourgeois, André Weiss, Lt.-Col. Requin, W. Ormsby Gore, el Vizconde de Eza, H. B. Butler, Richard P. Strong, J. A. Salter, A. Claveille, Henri La Fontaine, Paul Otlet. London, Macmillan, 1920, pp. 29—45.

1155 Salter, James Arthur. **Allied Shipping Control: An Experiment in International Administration.** New Haven, Conn., Yale University Press, 1921. 372 p.

1156 Trask, David T. **The United States in the Supreme War Council: American War Aims and Inter-Allied Strategy, 1917—1918.** Middletown, Conn., Wesleyan University Press, 1961. 244 p.

1157 Trueblood, Benjamin F. **The Development of the Peace Idea, and Other Essays.** Introduction by Edwin D. Mead. Boston, Plimpton, 1932. xxviii + 243 p.

1158 World Peace Foundation. **The Supreme War Council,** *World Peace Foundation Pamphlets*, I (October 1917), x + 345—416.

1159 Wright, Peter E. **At the Supreme War Council.** New York, Putnam, 1921. 201 p.

1160 Zimmern, Alfred E. **The League of Nations and the Rule of Law, 1918—1935.** 2d ed. London, Macmillan, 1939.
Part II — Chapters I, II.

3. VERSAILLES SYSTEM

The League of Nations was only facet of the peace settlement of 1919 that resulted in international institutions. Because the United States failed to join the League and yet was responsible for the supervision of the peace treaties, the Conference of Ambassadors was established. German war reparations, complicated first by the problem of inflation and later by the world economic depression, also became a subject for several international conferences held outside the League framework.

3.1 VERSAILLES CONFERENCE (1919)

1161 Albrecht-Carrié, René. **Italy at the Paris Peace Conference.** New York, Columbia University Press, 1938. 575 p.

1162 Angell, Norman. **Versailles and Geneva,** *The Treaty of Versailles and After*, George Riddel, C. K. Webster, Arnold J. Toynbee, Denis Saurat, Werner von Rheinbaben, Forges Davanzati, Tappan Hollond, Marquess of Reading, Norman Angell. London, Allen and Unwin, 1935, pp. 174—87.

1163 Armstrong, Hamilton Fish. **Power Politics and the Peace Machinery,** *Foreign Affairs*, XIV (October 1935), 1—11.

1164 ——. **Versailles: Retrospect,** *Foreign Affairs*, XI (October 1932), 173—89.

1165 Baker, Ray Stannard. **The Versailles Treaty and After,** *Current History*, XIX (December 1923), 547—59.

1166 ——. **Woodrow Wilson and World Settlement.** Garden City, N.Y., Doubleday, Page, 1922. 3 vols.

Part C. — League of Nations System

1167 Beer, George Louis. **African Question at the Paris Peace Conference, with Papers on Egypt, Mesopotamia, and the Colonial Settlement.** New York, Macmillan, 1923. 628 p.

1168 Benns, F. Lee. **The Two Paris Peace Conferences of the Twentieth Century,** *Essays in History and International Relations in Honor of George Hubbard Blakeslee*, Dwight E. Lee and George E. McReynolds (eds.). Worcester, Mass., Clark University Press, 1949, pp. 153–70.

1169 Binkley, Robert C. **New Light on the Paris Peace Conference, from the Armistice to the Organization of the Peace Conference,** *Political Science Quarterly*, XLVI (September 1931), 335–61; (December 1931), 509–47.

1170 Birdsall, Paul. **Versailles Twenty Years After.** New York, Reynal and Hitchcock, 1941. 350 p.

1171 Bliss, Tasker Howard. **The Problem of Disarmament,** *What Really Happened at Paris*, Edward M. House and Charles Seymour (eds.). New York, Scribner, 1921, pp. 370–97.

1172 Bonsal, Stephen. **Suitors and Suppliants: The Little Nations at Versailles.** Introduction by Arthur Krock. New York, Prentice-Hall, 1946. 301 p.

1173 — —. **Unfinished Business.** Introduction by Hugh Gibson. New York, Doubleday, Doran, 1944. xi + 313 p.

Excerpts from the author's diary, when he was President Wilson's confidential interpreter at the Paris Conference of 1919.

1174 Caldis, Calliope, **The Council of Four As a Joint Emergency Authority in the European Crisis at the Paris Peace Conference, 1919.** Annemasse, Impr. Franco-suisse, 1953. 228 p.

1175 Chase, Eugene P. **The United Nations: After San Francisco,** *Current History*, New Series, XXII (January 1952), 9—12.

1176 Curry, George. **Woodrow Wilson, Jan Smuts, and the Versailles Settlement,** *American Historical Review*, LXVI (July 1961), 968—86.

1177 Czernin, Ferdinand. **Versailles 1919: The Forces, Events and Personalities That Shaped the Treaty.** New York, Putnam, 1964. 437 p.

1178 Day, Clive. **The Atmosphere and Organization of the Peace Conference,** *What Really Happened at Paris*, Howard M. House and Charles Seymour (eds.). New York, Scribner, 1921, pp. 15—36.

1179 Dillon, Emile J. **The Inside Story of the Peace Conference.** New York, Harper, 1920. 512 p.

1180 Fenwick, Charles C. **Organization and Procedure of the Peace Conference,** *American Political Science Review*, XIII (May 1919), 199—212.

Connection between Hague Conference, Supreme War Command, and Versailles Conference in the development of procedures at conferences.

1181 Finch, George A. **The Peace Conference of Paris, 1919: Its Organization and Method of Work,** *American Journal of International Law*, XIII (April 1919), 159—86.

1182 Gompers, Samuel. **The Labor Clauses of the Treaty,** *What Really Happened at Paris*, Edward M. House and Charles Seymour (eds.). New York, Scribner, 1921, pp. 319—35.

1183 Hankey, Maurice. **The Supreme Council at the Paris Peace Conference 1919: A Commentary.** London, Allen and Unwin, 1963. 206 p.

1184 House, Edward M. **The Intimate Papers of Colonel House, Arranged As a Narrative by Charles Seymour.** Boston, Houghton, Mifflin, 1926—1928. 4 vols.

Part C. — League of Nations System

1185 House, Edward M. and Seymour, Charles (eds.). **What Really Happened at Paris: The Story of the Peace Conference, 1918–1919, by American Delegates.** New York, Scribner, 1921. xiv + 528 p.

1186 Howard-Ellis, C. **The Origin, Structure and Working of the League of Nations.** Boston, Houghton, Mifflin, 1928.
Chapter II.

1187 Hudson, Manley Ottmer. **The Protection of Minorities and Natives in Transferred Territories,** *What Really Happened at Paris*, Edward M. House and Charles Seymour (eds.). New York, Scribner, 1921, pp. 204–30.

1188 Kaliharvi, Thorsten V. **Settlements of World Wars I and II Compared,** *Annals of the American Academy of Political and Social Science*, CCLVII **(May 1948),** 194–202.

1189 Kepi. **Versailles—Before and After,** *Foreign Affairs*, II (December 1923), 193–210.

1190 Lansing, Robert. **The Big Four and Others of the Peace Conference.** Boston, Houghton, Mifflin, 1921. 212 p.

1191 — —. **The Peace Negotiations: A Personal Narrative.** Boston, Houghton, Mifflin, 1921. vi + 328 p.

1192 Lloyd George, David. **Memoirs of the Peace Conference.** New Haven, Conn., Yale University Press, 1939. 2 vols.

1193 Luckau, Alma. **The German Delegation at the Paris Peace Conference.** New York, Columbia University Press, 1941. xv + 522 p.

1194 Marston, Frank Swain. **The Peace Conference of 1919: Organization and Procedure.** London, Oxford University Press, 1944. 276 p.

Part C. — League of Nations System

1195 Miller, David Hunter. **The Drafting of the Covenant.** New York, Putnam, 1928. 2 vols.

   The standard work on the genesis of the Covenant.

1196 — —. **The Making of the League of Nations,** *What Really Happened at Paris*, Edward M. House and Charles Seymour (eds.). New York, Scribner, 1921. pp. 398—424.

1197 — —. **My Diary at the Conference of Paris.** New York, Appeal, 1924. 21 vols.

   The edition of this work consists of forty sets only.

1198 Moon, Parker Thomas. **More Light on the Peace Conference,** *Political Science Quarterly*, XXXVI (September 1921), 501—508.

1199 Morley, Felix. **The Society of Nations.** Washington, Brookings, 1932.
   Chapters I—VI.

1200 Nicolson, Harold George. **Peacemaking at Paris: Success, Failure, or Farce?** *Foreign Affairs*, XXV (January 1947), 190—203.

1201 — —. **Peacemaking, 1919: Being Reminiscences of the Paris Peace Conference.** Boston, Houghton, Mifflin, 1933. vii + 378 p.

1202 Noble, George Bernard. **Policies and Opinions at Paris, 1919: Wilsonian Diplomacy, the Versailles Peace, and French Public Opinion.** New York, Macmillan, 1935. x + 465 p.

1203 Riddell, George, Webster, C. K., Toynbee, Arnold J., Saurat, Denis, Rheinbaben, Werner von, Davanzati, Forges, Hollond, Tappan, Reading, Marquess of, Angell, Norman. **The Treaty of Versailles and After.** London, Allen and Unwin, 1935. 192 p.

1204 Schiff, Victor. **The Germans at Versailles.** London, Williams and Norgate, 1930. 208 p.

Part C. — *League of Nations System*

1205 Schwarzenberger, Georg. **Power Politics.** 3d ed. London, Stevens, 1964.

Chapter XVII.

1206 Sharp, Walter, and Kirk, Grayson. **Contemporary International Politics.** New York, Farrar and Rinehart, 1941.
Chapter XXI.

1207 Shotwell, James T. **At the Paris Peace Conference.** New York, Macmillan, 1937. 444 p.

1208 Slosson, Preston. **The Constitution of the Peace Conference,** *Political Science Quarterly,* XXXV (September 1920), 360–71.

1209 — —. **Unity and Division at Versailles,** *The Quest for Political Unity in World History,* Stanley Pargellis (ed.). Washington, U. S. Government Printing Office, 1944, pp. 159–62.

1210 Temperley, Harold W. V. (ed.). **A History of the Peace Conference of Paris.** London, Frowde, and Hodder and Stoughton, 1920–24. 6 vols.

1211 Toynbee, Arnold J. **The League of Nations,** *The Treaty of Versailles and After,* George Riddell, C. K. Webster, Arnold J. Toynbee, Denis Saurat, Werner von Rheinbaben, Forges Davanzati, Tappan Hollond, Marquess of Reading, Norman Angell. London, Allen and Unwin, 1935, pp. 24–41.

1212 United States, Department of State. **The Treaty of Versailles and After: Annotations of the Text of the Treaty.** Department of State Publication 2724, Conference Series 92. Washington, U. S. Government Printing Office, 1947. xiv + 1018 p.

Pages 69–122 deal with the Covenant of the League of Nations. This work was initiated by President Roosevelt in October 1943, and prepared by Denys P. Myers.

1213 Walters, Francis Paul. **A History of the League of Nations.** London, Oxford University Press, 1960.

Chapter IV.

1214 Webster, Charles Kingsley. **Patterns of Peacemaking,** *Foreign Affairs,* XXV (July 1947), 596–611.

1215 — —. **The Problem Before the Peacemakers,** *The Treaty of Versailles and After,* George Riddell, C. K. Webster, Arnold J. Toynbee, Denis Saurat, Werner von Rheinbaben, Forges Davanzati, Tappan Hollond, Marquess of Reading, Norman Angell. London, Allen and Unwin, 1935, pp. 24–41.

1216 Webster, Charles Kingsley and Temperley, Harold W. V. **The Congress of Vienna, 1814–1815, and the Conference of Paris, 1919.** London, H. M. Stationery Office, 1923. 28 p.

Contains two Parts: (1) a comparison of the organizations and their results by Webster; (2) attempts at international government in Europe: the period of the Congress of Vienna (1814–1825), and the period since the Treaty of Versailles (1919–1922), by Temperly.

1217 Webster, Charles Kingsley and Herbert, Sydney. **The League of Nations in Theory and Practice.** London, Allen and Unwin, 1933.

Chapter III.

1218 Willoughby, Westel W. **China at the Conference.** Baltimore, John Hopkins Press, 1922. 419 p.

1219 Wilson, Florence. **The Origins of the League Covenant: Documentary History of Its Drafting.** London, Hogarth Press, 1928. 260 p.

1220 Woolsey, Lester H. **The Personal Diplomacy of Colonel House,** *American Journal of International Law,* XXI (October 1927), 706–15.

1221 Wright, Quincy. **Where the League of Nations Stands Today.** Minneapolis, University of Minnesota Press, 1934. 25 p.

3.2 CONFERENCE OF AMBASSADORS (Paris)

1222 Pink, Gerhard P. **The Conference of Ambassadors (Paris 1920—1931),** *Geneva Studies,* XII (February 1942), 1—293.

3.3 REPARATIONS

1223 Alpha. **Reparations and the Policy of Repudiation: An American View,** *Foreign Affairs,* II (Summer 1923), 55—83.

1224 Anderson, C. P. **Final Liquidation of German War Reparations,** *American Journal of International Law,* XXV (January 1931), 97—101.

1225 Angell, J. W. **The Payment of Reparations and Inter-Ally Debts,** *Foreign Affairs,* IV (October 1925), 85—96.

1226 — —. **Reparation and the Inter-Ally Debts in 1931,** *Foreign Policy Reports,* VII (April 29, 1931), 83—100.

1227 Boyden, R. W. **The Dawes Report,** *Foreign Affairs,* II (June 1924), 583—97.

1228 — —. **Relation Between Reparations and the Interallied Debts,** *Academy of Political Science Proceedings,* XII (January 1928), 819—26.

1229 — —. **The United States and the Dawes Plan,** *Academy of Political Science Proceedings,* XI (January 1925), 343—53.

1230 Burnett, Philip M. **Reparation at the Paris Peace Conference from the Standpoint of the American Delegation.** New York, Columbia University Press, 1940. 2 vols.

1231 Dawes, Charles G. **A Journal of Reparations.** Foreword by Lord Stamp and H. Brüning. London, Macmillan, 1939. xxv + 527 p.

1232 Dulles, J. F. **The Reparation Problem,** *Economic Journal*, XXXI (June 1921), 179—86.

1233 Finch, G. A. **The Dawes Report on German Reparation Payments,** *American Journal of International Law*, XVIII (July 1924), 419—35.

1234 — —. **The Revision of the Reparation Clauses of the Treaty of Versailles and the Cancellation of Inter-Allied Indebtedness,** *American Journal of International Law*, XVI (October 1922), 611—27.

1235 — —. **The Settlement of the Reparation Problem,** *American Journal of International Law*, XXIV (April 1930), 339—50.

1236 Fraser, L. **Reparation Settlement Signed June 7, 1929; With Historical and Explanatory Introduction,** *International Conciliation*, CCLIII (October 1929), 429—521.

1237 Gilbert, S. P. **The Meaning of the Dawes Plan,** *Foreign Affairs*, IV (April 1926), i—xii (supplement).

1238 Hershey, A. S. **German Reparations,** *American Journal of International Law*, XV (July 1921), 411—18.

1239 Kuczynski, R. R. **A Year of the Dawes Plan,** *Foreign Affairs*, IV (January 1926), 254—63.

Part C. — League of Nations System

1240 Lamont, T. W. **The Dawes Plan and European Peace,** *Academy of Political Science Proceedings,* XI (January 1925), 325—32.

1241 Morgan, S. **Conditions Precedent to the Settlement,** *Academy of Political Science Proceedings,* XIV (January 1931), 215—26.

1242 Moulton, Harold G. **The Reparation Plan: An Interpretation of the Reports of the Expert Committees Appointed by the Reparation Commission, November 30, 1923.** New York, McGraw-Hill, 1924. x + 325 p.

1243 Myers, Denys P. **The Reparation Settlement, 1930.** Boston, World Peace Foundation, 1930. 252 + xiii p.

1244 Norton, H. K. **Germany and the Dawes Commission,** *World Today,* LIII (March 1929), 387—94.

1245 Williams, John F. **Reparations,** *International Affairs,* XI (March 1932), 183—98.
Comments by McFadyean, Sanders, Wise, Nissim, Lias, Bewes.

1246 — —. **The Tribunal for the Interpretation of the Dawes Plan,** *American Journal of International Law,* XXII (October 1928), 797—802.

1247 Young, A. A. **The United States and Reparations,** *Foreign Affairs,* I (March 1923), 35—47.

4. GENERAL COMENTARIES AND EVALUATIONS

See also A 4.2.

1248 Allen, Stephen H. **International Relations.** Princeton, N. J., Princeton University Press, 1920.

Chapter X.

1249 Ames, Herbert B. **What Is the League of Nations?** *American Political Science Review*, XXII (August 1928), 706–11.

1250 Angell, Norman. **Geneva and the Drift to War.** London, Allen and Unwin, 1938. 234 p.

1251 — —. **How May League Principles Be Made Political Realities?** *Problems of Peace*, Series 12 (1937), 133–46.

1252 Anon. **The League at Work,** *North American Review*, CCXI (April 1920), 444–56.

1253 Arnold-Forster, W. **The Elements of World Order,** *Problems of Peace*, Series 10 (1935), 19–36.

1254 Avenol, Joseph. **The Future of the League of Nations,** *International Affairs*, XIII (March 1934), 143–53.

Comments by Steed, Mander, Drury-Lowe, Power, Garnett, Nevinson, Macartney, Hutton, Murray.

1255 Beck, James M. **A World Association Impractical Under Present Conditions,** *Annals of the American Academy of Political and Social Science*, XCVI (July 1921), 146–52.

1256 Beer, Max. **The League on Trial: A Journey to Geneva.** W. H. Johnston (trans.). London, Allen and Unwin, 1933. 415 p.

1257 Beneš, Eduard. **The League of Nations: Successes and Failures,** *Foreign Affairs*, XI (October 1932), 66—80.

1258 — —. **Ten Years of the League,** *Foreign Affairs*, VIII (January, 1930), 212—24.

1259 Bourgeois, Léon V. A. **L'Oeuvre de la Société des Nations (1920— 1923).** Paris, Payot, 1923. 456 p.

1260 Bourquin, Maurice. **Dynamism and the Machinery of International Institutions,** *Geneva Studies*, XI (September 1940), 1—62.

1261 Bower, Graham. **Peace Versus the League of Nations: Avdi Alteram Partem,** *Transactions (Grotius Society)*, VII (1921), 89—108.

Comments by Hopkinson, Barratt, Darby, Knight, Woolf, Henriques and Bellot.

1262 Brown, Philip Marshall. **International Society.** New York, Macmillan, 1923.

Chapter X.

1263 Bryant, Stewart F. **The Stakes at Geneva,** *World Affairs Quarterly*, III (April 1932), 36—48.

1264 Buell, Raymond Leslie. **International Relations.** New York, Holt, 1929.

Chapter XXVIII.

1265 Butler, Harold B. **The Lost Peace: A Personal Impression.** London, Faber, 1942. 246 p.

Part C. — *League of Nations System*

1266 Butler, Nicholas M. **The Path to Peace: Essays and Addresses on Peace and Its Meaning.** New York, Scribner, 1930. xiii + 320 p.

1267 Carr, E. H. **International Relations Since the Peace Treaties.** London, Macmillan, 1937. viii + 284 p.

1268 Cecil, Robert A. **A Great Experiment.** New York, Oxford University Press, 1941. 390 p.
Autobiography.

1269 — —. **International Democracy,** *Political Quarterly*, V (1934), 323—41.

1270 Cohen, A. **La Société des Nations devant le conflict Italo-Ethopien.** Geneva, Droz, 1960. 144 p.

1271 Corbett, P. E. **What Is the League of Nations?** *British Yearbook of International Law*, IV (1924), 119—48.

1272 Cranston, Alan MacGregor. **The Killing of the Peace.** New York, Viking, 1945. 304 p.

1273 Crosby, Oscar T. **The Essentials of a World Organization for the Maintenance of Peace,** *Annals of the American Academy of Political and Social Science*, XCVI (July 1921), 153—59.

1274 Davis, Harriet Eager (ed.). **Pioneers in World Order: An American Appraisal of the League of Nations.** New York, Columbia University Press, 1944. 272 p.

1275 Duggan, Stephen Pierce. **Introduction,** *The League of Nations*, Stephen Pierce Duggan (ed.). Boston, Atlantic Monthly Press, 1919, pp. 1—17.

Part C. — *League of Nations System*

1276 — —. (ed.). **The League of Nations.** Boston, Atlantic Monthly Press, 1919. 357 p.

1277 Ewing, Alfred C. **The Individual, the State, and World Government.** New York, Macmillan, 1947. 322 p.

1278 Fanshawe, Maurice and Macartney, C. A. **What the League Has Done, 1920—1937.** London, League of Nations Union, 1937. 107 p.

1279 Fisher, Irving. **League or War?** New York, Harper, .923. xi + 2168 p.

1280 Foley, Hamilton (comp.). **Woodrow Wilson's Case for the League of Nations.** Princeton, N. J., Princeton University Press, 1923, 271 p.

1281 Fosdick, Raymond B. **The League of Nations After Three Years,** *Atlantic Monthly,* CXXX (August 1922), 256—68.

1282 — —. **Stabilization of Peace Through the League of Nations,** *Academy of Political Science Proceedings,* XVI, 2 (1935), 196—205.

1283 — —. **The Structure of the League,** *The League of Nations Starts,* Raymond B. Fosdick, George Rublee, J. T. Shotwell, Léon Bourgeois, André Weiss, Lt.-Col. Requin, W. Ormsby Gore, el Vizconde de Eza, H. B. Butler, Richard P. Strong, J. A. Salter, A. Claveille, Henri La Fontaine, Paul Otlet. London, Macmillan, 1920, pp. 1—28.

1284 Fosdick, Raymond B., Rublee, George, Shotwell, J. T., Bourgeois, Léon, Weiss, André, Requin, Lt-Col., Ormsby-Gore, W., Eza, El Vizconde de, Butler, H. B., Strong, Richard P., Salter, J. A., Claveille, A., La Fontaine, Henri, Otlet, Paul. **The League of Nations Starts: An Outline By Its Organizers.** London, Macmillan, 1920. 237 p.

1285 Gathorne-Hardy, Geoffrey N. **The League at the Cross-Roads,** *International Affairs,* XV (July 1936), 487—98.

Followed by comments of Garnett, Steed, Macartney, Rowan-Robinson, Atholl, Drury-Lowe, Hollingworth, Zimmern, Taylor.

Part C. — *League of Nations System*

1286 Gibberd, Kathleen. **The League in our Time.** New York, Smith, 1933. 238 p.

1287 Gilchrist, Huntington. **Political Disputes: Dumbarton Oaks and the Experience of the League of Nations,** *Academy of Political Science Proceedings,* XXI (May 1945), 404—14.

1288 Gonsiorowski, Miroslas. **Société des Nations et problème de la Paix.** Paris, Rousseau, 1927. 2 vols.

1289 Graham, Malbone W. **The Problem of World Organization,** *Problems of War and Peace in the Society of Nations,* University of California International Relations Committee (ed.). Berkeley, University of California Press, 1937, pp. 103—28.

1290 Grant, Arthur James. **The "Holy Alliance" and the League of Nations.** Foreword by Robert Cecil. London, League of Nations Union, 1923. 14 p.

1291 Haile, Pennington. **The League of Nations,** *Contemporary World Politics,* Francis J. Brown, Charles Hodges and Joseph S. Roucek (eds.). New York, Wiley, 1939, pp. 431—51.

1292 Harriman, Edward A. **The League of Nations, a Rudimentary Superstate,** *American Political Science Review,* XXI (February 1927), 137—40.

1293 Harvey, Paul. **World Policies of Co-operation,** *Institute of World Affairs Proceedings,* I (1926), 159—69.

1294 Hicks, Frederick Charles. **The New World Order: International Organization, International Law, International Cooperation.** Garden City, Doubleday, Page, 1920. 496 p.

1295 Hill, Norman L. **The Individual in International Organization,** *American Political Science Review,* XXVIII (April 1934), 276—87.

1296 Hillson, Norman. **Geneva Scene.** London, Routledge, 1936. 303 p.

1297 Hinsley, Francis H. **Power and the Pursuit of Peace.** Cambridge, Eng., Cambridge University Press, 1963.

Chapter XII.

1298 Hitchcock, Gilbert M. **In Defense of the League of Nations,** *Annals of the American Academy of Political and Social Science,* LXXXIV (July 1919), 201–207.

1299 Hitchner, Dell G. **The Failure of the League: Lesson in Public Relations,** *Public Opinion Quarterly,* VIII (Spring 1944), 61–71.

1300 Hoden, Marcel. **Europe Without the League,** *Foreign Affairs,* XVIII (October 1939), 13–28.

1301 Holt, Hamilton. **The League of Nations Effective,** *Annals of the American Academy of Political and Social Science,* XCVI (July 1921), 1–10.

1302 — —. **The League of Nations: What It Is Doing,** *Annals of the American Academy of Political and Social Science,* CVIII (July 1923), 193–95.

1303 Houghton, N. D. **The Present Status of the League of Nations,** *International Conciliation,* CCCXVII (February 1936), 67–108.

1304 Hudson, Manley O. **Postwar Progress Toward World Peace,** *Annals of the American Academy of Political and Social Science,* CLXXIV (July 1934), 141–49.

1305 Huston, Howard. **The League of Nations,** *Institute of World Affairs Proceedings,* III (1929), 185–92.

1306 Institute on World Organization. **World Organization: A Balance Sheet of the First Great Experiment.** Introduction by Carl J. Hambro. Washington, American Council on Public Affairs, 1942. 426 p.

1307 Jacks, Lawrence P. **Co-operation or Coercion?** New York, Dutton, 1938. xvii + 153 p.

1308 Jerrold, Douglas. **They That Take the Sword.** London, Lant, 1936. 247 p.

1309 Johnsen, Julia E. (comp.). **League of Nations.** New York, Wilson, 1924. 121 p.

Excerpts from various sources; a short bibliography.

1310 Joyce, James Avery. **The Story of International Cooperation.** New York, Watts, 1964.

Chapter IX.

1311 — —. **World in the Making.** New York, Schuman, 1953.

Chapter IX.

1312 Kendrick, B. B. **Thoughts on Permanent Peace,** *Political Science Quarterly,* XXXIV (May 1919), 127—40.

1313 Kertesz, Stephen D. **Diplomacy in the Atomic Age: I,** *Review of Politics,* XXI (January 1959), 151—87.

1314 Keynes, John Maynard. **The Economic Consequences of the Peace.** New York, Harcourt, Brace and Howe, 1920. 298 p.

A classic but harsh view of Wilson, written out of disgust and bitterness with the terms of the Treaty of Versailles.

1315 Lalovel, H. **Les conceptions politiques de la Société des Nations, et l'élaboration du pacte.** Paris, Pedone, 1923. 72 p.

Part C. — League of Nations System

1316 Lauterpacht, H. **Resurrection of the League,** *Political Quarterly,* XII (April—June 1941), 121—33.
Commentary on Cecil's **A Great Experiment.**

1317 League of Nations, Information Section. **The League of Nations and the Press.** Geneva, 1928. 64 p.

1318 Lenroot, Irvine L. **The Essentials of World Organization,** *Annals of the American Academy of Political and Social Science,* XCVI (July 1921), 138—40.

1319 Levermore, Charles H. **Achievements of the League of Nations in Its First Year,** *Annals of the American Academy of Political and Social Science,* XCVI (July 1921), 11—16.

1320 Lippmann, Walter. **Ten Years: Retrospect and Prospect,** *Foreign Affairs,* XI (October 1932), 51—53.

1321 Lothian, Lord. **New League or No League,** *International Conciliation,* CCCXXV (December 1936), 589—604.
Reprinted from *Observer* (London), August 16, 23 and 30, 1936.

1322 Lowell, A. Lawrence. **The Future of the League,** *Foreign Affairs,* IV (July 1926), 525—34.

1323 — —. **The League of Nations: Its Organization and Operation,** *The League of Nations,* Stephen Pierce Duggan (ed.). Boston, Atlantic Monthly Press, 1919, pp. 96—111.

1324 Lytton, Victor A. G. R. Bulwer-Lytton. **Conditions of International Order,** *World Affairs,* IV (September 1938), 119—30.

1325 McCallum, Ronald B. **Public Opinion and the Last Peace.** London, Oxford University Press, 1944. ix + 214 p.

Part C. — League of Nations System

1326 McCurdy, C. A. **The League of Nations—The Work of Lawyers,** *Transactions* (Grotius Society), V (1919), 119—23.

Comments by Ottley, Bellot, Keen, Henriques, Bewes and Whittuck.

1327 Madariaga, Salvador de. **The World's Design.** London, Allen and Unwin, 1938. xx + 291 p.

1328 Malik, Charles. **Man in the Struggle for Peace.** New York, Harper and Row, 1963. 242 p.

1329 Mander, L. A. **What Are the Essential Directions of Future International Organization,** *Institute of World Affairs Proceedings*, IX (July 1932), 97—98.

1330 Martin, Charles E. **The League of Nations as an Institution,** *Institute of World Affairs Proceedings*, I (1926), 70—76.

1331 Moore, John Bassett. **Some Essentials of a League for Peace,** *The League of Nations*, Stephen Pierce Duggan (ed.). Boston, Atlantic Monthly Press, 1919, pp. 64—81.

1332 Morley, Felix. **The Society of Nations.** Washington, Brookings, 1932.

Chapter XVI.

1333 Morrison, Herbert S. **A New Start with the League of Nations,** *Problems of Peace*, Series 11 (1936), 5—27.

1334 Mowat, R. B. **International Anarchy,** *Problems of Peace*, Series 10 (1935), 5—18.

Antecedents of the League.

1335 Munch, P. (ed.). **Les origines et l'oeuvre de la Société des Nations.** Copenhagen, Gyldendal, 1923—24. 2 vols.

Part C. — League of Nations System

1336 Murray, Gilbert. **From the League to U.N.** London, Oxford University Press, 1948. 217 p.

1337 — —. **The Ordeal of This Generation.** New York, Harper, 1929. ix + 276 p.

1338 — —. **A Survey of Recent World Affairs,** *Problems of Peace,* Series 8 (1933), 1—16.

1339 Myers, Denys P. **The League of Nations in Action,** *Current History,* XXI (November 1924), 181—88.

1340 — —. **Operation of the League of Nations,** *American Political Science Review,* XVIII (May 1924), 351—58.

1341 Newfang, Oscar. **World Federation,** P. Gault (trans.). New York, Barnes and Noble, 1939.

  Chapters IX—X.

1342 Niemeyer, Gerhart. **The Balance-Sheet of the League Experiment,** *International Organization,* VI (November 1952), 537—58.

1343 Noel-Baker, Philip J. **The League of Nations at Work.** London, Nisbet, 1926. 135 p.

1344 Oppenheim, Lassa F. L. **The League of Nations and Its Problems.** London, Longmans, Green, 1919. xii + 84 p.

1345 Oussky, Stephan. **Central Europe and the Future of the Collective System,** *Problems of Peace,* Series 11 (1936), 42—63.

1346 Phelan, E. J. **Public Opinion and the League of Nations,** *Problems of Peace,* Series 8 (1933), 80—99.

  On press coverage.

1347 Phelps, Edith M. (comp.). **Selected Articles on a League of Nations.** 4th ed. New York, Wilson, 1919. 362 p.

1348 Pipkin, Charles W. **The Machinery of Experiment at Geneva,** *Political Science Quarterly*, XLVII (June 1932), 274—81.

1349 Pollock, Frederick. **The League of Nations.** 2d ed. London, Stevens, 1922. 266 p.

1350 Potter, Pitman B. **An Introduction to the Study of International Organization.** 4th ed. New York, Appleton-Century, 1935.

Chapter XXIV.

1351 — —. **The League on the Development of International Organization,** *World Organization*, Institute on World Organization (ed.). Washington, American Council on Public Affairs, 1942, pp. 1—13.

1352 — —. **The League of Nations and Other International Organizations: An Analysis of the Evolution and Position of the League in Cooperation Among States,** *Geneva Studies*, V, 6 (1934), 1—22.

1353 — —. **Progress in International Cooperation,** *Political Science Quarterly*, L (September 1935), 377—404.

1354 — —. **This World of Nations.** New York, Macmillan, 1929.

Chapter XVII.

1355 Quigley, Harold S. **From Versailles to Locarno: A Sketch of the Recent Development of International Organization.** Minneapolis, University of Minnesota Press, 1927. 170 p.

1356 Ranshofen-Wertheimer, Egon. **Geneva and the Evolution of a New Diplomacy,** *World Organization*, Institute on World Organization (ed.). Washington, American Council of Public Affairs, 1942, pp. 14—29.

Part C. — League of Nations System

1357 Rappard, William E. **The Beginnings of International Government,** *American Political Science Review*, XXIV (November 1930), 1001–16.

   Published concurrently in *Problems of Peace*.

1358 — —. **The Evolution of the League of Nations,** *American Political Science Review*, XXI (November 1927), 792–826.

   Published concurrently in *Problems of Peace*.

1359 — —. **The Future of the League of Nations,** *Problems of Peace*, Series 3 (1928), 1–30.

1360 — —. **The Geneva Experiment.** London, Oxford University Press, 1931. 115 p.

1361 — —. **International Relations As Viewed from Geneva.** New Haven, Conn., Yale University Press, 1925. 228 p.

1362 — —. **The League in Relation to the World Crisis,** *Political Science Quarterly*, XLVII (December 1932), 481–512.

1363 — —. **The League of Nations As an Historical Fact,** *International Conciliation*, CCXXXI (June 1927), 9–32.

   "The League, as all living organisms, cannot remain as it is. It must either die, or grow and change."

1364 — —. **Nationalism and the League of Nations Today,** *American Political Science Review*, XXVII (October 1933), 721–37.

   Published concurrently in *Problems of Peace*.

1365 — —. **Le nationalisme économique et la Société des Nations,** *Recueil des Cours*, LXI (1937), 103–251.

1366 — —. **The Quest for Peace Since the World War.** Cambridge, Harvard University Press, 1940. 516 p.

1367 — —. **Vues retrospectives sur la Société des Nations,** *Recueil des Cours,* LXXI (1947), 117—225.

1368 — —. **What Is the League of Nations?,** *International Conciliation,* CCCXXXIX (April 1938), 123—42.
Trans. J. Mowat.

1369 — —. **Why Peace Failed,** *Annals of the American Academy of Political and Social Science,* CCX (July 1940), 1—6.

1370 Redslob, Robert. **The League As a Confederation,** *Problems of Peace,* Series 6 (1931), 1—14.

1371 — —. **Théorie de la Société des Nations,** Paris, Rousseau, 1927. 349 p.

1372 Reynolds, Ernest Edwin. **The League Experiment.** London, Nelson, 1939. 163 p.

1373 Riches, Cromwell. **The League of Nations and the Promotion of World Peace,** *Annals of the American Academy of Political and Social Science,* CLXXV (September 1934), 123—32.

1374 Riou, Gaston. **A French View of the League of Nations,** *Problems of Peace,* Series 11 (1936), 28—41.

1375 Russell, Frank M. **The League of Nations and World Peace,** *Institute of World Affairs Proceedings,* I (1926), 41—43.

1376 — —. **Postwar Tendencies in International Co-operation,** *Institute of World Affairs Proceedings,* VII (1930), 241—45.

Part C. — *League of Nations System*

1377 — —. **Theories of International Relations.** New York, Appleton-Century, 1936.

Chapter XV.

1378 Sainte-Aulaire, Auguste Felix Charles de Beaufoil. **Geneva Versus Peace.** London, Steed, 1937. 272 p.

1379 Schelle, Georges. **Théorie du governement international,** *World Affairs,* I (April—June 1935), 18—25.

1380 Schellenberg, T. R. **The League and the Status Quo,** *Annals of the American Academy of Political and Social Science,* CLXXV (September 1934), 28—32.

1381 Schwarzenberger, Georg. **Power Politics.** 3d ed. London, Stevens, 1964.

Chapter XVIII.

1382 Seignobos, M. **Obstacles Faced by the League of Nations,** *Current History,* XIII (October 1920), 28—29.

1383 Sharp, Walter and Kirk, Grayson. **Contemporary International Politics.** New York, Farrar and Rinehart, 1941.

Chapter XXII.

1384 Shaw, George Bernard. **The League of Nations.** London, Fabian Society, 1929. 11 p.

1385 Shotwell, J. T. **First Pages from the History of the League of Nations,** *The League of Nations Starts,* Raymond B. Fosdick, George Rublee, J. T. Shotwell, Léon Bourgeois, André Weiss, Lt.-Col. Requin, W. Ormsby-Gore, el Vizconde de Eza, H. B. Butler, Richard P. Strong, J. A. Salter, A. Claveille, Henri La Fontaine, Paul Otlet. London, Macmillan, 1920, pp. 46—58.

163

Part C. — League of Nations System

1386 — —. **Mechanism for Peace in Europe,** *Academy of Political Science Proceedings,* XVII, 3 (1936), 287—96.

1387 Slocombe, George E. **A Mirror to Geneva: Its Growth, Grandeur and Decay.** London, Cape, 1937. 348 p.

1388 Streit, Clarence K. **The League's Defenders Make Answer,** *International Conciliation,* (March 1934), 83—90.

Reprinted from *New York Times Magazine,* January 14, 1954.

1389 Sweetser, Arthur. **The Approach to World Unity, 1914—1919, 1920—1930.** Geneva, League of Nations Association, 1929. 50 p.

1390 — —. **The First Ten Years of the League of Nations,** *International Conciliation,* CCLVI (January 1930), 9—64.

1391 — —. **The First Year and a Half of the League of Nations,** *Annals of the American Academy of Political and Social Science,* XCVI (July 1921), 21—33.

1392 — —. **The Framework of Peace,** *Pioneers in World Order,* Harriet E. Davis (ed.). New York, Columbia University Press, 1944, pp. 1—26.

1393 — —. **The League of Nations and Associated Agencies,** *International Conciliation,* CCCXCVII (February 1944), 140—49.

1394 — —. **The League of Nations at Work.** New York, Macmillan, 1920. 215 p.

1395 — —. **The League of Nations in World Politics,** *World Organization,* Institute on World Organization (ed.). Washington, American Council on Public Affairs, 1942, pp. 30—49.

Part C. — League of Nations System

1396 — —. **What the League of Nations Has Accomplished.** New York, League of Nations Non-Partisan Association, 1924. 96 p.

1397 Taft, Henry M. **The Essentials in the League of Nations to a World Organization,** *Annals of the American Academy of Political and Social Science,* XCVI (July 1921), 159—60.

1398 Temperly, Arthur Cecil. **The Whispering Gallery of Europe.** Foreword by Anthony Eden. London, Collins, 1938. 359 p.

1399 Thompson, David. **International Democracy,** *Political Quarterly,* VIII (January—March 1937), 36—50.

1400 Vandenbosch, Amry and Hogan, Willard N. **Toward World Order.** New York, McGraw-Hill, 1963.

Chapter III.

1401 — —. **The United Nations.** New York, McGraw-Hill, 1952.

Chapter V.

1402 Van Langenhove, Fernand. **La crise du système de securité collective des Nations Unies 1946—1957.** La Haye, Nijhoff, 1958. 272 p.

1403 Varghese, Payappilly Itty. **International Law and Organization.** Lucknow, Eatern Book Company, 1952.

Chapters XX, XXI.

1404 Voorhees, Dayton, **The League of Nations: A Corporation, Not a Superstate.** *American Political Science Review,* XX (November 1926), 847—52.

1405 Waller, Bolton C. **Paths to World Peace.** London, Allen and Unwin, 1926. 224 p.

Part C. — League of Nations System

1406 Wallis, John Eyre W. **The Sword of Justice; or, the Christian Philosophy of War Completed in the Idea of a League of Nations.** Introduction by Ernest Barker. New York, Stokes, 1919. xii + 147 p.

1407 Walston, Charles. **Can the League of Nations Be Saved?** *International Conciliation*, CXCIII, special bulletin, (November 1923), 893—921.

1408 Walters, Francis Paulo. **Dumbarton Oaks and the League: Some Points of Comparison,** *International Affairs*, XXI (April 1945), 141—54.

1409 — —. **Introduction,** *Problems of Peace*, Series 12 (1937), 1—8.

1410 — —. **The Problem of Peace Today,** *Problems of Peace*, Series 13 (1938), 15—48.

1411 Whelen, F. **The League of Nations in Being,** *The Evolution of World-Peace*, Francis S. Marvin (ed.). London, Oxford University Press, 1921, pp. 146—58.

1412 Williams, Bruce S. **State Security and the League of Nations.** Baltimore, Johns Hopkins Press, 1927.

Chapters III, IV.

1413 Williams, Talcott. **The Misleading Myth of the Equality of Nations,** *Annals of the American Academy of Political and Social Science*, XCVI (July 1921), 124—28.

1414 Wilson, Duncan and Wilson, Elizabeth. **Federation and World Order.** London, 1939.

Chapter II.

1415 Woods, William Seaver. **Has the League Failed?** *Current History*, XLIV (June 1936), 71—76.

1416 Woolf, Leonard. **From Geneva to the Next War,** *Political Quarterly*, IV (January—March 1933), 30—43.

Part C. — League of Nations System

1417 — —. **From Serajevo to Geneva,** *Political Quarterly,* I (April—June 1930), 186—206.

1418 — —. **The Ideal of the League Remains,** *Political Quarterly,* VII (July—September 1936), 330—45.

1419 — —. **De Profundis,** *Political Quarterly,* X (October—December 1939), 463—76.

1420 — —. **The Resurrection of the League,** *Political Quarterly,* VIII (October—December 1937), 337—52.

1421 Wright, Quincy. **In Search of Peace: The Political Aims and Activities of the League of Nations,** *Windows on the World: American Attempts to Organize International Life,* League of Nations Pavilion, New York World's Fair of 1939 (ed.). New York, Columbia University Press, 1939, pp. 3—18.

1422 — —. **Is the League of Nations the Road to Peace?** *Political Quarterly,* V (1934), 92—106.

1423 Zilliacus, M. Konni. **The League and the World To-day,** *Problems of Peace,* Series 13 (1938), 258—84.

1424 — —. **The Nature and Working of the League of Nations,** *Problems of Peace,* Series 4 (1929), 1—21.

1425 Zimmern, Alfred E. **The League of Nations and the Rule of Law, 1918—1935.** 2d ed. London, Macmillan, 1939.
Part II — Chapters X, XI.

1426 — —. **Liberty, Democracy, and the Movement Towards World Order,** *Problems of Peace,* Series 10 (1935), 139—51.

1427 — —. **Organize the Peace World!** *Political Quarterly,* V (1939), 153—66.

Part C. — League of Nations System

5. COVENANT

The basic constitution of the League of Nations was set forth in the Covenant. What is often forgotten, however, is that on a number of occasions the Covenant was amended, despite the requirement that amendments and resolutions in the League had to be adopted unanimously.

5.1 MEANING AND INTERPRETATIONS

1428　Ames, C. B. **Article Eight of the League of Nations Covenant and the Washington Conference,** *Southwestern Social Science Quarterly,* II (March 1922), 302—10.

1429　Auer, Paul de. **Plebiscites and the League of Nations Covenant,** *Transactions,* (Grotius Society), VI (1920), 45—56.
Comments by Manisty, Davies, Bewes, Whittuck, Phillimore, Macdonell, Bellot.

1430　Bradley, Phillips. **Some Legislative and Administrative Aspects of the Application of Article XVI of the Covenant,** *Transactions* (Grotius Society), XXII (1936), 13—29.

1431　Brierly, James Leslie. **The Covenant and the Charter.** Cambridge, Cambridge University Press, 1947. 27 p.

1432　Derocque, Gilberte. **Le projet de paix perpétuelle de l'Abbé de Saint-Pierre comparé au Pacte de la Société des Nations.** Paris, Rousseau, 1929. 203 p.

1433　Eagleton, Clyde. **Covenant of the League of Nations and Charter of the United Nations: Points of Difference.** Washington, U. S. Government Printing Office, 1946. 14 p.
An expansion of his article, with the same title, in the *Department of State Bulletin,* August 19, 1945.

1434 Feinberg, Nathan. **The Legality of a "State of War" after the Cessation of Hostilities: Under the Charter of the United Nations and the Covenant of the League of Nations.** Jerusalem, Hebrew Univesity, 1961. 86 p.

1435 Gathorne-Hardy, G. M. and Mitrany, David. **Territorial Revision and Article 19 of the League Covenant,** *International Affairs*, XIV (November 1935), 818—36.

1436 Geneva Research Center. **The Covenant and the Pact,** *Geneva Studies*, I (December 1930), 1—23.

1437 Goodrich, Leland M. **From League of Nations to United Nations,** *International Organization*, I (February 1947), 3—21.

1438 Howard-Ellis, C. **The Origin, Structure and Working of the League of Nations.** Boston, Houghton, Mifflin, 1928.

Chapter V.

1439 Hudson, Manley O. **The Covenant of the League of Nations As a Pact of Peace,** *Southern Review*, I (July 1935), 120—38.

1440 Hughan, Jessie W. **A Study of International Government.** New York, Crowell, 1923.

Chapter VIII.

1441 Kellor, Frances A. and Hatvany, Antonia. **Security Against War.** New York, Macmillan, 1924.

Chapter I.

1442 Kelsen, Hans. **Legal Technique in International Law: A Textual Critique of the League Covenant,** *Geneva Studies*, X (December 1939), 1—178.

1443 — —. **The Old and the New League: The Covenant and the Dumbarton Oaks Proposals,** *American Journal of International Law,* XXXIX (January 1945), 45—83.

1444 Knudson, John I. **A History of the League of Nations.** Atlanta, Smith, 1938.
Chapter II.

1445 Kunz, Josef Laurenz. **L'Article XI du pacte de la Société des Nations,** *Recueil des Cours,* XXXIX (1932), 683—789.

1446 — —. **The Covenant of the League of Nations and Neutrality,** *American Society of International Law Proceedings,* XXIX (1935), 36—42.
Comments by M. O. Hudson.

1447 Lauterpacht, H. **The Covenant As the Higher Law,** *British Yearbook of International Law,* XVII (1936), 54—65.

1448 — —. **International Law After the Covenant,** *Problems of Peace,* Series 10 (1935), 37—56.

1449 League of Nations, Secretariat, Information Section. **The League of Nations: Its Constitution and Organisation.** Rev. ed. Geneva, 1926. 68 p.

1450 Lowell, A. Lawrence. **The Charter of the League of Nations and Corfu,** *World Peace Foundation Pamphlets,* VI, 3 (1923), 169—75.

1451 Madariaga, S. de. **The Cause and Cure of Article 16,** *Problems of Peace,* Series 13 (1938), 123—43.

1452 Magruder, Frank Abbott. **National Governments and International Relations.** Boston, Allyn and Bacon, 1929. xiv + 595 p.

1453 Mandelstam, André Nicolayevitch. **La conciliation internationale d'après le Pacte et la jurisprudence du conseil de la Société des Nations,** *Recueil des Cours,* XIV (1926), 337–643.

1454 Potter, Pitman B. **Article XIX of the Covenant of the League of Nations,** *Geneva Studies,* XXI (August 1941), 1–98.

1455 — —. **An Introduction to the Study of International Organization.** 4th ed. New York, Appleton-Century, 1935.

Chapters XV–XVII.

1456 Rauchberg, H. **Les obligations jurisdiques des membres de la Société des Nations pour le maintien de la paix,** *Recueil des Cours,* XXXVII (1930), 87–203.

1457 Ray, Jean. **Commentaire du Pacte de la Société des Nations selon la politique et la jurisprudence des organes de la Société.** Paris, Sirey. 1930. 717 p.

Supplementary issues were published in each of three succeeding years.

1458 Rutgers, V. H. **La mise en harmonie du Pacte de la Société des Nations avec le Pacte de Paris,** *Recueil des Cours,* XXXVIII (1931), 5–123.

1459 Schiffer, Walter. **L'Article 16 du Pacte de la Société des Nations.** Paris, Marchael et Villard, 1939. 69 p.

1460 Schücking, Walter M. A. and Wehberg, Hans. **Die Satzung des Völkerbundes.** 3d ed. Berlin, Wahlen, 1931. xxvii + 604 p.

1461 Scott, James Brown. **Interpretation of Article X of the Covenant of the League of Nations,** *American Journal of International Law,* XVIII (January 1924), 108–13.

1462   Spaight, James Molony. **Pseudo-Security.** New York, Longmans, 1928. 182 p.

    Examines clauses of the Covenant and finds them wanting in respect to security.

1463   Taft, William Howard. **The Paris Covenant for a League of Nations,** *American Political Science Review,* XIII (May 1919), 181—98.

1464   Vinson, John C. **Referendum for Isolation: Defeat of Article Ten of League of Nations Covenant,** Athens, University of Georgia Press, 1961. 148 p.

1465   Walters, Francis Paul. **A History of the League of Nations.** London, Oxford University Press, 1960.

    Chapter V.

1466   Williams, Bruce S. **State Security and the League of Nations.** Baltimore, Johns Hopkins Press, 1927.

    Chapters III, IV.

1467   Williams, John Fischer. **Some Aspects of the Covenant of the League of Nations.** London, Oxford University Press, 1934. vi + 322 p.

1468   Wilson, Florence. **The Origins of the League Covenant.** Introduction by P. J. Noel Baker. London, Hogarth, 1928. xiii + 260 p.

1469   Wright, Quincy. **Article 19 of the League Covenant and the Doctrine of Rebus Sic Stantibus,** *American Society of International Law Proceedings,* XXX (1936), 55—72.

    Comments by Tobin, Hill, Garner, Stowell, Martin, Deak, Fenwick, Wilson, Marburg, Finch, and Butler.

1470   — —. **Effects of the League of Nations Covenant,** *American Political Science Review,* XIII (November 1919), 556—76.

5.2 REVISIONS AND PROPOSED AMENDMENTS

1471 Auer, Paul de. **Proposals for the Reform of the Covenant,** *World Affairs*, II (September 1936), 111–64.

   Comments by Madariaga, Mitrany, Politis, Potter, Rappard, Salter, Temperley, Wehberg.

1472 Eagleton, Clyde. **Reform of the Covenant of the League of Nations,** *American Political Science Review*, XXXI (June 1937), 455–72.

1473 Engel, Salo. **League Reform.** New York, Columbia University Press, 1940. 282 p.

1474 — —. **League Reform: An Analysis of Official Proposals and Discussions, 1936–1939,** *Geneva Studies*, XI (August 1940), 1–282.

   The introduction describes briefly the years 1920–35.

1475 Harley, J. Eugene. **Should the League of Nations Be Reformed?** *World Affairs Quarterly*, VII (July 1936), 380–91.

1476 Heymann, Curt L. **Reforming the League: A Review of Proposals to Rejuvenate the Old Young Man of Geneva,** *Current History*, XLV (December 1936), 51–55.

1477 Hostie, Jan. **Revision of the League Covenant: I,** *World Organization*, Institute on World Organization (ed.). Washington, American Council on Public Affairs, 1942, pp. 345–91.

1478 Jacks, L. P. **Alexander Hamilton and the Reform of the League, an Historical Parallel,** *Hibbert Journal*, XXXV (October 1936), 1–19.

1479 Keen, Frank Noel. **A Better League of Nations.** New York, Smith, 1934. 160 p.

1480 — —. **Revision of the League of Nations Covenant,** *Transactions* (Grotius Society), V (1919), 95—108.

Comments by Bower, Whittuck, Knight, and Bellot.

1481 Kelsen, Hans. **Revision of the League Covenant: II,** *World Organization,* Institute on World Organization (ed.). Washington, American Council on Public Affairs, 1942, pp. 392—412.

1482 Kidd, George. **Reform of the League of Nations: Changes in the League, Past and Proposed,** *Geneva Studies,* VI (1934), 9—42.

1483 Kunz, J. L. **Observations on the** *de facto* **Revision to the Covenant,** *World Affairs,* IV (September 1938), 131—43.

1484 League of Nations Union. **The Reform and Development of the League of Nations.** London, League of Nations Union, 1936. 19 p.

1485 Llewellyn-Jones, F. **Treaty Revision and Article 17 of the Covenant of the League of Nations,** *Transactions* (Grotius Society), XIX (1933), 13—30.

Comments by J. Barratt.

1486 Manning, C. A. W. **The Proposed Amendments to the Covenant of the League of Nations,** *British Yearbook of International Law,* XI (1930), 158—71.

1487 Mowat, Robert Balmain. **The Reform of the League of Nations,** *Contemporary Review,* CXLVI (November 1934), 545—55.

1488 Myers, Denys P. **The League of Nations' Covenant—1939 Model,** *American Political Science Review,* XXXIII (April 1939), 193—218.

1489 Newfang, Oscar. **World Federation.** P. Gault (trans.). New York, Barnes and Noble, 1939.

Chapter XII.

Part C. — *League of Nations System*

1490 Potter, Pitman B. **Reform of the League,** *Geneva Studies,* VII (October 1936), 2–12.

1491 Ray, Jean. **L'Eventuelle reforme de la Société des Nations: quelques données et suggestions,** *Revue de Droit International et de Legislation Comparée,* XVII, 2 (1936), 225–56.

1492 Salter, Arthur. **Reform of the League,** *Political Quarterly,* VII (1936), 465–80.

1493 Schücking, W. **Le development du Pact de la Société des Nations,** *Recueil des Cours,* XX (1927), 353–457.

1494 Schwarzenberger, Georg. **The States Members of the League and the Reform of the Covenant,** *World Affairs,* II (December 1936), 351–59.

1495 Stephens, Waldo E. **Revisions of the Treaty of Versailles.** New York, Columbia University Press, 1939.

Chapter VII.

1496 Streit, Clarence K. **Reform of the Covenant Is Not Enough,** *Problems of Peace,* Series 11 (1936), 213–32.

1497 Walters, Francis Paul. **A History of the League of Nations.** London, Oxford University Press, 1960.

Chapter LVI.

1498 White, Thomas Raeburn. **The Amended Covenant of the League of Nations,** *Annals of the American Academy of Political and Social Science,* LXXXIV (July 1919), 177–93.

1499 Wilcox, Francis O. **Geneva's Future: Proposals for Reform Flood the League, For Peace Depends upon Its Continuance,** *Current History,* XLVI (April 1937), 73–77.

1500 Wright, Quincy. **Reform of the League of Nations: Introduction,** *Geneva Studies,* V (1934), 1–8.

Part C. — *League of Nations System*

6. CONSTITUTIONAL QUESTIONS

Were the bibliography to deal with all international legal aspects of the League of Nations, a much larger compilation would result. Instead, a number of the key issues in international law dealing with international organization are treated in this section.

6.1 GENERAL PROBLEMS

See also C 5.

1501 Alvarez, Alejandro. **Impressions Left by the First Hague Conference for the Codification of International Law,** *Transactions* (Grotius Society), XVI (1930), 119–29.

1502 Andrews, Fannie Fern. **Influence of the League of Nations on the Development of International Law,** *American Political Science Review,* XVIII (May 1924), 358–66.

1503 Barker, P. J. **The Codification of the International Law,** *British Yearbook of International Law,* IV (1924), 38–65.

1504 Dunn, Frederick S. **The Practice and Procedure of International Conferences.** Baltimore, Johns Hopkins Press, 1929. 232 p.

1505 Geneva Research Center. **The First Conference for the Codification of International Law,** *Geneva Studies,* I (March 1930), 1–25.

1506 Harriman, Edward A. **The Constitution at the Crossroads: A Study of the Legal Aspects of the League of Nations, the Permanent Organization of Labor and the Permanent Court of International Justice.** New York, Doran, 1925. 274 p.

1507 Hudson, Manley O. **Current International Co-operation.** Calcutta, Calcutta University Press, 1927. 149 p.

Part C. — League of Nations System

1508   Ray, Jean. **Commentaire du Pacte de la Société des Nations selon la politique et la jurisprudence des organes de la Société.** Paris, Sirey, 1930. 717 p.

   Supplements were issued for the years 1930—31 and 1931—32.

1509   Shenton, Herbert Newhard. **Cosmopolitan Conversation.** New York, Columbia University Press, 1933. 803 p.

1510   Starke, J. G. **The Contribution of the League of Nations to International Law,** *Indian Yearbook of International Affairs,* XIII (Part 2, 1964), 207—26.

1511   Walp, Paul K. **Constitutional Development of the League of Nations.** Lexington, University of Kentucky Press, 1931. 183 p.

1512   Williams, John Fischer. **Chapters on Current International Law and the League of Nations.** London, Longmans, Green, 1929. viii + 513 p.

6.2 DOMESTIC JURISDICTION

See also C 10.2.

1513   Andrassy, Georges. **La souveraineté et la Société des Nations,** *Recueil des Cours,* LXI (1937), 641—761.

1514   Bourquin, Maurice. **L'État souverain et l'organisation internationale.** New York, Manhattan, 1959. 237 p.

1515   Brierly, James Leslie. **Matters of Domestic Jurisdiction,** *British Yearbook of International Law,* VI (1925), 8—19.

1516   Butler, Geoffrey. **Sovereignty and the League of Nations,** *British Yearbook of International Law,* I (1920—21), 35—44.

Part C. — League of Nations System

1517 Hill, Martin. **Immunities and Privileges of International Officials.** Washington, Carnegie, 1947. xiv + 281 p.

1518 Hill, Norman L. **International Jurisdiction and Domestic Questions,** *Southwestern Social Science Quarterly,* X (June 1929), 22—32.

1519 Kimball, Everett. **The Monroe Doctrine and the League of Nations,** *The League of Nations,* Stephen Pierce Duggan (ed.). Boston, Atlantic Monthly Press, 1919, pp. 289—306.

1520 Knudson, John I. **A History of the League of Nations.** Atlanta, Smith, 1938.

Chapter VI.

1521 Lansing, Robert. **Notes on Sovereignty: From the Standpoint of the State and of the World.** Washington, Carnegie, 1921. 94 p.

1522 Laski, H. J. **International Government and National Sovereignty,** *Problems of Peace,* Series 1 (1926), 288—312.

1523 Madariaga, Salvador de. **The Monroe Doctrine and the League of Nations,** *Problems of Peace,* Series 4 (1929), 60—85.

Its meaning to the League.

1524 Schapiro, L. B. **Domestic Jurisdiction in the Covenant and the Charter,** *Transactions* (Grotius Society), XXXIII (1947), 195—211.

1525 Secretan, Jacques. **The Independence Granted to Agents of the International Community in Their Relations with National Public Authorities,** *British Yearbook of International Law,* XVI (1935), 56—78.

1526 Spencer, John H. **The Monroe Doctrine and the League Covenant,** *American Journal of International Law,* XXX (July 1936), 400—13.

Part C. — *League of Nations System*

1527 Stallybrass, William T. S. **A Society of States: Sovereignty, Independence, and Equality in a League of Victors.** New York, Dutton, 1919. xvii + 243 p.

1528 Vinacke, Harold M. **International Organization.** New York, Crofts, 1934.

Chapters XIV, XV.

1529 Wilcox, Francis D. **The Ratification of League Conventions: An Examination of the Problem of Giving Effect to Agreements Between States,** *Geneva Studies*, VI (1935), 1—35.

1530 Williams, John Fischer. **Sovereignty, Seisin, and the League,** *British Yearbook of International Law*, VII (1926), 24—42.

1531 Wood, Hugh McKinnon. **Legal Relations Between Individuals and a World Organization of States,** *Transactions* (Grotius Society), XXX (1944), 141—64.

1532 Wright, Quincy. **Sovereignty of the Mandates,** *American Journal of International Law*, XVII (October 1923), 691—703.

6.3 FINANCING

1533 Ames, Herbert Brown. **The League of Nations: Financial Administration and Apportionment of Expenses.** Geneva, Information Section, League of Nations Secretariat, 1923. 42 p.

1534 Howard-Ellis, C. **The Origin, Structure and Working of the League of Nations.** Boston, Houghton, Mifflin, 1928.

Chapter XI.

1535 Jacklin, Seymour. **The Finances of the League,** *International Affairs*, XIII (September 1934), 689—96.

Comments by Kisch, Parker, Reid, Chatterjee.

1536 Jenks, C. W. **Some Legal Aspects of the Financing of International Institutions,** *Transactions* (Grotius Society), XXVIII (1942), 87–132.

1537 League of Nations, Secretariat, Information Section. **Financial Administration and Apportionment of Expenses.** Rev. ed. Geneva, 1928. 41 p.

1538 Myers, Denys P. **Handbook of the League of Nations.** Boston, World Peace Foundation, 1935.

Chapter V.

1539 — —. **National Subsidy of International Organs,** *American Journal of International Law,* XXXIII (April 1939), 318–31.

1540 Singer, J. David. **The Finances of the League of Nations.** *International Organization,* XIII (Spring 1959), 255–73.

1541 Walters, Francis Paul. **A History of the League of Nations.** London, Oxford University Press, 1960.

Chapter XII.

6.4 MEMBERSHIP

See also C 13.1.

1542 Aufricht, Hans. **Principles and Practices of Recognition by International Organization,** *American Journal of International Law,* XLIII (October 1949), 679–704.

1543 Burns, Josephine J. **Conditions of Withdrawal from the League of Nations,** *American Journal of International Law,* XXIX (January 1935), 40–50.

Part C. — League of Nations System

1544 Feinberg, Nathan. **The Admission of New Members to the League of Nations and the United Nations Organisation,** *Recueil des Cours,* LXXX (1952), 293—391.

1545 Friedlander, Lilian M. **The Admission of States to the League of Nations,** *British Yearbook of International Law,* IX (1928), 84—100.

1546 Graham, Malbone W. **The League of Nations and the Recognition of States.** Berkeley, University of California Press, 1933. 79 p.

1547 Gross, Leo. **Was the Soviet Union Expelled from the League of Nations?** *American Journal of International Law,* XXXIX (January 1945), 35—44.

1548 Hudson, Manley O. **Membership in the League of Nations,** *American Journal of International Law,* XVIII (July 1924), 436—58.

1549 Rudzinski, Aleksander W. **Admission of New Members: The United Nations and the League of Nations,** *International Conciliation,* CDLXXX (April 1952), 143—96.

1550 Schwarzenberger, Georg. **The League of Nations and World Order: A Treatise on the Principle of Universality in the Theory and Practice of The League of Nations.** Preface by H. A. Smith. London, Constable, 1936. xvii + 191 p.

1551 Webster, Charles Kingsley and Herbert, Sydney. **The League of Nations in Theory and Practice.** London, Allen and Unwin, 1933.

Chapter IV.

1552 Wright, Quincy. **The Effect of Withdrawal from the League upon a Mandate,** *British Yearbook of International Law,* XVI (1935), 104—13.

6.5 VOTING

1553 Hill, Norman L. **Unanimous Consent in International Organization,** *American Journal of International Law,* XXII (April 1928), 319—29.

1554 Riches, Cromwell A. **Majority Rule in International Organizations.** Baltimore, Johns Hopkins Press, 1940. 322 p.

1555 — —. **The Unanimity Rule and the League of Nations.** Baltimore, Johns Hopkins Press, 1933. 224 p.

1556 Stone, Julius. **The Rule of Unanimity: The Practice of the Council and Assembly of the League of Nations,** *British Yearbook of International Law,* XIV (1933), 18—42.

1557 Williams, John Fischer. **The League of Nations and Unanimity,** *American Journal of International Law,* XIX (July 1925), 475—88.

7. MAIN ORGANS

7.1 ASSEMBLY

1558 Anon. **The Work of the Eleventh Assembly Relating to the Permanent Court of International Justice,** *British Yearbook of International Law,* XII (1931), 107—31.

Rapid extension of compulsory jurisdiction requires specific amendments.

1559 Berdahl, Clarence A. **Relations of the United States with the Assembly of the League of Nations,** *American Political Science Review,* XXVI (February 1932), 99—111.

Part C. — *League of Nations System*

1560 Brett, Oliver (ed.). **The First Assembly: A Study of the Proceedings of the First Assembly of the League of Nations.** London, Macmillan, 1921. viii + 277 p.

1561 Brierly, J. L. **The Legislative Functions in International Relations,** *Problems of Peace,* Series 5 (1930), 205—29.

1562 Burton, Margaret E. **The Assembly of the League of Nations.** Chicago, University of Chicago Press, 1941. 441 p.

1563 Calderwood, Howard B. **The General Committee and Other Auxiliary Committees of the League Assembly,** *American Journal of International Law,* XXXVIII (January 1944), 74—94.

1564 Cecil, Robert A. **Reflections on the First Assembly,** *The First Assembly,* Oliver Brett (ed.). London, Macmillan, 1921, pp. 231—51.

1565 — —. **The Tenth Assembly of the League of Nations,** *International Affairs,* VIII (November 1929), 541—52.

Comments by Bodington, Clark, Harley, Reed, Ali, Harris, Taylor, Drury-Lowe, Williams, Horsfall, Collingwood, Stavridi, Edinger, White.

1566 Cheever, Daniel S. and Haviland, H. Field, Jr. **Organizing for Peace.** Boston, Houghton, Mifflin, 1954.

Chapter IV.

1567 Dalton, Hugh and Hamilton, Mary. **The Eleventh Assembly of the League of Nations,** *International Affairs,* IX (November 1930), 758—74.

Comments by Zimmern, Williams, Drury-Lowe, Dewar, Nevinson, Mander, Harries.

1568 Geneva Research Center. **The Assembly of the League of Nations,** *Geneva Studies,* I (September 1930), 1—19.

1569 Hill, Norman L. **The Public International Conference.** Stanford, Stanford University Press, 1929. 267 p.

1570 Johnston, G. A. **Parliaments, National and International,** *Problems of Peace,* Series 5 (1930), 44—70.

1571 Kirkpatrick, Helen Paull. **The Sixteenth Assembly of the League of Nations,** *Geneva Studies,* VI (1935), 1—25.

1572 Lytton, Victor A. G. R. B. — L. **First Assembly: The Birth of the United Nations Organization.** New York, Hutchinson, 1946. 96 p.

1573 — —. **The Twelfth Assembly of the League of Nations,** *International Affairs,* X (November 1931), 740—53.

Comments by Garnett, Keen, Drury-Lowe, Lyttelton, Lytton.

1574 Morley, Felix. **The Society of Nations.** Washington, Brookings, 1932.

Chapters XIII—XV.

1575 Moulton, Mildred A. **A Structural View of the Conference As an Organ of International Cooperation.** Highland Park, N. J., n.p., 1930. 118 p.

An examination emphasizing postwar practice as shown in the organization of some typical conferences. Ph. D. dissertation, New York University.

1576 Myers, Denys P. **The League of Nations: Third Assembly,** *Current History,* XVII (November 1922), 194—201.

1577 — —. **Sixth Assembly of the League of Nations,** *Current History,* XXIII (November 1925), 222—26.

1578 Ormsby-Gore, W. **The Fourteenth Assembly of the League of Nations,** *International Affairs,* XIII (January 1934), 47—57.

Comments by Drury-Lowe, White, Keen, Wise, Webster, Cohen, Cecil.

Part C. — League of Nations System

1579 Potter, Pitman. B. **An Introduction to the Study of International Organization.** 4th ed. New York, Appleton-Century, 1935.

Chapter XIX.

1580 Steel-Maitland, A. **The Third Assembly of the League of Nations,** *International Affairs*, I (September 1922), 181—89.

1581 Streit, Clarence K. **The League of Nations Assembly in Action,** *Current History*, XXXIII (January 1931), 557—61.

1582 Walters, Francis Paul. **A History of the League of Nations.** London, Oxford University Press, 1960.

Chapter XI.

1583 Wambaugh, Sarah. **Two Accomplishments of the Existing League— The Secretariat and the Assembly,** *Annals of the American Academy of Political and Social Science*, XCVI (July 1921), 16—21.

1584 Webster, Charles Kingsley and Herbert, Sydney. **The League of Nations in Theory and Practice.** London, Allen and Unwin, 1933.

Chapter V.

1585 Young, Hilton. **The Work of the Eighth Assembly of the League of Nations,** *International Affairs*, VI (November 1927), 368—78.

Comments by Moore, Hancock, Keen, Reid, Elliot, Garnett, White, Dickinson, Lytton.

7.2 COUNCIL

1586 Berdahl, Clarence A. **Relations of the United States With the Council of the League of Nations,** *American Political Science Review*, XXVI (June 1932), 497—526.

1587 Cheever, Daniel S. and Haviland, H. Field, Jr. **Organizing for Peace.** Boston, Houghton, Mifflin, 1954.

Chapters V, VI.

Part C. — League of Nations System

1588 Conwell-Evans, Thomas P. **The League Council in Action: A Study of the Methods Employed by the Council of the League of Nations to Prevent War and to Settle International Disputes.** London, Oxford University Press, 1929. xix + 291 p.

1589 Deak, Francis. **The Hungarian-Rumanian Land Dispute: A Study of Hungarian Property Rights in Transylvania Under the Treaty of Trianon.** Introduction by George W. Wickersham. New York, Columbia University Press, 1928. xiv + 272 p.

1590 Mandelstam, André Nicolayevitch. **"La conciliation internationale d'après le Pacte et la jurisprudence du Conseil de la Société des Nations,** *Recueil des Cours*, XIV (1926), 337–643.

1591 Mantoux, Paul. **Action of the Council of the League of Nations in International Disputes,** *Problems of Peace*, Series 1 (1926), 90–109.

1592 — —. **On the Procedure of the Council of the League of Nations for the Settlement of Disputes,** *International Affairs*, V (January 1926), 16–31.

1593 — —. **The Working of the League Council,** *Problems of Peace*, Series 3 (1928), 31–50.

1594 Morley, Felix. **The Society of Nations.** Washington, Brookings, 1932.

Chapters X, XI.

1595 Mower, Edmund. **International Government.** Boston, Heath, 1931.

Chapter XXXIII.

1596 Myers, Denys P. **Representation in League of Nations Council,** *American Journal of International Law*, XX (October 1926), 689–713.

Part C. — League of Nations System

1597 Potter, Pitman B. **An Introduction to the Study of International Organization.** 4th ed. New York, Appleton-Century, 1935.

Chapter XVIII.

1598 Soward, Frederic H. **The Election of Canada to the League of Nations Council in 1927,** *American Journal of International Law*, XXIII (October 1929), 753–65.

1599 Walters, Francis Paul. **A History of the League of Nations.** London, Oxford University Press, 1960.

Chapters IX, X.

1600 Webster, Charles Kingsley and Herbert, Sydney. **The League of Nations in Theory and Practice.** London, Allen and Unwin, 1933.

Chapter VI.

1601 Williams, Bruce. **The League Commission on the Composition of the Council,** *American Political Science Review*, XX (August 1926), 643–46.

1602 Willoughby, Wester W. **The Sino-Japanese Controversy and the League of Nations.** Baltimore, Johns Hopkins Press, 1935. xxv + 733 p.

7.3 SECRETARIAT

7.3.1 GENERAL OBSERVATIONS

1603 Cheever, Daniel S. and Haviland, H. Field, Jr. **Organizing for Peace.** Boston, Houghton, Mifflin, 1954.

Chapter XIII.

1604 Drummond, Eric. **The Secretariat of the League of Nations,** *Public Administration*, IX (April 1931), 228–35.

Part C. — League of Nations System

1605 Howard-Ellis, C. **The Origin, Structure and Working of the League of Nations.** Boston, Houghton, Mifflin, 1928.

Chapter VII.

1606 League of Nations, Secretariat. **Ten Years of World Co-operation.** Geneva, 1930.

Chapter XIII.

1607 Morley, Felix. **The Society of Nations.** Washington, Brookings, 1932.

Chapters VIII, IX.

1608 Potter, Pitman B. **An Introduction to the Study of International Organization.** 4th ed. New York, Appleton-Century, 1935.

Chapter XX.

1609 Royal Institute of International Affairs. **The International Secretariat of the Future: Lessons from Experience by a Group of Former Officials of the League of Nations.** New York, Oxford University Press, 1944. 64 p.

1610 Walters, Francis Paul. **A History of the League of Nations.** London, Oxford University Press, 1960.

Chapters VII, XLV.

1611 Webster, Charles Kingsley and Herbert, Sydney. **The League of Nations in Theory and Practice.** London, Allen and Unwin, 1933.

Chapter VII.

1612 Ames, Herbert B. **The League of Nations Financial Administration and Apportionment of Expenses.** Geneva, Information Section, League Secretariat, 1923. 42 p.

7.3.2 INTERNATIONAL CIVIL SERVICE

1613 Boudreau, Frank G. **International Civil Service,** *Pioneers in World Order,* Harriet E. Davis (ed.). New York, Columbia University Press, 1944, pp. 76–86.

1614 Burns, C. Delisle. **International Administration,** *British Yearbook of International Law,* VII (1926), 54–72.

1615 Butler, H. B. **Some Problems of an International Civil Service,** *Public Administration,* X (October 1932), 377–87.

1616 Durant, E. Dana. **Standardizing World Statistics,** *Pioneers in World Order,* Harriet E. Davis (ed.). New York, Columbia University Press, 1944, pp. 178–81.

1617 Egger, Rowland. **The Administration of International Organizations.** New York, Carnegie, 1942. 103 p.

1618 Evans, Archibald A. **The International Secretariat of the Future,** *Public Administration,* XXII (November 1944), 64–74.

1619 Gascón y Marín, José. **Les transformations du droit administratif international,** *Recueil des Cours,* XXXIV (1930), 5–75.

1620 League of Nations, Secretariat, Information Section. **Financial Administration and Apportionment of Expenses.** Rev. ed. Geneva, 1928. 41 p.

1621 Mitrany, David. **Problems of International Administration,** *Public Administration,* XXIII (Spring 1945), 2–12.

1622 Phelan, Edward J. **International Administration,** *Problems of Peace,* Series 10 (1935), 126–38.

Part C. — *League of Nations System*

1623 — —. **The New International Civil Service,** *Foreign Affairs,* XI (January, 1933), 307—14.

1624 Purves, Chester. **The Internal Administration of an International Secretariat.** London, Royal Institute of International Affairs, 1945. 78 p.

1625 — —. **Personnel and Finance,** *Public Administration,* XXIII (Spring 1945), 12—20.

1626 Ranshofen-Wertheimer, Egon F. **International Administration: Lessons from the Experience of the League of Nations,** *American Political Science Review,* XXXVII (October 1943), 872—87.

1627 — —. **The International Civil Service of the Future,** *Civil Service in Wartime,* Leonard D. White (ed.). Chicago, University of Chicago Press, 1945, pp. 181—227.

1628 Sayre, Francis Bowers. **International Administration,** *The League of Nations,* Stephen Pierce Duggan (ed.). Boston, Atlantic Monthly Press, 1919, pp. 128—60.

1629 Walters, F. P. **Administrative Problems of International Organization.** London, Oxford University Press, 1941. 20 p.

1630 Wambaugh, Sarah. **Two Accomplishments of the Existing League— the Secretariat and the Assembly,** *Annals of the American Academy of Political and Social Science,* XCVI (July 1921), 16—21.

Part C. — League of Nations System

8. ECONOMIC AND SOCIAL ACTIVITIES

Because many of the institutions treated in this category were independent of the League of Nations, they are filed separately. In particular, the various councils supervising the prices and distribution of such commodities as tin and rubber, the Bank for International Settlements, public international unions concerned with communications and transportation, and the International Labor Organization operated autonomously, with their headquarters often outside Geneva.

8.1 GENERAL DISCUSSIONS

1631   Cheever, Daniel S. and Haviland, H. Field, Jr. **Organizing for Peace.** Boston, Houghton, Mifflin, 1954.

Chapter XXII.

1632   Dendias, Michel. **Les principes services internationaux administratifs,** *Recueil des Cours,* LXIII (1938), 247–365.

1633   Greaves, Harold R. **The League Committees and World Order: A Study of the Permanent Expert Committees of the League of Nations As an Instrument of International Government.** London, Oxford University Press, 1931. 266 p.

1634   Knudson, John I. **A History of the League of Nations.** Atlanta, Smith, 1938.

Chapters VII, VIII, X.

1635   La Fontaine, Henri and Otlet, Paul. **International Associations of Various Types, The League of Nations Starts,** Raymend B. Fosdick, George Rublee, J. T. Shotwell, Léon Bourgeois, André Weiss, Lt.-Col. Requin, W. Ormsby-Gore, el Vizconde de Eza, H. B. Butler, Richard P. Strong, J. A. Salter, A. Claveille, Henri La Fontaine, Paul Otlet. London, Macmillan, 1920, pp. 201–209.

Part C. — League of Nations System

1636 Middlebush, Frederick A. and Hill, Chesney. **Elements of International Relations.** New York, McGraw-Hill, 1940.

  Chapter XVI.

1637 Morley, Felix. **The Society of Nations.** Washington, Brookings, 1932.

  Chapter VII.

1638 Mower, Edmund. **International Government.** Boston, Heath, 1931.

  Chapter XXIX.

1639 Myers, Denys. **Handbook of the League of Nations.** Boston, World Peace Foundation, 1935.

  Chapter VIII.

1640 Pastuhov, Vladimir D. **Memorandum on the Composition, Procedure, and Functions of the Committees of the League of Nations.** Washington, Carnegie, 1943. 96 p.

1641 Potter, Pitman B. **Note on the Distinction Between Political and Technical Questions,** *Political Science Quarterly,* L (June 1935), 264–71.

  On the imprecise nature of the dichotomy.

1642 Rapisardi-Mirabelli, A. **La théorie générale des unions internationales,** *Recueil des Cours,* VII (1925), 345–93.

1643 Sweetser, Arthur. **The Non-Political Achievements of the League,** *Foreign Affairs,* XIX (October 1940), 179–92.

1644 Walters, Francis Paul. **A History of the League of Nations.** London, Oxford University Press, 1960.

  Chapter LX.

8.2 ECONOMIC FUNCTIONS

8.2.1. GENERAL OBSERVATIONS

1645 Cheever, Daniel S. and Haviland, H. Field, Jr. **Organizing for Peace.** Boston, Houghton, Mifflin, 1954.

Chapter XVII.

1646 Frank, Glenn. **The League of Nations and Economic Institutions,** *The League of Nations,* Stephen Pierce Duggan (ed.). Boston, Atlantic Monthly Press, 1919, pp. 184—200.

1647 Garvin, James L. **The Economic Foundations of Peace; Or, World-Partnership As the Truer Basis of the League of Nations.** London, Macmillan, 1919. xxiv + 574 p.

1648 Heilperin, Michael A. **Economic and Financial Issues,** *World Organization,* Institute on World Organization (ed.). Washington, American Council on Public Affairs, 1942, pp. 50—82.

1649 Hill, Martin. **The Economic and Financial Organization of the League of Nations: A Survey of Twenty-Five Years' Experience.** Washington, Carnegie, 1946. xv + 168 p.

1650 Howe, Frederic C. **Economic Foundations of the League of Nations,** *Annals of the American Academy of Political and Social Science,* LXXXIII (May 1919), 313—16.

1651 Kaufmann, Wilhelm. **Les unions internationales de nature économique,** *Recueil des Cours,* III (1924), 181—289.

1652 League of Nations, Secretariat, Information Section. **Economic and Financial Organisation.** Rev. ed. Geneva, 1928. 118 p.

Part C. — League of Nations System

1653   League of Nations, Secretariat. **Ten Years of World Co-operation.** Geneva, 1930.

      Chapter V.

1654   League of Nations, Secretariat, Information Section. **Work of the Financial and Economic Organisation.** Geneva, 1924. 69 p.

1655   Leonard, L. Larry. **International Organization.** New York, McGraw-Hill, 1951.

      Chapter XVIII.

1656   Loveday, Alexander. **The Economic and Financial Activities of the League,** *International Affairs*, XVII (November 1938), 788—803.

      Comments by Condliffe, Newbold, Bevin, Campbell, Lias.

1657   McClure, Wallace M. **World Prosperity As Sought Through the Economic Work of the League of Nations.** New York, Macmillan, 1933. xxxix + 613 p.

1658   Robinson, Henry M. **Some Lessons of the Economic Conference,** *Foreign Affairs*, VI (October 1927), 22—40.

1659   Salter, James Arthur. **The Economic Conference: Prospects of Practical Results,** *International Affairs*, VI (November 1927), 350—60.

      Comments by Layton, Aman, Power, Cohen, Reid, Goode, Williams, Bewes, Harris, Anderson.

1660   — —. (ed.). **The Economic Consequences of the League: The World Economic Conference.** London, Europa, 1927. ix + 235 p.

1661   — —. **The Economic Organization of Peace,** *Foreign Affairs*, IX (October 1930), 42—53.

Part C. — League of Nations System

1662 — —. **Economic Policy: The Way to Peace and Prosperity,** *Problems of Peace,* Series 2 (1927), 104–23.

Postwar economic recovery and effort of the League.

1663 — —. **Economics and Finance,** *The League of Nations Starts,* Raymond B. Fosdick, George Rublee, J. T. Shotwell, Léon Bourgeois, André Weiss, Lt-Col. Requin, W. Ormsby-Gore, el Vizconde de Eza, H. B. Butler, Richard P. Strong, J. A. Salter, A. Claveille, Henri La Fontaine, Paul Otlet. London, Macmillan, 1920, pp. 170–84.

1664 Smith, J. Russell. **Trade and a League of Nations or Economic Internationalism,** *Annals of the American Academy of Political and Social Science,* LXXXIII (May 1919), 287–305.

1665 Williams, Wythe. **The Geneva Conference on International Economic Problems,** *Current History,* XXVI (July 1927), 581–86.

Followed by documents.

1666 Young, Allyn A. and Fay, H. Van V. **The International Economic Conference,** *World Peace Foundation Pamphlets,* X, 4 (1927), 361–411.

8.2.2. EUROPEAN RECONSTRUCTION

1667 Aubert, Louis. **The Reconstruction of Europe: Its Economic and Political Conditions, Their Relative Importance.** New Haven, Yale University Press, 1925. 180 p.

1668 Brailsford, Henry N. **After the Peace.** New York, Seltzer, 1922. 185 p.

1669 Fraser, Leon. **The International Bank and Its Future,** *Foreign Affairs,* XIV (April 1936), 453–64.

1670 High, Stanley. **Europe Turns the Corner.** Introduction by Edward M. House. New York, Abingdon, 1925. 308 p.

Part C. — League of Nations System

1671 Institute of Pacific Relations. **Principles and Methods of Financial Reconstruction Work Undertaken Under the Auspices of the League of Nations.** Honolulu, Institute of Pacific Relations, 1929. 61 p.

1672 McFaydean, Andrew. **International Banking and Finance,** *Problems of Peace,* Series 5 (1930), 71—90.

1673 McIvor, Carlisle C. **The League and Economic Reconstruction,** *Geneva Studies,* III (1932), 1—28.

1674 Mackinder, Halford J. **Democratic Ideals and Reality: A Study in the Politics of Reconstruction.** Introduction by Edward Mead Earle; foreword by George F. Eliot. New York, Holt, 1942. xxvi + 219 p.

1675 Martin, Charles E. **The League of Nations and Economic Readjustments,** *Institute of World Affairs Proceedings,* I (1926), 125—34.

1676 Morgan, Shepard. **The Constructive Functions of the International Bank,** *Foreign Affairs,* IX (July 1931), 580—91.

1677 Myers, Margaret G. **The League Loans,** *Political Science Quarterly,* LX (December 1945), 492—526.

1678 Rogers, Lindsay (ed.). **The Problems of Reconstruction,** *International Conciliation,* CXXXV (February 1919), 5—45.

Excerpts from various sources.

1679 Salter, James Arthur. **The Progress of Economic Reconstruction in Europe,** *Problems of Peace,* Series 1 (1926), 110—26.

1680 Strakosch, Henry. **The Convention on Financial Assistance,** *International Affairs,* X (March 1931), 208—16.

Comments by Williams, Joseph, Drury-Lowe, Cox, Reid, Manning, Askew, Bewes, Hutton.

Part C. — *League of Nations System*

1681 Tyler, Royall. **The League of Nations Reconstruction Schemes in the Interwar Period.** Geneva, League of Nations, Secretariat, Economic, Financial and Transit Department, 1945. 171 p.

1682 Webster, Charles Kingsley and Herbert, Sydney. **The League of Nations in Theory and Practice.** London, Allen and Unwin, 1933.

Chapter XIV.

1683 Winkler, Max. **The Investor and League Loans,** *Foreign Policy Reports,* IV (June 1928), 15—26.

8.2.3 PROBLEMS CONNECTED WITH THE WORLD DEPRESSION OF THE 1930s

1684 Bailey, S. H. **International Economic Cooperation at the Cross-Roads,** *American Political Science Review*, XXVIII (October 1934), 807—24.

1685 Bresler, Harvey J. **Trade Barriers and the League of Nations,** *Foreign Policy Reports*, VII (August 5, 1931), 205—18.

1686 Douglas, Paul H. **World Unemployment and Its Reduction Through International Cooperation,** *Problems of Peace*, Series 6 (1931), 26—50.

1687 Geneva Research Center. **The Movement to Unify the Laws Regarding Bills of Exchange and Checks,** *Geneva Studies*, I (May 1930), 1—7.

1688 Grady, Henry F. **Attempts at Freer Trade: The Economic and Financial Work of the League of Nations,** *Windows on the World: American Attempts to Organize International Life,* League of Nations Pavilion, New York World's Fair of 1939 (ed.), New York, Columbia University Press, 1939, pp. 21—34.

1689 Layton, W. T. **The Forthcoming Economic Conference of the League of Nations and Its Possibilities,** *International Affairs,* VI (March 1927), 69—81.

Comments by Vyle, Salter, Bell, Alexander, Shaw, Goode, Stamp.

1690 MacIver, Robert. **National Economic Planning and International Organization,** *Problems of Peace,* Series 9 (1934), 205—25.

1691 Martin, P. W. **Public Works and the World Crisis,** *Problems of Peace,* Series 8 (1933), 226—45.

1962 Pasvolsky, Leo. **Problems of the World Economic Conference,** *Geneva Studies,* IV (1933), 1—18.

League resolution discussed.

1693 Phelan, E. J. **Industrial and Social Aspects of the Economic Crisis,** *Problems of Peace,* Series 7 (1932), 107—29.

1694 Robbins, Lionel. **Economic Planning and International Order.** London, Macmillan, 1936. xv + 330 p.

1695 Spates, Thomas G. **International Planning of Public Works,** *Geneva Studies,* III (March 1932), 1—24.

1696 — —. **Unemployment as an International Problem,** *Geneva Studies,* II (March 1931), 1—30.

1697 Walters, Francis Paul. **A History of the League of Nations.** London, Oxford University Press, 1960.

Chapters XXXVI, XLII.

1698 Winslow, Earle M. **The League and Concerted Economic Action,** *Geneva Studies,* II (February 1931), 1—19.

8.2.4 RAW MATERIALS AND COMMODITIES

1699   Elliot, W. Y., May, Elizabeth S., Rowe, J. W. F., Skelton, Alex, and Wallace, Donald H. **International Control in the Non-Ferrous Metals.** New York, Macmillan, 1937. xxi + 801 p.

1700   Hexner, Ervin. **The International Steel Cartel.** Chapel Hill, University of North Carolina Press, 1943. 339 p.

1701   Holland, William L. (ed.). **Commodity Control in the Pacific Area.** Stanford, Stanford University Press, 1935. 452 p.

1702   Kapp, Karl W. **The League of Nations and Raw Materials 1919—1939,** *Geneva Studies,* XII (September 1941), 9—64.

1703   Knorr, K. E. **Tin Under Control.** Stanford, Stanford University Press, 1945. 314 p.

1704   Political and Economic Planning. **Commodity Control Schemes,** *Planning,* IX (July 29, 1941), 2—19.

1705   Swerling, Boris C. **International Control of Sugar, 1918—1941.** Stanford, Stanford University Press, 1949. vii + 69 p.

1706   Wickizer, V. D. **Tea Under International Regulation.** Stanford, Food Research Institute, Stanford University, 1944. 198 p.

1707   Wilk, Kurt. **International Administrative Regulations: The Case of Rubber,** *American Political Science Review,* XXXVI (April 1942), 323—37.

1708   — —. **The International Sugar Regime,** *American Political Science Review,* XXXIII (October 1939), 860—78.

8.2.5 BANK FOR INTERNATIONAL SETTLEMENTS (Basel)

1709 Adam, H.-T. **Les organismes internationaux spécialisés.** Paris, Pinchon et Durand-Auzias, 1965.
Volume II, Chapter V.

1710 Dulles, Eleanor Lansing. **The Bank for International Settlements at Work.** New York, Macmillan, 1932. 631 p.

1711 Einzig, Paul. **The Bank for International Settlements.** New York, Macmillan, 1930. 179 p.

1712 Papi, G. U. **The First Twenty Years of the Bank for International Settlements; With a Bibliographical Appendix on the Bank and Cognate Subjects Compiled on the Basis of the Information Supplied by the BIS.** Rome, Bancaria, 1951. 270 p.

1713 Schloss, H. H. **The Bank for International Settlements.** Amsterdam, North-Holland, 1958. xi + 184 p.

1714 Smith, R. S. **Reparations and the Bank for International Settlements,** *South Atlantic Quarterly*, XXIX (July 1930), 304—20.

8.3 COMMUNICATIONS AND TRANSPORTATION

8.3.1 GENERAL OBSERVATIONS

1715 Clark, George Norman. **Unifying the World.** London, Swarthmore, 1920. 116 p.

1716 Claveille, A. **Transportation and Communications Between States,** *The League of Nations Starts,* Raymond B. Fosdick, George Rublee, J. T. Shotwell, Léon Bourgeois, André Weiss, Lt.-Col. Requin, W. Ormsby-Gore, el Vizconde de Eza, H. B. Butler, Richard P. Strong, J. A. Salter, A. Claveille, Henri La Fontaine, Paul Otlet. London, Macmillan, 1920, pp. 185—200.

Part C. — *League of Nations System*

1717 Haas, R. **World Transit and Communications,** *Problems of Peace,* Series 2 (1927), 212–20.

1718 Hostie, Jan. **Communications and Transit,** *World Organization,* Institute on World Organization (ed.). Washington, American Council on Public Affairs, 1942, pp. 158–88.

1719 Knudson, John I. **A History of the League of Nations.** Atlanta, Smith, 1938.

Chapter IX.

1720 League of Nations, Secretariat, Information Section. **Communications and Transit.** Geneva, 1924. 41 p.

1721 League of Nations, Secretariat. **Ten Years of World Co-operation.** Geneva, 1930.

Chapter VI.

1722 Mander, Linden A. **Foundations of Modern World Society.** Stanford, Stanford University Press, 1947.

Chapter VI.

1723 Middlebush, Frederick A. and Hill, Chesney. **Elements of International Relations.** New York, McGraw-Hill, 1940.

Chapter XIV.

1724 Webster, Charles Kingsley and Herbert, Sydney. **The League of Nations in Theory and Practice.** London, Allen and Unwin, 1933.

Chapter XVI.

8.3.2 COMMUNICATIONS

1725 Akzin, Benjamin. **Membership in the Universal Postal Union,** *American Journal of International Law,* XXVII (October 1933), 651–74.

Part C. — League of Nations System

1726   Bourquin, Maurice. **L'Organisation Internationale des Voies de Communication,** *Recueil des Cours,* V (1924), 163—209.

1727   Codding, George Arthur, Jr. **The International Telecommunication Union: An Experiment in International Cooperation.** Leyden, Brill, 1952. xvii + 505 p.

1728   — —. **The Universal Postal Union.** New York, New York University Press, 1964. 296 p.

1729   Grandin, Thomas. **The Political Use of the Radio,** *Geneva Studies,* X (August 1939), 1—116.

1730   Stewart, Irvin. **The International Telegraph Conference of Brussels and the Problem of Code Language,** *American Journal of International Law,* XXIII (April 1929), 292—306.

1731   Turkel, Harry Raymond. **International Postal Congresses,** *British Yearbook of International Law,* X (1929), 171—80.

1732   Williamson, F. H. **The International Postal Service and the Universal Postal Union,** *International Affairs,* IX (January 1930), 68—78.

8.3.3 TRANSPORTATION

1733   Blackburn, Glen A. **International Control of the River Danube,** *Current History,* XXXII (September 1930), 1154—59.

1734   Chamberlain, Joseph P. **International Control of International Waterways, Railways, and Highways,** *The League of Nations,* Stephen Pierce Duggan (ed.). Boston, Atlantic Monthly Press, 1919, pp. 218—236.

1735   — —. **The Regime of the International Rivers: Danube and Rhine.** New York, Columbia University Press, 1923. 317 p.

Part C. — League of Nations System

1736 Colegrove, Kenneth W. **International Control of Aviation.** Boston, World Peace Foundation, 1930. 234 p.

1737 Commission Européenne du Danube. **La Commission Européenne du Danube et son oeuvre de 1856 à 1931.** Paris, Impr. Nationale, 1931. viii + 526 p.

1738 Geneva Research Center. **International Aerial Navigation,** *Geneva Studies,* I (August 1930), 1–11.

1739 Hudson, Manley O. and Sohn, Louis B. **Fifty Years of Arbitration in the Union of International Transport by Rail,** *American Journal of International Law,* XXXVII (October 1943), 597–610.

1740 International Air Traffic Association. **International Collaboration in Civil Aviation, 1919–1939: A Description of IATA Activities.** Hague, International Air Traffic Association, 1939. 36 p.

1741 L., G. **Europe's International Waterways,** *World Today,* New Series, VII (October 1951), 419–29.

1742 Masters, Ruth D. **International Organization of European Rail Transport,** *International Conciliation,* CCCXXX (May 1937), 487–544.

Appendix contains documents.

1743 Miller, David Hunter. **The International Regime of Ports, Waterways and Railways,** *American Journal of International Law,* XIII (October 1919), 669–86.

1744 Sherman, Gordon E. **The International Organization of the Danube Under the Peace Treaties,** *Amrican Journal of International Law,* XVII (July 1923), 438–59.

1745 Tombs, Laurence C. **International Organization in European Air Transport.** Foreword by Joseph P. Chamberlain. New York, Columbia University Press, 1936. xvii + 219 p.

1746 Toulmin, G. E. **The Barcelona Conference on Communications and Transit and the Danube Statute,** *British Yearbook of International Law,* III (1922–23), 167–78.

1747 Warner, Edward P. **International Air Transport,** *Foreign Affairs,* IV (January 1926), 278–93.

1748 Wehle, Louis B. **International Administration of European Inland Waterways,** *American Journal of International Law,* XL (January 1946), 100–20.

8.4 INTERNATIONAL LABOR ORGANIZATION (Geneva)

8.4.1 GENERAL OBSERVATIONS

See also C 14.

1749 Andrews, John B. **Labor in the Peace Treaty,** *The League of Nations,* Stephen Pierce Duggan (ed.). Boston, Atlantic Monthly Press, 1919, pp. 237–52.

1750 Argentier, Clément. **Les résultats acquis par l'Organisation Permanente du Travail de 1919 à 1929.** Paris, Sirey, 1930. 592 p.

1751 Barnes, George Nicoll. **History of the International Labour Office.** London, Williams and Norgate, 1926. xvi + 106 p.

1752 Batler, H. B. **The Past, Present, and Future of the International Labour Organization,** *Problems of Peace,* Series 5 (1930), 29–43.

1753 Beddington-Behrens, Edward. **The International Labour Office (League of Nations): A Survey of Certain Problems of International Administration.** Foreword by H. J. Laski. London, Parsons, 1924. 230 p.

1754 — —. **The International Labor Office: A Survey of Certain Problems of International Administration.** London, Parsons, 1924. 220 p.

1755 Blelloch, David H. **The International Labor Organization: I,** *World Organization*, Institute on World Organization (ed.). Washington, American Council on Public Affairs, 1942, pp. 307–33.

1756 Burge, M. R. K. **Some Aspects of Administration in the I.L.O. Office,** *Public Administration*, XXIII (Spring 1945), 21–31.

1757 Butler, H. B. **The International Labour Organisation,** *The League of Nations Starts*, Raymond B. Fosdick, George Rublee, J. T. Shotwell, Léon Bourgeois, André Weiss, Lt.-Col. Requin, W. Ormsby-Gore, el Vizconde de Eza, H. B. Butler, Richard P. Strong, J. A. Salter, A. Claveille, Henri La Fontaine, Paul Otlet, London, Macmillan, 1920, pp. 140–54.

1758 Cheyney, Alice Squires. **The International Labor Organization,** *Foreign Policy Reports*, X (July 4, 1934), 110–20.

1959 — —. **International Labor Standards and American Legislation (A Comparison),** *Geneva Studies*, II (August 1931), 1–62.

1760 Custos. **The International Labour Code,** *Political Quarterly*, XIII (July–September 1942), 303–10.

1761 Dillon, Conley H. **International Labour Conventions.** Chapel Hill, University of North Carolina Press, 1942. 272 p.

1762 Ellison, W. J. **The Nature and Aims of the International Labour Organisation,** *Problems of Peace*, Series 1 (1926), 50–62.

1763 Eppstein, John (comp.). **Ten Years of the League of Nations.** London, Fair Press, 1929.

Chapter IV.

1764 Feis, Herbert. **The Attempt to Establish the Eight-Hour Day by International Action,** *Political Science Quarterly,* XXXIX (September 1924), 373–413.

1765 Follows, John W. **Antecedents of the International Labour Organisation.** Oxford, Clarendon, 1951. x + 234 p.

1766 Gilliard, Edward M. **The International Labor Organization,** *American Journal of Sociology,* XXXVI (September 1930), 233–40.

1767 Gompers, Samuel. **The Labor Clauses of the Treaty,** *What Really Happened at Paris,* Edward M. House and Charles Seymour (eds.). New York, Scribner, 1921, pp. 319–35.

1768 Goodrich, Carter. **The Conference of the International Labor Organization,** *International Conciliation,* CCCLXXVI (January 1942), 5–24.

1769 — —. **The International Labor Organization,** *Pioneers in World Order,* Harriet E. Davis (ed.). New York, Columbia University Press, 1944. pp. 87–106.

1770 Gregory, Charles Noble. **The International Labor Organization in the League of Nations,** *American Journal of International Law,* XV (January 1921), 42–50.

1771 Harley, John E. **The League of Nations and the New International Law.** New York, Oxford University Press, 1921.

Chapter IV.

1772 Harris, H. Wilson. **What the League of Nations Is.** London, Allen and Unwin, 1925,

Chapter IV.

1773 Hewes, Amy. **Functional Representation in the International Labor Organization,** *American Political Science Review,* XXII (May 1928), 324—38.

1774 Hiitonen, E. **La compétence de l'Organisation International du Travail.** Paris, Rousseau, 1929. xlvii + 356 p.

1775 Hohman, Elmo P. **The International Labour Organisation and the Seaman,** *Geneva Studies,* VIII, 1 (1937), 3—17.

1776 Howard-Ellis, C. **The Origin, Structure and Working of the League of Nations.** Boston, Houghton, Mifflin, 1928.

Chapter VIII.

1777 Hudson, Manley O. **Progress in International Organization.** Oxford, Oxford University Press, 1932.

Chapter V.

1778 Huntington, Henry Strong. **Work of the International Labor Organization,** *Current History,* XXVI (April 1927), 163—66.

1779 International Labour Office. **The International Labour Organisation: The First Decade.** Preface by Albert Thomas. London, Allen and Unwin, 1931. 382 p.

1780 — —. **International Labour Review.** Geneva, Monthly, 1921. —.

1781 Jenks, Clarence Wilfred. **The Contribution to International Legislation of the Nineteenth Session of the International Labor Conference,** *American Political Science Review,* XXX (August 1936), 742—53.

1782 — —. **The International Labour Organisation and Peaceful Change,** *World Affairs,* IV (March 1939), 361—79.

Part C. — *League of Nations System*

1783 — —. **The Origins of the International Labour Organisation,** *International Labour Review*, XXX (November 1934), 575—81.

1784 — —. **The Relation Between Membership of the League of Nations and Membership of the International Labour Organisation,** British *Yearbook of International* Law, XVI (1935), 79—83.

1785 — —. **The Revision of International Labour Conventions,** *British Yearbook of International Law*, XIV (1933), 43—65.

1786 — —. **The Significance for International Law of the Tripartite Character of the International Labour Organisation,** *Transactions* (Grotius Society), XXII (1936), 45—81.

1787 Johnston, George A. **International Social Progress: The Work of the International Labour Organisation of the League of Nations.** New York, Macmillan, 1924. 263 p.

1788 — —. **Labour and the World Community,** *Problems of Peace*, Series 6 (1931), 157—87.

1789 Kellor, Frances A. and Hatvany, Antonia. **Security Against War.** New York, Macmillan, 1924.

Chapter XXVII.

1790 Knudson, John I. **A History of the League of Nations.** Atlanta, Smith, 1938.

Chapter XIII.

1791 Lorwin, Lewis L. **Labor and Internationalism.** New York, Macmillan, 1929. xvii + 682 p.

1792 Lowe, Boutelle E. **International Aspects of the Labor Problem.** New York, Gray, 1918. 128 p.

Part C. — League of Nations System

1793 — —. **International Protection of Labor: International Labor Organization, History and Law.** New York, Macmillan, 1935. 594 p.

1794 Macdonell, John. **International Labour Conventions.** *British Yearbook of International Law*, I (1920—1921), 191—222.

1795 Mahaim, Ernest. **L'Organisation Permanente du Travail,** *Recueil des Cours*, IV (1924), 69—221.

1796 — —. **The Principles of International Labor Legislation,** *Annals of the American Academy of Political and Social Science*, CLXVI (March 1933), 10—17.

1797 Martin, William. **The International Labour Organisation,** *Academy of Political Science Proceedings*, XII, 1 (1926), 399—410.

1798 Meeker, Royal. **The International Labor Organization,** *Annals of the American Academy of Political and Social Science*, CVIII (July 1923), 206—10.

1799 Miller, David Hunter. **International Relations of Labor.** New York, Knopf, 1921. 77 p.

1800 Miller, Spencer, Jr. (ed.). **What the International Labor Organization Means to America.** Foreword by John G. Winant. New York, Columbia University Press, 1936. xiii + 108 p.

1801 Mills, D. Handel. **Industrial Cooperation,** *Ten Years of the League of Nations*, John Eppstein (ed.). London, Fair Press, 1929, pp. 139—47.

1802 Mower, Edmund. **International Government.** Boston, Heath, 1931.
Chapter XXXV.

1803 National Industrial Conference Board. **The Work of the International Labor Organization.** New York, National Industrial Conference Board, 1928. 197 p.

1804 Périgord, Paul. **The International Labor Organization: A Study of Labor and Capital in Cooperation.** New York, Appleton, 1926. 339 p.

1805 Phelan, Edward J. **The Admission of the Central Powers to the International Labor Organization,** *The Origins of the International Labor Organization,* James T. Shotwell (ed.). New York, Columbia University Press, 1935, Vol. I, pp. 259—84.

1806 — —. **Current Progress of International Labour Legislation,** *Problems of Peace,* Series 1 (1926), 63—89.

1807 — —. **The Future of the International Labour Organisation,** *Problems of Peace,* Series 4 (1929), 175—93.

1808 — —. **How the International Labour Organization Operates,** *Annals of the American Academy of Political and Social Science,* CLXVI (March 1933), 4—9.

1809 — —. **The International Labour Organisation and the Future of the Collective System,** *Problems of Peace,* Series 11 (1936), 128—44.

1810 — —. **The Progress and Problems of the International Labour Organisation,** *Problems of Peace,* Series 2 (1927), 46—70.

1811 — —. **Social Justice and World Peace,** *Problems of Peace,* Series 9 (1934), 174—89.

1812 — —. **Tendencies in International Labour Legislation,** *Problems of Peace,* Series 3 (1927), 96—129.

1813 — —. **Yes and Albert Thomas.** London, Cresset, 1949. xvi + 270 p.

1814 Pierre-Tixier, Andrien. **The International Labor Organization: II.** *World Organization,* Institute on World Organization (ed.). Washington, American Council on Public Affairs, 1942, pp. 334—44.

1815 Pribram, Karl. **The ILO: Present Functions and Future Tasks,** *Foreign Affairs,* XXI (October 1942), 158—67.

1816 Price, John. **The International Labour Movement.** London, Oxford University Press, 1945. 273 p.

1817 Potter, Pitman B. **An Introduction to the Study of International Organization.** 4th ed. New York, Appleton-Century, 1935.

Chapter XXI.

1818 Sanger, Sophy. **Labour Legislation Under the League of Nations,** *Transactions* (Grotius Society), V (1919), 145—53.

Comments by Goudy, Bisschop, Cole and Bellot.

1819 Schelle, Georges. **L'Organisation Internationale du Travail et le B.I.T.** Paris, Rivière, 1930. 333 p.

1820 Shotwell, James T. **International Labor Legislation and the Tariff,** *International Conciliation,* CCCIX (April 1935), 136—42.

1821 — —. **The International Labor Organization As an Alternative to Violent Revolution,** *Annals of the American Academy of Political and Social Science,* CLXVI (March 1933), 18—25.

1822 — —. (ed.). **The Origins of the International Labor Organization.** New York, Columbia University Press, 1934. 2 vols.

Volume I contains essays by various scholars, and sundry documents. Volume II contains documents exclusively. An indispensable guide.

1823 Simpson, Smith. **Constitutional Development of the I. L. O. As Affected by the Recent International Labor Conference,** *American Political Science Review,* XXXVIII (August 1944), 719—25.

1824 — —. **International Labor Conference: Twenty-sixth Session,** *American Journal of International Law,* XXXVIII (October 1944), 557—76.

1825 — —. **The International Labor Organization,** *International Conciliation,* CCCLV (December 1939), 594—601.

1826 — —. **Twenty-fifth Session of the International Labor Conference,** *American Journal of International Law,* XXXIII (October 1939), 716—25.

1827 Solano, E. John (ed.). **Labour As an International Problem: A Series of Essays Comprising a Short History of the International Labour Organisation and a Review of General Industrial Problems.** London, Macmillan, 1920. lx + 345 p.

1828 Stewart, Bryce M. **Canadian Labor Laws and the Treaty.** New York, Columbia University Press, 1926. 501 p.

1829 Sweetser, Arthur. **The United States and the League, the Labour Organisation, and the World Court During 1940,** *Geneva Studies,* XI (December 1940), 1—19.

1830 Tayler, William L. **Federal States and Labor Treaties: Relations of Federal States to the International Labor Organization (A Study of the Origin and Application of Art. 19, Par. 9, of Its Constitution).** Foreword by Samuel McCune Lindsay. New York, Apollo, 1935. 171 p.

1831 Tead, Ordway. **Labor and the League of Nations,** *International Conciliation,* CXXXI (October 1918), 21—32.

1832 Watt, Robert J. **The Present Day Significance of the International Labor Organization,** *International Conciliation,* CCCLV (December 1939), 602—608.

1833 Webster, Charles Kingsley and Herbert, Sydney. **The League of Nations in Theory and Practice.** London, Allen and Unwin, 1933.

Chapter XV.

1834 Wilson, Francis Graham. **The International Codification of the Law of Labor,** *Institute of World Affairs Proceedings,* V (1929), 129—40.

1835 — —. **The International Labour Organisation,** *International Conciliation,* CCLXXXIV (November 1932), 401—53.

1836 — —. **International Labor Relations of Federal Governments,** *Southwestern Social Science Quarterly,* X (September 1929), 190—216.

1837 — —. **Labor in the League System: A Study of the International Labor Organization in Relation to International Administration.** Stanford, Stanford University Press, 1934. 384 p.

1838 — —. **The Preparation of International Labor Conventions,** *American Journal of International Law,* XXVIII (July 1934), 506—26.

1839 Woll, Matthew. **The International Labor Office: A Criticism,** *Current History,* XXXI (January 1930), 683—89.

1840 Wright, Quincy (ed.). **Unemployment As a World Problem.** Chicago, University of Chicago Press, 1932. 261 p.

8.4.2 ROLE OF THE UNITED STATES

1841 Gathings, James A. **Appointment of American Delegates to the International Labor Organization,** *American Political Science Review,* XXIX (October 1935), 870—71.

1842 Geneva Research Center. **League of Nations, International Labour Organization and the United States,** *Geneva Studies,* X (March 1939), 1–66.

1843 — —. **The United States and the League, The Labour Organisation, and the World Court in 1939,** *Geneva Studies,* IX (February 1940), 1–67.

1844 — —. **The United States, League of Nations and International Labour Organisation During 1937,** *Geneva Studies,* IX (January 1938), 7–72.

1845 Hubbard, Ursula P. **The Cooperation of the United States with the League of Nations, and with the International Labour Organisation,** *International Conciliation,* CCLXXIV (November 1931), 9–159.

Contains an appendix of documents.

1846 Hudson, Manley O. **Membership of the United States in the International Labor Organization,** *American Journal of International Law,* XXVIII (October 1934), 669–84.

Condensed in *International Conciliation,* April 1935.

1847 Lindsay, Samuel McCune. **The Problem of American Cooperation,** *The Origins of the International Labor Organization,* James T. Shotwell (ed.). New York, Columbia University Press, 1935, Vol. I, pp. 331–70.

1848 Phelan, Edward J. **The United States and the International Labor Organization,** *Political Science Quarterly,* L (March 1935), 107–21.

1849 Richardson, J. Henry. **The Work of the International Labour Organisation,** *Political Quarterly,* VIII (October–December 1937), 417–29.

1850 Sweetser, Arthur. **The United States and the League, the Labour Organisation, and the World Court During 1940,** *Geneva Studies,* XI (December 1940), 1–19.

Part C. — League of Nations System

8.5 SOCIAL QUESTIONS

8.5.1 GENERAL OBSERVATIONS

1851 Abbott, Grace. **Social Welfare by Co-operation: The League's Advisory Committee on Social Questions,** *Windows on the World: American Attempts to Organize International Life*, League of Nations Pavilion, New York World's Fair of 1939 (ed.). New York, Columbia University Press, 1939, pp. 55—70.

1852 Aldous, Leslie R. **Social Services of the League,** *Ten Years of the League of Nations*, John Eppstein (ed.). London, Fair Press, 1929, pp. 165—71.

1853 Castendyck, Elsa. **Social Problems,** *Pioneers in World Order*, Harriet E. Davis (ed.). New York, Columbia University Press, 1944, pp. 229—39.

1854 — —. **Social Questions,** *World Organization*, Institute on World Organization (ed.). Washington, American Council on Public Affairs, 1942, pp. 112—20.

1855 Cheever, Daniel S. and Haviland, H. Field, Jr. **Organizing for Peace.** Boston Houghton, Mifflin, 1954.

Chapter XX.

1856 Crowdy, Rachel. **The Humanitarian Activities of the League of Nations,** *International Affairs*, VI (May 1927), 153—62.

Comments by Somerville, Hancock, Nettleford, Lyttelton, Currey, Bewes, Harris, Swanwick, Furse, Astor, Herford, Atholl.

1857 Dexter, Robert C. **International Social Adjustments,** *Social Forces*, VII (June 1929), 581—89.

1858 Harris, H. Wilson. **What the League of Nations Is.** London, Allen and Unwin, 1925.

Chapter XI.

1859 Johnston, George A. **International Social Progress.** New York, Macmillan, 1924. 263 p.

1860 League of Nations, Secretariat, Information Section. **Social and Humanitarian Work.** Geneva, 1924. 47 p.

1861 Mortished, R. J. P. **The Social Basis of World Order,** *Problems of Peace*, Series 10 (1935), 104—25.

1862 Mower, Edmund. **International Government.** Boston, Heath, 1931.

Chapter XXVII.

1863 Potter, Pitman B. **The Social Services of the League of Nations,** *Geneva Studies*, VI (1935), 1—16.

1864 Webster, Charles Kingsley and Herbert, Sydney. **The League of Nations in Theory and Practice.** London, Allen and Unwin, 1933.

Chapter XVII.

8.5.2 HEALTH AND NUTRITION

1865 Abt, G. **Vingt-cinq ans d'activité de l'Office International d'Hygiène Publique, 1900—1933.** Paris, Office International d'Hygiène Publique, 1933. 140 p.

1866 Boudreau, Frank G. **Ancient Diseases—Modern Defences: The Work of the Health Organization of the League of Nations,** *Windows on the World: American Attempts to Organize International Life*, League of Nations Pavilion, New York World's Fair of 1939 (ed.). New York, Columbia University Press, 1939, pp. 37—52.

Part C. — League of Nations System

1867 — —. **Health, Nutrition, and Housing,** *World Organization*, Institute on World Organization (ed.). Washington, American Council on Public Affairs, 1942, pp. 83—98.

1868 — —. **International Heath Work,** *Academy of Political Science Proceedings*, XII, 1 (1926), 379—98.

1869 — —. **International Health Work,** *Pioneers in World Order*, Harriet E. Davis (ed.). New York, Columbia University Press, 1944, pp. 193—207.

1870 — —. **World Public Health,** *Problems of Peace*, Series 5 (1930), 112—31.

1871 Buchanan, G. S. **International Cooperation in Public Health: Its Achievements and Prospects.** London, Lancet, 1934. 60 p.

1872 Harris, H. Wilson. **What the League of Nations Is.** London, Allen and Unwin, 1925.

Chapter X.

1873 League of Nations, Health Organisation. **Bibliography of the Technical Work of the Health Organisation of the League of Nations, 1920—1945.** Geneva, 1945. 235 p.

1874 League of Nations, Secretariat, Information Section. **The Health Organisation of the League of Nations.** Rev. ed. Geneva, 1926. 48 p.

1875 League of Nations, Secretariat. **Ten Years of World Co-Operation.** Geneva, 1930.

Chapter VII.

1876 McDougall, F. L. **Food and Welfare: League of Nations Studies of Nutrition and National Economic Policy,** *Geneva Studies*, IX (November 1938), 7—56.

Part C. — *League of Nations System*

1877 Mackenzie, M. D. **World Cooperation on Health,** *Problems of Peace,* Series 12 (1937), 75—98.

1878 Mander, Linden A. **Foundations of Modern World Society.** Rev. ed. Stanford, Stanford University Press, 1947.

Chapter IV.

1879 Merrill, Frederick T. **Nutrition: A League Project,** *Foreign Policy Reports,* XIV (January 15, 1939), 250—56.

1880 Mower, Edmund. **International Government.** Boston, Heath, 1931.

Chapter XXVI.

1881 Strong, Richard P. **Public Health, the League, and the Red Cross,** *The League of Nations Starts,* Raymond B. Fosdick, George Rublee, J. T. Shotwell, Léon Bourgeois, André Weiss, Lt.-Col. Requin, W. Ormsby-Gore, el Vizconde de Eza, H. B. Butler, Richard P. Strong, J. A. Salter, A. Claveille, Henri La Fontaine, Paul Otlet. London, Macmillan, 1920, pp. 155—69.

1882 White, Norman. **The League of Nations and the Health of the World,** *Problems of Peace,* Series 2 (1927), 221—36.

1883 Winslow, C. E. A. **International Organization for Health.** New York, Commission to Study the Organization of Peace, 1944. 32 p.

8.5.3 NARCOTIC DRUGS

1884 Aspland, W. H. Graham. **Opium Traffic's Stranglehold on China,** *Current History,* XXII (July 1925), 609—12.

1885 Azcárate y Flórez, Pablo de. **League of Nations and National Minorities.** Eileen E. Brooke (trans.). Washington, Carnegie, 1944. 208 p.

Part C. — League of Nations System

1886 Bailey, Helen Miller. **The Narcotic Convention Goes into Force,** *World Affairs Quarterly,* V (April 1934), 84—87.

1887 Bailey, S. H. **The International Drug Control at Work,** *Political Quarterly,* IX (1938), 86—98.

1888 Buell, Raymond Leslie. **The International Opium Conferences with Relevant Documents,** *World Peace Foundation Pamphlets,* VIII, 2—3 (1925), 39—119.

1889 Crowdy, Rachel. **The Opium Traffic and the Work of the Social Section of the League,** *Problems of Peace,* Series 2 (1927), 195—211.

1890 Eisenlohr, Louise E. S. **International Narcotics Control.** London, Allen and Unwin, 1934. 295 p.

1891 Farnham, John D. and Moorhead, Helen Howell. **International Limitation of Dangerous Drugs,** *Foreign Policy Reports,* VII (April 1, 1931), 19—47.

1892 Gavit, John P. **Opium.** New York, Brentano's, 1927. 308 p.

1893 May, Herbert L. **Dangerous Drugs,** *Pioneers in World Order,* Harriet E. Davis (ed.). New York, Columbia University Press, 1944, pp. 182—92.

1894 — —. **Fighting Dangerous Drugs: The Work of the League's Anti-Opium Agencies,** *Windows on the World: American Attempts to Organize International Life,* League of Nations Pavilion, New York World's Fair of 1939 (ed.). New York, Columbia University Press, 1939, pp. 73—88.

1895 Moorhead, Helen Howell. **International Administration of Narcotic Drugs, 1928—1934,** *Foreign Policy Reports,* X (February 27, 1935), 330—44.
Published concurrently in *Geneva Studies.*

1896 Morgan, Laura Puffer. **A Possible Technique of Disarmament Control: Lessons from League of Nations Experience in Drug Control,** *Geneva Studies,* XI (November 1940), 1—96.

1897 Renborg, Bertl A. **International Drug Control: A Study on International Administration by and Through the League of Nations.** Washington, Carnegie, 1947. 276 p.

1898 — —. **Narcotic Drugs—International Administration,** *World Organization,* Institute on World Organization (ed.). Washington, American Council on Public Affairs, 1942, pp. 99—111.

1899 Willoughby, Westel W. **Opium As an International Problem.** Baltimore, Johns Hopkins Press, 1925. 585 p.

1900 World Peace Foundation. **The International Opium Conference.** Boston, World Peace Foundation, 1925. 194 p.

8.5.4 MINORITIES

1901 Ammende, Ewald. **Die Nationalitäten in den Staaten Europas: Sammlung von Lagerberichten.** Vienna, Braumüller, 1931. 566 p.

1902 Azcárate y Florez, Pablo de. **League of Nations and National Minorities.** Eileen E. Brooke (trans.). Washington, Carnegie, 1945. ix + 216 p.

1903 Bentwich, Norman. **The League of Nations and Racial Persecution in Germany,** *Transactions* (Grotius Society), XIX (1933), 75—88.

1904 Bewes, Wyndham A. **The Working of the Minority Treaties,** *International Affairs,* V (March 1926), 79—95.

Part C. — League of Nations System

1905 Calderwood, Howard B. **The Proposed Generalization of the Minorities Regime,** *American Political Science Review,* XXVIII (December 1934), 1088—98.

1906 — —. **The Protection of Minorities,** *Geneva Studies,* II (September 1930), 1—28.

1907 — —. **Should the Council of the League of Nations Establish a Permanent Minorities Commission?** *American Political Science Review,* XXVII (April 1933), 250—59.

1908 Cheever, Daniel S. and Haviland, H. Field, Jr. **Organizing for Peace.** Boston, Houghton, Mifflin, 1954.
Chapter XXII.

1909 Eppstein, John (comp.). **Ten Years of the League of Nations.** London, Fair Press, 1929.
Chapter VIII.

1910 Feinberg, Nathan. **La juridiction et la jurisprudence en matière de mandats et de minorités,** *Recueil des Cours,* LIX (1937), 591—705.

1911 Foreign Policy Association. **Protection of Minorities in Europe,** *Foreign Policy Reports,* II (July 3, 1926), 104—16.

1912 Graham, Malbone W., Jr. **The League of Nations and the Protection of Minorities,** *Institute of World Affairs Proceedings,* I (1926), 51—56.

1913 Harris, H. Wilson. **What the League of Nations Is.** London, Allen and Unwin, 1925.
Chapter XIV.

Part C. — League of Nations System

1914 Heyking, Baron. **The International Protection of Minorities—The Achilles Heel of Nations,** *Transactions* (Grotius Society), XIII (1927), 31—49.

Comments by Jennings, Wolf, Bewes, Jelf, Grey, Fraser, Bellot and Goitein.

1915 Hudson, Manley Ottmer. **The League of Nations and the Protection of the Inhabitants of Transferred Territories,** *Annals of the American Academy of Political and Social Science,* XCVI (July 1921), 78—83.

1916 — —. **The Protection of Minorities and Natives in Transferred Territories,** *What Really Happened at Paris,* Edward M. House and Charles Seymour (eds.). New York, Scribner, 1921, pp. 204—30.

1917 Kershaw, Raymond N. **The League and the Protection of Linguistic, Racial, and Religious Minorities,** *Problems of Peace,* Series 3 (1928), 156—77.

1918 Ladas, Stephen P. **The Exchange of Minorities: Bulgaria, Greece, and Turkey.** New York, Macmillan, 1932. 849 p.

1919 League of Nations, Secretariat. **Ten Years of World Co-operation.** Geneva, 1930.

Chapter XI.

1920 League of Nations, Secretariat, Information Section. **The League of Nations and Minorities.** Geneva, 1923. 34 p.

1921 — —. **The League of Nations and the Protection of Minorities of Race, Language and Religion.** Rev. ed. Geneva, 1927. 78 p.

1922 Macartney, Carlile Aylmer. **National States and National Minorities.** London, Milford, 1934. ix + 553 p.

Part C. — League of Nations System

1923 Mair, Lucy P. **The League Council and a Minorities Commission,** *Political Quarterly,* I (July—September 1930), 410—22.

1924 — —. **The Machinery of Minority Protection,** *International Affairs,* VII (July 1928), 256—66.

1925 — —. **The Protection of Minorities.** London, Christophers, 1928. 244 p.

1926 Mander, Linden A. **Foundations of Modern World Society** Rev. ed. Stanford, Stanford University Press, 1947.

Chapter X.

1927 Mower, Edmund. **International Government.** Boston, Heath, 1931.

Chapter XXIV.

1928 Murray, Gilbert. **National Tolerance As an International Obligation,** *Problems of Peace,* Series 5 (1930), 167—87.

1929 Robinson, Jacob. **Das Minoritätenproblem und seine Literatur.** Berlin, Grurpter, 1928. 265 p.

1930 — —. **Minorities,** *World Organization,* Institute on World Organization (ed.). Washington, American Council on Public Affairs, 1942, pp. 231—42.

1931 Rosting, Helmer. **Protection of Minorities by the League of Nations,** *American Journal of International Law,* XVII (October 1923), 641—60.

1932 Roucek, Joseph S. **Procedure in Minorities Complaints,** *American Journal of International Law,* XXIII (July 1929), 538—51.

1933 — —. **The Working of the Minorities System Under the League of Nations.** Prague, Orbis, 1929. 122 p.

1934 Stone, Julius. **International Guarantees of Minority Rights: Procedure of the Council of the League of Nations in Theory and Practice.** London, Oxford University Press, 1932. 288 p.

1935 — —. **The Legal Nature of the Minorities Petition,** *British Yearbook of International Law,* XIII (1933), 76—94.

1936 — —. **Regional Guarantees of Minority Rights: A Study of Minorities Procedure in Upper Silesia.** New York, Macmillan, 1933. 313 p.

1937 Walters, Francis Paul. **A History of the League of Nations.** London, Oxford University Press, 1960.

Chapter XXXIV.

1938 Webster, Charles Kingsley and Herbert, Sydney. **The League of Nations in Theory and Practice.** London, Allen and Unwin, 1933.

Chapter XIII.

1939 Wilde, John C. de. **The Problem of Minorities,** *Foreign Policy Reports,* VII (November 25, 1931), 341—58.

8.5.5 REFUGEES

1940 Bentwich, Norman. **The International Problem of Refugees,** *Foreign Policy Reports,* XI (February 12, 1936), 306—16.

Published also in *Geneva Studies,* 1935.

Part C. — League of Nations System

1941 — —. **The League of Nations and Refugees,** *British Yearbook of International Law*, XVI (1935), 114—29.

1942 Childs, S. Lawford. **Refugees: A Permanent Problem in International Organization,** *Problems of Peace*, Series 13 (1938), 196—225.

1943 Eppstein, John (comp.). **Ten Years of the League of Nations.** London, Fair Press, 1929.

Chapter XIII.

1944 François, J.W.A. **Le problème des apatrides,** *Recueil des Cours*, LIII (1935), 287—375.

1945 Macartney, Carlile A. **Refugees: The Work of the League.** London, League of Nations Union, 1930. 127 p.

1946 McDonald, James G. **Refugees,** *Pioneers in World Order*, Harriet E. Davis (ed.). New York, Columbia University Press, 1944, pp. 208—28.

1947 Reynolds, Ernest Edwin. **Nansen.** London, Blis, 1932. xi + 274 p.

1948 Rubinstein, J. L. **The Refugee Problem,** *International Affairs*, XV (September 1936), 716—34.

1949 Simpson, John Hope. **The Refugee Problem,** *International Affairs*, XVII (September—October 1938), 607—20.

Comments by Malcolm, Marley, Bentwich, Ormerod, Hobman, Stewart, Smith, Williams, Cohen.

1950 — —. **The Refugee Problem: Report of a Survey.** New York, Oxford University Press, 1939. 637 p.

1951 — —. **The Work of the Greek Refugee Settlement Commission,** *International Affairs,* VIII (November 1929), 583—601.

Comments by Cunliffe-Owen, Garnett, Mance.

1952 Thompson, Dorothy. **Refugees: A World Problem,** *Foreign Affairs,* XVI (April 1938), 375—87.

1953 Toller, Ernst. **The Refugee Problem,** *Political Quarterly,* VI (1935), 386—99.

8.5.6 SLAVERY AND TRAFFIC IN WOMEN AND CHILDREN

1954 Coupland, Reginald. **The British Anti-Slavery Movement.** London, Butterworth, 1933, 255 p.

1955 Everett, R. H. **International Traffic in Women and Children,** *Journal of Social Hygiene,* XIII (May 1927), 65—75.

1956 Geneva Research Center. **The Suppression of Slavery,** *Geneva Studies,* II (April 1931), 1—31.

1957 Johnson, Bascom. **International Traffic in Women and Children,** *Journal of Social Hygiene,* (February 1928), 268—89.

1958 Klingberg, Frank J. **The Anti-Slavery Movement in England: A Study in English Humanitarianism.** New Haven, Conn., Yale University Press, 1926. xii + 390 p.

1959 Warnshuis, A. L., Chamberlain, Joseph P., and Wright, Quincy. **The Slavery Convention of Geneva, September 25, 1926,** *International Conciliation,* CCXXXVI (January 1928), 7—67.

Includes documents.

8.6 INTERNATIONAL INTELLECTUAL COOPERATION

See also F 4.

1960 Bonnet, Henri. **Intellectual Cooperation,** *World Organization*, Institute on World Organization (ed.). Washington, American Council on Public Affairs, 1942, pp. 189—210.

1961 — —. **L'oeuvre de l'Institut International de Cooperation Intellectuelle,** *Recueil des Cours*, LXI (1937), 461—539.

1962 Dowling, Evaline. **International Cooperation,** *Institute of World Affairs Proceedings*, V (1929), 216—21.

World Federation of Education Associations.

1963 Feis, Herbert. **Research Activities of the League of Nations: A Report Made to the Committee on International Relations of the Social Science Research Council on the Methods and Progress of Research in the League of Nations and International Labour Organization.** Old Lyme, Conn., Old Lyme Press, 1929. 27 p.

1964 Galabert, Henri. **La Commission de Coopération Intellectuelle de la Société des Nations.** Toulouse, Lion, 1931. 240 p.

1965 Garnett, J. C. Maxwell. **The Psychology of Patriotism and the Aims of the League of Nations Association,** *Problems of Peace*, Series 1 (1926), 326—51.

1966 Geneva Research Center. **International Research in Geneva,** *Geneva Studies*, II (1932), 1—24.

1967 Hale, George Ellery. **The International Organization of Scientific Research,** *International Organization*, CLIV (September 1920), 13—23.

Part C. — *League of Nations System*

1968 Hodges, Charles. **The World Union of Intellectual Forces,** *Current History*, XXIV (April 1926), 411—15.

1969 Institut International de Coopération Intellectuelle. **L'Institut International de Coopération Intellectuelle, 1925—1946.** Paris, 1946. 599 p.

1970 International Institute of Intellectual Cooperation. **International Institute of Intellectual Cooperation.** New York, Columbia University Press, 1934. 192 p.

1971 Jessup, Philip C. **L'exploitation des richesses de la mer,** *Recueil des Cours*, XXIX (1929), 405—508.

1972 Knudson, John I. **A History of the League of Nations.** Atlanta, Smith, 1938.

Chapter XI.

1973 Kolasa, Jan. **International Intellectual Cooperation (The League Experience and the Beginnings of UNESCO).** Warsaw, Nauk, 1962. 208 p.

1974 League of Nations, Secretariat, Information Section. **The League of Nations and Intellectual Cooperation.** Rev. ed. Geneva, 1927. 52 p.

1975 League of Nations, Secretariat. **Ten Years of World Co-operation.** Geneva, 1930.

Chapter VIII.

1976 Leland, Waldo G. **The International Union of Academies and the American Council of Learned Societies,** *International Conciliation*, CLIV (September 1920), 24—39.

1977 Mander, Linden A. **Foundations of Modern World Society.** Stanford, Stanford University Press, 1947.

Chapter XII.

1978 Mower, Edmund. **International Government.** Boston, Heath, 1931.
Chapter XXVIII.

1979 Murray, Gilbert. **Intellectual Cooperation,** *Agenda*, III (May 1944), 104–13.

1980 Pascal-Bonetti. **Intellectual Cooperation Among the Nations,** *Institute of World Affairs Proceedings*, VIII (1931), 234–39.

1981 Pham, Thi-Tu. **La Coopération Intellectuelle sous la Société des Nations.** Geneva, Postgraduate Institute of International Studies, 1962. 266 p.

1982 Shotwell, James T. **Where Minds Meet: The Intellectual Co-operation Organization of the League of Nations,** *Windows on the World: American Attempts to Organize International Life*, League of Nations Pavilion, New York World's Fair of 1939 (ed.). New York, Columbia University Press, 1939, pp. 91–103.

1983 Szinai, Miklos. **Béla Bartok and the Permanent Committee on Literature and Art of the League of Nations,** *New Hungarian Quarterly*, V (Autumn 1964), 143–45.

1984 Webster, Charles Kingsley and Herbert, Sydney. **The League of Nations in Theory and Practice.** London, Allen and Unwin, 1933.
Chapter XIX.

1985 Whitton, John B. **The Reorganisation of the Geneva Research Centre,** *Geneva Studies*, VII, 10 (1936–37), 3–13.

1986 Zimmern, Alfred. **The League and International Co-operation,** *Problems of Peace*, Series 1 (1926), 144–50.

Part C. — League of Nations System

9. MANDATES SYSTEM AND DEPENDENT PEOPLES

Though the mandates system gradually became coordinated by the League Mandates Commission, the League's sole function in relation to many of the "special areas" was to administer plebiscites and to hear minorities' positions. Shanghai, Suez, and Tangier never were brought within even partial League control, though various proposals for the extension of League jurisdiction were made from time to time.

9.1 STRUCTURE OF THE MANDATES SYSTEM

1987　Addams, Jane. **The Potential Advantages of the Mandate System,** *Annals of the American Academy of Political and Social Science,* XCVI (July 1921), 70—74.

1988　Amery, L. S. **The Problem of the Cessation of the Mandated Territories,** *International Affairs,* XVI (January 1937), 3—16.

　　　Comments by Garnett, Deverell, Miller, Scarman, Philipps, Clark, Malcolm.

1989　Ankers, P. M. **The Mandates System: Origin, Principles, Application.** Geneva, Secretariat of the League of Nations, 1945. 120 p.

1990　Barnes, Leonard. **The Future of Colonies. London,** Hogarth, 1936. 46 p.

1991　Bentwich, Norman. **Colonial Mandates and Trusteeships,** *Transactions* (Grotius Society), XXXII (1946), 121—34.

1992　— —. **Colonies, Mandates and Germany,** *World Affairs,* II (December 1936), 309—17.

Part C. — League of Nations System

1993 — —. **The Mandates System.** London, Longmans, Green, 1930. 200 p.

1994 — —. **Le système des mandats,** *Recueil des Cours,* XXIX (1929), 119–80.

1995 — —. **Ten Years of International Mandates,** *Political Quarterly,* II (October–December 1931), 564–76.

1996 Bonn, M. J. **The Future of Imperialism,** *Annals of the American Academy of Political and Social Science,* CCXXVIII (July 1943), 71–77.

1997 Borchard, Edwin M. **The Problem of Backward Areas and of Colonies,** *The League of Nations,* Stephen Pierce Duggan (ed.). Boston, Atlantic Monthly Press, 1919, pp. 201–17.

1998 Buell, Raymond Leslie. **'Backward' Peoples Under the Mandate System,** *Current History,* XX (June 1924), 386–95.

1999 — —. **The Mandate System After Ten Years,** *Current History,* XXXI (December 1929), 545–50.

2000 Cheever, Daniel S. and Haviland, H. Field, Jr. **Organizing for Peace.** Boston, Houghton, Mifflin, 1954.

Chapters X, XXII.

2001 Chowdhuri, R. N. **International Mandate and Trusteeship Systems: A Comparative Study.** Hague, Nijhoff, 1955. 328 p.

2002 Conover, Helen F. (comp.). **Non-Self-Governing Areas with Special Emphasis on Mandates and Trusteeships: A Selected List of References.** Washington, Library of Congress, 1947. ix + 467 p.

2003 Diena, Giulio. **Les mandats internationaux,** *Recueil des Cours,* V (1924), 215–65.

2004 Eppstein, John (comp.). **Ten Years of the League of Nations.** London, Fair Press, 1929.

Chapter XII.

2005 Evans, Luther Harris. **The General Principles Governing the Termination of a Mandate,** *American Journal of International Law,* XXVI (October 1932), 735–58.

2006 Feinberg, Nathan. **La juridiction et la jurisprudence en matière de mandats et de minorités,** *Recueil des Cours,* LIX (1937), 591–705.

2007 Foreign Policy Association. **Colonial vs. Mandate Administration,** *Foreign Policy Reports,* II (March 22, 1926), 12–24.

2008 — —. **Functions of the Permanent Mandates Commission,** *Foreign Policy Reports,* III (April 27, 1927), 45–60.

2009 Gerig, Benjamin. **Mandates and Colonies,** *World Organization,* Institute on World Organization (ed.). Washington, American Council on Public Affairs, 1942, pp. 211–30.

2010 — —. **The Open Door and the Mandates System: A Study of Economic Equality Before and Since the Establishment of the Mandates System.** Foreword by William E. Rappard. London, Allen and Unwin, 1930. 236 p.

2011 Gibbons, Herbert Adams. **The Defects of the System of Mandates,** *Annals of the American Academy of Political and Social Science,* XCVI (July 1921), 84–90.

Part C. — League of Nations System

2012 Gilchrist, Huntington. **Dependent Peoples and Mandates,** *Pioneers in World Order,* Harriet E. Davis (ed.). New York, Columbia University Press, 1944, pp. 121–55.

2013 — —. **The Operation of the Mandates System,** *Problems of Peace,* Series 2 (1927), 172–94.

2014 Gonsiorowski, Miroslas. **La Société des Nations et la problème de la paix.** Paris, Rousseau, 1927. 2 vols.

2015 Grinshaw, H. A. **The Mandates System,** *Problems of Peace,* Series 2 (1927), 143–71.

2016 — —. **The Mandates System and the Problem of Native Labour.** *Problems of Peace,* Series 3 (1928), 130–55.

2017 Gross, Leo. **United Nations Trusteeship and the League of Nations Mandate Systems,** *India Quarterly,* IV (July–September 1948), 224–39.

2018 Haas, Ernst B. **The Reconciliation of Conflicting Colonial Policy Aims: Aceptance of the League of Nations' Mandate System,** *International Organization,* VI (November 1952), 521–36.

2019 Hales, James C. **The Creation and Application of the Mandate System,** *Transactions* (Grotius Society), XXV (1939), 185–284.

2020 — —. **The Reform and Extension of the Mandate System,** *Transactions* (Grotius Society), XXVI (1940), 153–210.

2021 — —. **Some Legal Aspects of the Mandate System: Sovereignty, Nationality-Termination and Transfer,** *Transactions* (Grotius Society), XXII (1937), 85–126.

2022 Harris, H. Wilson. **What the League of Nations Is.** London, Allen and Unwin, 1925.

Chapter XII.

2023 Hill, Norman L. **International Administration.** New York, McGraw-Hill, 1931.

Chapter V.

2024 Hudson, Manley Ottmer. **The Protection of Minorities and Natives in Transferred Territories,** *What Really Happened at Paris,* Edward M. House and Charles Seymour (eds.). New York, Scribner's, 1921, pp. 204–30.

2025 Hughan, Jessie W. **A Study of International Government.** New York, Crowell, 1923.

Chapter XI.

2026 Kastl, L. **Colonial Administration As an International Trust,** *Problems of Peace,* Series 5 (1930), 132–66.

2027 League of Nations, Secretariat. **Ten Years of World Co-operation.** Geneva, 1930.

Chapter IX.

2028 League of Nations, Secretariat, Information Section. **The League of Nations and Mandates.** Geneva, 1924. 37 p.

2029 — —. **The Mandate System.** Rev. ed. Geneva, 1927. 40 p.

2030 Lee, Duncan Campbell. **Mandates and How They Are Working,** *Transactions* (Grotius Society), XII (1926), 31–47.

Comments by Manisty, Colombos, Sherwood, and Bewes.

Part C. — League of Nations System

2031 Louis, Wm. Roger. **African Origins of the Mandates Idea.** *International Organization*, XIX (Winter, 1965), 20–36.

2032 Macaulay, Neil. **Mandates: Reasons, Results, Remedies.** Foreword by Edward Grigg. London, Methuen, 1937. x + 213 p.

2033 Margalith, Aaron M. **The International Mandates.** Baltimore, Johns Hopkins Press, 1930. ix + 242 p.

2034 Miller, David Hunter. **The Origin of the Mandate System,** *Foreign Affairs*, VI (January 1928), 277–89.

2035 Mills, Mark Carter. **The Mandatory System,** *American Journal of International Law*, XVII (January 1923), 50–62.

2036 Moresco, Emanuel (ed.). **Colonial Questions and Peace.** Paris, Institute of Intellectual Co-operation, 1939. 345 p.

2037 Mower, Edmund. **International Government.** Boston, Heath, 1931.
Chapter XXIII.

2038 Myers, Denys P. **The Mandate System of the League of Nations,** *Annals of the American Academy of Political and Social Science*, XCVI (July 1921), 74–77.

2039 Myers, S. D., Jr. **The Permanent Mandates Commission and the Administration of Mandates,** *Southwestern Social Science Quarterly*, XI (December 1930), 213–46.

2040 O'Connell, D. P. **Nationality in "C" Class Mandates,** *British Yearbook of International Law*, XXXI (1954), 458–61.

Part C. — League of Nations System

2040a Ormsby-Gore, M. **Indirect International Supervision,** *The League of Nations Starts,* Raymond B. Fosdick, George Rublee, J. T. Shotwell, Léon Bourgeois, AndrÉ Weiss, Lt-Col. Requin, W. Ormsby-Gore, el Vizconde de Eza, H. B. Butler, Richard P. Strong, J. A. Salter, A. Claveille, Henri La Fontaine, Paul Otlet. London, Macmillan, 1920, pp. 101—25.

2041 Potter, Pitman B. **Origin of the System of Mandates Under the League of Nations,** *American Political Science Review,* XVI (November 1922), 563—83.

2042 — —. **Origin of the System of Mandates,** *American Political Science Review,* XX (November 1926), 842—46.

2043 Rappard, William E. **The Mandates and the International Trusteeship System,** *Political Science Quarterly,* LXI (September 1946), 408—19.

2044 — —. **The Practical Working of the Mandates System,** *International Affairs,* (September 1925), 205—26.

2045 Rolin, H. **La pratique des mandats internationaux,** *Recueil des Cours,* XIX (1927), 497—627.

2046 Sandhaus, Edith. **Les mandats dans l'Empire Britannique.** Grenoble, Saint-Bruno, 1931. 334 p.

2047 Van Rees, D. F. W. **Les mandats internationax: le controle internationale de l'administration mandataire.** Paris, Rousseau, 1927—28. 2 vols.

2048 Webster, Charles Kingsley and Herbert, Sydney. **The League of Nations in Theory and Practice.** London, Allen and Unwin, 1933.
Chapter XVIII.

2049 White, Freda. **The Mandate System,** *Ten Years of the League of Nations,* John Eppstein (ed.). London, Fair Press, 1929, pp. 150—56.

2050 — —. **Mandates.** London, Cape, 1926. 196 p.

2051 Wright, Quincy. **The Effect of Withdrawal from the League upon a Mandate,** *British Yearbook of International Law,* XVI (1935), 104—13.

2052 — —. **The Mandates System and Public Opinion,** *Southwestern Social Science Quarterly,* IX (March 1929), 369—406.

2053 — —. **Mandates Under the League of Nations.** Chicago, University of Chicago Press, 1930. 726 p.

2054 — —. **Sovereignty of the Mandates,** *American Journal of International Law,* XVII (October 1923), 691—703.

9.2 PARTICULAR MANDATES

9.2.1 AFRICAN MANDATES

2055 Datta, Ansu Kuman. **South-West Africa Under the Mandatory System,** *Africa Quarterly,* II (October 1962), 155—72.

2056 Ilsley, Lucretia L. **The Administration of Mandates by the British Dominions,** *American Political Science Review,* XXVIII (April 1934), 287—302.

Southwest Africa.

2057 Logan, Rayford W. **The Operation of the Mandate System in Africa, 1919—1927.** Washington, Foundation Publishers, 1942. xii + 50 p.

2058 Mitchell, Nicholas Pendleton. **Land Problems and Policies in the African Mandates of the British Commonwealth.** Baton Rouge, Louisiana State University Press, 1931. 155 p.

2059 Van Maanen-Helmer, Elizabeth. **The Mandate System in Relation to Africa and the Pacific Islands.** London, King, 1929. 331 p.

9.2.2 MIDDLE EASTERN MANDATES

9.2.2.1 GENERAL OBSERVATIONS

2060 Bentwich, Norman. **Nationality in Mandated Territories Detached from Turkey,** *British Yearbook of International Law,* VII (1926), 97–109.

9.2.2.2. IRAQ, LEBANON, SYRIA

2061 Andrews, Fannie Fern. **The Holy Land Under Mandate.** Boston, Houghton, Mifflin, 1931. 2 vols.

Excellent bibliography.

2062 Antonius, George. **Syria and the French Mandate,** *International Affairs,* XIII (July 1934), 523–35.

Followed by a discussion.

2063 Cardahi, Choucri. **Le mandat de la France sur la Syrie et le Liban,** *Recueil des Cours,* XXXXXIII (1933), 663–791.

2064 Davidson, Nigel. **The Termination of the Iraq Mandate,** *International Affairs,* XII (January 1933), 60–76.

Comments by Mumford, Bentwich, Cox.

2065 Emerson, Rupert. **Iraq: The End of a Mandate,** *Foreign Affairs,* XI (January 1933), 355–60.

2066 Evans, Luther H. **The Emancipation of Iraq from the Mandates System,** *American Political Science Review,* XXVI (December 1932), 1024—49.

2067 Foreign Policy Association. **The French Mandate in Syria,** *Foreign Policy Reports,* I (December 5, 1925), 1—8.

2068 Ireland, Philip W. **Iraq: A Study in Political Development.** London, Cape, 1937. 510 p.

2069 Longrigg, Stephen H. **Syria and Lebanon Under French Mandate.** London, Oxford University Press, 1958. 404 p.

2070 O'Zoux, Raymond. **Les états du Levant sous mandat français.** Paris, Larose, 1931. 329 p.

2071 Price, Clair. **Britain's White Elephant in Mesopotamia,** *Current History,* XVIII (April 1923), 40—43.

2072 Wright, Quincy. **Syrian Grievances Against French Rule,** *Current History,* XXIII (February 1926), 687—93.

9.2.2.3 PALESTINE

2073 Agronsky, G. **Lights and Shadows in Palestine Today.** *Current History,* XXI (October 1924), 75—80.

2074 al-Barghuthi, Omar Bey Salih. **Local Self-Government—Past and Present,** *Annals of the American Academy of Political and Social Science,* CLXIV (November 1932), 34—38.

Part C. — League of Nations System

2075 Antonius, George. **The Machinery of Government in Palestine,** *Annals of the American Academy of Political and Social Science,* CLXIV (November 1932), 55–61.

2076 Bentwich, Norman. **England in Palestine.** London, Paul, Trench, 1932. 358 p.

Appendix of documents.

2077 — —. **The Mandate for Palestine,** *British Yearbook of International Law,* X (1929), 137–43.

2078 — —. **The Palestine Mandate and the League of Arab States,** *World Affairs,* XI (July 1945), 131–37.

2079 — —. **Palestine's Progress and Problems,** *International Affairs,* XIV (May 1935), 369–84.

Comments by McFadyear, Snell, Hartog, Rathbone.

2080 Bentwich, Norman and Bentwich, Helen. **Mandate Memories, 1918–1948.** New York, Schocken, 1965. 231 p.

2081 Ben-Zwi, Isaac. **Local Autonomy in Palestine,** *Annals of the American Academy of Political and Social Science,* CLXIV (November 1932), 27–33.

2082 Cunningham, Alan. **Palestine: The Last Days of the Mandate,** *International Affairs,* XXIV (October 1948), 481–90.

2083 Frankfurter, Felix. **The Palestine Situation Restated,** *Foreign Affairs,* IX (April 1931), 409–34.

2084 Garratt, G. T. **Palestine Before the Commission,** *Political Quarterly,* VII (1936), 509–21.

Part C. — League of Nations System

2085 Gelber, Marvin B. **The Palestine Mandate: Story of a Fumble,** *International Journal,* I (October 1946), 302–16.

2086 Geneva Research Center. **The Palestine Mandate,** *Geneva Studies,* I (June 1930), 1–20.

2087 — —. **The Palestine Mandate (Revised),** *Geneva Studies,* II (October 1930), 1–26.

2088 Ghory, Emile. **An Arab View of the Situation in Palestine,** *International Affairs,* XV (September 1936), 684–99.

2089 H., G. S. **The Problem of Palestine,** *World Today,* New Series, I (November 1945), 195–204.

2090 Hadi, Aouni Bey Abdul. **The Balfour Declaration,** *Annals of the American Academy of Political and Social Science,* CLXIV (November 1932), 12–21.

2091 Hanna, Paul L. **British Policy in Palestine.** Introduction by Josephus Daniels. Washington, American Council on Public Affairs, 1942. xiii + 214 p.

2092 Hill, John G. **The Twisted Triangle in Palestine,** *World Affairs Quarterly,* IX (October 1938), 298–306.

2093 Husseini, Jamaal Bey. **The Proposed Palestine Constitution,** *Annals of the American Academy of Political and Social Science,* CLXIV (November 1932), 22–26.

2094 Hyamson, Albert M. **Palestine Under the Mandate, 1920–1948.** London, Methuen, 1950. ix + 210 p.

2095 Joseph, Bernard. **Palestine Legislation Under the British,** *Annals of the American Academy of Political and Social Science,* CLXIV (November 1932), 39—46.

2096 McQueen, Elizabeth L. **A History Event in Palestine,** *Current History,* XIV (July 1921), 583—86.

2097 Marcus, Ernst. **Palästina—Ein Werdender Staat,** Leipzig, Noske, 1929. xix + 328 p.

2098 Mogannam, Mogannam E. **Palestine Legislation under the British,** *Annals of the American Academy of Political and Social Science,* CLXIV (November 1932), 47—54.

2099 Myres, S. D., Jr. **Constitutional Aspects of the Mandate for Palestine,** *Annals of the American Academy of Political and Social Science,* CLXIV (November 1932), 1—11.

2100 Peel, V. N. **The Report of the Palestine Commission,** *International Affairs,* XVI (September 1937), 761—73.
Comments by Macfadyear, Philby, Kisch, Ali, Storrs.

2101 Philby, H. **The Palestine Report: The Arabs and the Future of Palestine,** *Foreign Affairs,* XVI (October 1937), 156—66.

2102 Popper, David H. **Liquidating the Palestine Mandate,** *Foreign Policy Reports,* XIII (November 1, 1937), 194—204.

2103 Rappard, William E. **Mandates and Trusteeships: With Particular Reference to Palestine,** *Journal of Politics,* VIII (November 1946), 520—30.

2104 Royal Institute of International Affairs. **Great Britain and Palestine, 1915—1945.** London, Royal Institute of International Affairs, 1946. xii + 177 p.

2105 Samuel, Herbert. **Building a Nation in Palestine,** *Current History,* XV (November 1921), 325—29.

2106 — —. **The Palestine Report: Alternatives to Partition,** *Foreign Affairs,* XVI (October 1937), 143—55.

2107 — —. **Palestine: The Present Position,** *Contemporary Review,* CLVI (July 1939), 9—17.

2108 Sidebotham, Herbert. **Great Britain and Palestine.** London, Macmillan, 1937. ix + 310 p.

2109 Stoyanovsky, J. **The Mandate of Palestine.** New York, Longmans, Green, 1928. 414 p.

2110 Toynbee, Arnold J. **The Present Situation in Palestine,** *International Affairs,* X (January 1931), 38—59.

Followed by discussion of Kenwarthy, Stein, Lamington, Gibb, Nissim, Jeffries, White, Dugdale, Nevinson.

2111 Weizmann, Chaim. **Palestine Today,** *International Affairs,* XV (September 1936), 671—78.

Comments by Steed, Nevinson, Angell, Smith, Hartog.

2112 Woodhead, John. **The Report of the Palestine Partition Commission,** *International Affairs,* XVIII (May 1939), 171—85.

Comments by Coupland, Todd, Pilkington, Cust, Stark, Hammond, Woodhead, Stein.

2113 Woolbert, Robert Gale. **Pan Arabism and the Palestine Problem,** *Foreign Affairs,* XVI (January 1938), 309—22.

2114 Worsfold, William Basil. **Palestine of the Mandate.** London, Allen and Unwin, 1925. 275 p.

2115 Wright, Quincy. **The Palestine Problem,** *Political Science Quarterly,* XLI (September 1926), 384—412.

2116 "Xenophon." **Seven Years of History in New Palestine,** *Current History,* XXI (March 1925), 907—14.

9.2.3 PACIFIC MANDATES

2117 Blakeslee, George H. **The Mandates of the Pacific,** *Foreign Affairs,* I (September 1922), 98—115.

2118 Bryant, Stewart F. **The Mandate Islands of Japan,** *World Affairs Quarterly,* IV (October 1933), 256—62.

2119 Clyde, Paul Hibbert. **Japan's Pacific Mandates.** New York, Macmillan, 1935. vi + 244 p.

2120 Eggleston, Frederic. **The Australian Mandate for New Guinea.** Melbourne University Press, 1928. 149 p.

2121 Evans, Luther Harris. **The Japanese Mandate Naval Base Question,** *American Political Science Review,* XXIX (August 1935), 482—87.

2122 — —. **New Guinea Under Australian Mandate Rule,** *Southwestern Social Science Quarterly,* X (June 1929), 1—21.

2123 Fifield, Russell H. **Disposal of the Carolines, Marshalls, and Marianas at the Paris Peace Conference,** *American Historical Review,* LI (April 1946), 472—79.

2124 Harris, Walter B. **The South Sea Islands Under Japanese Mandate,** *Foreign Affairs,* X (July 1932), 691—97.

Part C. — League of Nations System

2125 Heneman, Harlow J. **The Administration of Japan's Pacific Mandate,** *American Political Science Review*, XXV (November 1931), 1029—44.

2126 Ilsley, Lucretia L. **The Administration of Mandates by the British Dominions,** *American Political Science Review*, XXXVIII (April 1934), 287—302.

Naura, New Guinea, Western Samoa.

2127 Johnstone, William C. **Future of the Japanese Mandated Islands,** *Foreign Policy Reports*, XXI (September 15, 1945), 190—99.

2128 Jones, F. Llewellyn. **Plebiscites,** *Transactions* **(Grotius Society),** XIII (1927), 165—85.

Comments by Baty, Bisschop, Gahan, Pratt, Bourdillon.

2129 Kellor, Frances A. and Hatvany, Antonia. **Security Against War.** New York, Macmillan, 1924. 2 vols.

Chapters V—VII.

2130 League of Nations, Secretariat. **Ten Years of World Co-operation.** Geneva, 1930.

Chapter XII.

2131 Maanen-Helmer, Elizabeth van. **The Mandate System in Relation to Africa and the Pacific Islands.** London, King, 1929. 331 p.

2132 Mander, Linden A. **The Future of the Pacific Islands,** *Institute of World Affairs Proceedings*, XXI (1944—45), 92—102.

2133 Mower, Edmund. **International Government.** Boston, Heath, 1931.

Chapter XXV.

2134 Pauwels, Peter C. **The Japanese Mandate Islands.** Bandung, Van Dorp, 1936. 157 p.

2135 Wambaugh, Sarah. **A Monograph on Plebiscites, with a Collection of Official Documents and a Chronological List of Cases of Change of Sovereignty in Which the Right to Self-Determination Has Been Recognized.** New York, Oxford University Press, 1920. 1088 p.

2136 — —. **Plebiscites Since the War, with a Collection of Official Documents.** Washington, Carnegie, 1933. 2 vols.

2137 Yanaihara, Tadao. **Pacific Islands Under Japanese Mandate.** New York, Institute of Pacific Relations, 1940. 312 p.

9.3 ROLE OF THE UNITED STATES

2138 Andrews, Fannie Fern. **American Rights and Interests in the Mandatory System,** *Annals of the American Academy of Political and Social Science,* XCVI (July 1921), 95–97.

2139 Batsell, Walter Russell. **The United States and the System of Mandates,** *International Conciliation,* CCXIII (October 1925), 5–24.

Issue contains general information regarding the procedure and operations of the mandates system.

2140 Logan, Rayford W. **The Senate and the Versailles Mandate System.** Washington, Minorities Publisher, 1945. 112 p.

2141 McDonald, James G. **Mandates: America's Opportunity,** *Annals of the American Academy of Political and Social Science,* XCVI (July 1921), 90–94.

Part C. — *League of Nations System*

9.4 ADMINISTRATION OF "SPECIAL AREAS"

9.4.1 GENERAL OBSERVATIONS

2142 Anon. **Direct International Administration,** *The League of Nations Starts*, Raymond B. Fosdick, George Rublee, J. T. Shotwell, Léon Bourgeois, André Weiss, Lt.-Col. Requin, W. Ormsby-Gore, el Vizconde de Eza, H. B. Butler, Richard P. Strong, J. A. Salter, A. Claveille, Henri La Fontaine, Paul Otlet, London, Macmillan, 1920, pp. 91–100.

2143 Auer, Paul de. **Plebiscites and the League of Nations Covenant,** *Transactions* (Grotius Society), VI (1920), 45–56.

Comments by Manisty, Davies, Bewes, Whittuck, Phillimore, Macdonell, Bellot.

2144 Great Britain, Foreign Office, Historical Section. **Plebiscite and Referendum.** London, 1920. 151 p.

History of plebiscites.

2145 Harris, H. Wilson. **What the League of Nations Is.** London, Allen and Unwin, 1925.

Chapter XIII.

2146 Wambaugh, Sarah. **Control of Special Areas,** *Pioneers in World Order*, Harriet E. Davis (ed.). New York, Columbia University Press, 1944, pp. 107–20.

2147 — —. **New Tools for Peaceful Settlement,** *Annals of the American Academy of Political and Social Science*, CCXL (July 1945), 1–6.

Saar Governing Commission is used as an example that the four-power occupation of Germany could follow.

2148 — —. **The Plebiscite and Peaceful Change,** *World Affairs*, IV (June 1938), 16–25.

2149 Ydit, Meir. **Internationalised Territories from the "Free City of Cracow" to the "Free City of Berlin."** Leyden, Sythoff, 1961. 323 p.

9.4.2 DANZIG

2150 League of Nations, Secretariat, Information Section. **Saar Basin and Free City of Danzig.** Geneva, 1924. 34 p.

2151 Lewis, Malcolm M. **The Free City of Danzig,** *British Yearbook of International Law*, IV (1924), 89–102.

2152 Mason, John Brown. **Danzig Dilemma: A Study in Peacemaking by Compromise.** London, Oxford University Press, 1946. 377 p.

2153 — —. **The Free City of Danzig—A Noble Experiment,** *World Affairs Quarterly*, IX (July 1938), 168–73.

2154 Morrow, Ian F. D. **The International Status of the Free City of Danzig,** *British Yearbook of International Law*, XVIII (1951), 114–26.

2155 Morrow, Ian F. D., assisted by Sieveking, L. M. **The Peace Settlement in the German Polish Borderlands: A Study of Conditions To-day in the Pre-War Prussian Provinces of East and West Prussia.** London, Oxford University Press, 1936. xiv + 558 p.

2156 Reid, Helen Dwight. **Danzig,** *World Organization*, Institute on World Organization (ed.). Washington, American Council on Public Affairs, 1942, pp. 243–59.

2157 van Jarnel, J. A. **Danzig and the Polish Problem,** *International Conciliation*, CCLXXXVIII (March 1933), 9–33.

2158 Wertheimer, Mildred S. **Nazi Pressure in Danzig,** *Geneva Studies*, VII (May 1936), 2–16.

2159 — —. **The Nazification of Danzig,** *Foreign Policy Reports,* XII (June 1, 1936), 66–76.

9.4.3 SAAR

2160 Bassett, John S. **The League of Nations.** New York, Longmans, Green, 1938.
Chapter IX.

2161 Buchanan, R. M. K. **The Saar Problem,** *World Affairs Quarterly,* V (January 1935), 301–306.

2162 Fay, Sidney B. **The Fate of the Saar,** *Current History,* XLI (January 1935), 399–406.

2163 Florinsky, Michael T. **The Saar Strategy.** New York, Macmillan, 1934. xiv + 191 p.

2164 Haskins, Charles H. **The Saar Territory As It Is Today,** *Foreign Affairs,* I (December 15, 1922), 46–58.

2165 League of Nations, Secretariat, Information Section. **Saar Basin and Free City of Danzig.** Geneva, 1924. 34 p.

2166 Osborne, Sidney. **The Saar Question: A Disease Spot in Europe.** London, Allen and Unwin, 1923. 384 p.

2167 Pollock, James K. **The Saar Plebiscite,** *American Political Science Review,* XXIX (April 1935), 275–327.

2168 Russell, Frank M. **The International Government of the Saar.** Berkeley, University of California Press, 1926. 249 p.

2169 — —. **The Saar Basin Governing Commission,** *Political Science Quarterly,* XXXVI (June 1921), 169–83.

2170 — —. **The Saar: Battleground and Pawn.** Stanford, Stanford University Press, 1951. 204 p.

2171 Stone, Julius. **Regional Guarantees of Minority Rights: A Study of Minorities Procedure in Upper Silesia.** New York, Macmillan, 1933. 313 p.

2172 Straznicky, Milorad. **Jurisprudence de la Cour Suprême de Plébiscite du Bassin de la Sarre,** *Recueil des Cours,* LXIX (1939), 353–445.

2173 Walters, Francis Paul. **A History of the League of Nations.** London, Oxford University Press, 1960.

Chapter XLIX.

2174 Wambaugh, Sarah. **International Administration of the Saar Territory: 1920–1935,** *Iowa Law Review,* XXX (May 1945), 539–43.

2175 — —. **The Saar Plebiscite, with a Collection of Official Documents.** Cambridge, Harvard University Press, 1940. 487 p.

2176 — —. **The Saar,** *World Organization,* Institute on World Organization (ed.). Washington, American Council on Public Affairs, 1942, pp. 260–70.

2177 Wilde, John C. de. **The Future of the Saar,** *Foreign Policy Reports,* X (January 2, 1935), 282–92.

2178 Wiskemann, Elizabeth. **The Saar Plebiscite,** *Political Quarterly,* VI January–March 1935), 49–59.

9.4.4 SHANGHAI COURT

2179 Hudson, M. O. **The Rendition of the International Mixed Court at Shanghai,** *American Journal of International Law,* XXI (July 1927), 451–71.

2180 Kotenev, Anatol M. **Shanghai: Its Mixed Court and Council; Material Relating to the History, Practice and Statistics of the International Mixed Court.** Shanghai, North-China Daily News and Herald, 1925. xxvi + 588 p.

2181 — —. **Shanghai: Its Municipality and the Chinese; Being the History of the Shanghai Municipal Council and Its Relations with the Chinese, the Practice of the International Mixed Court, and the Inauguration and Constitution of the Shanghai Provisional Court.** Shanghai, North-China Daily News and Herald, 1927, xvii + 548 p.

2182 Quigley, H. S. **Extraterritoriality in China,** *American Journal of International Law*, XX (January 1926), 46–68.

9.4.5 SILESIA

2183 Hershey, Burnet. **An Inside View of the Silesian Peril,** *Current History*, XIV (July 1921), 556–61.

2184 Kaeckenbeeck, Georges **The International Experiment of Upper Silesia: A Study in the Working of the Upper Silesian Settlement, 1922–37.** London, Oxford University Press, 1942. 867 p.

2185 Osborne, Sidney. **The Upper Silesian Question and Germany's Coal Problem.** London, Allen and Unwin, 1920. 285 p.

2186 Paton, H. J. **Upper Silesia,** *International Affairs*, I (January 1922), 14–28.

2187 Rose, William J. **The Drama of Upper Silesia: A Regional Study.** Brattleboro, Vt., Daye, 1935. 349 p.

9.4.6 SUEZ CANAL

2188 Buell, Raymond Leslie. **The Suez Canal and League Sanctions,** *Geneva Studies*, VI, 3 (1935), 1–18.

2189 Hallberg, Charles W. **The Suez Canal: Its History and Diplomatic Importance.** New York, Columbia University Press, 1931. 434 p.

2190 Lesseps, Ferdinand M. de. **Recollections of Forty Years.** New York, Appleton, 1888. 2 vols.

2191 Mack, Gerstle. **The Land Divided: A History of the Panama Canal and Other Isthmian Canal Projects.** New York, Knopf, 1944. xv + 650 p.

2192 Siegfried, André. **Suez and Panama,** H. H. Hemming and Doras Hemming (trans.). New York, Harcourt, Brace, 1940. 400 p.

9.4.7 TANGIER

2193 Blix, H. **The Rule of Unanimity in the Revision of Treaties: A Study of the Treaties Governing Tangier,** *International and Comparative Law Quarterly,* V (July 1956), 447–65; (October 1956), 581–96.

2194 Gutteridge, J. A. C. **The Dissolution of the International Régime in Tangier,** *British Yearbook of International Law,* XXXIII (1957), 296–302.

2195 Harris, Walter B. **Tangier and Internationalism,** *International Affairs,* II (November 1923), 232–50.

A plea for League supervision.

2196 Stuart, Graham H. **The International City of Tangier,** *Institute of World Affairs Proceedings,* VIII (1931), 202–10.

2197 — —. **The International City of Tangier.** 2d ed. Stanford, Stanford University Press, 1955. xv + 270 p.

2198 T., I. **The Status of Tangier,** *World Today,* New Series, I (November 1945), 221–29.

Part C. — League of Nations System

10. PERMANENT COURT OF INTERNATIONAL JUSTICE (Hague)

Another organ that operated autonomously, the Permanent Court of Justice, eventually had the United States as a member.

10.1 GENERAL OBSERVATIONS

2199 Anon. **The Work of the Eleventh Assembly Relating to the Permanent Court of International Justice,** *British Yearbook of International Law,* XII (1931), 107–31.

Rapid extension of compulsory jurisdiction requires specific amendments.

2200 Borchard, Edwin M. **The Permanent Court of International Justice,** *Academy of Political Science Proceedings,* X, 3 (1923), 430–45.

2201 Bourgeois, Léon and Weiss, André. **The Permanent Court of International Justice,** *The League of Nations Starts,* Raymond B. Fosdick, George Rublee, J. T. Shotwell, Léon Bourgeois, André Weiss, Lt.-Col. Requin, W. Ormsby-Gore, el Vizconde de Eza, H. B. Butler, Richard P. Strong, J. A. Salter, A. Claveille, Henri La Fontaine, Paul Otlet. London, Macmillan, 1920, pp. 59–80.

2202 Bradley, Phillips. **The Permanent Court of International Justice,** *Contemporary World Politics,* Francis J. Brown, Charles Hodges and Joseph S. Roucek (eds.). New York, Wiley, 1939, pp. 471–86.

2203 Brierly, J. L. **The Judicial Settlement of International Disputes,** *International Affairs,* IV (September 1925), 227–41.

Comments by P. J. Noel Baker.

2204 Buell, Raymond Leslie. **International Relations.** New York, Holt, 1929.

Chapter XXV.

2205 — —. **The World Tribunal in Action,** *Current History,* XVII (December 1922), 411—18.

2206 Burns, Viktor. **La Cour Permanente de Justice Internationale, son organisation et sa procédure,** *Recueil des Cours,* LXII (1937), 551—670.

2207 Bustamente y Sirvén, Antonio Sánchez de. **The World Court,** Elizabeth F. Read (trans.). New York, Macmillan, 1925. xxv + 379 p.

2208 Caloyanni, Mégalos A.**The Organisation of International Justice, Justiciable and Political Disputes, and the Prospects Thereof,** *Transactions,* (Grotius Society), XXIII (1937), 71—84.

2209 Caloyanni, Mégalos A. **L'organisation de la Cour Permanente de Justice et son avenir,** *Recueil des Cours,* XXXVIII (1931), 655—785.

2210 Cheever, Daniel S. and Haviland, H. Field, Jr. **Organizing for Peace.** Boston, Houghton, Mifflin, 1954.

Chapter XII.

2211 Dean, Vera Micheles. **The Permanent Court of International Justice,** *Foreign Policy Reports,* V (December 25, 1929), 393—410.

2212 du Puy, William Atherton. **The New Hague Court at Work,** *Current History,* XVII (October 1922), 92—95.

2213 Fachiri, Alexander P. **International Law and the Permanent Court,** *Problems of Peace,* Series 2 (1927), 71—93.

2214 — —. **The Permanent Court of International Justice: Its Constitution, Procedure, and Work.** 2d ed. New York, Oxford University Press, 1932. 416 p.

2215 Fanshawe, Maurice. **The Permanent Court of International Justice,** *Ten Years of the League of Nations,* John Eppstein (ed.). London, Fair Press, 1929, pp. 43—53.

2216 Fenwick, Charles G. **Law the Prerequisite of an International Court,** *Annals of the American Academy of Political and Social Science,* XCVI (July 1921), 118—23.

2217 Fess, Simeon D. **The Movement Toward an International Court,** *Annals of the American Academy of Political and Social Science,* CXIV (July 1924), 135—43.

2218 Fosdick, Raymond B. **A Way of Escape from War,** *International Concilliation,* CCLXXVII (February 1932), 7—19; 53—65.

2219 Francqueville, Bernard de. **L'oeuvre de la Cour Permanente de Justice Internationale.** Paris, Les Éditions Internationales, 1928. 2 vols.

2220 Goodrich, Leland M. **The Nature of the Advisory Opinions of the Permanent Court of International Justice,** *American Journal of International Law,* XXXII (October 1939), 738—58.

2221 Hammarskjöld, Åke. **The Permanent Court of International Justice and Its Place in International Relations,** *International Affairs,* IX (July 1930), 467—94.

Comments by Fachiri, Harris, Bewes, Dent.

2222 — —. **The Permanent Court of International Justice and the Development of International Law,** *International Affairs,* XIV (November 1935), 797—817.

2223 — —. **Sidelights on the Permanent Court of International Justice,** *Michigan Law Review,* XXV (February 1927), 327—53.

2224 Hammond, John Hays. **A World Court,** *Annals of the American Academy of Political and Social Science,* XCVI (July 1921), 98—99.

2225 Harris, H. Wilson. **What the League of Nations Is.** London, Allen and Unwin, 1925.

Chapter V.

2226 Hill, David Jayne. **The Problem of a World Court: The Story of an Unrealized American Idea.** New York, Longmans, Green, 1927. 204 p.

2227 Hill, N. L. **National Judges in the Permanent Court of International Justice,** *American Journal of International Law,* XXV (October 1931), 670—83.

2228 Hinckley, Frank E. **Tendencies Towards Establishing a Permanent Parliament of International Law,** *Institute of World Affairs Proceedings,* V (1929), 141—45.

2229 Hostie, Jan. **The Statute of the Permanent Court of International Justice,** *American Journal of International Law,* XXXVIII (July 1944), 407—33.

2230 Howard-Ellis, C. **The Origin, Structure and Working of the League of Nations.** Boston, Houghton, Mifflin, 1928.

Chapter X.

2231 Hudson, Manley O. **The Administration of International Justice,** *Problems of Peace,* Series 5 (1930), 183—204.

2232 — —. **The Advisory Opinions of the Permanent Court of International Justice,** *International Conciliation,* CCXIV (November 1925), 5—58.

2233 — —. **Amended Rules of Permanent Court of International Justice,** *American Journal of International Law,* XXV (July 1931), 427—35.

Part C. — League of Nations System

2234 — —. **The Election of Members of the Permanent Court,** *American Journal of International Law,* XXIV (October 1930), 718-27.

2235 — —. **The First Conference for Codification of International Law,** *American Journal of International Law,* XXIV (July 1930), 447—66.

2236 — —. **The First Year of the Permanent Court of International Justice,** *American Journal of International Law,* XVII (January 1923), 15—28.

Professor Hudson continued these articles in subsequent years with each January issue, his last in 1959, "The Thirty-Seventh Year of the World Court." Manley Hudson was Professor of Law at Harvard University and subsequently a member of the World Court.

2237 — —. **The Independence of the Permanent Court of International Justice,** *American Society of International Law Proceedings,* XXV (1931), 92—102.

Comments by P. B. Potter.

2238 — —. **International Tribunals, Past and Future.** Washington, Carnegie, 1944. 287 p.

2239 — —. **The 1936 Rules of the Permanent Court of International Justice,** *American Journal of International Law,* XXX (July 1936), 463—70.

2240 — —. **The Permanent Court of International Justice.** New York, Macmillan, 1934. xxvii + 731 p.

2241 — —. **The Permanent Court of International Justice—An Indispensable First Step,** *Annals of the American Academy of Political and Social Science,* CVIII (July 1923), 188—92.

2242 — —. **The Permanent Court of International Justice and World Peace,** *Annals of the American Academy of Political and Social Science,* CXIV (July 1924), 122—25.

2243 — —. **The Permanent Court of International Justice,** 1920—1942. New York, Macmillan, 1943. xxiv + 807 p.

2244 — —. **Progress in International Organization.** Oxford, Oxford University Press, 1932.

Chapter VI.

2245 — —. **The Progressive Codification of International Law,** *American Journal of International Law*, XX (October 1926), 655—69.

2246 — —. **The Revision of the Statute of the World Court,** *Foreign Affairs*, IX (January 1931), 341—45.

2247 — —. **Ten Years of the World Court,** *Foreign Affairs*, XI (October 1932), 81—92.

2248 — —. **A Tribunal of Nations: The Permanent Court of International Justice, 1920—1939,** *Windows on the World: American Attempts to Organize International Life*, League of Nations Pavilion, New York World's Fair of 1939 (ed.). New York, Columbia University Press, 1939, pp. 107—17.

2249 — —. **The Work of the Permanent Court of International Justice During Its First Four Years,** *World Peace Foundation Pamphlets*, IX, 2 (1926), 80—136.

2250 — —. **The Work of the Permanent Court of International Justice During Its First Three Years,** *World Peace Foundation Pamphlets*, VIII, 7 (1925), 330—74.

2251 — —. **The Work of the Permanent Court of International Justice During Its First Two Years,** *World Peace Foundation Pamphlets*, VI, 6 (1923), 504—27.

Part C. — *League of Nations System*

2252 — —. **The World Court,** *Pioneers in World Order,* Harriet E. Davis (ed.). New York, Columbia University Press, 1944, pp. 65—75.

2253 — —. **The World Court, 1921—1938: A Handbook of the Permanent Court of International Justice.** 5th ed. Boston, World Peace Foundation, 1938. 345 p.

2254 — —. **The World Court 1922—1928,** *World Peace Foundation Pamphlets,* XI, 1 (1928), 1—156.

2255 Hughes, Charles Evans. **The Permanent Court of International Justice,** *Academy of Political Science Proceedings,* X, 3 (1923), 446—65.

Published concurrently in *American Society of International Law Proceedings,* 1923.

2256 — —. **World Court Not Controlled by League,** *Permanent Court of International Justice,* Julia E. Johnsen (ed.). New York, Wilson, 1924, pp. 48—68.

Reprinted from *Commercial and Financial Chronicle,* May 5, 1923.

2257 Hutcheson, Austin E. **The World Court and Peace,** *Annals of the American Academy of Political and Social Science,* CLXXV (September 1934), 133—37.

2258 Hyde, Charles Cheney. **The Interpretation of Treaties by the Permanent Court of International Justice,** *American Journal of International Law,* XXIV (January 1930), 1—19.

2259 Jessup, Philip C. **Revising the Statute of the Permanent Court of International Justice,** *American Journal of International Law,* XXIV (April 1930), 353—56.

2260 Johnsen, Julia E. (comp.). **Permanent Court of International Justice.** New York, Wilson, 1924. 118 p.

Excerpts from various sources and an excellent bibliography.

Part C. — *League of Nations System*

2261 Kellor, Frances A. and Hatvany, Antonia. **Security Against War.** New York, Macmillan, 1924.

Chapters XXIV, XXV.

2262 Knudson, John I. **A History of the League of Nations.** Atlanta, Smith, 1938.

Chapter XIV.

2263 Lauterpacht, Hersh. **The Development of International Law by the Permanent Court of Justice.** London, Longmans, Green, 1934. ix + 111 p.

2264 League of Nations, Secretariat. **Ten Years of World Co-operation.** Geneva, 1930.

Chapter III.

2265 — —. Information Section. **The Permanent Court of International Justice.** Rev. ed. Geneva, 1926. 62 p.

2266 Lindsey, Edward. **The International Court.** New York, Crowell, 1931. xix + 347 p.

2267 McNair, Arnold D. **The Council's Request for an Advisory Opinion from the Permanent Court of International Justice,** *British Yearbook of International Law*, VII (1926), 1—13.

2268 Mandere, H. C. G. J. van der. **Work of the Hague Tribunals,** *Current History*, XXI (December 1924), 383—90.

2269 Middlebush, Frederick A. and Hill, Chesney. **Elements of International Relations.** New York, McGraw-Hill, 1940.

Chapter XXIII.

2270 Miller, David Hunter. **The Hague Codification Conference,** *American Journal of International Law*, XXIV (October 1930), 674—93.

2271 Moore, John Bassett. **The Permanent Court of International Justice,** *International Conciliation,* CXCVII (April 1924), 5—20.

Reprinted from *Columbia Alumni News,* February 29, 1924.

2272 Mower, Edmund. **International Government.** Boston, Heath, 1931.

Chapter XXXIV.

2273 Myers, Dennis P. **The Modern System of Pacific Settlement of International Disputes,** *Political Science Quarterly,* XLVI (December 1931), 548—88.

Historical review of disputes settled by arbitration. Author sees the PCIJ as progress along that road. Shows how League of Nations and PCIJ work towards pacific settlement.

2274 Negulesco, Démètre. **L'evolution de la procédure des avis consultatifs de la Cour Permanente de Justice Internationale,** *Recueil des Cours,* LVII (1936), 5—95.

2275 Oppenheim, L. **The Future of International Law.** Oxford, Clarendon Press, 1921. 68 p.

2276 Pepper, George Wharton. **The Permanent Court of International Justice,** *Academy of Political Science Proceedings,* X, 3 (1923), 466—76.

2277 Permanent Court of International Justice. **Ten Years of International Jurisdiction (1922—1932).** Leyden, Sijhoff, 1932. 74 p.

2278 Phillimore, Walter G.F. **The Permanent Court of International Justice,** *International Affairs,* I (July 1922), 113—23.

2279 — —. **Scheme for the Permanent Court of International Justice,** *Transactions* (Grotius Society), VI (1920), 89—96.

Comments by Baratt, Henriques, Hopkinson, Pollock, Barclay, Jelf and Bower.

2280 Politis, Nicolas. **How the World Court Has Functioned,** *Foreign Affairs,* IV (April 1926), 443—53.

2281 Potter, Pitman B. **An Introduction to the Study of International Organization.** 4th ed. New York, Appleton-Century, 1935.

Chapter XXII.

2282 Reut-Nicolussi, E. **Reform of the Permanent Court of International Justice,** *Transactions* (Grotius Society), XXV (1939), 135—49.

2283 Root, Elihu. **The Permanent Court of International Justice,** *American Society of International Law Proceedings,* XVII (1923), 1—14.

2284 Rundestein, Simon. **La Cour Permanente de Justice Internationale comme instance de recours,** *Recueil des Cours,* XXXXIII (1933), 5—113.

2285 Salvioli, Gabriele. **La jurisprudence de la Cour Permanente de Justice Internationale,** *Recueil des Cours,* XII (1926), 5—113.

2286 Scerni, Mario. **La procédure de la Cour Permanente de Justice Internationale,** *Recueil des Cours,* LXV (1938), 565—681.

2287 Schachter, Oscar. **Enforcement of International Judicial and Arbitration Decisions,** *American Journal of International Law,* LIV (January 1960), 1—24.

2288 Scott, James Brown. **Aim and Purpose of an International Court of Justice,** *Annals of the American Academy of Political and Social Science,* XCVI (July 1921), 100—107.

2289 — —. **The Judicial Settlement of International Disputes. (Addresses at the Geneva Institute of International Relations, August 16th and 17th, 1926.)** London, Oxford University Press, 1927. 79 p.

Discusses the role of the U.S. Supreme Court in the settlement of inter-state disputes and the origin and nature of the Permanent Court of International Justice.

2290 — —. **The Judicial Settlement of International Disputes,** *Problems of Peace,* Series 1 (1926), 209—87.

2291 — —. **The Project of a Permanent Court of International Justice and Resolutions of the Advisory Committee of Jurists.** Washington, Carnegie, 1920. 235 p.

2292 Steiner, H. Arthur. **Fundamental Conceptions of International Law in the Jurisprudence of the Permanent Court of International Justice,** *American Journal of International Law,* XXX (July 1936), 414—38.

2293 Torriente, Cosme de la. **Cuba, Bustamente and the Permanent Court of International Justice,** *International Conciliation,* CLXXVIII (September 1922), 349—76.

2294 Vinacke, Harold M. **International Organization.** New York, Crofts, 1934.

Chapter X.

2295 Visscher, Charles de. **Les avis consultatifs de la Cour Permanente de Justice Internationale,** *Recueil des Cours,* XXVI (1929), 5—75.

2296 Warren, Charles. **The Supreme Court and the World Court 1832 and 1932,** *International Conciliation,* CCLXXXIX (April 1933), 9—24.

Reprinted from *Harvard Graduate's Magazine,* September 1932.

2297 Webster, Charles Kingsley and Herbert, Sydney. **The League of Nations in Theory and Practice.** London, Allen and Unwin, 1933.

Chapter VIII.

2298 Wheeler-Bennett, J. W. **Information on the Permanent Court of International Justice.** London, Association for International Understanding, 1924. 75 p.

Part C. — *League of Nations System*

2299 Wheeler-Bennett, John W. and Fanshawe, Maurice. **Information on the World Court, 1918—1928.** London, Allen and Unwin, 1929. 208 p.

2300 Whittuck, B. C. L. **A Court of International Justice,** *Transactions* (Grotius Society), V (1919), 39—46.

Comments by J. E. G. Montmorency, H. C. Dowdall, H. S. Q. Henriques.

2301 Wickersham, George W. **The Codification of International Law,** *Foreign Affairs*, IV (January 1926), 237—47.

An interesting analogy to American experience.

2302 Wood, Hugh McKinnon. **The World Court,** *World Organization*, Institute on World Organization (ed.). Washington, American Council on Public Affairs, 1942, pp. 271—306.

10.2 JURISDICTIONAL PROBLEMS

2303 Baker, P. J. **The Obligatory Jurisdiction of the Permanent Court of International Justice,** *British Yearbook of International Law*, V (1925), 68—102.

2304 Borchard, Edwin M. **Limitations on the Functions of International Courts,** *Annals of the American Academy of Political and Social Science*, XCVI (July 1921), 132—37.

2305 Fachiri, Alexander P. **Repudiation of the Optional Clause,** *British Yearbook of International Law*, XX (1939), 52—57.

Paraguay withdraws from League on basis of legal hassle over "optional clause" of the International Court of Justice.

2306 Hudson, Manley O. **The Permanent Court of International Justice: The Independence of the Court in Its Constitution, in Its Jurisdiction, and in Its Application to Law,** *American Society of International Law Proceedings*, XXV (1931), 92—102.

Comments by Potter, Hill, Jessup, Finch, Wright, Warren, Feller, Fenwick and Myers.

Part C. — *League of Nations System*

2307 — —. **The Work and the Jurisdiction of the Permanent Court of International Justice,** *Academy of Political Science Proceedings,* X, 3 (1923), 421–29.

2308 Jacoby, Sidney B. **Some Aspects of the Jurisdiction of the Permanent Court of International Justice,** *American Journal of International Law,* XXX (April 1936), 233–55.

2309 Kellogg, F. B. **Jurisdiction of the Permanent Court of International Justice,** *American Journal of International Law,* XXV (April 1931), 203–13.

2310 Kelsen, Hans. **Compulsory Adjudication of International Disputes,** *American Journal of International Law,* XXXVII (July 1943), 397–406.

2311 Peaslee, Amos J. **Obligatory Jurisdiction of the Permanent Court of International Justice,** *American Society of International Law Proceedings,* XXV (1931), 48–57.

Comments by Allen and Wright.

2312 Schindler, D. **Les progrès de l'arbitrage obligatoire depuis la création de la Société des Nations,** *Recueil des Cours,* XXV (1928), 237–361.

2313 Smith, Herbert A. **The Jurisdiction and Powers of an International Court,** *Annals of the American Academy of Political and Social Science,* XCVI (July 1921), 107–14.

2314 Wickersham, George W. **Compulsory Arbitration Not Essential to an Effective World Organization,** *Annals of the American Academy of Political and Social Science,* XCVI (July 1921), 114–18.

2315 Wilson, Robert R. **Reservation Clauses in Agreements for Obligatory Arbitration,** *American Journal of International Law,* XXIII (January 1929), 68–93.

10.3 ROLE OF THE UNITED STATES

2316 Anand, R. P. **The United States and the World Court,** *International Studies,* VI (January 1965), 254–84.

2317 Borel, Eugène. **The United States and the Permanent Court of International Justice,** *American Journal of International Law,* XVII (July 1923), 429–37.

2318 Calhoun, Harold. **Should the United States Enter the World Court?** *World Affairs Quarterly,* V (October 1934), 223–37.

2319 Clarke, John H. **The Relation of the United States to the Permanent Court of International Justice,** *Annals of the American Academy of Political and Social Science,* CXX (July 1925), 115–24.

2320 Fachiri, Alexander P. **The International Court: American Participation; Statute Revision,** *British Yearbook of International Law,* XI (1930), 85–99.

2321 Fleming, Denna Frank. **The United States and the World Court.** Garden City, Doubleday, Doran, 1945. 206 p.

2322 Foreign Policy Association. **The United States and the World Court,** *Foreign Policy Reports,* II (December 8, 1926), 230–41.

2323 Geneva Research Center. **The United States and the League, the Labour Organization, and the World Court in 1939,** *Geneva Studies,* XI (February 1940), 1–67.

2324 Hudson, Manley O. **The American Reservations and the Permanent Court of International Justice,** *American Journal of International Law,* XXII (October 1928), 776–96.

2325 — —. **The Permanent Court of International Justice, and the Question of American Participation, with a Collection of Documents.** Cambridge, Harvard University Press, 1925. 389 p.

2326 — —. **The Post-War Development of International Law and Some Contributions by the United States,** *Canadian Bar Review,* XII (April 1934), 191—208.

2327 — —. **The United States and the New International Court,** *Foreign Affairs,* I (December 1922), 71—82.

2328 — —. **The United States and the Permanent Court of International Justice,** *Institute of World Affairs Proceedings,* VIII (1931), 211—20.

2329 Hull, William I. **The Permanent Court of International Justice As an American Proposition,** *Annals of the American Academy of Political and Social Science,* CXIV (July 1924), 147—49.

2330 Jessup, Philip C. **The Acceptance of the Senate Reservations,** *International Conciliation,* CCLXXIII (October 1931), 9—28.

Appendix contains a documentary record of negotiation for the accession of the United States to the Court.

2331 — —. **Mr. Root, the Senate and the World Court,** *Foreign Affairs,* VII (July 1929), 585—99.

2332 — —. **The Permanent Court of International Justice: American Accession and Amendments to the Statute,** *International Conciliation,* CCLIV (November 1929), 527—51.

2333 — —. **The Root Formula for the Accession of the United States to the Permanent Court of International Justice,** *American Society of International Law Proceedings,* XXV (1931), 61—67.

Comments by Kingsbury, White, Hudson, Allen, Thompson, Peaslee, Borchard, Wright, Nicolson, Randolph, Bailey and Hill.

2334 — —. **The United States and the World Court,** *World Peace Foundation Pamphlets,* XII, 4 (1929), 1—156.

Part C. — *League of Nations System*

2335 Martin, Clarence E. **The United States and the World Court,** *Annals of the American Academy of Political and Social Science,* CLXXIV (July 1934), 134–40.

2336 Meyer, Carl L. W. **The United States and the World Court,** *Current History,* XXXII (August 1930), 889–93.

2337 Mills, Ogden. **The Obligation of the United States Toward the World Court,** *Annals of the American Academy of Political and Social Science,* CXIV (July 1924), 128–31.

2338 Myers, Denys P. **America's Unfavorable Attitude Toward Arbitration Treaties,** *Current History,* XXIII (February 1926), 656–62.

2339 Parker, Edwin B. **America's Part in Advancing the Administration of International Justice,** *International Conciliation,* CCIII (October 1924), 3–34.

Address before the Texas Bar Association, July 2, 1924.

2340 Sweetser, Arthur. **The United States and the League, the Labour Organization, and the World Court During 1940,** *Geneva Studies,* XI (December 1940), 1–19.

2341 Taft, Henry W. **The World Court: Something the United States Can Contribute to Create a Feeling of Security in Europe,** *Annals of the American Academy of Political and Social Science,* CXX (July 1925), 125–28.

2342 Wright, Quincy. **The United States and the Permanent Court of International Justice,** *International Conciliation,* CCXXXII (September 1927), 9–42.

Reprinted from *American Journal of International Law,* January 1927, with additions based on new material. Also discusses the international courts of Tangier and Shanghai.

10.4 PERMANENT COURT OF ARBITRATION (Hague)

See B 6.3.

11. POLITICAL ACTIVITIES: GENERAL ISSUES

11.1 COLLECTIVE SECURITY AND SANCTIONS
See also C 12.2 and C 12.3.

2343 Arnold-Forster, W. **Sanctions,** *International Affairs,* V (January 1926), 1—15.

2344 Aver, Paul von. **Die Lehren des Konflikts zwischen Italien und dem Völkerbund,** *World Affairs,* I (March 1936), 281—98.

2345 Ball, Joseph H. **Collective Security: The Why and How.** Boston, World Peace Foundation, 1943. 63 p.

2346 Beneš, Eduard. **The Problem of Collective Security in European Post-War Policy,** *International Security,* Walter H. C. Laves (ed.). Chicago, University of Chicago Press, 1939, pp. 3—76.

2347 Berdahl, Clarence A. **Disarmament and Equality,** *Geneva Studies,* III (April 1932), 1—16.
Possible use of sanctions.

2348 Bouché, Henri. **La guerre moderne et la sécurité collective,** *World Affairs,* IV (September 1938), 166—76.

2349 Bourquin, Maurice (ed.). **Collective Security: A Record of the Seventh and Eighth International Studies Conferences, Paris, 1934, London, 1935.** Paris, International Institute of Intellectual Cooperation, 1936. 514 p.

2350 Buell, Raymond Leslie. **Are Sanctions Necessary for a Successful International Organization?** *Annals of the American Academy of Political and Social Science,* CLVII (July 1932), 93–99.

2351 — —. **International Action on the Lytton Report,** *Foreign Policy Reports,* VIII (November 9, 1932), 208–18.

2352 — —. **The Weakness of Peace Machinery,** *Foreign Policy Reports,* VIII (September 14, 1932), 160–70.

2353 Buss, Claude A. **The Far East and the System of Collective Security,** *World Affairs Quarterly,* VIII (January 1938), 340–52.

2354 Chaput, R. A. **The Traditions of British Foreign Policy and Collective Security,** *World Affairs,* IV (March 1939), 399–409.

2355 Clark, Evans (ed.). **Boycotts and Peace.** New York, Harper, 1932. xx + 381 p.

2356 Cowie, Donald. **A New Move Towards Collective Security in the Pacific,** *World Affairs,* III (September 1937), 136–47.

2357 Davies, David. **The Case for an International Police Force,** *Free World,* II (April 1942), 211–15.

2358 — —. **An International Police Force,** *International Affairs,* XI (January 1932), 76–90.

Comments by Drury-Lowe, Williams, Carnegie, Smith, Reid, Barnes, Keen, Bewes.

2359 — —. **The Lessons of the Italo-Abyssinian Dispute,** *World Affairs,* II (June 1936), 5–24.

2360 Dobie, Edith. **The Nature and Ideals of Collective Security,** *Institute of World Affairs Proceedings,* XVI (1938), 133–36.

2361 Dulles, Allen W. **Collective Security,** *American Society of International Law Proceedings,* XXXIII (1939), 118–24.

2362 Fiédorowicz, George de. **Historical Survey of the Application of Sanctions,** *Transactions* (Grotius Society), XXII (1936), 117–31.

2363 Feis, Herbert. **A Successful League of Nations the Basis of European Security,** *Annals of the American Academy of Political and Social Science,* CXXVI (July 1926), 65–67.

2364 Foster, Homer P. **International Sanctions: Two Old Views and a New One,** *Political Science Quarterly,* XLIX (September 1934), 372–85.

2365 Gooch, G. P. **The Breakdown of the System of Collective Security,** *Problems of Peace,* Series 12 (1937), 58–74.

2366 — —. **Some Consequence of the Sino-Japanese Dispute,** *Problems of Peace,* Series 7 (1932), 252–63.

2367 Harley, J. Eugene. **The Outlook for Collective Security,** *Institute of World Affairs Proceedings,* XVI (1938), 141–50.

2368 Hart, Captain B. H. Liddell. **An International Force,** *International Affairs,* XII (March 1933), 205–19.

Various proposals. Comments by Nevinson, Hart, Garnett, Fremantle, Smith, Mallory, Davies.

2369 — —. **Military and Strategic Advantages of Collective Security in Europe,** *World Affairs,* IV (September 1938), 144–58.

Part C. — League of Nations System

2370 Hartmann, Frederick H. **The Relations of Nations** 3d ed. New York, Macmillan, 1967.

Chapter XX.

2371 Highley, Albert E. **The Actions of the States Members of the League of Nations in Application of Sanctions Against Italy, 1935–1936.** Geneva, Impr. du *Journal de Genève,* 1938. 251 p.

2372 — —. **The First Sanctions Experiment (A Study of League Procedures),** *Geneva Studies,* IX (July 1938), 7–141.

2373 Hill, Chesney. **Recent Policies of Non-Recognition,** *International Conciliation,* CCXCIII (October 1933), 9–127.

Contains documents.

2374 Hindsmarsh, Albert E. **Force in Peace: Force Short of War, in International Relations.** Cambridge, Harvard University Press, 1933. xii + 249 p.

2375 Holcombe, Arthur N. **The Far Eastern Conflict: II—The Peacemakers' Task,** *Current History,* XXXVI (April 1932), 52–57.

2376 Jacks, L. P. **Collective Security,** *Hibbert Journal,* XXXIV (January 1936), 161–77.

2377 — —. **A Demilitarized League of Nations,** *Hibbert Journal,* XXIV (July 1936), 493–509.

2378 Jebb, Gladwyn. **The Role of the United Nations,** *International Organization,* VI (November 1952), 509–20.

Conditions under which collective security operates.

2379 Kopelmanas, L. **The Problem of Aggression and the Prevention of War,** *American Journal of International Law,* XXI (April 1937), 244–57.

Examines League actions in various situations. Calls for international police force.

Part C. — League of Nations System

2380   Lester, Sean. **The Far East Dispute from the Point of View of the Small States,** *Problems of Peace,* Series 8 (1933), 120—35.

2381   Lowell, A. Lawrence. **Alternatives Before the League,** *Foreign Affairs,* XV (October 1936), 102—11.

2382   Lytton, Earl of. **The Lessons of the League of Nations Commission of Enquiry in Manchuria,** *World Affairs,* III (December 1937), 210—27.

2383   McNair, Arnold D. **Collective Security,** *British Yearbook of International Law,* XVII (1936), 150—64.

2384   Mander, Linden A. **Present Problems of Universal Peace,** *Institute of World Affairs Proceedings,* XV (1937), 199—205.

2385   Manning, C. A. W. **The Future of the Collective System,** *Problems of Peace,* Series 10 (1935), 152—77.

2386   Middlebush, Frederick A. and Hill, Chesney. **Elements of International Relations.** New York, McGraw-Hill, 1940.

       Chapter XX.

2387   Millward, Alex. **Only Yesterday: Some Reflections on the "Thirties," With Particular Reference to Sanctions,** *International Relations,* I (April 1957), 281—90.

2388   Mitrany, David. **The Problem of International Sanctions.** New York, Oxford University Press, 1925. 88 p.

2389   Nathan, Otto. **International Economic Action and Peace,** *Problems of Peace,* Series 11 (1936), 163—79.

       Use of economic sanctions.

2390 Noel-Baker, P. J. **The Future of the Collective System,** *Problems of Peace,* Series 10 (1935), 178–98.

On collective security.

2391 Potter, Pittman B. **Sanctions and Guaranties in International Organization,** *American Political Science Review,* XVI (May 1922), 297–303.

2392 — —. **Sanctions and Security: An Analysis of the French and American Views,** *Geneva Studies,* III (February 1932), 7–21.

Preceded by a six-page introduction.

2393 Rappard, W. E. **Cinq siècles de sécurité collective (1291–1798): Les experiences de la Suisse sous le régime des pactes de secours mutuel.** Paris, Recueil Sirey, 1945. ix + 606 p.

2394 Rothstein, Andrew. **How Can the Aggressor Be Stopped?** *Problems of Peace,* Series 13 (1938), 144–64.

On collective security.

2395 Rowell, Chester. **The Essential Conditions of Collective Security,** *Institute of World Affairs Proceedings,* XVI (1938), 160–62.

2396 Royal Institute of International Affairs. **The Character of International Sanctions and Their Application.** 2d ed. London, Oxford University Press, 1938. 247 p.

2397 Russell, Frank M. **Ethiopia and the Question of Collective Security,** *Institute of World Affairs Proceedings,* XIV (1936), 165–69.

2398 Sait, Edward M. **The Failure of Collective Security,** *Institute of World Affairs Proceedings,* XVI (1938), 137–40.

2399 Schick, Franz B. **Peace on Trial: A Study of Defense in International Organization,** *Western Political Quarterly,* II (March 1949), 1–44.

Historical survey of collective security from League of Nations and Kellogg Pact to NATO.

2400 Schalefield, Guy H. **Peace in the Far East and the Collective Security System,** *Problems of Peace,* Series 10 (1935), 82—103.

2401 Sharp, Walter and Kirk, Grayson. **Contemporary International Politics.** New York, Farrar and Rinehart, 1941.

Chapter XXV.

2402 Shotwell, James T. and Salvin, Marina. **Lessons on Security and Disarmament from the History of the League of Nations.** New York, King's Crown, 1949. 149 p.

Section on the Ethiopian war was written by Robert K. Webb.

2403 Stuart, Graham H. **Postwar Quest for Collective Security,** *Institute of World Affairs Proceedings,* XVI (1938), 151—53.

2404 Swanwick, Helena Maria. **Collective Insecurity.** London, Cape, 1937. 285 p.

2405 Taubenfeld, Howard J. **The "Economic Weapons": The League and the United Nations,** *American Society of International Law Proceedings,* LVIII (1964), 183—204.

On economic sanctions.

2406 Thomas, Bryn W. **An International Police Force.** Foreword by Arthur Henderson. London, Allenson, 1936. 172 p.

2407 Virgin, E. de. **Les expériences des dernières guerres et leur application au problème de la sécurité collective,** *World Affairs,* IV (June 1938), 26—34.

2408 Wehberg, Hans. **La police internationale,** *Recueil des Cours,* XLVII (1934), 7—131.

2409 — —. **Theory and Practice of International Policing.** London, Constable, 1935. 100 p.

2410 Wild, Payson S. **Sanctions and Treaty Enforcement.** Cambridge, Harvard University Press, 1934. xv + 231 p.

2411 Wilde, John C. de. **Testing League Sanctions,** *Foreign Policy Reports,* XI (December 4, 1935), 238—48.

2412 Williams, John Fischer. **Sanctions Under the Covenant,** *British Yearbook of International Law,* XVII (1936), 130—49.

2413 Wright, Quincy (ed.). **Neutrality and Collective Security.** Chicago, University of Chicago Press, 1936. xvii + 276 p.

2414 Zimmern, Alfred E. **The Problem of Collective Security,** *Neutrality and Collective Security,* Quincy Wright (ed.). Chicago, University of Chicago Press, 1936, pp. 3—92.

2415 — —. **The Testing of the League,** *Foreign Affairs,* XIV (April 1936), 373—88.

11.2 DISARMAMENT

2416 Abbott, Alden, H. **The League's Disarmament Activities—and the Washington Conference,** *Political Science Quarterly,* XXXVII (March 1922), 1—24.

2417 Ames, C. B. **Article Eight of the League of Nations Covenant and the Washington Conference,** *Southwestern Social Science Quarterly,* II (March 1922), 302—10.

Part C. — *League of Nations System*

2418 Arnold-Forster, William. **British Policy at the Disarmament Conference,** *Political Quarterly,* III (July—September 1932), 365—80.

2419 — —. **Disarmament and Security,** *Problems of Peace,* Series 8 (1933), 41—63.

2420 — —. **The Disarmament Conference.** London, National Peace Council, 1931. 91 p.

2421 — —. **The Disarmament Resolution of July, 1932,** *Problems of Peace,* Series 7 (1932), 130—55.

2422 — —. **The First Stage in Disarmament: A Commentary on the Continuing Programme of the Conference,** *Geneva Studies,* III, 8 (1932), 1—54.
League of Nations Society Conference.

2423 — —. **Policy for the Disarmament Conference,** *Political Quarterly,* II (July—September 1931), 378—93.

2424 Berdahl, Clarence A. **Disarmament and Equality,** *Geneva Studies,* III (April 1932), 1—16.
Possible use of sanctions.

2925 Bliss, Tasker H. **What Is Disarmament?** *Foreign Affairs,* IV (April 1926), 352—68.

2426 Brouckère, Louis de. **Les travaux de la Société des Nations en matière de désarmement,** *Recueil des Cours,* (1928), 365—450.

2427 Buell, Raymond Leslie. **The Washington Conference.** New York, Appleton, 1922. 461 p.

2428 Bullard, Robert Lee. **The Possibility of Disarmament by International Agreement,** *Annals of the American Academy of Political and Social Science,* XCVI (July 1921), 49—52.

2429 Butler, Geoffrey. **A Handbook to the League of Nations.** London, Longmans, Green, 1925.

Chapter X.

2430 Cecil, Viscount. **Facing the World Disarmament Conference,** *Foreign Affairs,* X (October 1931), 13—22.

2431 Cot, Pierre. **Disarmament and French Public Opinion,** *Political Quarterly,* II (July—September 1931), 367—77.

2432 Cushendun, Lord. **Disarmament,** *International Affairs,* VII (March 1928), 77—90.

Comments by Noel-Baker, Steed, Arnold-Forster, Kennedy, Deverell, Power, Aston.

2433 Davies, David. **Disarmament,** *Transactions* (Grotius Society), V (1919), 109—17.

Comments by Omond, Manisty, Hopkinson, and Bellot.

2434 — —. **The Problem of the Twentieth Century: A Study of International Relationships.** London, Benn, 1934. 795 p.

2435 Davis, Malcolm W. **The Draft Disarmament Convention: A Synthesis of Conference Decisions,** *Geneva Studies,* IV, 1 (1933), 1—16.

2436 Davis, Norman H. **The Disarmament Conference,** *International Conciliation,* CCLXXXV (December 1932), 470—76.

Issue contains various statements from delegates at the 1932 General Disarmament Conference.

Part C. — League of Nations System

2437 Dell, Robert Edward. **The Geneva Racket, 1920–1939.** London, Hale, 1940. 375 p.

2438 Dulles, Allen Welsh. **The Disarmament Puzzle,** *Foreign Affairs,* IX (July 1931), 605–16.

2439 — —. **Progress Toward Disarmament,** *Foreign Affairs,* XI (October 1932), 54–65.

2440 Erzberger, Matthias. **The League of Nations.** New York, Holt, 1919.
Chapter VIII.

2441 Eza, el Vizconde de. **Reduction of Armaments,** *The League of Nations Starts,* Raymond B. Fosdick, George Rublee, J. T. Shotwell, Léon Bourgeois, André Weiss, Lt.-Col. Requin, W. Ormsby-Gore, el Vizconde de Eza, H. B. Butler, Richard P. Strong, J. A. Salter, A. Claveille, Henri La Fontaine, Paul Otlet. London, Macmillan, 1920, pp. 126–39.

2442 Foreign Policy Association. **Disarmament and the Five Naval Powers,** *Foreign Policy Reports,* III (March 30, 1917), 17–32.

2443 — —. **Disarmament Projects and Agreements (1899–1926),** *Foreign Policy Reports,* I (January 29, 1926), 1–9.

2444 Fuller, J. F. C. **Disarmament and Delusion,** *Current History,* XXXVI (September 1932), 649–54.

2445 Géraud, André. **The London Naval Conference: A French View,** *Foreign Affairs,* VIII (July 1930), 519–32.

2446 Harley, Eugene. **Selected Bibliography on the Limitation of Armament,** *Institute of World Affairs Proceedings,* I (December 5–12, 1926), 31–33.

2447 Harris, H. Wilson. **What the League of Nations Is.** London, Allen and Unwin, 1925.

Chapter VII.

2448 Hicks, Frederick C. **Curtailment of Armament,** *Annals of the American Academy of Political and Social Science,* XCVI (July 1921), 56–62.

2449 Hoag, Charles L. **Preface to Preparedness: The Washington Disarmament Conferences and Public Opinion.** Introduction by H. E. Yarnell. Washington, American Council on Public Affairs, 1941. 205 p.

2450 Hosono, Gunji. **Histoire du désarmement.** Paris, Pedone, 1933. 253 p.

A translation of the author's Ph.D. thesis, Columbia University.

2451 Ichihashi, Yamato. **The Washington Conference and After: A Historical Survey.** Stanford, Stanford University Press, 1928. 443 p.

2451a Ito, Masanori. **Readings on the Naval Disarmament Problem.** Tokyo, Chuo Koron Sha, 1934. 458 p.

2452 Jackh, Ernst. **Disarmament,** *World Affairs Quarterly,* III (October 1932), 45–74.

2453 Kellor, Frances A. and Hatvany, Antonia. **Security Against War.** New York, Macmillan, 1924.

Chapter XXXVI.

2454 Knudson, John I. **A History of the League of Nations.** Atlanta, Smith, 1938.

Chapter V.

2455 Lavallaz, Maurice de. **Essai sur le désarmement et le Pacte de la Société des Nations.** Paris, Rousseau, 1926. 505 p.

2456 League of Nations, Secretariat. **Ten Years of World Co-operation.** Geneva, 1930.

Chapter II.

2457 — —. Information Section. **The League of Nations and Reduction of Armaments.** Geneva, 1923. 59 p.

2458 — —. **The Reduction of Armaments and Organisation of Peace.** Rev. ed. Geneva, 1928. 166 p.

2459 Lippmann, Walter. **The London Naval Conference: An American View,** *Foreign Affairs,* VIII (July 1930), 499—518.

2460 Madariaga, Salvador de. **Current Problems and Progress in Disarmament,** *Problems of Peace,* Series 1 (1926), 127—43.

2461 — —. **The Difficulties of Disarming,** *Problems of Peace,* Series 5 (1930), 284—303.

2462 — —. **Disarmament: The Role of the Anglo-Saxon Nations,** *Problems of Peace,* Series 3 (1928), 51—74.

2463 — —. **The Preparation of the First General Disarmament Conference,** *Problems of Peace,* Series 2 (1927), 124—42.

2464 Maurice, Frederick. **Disarmament,** *International Affairs,* V (May 1926), 117—31.

Comments by Richmond, Noel-Baker, Drury-Lowe, Kennedy.

2465 Mead, Nelson P. **The Locarno Pacts and the Movement for Disarmament,** *Annals of the American Academy of Political and Social Science,* CXXVI (July 1926), 62—64.

2466 Mondell, Frank W. **Limitation of Armaments by International Agreement,** *Annals of the American Academy of Political and Social Science,* XCVI (July 1921), 53—56.

2467 Morgan, Laura Kuffer. **Armament and Measures of Enforcement,** *World Organization,* Institute on World Organization (ed.). Washington, American Council on Public Affairs, 1942, pp. 121—57.

2468 — —. **Disarmament,** *Pioneers in World Order,* Harriet E.Davis (ed.). New York, Columbia University Press, 1944, pp. 42—64.

2469 Mower, Edmund. **International Government.** Boston, Heath, 1931.

Chapter XXXI.

2470 Myers, Denys P. **Handbook of the League of Nations.** Boston, World Peace Foundation, 1935.

Chapter XI.

2471 — —. **League of Nations Works for Disarmament,** *Current History,* XIX (November 1923), 180—84.

2472 — —. **World Disarmament: Its Problems and Prospects.** Boston, World Peace Foundation, 1932. 370 p.

2473 Noel-Baker, Philip J. **Disarmanent.** New York, Harcourt, Brace, 1926. 352 p.

2474 Ogg, Frederic Austin. **International Sanctions and the Limitation of Armaments,** *The League of Nations,* Stephen Pierce Duggan (ed.). Boston, Atlantic Monthly Press, 1919. pp. 112—27.

2475 Politis, Nicholas S. **The Problem of Disarmament,** *International Conciliation,* CCXCVIII (March 1934), 59—80.

Reprinted from *L'Esprit International* (Paris), January 1934.

Part C. — *League of Nations System*

2476 Riddell, Walter A. **World Security by Conference.** Toronto, Ryerson, 1947.

Part I, Chapter IX.

2477 Rogers, John Jacob. **Reduction of Armaments,** *Annals of the American Academy of Political and Social Science,* XCVI (July 1921), 62–67.

2478 Rogers, Lindsay. **The Struggle for Disarmament,** *Current History,* XXXV (February 1932), 629–37.

2479 Rolin, Henri. **The First General Disarmament Conference,** *Problems of Peace,* Series 6 (1931), 51–69.

2480 — —. **The Manufacture of Arms and the Arms Traffic,** *Problems of Peace,* Series 8 (1933), 64–79.

2481 Russell, Frank M. **Theories of International Relations.** New York, Appleton-Century, 1936.

Chapter XIX.

2482 Scialoja, Vittorio. **Obstacles to Disarmament,** *Foreign Affairs,* X (January 1932), 212–19.

2483 Scott, James Brown. **Disarmament Through International Organization,** *Annals of the American Academy of Political and Social Science,* CXXVI (July 1926), 146–50.

2484 Shillock, John C., Jr. **The Post-War Movements to Reduce Naval Armaments,** *International Conciliation,* CCXLV (December 1928), 9–92.

2485 Shotwell, James T. **On the Rim of the Abyss.** New York, Macmillan, 1936.

Chapter X.

2486 Shotwell, James T. and Salvin, Marina. **Lessons on Security and Disarmament from the History of the League of Nations.** New York, King's Crown, 1949. 149 p.

2487 Smith, H. A. **The Problem of Disarmament in the Light of History,** *International Affairs*, X (September 1931), 600–13.

Comments by Steed, Garnett, Carter, Fremantle, Dewar, Bewes, Henty.

2488 Stone, William T. **The Disarmament Crisis—1933,** *Foreign Policy Reports*, IX (October 25, 1933), 186–96.

2489 — —. **The Draft Treaty for the World Conference,** *Foreign Policy Reports*, VI (February 18, 1931), 471–88.

2490 — —. **The London Naval Conference,** *Foreign Policy Reports*, VI (May 28, 1930), 101–30.

2491 — —. **The World Disarmament Conference, First Stage, February 2– March 17, 1932,** *Foreign Policy Reports*, VIII (May 11, 1932), 60–66.

2492 — —. **The World Disarmament Conference: Second Stage, March 17, 1932–January, 1933,** *Foreign Policy Reports*, VIII (January 18, 1933), 268–78.

2493 Tarbell, Ida Minerva. **Peacemakers: Blessed and Otherwise.** New York, Macmillan, 1922. 227 p.

Washington Conference.

2494 Tate, Merze. **The Disarmament Illusion: The Movement for a Limitation of Armaments to 1907.** New York, Macmillan, 1942. xiv + 398 p.

2495 Walsh, Thomas J. **The Urge for Disarmament,** *Annals of the American Academy of Political and Social Science*, XCVI (July 1921), 45–48.

Part C. — *League of Nations System*

2496 Walters, Francis Paul. **A History of the League of Nations.** London, Oxford University Press, 1960.

Chapters XVIII, XXXI, XLI, XLIV.

2497 Webster, Charles Kingsley and Herbert, Sydney. **The League of Nations in Theory and Practice.** London, Allen and Unwin, 1933.

Chapter XII.

2498 Wehberg, Hans. **The Limitation of Armaments: A Collection of the Projects for the Solution of the Problem (Preceded by an Historical Introduction).** Washington, Carnegie, 1921. 104 p.

2499 Wheeler-Bennett, John W. **Disarmament and Security Since Locarno, 1925–1931: Being the Political and Technical Background of the General Disarmament Conference, 1932.** Introduction by Neill Malcolm. New York, Macmillan, 1932. 383 p.

2500 — —. **The Disarmament Deadlock.** London, Routledge, 1934. xii + 302 p.

2501 Williams, Benjamin H. **The United States and Disarmament.** New York, McGraw-Hill, 1931. 361 p.

2502 Wilson, Hugh R. **Disarmament and the Cold War in the Thirties.** New York, Vantage, 1963. 87 p.

2503 Woodward, David. **Limitation of Air Armaments,** *Foreign Policy Reports,* VI (October 29, 1930), 297–313.

2504 — —. **Limitation of Land Armaments,** *Foreign Policy Reports,* VI (April 2, 1930), 19–35.

Part C. — *League of Nations System*

11.3 LEGAL ATTEMPTS TO "OUTLAW" WAR

11.3.1 GENERAL OBSERVATIONS

2505 Ball, M. Margaret and Killough, Hugh B. **International Relations.** New York, Ronald, 1956.

Chapter XVIII.

2506 Cecil, Robert. **The Draft Treaty of Mutual Assistance,** *International Affairs*, III (March 1924), 45—60.

Comments by Amery, Maurice, Swanwick, Drury-Lowe, Zimmern, Balfour.

2507 Cruickshank, Earl F. **Supplementary International Organization,** *Annals of the American Academy of Political and Social Science*, CLXXV (September 1934), 138—42.

2508 Eagleton, Clyde. **The Attempt to Define Aggression,** *International Conciliation*, CCLXIV (November 1930), 7—76.

2509 Foreign Policy Association. **The League of Nations and Outlawry of War,** *Foreign Policy Reports*, III (February 17, 1928), 398—417.

2510 Jessup, Philip C. **American Neutrality and International Police,** *World Peace Foundation Pamphlets*, XI 3 (1928), 355—524.

2511 — —. **The United States and Treaties for the Avoidance of War,** *International Conciliation*, CCXXXIX (April 1928), 7—71.

Arbitration and conciliation treaties as preludes to the Kellogg-Briand Pact.

2512 Kellor, Frances A. and Hatvany, Antonia. **Security Against War.** New York, Macmillan, 1924.

Chapter XXXIX.

2513 Korovine, E. **Les pactes de non-agression économique et la préservation de la paix,** *World Affairs,* I (October—December 1935), 213-14.

2514 Ogg, Frederic Austin. **International Sanctions and the Limitation of Armaments,** *The League of Nations,* Stephen Pierce Duggan (ed.). Boston, Atlantic Monthly Press, 1919. pp. 112—127.

2515 Potter, Pitman B. **International Regulation of National Action for Self-Defense,** *Southwestern Social Science Quarterly,* X (December 1929), 279—89.

2516 Sharp, Walter and Kirk, Grayson. **Contemporary International Politics.** New York, Farrar and Rinehart, 1941.

Chapters XXIII, XXIV.

2517 Shotwell, James T. **The League's Work for Peace,** *Current History,* XLIII (November 1935), 119—24.

2518 — —. **The Movement to Renounce War As a Diplomatic Weapon,** *Current History,* XXVII (October 1927), 62—64.

2519 — —. **Plans and Protocols to End War, Historical Outline and Guide,** *International Conciliation,* CCVIII (March 1925), 5—34.

2520 Vinacke, Harold M. **International Organization.** New York, Crofts, 1934.

Chapter XII.

2521 Vinson, John C. **William E. Borah and the Outlawry of War.** Athens, University of Georgia Press, 1957. 212 p.

2522 Wertheimer, Mildred S. **The League of Nations and Prevention of War,** *Foreign Policy Reports,* VI (August 6, 1930), 207—24.

2523 Wheeler-Bennett, John W. and Langermen, F. E. **Information on the Problem of Security, 1917—1926.** Introduction by H. A. L. Fisher. London, Allen and Unwin, 1927. 272 p.

2524 Williams, Bruce S. **State Security and the League of Nations.** Baltimore, Johns Hopkins Press, 1927.

Chapters V, VI.

2525 Williams, John Fischer. **Treaties for the Pacific Settlement of Disputes—Mutual Assistance and Non-Aggression,** *International Affairs,* VII (November 1928), 407—21.

2526 — —. **Treaty Revision and the Future of the League,** *International Affairs,* X (May 1931), 326—47.

Comments by Keen, Higgins, Hailsham.

2527 Wright, Quincy. **The Concept of Aggression in International Law,** *American Journal of International Law,* XXIX (July 1935), 373—95.

11.3.2 GENEVA PROTOCOL (1924)

2528 Bassett, John S. **The League of Nations.** New York, Longmans, Green, 1938.

Chapter XI.

2529 Borel, Eugène. **L'Acte Général de Genève,** *Recueil des Cours,* XXVII (1929). 501—95.

2530 Burks, David D. **The United States and the Geneva Protocol of 1924: "A New Holy Alliance"?** *American Historical Review,* LXIV (July 1959), 891—905.

2531 Calderon, Francisco Garcia. **Geneva Protocol As It Affects the Monroe Doctrine,** *Current History,* XXI (December 1924), 506–11.

2532 Clarke, John H. **America and World Peace.** New York, Holt, 1925. vii + 145 p.

2533 — —. **A Popular Discussion of the Protocol,** *World Peace Foundation Pamphlets,* VII, 9 (1924), 509–17.

2534 Hudson, Manley O. **The Geneva Protocol,** *Foreign Affairs,* III (December 1924), 226–35.

2535 Lowell, A. Lawrence. **The Protocol and Its Implications,** *World Peace Foundation Pamphlets,* VII, 9 (1924), 518–25.

2536 Manisty, Herbert F. **Effect of the Protocol and the Covenant,** *Transactions* (Grotius Society), X (1924), 159–67.

Comments by Jelf, Bewes, Bisschop and Bellot.

2537 Mead, Nelson P. **The Locarno Pacts and the Movement for Disarmament,** *Annals of the American Academy of Political and Social Science,* CXXVI (July 1926), 62–64.

2538 Miller, David Hunter. **The Geneva Protocol.** New York, Macmillan, 1925. 279 p.

2539 Noel-Baker, P. J. **The Geneva Protocol for the Pacific Settlement of International Disputes.** London, King, 1925. x + 228 p.

2540 Politis, N. and Beneš, E. **Arbitration, Security and Reduction of Armaments,** *World Peace Foundation Pamphlets,* VII, 7 (1924), 414–52.

Part C. — League of Nations System

2541 Shotwell, James T. **Introduction,** *International Conciliation,* CCV (December 1924), 5—8.

Issue contains the text of the Geneva Protocol and the official analysis by the First Committee of the League Assembly.

2542 Walters, Francis Paul. **A History of the League of Nations.** London, Oxford University Press, 1960.
Chapter XXII.

2543 **What the Protocol Does,** *World Peace Foundation Pamphlets,* VII, 7 (1924), 391—400.

2544 Williams, John Fischer. **The Geneva Protocol of 1924.** London, Allen and Unwin, 1925. 18 p.

2545 — —. **The Geneva Protocol of 1924 for the Pacific Settlement of International Disputes,** *International Affairs,* III (November 1924), 288—304.

2546 Williams, Roth (pseud.). **The League, the Protocol, and the Empire.** London, Allen and Unwin, 1925. 174 p.

11.3.3 LOCARNO AGREEMENTS (1925)

2547 Bassett, John S. **The League of Nations.** New York, Longmans, Green, 1938.
Chapter XII.

2548 **Beneš, Eduard. After Locarno: The Security Problem Today,** *Foreign Affairs,* IV (January 1926), 195—210.

2549 — —. **The Problem of Collective Security in European Post-War Policy,** *International Security,* Walter H. C. Laves (ed.). Chicago, University of Chicago Press, 1939, pp. 3—76.

Part C. — *League of Nations System*

2550 Berber, F. J. **Locarno: A Collection of Documents.** London, Hodge, 1936. 405 p.

2551 Bisschop, W. R. **The Locarno Pact,** *Transactions* (Grotius Society), XI (1925), 79—112.

Comments by Manisty, McNair, Bewes, Jacobs, Hewitt, Jelf, Dent, Toye.

2552 Davis, Norman H. **The Locarno Pacts: Their Meaning to Europe and to America,"** *Current History,* XXIII (December 1925), 316—20.

2553 Dexter, Byron. **Locarno Again,** *Foreign Affairs,* XXXII (October 1953), 24—47.

2554 Fabre-Luce, Alfred. **Locarno: The Reality,** C. Vesey (tr.). New York, Knopf, 1928. viii + 209 p.

2555 Foreign Policy Association. **The Locarno Security Conference,** *Foreign Policy Reports,* I (October 5, 1925), 1—8.

2556 Freytagh-Loringhoven, Axel von. **Les ententes regionales,** *Recueil des Cours,* LVI (1936), 589—677.

2557 Gasiorowski, Zygmunt T. **Benes and Locarno: Some Unpublished Documents,** *Review of Politics,* XX (April 1958), 209—24.

2558 Glasgow, George. **From Dawes to Locarno: 1924—1925.** London, Benn, 1925. 202 p.

2559 Grigg, Edward. **The Merits and Defects of the Locarno Treaty As a Guarantee of World Peace,** *International Affairs,* XIV (March—April 1935), 176—86.

Comments by Chamberlain, Garnett, Webster, Nissim, Drury-Lowe, Steed.

2560 Grun, George A. **Locarno: Idea and Reality,** *International Affairs,* XXXI (October 1955), 477—85.

2561 Harris, H. Wilson. **Locarno: A European View,** *Annals of the American Academy of Political and Social Science,* CXXVI (July 1926), 160—63.

2562 MacDonald, William. **The Conference at Locarno,** *Current History,* XXIII (December 1925), 321—23 ff.

Followed by text of security treaties.

2563 — —. **The Locarno Agreements,** *Annals of the American Academy of Political and Social Science,* CXXVI (July 1926), 59—61.

2564 Mead, Nelson P. **The Locarno Pacts and the Movement for Disarmament,** *Annals of the American Academy of Political and Social Science,* CXXVI (July 1926), 62—64.

2565 Steed, Wickham. **Locarno and British Interests,** *International Affairs,* IV (November 1925), 286—99.

Comments by Pearce-Higgins, Elliot, Kennedy, Swanwick, Malcolm, Sanderson.

2566 Walters, Francis Paul. **A History of the League of Nations.** London, Oxford University Press, 1960.

Chapters XXIV, XXIX, LIV.

11.3.4 KELLOGG-BRIAND PACT (1928)

2567 Brown, Philip Marshall. **Difficulties of Implementing the Kellogg Pact,** *Current History,* XXXIII (January 1931), 493—97.

2568 Butler, Nicholas Murray. **The Path to Peace.** New York, Scribner, 1930. 333 p.

Part C. — *League of Nations System*

2569 Capper, Arthur. **Making the Peace Pact Effective,** *Annals of the American Academy of Political and Social Science,* CXLIV (July 1929), 40 —50.

2570 Colombos, C. J. **The Paris Pact, Otherwise Called the Kellogg Pact,** *Transactions* (Grotius Society), XIV (1928), 87—99.

Comments by Jelf, Fraser, Lauterpacht, Bewes, Jacobs, Latey, Pratt, Lee, Bisschop and Goitein.

2571 Geneva Research Center. **The Covenant and the Pact,** *Geneva Studies,* I (December 1930), 1—23.

2572 Gonsiorowski, Miroslas. **The Legal Meaning of the Pact for the Renunciation of War,** *American Political Science Review,* XXX (August 1936), 653—80.

2573 Hudson, Manley O. **By Pacific Means: The Implementation of Article Two of the Pact of Paris.** New Haven, Yale University Press, 1935. 200 p.

2574 Keen, F. N. **The Preamble to the Pact of Paris,** *Transactions* (Grotius Society), XXI (1935), 177—90.

2575 Kerr, Philip. **The Outlawry of War,** *International Affairs,* VII (November 1928), 361—77.

Comments by Spender, King-Hall, Buxton, Rooker, Swanwick, Steed, Grey.

2576 Lauterpacht, T. **The Pact of Paris and the Budapest Articles of Interpretation,** *Transactions* (Grotius Society), XX (1934), 178—202.

Comments by Baty and Keen.

2577 Leebrick, Karl C. **The Paris Pacts,** *Institute of World Affairs Proceedings,* IV (December 1928), 224—27.

Part C. — *League of Nations System*

2578 Miller, David Hunter. **The Peace Pact of Paris: A Study of the Briand-Kellogg Treaty.** New York, Putnam, 1928. 287 p.

2579 Morris, Roland S. **The Pact of Paris for the Renunciation of War: Its Meaning and Effect in International Law,** *American Society of International Law Proceedings*, XXIII (1929), 88—91.

Comments by Chamberlain, Latane, McKenney, Fenwick, Hull, Ralston, Havighurst, Kingsbury, Potter, Borchard, and Kuhn.

2580 Myers, Denys P. **Origin and Conclusion of the Paris Pact,** *World Peace Foundation Pamphlets*, XII (2, 1929), 1—196.

2581 Myers, William Starr. **The Kellogg Pact — The Question of Sanction,** *Annals of the American Academy of Political and Social Science*, CXLIV July 1929), 59—62.

2582 Rogers, Edith Nourse. **How the Kellogg Peace Pact Can Be Made Effective,** *Annals of the American Academy of Political and Social Science*, CXLIV (July 1929), 51—54.

2583 Rutgers, V. H. **La mise en harmonie du Pacte de la Société des Nations avec le Pacte de Paris,** *Recueil des Cours*. XXXVIII (1931), 5—123.

2584 Shotwell, James T. **The American Problem,** *World Affairs*, I (July—September 1935), 116—28.

2585 — —. **On the Rim of the Abyss.** New York, Macmillan, 1936.

Chapter IV.

2586 — —. **The Pact of Paris, With Historical Commentary,** *International Conciliation*, CCXLIII (October 1928), 11—23.

Issue contains various documents.

Part C. — *League of Nations System*

2587 — —. **War As an Instrument of National Policy and Its Renunciation in the Pact of Paris.** New York, Harcourt, Brace, 1929. 310 p.

2588 Stimson, Henry L. **The Pact of Paris: Three Years of Development,** *Foreign Affairs,* XI (October 1932), i—ix.

2589 Watkins, Arthur C. **The Paris Pact: A Textbook for Schools and Colleges.** New York, Harcourt Brace, 1932. vii + 120 p.

2590 Wheeler-Bennett, John W. **Information on the Renunciation of War, 1927—1928.** Introduction by Philip H. Kerr. London, Allen and Unwin, 1928. 191 p.

2591 Whitton, John B. **What Follows the Pact of Paris?** *International Conciliation,* CCLXXVI (January 1932), 3—48.

2592 Wickersham, George W. **The Pact of Paris: A Gesture or a Pledge?** *Foreign Affairs,* VII (April 1929), 356—71.

2593 Williams, John Fischer. **Recent Interpretations of the Briand-Kellogg Pact,** *International Affairs,* XIV (May 1935), 346—60.

Comments by Bewes, Lauterpacht, Coulton, Drury-Lowe, Garnett, Howad.

2594 Wright, Quincy. **The Meaning of the Pact of Paris,** *American Journal of International Law,* **XXVII** (January 1933), 39—61.

11.4 PEACEFUL CHANGE AND PACIFIC SETTLEMENT

2595 Abraham, G. **The Settlement of Non-justiciable Disputes Through the League,** *Problems of Peace,* Series 2 (1927), 94—103.

Part C. — League of Nations System

2596 Arnold-Forster, W. **Order and Self-Defense in the World Community,** *Problems of Peace,* Series 5 (1930), 230—55.
On pacific settlement and peaceful change.

2597 Bourquin, Maurice (ed.). **Peaceful Change.** Paris, International Institute of Intellectual Co-operation, 1937. 684 p.

2598 Caloyanni, M. A. **The Montreux Capitulations Conference and the Process of Peaceful Change,** *World Affairs,* III (March 1938), 328—41.

2599 Condliffe, John B. **Markets and the Problem of Peaceful Change.** Paris International Institute of Intellectual Cooperation, 1938. 63 p.

2600 Cruttwell, C. R. M. F. **A History of Peaceful Change in the Modern World.** London, Oxford University Press, 1937. 221 p.

2601 Davis, Malcolm M. **Councils Against War: A Comparison of Cases in Third-Party Dealing with Disputes Between Nations,** *Geneva Studies,* III, 11 (1932, 1—14.

2602 — —. **Peaceful Change: An Analysis of Current Proposals,** *Problems of Peace,* Series 12 (1937), 46

2603 Dunn, Frederick S. **Peaceful Change.** New York, Council on Foreign Relations, 1937. v + 156 p.

2604 Friedensburg, Ferdinand. **Rohstoffe and "Peaceful Change,"** *World Affairs,* III (December 1937), 242—56.

2605 Hall, H. Duncan. **Pacific Settlement of International Disputes: Recent Trends,** *American Society of International Law Proceedings,* XXXIV (1940), 115—25.

Part C. — League of Nations System

2606 Hedges, R. Yorke. **Some Aspects of Peaceful Change,** *World Affairs,* I (March 1936), 271—80.

2608 Hudson, M. P. **Recent Territorial Disputes Before the League of Nations,** *Problems of Peace,* Series 8 (1933), 100—19.

2609 Jenks, C. Wilfred. **The International Labour Organisation and Peaceful Change,** *World Affairs,* IV (March 1939), 361—79.

2610 — —. **The Montreux Conference and the Law of Peaceful Change,** *World Affairs,* II (September 1936), 242—53.
Chapter III.

2611 Knudson, John I. **A History of the League of Nations.** Atlanta, Smith, 1938. 445 p.

2612 Manning, C. A. W. **Some Suggested Conclusions,** *Peaceful Change,* C. A. W. Manning (ed.). London, Macmillan, 1937, pp. 169—90.

2613 Myers, Denys P. **The Modern System of Pacific Settlement of International Disputes,** *Political Science Quarterly,* XLVI (December 1931), 548—88.

2614 Potter, Pitman B. **Article XIX of the Covenant of the League of Nations: A Study in the Problem of International Government,** *Geneva Studies,* XII (August 1941), 9—98.

2615 Rolin, Henri. **The Peaceful Settlement of Disputes,** *Problems of Peace,* Series 4 (1929), 22—38.
Procedures.

2616 Stone, William T. and Eichelberger, Clark M. **Peaceful Change, the Alternative to War.** New York, Foreign Policy Association, 1937. 46 p.

2617 Strupp, Karl. **Legal Machinery for Peaceful Change.** Preface by George Scelle. London, Constable, 1937. xxvi + 85 p.

2618 Toynbee, Arnold J. **The Lessons of History,** *Peaceful Change,* C. A. W. Manning (ed.). London, Macmillan, 1937, pp. 27–38.

2619 Wambaugh, Sarah. **The Plebiscite and Peaceful Change,** *World Affairs,* IV (June 1938), 16–25.

2620 Webster, C. K. **What Is the Problem of Peaceful Change?** *Peaceful Change,* C. A. W. Manning (ed.). London, Macmillan, 1937, pp. 3–24.

2621 Williams, John Fischer. **The Pan American and League of Nations Treaties of Arbitration and Conciliation,** *British Yearbook of International Law,* X (199), 14–31.

Part C. — *League of Nations System*

12. POLITICAL ACTIVITIES: PARTICULAR DISPUTES

Although the League of Nations was able to handle successfully a number of minor disputes, the reasons for its ultimate failure can be traced in detail in the reluctance of its members to use the machinery available to them in dealing with disputes on three continents — in Manchuria, in Chaco and in Ethiopia.

12.1 SINO-JAPANESE CONFLICT (1931—1945)

2622   Burton, Wilbur. **Japan's Bid for Far East Supremacy,** *Current History,* XXXV (February 1932), 650—54.

2623   Buss, Claude A. **Japan in China,** *World Affairs Quarterly,* IX (July 1938), 125—41.

2624   Chamberlin, William Henry. **Asia's Irrepressible Conflict: A Distinguished Correspondent Analyzes the Background of the Present Battles,** *Current History,* XLVII (October 1937), 29—34.

2625   Current, Richard N. **The Stimson Doctrine and the Hoover Doctrine,** *American Historical Review,* LIX (April 1954), 513—42.

2626   Eddy, Sherwood. **The Sino-Japanese Dispute: Impressions of an Eye-Witness,** *Problems of Peace,* Series 7 (1932), 135—51.

2627   Geneva Research Center. **The League and Manchukuo,** *Geneva Studies,* V (1934), 1—40.

Part C. — League of Nations System

2628 — —. **The League and Manchuria: The First Phase of the Chinese-Japanese Conflict (September 18—20, 1931)**, *Geneva Studies*, II (October 1931), 1—34.

2629 — —. **The League and Manchuria: The Second Phase of the Chinese-Japanese Conflict (October 1—24, 1931)**, *Geneva Studies*, II (November 1931), 1—60.

2630 — —. **The League and Manchuria: The Third Phase of the Chinese-Japanese Conflict (October 25—December 31, 1931)**, *Geneva Studies*, II (December 1931), 1—91.

2631 — —. **The League and Shanghai: The Fourth Phase of the Chinese-Japanese Conflict (January 1—April 20, 1932)**, *Geneva Studies*, III (May 1932), 1—104.

2632 Geneva Research Committee. **The League and the Lytton Reports: The Fifth Phase of the Chinese-Japanese Conflict (May 1—December 31, 1932)**, *Geneva Studies*, III (1932), 1—32.

2633 Harley, John Eugene. **The Role of the League of Nations in the Sino-Japanese Controversy**, *World Affairs Quarterly*, III (October 1932), 31—44.

2634 Hishida, Seiji G. **Comments on John Bassett Moore's Discussion, with Reference to the Manchurian Incident, Embargo and Neutrality, "Aggression", Kellogg Pact, League, American "Birthright", etc.** Tokyo, Maruzen, 1933. viii + 67 p.

2635 Hsü, Shu-hsi. **An Introduction to Sino-Foreign Relations.** Shanghai, Kelly and Walsh, 1941. 165 p.

2636 International Relations Committee. **Public Opinion Towards the Report of the League Enquiry Commission on Sino-Japanase Dispute.** Nanking, International Relations Committee, 1932. vi + 105 p.

Part C. — League of Nations System

2637 Johnson, Grace Allen and Ames, Herbert B. **The Case of China and Japan Before the League of Nations: A Dramatization of the Events of 1931–1933.** Boston, Peabody Fund, 1933. x + 50 p.

2638 Kawakami, K. K. **Japan Seeks Economic Empire in Manchuria,** *Current History,* XXX (September 1929), 1111–18.

2639 Lauterpacht, H. **Japan and the Covenant,** *Political Quarterly,* III (April–June 1932), 174–93.

2640 Lohman, Philipp H. **The Background of the Sino-Japanese Conflict,** *World Affairs Quarterly,* X (October 1939), 246–57.

2641 Lowell, A. Lawrence. **Manchuria, the League, and the United States,** *Foreign Affairs,* X (April 1932), 351–68.

2642 Lytton, Earl of Victor A. G. R. **The Problem of Manchuria,** *International Affairs,* XI (November 1932), 737–49.

Comments by Steed, Green, Bland.

2643 MacMurray, John V. A. **The Treaty Status of Manchuria,** *Annals of the American Academy of Political and Social Science,* CLXV (January 1933), 146–53.

2644 Mah, N. Wing. **The Manchurian Crisis,** *Institute of World Affairs Proceedings,* VIII (1931), 91–98.

2645 — —. **The Sino-Japanese Controversy,** *World Affairs Quarterly,* III (July 1932), 27–34.

2646 Mallory, Walter H. **The Permanent Conflict in Manchuria,** *Foreign Affairs,* X (January 1932), 220–29.

2647 Middlebush, Frederick A. **The Effect of the Non-Recognition of Manchukuo,** *American Political Science Review,* XXVIII (August 1934), 677–83.

2648 Mogi, Sobi. **The Manchurian Problem,** *Political Quarterly,* III (January–March 1932), 97–107.

2649 Morley, Felix. **The Society of Nations.** Washington, Brookings, 1932.
Chapter XII.

2650 Nakazawa, Ken. **Manchuria — Past and Present,** *Institute of World Affairs Proceedings,* VIII (1931), 99–107.

2651 — —. **The Sino-Japanese Controversy,** *World Affairs Quarterly,* III (July 1932), 35–51.

2652 Nikolaieff, A. M. **Rivalry of Russia, China and Japan in Manchuria,** *Current History,* XXVII (February 1928), 669–75.

2653 Peake, Cyrus H. **The Clash of Arms in Manchuria,** *Current History,* XXXV (January 1932), 507–12.

2654 Perkins, E. R. **The Non-Application of Sanctions Against Japan, 1931–1932,** *Essays in History and International Relations: In Honor of George Hubbard Blakeslee,* Dwight E. Lee and George E. McReynolds (eds.). Worcester, Mass., Clark University Press, 1949. Pp. 215–32.

2655 Rappaport, Armin. **Henry L. Stimson and Japan, 1931–33.** Chicago, University of Chicago Press, 1963. 238 p.
Part I, Chapter X.

2656 Riddell, Walter A. **World Security by Conference.** Toronto, Ryerson, 1947.

Part C. — League of Nations System

2657 Rowell, Chester G. **The Critical Situation in the Orient,** *Institute of World Affairs Proceedings,* VIII (1931), 83—90.

2658 Rubinow, Edward S. **Sino-Japanese Warfare and the League of Nations,** *Geneva Studies,* IX (May 1938), 11—93.

Preface by Malcolm W. Davis.

2659 Saito, Hirosi. **A Japanese View of the Manchurian Situation,** *Annals of the American Academy of Political and Social Science,* CLXV (January 1933), 159—66.

2660 Smith, Sara Rector. **The Manchurian Crisis, 1931—1932: A Tragedy in International Relations.** New York, Columbia University Press, 1948. ix + 281 p.

2661 Stimson, Henry L. **The Far Eastern Crisis: Recollections and Observations.** New York, Harper, 1936. 293 p.

2662 Sze, Sao-Ke Alfred. **A Chinese View of the Manchurian Situation,** *Annals of the American Academy of Political and Social Science,* CLXV (January 1933), 154—58.

2663 Walters, Francis Paul. **A History of the League of Nations.** London, Oxford University Press, 1960.

Chapter XL.

2664 Wilde, John C. de. **The League and the Sino-Japanese Dispute,** *Foreign Policy Reports,* VIII (July 20, 1932), 108—18.

2665 Willoughby, Westel W. **The Sino-Japanese Controversy and the League of Nations.** Baltimore, Johns Hopkins Press, 1935. xxv + 733 p.

2666 Zimmern, Alfred. **The Manchurian Question,** *Political Quarterly,* III (January—March 1932), 88—96.

12.2 CHACO CONFLICT (1932–1935)

2667 Adorno Benítez, Félix. **Relato de episodos de la guerra del Paraguay con Bolivia, 1932–1935.** Asunción, Arte, 1963. 171 p.

2668 Alvarez del Vayo. **The Chaco War.** *Problems of Peace,* Series 9 (1934), 150–73.

2669 Chamberlain, Joseph P. **Equality of Belligerents and the Embargo Resolutions,** *Annals of the American Academy of Political and Social Science,* CXLIV (July 1929), 55–58.

2670 Cooper, Russell M. and Mattison, Mary. **The Chaco Dispute,** *Geneva Studies,* V (1934), 1–26.

2671 Del Rio, F. Nieto. **Chile's Conflict With Bolivia and Peru,** *Current History,* XV (December 1921), 449–53.

2672 Hudson, Manley O. **The Chaco Arms Embargo,** *International Conciliation,* CCCXX (May 1936), 217–46.

2673 Kain, Ronald Stuart. **Behind the Chaco War,** *Current History,* XLII (August 1935), 468–74.

2674 — —. **The Chaco Dispute and the Peace System,** *Political Science Quarterly,* L (September 1935), 321–42.

2675 Kirkpatrick, Helen Paull. **The League and the Chaco Dispute,** *Foreign Policy Reports,* XII (July 15, 1936), 110–20.
Published concurrently in *Geneva Studies.*

2676 La Foy, Margaret. **The Chaco Dispute and The League of Nations.** Bryn Mawr, Pa., Bryn Mawr Press, 1941. 157 p.

Part C. — *League of Nations System*

2677 Lindsay, J. W. **The War Over the Chaco: A Personal Account,** *International Affairs*, XIV (March—April 1935), 231—40.

2678 Mattison, Mary. **The Chaco Arms Embargo,** *Geneva Studies*, V, 5 (1934), 1—16.

2679 Schurz, William L. **The Chaco Dispute Between Bolivia and Paraguay,** *Foreign Affairs*, VII (July 1929), 650—55.

2680 Sweetser, Arthur. **The Practical Working of the League of Nations: A Concrete Example,** *International Conciliation*, CCXLIX (April 1929), 197—217.

2681 White, John W. **Warfare in the Chaco Jungle,** *Current History*, XXXVIII (April 1933), 41—46.

2682 Wilde, John C. de. **South American Conflicts: The Chaco and Leticia,** *Foreign Policy Reports*, IX (May 24, 1933), 58—68.

2683 Zook, David H. **The Conduct of the Chaco War.** Preface by Pablo Max Ynsfran; foreword by Charles W. Arnade. New York, Bookman, 1960. 280 p.

12.3 ITALO-ETHIOPIAN CONFLICT (1934—1936)

2684 Anon. **Sanctions in the Italo-Ethiopian Conflict,** *International Conciliation*, CCCXV (December 1935), 539—44.

2685 Atwater, Elton. **Administration of Export and Import Embargoes by Member States of the League of Nations, 1935—1936: With Special Reference to Great Britain, France, Belgium, the Netherlands, Denmark, Norway, and Sweden,** *Geneva Studies*, IX (December 1938), 7—64.

2686 Bonn, M. J. **How Sanctions Failed,** *Foreign Affairs*, XV (January 1937), 350—61.

Part C. — *League of Nations System*

2687   Bradley, Phillips. **The United States of America and Sanctions,** *Problems of Peace,* Series 11 (1936), 104—27.

2688   Davies, David. **Nearing the Abyss: The Lesson of Ethiopia.** London, Constable, 1936. 182 p.

2689   Dean, Vera Micheles. **The League and the Italian-Ethiopian Dispute,** *Geneva Studies,* VI, 8 (1935), 1—16.

2690   — —. **The League and the Italo-Ethiopian Crisis,** *Foreign Policy Reports,* XI (November 6, 1935), 214—24.

2691   — —. **The Quest for Ethiopian Peace,** *Foreign Policy Reports,* XI (February 26, 1936), 318—32.
Published concurrently in *Geneva Studies,* March 1936.

2692   Feis, Herbert. **Seen From E. A.: Three International Episodes.** New York, Knopf, 1947. xi + 313 p.

2693   Forges-Davanzati, Roberto. **Italy's Case Against Ethiopia,** *Current History,* XLIII (October 1935), 8—14.

2694   Hiett, Helen. **Public Opinion and the Italo-Ethiopian Dispute: The Activity of Private Organizations in the Crisis,** *Geneva Studies,* VII (February 1936), 3—28.

2695   Highley, Albert E. **The Actions of the States Members of the League of Nations in Application of Sanctions Against Italy, 1935—1936.** Geneva, Imprimerie du *Journal de Genève,* 1938. 251 p.

2696   — —. **The First Sanctions Experiment (A Study of League Procedures),** *Geneva Studies,* IX (July 1938), 7—141.
Contains an excellent bibliography.

Part C. — League of Nations System

2697 Isaacs, Leo. **Italy's Record in Ethiopia,** *Current History,* XLIX (September 1938), 25–28.

2698 Koren, William, Jr. **Imperialist Rivalries in Ethiopia,** *Foreign Policy Reports,* XI (September 11, 1935), 170–80.

2699 — —. **The Italian-Ethiopian Dispute,** *Geneva Studies,* VI, 4, 1935), 1–16.

2700 Martelli, George. **Italy Against the World: The First Complete and Impartial Account of Italy's Repudiation of the League and Her Conquest of Abyssinia.** New York, Harcourt, Brace, 1938. xii + 316 p.

2701 Melley, John M. **Ethiopia and the War from the Ethiopian Point of View,** *International Affairs,* XV (January 1936), 103–16.
Comments by Reid, Steed, White, Lias.

2702 Mower, Edmund. **International Government.** Boston, Heath, 1931.
Chapter XXX.

2703 Polyzoides, Adamatios. **Ethiopia—A Milestone in World Affairs,** *World Affairs Quarterly,* VI (October 1935), 217–28.

2704 Potter, Pitman B. **Lessons from the Wal-Wal Arbitration Between Ethiopia and Italy,** *World Affairs,* I (October–December 1935), 179–88.

2705 — —. **The Wal Wal Arbitration.** Washington, Carnegie, 1938. 182 p.

2706 — —. Riddell, Walter A. **World Security by Conference.** Toronto, Ryerson, 1947.
Part I—Chapters XIII, XVII.

2707 Rowell, Chester. **Geneva, Rome, and Addis Ababa: An Analysis and Appraisal,** *Institute of World Affairs Proceedings,* XIII (1935) 35–42.

2708 Royal Institute of International Affairs. **Abyssina and Italy.** New York, Oxford University Press, 1935. 48 p.

2709 Sandford, D. A. **Ethiopia: Reform from Within Versus Foreign Control,** *International Affairs,* XV (March 1936), 183—210.

2710 Schwarzenberger, Georg. **The Italo-Abyssinian Dispute,** *World Affairs,* I (July—September 1935); I (October—December 1935), 231—46; I (March 1936), 332—39; II (June 1936), 75—79; II (September 1936), 254—61.

2711 Shotwell, James T. and Salvin, Marina. **Lessons on Security and Disarmament from the History of the League of Nations.** New York, King's Crown, 1949. 149 p.

Section on the Ethiopian war was written by Robert K. Webb.

2712 Spencer, John H. **The Italian-Ethiopian Dispute and the League of Nations,** *American Journal of International Law,* XXXI (October 1937), 614—41.

2713 Stern, W. B. **The Treaty Background of the Italo-Ethiopian Dispute,** *American Journal of International Law,* XXX (April 1936), 189—203.

2714 Walters, Francis Paul. **A History of the League of Nations.** London, Oxford University Press, 1960.

Chapter LIII.

2715 Woolf, Leonard. **Meditation on Abyssinia,** *Political Quarterly,* VII (January—March 1936), 16—32.

2716 Work, Ernest. **Ethiopia: A Pawn in European Diplomacy.** New York, Macmillan, 1935. xii + 354 p.

2717 Wright, Quincy. **The Test of Aggression in the Italo-Ethiopian War,** *American Journal of International Law,* XXX (January 1936), 45—56.

2718 Zimmern, Alfred. **The League's Handling of the Italo-Abyssinian Dispute,** *International Affairs,* XIV (November 1935), 751—68.

12.4 OTHER QUESTIONS

2719 Barros, James. **The Corfu Incident of 1923: Mussolini and the League of Nations.** Princeton, Princeton University Press, 1965. 339 p.

2720 — —. **The Greek-Bulgarian Incident of 1925: The League of Nations and the Great Powers,** *Proceedings of the American Philosophical Society,* CVIII (August 27, 1964), 354–85.

2721 Brockelbank, W. J. **The Vilna Dispute,** *American Journal of International Law,* XX (July 1926), 483–501.

2722 Deák, Francis. **The Hungarian-Rumanian Land Dispute: A Study of Hungarian Property Rights in Transylvania Under the Treaty of Trianon.** Introduction by George W. Wickersham. New York, Columbia University Press, 1928. xiv + 272 p.

2723 Hudson, Manley O. **How the League of Nations Met the Corfu Crisis,** *World Peace Foundation Pamphlets,* VI, 3 (1923), 176–98.

2724 LeFur, Louis. **The League of Nations and the Present Crisis,** *International Conciliation,* CCCIII (October 1934), 326–43.
Concerning the German resurgence.

2725 Lowell, A. Lawrence. **The Charter of the League of Nations and Corfu,** *World Peace Foundation Pamphlets,* VI, 3 (1923), 169–75.

2726 Padelford, Norman J. and Anderson, K. Gosta A. **The Aaland Islands Question,** *American Journal of International Law,* XXXIII (July 1939), 465–87.

2727 Wilcox, Francis O. **The League of Nations and the Spanish Civil War,** *Annals of the American Academy of Political and Social Science,* CXCVIII (July 1938), 65–72.

2728 Wright, Quincy. **The Mosul Dispute,** *American Journal of International Law,* XX (July 1926), 453–64.

13. NATIONAL ACTORS AND THE LEAGUE SYSTEM

See also C 9.2 and C 12.

13.1 GENERAL DISCUSSIONS

2729 Barnes, Harry E. **National Self-Determination and the Problems of the Small Nations,** *The League of Nations,* Stephen Pierce Duggan (ed.). Boston, Atlantic Monthly Press, 1919, pp. 161—83.

2730 Hambro, Carl J. **The Role of Smaller Powers in international Affairs Today,** *International Affairs,* XV (March 1936), 167—77.

Comments by Ross, White, Zimmern, Knudsen, Lyttleton, Lytton.

2731 Hudson, Manley O. **The Members of the League of Nations,** *British Yearbook of International Law,* XVI (1935), 130—52.

2732 Myers, Denys. **Handbook of the League of Nations.** Boston, World Peace Foundation, 1935.

Chapter I.

2733 Potter, Pitman B. **An Introduction to the Study of International Organization.** 4th ed. New York, Appleton-Century, 1935.

Chapter XXIII.

2734 — —. **Permanent Delegations to the League of Nations,** *American Political Science Review,* XXV (February 1931), 21—44.

Published concurrently in *Geneva Studies,* November 1930.

2735 — —. **This World of Nations.** New York, Macmillan, 1929.

Chapter XIX.

2736 Rappard, William E. **Small States in the League of Nations,** *Political Science Quarterly*, XLIX (December 1934), 544—75.

2737 Requin, Lt.-Colonel. **Offical National Co-operation,** *The League of Nations Starts*, Raymond B. Fosdick, George Rublee, J. T. Shotwell, Léon Bourgeois, André Weiss, Lt.-Col. Requin, W. Ormsby-Gore, el Vizconde de Eza, H. B. Butler, Richard P. Strong, J. A. Salter, A. Claveille, Henri La Fontaine, Paul Otlet. London, Macmillan, 1920, pp. 81—90.

2738 Rodgers, Lindsay. **The League of Nations and the National States,** *The League of Nations*, Stephen Pierce Duggan (ed.). Boston, Atlantic Monthly Press, 1919, pp. 82—95.

2739 Tchernoff, J. **Les nations et la Société des Nations dans la politique moderne.** Foreword by Albert Thomas. Paris, Alcan, 1919. 200 p.

2740 Tobin, Harold. **The Problem of Permanent Representation at the League of Nations,** *Political Science Quarterly*, XLVIII (December 1933), 481—512.

2741 Vandenbosch, Amry. **Small States in International Politics and Organization,** *Journal of Politics*, XXVI (May 1964), 293—312.

Surveys the role of small states from the Congress of Vienna to the United Nations.

2742 Walston, Charles. **The English-Speaking Brotherhood and the League of Nations.** Cambridge, Cambridge University Press, 1919. xxi + 224 p.

2743 Walters, Francis Paul. **A History of the League of Nations.** London, Oxford University Press, 1960.

Chapters LXVI, LXVII.

2744 Zimmern, Alfred. **The Great Powers in the League of Nations,** *Problems of Peace*, Series 9 (1934), 54—73.

13.2 PARTICULAR COUNTRIES

13.2.1 BRITISH COMMONWEALTH COUNTRIES

2745 Adam, George B. **The British Empire and a League of Peace, Together with an Analysis of Federal Government, Its Function and Its Method.** New York, Putnam, 1919. iii + 115 p.

2746 Burns, C. Delisle. **The British Commonwealth and the League of Nations,** *Problems of Peace*, Series 3 (1928), 208—42.
Effect of membership upon foreign policy in the dominions.

2747 Charvet, Jean-Félix. **L'influence britannique dans la S.D.N. (Des origines de la S.D.N. jusqu'a nos jours).** Preface by Gilbert Gidel. Paris, Rodstein, 1938. 189 p.

2748 Dafoe, J. W. **Canada, the Empire and the League,** *Foreign Affairs*, XIV (January 1936), 297—308.

2749 Eastman, Samuel Mack. **Canada at Geneva.** Toronto, Ryerson, 1946. 117 p.

2750 Ellis, A. D. **Australia and the League of Nations.** New York, Macmillan, 1922. 62 p.

2751 Manning, C. A. **The Policies of the British Dominions in the League of Nations.** Geneva, Kundig, 1932. 159 p.

2752 Moore, William Harrison. **The Dominions of the British Commonwealth in the League of Nations,** *International Affairs*, X (May 1931), 372—91.

2753 Potter, Pitman B. **The League of Nations and Other International Organizations: An Analysis of the Evolution and Position of the League in Cooperation Among States,** *Geneva Studies,* V, 6 (1934), 1—22.

2754 Ram, Vangala S. and Sharma, Brij. **India and the League of Nations.** Lucknow, Upper India Publishing House, 1932. 239 p.

2755 Rovell, Newton Wesley. **The British Empire and World Peace.** New York, Oxford University Press, 1922. 307 p.

2756 Soward, Frederic H. **Canada and the League of Nations,** *International Conciliation,* CCLXXXIII (October 1932), 359—95.

2757 — —. **The Election of Canada to the League of Nations Council in 1927,** *American Journal of International Law,* XXIII (October 1929), 753—65.

2758 Stewart, Bruce M. **Canadian Labor Laws and the Treaty.** New York, Columbia University Press, 1926. 501 p.

2759 Wallbank, T. Walter. **The League and Britain's Foreign Policy,** *World Affairs Quarterly,* VIII (April 1937), 33—42.

2760 Williams, John Fischer. **Great Britain and the League,** *International Affairs,* XVII (March 1938), 187—205.

Comments by Garnett, Keen, Robinson, Dunbabin, Zvegintzov, Grigg, Arnold.

2761 Williams, Roth (pseud.). **The League of Nations Today: Its Growth, Record and Relation to British Foreign Policy.** London, Allen and Unwin, 1923. 223 p.

2762 Wolfsohn, H. **The Evolution of Australia in World Affairs,** *Australian Outlook,* VII (March 1953), 5—21.

2763 Zimmern, Alfred. **The British Commonwealth and the League of Nations,** *Problems of Peace,* Series 2 (1927), 295—317.

13.2.2 EUROPEAN COUNTRIES

2764 Aubert, Louis. **France and the League,** *Foreign Affairs,* III (July 1925), 637—52.

2765 Bassett, John S. **The League of Nations.** New York, Longmans, Green, 1938.
Chapter XIV: Germany.

2766 Berber, Fritz. **The Third Reich and the Future of the Collective System,** *Problems of Peace,* Series 11 (1936), 64—83.

2767 Bernstorff, Count von. **Germany and the League,** *Foreign Affairs,* II (March 1924), 390—96.

2768 Brooks, Robert C. **Swiss Referendum on the League of Nations,** *American Political Science Review,* XIV (August 1920), 477—80.

2769 Brouckère, L. de. **Germany and Geneva: III, A Belgian View,** *Political Quarterly,* V (January—March 1934), 13—17.

2770 Gerould, James Thayer. **Germany's Admission to the League of Nations,** *Current History,* XXV (October 1926), 237—43.

2771 Marley, J. Eugene. **The Significance of Germany's Admission Into the League,** *Institute of World Affairs Proceedings,* I (1926), 76—80.

2772 Herz, John H. **The National Socialist Doctrine of International Law and the Problems of International Organization,** *Political Science Quarterly,* LIV (December 1939), 536—54.

2773 Jäckh, Ernest. **Die Politik Deutschlands im Völkerbund.** Geneva, Kundig, 1932. 96 p.

2774 Jones, Samuel S. **Scandinavian States and the League of Nations.** Princeton, Princeton University Press, 1939. 298 p.

2775 Kayser, Jacques. **French Policy and the Resurrection of the League,** *Problems of Peace,* Series 12 (1937), 162—75.

2776 Lange, Chr. **Germany and Geneva: II, A Norwegian View,** *Political Quarterly,* V (January—March 1934), 7—12.

2777 Munch, Peter. **La politique du Danmark dans la Société des Nations.** Geneva, Kundig, 1931. 43 p.

2777a Pasvolsky, Leo. **Bulgaria's Economic Position, with Special Reference to the Reparation Problem and the Work of the League of Nations.** Washington, Brookings, 1930. xiii + 409 p.

2778 Patterson, Caleb Perry. **The Admission of Germany to the League of Nations and Its Probable Significance,** *International Conciliation,* CCXXXI (June 1927), 33—52.

2779 Piip, A. **Esthonia and the League of Nations,** *Transactions* (Grotius Society), VI (1920), 35—43.

Comments by Macdonell, Bower, Manisty, Henriques and Jelf.

2780 Oussky, Stefan. **The Little Entente and the League of Nations,** *International Affairs,* XIII (May 1934), 378—88.

Comments by White, Goode, Mander, Seton-Watson, Smith.

2781 Rappard, William E. **Germany and Geneva,** *Foreign Affairs,* IV (July 1926), 535—46.

Part C. — League of Nations System

2782 — —. **Germany and Geneva: I, A Swiss View,** *Political Quarterly,* V (January—March 1934), 1—6.

2783 Rolin, Henri A. **La politique de la Belgique dans la Société des Nations.** Geneva, Kundig, 1931. 87 p.

2784 — —. **The View Point of the Smaller European States,** *Problems of Peace,* Series 13 (1938), 165—77.
   The Oslo Group—Scandinavia and Benelux countries.

2785 Schwarz, Wolfgang. **Germany and the League of Nations,** *International Affairs,* X (March 1931), 197—203.
   Followed by discussion by Steed and others.

2786 Schwendemann, Karl von. **Deutschland und das Kollektivsystem,** *World Affairs,* I (July-September 1935), 100—15.

2787 Waller, Bolton C. **Ireland and the League of Nations.** Dublin, Talbot, 1925. 74 p.

2788 Wolfers, Arnold. **Germany in the League — A Survey and a Forecast,** *Problems of Peace,* Series 2 (1927), 237—49.

2789 Zahler, Walter R. **Switzerland and the League of Nations,** *American Political Science Review,* XXX (August 1936), 753—57.

13.2.3 FAR EASTERN COUNTRIES

2790 Fujii, Shin'ichi. **Views of League of Nations and Japan.** Tokyo, Mangetsudo, 1925.
   Part I.

Part C. — League of Nations System

2791 Hsia, Chi-feng. **China and The League; And My Experiences in the Secretariat.** Shanghai, Commercial Press, 1928. viii + 163 p.

2792 Kawakami, K. K. **Japan and World Peace.** New York, Macmillan, 1919. xv + 196 p.

2793 Matsushita, Masatoshi. **Japan in the League of Nations.** New York, Columbia University Press, 1929. 177 p.

2794 Miyaoka, Tsunejiro. **The Foreign Policy of Japan,** *International Conciliation*, CCCVII (February 1935), 31–42.

2795 Nitobe, Inazo. **Japan in the League of Nations,** *World Affairs Quarterly*, IV (April 1933), 61–69.

2796 Oliver, Lord. **Asia and the League,** *Problems of Peace*, Series 3 (1928), 242–77.

2797 Quan, Lau-king. **China's Relations with the League of Nations, 1919–1936.** Hong Kong, Asiatic, 1939 xviii + 414 p.

2798 Walters, Francis Paul. **A History of the League of Nations.** London, Oxford University Press, 1960.

Chapter XXVIII: China.

13.2.4 LATIN AMERICAN COUNTRIES

2799 Alfaro, Ricardo J. **The American Continent and the League,** *World Organization*, Institute on World Organization (ed.). Washington, American Council on Public Affairs, 1942, pp. 413–26.

2800 Edwards, Agustin. **Latin-America and the League of Nations,** *Current History,* XVIII (May 1923), 181—84.

2801 — —. **Latin America and the League of Nations,** *International Affairs,* VIII (March 1929), 134—49.
Comments by Wilson, Harris, Bewes, Manning.

2802 Kelchner, Warren H. **Latin American Relations with the League of Nations.** Boston, World Peace Foundation, 1930. 207 p.

2803 Macedo Soares, José Carlos de. **Le Brésil et la Société des Nations.** Preface by Gabriel Hanotaux. Paris, Pedone, 1927. xiv + 278 p.

2804 Martin, Percy Alvin. **Latin America and the League of Nations,** *American Political Science Review,* XX (February 1926), 14—30.

2805 Matos, José. **L'Amérique et la Société des Nations,** *Recueil des Cours,* XXVIII (1929), 5—103.

2806 Torriente, Cosme de la. **Cuba, Bustamente and the Permanent Court of International Justice,** *International Conciliation,* CLXXVIII (September 1922), 349—76.

2807 — —. **Cuba, the United States of America and the League of Nations,** *International Conciliation,* CLXXVIII (September 1922), 361—76.

13.2.5 LIBERIA

2808 Du Bois, W. E. Burghardt. **Liberia, the League and the United States,** *Foreign Affairs,* XI (July 1933), 682—95.

2809 Koren, William, Jr. **Liberia, the League and the United States,** *Foreign Policy Reports,* X (November 21, 1934), 239—48.

Part C. — *League of Nations System*

13.2.6 SOVIET UNION

2810 Davis, Kathryn W. **The Soviet Union and the League of Nations 1919–1933,** *Geneva Studies,* V (1934), 1–23.

2811 — —. **The Soviets at Geneva.** Geneva, Kundig, 1934. 315 p.

2812 Eddy, Sherwood. **Russia and the World Community,** *Problems of Peace,* Series 6 (1931), 210–35.

2813 Nevins, Allan. **League Gains from Russia,** *Current History,* XLI (November 1934), 143–48.

2814 Prince, Charles. **The USSR and International Organizations,** *American Journal of International Law,* XXXVI (July 1942), 425–45.

2815 Rothstein, Andrew. **Soviet Policy and the Reconstruction of the League,** *Problems of Peace,* Series 12 (1937), 176–98.

2816 Walters, Francis Paul. **A History of the League of Nations.** London, Oxford University Press, 1960.

Chapter XLVIII.

13.2.7 UNITED STATES

See also C 8.4.2, C 9.3, C 10.3.

2817 Bailey, Thomas A. **Woodrow Wilson and the Lost Peace.** New York, Macmillan, 1944. 381 p.

2818 Bassett, John S. **The League of Nations.** New York, Longmans, Green, 1938.

Chapter XV.

2819 Berdahl, Clarence A. **The Policy of the United States with Respect to the League of Nations.** Geneva, Kundig, 1932. 129 p.

2820 — —. **Relations of the United States with the Assembly of the League of Nations,** *American Political Science Review,* XXVI (February 1932), 99—111.

2821 — —. **Relations of the United States with the Council of the League of Nations,** *American Political Science Review,* XXVI (June 1932), 497—526.

2822 Borg, Dorothy. **The United States and the Far Eastern Crisis of 1933—1938: From the Manchurian Incident Through the Initial Stage of the Undeclared Sino-Japanese War.** Cambridge, Harvard University Press, 1964. x + 674 p.

2823 Bradley, Phillips. **The United States of America and Sanctions,** *Problems of Peace,* Series 11 (1936), 104—27.

2824 Brown, Philip Marshall. **Fundamentals in the Foreign Policy of the United States,** *Annals of the American Academy of Political and Social Science,* CXIV (July 1924), 97—101.

2825 Buell, Raymond Leslie. **American Neutrality and Collective Security,** *Geneva Studies,* VI, 6 (1935), 1—29.

2826 — —. **The United States and the League of Nations,** *Foreign Policy Reports,* VI (July 9, 1930), 167—84.

2827 Bullard, Arthur. **American Diplomacy in the Modern World.** Foreword by Roland S. Morris. Philadelphia, University of Pennsylvania Press, 1928. 127 p.

2828 Charnwood, Lord. **Relations of the United States to the League of Nations,** *Transactions (Grotius Society),* X (1924), 11—26.

Comments by Cave, Whittuck, Bellot, Charnwood, Latey, Bewes, Barrat, Petrie, and Bisschop.

Part C. — *League of Nations System*

2829 Clark, Keith. **International Communications: The American Attitude,** New York, Columbia University Press, 1931. 261 p.

American policy in the evolution of international unions dealing with posts, telegraph and wireless.

2830 Clarke, John H. **America and World Peace.** New York, Holt, 1925. vii + 145 p.

2831 Cooper, Russell M. **American Consultation in World Affairs for the Preservation of Peace.** Introduction by James T. Shotwell. New York, Macmillan, 1934. xiv + 406 p.

2832 Darling, Arthur B. **America's Way with the League,** *Current History,* XXXIX (November 1933), 173–79.

2833 Dickinson, Edwin D. **The United States and World Organization,** *American Political Science Review,* XVI (May 1922), 183–93.

2834 Dickinson, Thomas H. **The United States and the League.** New York, Dutton, 1923. 151 p.

2835 Du Bois, W. E. Burghardt. **Liberia, the League and the United States,** *Foreign Affairs,* XI (July 1933), 682–95.

2836 Fisher, Irving. **America's Interest in World Peace.** New York, Funk and Wagnalls, 1924. 123 p.

2837 Fleming, Denna Frank. **The United States and the League of Nations, 1918–1920.** New York, Putnam, 1932. 559 p.

2838 — —. **The United States and World Organization, 1920–1933.** New York, Columbia University Press, 1938. 569 p.

Part C. — League of Nations System

2839 Foreign Policy Association. **American Neutrality and League Wars,** *Foreign Policy Reports,* IV (March 30, 1928), 19—34.

2840 France, Joseph Irwin. **The Concert of Nations,** *Annals of the American Academy of Political and Social Science,* XCVI (July 1921), 141—46.

2841 Garner, James W. **America and the World Community,** *Problems of Peace,* Series 6 (1931), 236—52.

2842 Garvin, J. L. **The League of Nations and the English Speaking World,** *Problems of Peace,* Series 5 (1930), 256—83.

2843 Geneva Research Center. **American Cooperation with the League of Nations,** *Geneva Studies,* I (July 1930), 1—44.

2844 — —. **American Cooperation with the League of Nations, 1919—1931 (Revised),** *Geneva Studies,* II (July 1931), 1—50.

2845 — —.**The United States and the League of Nations During 1930,** *Geneva Studies,* II (January 1931), 1—27.
Articles on American relations with the League appeared, usually in the January issue, in subsequent years through Volume 11, with the exception of Volume 8.

2846 Hard, William. **Why Enter Europe?** *Annals of the American Academy of Political and Social Science,* CXIV (July 1924), 115—19.

2847 Harley, John Eugene. **America Joins the Quest for Peace,** *World Affairs Quarterly,* V (January 1935), 341—54.

2848 Hill, David Jayne. **American Cooperation for World Peace,** *International Conciliation,* CXCIV (January 1924), 23—49.
Reprinted from *Saturday Evening Post,* October 27 and November 3, 1923.

2849 — —. **American World Policies.** New York, Doran, 1920. 257 p.

Part C. — League of Nations System

2850 — —. **Present Problems in Foreign Policy.** New York, Appleton, 1919. xii + 360 p.

2851 Hopkinson, Alfred, **America and the League of Nations,** *Transactions* (Grotius Society), X (1924), 1—6.

Comments by Manisty, Schuster, Jelf, Jacobs, Keen, Bewes, Jaffe, Whittuck, Henriques and Bellot.

2852 Hubbard, Ursula P. **The Cooperation of the United States with the League of Nations, 1931—1936,** *International Conciliation*, CCCXXIX (April 1937), 295—468.

2853 Hudson, Manley O. **American Cooperation with the League of Nations,** *World Peace Foundation Pamphlets*, VII, 1 (1924), 4—26.

2854 — —. **America's Participation in World Organization,** *Problems of Peace*, Series 7 (1932), 174—92.

2855 — —. **America's Relation to World Peace,** *Problems of Peace*, Series 3 (1928), 178—207.

2856 — —. **America's Role in the League of Nations,** *American Political Science Review*, XXIII (February 1929), 17—32.

2857 — —. **The Effect of the Present Attitude of the United States Toward the League of Nations,** *Annals of the American Academy of Political and Social Science*, CXX (July 1925), 112—14.

2858 — —. **Our Attitude Toward the League of Nations,** *Annals of the American Academy of Political and Social Science*, CLVI (July 1931), 147—52.

2859 — —. **Progress in International Organization.** Oxford, Oxford University Press, 1932.

Chapter IX.

2860 Hull, William I. **The United States and International Government,** *Annals of the American Academy of Political and Social Science,* XCVI (July 1921), 128—32.

2861 Jessup, Phillip C. **The United States and Treaties for the Avoidance of War,** *International Conciliation,* CCXXXIX (April 1928), 7—71.

Arbitration and conciliation treaties as preludes to the Kellogg- Briand Pact.

2862 Knudson, John I. **A History of the League of Nations.** Atlanta, Smith, 1938.

Chapter XII.

2863 Koren, William, Jr. **Liberia, the League and the United States,** *Foreign Policy Reports,* X (November 21, 1934), 239—48.

2864 Lindsay, Samuel McCune. **The Problem of American Cooperation,** *The Origins of the International Labor Organization,* James T. Shotwell (ed.). New York, Columbia University Press, 1935, 331—70.

2865 Lingelbach, William E. **The Monroe Doctrine and American Participation in European Affairs,** *Annals of the American Academy of Political and Social Science,* XCVI (July 1921), 33—41.

2866 Lodge, Henry Cabot. **The Senate and The League of Nations.** New York, Scribner's, 1925. 424 p.

2867 Lowell, A. Lawrence. **Manchuria, the League, and the United States,** *Foreign Affairs,* X (April 1932), 351—68.

2868 Malin, James C. **The United States After the World War.** Boston, Ginn, 1930. vi + 584 p.

2869 Marshall, Thomas R. **America, the Nations and the League,** *Annals of the American Academy of Political and Social Science* LXXXIV (July 1919), 194—200.

Part C. — *League of Nations System*

2870 Meaney, N. K. **The British Empire in the American Rejection of the Treaty of Versailles,** *Australian Journal of Politics and History,* IX (November 1963), 213—34.

2871 Morgenthau, Henry. **The Attitude of the United States Toward Europe,** *Annals of the American Academy of Political and Social Science,* XCVI (July 1921), 68—69.

2872 Munro, Henry F. **The United States — and the Policy of Isolation,** *The League of Nations,* Stephen Pierce Duggan (ed.). Boston, Atlantic Monthly Press, 1919, pp. 273—288.

2873 Nevins, Allan. **Why America Rejected the League,** *Current History,* XXXVI (April 1932), 20—26.

2874 Pepper, George W. **America and the League of Nations,** *Journal of Comparative Legislation and International Law,* III (January 1921), 21—30.

2875 Reiff, Henry. **The United States and International Administrative Unions: Some Historical Aspects,** *International Conciliation,* CCCXXXII (September 1937), 627—57.

2876 Schmeckebier, Laurence Frederick. **International Organizations in Which the United States Participates.** Washington, Brookings, 1935. 370 p.

2877 Shotwell, James T. **On the Rim of the Abyss.** New York, Macmillan, 1936.

Chapter XII.

2878 Snow, Alpheus H. **The American Philosophy of Government.** New York, Putnam, 1921. iii + 485 p.

2879 Sweetser, Arthur. **The United States and World Organization in 1944,** *International Conciliation,* CDIX, Section Two (March 1945), 193–200.

2880 — —. **The United States, the United Nations and the League of Nations,** *International Conciliation,* CDXVIII (February 1946), 51–59.

2881 Taft, Henry W. **The Monroe Doctrine and a World Organization,** *Annals of the American Academy of Political and Social Science,* XCVI (July 1921), 41–44.

2882 Taubenfeld, Howard J. **The "Economic Weapon": The League and the United Nations,** *American Society of International Law Proceedings,* LVIII (1964), 183–204.

2883 Trask, David T. **The United States in the Supreme War Council: American War Aims and Inter-Allied Strategy,** 1917–1918. Middletown, Wesleyan University Press, 1961. 244 p.

2884 Wallace, Benjamin B. **How the United States Led the League in 1931,** *American Political Science Review,* XXXIX (February 1945), 101–16.

2885 Walters, Francis Paul. **A History of The League of Nations.** London, Oxford University Press, 1960.

Chapter VI.

2886 Williams, Benjamin H. **The United States and Disarmament.** New York, McGraw-Hill, 1931. 361 p.

2887 Wright, Q. **Woodrow Wilson and the League of Nations,** *Social Research,* XIV (Spring, 1957), 65–86.

2888 Zimmern, Alfred E. **The American Road to World Peace.** New York, Dutton, 1953.

Section V.

Part C. — *League of Nations System*

14. FINAL YEARS OF THE LEAGUE OF NATIONS

While World War II was being fought, the League of Nations maintained a nominal existence. Organs of the new United Nations were established outside Geneva during the war, and some League bodies either moved their headquarters as well or became inactive.

2889 An Observer. **The Future of the International Labour Organisation,** *Political Quarterly*, XV (January-March 1944), 66–76.

2890 Bentwich, Norman. **The Mandated Territories During the Second World War, 1939–42,** *British Yearbook of International Law*, XXI (1944), 164–68.

2891 Boudreau, Frank G. **Public Health and Nutrition in the Period of Transition,** *The Transitional Period: Second Report and Papers Presented to the Commission,* Commission to Study the Organization of Peace (ed.). New York, Commission to Study the Organization of Peace, 1942, pp. 170–78.

2892 Frankel, W. **The Future of the Permanent Court of International Justice,** *World Affairs*, X (January 1945), 116–20.

2893 Hall, H. Duncan. **The Belligerency of the Mandated Territories During the Second World War,** *British Yearbook of International Law*, XXIV (1947), 389–92.

2894 Hediger, Ernest S. **Geneva Institutions in Wartime,** *Foreign Policy Reports*, XIX (May 1, 1943), 38–48.

2895 International Labor Office. **A New Era: The Philadephia Conference and the Future of the I. L. O.** Montreal, 1944. 145 p.

Contains all those speeches or parts of speeches delivered by members of the International Labor Conference, on the subject of the I.L.O. meeting in Philadelphia, April-May, 1944.

2896 Moorhead, Helen Howell. **International Narcotics Control: 1939—1946,** *Foreign Policy Reports,* XXII (July 1, 1946), 94—103.

2897 Myers, Denys P. **Liquidation of League of Nations Functions,** *American Journal of International Law,* XLII (April 1948), 320—54.

2898 Simpson, Smith. **The International Labor Conference, 1941,** *American Political Science Review,* XXXVI (February 1942), 102—104.

2899 — —. **International Labor Organization at Montreal,** *American Political Science Review,* XXXV (February 1941), 112—14.

2900 Sweetser, Arthur. **The United States and World Organization in 1944,** *International Conciliation,* CDIX, Section Two (March 1945), 193—200.

2901 Winant, John G. **The International Labour Organisation in Wartime and After,** *Foreign Affairs,* XIX (April 1941), 633—40.

2902 Wood, H. McKinnon. **The Dissolution of the League of Nations,** *British Yearbook of International Law,* XXIII (1946), 317—23.

Part D.

UNITED NATIONS SYSTEM

Part D. — *United Nations System*

The "United Nations system" includes the main political organs and various specialized agencies, in addition to the social, economic and administrative functions of the United Nations. The main difference from the League system, structurally speaking, is that organs formerly independent of the League are integrally a part of the UN.

1. BIBLIOGRAPHIES AND DOCUMENTS

See A 3.3. and A 5.3.

2. WORLD WAR II EFFORTS

During World War II, from the Atlantic Charter declaration until the San Francisco Conference, the assumption among Allied leaders was that a new international organization would be established as a replacement for the League. Details were discussed in a number of conferences, but the actual conduct of the war and the execution of the peace were matters handled quite separately from the plans for the United Nations.

2.1 PLEAS FOR A POSTWAR INTERNATIONAL ORGANIZATION

2903 Adler, Mortimer J. **How to Think About War and Peace.** New York, Simon and Schuster, 1944. xxiii + 307 p.

2904 Agar, Herbert; Aydelotte, Frank; Borgese, G. A.; Broch, Hermann; Brooks, Van Wyck; Comstock, Ada L.; Elliott, William Yandell; Fisher, Dorothy Canfield; Gauss, Christian; Jászi, Oscar; Johnson, Alvin; Kohn, Hans; Mann, Thomas; Mumford, Lewis; Neilson, Allen William; Niebuhr, Reinhold; and Salvemini, Gaetano. **The City of Man: A Declaration of World Democracy.** New York, Viking, 1940. 113 p.

> The names given on the title page are those of a "Committee on Europe" which had its inception in 1938. The first conference of the Committee was held at Atlantic City in May 1940, at which time "it seemed too late... for a 'Committee on Europe' and on Europe alone. It became as a temporary nucleus, with any further specification, a 'Committee,' tentatively, 'of fifteen.'" At the second conference, held at Sharon, Connecticut, in August 1940, William Allen Neilson was elected chairman and G. A. Borgese secretary.

Part D. — United Nations System

2905 Agar, William. **International Co-operation or World War III,** *Annals of American Academy of Political and Social Science,* CCXXVIII (July 1943), 47–51.

2906 Bain, Read. **Sociopathy and World Organization,** *American Sociological Review,* IX (April 1944), 127–38.

2907 Berdahl, Clarence A. **The Leadership of the United States in the Post-War World,** *American Political Science Review,* XXXVIII (April 1944), 235–48.

2908 Bonn, M. J. **The New World Order,** *Annals of the American Academy of Political and Social Science,* CCXVI (July 1941), 163–77.

2909 — —. **The Structure of Society and Peace,** *Annals of the American Academy of Political and Social Science,* CCX (July 1949), 7–13.

2910 Bonnet, Henri. **Outlines of the Future: World Organization Emerging From the War.** Chicago, World Citizens Association, 1943. vii + 128 p.

2911 — —. **The United Nations on the Way.** Chicago, World Citizens Association, 1942. 170 p.

2912 — —. **The United Nations: What They Are; What They May Become.** Chicago, World Citizens Association, 1942. 100 p.

2913 Bordwell, Percy. **A Constitution for the United Nations,** *Iowa Law Review,* XXVIII (March 1943), 387–421.

2914 Brunaer, Esther Caukin. **Building on League Foundations,** *Reconstituting the League of Nations,* Julia E. Johnsen (ed.). New York, Wilson, 1943, pp. 127–35.

From her pamphlet, *Building of the New World Order.*

2915 Bunge, Alejandro E. **The Foundations of Peace,** *Annals of the American Academy of Political and Social Science,* CCX (July 1949), 14—18.

2916 Butler, Nicholas Murray. **The Hope of the World,** *International Conciliation,* CDIII (September 1944), 576—85.

2917 Byng, Edward J. **The Status of the Union: International or Supra-National,** *Reconstituting the League of Nations,* Julia E. Johnsen (ed.). New York, Wilson, 1943, pp. 243—46.

2918 Carr, E. H. and Madariaga, S. de. **The Future of International Government.** London, National Peace Council, 1941. 24 p.

2919 Cassel, Gustav. **Reflections on Postwar Reconstruction,** *Annals of the American Academy of Political and Social Science,* CCX (July 1940), 24—28.

2920 Cecil, Robert. **Peace Through International Co-Operation,** *Annals of the American Academy of Political and Social Science,* CCX (July 1940), 57—65.

2921 Chaffee, Zechariah, Jr. **International Utopias,** *Daedalus,* LXXV (October 1942), 39—53.

2922 Chamberlain, Joseph P. **International Organization,** *International Conciliation,* CCCLXXXV (December 1942), 459—523.

2923 Colombos, C. John. **The Shape of Things to Come,** *Transactions* (Grotius Society), XXX (1944), 83—95.

Comments by Goodhart, Dehn, Nagórski, Keen, Murray, Hutton-Ashkenny, Frascona, Wilenkin and Moore.

2924 Commission to Study the Organization of Peace. **Fundamentals of the International Organization.** New York, Commission to Study the Organization of Peace, 1943. 27 +36 + 40 + 24 p.

Contains the Commission's fourth report and is divided into four sections: General Statements, Security and World Organizations, The Economic Organization of Welfare, International Safeguard of Human Rights.

Part D. — *United Nations System*

2925 — —. **Preliminary Report.** New York, Commission to Study the Organization of Peace, 1940. 14 p.

Contains the Commission's first report.

2926 Condliffe, J. B. **Agenda for a Postwar World.** New York, Norton, 1942. 232 p.

2927 Corbett, Percy E. **Post-War Worlds.** New York, Farrar and Rinehart, 1942. xv + 211 p.

2928 Cousins, Norman. **Modern Man Is Obsolete.** New York, Viking, 1945. 59 p.

2929 Dean, Vera Micheles. **Toward a New World Order,** *Foreign Policy Reports,* XVII (May 15, 1941), 50–68.

2930 — —. **U. S. Plans for World Organization,** *Foreign Policy Reports,* XX (August 15, 1944), 130–36.

2931 Dolivet, Louis. **Educating Public Opinion for World Organization,** *Annals of the American Academy of Political and Social Science,* CCXXII (July 1942), 84–89.

2932 Douglas, Emily Taft. **America's Second Chance,** *Annals of the American Academy of Political and Social Science,* CCXL (July 1945), 7–10.

2933 Eagleton, Clyde. **Organization of the Community of Nations,** *American Journal of International Law,* XXXVI (April 1942), 229–41.

2934 — —. **Peace Means More Than Political Adjustment,** *Annals of the American Academy of Political and Social Science,* CCX (July 1940), 35–42.

Part D. — United Nations System

2935 — —. **World Government Discussion in the United States,** *World Affairs,* XII (October 1946), 251–58.

2936 Einaudi, Luigi. **The Nature of a World Peace,** *Annals of the American Academy of Political and Social Science,* CCX (July 1940), 66–67.

2937 Evans, Archibald A. **Characteristics of International Organization,** *Public Administration,* XXIII (Spring, 1945), 31–38.

2938 Fike, Linus R. **No Nation Alone: A Plan for Organized Peace.** New York, Philosophical Library, 1943. 96 p.

2939 Finer, Herman, **The TVA: Lessons for International Application.** Montreal, International Labor Office, 1944. viii + 289 p.

2940 Fleming, D. F. **Coming World Order, Closed or Free,** *Journal of Politics,* IV (May 1942), 250–63.

2941 Freeman, Harrop A. (ed.). **Peace Is the Victory.** New York, Harper, 1944. x + 253 p.

2942 Gamio, Manuel. **War and the Acculturation of the Masses,** *Annals of the American Academy of Political and Social Science,* CCX (July 1940), 28–34.

2943 Gurian, Waldemar. **Perpetual Peace? Critical Remarks on Mortimer Adler's Book,** *Review of Politics,* VI (April 1944), 228–38.

2944 Hambro, Carl J. **How to Win the Peace.** Philadelphia, Lippincott, 1942. 384 p.

2945 — —. **Postwar Political Organization of the World,** *Annals of the American Academy of Political and Social Science,* CCXXII (July 1942), 109–16.

2946 Hambro, Edvard. **Small States and a New League, from the Viewpoint of Norway,** *American Political Science Review,* XXXVII (October 1943), 903–909.

2947 Harley, J., Eugene. **The Coming Revival of the League of Nations,** *World Affairs Quarterly,* XII (October 1941), 235–46.

2948 — —. **Post-War International Organization,** *American Society of International Law Proceedings,* XXXIV (1940), 104–15.

2949 Herz, John H. **Power Politics and World Organization,** *American Political Science Review,* XXXVI (December 1942), 1139–52.

2950 Heyting, W. J. **The Organization of Post-War Peace,** *Transactions* (Grotius Society), XXX (1944), 209–38.

2951 Hirsch, Joseph and Allen, Leonard. **America Looks Beyond the War,** *Southwestern Social Science Quarterly,* XXII (March 1942), 317–23.

2952 Hoover, Herbert Clark and Gibson, Hugh. **The Basis of a Lasting Peace.** New York, Van Nostrand, 1945. 44 p.

2953 — —. **The Problems of Lasting Peace.** Garden City, Doubleday, Doran, 1942. 295 p.

2954 Hudson, Manley O. **International Courts in the Postwar World,** *Annals of the American Academy of Political and Social Science,* CCXXII (July 1942), 117–23.

2955 — —. **The International Law of the Future,** *International Conciliation,* CDVI (December 1944), 757–73.

2956 Hughan, Jessie W. **New Leagues for Old: Blueprints or Foundations?** New York, Plowshare, 1945. 32 p.

2957 Huszar, George B. de. **The United Nations in War and Peace,** *World Affairs,* CVI (June 1943), 98–104.

2958 Huxley, Julian. **Armaments and Security,** *New Republic,* CIV (June 2, 1941), 750–52.

2959 Jackson, Robert H. **The Challenge of International Lawlessness,** *International Conciliation,* CCCLXXIV (November 1941), 683–91.

2960 Johnsen, Julia E. (comp.). **Plans for a Post-War World.** New York, Wilson, 1942. 238 p.

A collection of readings with a comprehensive bibliography.

2961 — —. **Reconstituting the League of Nations.** New York, Wilson, 1943. 304 p.

Excellent bibliography.

2962 — —. **World Peace Plans.** New York, Wilson, 1943. 304 p.

Excellent bibliography.

2963 Kelsen, Hans. **Peace Through Law.** Chapel Hill, University of North Carolina Press, 1944. 155 p.

2964 — —. **The Principle of Sovereign Equality of States As a Basis for International Organization,** *Yale Law Review,* LIII (March 1944), 207–20.

2965 Lanux, Pierre de. **France and a Durable Peace,** *Annals of the American Academy of Political and Social Science,* CCX (July 1940), 82–88.

2966 Lerner, Max and Lerner, Edna. **International Organization After the War,** *Problems in American Life Series,* XV (1943), 10–13.

2967 Lorwin, Lewis L. **Postwar Plans of the United Nations.** New York, Twentieth Century Fund, 1943. 307 p.

2968 McKenzie, Vernon. **United Nations Propaganda in the United States,** *Public Opinion Quarterly*, VI (Fall, 1942), 351–66.

2969 Mackinder, Halford F. **The Round World and the Winning of the Peace,** *Foreign Affairs*, XXI (July 1943), 595–605.

2970 Macready, Gordon N. **The Provision of Military Forces for Use by the World Organization,** *Academy of Political Science Proceedings*, XXI (May 1945), 340–46.

2971 Malcolm, Roy. **Another Chance,** *World Affairs Quarterly*, XV (January 1944), 354–61.

2972 Mallery, Otto Tod. **Economic Union and Durable Peace.** 2d ed. New York, Harper, 1943. xvi + 183 p.

2973 Millspaugh, Arthur C. **Peace Plans and American Choices: The Pros and Cons of World Order.** Washington, Brookings, 1942. vii + 107 p.

2974 Mitrany, David. **The Road to Security.** London, National Peace Council, 1944. 20 p.

2975 Najera, Francisco Castillo. **Organization of Peace,** *Annals of the American Academy of Political and Social Science*, CCXXII (July 1942), 60–73.

2976 Nearing, Scott. **United World: The Road to International Peace.** New York, Island Press, 1945. 265 p.

2977 Niemeyer, Gerhart. **World Order and the Great Powers,** *The Second Chance: America and the Peace*, John B. Whitton (ed.). Princeton, Princeton University Press, 1944, pp. 30–67.

2978 O'Brien, John A. **The Pope's Way to Peace,** *International Conciliation,* CDIV (October 1944), 647—63.

2979 Page, Ralph W. **Designs for a World Order,** *Annals of the American Academy of Political and Social Science,* CCX (July 1940), 50—56.

2980 Parker, John J. **World Organization,** *American Bar Association Journal,* XXIX (November 1943), 617—22.

2981 Parkes, Henry B. **The World After the War.** New York, Crowell, 1943. vii + 240 p.

2982 Patterson, George Stuart. **A Peace and Sound Economics,** *Annals of the American Academy of Political and Social Science,* CCX (July 1940), 68—72.

2983 Peaslee, Amos J. **A Permanent United Nations.** New York, Putnam, 1942. 146 p.

2984 — —. **A United and Universal Society of Nations,** *Reconstituting the League of Nations,* Julia E. Johnsen (ed.). New York, Wilson, 1943, pp. 259—62.
Address before the Institute of Foreign Affairs, Earlham College.

2985 Perry, Ralph B. **One World in the Making.** New York, Wyn, 1945. 275 p.

2986 Pink, Louis H. **Toward International Economic Organization,** *Annals of the American Academy of Political and Social Science,* CCXXXIV (July 1944), 91—95.

2987 Potter, Pitman B. **Postwar International Organization and Administration,** *Institute of World Affairs Proceedings,* XXI (1944—45), 27—32.

2988 Ralston, Jackson H. **A Quest for International Order.** Washington, Byrne, 1941. 205 p.

2989 Ranshofen-Wertheimer, Egon. F. **Power in International Government,** *Free World,* III (June 1942), 78—82.

2990 — —. **Victory Is Not Enough: The Strategy for a Lasting Peace.** New York, Norton, 1942. 322 p.

2991 Riddle, J. H. **International Financial Organization,** *Academy of Political Science Proceedings,* XXI (May 1944), 29—40.

2992 Robinson, Howard; Wooster, Harvey Alden; Lerner, Max; Eliot, George Fielding; Viner, Jacob; Wright, Quincy; Hocking, William Ernest; Jászi, Oscar. **Toward International Organization.** New York, Harper, 1942. viii + 218 p.

2993 Rugg, Harold O. **Now Is the Moment.** New York, Duell, Sloan and Pearce, 1943. xii + 269 p.

2994 Schuman, Frederick L. **War, Peace, and the Balance of Power,** *Annals of the American Academy of Political and Social Science,* CCX (July 1940), 73—81.

2995 Shotwell, James T. **The Great Decision.** New York, Macmillan, 1944. 268 p.

2996 — —. **International Organization,** *Annals of the American Academy of Political and Social Science,* CCX (July 1940), 19—23.

2997 Straight, Michael W. **Make This the Last War: The Future of the United Nations.** New York, Harcourt, Brace, 1943. x + 417 p.

2998 — —. **The United Nations,** *Annals of the American Academy of Political and Social Science,* CCXXII (July 1942), 32—37.

2999 Sturzo, Luigi. **The New League of Nations,** *Contemporary Review,* CLXIII (February 1943), 71—77.

3000 Talbott, E. Guy. **The Need for World Organization,** *World Affairs Quarterly,* XI (October 1940), 287—95.

3001 Temple, William. **Christianity and Social Order.** New York, Penguin, 1942. 93 p.

The author was Archbishop of Canterbury.

3002 Thomas, Norman. **America's Contribution to an Enduring Peace,** *Annals of the American Academy of Political and Social Science,* CCX (July 1940), 43—49.

3003 Tiwari, S. C. **The Attitude of the Republican Party Towards the Creation of the United Nations During the Second World War,** *International Studies,* III (January 1962), 325—48.

3004 United States, Department of State. **Organizing the United Nations: A Series of Articles from the Department of State Bulletin.** United States-United Nations Information Series 6. Department of State Publication 2573. Washington. U. S. Government Printing Office, 1946. 57 p.

3005 Vandenberg, Arthur Hendrik. **The Private Papers of Senator Vandenberg,** Arthur Hendrik Vandenberg, Jr. (ed.), with the collaboration of Joe Alex Morris. Boston, Houghton, Mifflin, 1952. 599 p.

3006 Villari, Luigi. **Foundations of a Durable Peace,** *Annals of the American Academy of Political and Social Science,* CCX (July 1940), 89—97.

3007 Viner, Jacob. **The International Economic Organization of the Future,** *Toward International Organization,* Howard Robinson, Harvey Alden Wooster, Max Lerner, George Fielding Eliot, Jacob Viner, Quincy Wright, William Ernest Hocking, Oscar Jászi. New York, Harper, 1942, pp. 110–37.

3008 Wells, H. G. **Ten Points for World Peace: A "Declaration of the Rights of Man" Should Be the Foundation of Any Post-War World,** *Current History,* LI (March 1940), 16–18.

3009 Whitton, John B. **Institutions of World Order,** *The Second Chance: America and the Peace,* John B. Whitton (ed.). Princeton, Princeton University Press, 1944, pp. 68–114.

3010 — —. (ed.). **The Second Chance: America and the Peace.** Princeton, Princeton University Press, 1944. vi + 235 p.

3011 Woody, Thomas. **World Integration and Education,** *Political Science Quarterly,* LX (September 1945), 385–411.

3012 Woolf, Leonard Sidney. **The War for Peace.** London, Routledge, 1940. 224 p.

3013 Wright, Quincy. **Dilemmas for a Post-War World,** *Free World,* I (October 1940), 14–16.

3014 — —. **International Justice,** *Toward International Organization,* Howard Robinson, Harvey Alden Wooster, Max Lerner, George Fielding Eliot, Jacob Viner, Quincy Wright, William Ernest Hocking, Oscar Jászi. New York, Harper, 1942, pp. 139–60.

3015 — —. **Peace Problems of Today and Yesterday,** *American Political Science Review,* XXXVIII (June 1944), 512–20.

2.2 NEGOTIATIONS LEADING UP TO THE UNITED NATIONS

3016 Adams, James Truslow. **The Atlantic Charter: Some of the Consequences If Its Aims Are Adopted,** *Barron's* XXI (October 13, 1941), 3.

3017 Appadorai, A. **Dumbarton Oaks,** *India Quarterly*, I (April 1945), 139–45.

3018 Arnold-Forster, W. **The Atlantic Charter,** *Political Quarterly*, XIII (April–June 1942), 144–59.

3019 Benson, Oliver. **United Nations Diplomatic Front,** *Current History*, New Series, II (June 1942), 241–46.

3020 Bregman, Alexander. **Appeasement Charter? A Study of the Dumbarton Oaks Proposals.** London, Love, 1945. 74 p.

3021 Chase, Eugene P. **The United Nations in Action.** New York, McGraw-Hill, 1950.
Chapter II.

3022 Comstock, Alzada. **Bretton Woods and After,** *Current History*, New Series, VII (September 1944), 161–66.

3023 — —. **Reconstruction and World Exchange,** *Current History*, New Series, VII (August 1944), 81–88.

3024 Cooper, John C. **The Bermuda Plan: World Pattern for Air Transport,** *Foreign Affairs*, XXV (October 1946), 59–71.

3025 Dean, Vera Micheles. **The Four Cornerstones of Peace.** New York, McGraw-Hill, 1946. 267 p.

Part D. — United Nations System

3026 Eagleton, Clyde. **The Atlantic Charter,** *World Affairs,* VII (January 1942), 172–82.

3027 Ellis, Ellen D. **The Great Debate Is On,** *Current History,* New Series VIII, (April 1945), 299–309.

3028 Fay, Sidney B. **The Dumbarton Oaks Conference,** *Current History,* New Series, VII (October 1944), 257–64.

3029 — —. **The Meaning of the Moscow Conference,** *Current History,* New Series, V (December 1943), 289–94.

3030 — —. **Moscow, Cairo and Teheran,** *Current History,* New Series, VI (February 1944), 97–103.

3031 Fisher, Allan G. B. **International Institutions in a World of Sovereign States,** *Political Science Quarterly,* LIX (March 1944), 1–14.

   Discusses structure and functions of proposed United Nations agencies. Concerned with historical comparisons between those and previous League of Nations ones. Notes conflict between notion of nation-state and internationalism.

3032 Freeman, Harrop A. **Principles and Practice from Delaware to Dumbarton Oaks.** Philadelphia, Pacifist Research Bureau, 1945. 63 p.

3033 Harley, J. Eugene. **Dumbarton Oaks and World Security,** *World Affairs Quarterly,* XV (October 1944), 234–52.

3034 Holborn, Louise W. (ed.). **War and Peace Aims of the United Nations.** Boston, World Peace Foundation, 1943–48. 2 vols.

3035 Hull, Cordell. **The Memoirs of Cordell Hull.** New York, Macmillan, 1948. 2 vols.

   See especially Volume II, pp. 1625–1742, on the emergence of the United Nations

Part D. — United Nations System

3036 Johnsen, Julia E. (comp.). **The "Eight Points" of Post-War World Reorganization.** New York, Wilson, 1942. 126 p.

Extensive bibliography.

3037 Kelsen, Hans. **The Old and the New League: The Covenant and the Dumbarton Oaks Proposals,** *American Journal of International Law,* XXXIX (January 1945), 45—83.

3038 Leonard, L. Larry. **International Organization.** New York, McGraw-Hill, 1951.

Chapter XIX.

3039 Loewenstein, Karl. **The Serpent in Dumbarton Oaks,** *Current History,* New Series, VIII (April 1945), 310—16.

3040 McKelvey, Raymond D. **The Big Power Conferences,** *Institute of World Affairs Proceedings,* XXI (1945), 143—48.

3041 Mason, Edward S. **Reflections on the Moscow Conference,** *International Organization,* I (September 1947), 475—87.

3042 Nash, Philip C. **Spring Leaves on Dumbarton Oaks,** *Annals of the American Academy of Political and Social Science,* CCXL (July 1945), 11—19.

3043 O., A. N. **Impressions of the Moscow Conference,** *World Today,* New Series, III (June 1947), 248—54.

3044 Opie, Redvers; Ballantine, Joseph W.; Birdsall, Paul; Muther, Jeannette E.; and Thurber, Clarence E. **The Search for Peace Settlements.** Washington, Brookings, 1951.

Chapter III.

3045 Pasvolsky, Leo. **Dumbarton Oaks Proposals for Economic and Social Cooperation,** *International Conciliation,* CDIX, Section Two (March 1945), 201—208.

Part D. — United Nations System

3046 Redmond, D. G. **Quebec and Woodrow Wilson,** *Current History,* New Series, V (October 1943), 97—102.

3047 Riddell, Walter A. **World Security by Conference.** Toronto, Ryerson, 1947.

Part II, Chapter I.

3048 Russell, Ruth B. and Mather, Jeanette E. **A History of the United Nations Charter: The Role of the United States, 1940—45.** Washington, Brookings, 1958. 1,140 p.

3049 Schwarzenberger, Georg. **Power Politics.** 3d ed. London, Stevens, 1964.

Chapter XIX.

3050 Sherwood, Robert E. **Roosevelt and Hopkins.** Rev. ed. New York, Harper, 1950. 779 p.

3051 Summers, Robert E. (comp.). **Dumbarton Oaks.** New York, H. W. Wilson, 1945. 267 p.

Excerpts from various writings and documents with a short bibliography.

3052 Thompson, David. **The Undertones of Dumbarton Oaks,** *World Affairs,* XI (April 1945), 12—19.

3053 Traynor, Elisabeth. **International Monetary and Financial Conferences in the Interwar Period.** Washington, Catholic University of America Press, 1949. ix + 196 p.

3054 Truman, Harry S. **Memoirs.** 1st ed. Garden City, Doubleday, 1955—56. 2 vols.

3055 Van Zandt, J. Parker. **The Chicago Civil Aviation Conference — With Texts of Convention on International Civil Aviation and International Air Transport Agreement,** *Foreign Policy Reports,* XX (February 15, 1945), 290—308.

Part D. — United Nations System

3056 Walters, Francis P. **Dumbarton Oaks and the League: Some Points of Comparison,** *International Affairs,* XXI (April 1945), 141–54.

3057 Warner, Edward. **The Chicago Air Conference,** *Foreign Affairs,* XXIII (April 1945), 406–21.

3058 Woolf, Leonard. **The United Nations,** *Political Quarterly,* XVI (January–March 1945), 12–20.

Discusses Dumbarton Oaks proposals.

3059 Zimmern, Alfred E. **The American Road to World Peace.** New York, Dutton, 1953.

Section IX.

2.3 WARTIME COLLABORATIVE MACHINERY

See also C 8.2.4.

3060 A., A. S. **The European Coal Organization: International Cooperation in Practice,** *World Today,* New Series, II (March 1946), 97–105.

3061 Blumenson, M. **Politics and the Military in the Liberation of Paris,** *Yale Review,* L (December 1960), 271–86.

3062 Gilchrist, Huntington. **Political Disputes: Dumbarton Oaks and the Experience of the League of Nations,** *Academy of Political Science Proceedings,* XXI (May 1945), 404–14.

3063 Hall, H. Duncan. **The Combined Raw Materials Board,** *British Yearbook of International Law,* XXI (1944), 168–71.

3064 Leighton, Richard M. **Allied Unity of Command in the Second World War: A Study in Regional Organization,** *Political Science Quarterly,* LXVII (September 1952), 339–425.

3065 Maurice, Frederick. **Unity of Policy Among Allies,** *Foreign Affairs,* XXI (January 1943), 322–30.

3066 Pogue, Forrest C. **The Supreme Allied Command in Northern Europe, 1944–1945: Essays in History and International Relations in Honor of George Hubbard Blakeslee,** Dwight E. Lee and George E. McReynolds (eds.). Worcester, Mass., Clark University Press, 1949, pp. 171–92.

3067 Rosen, S. McKee. **Combined Boards of the Second World War: An Experiment in International Administration.** New York, Columbia University Press, 1951. 288 p.

3068 Samuels, Nathaniel. **The European Coal Organization,** *Foreign Affairs,* XXVI (July 1948), 728–36.

3069 Tyler, J. E. **Military Aspects of Anglo-French Union,** *World Affairs,* VI (July 1940), 50–56.

2.4 SAN FRANCISCO CONFERENCE (1945)

3070 Amerasinghe, C. F. **The Use of Armed Force by the United Nations in the Charter Travaux Preparatoires,** *Indian Journal of International Law,* V (July 1965), 305–33.

Charter Travaux Preparatoires consist of materials connected with the making of the charter, such as preliminary exchanges of notes between great powers and records of proceedings at the Conference on International Organization.

3071 Baker, Alonzo L. **One Month of San Francisco,** *World Affairs Quarterly,* XVI (July 1945), 155–61.

3072 Benns, F. Lee. **The Two Paris Peace Conferences of the Twentieth Century,** *Essays in History and International Relations in Honor of George Hubbard Blakeslee,* Dwight E. Lee and George E. McReynolds (eds.). Worcester, Mass., Clark University Press, 1949, pp. 153–70.

Part D. — *United Nations System*

3073 Chase, Eugene P. **The United Nations in Action.** New York, McGraw-Hill, 1950.

Chapters III, IV.

3074 Dean, Vera Micheles. **The San Francisco Conference — With Text of Charter,** *Foreign Policy Reports,* XXI (July 15, 1945), 110—36.

3075 E., D. P. **International Economic and Social Co-operation: The San Francisco Proposals,** *World Today,* New Series, I (November 1945), 230—40.

3076 Fox, William T. R. **The Super-Powers at San Francisco,** *Review of Politics,* VIII (January 1946), 115—27.

3077 Gilchrist, Huntington. **Colonial Question at the San Francisco Conference,** *American Political Science Review,* XXXIX (October 1945) 982—92.

3078 Goodrich, Leland M. **The United Nations.** New York, Crowell, 1963.

Chapter II.

3079 Goodspeed, Stephen S. **The Nature and Function of International Organization.** New York, Oxford University Press, 1963.

Chapter IV.

3080 K., D. **The Trusteeship Proposals at San Francisco,** *World Today,* New Series, I (August 1945), 76—86.

3081 Kirk, Grayson and Chamberlain, Lawrence. **The Organization of the San Francisco Conference,** *Political Science Quarterly,* LX (September 1945), 321—42.

3082 Leonard, L. Larry. **International Organization.** New York, McGraw-Hill, 1951.

Chapter III.

8083 Morgenthau, Hans J. (ed.). **Peace, Security, and the United Nations.** Chicago, University of Chicago Press, 1946. 133 p.

3084 Moseley, Philip E. **Peace-Making, 1946,** *International Organization,* I (February 1947), 22—32.

3085 Plaza, Galo. **Latin America's Contribution to the United Nations Organization,** *International Conciliation,* CDXIX (March 1946), 150—57.

3086 Polyzoides, A. T. **From League to Charter: The Story of San Francisco,** *World Affairs Quarterly,* XVI (July 1945), 173—83.

3087 — —. **The United Nations Conference Meets in San Francisco,** *World Affairs Quarterly,* XVI (April 1945), 65—77.

3088 Starr, Mark. **Labor Issues at San Francisco,** *Current History,* New Series, VIII (June 1945), 517—21.

3089 Thomson, David, Meyer, E., and Briggs, A. **Patterns of Peacemaking.** New York, Oxford University Press, 1946. vii + 399 p.

3090 Vandenbosch, Amry and Hogan, Willard N. **Toward World Order.** New York, McGraw-Hill, 1963.

Chapter IV.

2.5 INSTITUTIONS TO EXECUTE THE PEACE

3091 Appleman, John Alan. **Military Tribunals and International Crimes.** Indianapolis, Bobbs-Merrill, 1954. 421 p.

Part D. — United Nations System

3092 Balfour, Michael and Mair, John. **Four-Power Control in Germany and Austria: 1945–1946.** New York, Oxford University Press, 1956. 390 p.

3093 Birkett, Justice. **International Legal Theories Evolved at Nuremberg,** *International Affairs,* XXIII (July 1947), 317–25.

3094 Blakeslee, George H. **The Establishment of the Far Eastern Commission,** *International Organization,* V (August 1951), 499–514.

3095 Borton, Hugh. **United States Occupation Policies in Japan Since Surrender,** *Political Science Quarterly,* LXII (June 1947), 250–57.

3096 Doman, Nicholas. **Political Consequences of the Nuremberg Trial,** *Annals of the American Academy of Political and Social Science,* CCXLVI (July 1946), 81–90.

3097 Dull, Paul S. and Umemura, Michael T. **The Tokyo Trials: A Functional Index to the Proceedings of the International Military Tribunal for the Far East.** Ann Arbor, University of Michigan Press, 1957. vi + 94 p.

3098 Freymond, Jacques. **The Saar Conflict, 1945–1955.** Foreword by John Goormaghtigh. New York, Praeger, 1961. xxviii + 395 p.

3099 Friedmann, W. **The Allied Military Government of Germany.** London, Stevens, 1947. 362 p.

3100 Friters, G. M. **The International Authority for the Ruhr,** *World Affairs,* New Series, III (October 1949), 378–89.

3101 G., I. L. **The Allied Commission for Austria,** *World Today,* New Series, I (November 1945), 204–13.

3102 Glueck, Sheldon. **The Nuremberg Trial and Aggressive War.** New York, Knopf, 1946. xv + 121 p.

3103 Green, L. C. **Berlin and the United Nations,** *World Affairs*, New Series, III (January 1949), 23—42.

3104 H., H. **Allied Administration in Germany,** *World Today*, New Series, IV (April 1948), 160—72.

3105 Harris, Charles R. S. **Allied Military Administration of Italy, 1943—1945.** London, H. M. Stationery Office, 1957. xv + 479 p.

3106 Hirsch, Felix. **Lessons of Nuremberg,** *Current History*, New Series, XI (October 1946), 312—18.

3107 Holborn, Hajo. **American Military Government: Its Organization and Politics.** Washington, Infantry Journal Press, 1947. xiii + 243 p.

3108 Jackson, Robert H. **The Nürnberg Case.** New York, Knopf, 1947. xviii + 268 p.

3109 Jackson, William Eldred. **Putting the Nuremberg Law to Work,** *Foreign Affairs*, XXV (July 1947), 550—65.

3110 Kaeckenbeeck, H. E. Georges. **The International Authority for the Ruhr and the Schuman Plan,** *Transactions* (Grotius Society), XXXVII (1951), 4—13.

Comments by Green, Goitein, Elkin, Jaffé, Loewenfeld, Moore, Adamkiewicz, Zaslawski.

3111 Levy, Albert G. D. **The Law and Procedure of War Crime Trials,** *American Political Science Review*, XXXVII (December 1943), 1052—81.

3112 Lozier, Marion E. **Nuremberg: A Reappraisal,** *Columbia Journal of Transnational Law,* II (Fall 1962), 22–33.

3113 Martin, Edwin M. **The Allied Occupation of Japan.** Stanford, Stanford University Press, 1948. xvi + 155 p.

3114 Maugham, Viscount. **U.N.O. and War Crimes.** London, Murray, 1951. 143 p.

3115 Muhlen, N. **America and American Occupation in German Eyes,** *Annals of the American Academy of Political and Social Science,* CCXCV (September 1954), 52–61.

3116 Radin, Max. **Justice at Nuremberg,** *Foreign Affairs,* XXIV (April 1946), 369–84.

3117 Schwarzenberger, G. **The Judgment of Nuremberg,** *Year Book of World Affairs,* II (1948), 94–124.

3118 Sebald, William J. and Brines, Russell. **With MacArthur in Japan: A Personal History of the Occupation.** New York, Norton, 1965. 318 p.

3119 Stimson, Henry L. **The Nuremberg Trial: Landmark in Law,** *Foreign Affairs,* XXV (January 1947), 179–89.

3120 Stratton, Samuel S. **The Far Eastern Commission,** *International Organization,* II (February 1948), 1–18.

3121 Taylor, Philip H. and Braibanti, Ralph J. D. **Administration of Occupied Areas: A Study Guide.** Syracuse, Syracuse University Press, 1948. iv + 111 p.

Part D. — United Nations System

3122 W., J. E. and L., H. G. **The Breakdown of Four-Power Rule in Berlin,** *World Today,* New Series, IV (August 1948), 322—31.

3123 Wechsler, Herbert. **The Issues of the Nuremberg Trial,** *Political Science Quarterly,* LXII (March 1947), 11—26.

3124 Wilcox, Francis O. **The United Nations and the Peace Treaties,** *Annals of the American Academy of Political and Social Science,* CCLVII (May 1948), 175—83.

3125 Woetzel, Robert K. **The Nuremberg Trials in International Law.** London, Stevens, 1960. 287 p.

3126 — —. **The Nuremberg Trials in International Law: With a Postscript on the Eichmann Case.** New York, Praeger, 1962. 317 p.

3127 Wright, Quincy. **The Nuremberg Trial,** *Annals of the American Academy of Political and Social Science,* CCXLVI (July 1946), 72—80.

3128 Ydit, Méir. **Internationalised Territories from the "Free City of Cracow" to the "Free City of Berlin."** Leyden, Sythoff, 1961. 323 p.

3. GENERAL COMMENTARIES AND EVALUATIONS

See also A 4.3.

3129 Ames, Herbert B. **Seven Years with the League of Nations.** New York, Herald-Nathan, 1928, 62 p.

3130 Anderson, Violet (ed.). **The United Nations Today and Tomorrow.** Boston, Humphries, 1943. 166 p.

3131 Armstrong, Hamilton Fish. **The Calculated Risk.** New York, Macmillan, 1947. xii + 68 p.

3132 — —. **Coalition for Peace,** *Foreign Affairs,* XXVII (October 1948), 1–16.

3133 — —. **UN on Trial,** *Foreign Affairs,* XXXIX (April 1961), 388–415.

3134 Attlee, C. R **The Future of the United Nations.** New Delhi, Indian Council for Cultural Relations, 1961. 29 p.

3135 Atwater, Elton; Butz, William; Forster, Kent; and Riemer, Neal. **World Affairs.** New York, Appleton-Century-Crofts, 1958.
Chapter XIII.

3136 Barron, Bryton. **Dream Becomes a Nightmare: The UN Today.** Springfield, Virginia, Crestwood, 1964. 188 p.

3137 Bell, Coral. **The United Nations and the West,** *International Affairs,* XXIX (October 1953), 464–72.

3138 Beloff, Max. **Problems of International Government,** *Year Book of World Affairs,* VIII (1954), 1–20.

3139 Berkes, Ross N. **Can We Count on the United Nations?** *Current History,* XXXVIII (June 1960), 321–25.

3140 — —. **The New Frontier in the U.N.,** *Current History,* XLII (January 1962), 43–48.

3141 — —. **The United Nations and the Cold War Conflict,** *Current History,* New Series, XXXVII (October 1959), 228–32.

3142 Berle, A. A., Jr. **Our Best Guarantee of National Security,** *Reporter,* XI (December 2, 1954), 10–13.

3143 Bloomfield, Lincoln P. **The New Diplomacy in the United Nations,** *The United States and The United Nations,* Francis O. Wilcox and H. Field Haviland, Jr. (eds.). Baltimore, Johns Hopkins Press, 1961, pp. 49–74.

3144 Boasson, Charles. **International Organization Examined and Appraised,** *World Politics,* VIII (July 1956), 579–87.

3145 Bogardus, Emory S. **The Sociology of a Structured Peace,** *Sociology and Social Research,* XLIV (May-June 1960), 352–56.

3146 Bokhari, Ahmed S. **Parliaments, Priests and Prophets,** *Foreign Affairs,* XXXV (April 1957).

3147 Boyd, Andrew K. H. **United Nations: Piety, Myth and Truth.** Harmondsworth, Penguin, 1964. 200 p.

Part D. — *United Nations System*

3148 — —. **The Unknown United Nations,** *International Journal,* XIX (Spring, 1964), 202–12.

3149 Boyd, Andrew and Graecen, Robert. **World Front, 1950: A Survey of the United Nations at Work.** London, United Nations Association, 1950. 63 p.

3150 Brackett, Russell D. **Pathways to Peace.** Minneapolis, Denison, 1965.
Chapter III.

3151 Brohi, A. K. **The Future of the United Nations,** *Pakistan Horizon,* IX (March 1956), 3–10.

3152 Bryson, Lyman, Finkelstein, Louis, Lasswell, Harold D., and MacIver, R. M. (eds.). **Foundations of World Organization: A Political and Cultural Appraisal.** New York, Harper, 1952. xiv + 498 p.

3153 Burnham, James. **What is the Purpose of the United Nations?** *Annals of the American Academy of Political and Social Science,* CCLII (July 1947), 1–10.

3154 Carnegie Endowment for International Peace (ed.). **Perspectives on Peace 1910–1960.** New York, Praeger, 1960. viii + 202 p.

3155 Carpenter, Francis W. **Men in Glass Houses.** New York, McBride, 1951. 300 p.

3156 Carr, William G. **One World in the Making: The United Nations.** Boston, Ginn, 1946. v + 100 p.

3157 Castren, Erik. **Some Aspects of the Future Activity of the United Nations,** *Indian Journal of International Law,* I (1960–61), 178–83.

3158 Chaumont, Charles. **A French View on Security Through International Organization,** *International Organization,* IV (May 1950), 236—46.

3159 Cherwell, Viscount. **The United Nations Organization: In Its Present Form It Cannot Work,** *The United Nations: The Continuing Debate,* Charles A. McClelland (ed.). San Francisco, Chandler, 1960, pp. 23—31.

A speech delivered in the House of Lords, London, December 11, 1956.

3160 Christol, Carl Q. **Adjusting to the New United Nations,** *Institute of World Affairs Proceedings,* XXXVIII (1962), 248—61.

3161 Clark, William. **New Forces in the United Nations,** *International Affairs,* XXXVI (July 1960), 322—29.

3162 Claude, Inis L., Jr. **Conflict, Cooperation, and Consensus — The Role of the U.N.: A Review,** *Journal of Conflict Resolution,* VI (June 1962), 166—68.

3163 — —. **The Containment and Resolution of Disputes,** *The United States and the United Nations,* Francis O. Wilcox and H. Field Haviland, Jr. (eds.). Baltimore, Johns Hopkins Press, 1961, pp. 101—28.

3164 — —. **Implications and Questions for the Future,** *International Organization,* XIX (Summer, 1965), 835—46.

3165 Cleveland, Harlan. **The Capacities of the United Nations,** *The United States and the United Nations,* Francis O. Wilcox and H. Field Haviland, Jr. (eds.). Baltimore, Johns Hopkins Press, 1961, pp. 129—50.

3166 — —. **The Evolution of Rising Responsibility,** *International Organization,* XIX (Summer, 1965), 828—34.

3167 — —. **The Road Around Stalemate,** *Foreign Affairs,* XL (October 1961), 28—38.

Part D. — *United Nations System*

3168 Cohen, Benjamin A. **The United Nations and the Individual,** *Journal of International Affairs*, IX, 2 (1955), 90—94.

3169 Comay, Joan. **The UN in Action.** New York, Macmillan, 1965. 150 p.

3170 Commission to Study the Organization of Peace. **Peaceful Coexistence: A New Challenge to the United Nations.** New York, Commission to Study the Organization of Peace, 1960. 47 p.

Contains the Commission's twelfth report.

3171 — —. **Strengthening the United Nations.** New York, Harper, 1957. 276 p.

Contains the tenth report of the Commission and reports of the Special Study Committees.

3172 Cordier, Andrew W. and Foote, Wilder (eds.). **The Quest for Peace: The Dag Hammarskjold Memorial Lectures.** New York, Columbia University Press, 1965. xxiv + 310 p.

3173 Courtney, Kathleen D. **The United Nations in a Divided World,** *International Affairs*, XXV (April 1949), 168—74.

Comment by Viscount Cecil of Chelwood.

3174 Dawson, Kenneth H. **The United Nations in a Disunited World,** *World Politics*, VI (October 1953), 209—35.

3175 Dean, Vera M. **The U.N. Today.** New York, Holt, Rinehart and Winston, 1965. 112 p.

3176 Dhadwal, N. S. **United Nations at Work,** *Indian Journal of Political Science*, XIII (April 1952), 6—15.

3177 Dixon, Pierson. **Diplomacy at the United Nations,** *International Relations*, I (October 1958), 457—66.

Part D. — *United Nations System*

3178 Dolivet, Louis. **The United Nations Is Here to Stay**, *Federal World Government*, Julia E. Johnson (ed.). New York, Wilson, 1948, pp. 192–99.

Reprinted from *Chamber of Commerce Monthly Bulletin* (New York), April 1948.

3179 Douglas, Helen Gahagan. **Impressions of the United Nations**, *Annals of the American Academy of Political and Social Science*, CCLII (July 1947), 45–52.

3180 Drury, Allen. **A Shade of Difference.** Garden City, Doubleday, 1962. 603 p.

A novel concerning the United Nations.

3181 Dulles, Allen W. and Lamb, Beatrice P. **The United Nations: An Appraisal.** With a statement by Edward R. Stettinius, Jr. New York, Foreign Policy Association, 1946. 96 p.

3182 Dulles, John Foster. **The Future of the United Nations**, *International Conciliation*, CDXLV (November 1948), 579–90.

3183 Eagleton, Clyde. **The Forces That Shape Our Future.** New York, Oxford University Press, 1945. 200 p.

3184 ― ―. **The United Nations: Aims and Structure**, *Yale Law Journal*, LV (August 1946), 974–96.

3185 ― ―. **The United Nations: Policies That Backfired**, *Current History*, New Series, XXII (January 1952), 26–29.

3186 ― ―. **What Shall We Do with the United Nations?** *World Affairs Quarterly*, XXV (January 1955), 361–84.

3187 Eggleston, Frederic. **The United Nations As an Instrument for Preserving Peace**, *Paths to Peace*, Victor H. Wallace (ed.). Melbourne, Melbourne University Press, 1957, pp. 317–35.

Part D. — United Nations System

3188 Elliott, William Y. **A Time for Peace?** *Virginia Quarterly Review,* XXII (Spring, 1946), 161–178.

3189 Evatt, Herbert V. **The Task of Nations.** New York, Duell, Sloan and Pearce, 1949. 279 p.

3190 — —. **The United Nations.** Cambridge, Harvard University Press, 1948. 154 p.

3191 Feller, Abraham H. **United Nations and World Community.** Boston, Little, Brown, 1953. 153 p.

3192 — —. **The United Nations: Appraisal and Forecast,** *Zeitschrift für Ausländisches Öffentliches Recht und Völkerrecht,* XIII (February 1950), 57–66.

3193 Fenichell, Stephen S. **The United Nations: Design for Peace.** New York, Holt, Rinehart and Winston, 1960. 144 p.

3194 Finkelstein, Lawrence S. **The United Nations: Then and Now,** *International Organization,* XIX (Summer, 1965), 367–93.

3195 Forsyth, W. D. **Whither U.N.?** *Australian Journal of Politics and History,* IX (May 1963), 39–58.

3196 Fouques-Duparc, Jacques. **A European Point of View on the United Nations,** *International Conciliation,* CDXLIII (September 1948), 453–57.

3197 Fox, William T. R. **The United Nations in the Era of Total Diplomacy,** *International Organization,* V (May 1951), 265–73.

3198 Frye, William R. **Press Coverage of the UN,** *International Organization,* X (May 1956), 276–81.

3199 Fuchs, Lawrence H. **Nations In the Future: Organization for Survival,** *Western Political Quarterly,* IX (March 1956), 11—20.

3200 Goldstein, Walter. **The U.N. and Its Detractors,** *Bulletin of the Atomic Scientists,* XVIII (April 1962), 12—17.

3201 Goodrich, Leland M. **International Organization,** *World Politics,* III (April 1951), 408—16.

3202 — —. **The United Nations: Its Records of Achievement,** *Foreign Policy Reports,* XXIII (September 15, 1947), 162—72.

3203 Goodwin, Geoffrey. L. **The Expanding United Nations: Diplomatic Pressures and Techniques,** *International Affairs,* XXXVII (April 1961), 170—80.

3204 — —. **The Political Role of the United Nations: Some British Views,** *International Organization,* XV (Autumn, 1961), 581—602.

3205 — —. **The Role of the United Nations in World Affairs,** *International Affairs,* XXXIV (January 1958), 25—37.

3206 Gordenker, Leon. **The Political Process in International Organizations,** *World Politics,* XIV (April 1962), 519—31.

3207 Green, L. C. **Recent Issues at Lake Success,** *World Affairs,* New Series, I (October 1947), 340—56.

3208 Gross, Ernest A. **Shifting Institutional Pattern of the United Nations,** *The United States and the United Nations,* Francis O. Wilcox and H. Field Haviland, Jr. (eds.). Baltimore, Johns Hopkins Press, 1961, pp. 75—100.

Part D. — United Nations System

3209 — —. **United Nations Record and United Nations Dilemma,** *The United Nations: The Continuing Debate*, Charles A. McClelland (ed.). San Francisco, Chandler, 1960, pp. 97—105.

Reprinted from *New York Times Magazine*, September 21, 1958, pp. 12ff.

3210 Hammarskjöld, Dag. **Markings,** Leif Sjobert and W. H. Auden (trans.). Foreword by W. H. Auden. New York, Knopf, 1964. xxiii + 221 p.

3211 — —. **The United Nations and the Political Scientist,** *American Political Science Review*, XLVII (December 1953), 975—79.

3212 — —. **The United Nations in the Modern World,** *Journal of International Affairs*, IX, 2 (1955), 7—11.

3213 Harley, J. Eugene. **Achievements of the United Nations,** *World Affairs Quarterly*, XXII (October 1951), 280—95.

3214 Harris, Robert E. G. **The Outlook for UNO,** *World Affairs Quarterly*, XVII (April 1946), 9—24.

3215 Henkin, Louis. **The United Nations and Its Supporters: A Self-Examination,** *Political Science Quarterly*, LXXVIII (December 1963), 504—36.

3216 Hinsley, Francis H. **Power and the Pursuit of Peace.** Cambridge, Cambridge University Press, 1963.

Chapter XVI.

3217 Hoffmann, Stanley. **An Evaluation of the U. N.,** *Ohio State Law Journal*, XXII (Summer 1961), 472—94.

3218 Holcombe, Arthur N. **The Role of Politics in the Organization of Peace,** *Organizing Peace in the Nuclear Age*, Commission to Study the Organization of Peace (ed.). New York, New York University Press, 1959, pp. 50—116.

3219 Hula, Eric. **Four Years of the United Nations,** *Social Research,* XVI (December 1949), 395—415.

3220 — —. **The United Nations in Crisis,** *Social Research,* XXVII (Winter, 1960), 387—420.

3221 Huszar, George B. de (ed.). **Persistent International Issues.** New York, Harper, 1947. 62 p.

3222 Huth, Arno G. **International Organizations and Conferences — Experiences and Lessons,** *Foundations of World Organization,* Lyman Bryson, Louis Finkelstein, Harold D. Lasswell, and R. M. MacIver (eds.). New York, Harper, 1950, pp. 261—80.

3223 Hyder, Khurshid. **United Nations — Problems and Prospects,** *Pakistan Horizon,* XVII, 4 (1964), 329—41.

3224 Ibrahim, A. Rashid. **The United Nations: An Assessment,** *Pakistan Horizon,* XIV, 2 (1961), 112—20.

3225 Jackson, Elmore. **The Future Development of the United Nations: Some Suggestions for Research,** *Journal of Conflict Resolution,* V (June 1961), 119—27.

3226 Jaspers, Karl. **The Future of Mankind,** E. B. Ashton (trans.). Chicago, University of Chicago Press, 1961.
Chapter IX.

3227 Jászi, Oscar. **The Political Organization of the Future,** *Toward International Organization,* Howard Robinson, Harvey Alden Wooster, Max Lerner, George Fielding Eliot, Jacob Viner, Quincy Wright, William Ernest Hocking, Oscar Jászi. New York, Harper, 1942, pp. 190—217.

Part D. — *United Nations System*

3228 Jebb, Gladwyn. **The Free World and the United Nations,** *Foreign Affairs*, XXI (April 1953), 382–91.

3229 Jones, Goronwy J. **Challenge to the Peacemakers.** London, Wingate, 1951. 173 p.

3230 Jordan, William M. **Concepts and Realities in International Political Organization,** *International Organization*, XI (Autumn, 1957), 587–96.

3231 Joyce, J. A. **The Story of International Cooperation.** New York, Watts, 1964.

Chapter X.

3232 Katz-Suchy, Juliusz. **One World Through the United Nations,** *Annals of the American Academy of Political and Social Science*, CCLVIII (July 1948), 90–100.

3233 Kenworthy, L. S. **Telling the UN Story: New Approaches to Teaching About the UN and Its Related Agencies.** Dobbs Ferry, Oceana, 1963. 166 p.

3234 Kertesz, Stephen D. **Diplomacy in the Atomic Age: II,** *Review of Politics*, XXI (April 1959), 357–88.

3235 Kintner, William R. **The United Nations Record of Handling Major Disputes,** *The United States and the United Nations*, Franz B. Gross (ed.). Norman, University of Oklahoma Press, 1964, pp. 87–124.

3236 Kirk, Grayson L. **The United Nations and Maintaining Peace,** *Academy of Political Science Proceedings*, XXII (January 1947), 110–19.

3237 van Kleffens, Eelco N. **The United Nations and Some Main Trends of Our Time,** *Annals of the American Academy of Political and Social Science*, CCLII (July 1947), 71–77.

3238 Koo, V. K .Wellington. **Basic Problems of the United Nations,** *Annals of the American Academy of Political and Social Science,* CCLII (July 1947), 78—83.

3239 Larson, Arthur. **Common Sense and the United Nations,** *Saturday Review,* XLV (February 24, 1962), 17—20 ff.

3240 Lasswell, Harold D. **The Interrelations of World Organization and Society,** *Yale Law Journal,* LV (August 1946), 889—909.

3241 Lawson, Ruth C. **The United Nations: Dilemmas and Discords,** *Current History,* New Series, XXIV (February 1953), 205—209.

3242 — —. **United Nations: II, The Influence of Power Politics,** *Current History,* New Series, XIV (January 1948), 20—26.

3243 — —. **The United Nations: III, Brighter Hopes?** *Current History,* New Series, XVII (July 1949), 11—14.

3244 — —. **The United Nations: II, "Major Disputes and Minor Agreements,"** *Current History,* New Series, XVI (February 1949), 79—82.

3245 Lee, Marc J. **The United Nations and World Realities.** Oxford, Pergamon, 1965. viii + 255 p.

3246 L'Huillier, Fernand. **L'organisation des Nations Unies,** *Les institutions intrenationales et transnationales,* Fernand L'Huillier (ed.). Paris, Presses Universitaires, 1961, pp. 15—27.

3247 Lie, Trygve. **In the Cause of Peace: Seven Years in the United Nations.** New York, Macmillan, 1954. xiii + 473 p.

Part D. — *United Nations System*

3248 Lie, Trygve; Evatt, Herbert V.; Malik, Charles; Roosevelt, Eleanor; Bodet, Jaime Torres; Chisholm, Brock; Boyd-Orr, John; Bunche, Ralph; Cohen, Benjamin; Rajchman, Ludwick; and Romulo, Carlos P. **Peace on Earth.** Introduction by Robert E. Sherwood. New York, Hermitage, 1949. 251 p.

3249 Lodge, H. C. **The Task of Waging Peace: The UN Balance Sheet After Eleven Years,** *American Bar Association Journal*, XLII (November 1956), 1027–31.

3250 Luns, J. M. A. H. **Town Meeting of the World,** *Pakistan Horizon*, VI (September 1953), 93–99.

3251 McGuire, Paul. **Experiment in World Order.** New York, Morrow, 1948. 412 p.

3252 McHenry, Dean E. **The United Nations After Three Years,** *Institute of World Affairs Proceedings*, XXV (1949), 113–18.

3253 Mackay, R. W. G. **NATO and U. N.,** *Annals of the American Academy of Political and Social Science*, CCLXXXVIII (July 1953), 119–25.

3254 Malik, Charles. **Man in the Struggle for Peace.** New York, Harper and Row, 1963. 242 p.

3255 Mander, Linden A. **The United Nations in Action Today,** *World Affairs Quarterly*, XIX (April 1948), 25–32.

Published concurrently in the *Institute of World Affairs Proceedings*.

3256 Manly, Chesly. **The UN Record: Ten Fateful Years for America.** Chicago, Regnery, 1955. 256 p.

3257 Meigs, Cornelia. **The Great Design: Men and Events in the United Nations from 1945 to 1963.** Boston, Little, Brown, 1965. 319 p.

3258 Meyer, Cord, Jr. **The United Nations Lacks Authority and Power,** *Federal World Government,* Julia E. Johnsen (ed.). New York, Wilson, 1948, pp. 86–94.

3259 Moore, Bernard. **The Second Lesson: Seven Years at the United Nations.** London, Macmillan, 1957. ix + 228 p.

3260 Moore, Harry H. **The United Nations, Survival or Suicide,** Harry H. Moore (ed.). New York, Harper, 1948, pp. 105–14.

3261 Moore, Raymond A., Jr. **Introduction,** *The United Nations Reconsidered,* Raymond A. Moore, Jr. (ed.). Columbia, University of South Carolina Press, 1963, pp. 1–24.

3262 — —. (ed.). **The United Nations Reconsidered.** Columbia, University of South Carolina Press, 1963. 158 p.

3263 Morgenthau, Hans J. **Diplomacy,** *Yale Law Journal,* LV (August 1946), 1067–80.

3264 — —. **Politics Among Nations.** 14th ed. New York, Knopf, 1967.
Chapter XXVIII.

3265 — —. **The Yardstick of National Interest,** *Annals of the American Academy of Political and Social Science,* CCXCVI (November 1954), 77–84.

3266 Mudaliar, Ramaswami. **The United Nations and the World,** *Pakistan Horizon,* XIII, 4 (1960), 300–303.

3267 Munro, Leslie. **United Nations: Hope for a Divided World.** New York, Holt, 1960. 185 p.

3268 Nolde, O. F. **Power for Peace: The Way of the UN and the Will of the Christian People.** Philadelphia, Muhlenberg, 1946. 138 p.

3269 Nordskog, John Eric. **Cultural Lag and World Organization,** *Sociology and Social Research,* XXXI (September 1946), 21—29.

3270 Padelford, Norman J. and Goodrich, Leland M. (ed.). **The United Nations in the Balance.** New York, Praeger, 1965. x + 482 p.
Reprint of *International Organization,* Summer, 1965.

3271 Paparao, A. **United Nations at Work,** *Indian Journal of Political Science,* XIII (April 1952), 1—5.

3272 Pearson, Lester B. **The Present Position of the United Nations,** *International Relations,* I (October 1957), 324—38.

3273 Petersen, Keith S. **The Uses of the United Nations,** *Southwestern Social Science Quarterly,* XLIV (June 1963), 51—61.

3274 Polyzoides, A. T. **The United Nations in the Second Year,** *World Affairs Quarterly,* XVII (October 1946), 306—15.

3275 — —.**The United Nations in the Seventh Year,** *World Affairs Quarterly,* XXIII (October 1952), 294—303.

3276 — —. **The United Nations — Two Years After San Francisco,** *World Affairs Quarterly,* XVIII (April 1947), 83—96.

3277 Potter, Pitman B. **The Challenge of World Organization,** *Institute of World Affairs Proceedings,* XXII (1946), 164—74.

3278 Purcell, Royal. **United Nations Progress Report,** *World Affairs Quarterly,* each quarterly issue from January 1948 to January 1950.

Part D. — *United Nations System*

3279 Rabe, Olive. **United Nations Day.** New York, Crowell, 1965. n. p.

3280 Rappard, William E. **The United Nations As Viewed from Geneva,** *American Political Science Review*, XL (June 1946), 545—51.

3281 — —. **The United Nations from a European Point of View,** *Yale Law Journal*, LV (August 1946), 1036—48.

3282 Reed, Edward (ed.). **Pacem in Terris [Peace on Earth].** Preface by Robert M. Hutchins; introduction by John K. Jessup. New York, Pocket Books, 1965. xxv + 260 p.

Proceedings of an International Convocation on the Requirements of Peace sponsored by the Center for the Study of Democratic Institutions.

3283 Reiff, Henry. **Transition from League of Nations to United Nations.** Washington, U. S. Government Printing Office, 1946. 18 p.

3284 Rider, Fremont. **The Great Dilemma of World Organization.** New York, Reynal and Hitchcock, 1946. 85 p.

3285 Rienow, Robert. **Contemporary International Politics.** New York, Crowell, 1961.

Chapter XVI.

3286 Riggs, Robert E. **The United Nations As a Policy Instrument,** *Brigham Young University Studies*, II (Spring-Summer, 1960), 149—75.

3287 Robins, Dorothy B. **The U. N. Story: Toward a More Perfect World.** New York, American Association for the United Nations, 1950. 104 p.

3288 Robinson, Joseph William. **College Students Ask About the United Nations,** *World Affairs Quarterly*, XXIX (April 1958), 53—64.

Part D. — *United Nations System*

3289 Robinson, Jacob. **Metamorphosis of the United Nations,** *Recueil des Cours*, XCIV (1958), 497—589.

3290 Romulo, Carlos P. **New Aspects of Peace,** *Peace on Earth*, Trygve Lie, Herbert V. Evatt, Charles Malik, Eleanor Roosevelt, Jaime Torres Bodet, Brock Chisholm, John Boyd-Orr, Ralph Bunche, Benjamin Cohen, Ludwick Rajchman, and Carlos P. Romulo. New York, Hermitage, 1949, pp. 149—58.

3291 — —. **Strengthening the United Nations,** *Annals of the American Academy of Political and Social Science*, CCXCVI (November 1954), 14—19.

3292 Roosevelt, Eleanor, and Witt, William De. **U. N.: Today and Tomorrow.** New York, Harper, 1953. xiv + 236 p.

3293 Rosenthal, Abraham Michael. **The United Nations: Its Record and Prospects.** New York, Manhattan, 1953. 64 p.

3294 Rubin, Ronald. **The U. N. Correspondent,** *Western Political Quarterly*, XVII (December 1964), 615—31.

3295 Rusett, Alan W. de. **Reflections on the Expanding Membership of the United Nations,** *International Relations*, I (April 1958), 401—15.

3296 Sandler, Åke. **After the U. N. — What?** *Western Political Quarterly*, XVI (September 1963), Supplement, 28—30.

3297 Shotwell, James T. **The United Nations: Strengthening World Government,** *Current History*, New Series, XXII (January 1952), 30—34.

3298 Silvercruys, Baron. **The U. N.: Prospects of Immediate Realization,** *Annals of the American Academy of Political and Social Science*, CCXLVI (July 1946), 19—23.

Part D. — *United Nations System*

3299 Singh, Sushil Chandra. **The Difficulties of the United Nations,** *Political Scientist*, I (July-December 1964), 27—32.

3300 Soule, George. **U. N.'s Purpose: Another View,** *Annals of the American Academy of Political and Social Science*, CCLII (July 1947), 11—15.

3301 Soward, F. H. **The Changing Balance of Power in the United Nations,** *Political Quarterly*, XXVIII (October-December 1950), 316—27.

3302 Sparkman, John J. **The United Nations and the Future,** *American Society of International Law Proceedings*, XLIX (1955), 136—45.

3303 Stevenson, Adlai. **Looking Outward: Years of Crisis at the United Nations.** New York, Harper and Row, 1963. 295 p.

3304 Strausz-Hupé, Robert. **Introduction,** *The United States and the United Nations*, Franz B. Gross (ed.). Norman, University of Oklahoma Press, 1964, pp. 3—21.

3305 Sweetser, Arthur. **From the League to the United Nations,** *Annals of the American Academy of Political and Social Science*, CCXLVI (July 1946), 1—8.

3306 — —. **The United Nations and World Peace,** *Institute of World Affairs Proceedings*, XXIII (1946), 197—211.

3307 Theobald, Robert (ed.). **The UN and Its Future.** New York, Wilson, 1963. 190 p.
Collection of readings with a short bibliography.

3308 Thompson, Francis Willard. **The Warp Shows; The Weft Is Yet to Be,** *Institute of World Affairs Proceedings*, XXXIX (1963), 274—79.

3309 Thompson, Kenneth W. **The New Diplomacy and the Quest for Peace,** *International Organization,* XIX (Summer, 1965), 394—409.

3310 Tiner, Hugh M. **What Does the United Nations Mean to Us?** *World Affairs Quarterly,* XIX (January 1949), 398—402.

3311 Uhl, Alexander. **The Assault on the U. N.** Washington, Public Affairs Institute, 1953. iii + 35 p.

3312 UNESCO, Youth Institute. **World Peace and the United Nations.** Dobbs, Ferry, Oceana, 1962. 112 p.

3313 Van Wagenen, R. W. **Expanding the United Nations Community: Analysis and Proposition,** *Annals of the American Academy of Political and Social Science,* CCXCVI (November 1954), 93—96.

Comments by Heinrich von Brentano, Clement Davies, Rajeshwar Dayal, R. W. G. Mackay, Lester B. Pearson, and You Chan Yang.

3314 Varghese, Payappilly Itty. **International Law and Organization.** Lucknow, Eastern Book Company, 1952.

Chapters XXII, XXIII.

3315 Verdross, Alfred von. **Fundamental Principles of the United Nations Organisation,** *Recueil des Cours,* LXXXIII, (1953), 1—77.

3316 Wadsworth, J. J. **The United Nations: An American View of the World Organization,** *American Bar Association Journal,* XLIII (November 1957), 989—92.

3317 Watkins, James T. **United Nations — A Perspective for Americans,** *Institute of World Affairs Proceedings,* XXIV (1948), 174—80.

Part D. — United Nations System

3318 Watts, V. Orval. **The United Nations: Planned Tyranny.** Foreword by Clarence Manion. New York, Devin-Adair, 1955. 149 p.

3319 Webster, Charles. **The United Nations Reviewed,** *International Conciliation,* CDXLIII (September 1948), 441–52.

Comparison with the League of Nations.

3320 Wight, Martin. **The Power Struggle Within the United Nations,** *Institute of World Affairs Proceedings,* XXXII (1956), 247–59.

3321 Wilcox, Francis O. **The Soviet Challenge and the United Nations,** *The United Nations: The Continuing Debate,* Charles A. McClelland (ed.). San Francisco, Chandler, 1960, pp. 77–80.

Excerpts from a speech before the Annual Convention of the American Association of Junior Colleges at New York City on March 9, 1956.

3322 — —. **United Nations: Challenges of a New Age.** Washington, Government Printing Office, 1958. 18 p.

3323 — —. **The United Nations in an Interdependent World.** Washington, U. S. Government Printing Office, 1958. 20 p.

3324 — —. **The United Nations in the Mainstream of History,** *American Society of International Law Proceedings,* L (1956), 187–98.

3325 — —. **The United Nations: Its Issues and Responsibility.** Washington, U. S. Government Printing Office, 1957. 20 p.

3326 Windass, Stanley. **The Vitality of the United Nations,** *Yale Review,* LIII (June 1964), 481–96.

3327 Wood, Bryce. **The Court, the Charter and the Secretariat: Recent Books on International Organization,** *International Organization,* VII (February 1953), 35–46.

3328 Woodside, Wilson. **UN Progress?** *International Journal,* II (Spring, 1947), 118–23.

3329 Wortley, Ben Atkinson (ed.). **The United Nations: The First Ten Years.** New York, Oceana, 1957. 206 p.

3330 Wright, Quincy. **Accomplishments and Expectations of World Organization,** *Yale Law Journal,* LV (August 1946), 870–88.

3331 — —. **Making the United Nations Work,** *Review of Politics,* VII (October 1946), 528–32.

3332 — —. **Problems of Stability and Progress in International Relations.** Berkeley, University of California Press, 1954.

Chapters IV, V, XVIII.

3333 — —. **Recent Trends in the Evolution of the United Nations,** *International Organization,* II (November 1948), 617–31.

3334 Yalem, R. J. **Law, Organization, and Politics in the International Community,** *Washington University Law Quarterly,* II (April 1957), 110–17.

3335 Yearley, C. K., Jr. **Self-Interest and the UN,** *Commonweal,* LXXV (March 1962), 659–62.

Part D. — United Nations System

4. CHARTER

Changes in the Charter of the United Nations, in contrast to those of the League's Covenant, have been the result of a revision of procedural rules in the principal organs. No proposed amendments have obtained the consent of both the United States and the Soviet Union.

4.1 MEANING AND INTERPRETATIONS

3336 Aaronson, Michael. **Some Procedural Aspects of Article 2 (7),** *International Relations,* II (October 1960), 80–85.

3337 Anon. **International Responsibility for Colonial Peoples: The United Nations and Chapter XI of the Charter,** *International Conciliation,* CDLVIII (February 1950), 51–112.
Contains commentary, documents, reading list.

3338 Bailey, Kenneth. **Some Thoughts on the Place of the United Nations Charter in the International Law of Today,** *Columbia Journal of Transnational Law,* I (Fall, 1962), 8–13.

3339 Bentwich, Norman. **From Geneva to San Francisco: An Account of the International Organization of the New Order.** London, Gollancz, 1946. 111 p.

3340 Bentwich, Norman and Martin, Andrew. **A Commentary on the Charter of the United Nations.** London, Routledge and Paul, 1950. xxviii + 239 p.

3341 Bowett, Derek William. **Self-Defense in International Law.** New York, Praeger, 1958. xv + 294 p.

3342 Brandon, Michael. **Analysis of the Terms "Treaty" and "International Agreement" for Purposes of Registration under Article 102 of the United Nations Charter,** *American Journal of International Law,* XLVII (January 1953), 49–69.

3343 Brierly, James Leslie. **The Covenant and the Charter.** Cambridge, Cambridge University Press, 1947. 27 p.

3344 Briggs, Herbert W. **Power Politics and International Organization,** *American Journal of International Law,* XXXIX (October 1945), 664–79.

A historical survey of the influence of state power on interstate arrangement since the Congress of Vienna, with a detailed analysis of U.N. Charter provisions.

3345 Cavers, David F. **Disarmament and the Charter,** *Charter Review Conference: Ninth Report and Papers Presented to the Commission,* Commission to Study the Organization of Peace (ed.). New York, Commission to Study the Organization of Peace, 1955, pp. 130–52.

3346 Chakste, Mintauts. **Justice and Law in the Charter of the United Nations,** *American Journal of International Law,* XLII (July 1948), 590–600.

3347 Chase, Eugene P. **The United Nations in Action.** New York, McGraw-Hill, 1950.

Chapter V.

3348 Chevalier, Stuart. **The World Charter and the Road to Peace.** Los Angeles, Anderson, 1946. 179 p.

3349 Cohen, Benjamin V. **Principles Governing the Imposition of Sanctions Under the United Nations Charter,** *American Society of International Law Proceedings,* XLV (1951), 153–59.

3350 Colombos, John C. **The United Nations Charter,** *International Law Quarterly,* I (Spring, 1947), 20–33.

3351 Davis, Malcolm W. **The United Nations Charter: Development and Text,** *International Conciliation,* CDXIII (September 1945), 441—50.

3352 Eagleton, Clyde. **The Charter Adopted at San Francisco,** *American Political Science Review,* XXXIX (October 1945), 934—42.

3353 — —. **Covenant of the League of Nations and Charter of the United Nations: Points of Difference.** Washington, U. S. Government Printing Office, 1946. 14 p.

An expansion of his article which appeared in the *Department of State Bulletin,* August 19, 1945.

3354 — —. **The Pacific Settlement of Disputes Under the Charter,** *Annals of the American Academy of Political and Social Science,* CCXLVI (July 1946), 24—29.

3355 Eichelberger, Clark M. **U. N.: The First Twenty Years.** New York, Harper, 1965.

Chapter VIII.

3356 Fanshawe, Maurice. **The Charter Explained.** London, United Nations Association, 1945. 39 p.

3357 Feinberg, Nathan. **The Legality of a "State of War" After the Cessation of Hostilities: Under the Charter of the United Nations and the Covenant of the League of Nations.** Jerusalem, Hebrew University, 1961. 86 p.

3358 Friedrich, Carl J. **The Ideology of the United Nations Charter and the Philosophy of Peace of Immanuel Kant 1795—1945,** *Journal of Politics,* IX (February 1947), 10—30.

3359 Gibson, John S. **Article 51 of the Charter of the United Nations,** *India Quarterly,* XIII (April-June 1957), 121—37.

3360 Goodrich, Leland M. **From League of Nations to United Nations,** *International Organization,* I (February 1947), 3—21.

3361 Goodrich, Leland M. and Hambro, Edvard. **Charter of the United Nations: Commentary and Documents.** 2d ed. Boston, World Peace Foundation, 1949. xvi + 710 p.

3362 Gouré, Léon. **The Eastern European Bloc and the United Nations Charter,** *Journal of International Affairs,* III (Spring, 1949), 36—46.

3363 Gross, Leo. **Charter of the United Nations and the Lodge Reservations,** *American Journal of International Law* XLI (July 1947), 531—54.

3364 Kaeckenbeeck, Georges. **La Charte de San Francisco dans ses rapports avec le droit international,** *Recueil des Cours,* LXX (1947), 113—329.

3365 Kelsen, Hans. **Collective Security and Collective Self-Defense Under the Charter of the United Nations,** *American Journal of International Law,* XLII (October 1948), 783—96.

3366 — —. **The Preamble of the Charter: A Critical Analysis,** *Journal of Politics,* VIII (May 1946), 134—59.

3367 — —. **Sanctions in International Law Under the Charter of the United Nations,** *Iowa Law Review,* XXXI (May 1946), 499—543.

3368 Kerno, I. S. **The Organisation of the United Nations and of the International Court of Justice,** *Recueil des Cours,* LXXVIII (1951), 511—74.

3369 Khan, Rahmatulla. **Cuban Quarantine and the Charter of the U. N.,** *Indian Journal of International Law,* IV (1964), 107—23.

3370 Komarnicki, T. **The Problem of Neutrality Under the United Nations Charter,** *Transactions* (Grotius Society), XXXVIII (1952), 77—91.

3371 Lakshminarayan, C. V. **Analysis of the Principles and System of International Trusteeship in the Charter.** Geneva, Imprimeries Populaires, 1951. 206 p.

3373 Lie, Trygve. **The Charter,** *Peace on Earth*, Trygve Lie, Herbert V. Evatt, Charles Malik, Eleanor Roosevelt, Jaime Torres Bodet, Brock Chisholm, John Boyd-Orr, Ralph Bunche, Benjamin Cohen, Ludwick Rajchman, and Carlos P. Romulo. New York, Hermitage, 1949, pp. 7—26.

3374 Morley, Felix. **Humanity Tries Again: An Analysis of the United Nations Charter.** Washington, Human Events, 1946. 77 p.

3375 Mukerjee, S. **Nehru-Chou Principles and the Law of the UN Charter,** *Calcutta Review*, CXXXVII (October 1955), 46—75.

3376 Nicholas, Herbert George. **The United Nations As a Political Institution.** 2d ed. London, Oxford University, Press, 1962.

Chapter II.

3377 Nordskog, John Eric. **Collective Functions and Powers of the United Nations,** *World Affairs Quarterly*, XVIII (April 1947), 97—107.

3378 Pollux. **The Interpretation of the Charter of the United Nations,** *British Yearbook of International Law*, XXIII (1946), 54—82.

3379 Possony, Stefan T. **Peace Enforcement: The United Nations Charter,** *Yale Law Journal*, LV (August 1946), 937—49.

3380 Price, David B. **The Charter of the United Nations and the Suez War,** *International Relations*, I (October 1958), 494—511.

3381 Riggs, Robert E. **Overselling the UN Charter — Fact and Myth,** *International Organization*, XIV (Spring, 1960), 277—90.

3382 Ross, Alf. **Constitution of the United Nations: Analysis of Structure and Function.** Foreword by Trygve Lie. Copenhagen, Munksgaard, 1950. 236 p.

3383 Rotary International. **From Here On: The Charter of the United Nations with Interpretive Comments and Pertinent Discussion Questions.** 6th ed. Chicago, Rotary International, 1949. 106 p.

3384 Salvemini, Gaetano. **From the League to the UN,** *Atlantic Monthly*, CLXXVIII (August 1946), 56—60.

3385 Schachter, Oscar. **Interpretation of the Charter in the Political Organs of the United Nations,** *Law, State, and International Legal Order*, Salo Engel (ed.). Knoxville, University of Tennessee Press, 1964, pp. 269—84.

3386 Schwarzenberger, Georg. **The Charter of the United Nations,** *World Affairs*, XI (October 1945), 206—18.

3387 Skubiszewski, Krzysztof. **The Postwar Alliances of Poland and the United Nations Charter,** *American Journal of International Law*, LIII (July 1959), 613—34.

3388 United Nations, Library (New York). **A Bibliography of the Charter of the United Nations.** New York, 1955. 128 p.

3389 Vandenbosch, Amry and Hogan, Willard N. **The United Nations.** New York, McGraw-Hill, 1952.

Chapter VI.

3390 Verdross, Alfred. **General International Law and the United Nations Charter,** *International Affairs*, XXX (July 1954), 342—48.

3391 Wolfe, George V. **The States Directly Concerned: Article 79 of the United Nations Charter,** *American Journal of International Law,* XLII (April 1948), 368–88.

3392 Wortley, B. A. **The Veto and the Security Provisions of the Charter,** *British Yearbook of International Law,* XXIII (1946), 95–111.

3393 Wright, Quincy. **Human Rights and Charter Revision,** *Annals of the American Academy of Political and Social Science,* CCXCVI (November 1954), 46–55.

3394 Zimmern, Alfred E. **The American Road to World Peace.** New York, Dutton, 1953.

Section XII.

4.2 REVISIONS: PROPOSED, ADOPTED AND BY EVOLUTION

3395 Andrassy, Juraj. **Uniting for Peace,** *American Journal of International Law,* L (July 1956), 563–82.

3396 Arcé, José. **Right Now.** Madrid, Blass, 1951. 180 p.

3397 Bauer, John. **Make the UN Effective for Peace.** New York, Smith, 1952. 160 p.

3398 Black, J. E. **The United Nations Charter: Problems of Review and Revision,** *University of Cincinnati Law Review,* XXIV (Winter, 1955), 26–29.

3399 Boeg, N. V. **Review of the Charter of the United Nations,** *Transactions* (Grotius Society), XL (1954), 5–14.

Comments by Moore, Green, Freitas, Murray, Khambatta, Habicht.

Part D. — United Nations System

3400 Bradley, Rolland. **Amendments for the Charter of the United Nations,** *World Affairs Quarterly,* XVIII (July 1947), 172–76.

3401 — —. **Safe Revision of the Charter of the United Nations,** *World Affairs Quarterly,* XX (July 1949), 190–94.

3402 Brown, Benjamin H. (ed.). **The U. S. Stake in the UN: Problems of United Nations Charter Review.** New York, American Assembly, Graduate School of Business, Columbia University, 1954. 139 p.

3403 Cranston, Alan. **The Strengthening of the UN Charter,** *Political Quarterly,* XVII (July-September 1946), 187–200.

3404 Eagleton, Clyde. **Proposals for Strengthening the United Nations,** *Foreign Policy Reports,* XXV (September 15, 1949), 102–11.

3405 Martin, Andrew and Edwards, John B. S. **The Changing Charter: A Study in the Reform of the United Nations.** London, Sylvan, 1955. 128 p.

3406 Eichelberger, Clark M. **The United Nations Charter: A Growing Document,** *Annals of the American Academy of Political and Social Science,* CCLII (July 1947), 97–105.

3407 Ely, R. B. **The United Nations Charter: Review and Revision,** *Temple Law Quarterly,* XXVIII (Fall, 1954), 185–98.

3408 Engel, Salo. **De Facto Revision of the Charter of the United Nations,** *Journal of Politics,* XIV (February 1952), 132–44.

3409 Farran, C. D'O. **Proposals for UN Charter Revision,** *International and Comparative Law Quarterly,* II (July 1953), 383–86.

3410 Finkelstein, Lawrence S. **Reviewing the United Nations Charter,** *International Organization,* IX (May 1955), 213–31.

3411 — —. **United Nations Charter Review,** *Pakistan Horizon,* VIII (March 1955), 269–77.

3412 Fischer, Georges. **France and the Proposed Revision of the UN Charter,** *India Quarterly,* XI (October-December 1955), 365–75.

3413 Ghoshal, A. K. **Some Reflections of the Mode of Revision of the Charter,** *Indian Journal of Political Science,* XV (October 1954), 289–98.

3414 Giraud, Émile. **The Revision of the United Nations Charter,** *Recueil des Cours,* XC (1956), 307–463.

3415 Goodspeed, Stephen S. **Action Under the 'Uniting for Peace' Resolution,** *World Affairs Quarterly,* XXX (October 1959), 266–78.

3416 — —. **Reflections on Security Through the United Nations,** Il Politico, XXIII (March 1958), 27–38.

3417 Goswami, B. N. **The Commonwealth and the "Uniting for Peace" Resolution: A Study of the Legal Stand of Some Commonwealth Countries,** *International Studies,* III (April 1962), 451–60.

3418 Gross, Ernest A. **Revising the Charter,** *Foreign Affairs,* XXXII (January 1954), 203–16.

3419 Harper, Norman D. **Revision of the United Nations Charter: An Australian View,** *India Quarterly,* XI (July-September 1955), 236–47.

3420 Hevesy, P. De. **The Reform of the United Nations and the Transformation of the British Empire,** *Friedens-Warte,* LIV, 2 (1957), 139–45.

Part D. — *United Nations System*

3421 Hostie, J. F. **Reflections of an European Lawyer on Revision of the United Nations Charter,** *Tulane Law Review*, XXIX (April 1955), 473–90.

3422 Kelsen, Hans. **The Law of the United Nations.** New York, Praeger, 1951.

Chapter XX.

3423 Key, David McKendree. **United States Planning for Charter Review,** *Annals of the American Academy of Political and Social Science*, CCXCVI (November 1954), 151–55.

3424 Kohn, W. S. G. **Collective Self-Defense Under a Revised UN Charter,** *Social Research*, XXII (Summer, 1955), 231–41.

3425 Kopal, V. and Mrózek, I. **Problems of the Revision of the UN Charter.** Prague, Czechoslovak Academy of Sciences, 1957. 242 p.

3426 McInnis, Edgar. **Revision of the Charter: A Canadian View,** *India Quarterly*, XI (April-July 1955), 116–24.

3427 Martin, Andrew and Edwards, John B. S. **The Changing Charter: A Study in Reform of the United Nations.** London, Sylvan, 1955. 128 p.

3428 Millard, Everett L. **On Charter Review,** *Background*, IX (February 1966), 319–38.

3429 Moore, Arthur. **Revision of the United Nations Charter,** *India Quarterly*, IV (April-June 1948), 133–37.

3430 Morgenthau, Hans J. **The New United Nations and the Revision of the Charter,** *Review of Politics*, XVI (January 1954), 3–21.

3431 Morozov, P. D. **Soviet Policy Toward Revision,** *Annals of the American Academy of Political and Social Science*, CCXCVI (November 1954), 157–60.

3432 Neal, Marian. **United States Attitude Towards Charter Review,** *India Quarterly,* XI (October-December 1955), 354—64.

3433 Pal, K. C. **Revision of the UN Charter,** *Indian Journal of Political Science,* XV (October 1954), 313—26.

3434 Petersen, Keith S. **The Uses of the Uniting for Peace Resolution Since 1950,** *International Organization,* XIII (Spring, 1959), 219—32.

3435 Plaza, Galo. **Should the Charter Be Amended?** *Annals of the American Academy of Political and Social Science,* CCXLVI (July 1946), 30—35.

3436 Plimsoll, James. **The United Nations Character: 1945 and 1962,** *American Society of International Law Proceedings,* LVI (1962), 162—74.

3437 Rao, K. K. **The General Conference for the Review of the Charter of the United Nations,** *Fordham Law Review,* XXIV (Autumn, 1955), 356—68.

3438 Robinson, Jacob. **The General Review Conference,** *International Organization,* VIII (August 1954), 316—30.

3439 — —. **Revision of the Charter,** *The United Nations: Ten Years, Legal Progress,* Gezina J. H. Van Der Molen, W. P. J. Pompe and J. H. W. Verzijl (eds.). Hague, Nederlandse Studentenvereniging Voor Wereldrechtsorde, 1956, pp. 166—90.

3440 Roling, B. V. A. **Some Observations on the Review of the Charter,** *India Quarterly,* XII (January-March 1956), 54—64.

3441 Rusett, Alan de. **Strengthening the Framework of Peace: A Study of Current Proposals for Amending, Developing, or Replacing Present International Institutions for the Maintenance of Peace.** London, Royal Institute of International Affairs, 1950. xiii + 225 p.

3442 Russell, Ruth B. **Changing Patterns of Constitutional Development,** *International Organization,* XIX (Summer, 1965), 410—28.

Part D. — United Nations System

3443 Schick, F. B. **Towards a Living Constitution of the United Nations,** *International Law Quarterly,* II (Spring, 1948), 1—20.

3444 Schlochauer, Hans-Jurgen. **Problems of Reviewing the United Nations Charter,** *India Quarterly,* XII (January-March 1956), 65—75.

3445 Schwarzenberger, Georg. **An Analysis of the Replies to Our Questionnaire on the De Facto Revision of the Covenant,** *World Affairs,* IV (June 1938), 60—74.

3446 — —. **Committee on the Review of the Charter of the United Nations Report.** London, International Law Association, 1954. 98 p.

3447 — —. **Power Politics.** 3d ed. London, Stevens, 1964.
Chapter XXXIV.

3448 Schwelb, Egon. **The Amending Procedure of Constitutions of International Organizations,** *British Yearbook of International Law,* XXXI (1954), 49—95.

3449 — —. **Charter Review and Charter Amendment — Developments in 1958 and 1959,** *International and Comparative Law Quarterly,* IX (April 1960), 237—52.

3450 — —. **Charter Review and Charter Amendment — Recent Developments,** *International and Comparative Law Quarterly,* VII (April 1958), 303—33.

3451 — —. **Time Limit for the Ratification of Amendments to the UN Charter,** *International and Comparative Law Quarterly,* IV (July 1955), 475—83.

3452 Scott, R. F. **Revision of the United Nations Charter: A Study of Various Approaches,** *Michigan Law Review,* LIII (November 1954), 39—68.

3453 Shotwell, James T. **Implementing and Amending the Charter,** *International Conciliation*, CDXV (December 1945), 811—23.

3454 Sohn, L. B. **United Nations Charter Revision and the Rule of Law: A Program for Peace,** *Northwestern University Law Review*, L (January 1956), 709—25.

3455 Tarazi, Salah el dine. **The Risks of Revision: Appraisal of United Nations Preparations for Charter Review,** *Annals of the American Academy of Political and Social Science*, CCXCVI (November 1954), 140—46.

3456 Wilcox, Francis O. **How the United Nations Charter Has Developed,** *Annals of the American Academy of Political and Social Science*, CCXCVI (November 1954), 1—13.

3457 Wilcox, Francis O. and Marcy, Carl M. **Proposals for Changes in the United Nations.** Washington, Brookings,, 1955. xiv + 357 p.

3458 Wiley, Alexander. **The Senate and the Review of the United Nations Charter,** *Annals of the American Academy of Political and Social Science*, CCXCVI (November 1954), 156—62.

3459 Woolsey, L. H. **The Uniting for Peace Resolution of the United Nations,** *American Journal of International Law*, XLV (January 1951), 129—37.

3460 Wynner, Edith. **World Federal Government: Why? What? How? In Maximum Terms; Proposals for United Nations Charter Revision.** Afton, N. Y., Fedonat, 1954. 84 p.

3461 Younger, Kenneth. **United Nations Charter Review: A British Opinion,** *India Quarterly*, XI (April-July 1955), 105—15.

Part D. — *United Nations System*

5. CONSTITUTIONAL QUESTIONS

Legal issues in the United Nations have assumed proportions very different from those of the League. Deadlock exists on the questions of Chinese representation and the so-called great power veto. Similarly, the relationship between the UN and regional organizations has not been fully clarified.

5.1 GENERAL DISCUSSIONS

See also D 4.

3462 Ahluwalia, Kuljit. **The Legal Status, Privileges and Immunities of the Specialized Agencies of the United Nations and Certain Other International Organizations.** Foreword by Leland Goodrich. Hague, Nijhoff, 1964. xiii + 230 p.

3463 Aikman, C. C. **Law in the World Community,** *Political Science*, IX (March 1957), 3–21.

3464 Bloomfield, Lincoln. **Law, Politics, and International Disputes,** *International Conciliation*, DXVI (January 1958), 257–316.

3465 Bowett, D. W. **The Law of International Institutions.** New York, Praeger, 1963. xviii + 347 p.

3466 Briggs, Herbert W. **The International Law Commission.** Ithaca, N. Y., Cornell University Press, 1965. xv + 380 p.

3467 Cheng, Bin. **International Law in the United Nations,** *Year Book of World Affairs*, VIII (1954), 170–95.

3468 Claude, Inis L., Jr. **Swords Into Plowshares.** 3d ed. New York, Random House, 1964.

Chapter IX.

3469 Cohen, Benjamin V. **The United Nations: Constitutional Developments, Growth and Possibilities.** Cambridge, Harvard University Press, 1961. 106 p.

3470 Detter, Ingrid. **Lawmaking by International Organizations.** Stockholm, Norstedt, 1965. 353 p.

3471 — —. **The Organs of International Organizations Exercising Their Treaty-Making Power,** *British Yearbook of International Law,* XXXVIII (1962), 421–44.

3472 Eagleton, Clyde. **The Role of International Law,** *Charter Review Conference: Ninth Report and Papers Presented to the Commission.* Commission to Study the Organization of Peace (ed.). New York, Commission to Study the Organization of Peace, 1955, pp. 183–97.

3473 — —. **The Yardstick of International Law,** *Annals of the American Academy of Political and Social Science,* CCXCVI (November 1954), 68–76.

3474 Fakher, Hossein. **The Relationships Among the Principal Organs of the United Nations.** Geneva, Post-Graduate Institute of International Studies, 1950. ix + 200 p.

3475 Fawcett, J. E. S. **The Place of Law in an International Organization,** *British Yearbook of International Law,* XXXVI (1960), 321–42.

International Monetary Fund.

3476 Fitzmaurice, G. G. **The United Nations and the Rule of Law,** *Transactions* (Grotius Society), XXXVIII (1952), 135–50.

3477 Florio, Francesco. **La natura giuridica delle organizzazioni internazionali.** Milano, Giuffrè, 1949. 156 p.

3478 Freeman, Harrop A. **The United Nations Organization and International Law,** Cornell Law Quarterly, XXXI (March 1946), 259—84.

3479 Govindaraj, V. C. **The Law of International Institutions,** Indian Journal of International Law, I (1960—61), 484—95.

3480 Gross, Leo. **The United Nations and the Role of Law,** International Organization. XIX (Summer, 1965), 537—61.

3481 Hammarskjöld, D. **International Law and the United Nations,** Record of the Association of the Bar of the City of New York, X (October 1955), 322—31.

3482 Hexner, Ervin P. **Teleological Interpretation of Basic Instruments of Public International Organizations,** Law, State, and International Legal Order, Salo Engel (ed.). Knoxville, University of Tennessee Press, 1964, pp. 119—38.

3483 Higgins, Rosalyn. **The Development of International Law Through the Political Organs of the United Nations.** London, Oxford University Press, 1963. xxi + 402 p.

3484 Jenks, Clarence Wilfred. **The Common Law of Mankind.** New York, Praeger, 1958.

Chapter III.

3485 — —. **Due Process of Law in International Organizations,** International Organization, XIX (Spring, 1965), 163—76.

3486 — —. **The Impact of International Organisations on Public and Private International Law,** Transactions (Grotius Society), XXXVII (1951), 23—49.

Comments by Bentwich, Keen, Pollard, Lloyd, Stark, Chatterjee, Adamkiewicz, Elkin, Zaslawski, Piercy.

3487 — —. **The Proper Law of International Organisations.** London, Stevens, 1962. 282 p.

> The author emphasizes that international organizations bring up practical legal problems deserving the close attention of every lawyer. In the early pages he furnishes an impressive list of the transactions made daily by such organizations. The reader is reminded that these organizations make contracts of all descriptions; they acquire, occupy and dispose of all types of property; they effect insurances; they charter all forms of transport for use on land, sea and air; and they are free to sue and be sued in tort.

3488 — —. **Some Constitutional Problems of International Organizations,** *British Yearbook of International Law*, XXII (1945), 11—72.

3489 Jessup, Philip C. **Diplomatie parlementaire: Une étude de la qualité juridique des règles de procédure des organes des Nations Unies,** *Recueil des Cours*, LXXXIX (1956), 185—319.

3490 Kasme, Badr. **La capacité de l'organisation Nations Unies de conclure des traites.** Paris, Librairie Générale de Droit et de Jurisprudence, 1960. 214 p.

3491 Kelsen, Hans. **General International Law and the Law of the United Nations,** The United Nations: Ten Years, Legal Progress, Gezina J. H. Van Der Molen, W. P. J. Prompe and J. H. W. Verzijl (eds.). Hague, Nederlandse Studentenvereniging Voor Wereldrechtsorde, 1956, pp. 1—16.

3492 — —. **The Law of the United Nations.** New York, Praeger, 1951. xvii + 903 p.

3493 — —. **Recent Trends in the Law of the United Nations: A Supplement to the Law of the United Nations.** New York, Praeger, 1951.

3494 Lachs, Manfred. **The Law In and Of the United Nations,** *Indian Journal of International Law*, I (1960—61), 429—42.

3495 Lauterpacht, Hersch. **Codification and Development of International Law,** *American Journal of International Law,* XLIX (January 1955), 16—43.

3496 McClure, Wallace. **World Legal Order.** Chapel Hill, University of North Carolina Press, 1960.

Chapters IX—XI.

3497 Parry, Clive. **The Treaty-Making Power of the United Nations,** *British Yearbook of International Law,* XXVI (1949), 108—49.

3498 Rosenne, Shabtai. **United Nations Treaty Practice,** *Recueil des Cours,* LXXXVI (1954), 281—443.

3499 Rouyer-Hameray, Bernard. **Les compétences implicites des organisations internationales.** Paris, Librairie Générale de Droit et de Jurisprudence, 1962. 110 p.

3500 Scelle, George. **The Evolution of International Conferences,** *International Social Science Journal,* V, 2 (1953), 241—57.

3501 Schachter, O. **The Relation of Law, Politics and Action in the United Nations,** *Recueil des Cours,* CIX (1963), 169—256.

3502 Schiffer, Walter. **The Legal Community of Mankind: A Critical Analysis of the Modern Concept of World Organization.** New York, Columbia University Press, 1954. 367 p.

3503 Schneider, J. W. **Treaty-Making Power of International Organizations.** Geneva, Droz 1959. 150 p.

3504 Schwarzenberger, Georg. **Power Politics.** 3d ed. London, Stevens, 1964.

Chapter XXI.

3505 Sharp, Walter R. **A Checklist of Subjects for the Systematic Study of International Conferences,** *International Social Science Bulletin,* V, 2 (1953), 311—39.

3506 Skubiszewski, Krzysztof. **Forms of Participation of International Organizations in the Lawmaking Process,** *International Organization,* XVIII (Autumn, 1964), 790—805.

3507 Tammes, A. J. P. **Decisions of International Organs As a Source of International Law,** *Recueil des Cours* XCIV (1958), 265—363.

3508 Watt, Robert J. **Democracy in International Administration,** *Iowa Law Review,* XXX (May 1945), 515—20.

3509 Weissberg, Guenter. **The International Status of the United Nations.** New York, Oceana, 1961. xii + 228 p.

3510 Wright, Quincy. **International Law and the United Nations.** New York, Asia Publishing House, 1960. 134 p.

3511 — —. **The Role of Law in the Organization of Peace,** *Organizing Peace in the Nuclear Age,* Commission to Study the Organization of Peace (ed.). New York, New York University Press, 1959, pp. 27—49.

5.2 DOMESTIC JURISDICTION

See also D 9.2.

3512 Ago, R. **Internationale Organisationer og Deres Funktioner i Forhold til Staternes Indre Anliggender,** *Økonomi og Politik,* XXIX, 2—4 (1955), 105—20.

3513 Ahluwalia, Kuljit. **The Legal Status, Privileges, and Immunities of the Specialized Agencies of the United Nations and Certain Other International Organizations.** Foreword by Leland M. Goodrich. Hague, Nijhoff, 1964. xiii + 230 p.

3514 Bentwich, Norman. **The Limits of the Domestic Jurisdiction of the State,** *Transactions* (Grotius Society), XXXI (1945), 59—65.

Comments by Goodhart, Drucker, Hurst, Gleason, Zaslawski, Feist, Bresch, Neugroschel, Piercey, and Weis.

3515 Bernier, Robert. **L'autorité politique internationale et la sourveraineté des états: fondements philosophiques de l'ordre politique.** Montreal, Institut Social Populaire, 1951. 201 p.

3516 Bindschedler, R. **The Delimitation of Powers in the United Nations,** *Recueil des Cours,* CVIII (1963), 305—423.

3517 Brandon, M. **The Legal Status of the Premises of the United Nations,** *British Yearbook of International Law,* XXVIII (1951), 90—113.

3518 Corwin, Edward S. **The Constitution and World Organization.** Princeton University Press, 1944. xiii + 64 p.

3519 Drucker, Alfred. **The Nationalisation of United Nations Property in Europe,** *Transactions* (Grotius Society), XXXVI (1950), 75—114.

3520 Eagleton, Clyde. **International Government.** 3d ed. New York, Ronald, 1957.

Chapter IV.

3521 Eeckman, Paul. **The Domestic Jurisdiction Clause of the Charter: A Belgian View,** *International Organization,* IX (November 1955), 477—85.

3522 Ehrenfeld, Alice. **United Nations Immunity Distinguished from Sovereign Immunity,** *American Society of International Law Proceedings,* LII (1958), 88—94.

3523 Falk, Richard A. **The Authority of the United Nations over Non-Members.** Princeton, Center of International Studies, 1965. 101 p.

3524 Fawcett, J. E. S. **Détournement de Pouvoir by International Organizations,** *British Yearbook of International Law*, XXXIII (1957), 311–16.

3525 Friedmann, Wolfgang. **National Sovereignty, International Cooperation and the Reality of International Law,** *UCLA Law Review*, X (May 1963), 739–53.

3526 — —. **UNRRA and National Sovereignty,** *Fortnightly*, New Series, CLV (January 1944), 17–25

3527 Goodrich, Leland M. **The United Nations and Domestic Jurisdiction,** *International Organization*, III (February 1949), 14–28.

3528 Gros, André. **The Problem of Redress Against the Decisions of International Organisations,** *Transactions* (Grotius Society), XXXVI (1950), 30–37.

Comments by Adamkiewicz, Shelly, Culbertson, Zaslawski, Boeg.

3529 Harley, J. Eugene. **Sovereignty, Equality, and Force As Factors in a World Security Organization,** *World Affairs Quarterly*, XVI (October 1945), 253–74.

3530 Hexner, Ervin P. **Interpretation by International Organizations of Their Basic Instruments,** *American Journal of International Law*, LIII (April 1959), 341–70.

Discusses need for U.S. Supreme Court-like "final" court of appeals to define basic charters or constitutions of international organizations. Case study of IMF, IFC, IBRD.

3531 Hoffman, Paul G. **The United Nations and the Bricker Amendment,** *World Affairs Quarterly*, XXIV (January 1954), 348–56.

3532 Hoffmann, Stanley. **Organisations internationales et pouvoirs politiques des états.** Paris, Colin, 1954. 427 p.

3533 Howell, John M. **Delimiting "Domestic Jurisdiction."** *Western Political Quarterly*, X (September 1957), 512–26.

3534 — —. **The French and South African Walkouts and Domestic Jurisdiction,** *Journal of Politics*, XVIII (February 1956), 95–104.

3535 Ivrakis, S. C. **The Regulation-Making Power of the United Nations,** *Revue Hellénique de Droit International*, IX (January 1956), 80–92.

3536 Jenks, Clarence Wilfred. **The Headquarters of International Institutions: A Study in Their Location and Status.** London, Royal Institute of International Affairs, 1945. 102 p.

3537 Joyce, James Avery. **Revolution on East River: The Twilight of National Sovereignty.** New York, Abelard-Schuman, 1953. 244 p.

3538 Kass, Stephen L. **Obligatory Negotiations in International Organizations,** *Canadian Yearbook of International Law*, III (1965), 36–72.

3539 Keeton, George W. **National Sovereignty and International Order: An Essay upon the International Community and International Order.** London, Peace Book Company, 1939. 191 p.

3540 Kelsen, Hans. **The Law of the United Nations.** New York, Praeger, 1951.

Chapter XIX.

3541 — —. **Limitations on the Functions of the United Nations,** *Yale Law Journal*, LV (August 1946), 997–1015.

3542 King, John Kerry. **International Administrative Jurisdiction with Special Reference to the Domestic Laws of the United States of America.** Brussels, International Institute of Administrative Science, n. d. 288 p.

3543 Kunz, Josef L. **Privileges and Immunities of International Organizations,** *American Journal of International Law,* XLI (October 1947), 828–62.

3544 Preuss, Lawrence. **Article 2, Par. 7, of the Charter of the United Nations and Matters of Domestic Jurisdiction,** *Recueil des Cours,* LXXIV (1949), 535–651.

3545 — —. **The International Organization Immunities Act,** *American Journal of International Law,* XL (April 1946), 332–45.

3546 Rajan, M. S. **United Nations and Domestic Jurisdiction.** Bombay, Longmans, Green, 1958. 464 p.

3547 — —. **United States Attitude Toward Domestic Jurisdiction in the United Nations,** *International Organization,* XIII (Winter, 1959), 19–37.

3548 Rouyer-Hameray, Bernard. **Les compétences implicites des organisations internationales.** Paris, Librairie Générale de Droit et de Jurisprudence, 1962. 110 p.

3549 Rudzinski, Aleksandr Witold. **Domestic Jurisdiction in United Nations Practice,** *India Quarterly,* IX (October-December 1953), 313–54.

3550 Schapiro, L. B. **Domestic Jurisdiction in the Covenant and the Charter,** *Transactions* (Grotius Society), XXXIII (1947), 195–211.

3551 Scheuner, U. **Sovereignty and the United Nations,** *The United Nations: Ten Years, Legal Progress,* Gezina J. H. Van Der Molen, W. P. J. Pompe and J. H. W. Verzijl (eds.). Hague, Nederlandse Studentenvereniging Voor Wereldrechtsorde, 1956, pp. 17–42.

3552 Seyersted, Finn. **International Personality of Intergovernmental Organization: Do Their Capacities Really Depend upon Their Constitutions?** *Indian Journal of International Law,* IV (1964), 1–74.

3553 — —. **Is the International Personality of Intergovernmental Organizations Valid Vis-à-Vis Non-Members?** *Indian Journal of International Law*, IV (1964), 233—65.

3554 Surr, J. V. **American Taxation of the United Nations,** *Harvard International Law Club Journal*, V (Spring, 1964), 195—208.

3555 Visscher, Charles de. **Theory and Reality in International Law,** P. E. Corbett (trans.). Princeton, Princeton University Press, 1957.

Book II, Chapter III.

3556 Wright, Quincy. **Domestic Jurisdiction and the Competence of United Nations Organs,** *Charter Review Conference: Ninth Report and Papers Presented to the Commission,* Commission to Study the Organization of Peace (ed.). New York, Commission to Study the Organization of Peace, 1955, pp. 42—62.

3557 Yuen-Li, Liang. **The Legal Status of the United Nations in the U. S. A.,** *International Law Quarterly*, II (Winter, 1948—49), 577—602.

5.3 FINANCING

3558 Ali, Syed Amjad. **Implications of the United Nations Financial Crisis,** *Pakistan Horizon*, XVIII, 1 (1965), 20—27.

3559 Amerasinghe, C. F. **The United Nations Expenses Case — A Contribution to the Law of International Organization.** *Indian Journal of International Law*, IV (1964), 177—232.

3560 Bishop, Peter V. **Canada's Policy on the Financing of UN Peace-Keeping Operations,** *International Journal*, XX (Autumn, 1965), 463—83.

3561 Buchanan, W. H. **Expenses of the United Nations: Their Limits and the Financial Obligations Created,** *Harvard International Law Club Journal,* V (Spring, 1964), 165–94.

3562 Claude, Inis L., Jr. **The Political Framework of the United Nations' Financial Problem,** *International Organization,* XVII (Autumn, 1963), 831–59.

3563 Dravis, Irving B. and Davenport, W. S. **The Political Arithmetic of International Burden-Sharing,** *Journal of Political Economy,* LXXI (August 1963), 309–30.

A consideration of whether the United States finances international projects disproportionately.

3564 Gardner, Richard N. **United Nations Procedures and Power Realities: The International Apportionment Problem,** *American Society of International Law Proceedings,* LIX (1965), 232–46.

3565 Gross, Ernest A. **The United Nations.** New York, Harper, 1962.

Chapter V.

3566 Gross, Leo. **Expenses of the United Nations for Peace-Keeping Operations: The Advisory Opinion of the International Court of Justice,** *International Organization,* XVII (Winter, 1963), 1–35.

3567 Higgins, Terence. **The Politics of United Nations Finance,** *World Today,* New Series, XIX (September 1963), 380–89.

3568 Hill, Norman L. **The Allocation of Expenses in International Organization,** *American Political Science Review,* XXI (February 1927), 128–37.

3569 Malenbaum, Wilfred. **International Public Financing,** *International Conciliation,* DII (March 1955), 315–39.

3570 Mangone, Gerard J. and Srivastava, Anand K. **Budgeting for the United Nations,** *International Organization,* XII (Autumn, 1959), 473–854.

3571 Nichols, Calvin J. **Financing the UN: Problems and Prospects.** Cambridge, MIT Center for International Studies, 1961. 36 p.

3572 Padelford, Norman J. **Debt and Dilemma: The United Nations Crisis,** *India Quarterly,* XIX (October-December 1963), 311–34.

3573 — —. **Financial Crisis and the Future of the United Nations,** *World Politics,* XV (July 1963), 531–68.

3574 — —. **Financing Peace-Keeping: Politics and Crisis,** *International Organization,* XIX (Summer, 1965), 444–62.

3575 Pharand, A. Donat. **Analysis of the Opinion of the International Court of Justice on Certain Expenses of the United Nations,** *Canadian Yearbook of International Law,* I (1963), 272–97.

3576 Raju, G. S. **The Expenses of the United Nations Organisation,** *Indian Journal of International Law,* II (1962), 485–90.

3577 Rao, T. S. Rama. **The Expenses Judgment of the International Court of Justice — A Critique,** *Indian Year Book of International Affairs,* XII (1963), 134–60.

3578 Rössel, Agda. **Financing the United Nations: Its Economic and Political Implications,** *The Quest for Peace,* Andrew W. Cordier and Wilder Foote (eds.). New York, Columbia University Press, pp. 139–48.

3579 Simmonds, K. R. **The UN Assessments Advisory Opinion,** *International and Comparative Law Quarterly,* XIII (July 1964), 854–91.

3580 Singer, J. David. **Financing International Organization: The United Nations Budget Process.** Hague, Nijhoff, 1961. xvi + 185 p.

3581 — —. **The United Nations Advisory Committee on Administrative and Budgetary Questions,** *Public Administration*, XXXV (Winter, 1957), 395–416.

3582 Siotis, Jean. **A Review of John Stoessinger et al., Financing the United Nations System,** *Journal of Conflict Resolution*, IV (June 1965), 288–92.

3583 Stoessinger, John G. **Financing Peace-Keeping Operations,** *Power and Order: Six Cases in World Politics*, John G. Stoessinger and Alan F. Westin (eds.). New York, Harcourt, Brace and World, 1964, pp. 140–78.

3584 — —. **Financing the United Nations,** *International Conciliation*, DXXXV (November 1961), 3–36.

3585 Stoessinger, John G., with the collaboration of Lande, Gabriella Rosner; Claude, Inis L., Jr.; Egger, Rowland; Fried, John H. E.; Hoffmann, Stanley; Padelford, Norman J.; Pollis, Admantia; Rosenfeld, Marcia; Sharp, Walter R.; and Taubenfeld, Howard J. **Financing the United Nations System.** Washington, Brookings, 1964. 348 p.

3586 Szawlowski, Richard. **Recent Financial Problems of the UN,** *Public Finance*, XVIII (1963), 148–81.

3587 Taubenfeld, Rita Falk and Taubenfeld, Howard J. **Independent Revenue for the UN,** *International Organization*, XVIII (Spring, 1964), 241–67.

3588 West, Robert L. **The United Nations and the Congo Financial Crisis: Lessons of the First Year,** *International Organization*, XV (Autumn, 1961), 603–17.

5.4 MEMBERSHIP

5.4.1 GENERAL OBSERVATIONS

See also D 12.1.

3589 Ahmad, Mushtaq. **Admission of New Members to the United Nations,** *Pakistan Horizon,* VI (December 1953), 161–70.

3590 Aufricht, Hans. **Principles and Practices of Recognition by International Organizations,** *American Journal of International Law,* XLIII (October 1949), 679–704.

3591 Barabas, Frank. **Membership and Representation,** *Journal of International Affairs,* IX, 2 (1955), 31–38.

3592 Claude, Inis L., Jr. **Swords Into Plowshares.** 3d ed. New York, Random House, 1964.

Chapter V.

3593 Eagleton, Clyde. **International Government.** 3d ed. New York, Ronald, 1957.

Chapter III.

3594 Feinberg, Nathan. **The Admission of New Members to the League of Nations and the United Nations Organisation,** *Recueil des Cours,* LXXX (1952), 293–391.

3595 Goodrich, Leland M. **The United Nations.** New York, Crowell, 1963.

Chapter V.

3596 Gross, Leo. **Election of States to United Nations Membership,** *American Society of International Law Proceedings,* XLVIII (1954), 37–60.

3597 — —. **Progress Toward Universality of Membership in the United Nations,** *American Journal of International Law,* L (October 1956), 791–827.

3598 Hill, Norman L. **International Organization.** New York, Harper, 1952.
Chapter III.

3599 Holcombe, Arthur N. **The Problem of Membership,** *Charter Review Conference: Ninth Report and Papers Presented to the Commission,* Commission to Study the Organization of Peace (ed.). New York, Commission to Study the Organization of Peace, 1955, pp. 63–76.

3600 Humber, P. O. **Admission to the United Nations,** *British Yearbook of International Law,* XXIV (1947), 90–115.

3601 Kelsen, Hans. **The Law of the United Nations.** New York, Praeger, 1951.
Chapters IV, VII.

3602 — —. **Withdrawal from the United Nations,** *Western Political Quarterly,* I (March 1948), 29–43.

3603 Klooz, Marie S. **The Role of the General Assembly of the United Nations in the Admission of Members,** *American Journal of International Law,* XLIII (April 1949), 246–61.

3604 Liang, Yuen-li. **Conditions of Admission of a State to Membership in the United Nations,** *American Journal of International Law,* LIII (April 1959), 288–302.

3605 Livingstone, F. **Withdrawal from the United Nations – Indonesia,** *International and Comparative Law Quarterly,* XIV (April 1965), 637–45.

3606 Manno, Catherine Serf. **Problems and Trends in the Composition of Nonplenary UN Organs,** *International Organization,* XIX (Winter, 1965), 37–55.

3607 Rosenne, S. **Recognition of States by the United Nations,** *British Yearbook of International Law,* XXVI (1949), 437—47.

3608 Rudzinski, Aleksander W. **Admission of New Members: The United Nations and the League of Nations,** *International Conciliation,* CDLXXX (April 1952), 143—96.

3609 Singh, Nagendra. **Termination of Membership of International Organisations.** New York, Praeger, 1958. xv + 209 p.

3610 Sohn, Louis B. **Expulsion or Forced Withdrawal from an International Organization,** *Harvard Law Review,* LXXVII (June 1964), 1381—1425.

3611 — —. **Multiple Representation in International Assemblies,** *American Journal of International Law,* XL (January 1946), 71—99.

3612 Wilcox, Francis O. **Representation and Voting in the United Nations General Assembly,** *The United Nations,* Richard A. Falk and Saul H. Mendlovitz (eds.). New York, World Law Fund, 1966, pp. 272—94.

5.4.2 REPRESENTATION OF CHINA

3613 Appleton, Sheldon. **The Eternal Triangle: Communist China, the United States and the United Nations.** East Lansing, Michigan State University Press, 1961. 264 p.

3614 — —. **The United Nations, "China Tangle",** *Pacific Affairs,* XXXV (Summer, 1962), 160—67.

3615 Boyer, William W. and Akra, Neylan. **The United States and the Admission of Communist China,** *Political Science Quarterly,* LXXVI (September 1961), 332—53.

3616 Briggs, Herbert W. **Chinese Representation in the United Nations,** *International Organization,* VI (May 1952), 192—209.

Part D. — *United Nations System*

3617 Brook, David. **The UN and the China Dilemma.** New York, Vantage, 1956. 87 p.

3618 Brown, Benjamin H. and Greene, Fred. **Chinese Representation: A Case Study in United Nations Political Affairs.** New York, Woodrow Wilson Foundation, 1955. 52 p.

3619 Claude, Inis L., Jr. **Chinese Representation in the United Nations,** *Foundations of U. S. China Policy*, Urban G. Whitaker (ed.). Berkeley, Pacifica Foundation, 1959, pp. 122—29.

3620 Cohen, Maxwell. **Communist China: To Recognize or Not to Recognize,** *International Journal*, VIII (Autumn, 1953), 266—73.

3621 Halpern, A. M. **China, the United Nations and Beyond,** *China Quarterly*, X (April—June 1962), 72—77.

3622 Khan, Mohamed Samih. **Legal Aspects of the Problem of China's Representation in the United Nations,** *Pakistan Horizon*, X (September 1957), 134—43.

3623 Leyser, J. **The United Nations and the Question of China's Representation,** *Australian Outlook*, X (March 1956), 30—36.

3624 Mezeris, A. G. (ed.). **China Representation in the UN.** New York, International Review Service, 1965. 116 p.

3625 Newman, Robert P. **Recognition of Communist China?** New York, Macmillan, 1961.
Chapter X.

3626 Niebuhr, Reinhold. **China and the United Nations,** *Journal of International Affairs*, XI, 2 (1957), 187—89.

3627 Schick, F. B. **The Question of China in the United Nations,** *International and Comparative Law Quarterly*, XII (October 1963), 1232—50.

Part D. — *United Nations System*

3628 Tabata, Shigejiro. **Admission to the United Nations and Recognition of States — In Connection with the Matter of Chinese Representation,** *Japanese Annual of International Law*, V (1960), 1—14.

5.5 REGIONALISM

See E 3.

5.6 VOTING

5.6.1 GENERAL OBSERVATIONS

3629 Claude, Inis L., Jr. **Swords Into Plowshares.** 3d ed. New York, Random House, 1964.

Chapter VII.

3630 Crocker, W. R. **Voting in the International Institutions,** *Australian Outlook*, V (September 1951), 158—64.

3631 Greaves, H. R. G. **International Voting Procedures,** *Political Quarterly*, XVIII (October-December 1948), 331—40.

3632 Henig, Stanley. **Voting Procedures — A Reply,** *Journal of Common Market Studies*, I (May 1953), 219—23.

3633 Koo, Wellington, Jr. **Voting Procedures In International Political Organizations.** New York, Columbia University Press, 1947. vii + 349 p.

3635 McIntyre, Elizabeth. **Weighted Voting in International Organizations,** *International Organization*, VII (November 1954), 484—97.

3636 Maclaurin, John (pseud.). **The United Nations and Power Politics.** New York, Harper, 1951.

Chapter VII.

3637 Riches, Cromwell A. **Majority Rule in International Organization: A Study of the Trend from Unanimity to Majority Decision.** Baltimore, Johns Hopkins Press, 1958. viii + 322 p.

3638 Rudzinski, Aleksander W. **Election Procedure in the United Nations,** *American Journal of International Law,* LIII (January 1959), 81–111.

3639 — —. **Majority Rule vs. Great Power Agreement in the UN,** *International Organization,* IX (August 1955), 366–75.

3640 Rusett, Alan de. **Large and Small States in International Organization: Present Attitudes to the Problem of Weighted Voting,** *International Affairs,* XXX (October 1954), 463–74.

3641 — —. **Large and Small States in International Organization: The Need for a New Approach to the Question of Weighting Votes in the General Assembly,** *International Affairs,* XXXI (April 1955), 192–202.

3642 Senf, Catherine. **A Proposal for Weighting Votes in the UN Assembly,** *Charter Review Conference: Ninth Report and Papers Presented to the Commission,* Commission to Study the Organization of Peace (ed.). New York, Commission to Study the Organization of Peace, 1955, pp. 107–29.

3643 Sohn, Louis B. **Weighting of Votes in an International Assembly,** *American Political Science Review,* XXXVIII (December 1944), 1192–1203.

3644 Trinker, Frederick W. **The Anatomy of World Order.** Mexico City, Costa-Amic, 1946.

Chapter IV.

3645 Weinschel, Herbert. **The Doctrine of the Equality of States and Its Recent Modifications,** *American Journal of International Law,* XLV (July 1951), 417–42.

5.6.2 GENERAL ASSEMBLY VOTING PROCEDURE

3646 Hovey, Allan, Jr. **Voting Procedures in the General Assembly,** *International Organization,* IV (August 1950), 412–27.

3647 Kerley, Ernest L. **Voting on Important Questions in the United Nations General Assembly,** *American Journal of International Law,* LIII (April 1959), 324–40.

3648 Vallat, F. A. **Voting in the General Assembly of the United Nations,** *British Yearbook of International Law,* XXXI (1954), 273–98.

3649 Vandenbosch, Amry and Hogan, Willard N. **The United Nations.** New York, McGraw-Hill, 1952.

Chapter VIII.

3650 Wilcox, Francis O. **Representation and Voting in the United Nations General Assembly,** *The United Nations,* Richard A. Falk and Saul H. Mendlovitz (eds.). New York, World Law Fund, 1966, pp. 272–94.

5.6.3 VETO IN THE SECURITY COUNCIL

3651 Arnold-Forster, W. **The Great Powers' Veto: What Should Be Done?** *Political Quarterly,* XIX (January-March 1948), 40–49.

Chapter IX.

3652 Claude, Inis L., Jr. **Swords Into Plowshares.** 3d ed. New York, Random House, 1964.

Chapter VIII.

3653 Jiménez de Aréchaga, Eduardo. **Voting and the Handling of Disputes in the Security Council.** New York, Carnegie, 1950. 189 p.

3654 Lee, Dwight E. **The Genesis of the Veto,** *International Organization,* I (February 1947), 33–42.

3655 Liang, Yuen-Li. **The Settlement of Disputes in the Security Council: The Yalta Voting Formula,** *British Yearbook of International Law,* XXIV (1947), 330–59.

3656 M., B. **The Veto at Lake Success,** *World Today,* New Series, III (February 1947), 82–90.

3657 Moldaver, Arlette. **Repertoire of the Veto in the Security Council, 1946–1956,** *International Organization,* XI (Spring, 1957), 261–74.

3658 Padelford, Norman J. **The Use of the Veto,** *International Organization,* II (June 1948), 227–46.

3659 Reston, James B. **Votes and Vetoes,** *Foreign Affairs,* XXV (October 1946), 13–22.

3660 Rudzinski, Alexander. **The So-Called Double Veto: Some Changes in the Voting Practice of the Security Council,** *American Journal of International Law,* XLV (July 1951), 443–61.

3661 Vandenbosch, Amry and Hogan, Willard N. **The United Nations.** New York, McGraw-Hill, 1952.
Chapter IX.

3662 Wilcox, Francis O. **The Rule of Unanimity in the Security Council,** *American Society of International Law Proceedings,* XL (1946), 51–63.

3663 — —. **The Yalta Voting Formula,** *American Political Science Review,* XXXIX (October 1945), 943–56.

3664 Wortley, B. A. **The Veto and the Security Provisions of the Charter,** *British Yearbook of International Law,* XXIII (1946), 95–111.

6. MAIN ORGANS

Although the principal organs of the UN are the General Assembly, the Security Council, the Secretariat, the Economic and Social Council, the Trusteeship Council, and the International Court of the Justice, the latter three are filed separately to maintain consistency with the enumeration of categories in Part C.

6.1 GENERAL ASSEMBLY

See also D 5.6.2.

3665 Asamoah, Obed. **The Legal Effect of the Resolutions of the General Assembly,** *Columbia Journal of Transnational Law,* III, 2 (1965), 210—30.

3666 B., E. **The Fourth Assembly of the United Nations,** *World Today,* New Series, VI (February 1950), 64—73.

Articles on the General Assembly follow in each succeeding February issue until 1956.

3667 Bailey, Sydney D. **The General Assembly of the United Nations: A Study of Procedure and Practice.** Rev. ed. New York, Praeger, 1964. xv + 374.

3668 Chase, Eugene P. **The United Nations in Action.** New York, McGraw-Hill, 1950.

Chapters VII, VIII.

3669 Cheever, Daniel S. and Haviland, H. Field, Jr. **Organizing for Peace.** Boston, Houghton, Mifflin, 1954.

Chapter IV.

3670 Claude, Inis L., Jr. **Swords Into Plowshares.** 3d ed. New York, Random House, 1964.

Chapter XVI.

3671 Cocke, Erle, Jr. **United Nations General Assembly — A Captive of Its Own Procedures,** *Vanderbilt Law Review,* XIII (June 1960), 651–62.

3672 Coster, Douglas W. **The Interim Committee of the General Assembly,** *International Organization,* III (August 1949), 444–58.

3673 Dejany, Aouney W. **Competence of the United Nations General Assembly in the Tunisian-Moroccan Questions,** *American Society of International Law Proceedings,* XLVII (1953), 53–59.

3674 Dolivet, Louis. **The United Nations.** New York, Farrar, Straus, 1946.

Chapter III.

3675 Dulles, John Foster. **The General Assembly,** *Foreign Affairs,* XXIV (October 1945), 1–11.

3676 Evatt, Herbert V. **The General Assembly,** *Peace on Earth,* Trygve Lie, Herbert V. Evatt, Charles Malik, Eleanor Roosevelt, Jaimes Torres Bodet, Brock Chisholm, John Boyd-Orr, Ralph Bunche, Benjamin Cohen, Ludwick Rajchman, and Carlos P. Romulo. New York, Hermitage, 1949, pp. 89–101.

3677 Freedman, Max. **The General Assembly,** *International Journal,* II (Spring, 1947), 106–17.

3678 Gilchrist, Huntington. **Second Commission: The General Assembly,** *International Conciliation,* CDXIII (September 1945), 451–60.

3679 Goodrich, Leland M. **Development of the General Assembly,** *International Conciliation,* CDLXXI (May 1951), 231–81.

Part D. — United Nations System

3680 — —. **Development of the General Assembly.** New York, Carnegie, 1951. 281 p.

3681 Gordenker, Leon. **Policy-Making and Secretariat Influence in the UN General Assembly: The Case of Public Information,** *American Political Science Review,* LIV (June 1960), 359–73.

3682 Green, L. C. **The "Little Assembly,"** *Year Book of World Affairs,* III (1949), 169–87.

3683 Gross, Ernest A. **The United Nations.** New York, Harper, 1962.

Chapter III.

3684 Haviland, Henry Field, Jr. **Improving the Policy-Making Processes: Analysis and Proposition,** *Annals of the American Academy of Political and Social Science,* CCXCVI (November 1954), 106–9.

Comments by Lawrence S. Finkelstein, G. A. Lincoln, Louis B. Sohn, and Kenneth Younger.

3685 — —. **The Political Role of the General Assembly.** New York, Carnegie, 1951. 190 p.

3686 Hovey, Allan, Jr. **Obstructionism and the Rules of the General Assembly,** *International Organization,* V (August 1951), 515–30.

3687 Jessup, Philip C. **The UN General Assembly As a Parliamentary Body,** *Pakistan Horizon,* XIV, 1 (1961), 3–9.

3688 Johnson, D. H. N. **The Effect of Resolutions of the General Assembly of the United Nations,** *British Yearbook of International Law,* XXXII (1955–56), 97–122.

3689 Kelsen, Hans. **The Law of the United Nations.** New York, Praeger, 1951.

Chapter IX.

Part D. — United Nations System

3690 Khan, Muhammed Zafrulla. **The President of the General Assembly of the United Nations,** *International Organization,* XVIII (Spring, 1964), 231–40.

3691 Klooz, Marie S. **The Role of the General Assembly of the United Nations in the Admission of Members,** *American Journal of International Law,* XLIII (April 1949), 246–61.

3692 Ladame, Paul A. **L'Assemblée Général des Nations Unies.** Paris, Montargis, 1949. xv + 214 p.

3693 Lande, Gabriella Rosner. **The Changing Effectiveness of General Assembly Resolutions,** *American Society of International Law Proceedings,* LVIII (1964), 162–70.

3694 Laves, Walter H. C. and Wilcox, Francis O. **The First Meeting of the General Assembly,** *American Journal of International Law,* XL (April 1946), 346–71.

3695 Lawson, Ruth C. **The General Assembly in New York,** *Current History,* New Series, XII (January 1947), 1–7.

3696 — —. **United Nations: I, Second Assembly at Work,** *Current History,* New Series, XIII (December 1947), 325–29.

3697 — —. **The United Nations: I, The Fourth Assembly,** *Current History,* New Series, XVIII (January 1950), 16–22.

3698 — —. **The United Nations: I, Third Assembly at Work,** *Current History,* New Series, XV (December 1948), 329–33.

3699 — —. **The United Nations: II, "The Peace Assembly"?** *Current History,* New Series, XVIII (February 1950), 84–87.

3700 — —. **The Work of the General Assembly,** *Current History*, New Series, XII (February 1947), 106—16.

3701 Leonard, L. Larry. **International Organization.** New York, McGraw-Hill, 1951.

Chapter XIII.

3702 Liang, Yuen-Li. **The General Assembly and the Progressive Development and Codification of International Law,** *American Journal of International Law*, XLII (January 1948), 66—97.

3703 Maclaurin, John (pseud.). **The United Nations and Power Politics.** New York, Harper, 1951.

Chapter V.

3704 Macquarrie, Heath. **The Thirteenth General Assembly,** *International Journal*, XIV (Spring, 1959), 122—30.

3705 Moore, Bernard. **United Nations: First Assembly, New York, 1948.** London, United Nations Association, 1947. 107 p.

3706 Mower, A. Glenn, Jr. **The Sponsorship of Proposals in the United Nations General Assembly,** *Western Political Quarterly*, XV (December 1962), 661—66.

3707 Munro, Leslie. **Recent Developments in the Role of the General Assembly in the Maintenance of Peace,** *American Society of International Law Proceedings*, LII (1958), 34—45.

3708 Nicholas, Herbert George. **The United Nations As a Political Institution.** 2d ed. London, Oxford University Press, 1962.
Chapter V.

3709 Northedge, F. S. **The Authority of the United Nations General Assembly,** *International Relations,* I (October 1957), 349–61ff.

3710 Peterson, Keith S. **The Agendas of the United Nations General Assembly: A Content Analysis,** *Southwestern Social Science Quarterly,* XXXIX (December 1958), 232–41.

3711 Purcell, Royal. **1947's Town Meeting of the World,** *World Affairs Quarterly,* XVIII (October 1947), 297–304.

3712 Ragonette, Marie. **The United Nations: Report No. 1, The London Session.** New York, American Association for the United Nations, 1946. 32 p.

3713 Rivlin, Benjamin. **The Italian Colonies and the General Assembly,** *International Organization,* III (August 1949), 459–70.

3714 Shwadran, Benjamin. **The Seventh United Nations Assembly and the Palestine Question,** *Middle Eastern Affairs,* IV (April 1953), 113–26.

3715 Skubiszewski, Krzysztof. **The General Assembly of the United Nations and Its Power to Influence National Action,** *American Society of International Law Proceedings,* LVIII (1964), 153–61.

3716 Sloan, F. Blaine. **The Binding Force of a 'Recommendation' of the General Assembly of the United Nations,** *British Yearbook of International Law,* XXV (1948), 1–33.

3717 Smith, Herbert A. **The United Nations Assembly: Analysis of Aspects of International Legal Interest,** *International Affairs,* XXIII (April 1947), 228–37.

3718 Soward, F. H. **Canada, the Eleventh General Assembly and Trusteeship,** *Internaitonal Journal,* XII (Summer, 1957), 167–81.

3719 Spaak, Paul-Henri. **The Role of the General Assembly,** *International Conciliation,* CDXLV (November 1948), 591–615.

3720 Stevenson, Adlai E. **Major Accomplishments of the UN General Assembly: 17th Session.** Washington, U. S. Government Printing Office, 1963. 15 p.

3721 Talmadge, I. D. W. **The UNO's First Test,** *Current History,* New Series, X (March 1946), 193–98.

3722 Vallat, F. A. **The Competence of the United Nations General Assembly,** *Recueil des Cours,* XCVIII (1959), 203–91.

3723 — —. **The General Assembly and the Security Council of the United Nations,** *British Yearbook of International Law,* XXIX (1952), 63–104.

3724 Varma, S. N. **The Political Role of the General Assembly of the United Nations,** *D. A. V. College Research Journal* (Kanpur), I (April 1954), 1–19.

3725 Western, Maurice. **Canada's Role in the Second Assembly,** *International Journal,* III (Spring, 1948), 12–31.

3726 White, Freda. **The United Nations: The First Assembly, London 1946.** London, United Nations Association of Great Britain and Northern Ireland, 1946. 93 p.

3727 Williams, Wayne D. **What Instrumentality for the Administration of International Justice Will Most Effectively Promote the Establishment and Maintenance of International Law and Order?** *American Bar Association Journal,* XXX (September 1944), 489–96.

3728 Zaidi, Manzor. **The Seventeenth Session of the General Assembly,** *Pakistan Horizon,* XV, 4 (1962), 270–84; XVI, 2 (1963), 113–22.

6.2 SECURITY COUNCIL

See also D 5.6.3.

3729 Arechaga, Eduardo Jimenez de. **The Handling of International Disputes by the Security Council,** *Recueil des Cours,* LXXXV (1954), 5—105.

3730 Bennett, A. Leroy. **The Rejuvenation of the Security Council — Evidence and Reality,** *Midwest Journal of Political Science,* IX (November 1965), 361—75.

3731 Chase, Eugene P. **The United Nations in Action.** New York, McGraw-Hill, 1950.

Chapter X.

3732 Dennett, Raymond. **Politics in the Security Council,** *International Organization,* III (August 1949), 421—33.

3733 Dixit, R. K. **Non-Member States and the Settlement of Disputes in the Security Council,** *University of Toronto Law Journal,* XII, 2 (1958), 246—81.

3734 Dolivet, Louis. **The United Nations.** New York, Farrar, Straus, 1946.

Chapter IV.

3735 Eagleton, Clyde. **The Jurisdiction of the Security Council over Disputes,** *American Journal of International Law,* XL (July 1946), 513—62.

3736 Goodrich, Leland M. **The UN Security Council,** *International Organization,* XII (Summer, 1958), 273—87.

3737 — —. **Representation in the Security Council — A Survey,** *Indian Year Book of International Affairs,* XI (1962), 48—75.

3738 Green, L. C. **The Security Council in Action,** *Year Book of World Affairs,* II (1948), 125—61.

3739 — —. **The Security Council in Retreat,** *Year Book of World Affairs,* VIII (1954), 95—117.

3740 Gross, Ernest A. **The United Nations.** New York, Harper, 1962.
Chapter II.

3741 Hasluck, Paul. **Workshop of Security.** Melbourne, Cheshire, 1948. 181 p.

3742 Kahng, Tae Jin. **Law, Politics, and the Security Council.** Hague, Nijhoff, 1964. xiv + 252 p.

3745 Kane, R. Keith. **The Security Council,** *Foreign Affairs,* XXIV (October 1945), 12—25.

3744 Kelsen, Hans. **The Law of the United Nations.** New York, Praeger, 1951.
Chapter X.

3745 — —. **Organization and Procedure of the Security Council of the United Nations,** *Harvard Law Review,* LIX (September 1946), 1087—1121.

3746 — —. **The Settlement of Disputes by the Security Council,** *International Law Quarterly,* II (Summer, 1948), 173—213.

3747 Kerley, Ernest L. **The Powers of Investigation of the United Nations Security Council,** *American Journal of International Law,* LV (October 1961), 892—918.

Part D. — *United Nations System*

3748 Kirk, Grayson. **Third Commission: The Security Council,** *International Conciliation,* CDXIII (September 1945), 461–68.

3749 Leonard, L. Larry. **International Organization.** New York, McGraw-Hill, 1951.

Chapters XI, XII.

3750 Maclaurin, John (pseud.). **The United Nations and Power Politics.** New York, Harper, 1951.

Chapter VI.

3751 Makin, Norman J. O. **An Evaluation of the Security Council,** *Annals of the American Academy of Political and Social Science,* CCLII (July 1947), 93–96.

3752 Munro, Leslie. **The Present-Day Role of the Security Council in the Maintenance of Peace,** *American Society of International Law Proceedings,* XLIX (1955), 131–36.

3753 Nicholas, Herbert George. **The United Nations As a Political Institution.** 2d ed. London, Oxford University Press, 1962.

Chapter IV.

3754 Padelford, Norman J. **Politics and Change in the Security Council,** *International Organization,* XIV (Summer, 1960), 381–401.

3755 Petersen, Keith S. **The Business of the United Nations Security Council: History (1946–1963) and Prospects,** *Journal of Politics,* XVII (November 1965), 818–38.

3756 Shwadran, Benjamin. **Egypt Before the Security Council,** *Middle Eastern Affairs,* II, (December 1951), 383–400.

3757 Vallat, F. A. **The General Assembly and the Security Council of the United Nations,** *British Yearbook of International Law,* XXIX (1952), 63–104.

Part D. — United Nations System

3758 Walters, F. P. **UN Reform: Responsibility at the Centre,** *International Relations,* I (October 1957), 339—48.

6.3 SECRETARIAT

6.3.1 GENERAL OBSERVATIONS

3759 Bailey, Sydney D. **The Secretariat of the United Nations.** Rev. ed. New York, Praeger, 1964. x + 128 p.

3760 Chamberlin, Waldo. **Strengthening the Secretariat: Analysis and Proposition,** *Annals of the American Academy of Political and Social Science,* CCXCVI (November 1954), 131—33.

Comments by W. Friedmann, Awni Khalidy, Jacob Robinson, and Wallace S. Sayre.

3761 Chase, Eugene P. **The United Nations in Action.** New York, McGraw-Hill, 1950.

Chapter XVI.

3762 Cheever, Daniel S. and Haviland, H. Field, Jr. **Organizing for Peace.** Boston, Houghton, Mifflin, 1954.

Chapters XI, XXIII.

3763 Cohen, M. **The United States and the United Nations Secretariat: A Preliminary Appraisal,** *McGill Law Journal,* I (Autumn, 1953), 169—98.

3764 Crocker, Walter R. **Some Notes on the United Nations Secretariat,** *International Organization,* IV (November 1950), 598—613.

3765 Dean, Vera Micheles. **The UN Today.** New York, Holt, Rinehart and Winston, 1965.

Chapter IV.

Part D. — *United Nations System*

3766 Dolivet, Louis. **The United Nations.** New York, Farrar, Straus, 1946.
Chapter VIII.

3767 Giraud, E. **The Secretariat of International Institutions,** *Recueil des Cours,* LXXIX (1951), 373–507.

3768 Goodrich, Leland M. **The United Nations.** New York, Crowell, 1963.
Chapter VII.

3769 Goodspeed, Stephen S. **The Nature and Function of International Organization.** New York, Oxford University Press, 1963.
Chapter XI.

3770 Hill, Norman L. **International Organization.** New York, Harper, 1952.
Chapters XV, XVI.

3771 Irving, Clifford. **The Thirty-Eighth Floor.** New York, McGraw-Hill, 1965. 317 p.

3772 Jeanneret-Gris, Charles Edouard. **UN Headquarters.** New York, Reinhold, 1947. 79 p.

3773 Laves, Walter H. C. **The United Nations: Reorganizing the World's Governmental Institutions,** *Public Administration Review,* V (Summer, 1945), 183–93.

3774 Laves, Walter H. C. and Stone, Donald C. **The United Nations Secretariat,** *Foreign Policy Reports,* XXII (October 15, 1946), 182–91.

3775 Leonard, L. Larry. **International Organization.** New York, McGraw-Hill, 1951.
Chapter VI.

Part D. — *United Nations System*

3776 Maclaurin, John (pseud.). **The United Nations and Power Politics.** New York, Harper, 1951.

Chapter XI.

3777 Mangone, Gerard J. **A Short History of International Organization.** New York, McGraw-Hill, 1954.

Chapter VII.

3778 Masland, John W. **The Secretariat of the United Nations,** *Public Administration Review*, VI (Autumn, 1945), 364–72.

3779 Nicholas, Herbert George. **The United Nations As a Political Institution.** 2d ed. London, Oxford University Press, 1962.

Chapter VII.

3780 Parry, Clive. **The Secretariat of the United Nations,** *World Affairs*, IV (July 1950), 350–64.

3781 Ranshofen-Wertheimer, E. **The International Secretariat.** Washington, Carnegie, 1945. 500 p.

3782 Schachter, Oscar. **The Development of International Law Through the Legal Opinions of the United Nations Secretariat,** *British Yearbook of International Law*, XXV (1948), 91–132.

3783 Schwebel, Stephen M. **Secretary-General and Secretariat,** *Charter Review Conference: Ninth Report and Papers Presented to the Commission*, Commission to Study the Organization of Peace (ed.). New York, Commission to Study the Organization of Peace, 1955, pp. 198–211.

3784 Siotis, Jean. **Essai sur le Secrétariat International.** Geneva, Droz, 1963. 272 p.

3785 Stone, Donald C. **Organizing the United Nations,** *Public Administration Review,* VI (Spring, 1946), 115–29.

3786 Vandenbosch, Amry and Hogan, Willard N. **The United Nations.** New York, McGraw-Hill, 1952.
Chapter XII.

3787 Virally, Michel. **Vers une réforme du Secrétariat des Nations Unies?** *International Organization,* XV (Spring, 1961), 236–55.

3788 Wilson, J. V. **Problems of an International Secretariat,** *International Affairs,* XX (October 1944), 542–54.

3789 Winchmore, Charles. **The Secretariat: Retrospect and Prospect,** *International Organization,* XIX (Summer, 1965), 622–42.

3790 Wriggins, Howard and Bock, Edwin A. **The Status of the United Nations Secretariat.** New York, Woodrow Wilson Foundation, 1954. 30 p.

3791 Young, Tien Cheng. **International Civil Service: Principles and Problems.** Brussels, International Institute of Administrative Sciences, 1958. 268 p.

6.3.2 SECRETARY GENERAL

3792 Alexandrowicz, Charles Henry. **The Secretary-General of the United Nations,** *International and Comparative Law Quarterly,* XI (October 1962), 1109–30.

3793 Anglin, Douglas G. **Lester Pearson and the Office of Secretary-General,** *International Journal,* XVII (Spring, 1962), 145–50.

Part D. — United Nations System

3794 Bailey, Sydney D. **The Secretariat of the United Nations.** Rev. ed. New York, Praeger, 1964.

Chapter III.

3795 — —. **The Secretary-General of the United Nations,** *World Today,* New Series, XVII (January 1961), 2–11.

3796 — —. **The Troika and the Future of the UN,** *International Conciliation,* DXXXVIII (May 1962), 3–62.

3797 Commission to Study the Organization of Peace. **The UN Secretary-General: His Role in World Politics.** New York, Commission to Study the Organization of Peace, 1962. 63 p.

3798 Foote, Wilder (ed.). **Dag Hammarskjold: Servant of Peace.** New York, Harper and Row, 1962. 388 p.

3799 Goodrich, Leland M. **The Political Role of the Secretary-General,** *International Organization,* XVI (Autumn, 1962), 720–35.

3800 Gross, Ernest A. **The United Nations.** New York, Harper, 1962.

Chapter I.

3801 Hamilton, Thomas J. **The UN and Trygve Lie,** *Foreign Affairs,* XXIX (October 1950), 67–77.

3802 Hammarskjöld, Dag. **Two Differing Concepts of the United Nations Assayed: Introduction to the Annual Report of the Secretary-General on the Work of the Organization, 16 June 1960 – June 1961,** *International Organization,* XV (Autumn, 1961), 549–63.

3803 Hill, Norman L. **International Organization.** New York, Harper, 1952.
Chapter XVII.

3804 Jackson, Elmore. **Constitutional Developments of the United Nations: The Growth of Its Executive Capacity,** *American Society of International Law Proceedings,* LV (1961), 78—84.
Comments by Sohn, Schachter, and Schwebel.

3805 — —. **The Developing Role of the Secretary-General,** *International Organization,* XI (Summer, 1957), 431—45.

3806 James, A. M. **The Role of the Secretary-General of the United Nations in International Relations,** *International Relations,* I (October 1959), 620—38.

3807 Joyce, J. A. **The Strength of U Thant,** *Christian Century,* LXXX (August 28, 1963), 1047—50.

3808 Kelsen, Hans. **The Law of the United Nations.** New York, Praeger, 1951.
Chapter XI.

3809 Lash, Joseph P. **Dag Hammarskjold: Custodian of the Brushfire Peace.** Garden City, Doubleday, 1961. 304 p.

3810 — —. **Dag Hammarskjold's Conception of His Office,** *International Organization,* XVI (Summer, 1962), 542—66.

3811 Lentner, Howard H. **The Diplomacy of the United Nations Secretary General,** *Western Political Quarterly,* XVIII (September 1965), 531—50.

3812 — —. **The Political Responsibility and Accountability of the United Nations Secretary General,** *Journal of Politics,* XXVII (November 1965), 839—60.

3813 Leonard, L. Larry. **International Organization.** New York, McGraw-Hill, 1951.
Chapter XIV.

3814 Lippmann, Walter. **Dag Hammarskjold, United Nations Pioneer,** *International Organization*, XV (Autumn, 1961), 547—63.

3815 Miller, Richard I. **Dag Hammarskjold and Crisis Diplomacy.** Dobbs Ferry, Oceana, 1961. 344 p.

3816 Pyman, T. A. **The United Nations Secretary-Generalship,** *Australian Outlook*, XV (December 1961), 240—59.

3817 Schwebel, Stephen M. **The Secretary-General of the United Nations: His Political Powers and Practice.** Cambridge, Harvard University Press, 1952. xiv + 299 p.

3818 Singh, Jitendra. **The Position and Role of the Secretary-General of the United Nations,** *Indian Journal of Public Administration*, IX (April-June 1963), 212—37.

3819 Stein, Eric. **Mr. Hammarskjold, the Charter Law and the Future Role of the United Nations Secretary General,** *American Journal of International Law*, LVI (January 1962), 9—32.

3820 Van Langenhove, Fernand. **La role prominent du Secrétaire Général dans l'opérations des Nations Unies au Congo.** Hague, Nijoff, 1964. 260 p.

3821 Wadsworth, James J. **The Glass House: The United Nations in Action.** New York, Praeger, 1965. 224 p.

6.3.3. INTERNATIONAL CIVIL SERVICE

See also D 7.2.3. and D 7.3.4.3.

3822 Ahmed, Latheef N. **The Organization and Methods of the United Nations Administrative Committee on Coordination,** *Revue Internationale des Sciences Administratives,* XXIV, 3 (1958), 333—46.

3823 — —. **The Role of the United Nations Administrative Committee on Co-ordination in the Co-ordination of the Programmes and Activities of the United Nations and the Specialised Agencies,** *Revue Internationale des Sciences Administratives,* XXII, 3 (1956), 95—118.

3824 Angus, N. C. **United Nations and Public Administration,** *New Zealand Journal of Public Administration,* XXII (September 1959), 13—24.

3825 Basu, R. K. **Public Administration Under UN Technical Assistance Programme,** *Indian Journal of Public Administration,* IV (October-December 1958), 420—34.

3826 Behanan, K. T. **Realities and Make-Believe: Personnel Policy in the UN Secretariat.** New York, William-Frederick, 1952. 70 p.

3827 Block, Roger and Lefrevre, Jacqueline. **La fonction publique internationale et européenne.** Paris, Librairie Générale de Droit et de Jurisprudence, 1963. 219 p.

3828 Booth, D. A. **The United Nations, the United States and the International Civil Service,** *Revue Internationale des Sciences Administratives,* XXI, 4 (1955), 703—40.

3829 Claude, Inis L., Jr. **Swords Into Plowshares.** 3d ed. New York, Random House, 1964.

Chapter X.

3830 Cohen, Maxwell. **The United Nations Secretariat: Some Constitutional and Administrative Developments,** *American Journal of International Law,* XLIX (July 1955), 295–319.

3831 Crosswell, Carol McCormick. **Protection of International Personnel Abroad: Law and Practice Affecting the Privileges and Immunities of International Organization.** New York, Oceana, 1952. x + 198 p.

3832 Evans, Luther H. **Problems of Administration in International Affairs — A Memorandum,** *Foundations of World Organization,* Lyman Bryson, Louis Finkelstein, Harold D. Lasswell, and R. M. MacIver (eds.). New York, Harper, 1950, pp. 331–36.

3833 Fedder, Edwin H. **United States Loyalty Procedures and the Recruitment of International Personnel,** *Western Political Quarterly,* XV (December 1962), 705–12.

3834 Friedmann, Wolfgang and Fatouros, Arghyrios A. **The United Nations Administration Tribunal,** *International Organization,* XI (Winter, 1957), 13–29.

3835 Gaudemet, Paul Marie. **The Status of International Civil Servants in National Law,** *International Review of Administrative Sciences,* XXV, 1 (1959), 34–42.

3836 Goodrich, Leland M. **Geographical Distribution of the UN Secretariat,** *International Organization,* XVI (Summer, 1962), 465–82.

3837 Green, L. C. **The International Civil Servant, His Employer and His State,** *Transactions* (Grotius Society), XL (1954), 147–74.

3838 Hammarskjöld, Dag. **The International Civil Servant in Law and Fact.** Oxford, Clarendon Press, 1961. 28 p.

3839 — —. **The International Civil Service,** *EROPA Review,* II (December 1962), 55—82.

3840 Hardy, M. J. L. **Claims by International Organizations in Respect of Injuries to Their Agents,** *British Yearbook of International Law,* XXXVII (1961), 516—26.

3841 Harris, Joseph P. **Some Problems of International Administration, Illustrated by UNRA,** *Institute of World Affairs Proceedings,* XXI (1945), 85—86.

3842 Hill, Norman L. **The Personnel of International Administration,** *American Political Science Review,* XXIII (November 1929), 972—88.

3843 Honig, F. **The International Civil Service: Basic Problems and Contemporary Difficulties,** *International Affairs,* XXX (April 1954), 174—85.

3844 Hosch, Louis E. **The Public Administration Division of the United Nations: A Brief History,** *International Review of Administrative Sciences,* XXX, 3 (1964), 231—41.

3845 Howe, John M. **The Geographic Composition of International Secretariats,** *Journal of International Affairs,* II (Spring, 1948), 46—56.

3846 Ivrakis, Solon Cleanthe. **Speculations Round the Privileges and Immunities of the United Nations,** *Revue Hellénique de Droit International,* VII (April 1954), 175—93.

3847 Jenks, C. Wilfred. **Co-ordination in International Organization: An Introductory Survey,** *British Yearbook of International Law,* XXVIII (1951), 29—89.

General discussion of post—1945 world and international organizations, ECSC, NATO, UN, OAS.

Part D. — United Nations System

3848 — —. **La coordination: Nouveau problème d'organisation internationale,** *Recueil des Cours,* LXXVII (1950), 157—302.

3849 — —. **International Immunities.** London, Stevens, 1961. 178 p.

This book, wider in coverage than its title indicates, covers the privileges, immunities, and even status of international organizations and their personnel.

3850 — —. **Some Problems of an International Civil Service,** *Public Administration Review,* III (Spring, 1943), 93—105.

3851 Jessup, Philip C. **The International Civil Servant and His Loyalties,** *Journal of International Affairs,* IX, 2 (1955), 55—61.

3852 Kaplan, Robert. **Some Problems in the Administration of an International Secretariat,** *Journal of International Affairs,* II (Spring, 1948), 35—45.

3853 Kennedy, Donald B. **A Note on the Salary, Allowance, and Leave System of the UN,** *Public Administration Review,* XI (Summer, 1951), 199—202.

3854 Kindleberger, Charles P. **Economists in International Organizations,** *International Organization,* IX (August 1955), 338—52.

3855 King, John K. **The Privileges and Immunities of the Personnel of International Organizations.** Odense, Denmark, Strandberg, 1949. xiv + 282 p.

3856 Lall, S. **The International Civil Servant,** *Indian Journal of Public Administration,* II (January 1956), 12—17.

3857 Langrod, Georges. **The International Civil Service: Its Nature and Evolution,** F. G. Berthoud (trans.). Preface by Paul Guggenheim. Dobbs Ferry, Oceana, 1963. 358 p.

3858 Latheef, N. Ahmed. **The Role of the United Nations Administrative Committee on Coordination in the Coordination of the Programmes and Activities of the United Nations and the Specialized Agencies,** *Revue International des Sciences Administratives,* XXII (1956), 95–118.

3859 Lengyel, Peter. **Some Trends in the International Civil Service,** *International Organization,* XIII (Autumn, 1959), 520–37.

3860 Lewis, G. **The Selection and Training of International Civil Servants,** *Cahiers de Bruges,* VII, 2 (1957), 67–76.

3861 Loveday, A. **Reflections on International Administration.** London, Oxford University Press, 1956. x + 334 p.

3862 — —. **Staff Salaries in the UN Family,** *International Organization,* XI (Autumn, 1957), 635–48.

3863 M., B. **Geneva in 1947: A Centre for International Activities,** *World Today,* New Series, III (June 1947), 261–68.

3864 M., L. **Some Functions and Problems of the International Civil Servant,** *Indian Year Book of International Affairs,* V (1956), 229–53.

3865 Pelt, Adrian. **Peculiar Characteristics of an International Administration,** *Public Administration Review,* VI (Spring, 1946), 108–14.

3866 Potter, Pitman B. **What International Administrative Agencies Actually Do,** *Iowa Law Review,* XXX (July 1945), 544–47.

3867 Preuss, Lawrence. **Immunity of Officers and Employees of the United Nations for Official Acts: The Ranallo Case,** *American Journal of International Law,* XLI (July 1947), 555–78.

3868 Projansky, Sonia. **The Internship Program of the United Nations Secretariat,** *Journal of International Affairs*, II (Spring, 1948), 24–34.

3869 Purves, Chester. **The Internal Administration of an International Seccretariat.** London, Royal Institute of International Affairs, 1945. 78 p.

3870 Sbarounis, Athanase J. **Taxation of the United Nations Officials,** *Revue Hellénique de Droit International*, VII (January 1954), 1–19.

3871 Schwebel, S. M. **The International Character of the Secretariat of the United Nations,** *British Yearbook of International Law*, XXX (1953), 71–115.

3872 Scott, F. R. **The World's Civil Service,** *International Conciliation*, CDXCVI (January 1954), 259–320.

3873 Shafqat, C. M. **The United Nations and Its Agents,** *Papistan Horizon*, III (March 1950), 45–48.

3874 Sharp, Walter R. **Trends in United Nations Administration,** *International Organization*, XV (Summer, 1961), 393–407.

3874a — —. **International Bureaucracies and Political Development,** *Bureaucrary and Political Development*, Joseph La Palombara (ed.). Princeton, Princeton University Press, 1963, pp. 441–74.

3875 Singer, J. D. **The United Nations Advisory Committee on Administrative and Budgetary Questions,** *Public Administration*, XXXV (Winter, 1957), 395–416.

3876 Siotis, Jean. **Some Problems of European Secretariats,** *Journal of Common Market Studies*, II (May 1964), 222–50.

3877 Srivastava, A. K. **Geographical Distribution of Personnel in the United Nations,** *Indian Journal of Public Administration,* III (October 1957), 357—70.

3878 — —. **The Problem of Loyalty in International Organizations,** *India Quarterly,* XIV (January-March 1958), 77—86.

3879 Stein, Eric and Sharp, Walter R. **Some Implications of Expanding Membership for United Nations Administration and Budget.** New York, Carnegie, 1956. 77 + 34 p.

Two essays in one volume.

3880 Stone, Donald C. **Administrative Achievement in World Organization,** *Perspectives on a Troubled Decade,* Lyman Bryson, Louis Finkelstein, and R. M. MacIver (eds.). New York, Harper, 1950, pp. 423—34.

3881 — —. **The Application of Scientific Management Principles to International Administration,** *American Political Science Review,* XLII (October 1948), 915—27.

3882 Sweetser, Arthur. **The World's Civil Service,** *Iowa Law Review,* XXX (May 1945), 478—88.

3883 Swift, Richard N. **Personnel Problems of the United Nations Secretariat,** *International Organization,* XI (Spring, 1957), 228—47.

3884 Torre, Mottran (ed.). **The Selection of Personnel for International Service.** New York, World Federation for Mental Health, United States Committee, 1963. xxii + 161 p.

3885 Weis, G. **Training an International Civil Service,** *World Affairs,* X (January 1945), 112—15.

3886 Witmer, John D., II. **The United Nations Intern Program,** *Journal of International Affairs,* IX, 2 (1955), 62—66.

7. ECONOMIC AND SOCIAL ACTIVITIES

Because of the greater number of economic and social service agencies under the United Nations, coordination of their field operations requires a much larger bureaucratic staff in New York than was the case in Geneva. To compound the problem of supervision, the headquarters of many specialized agencies are located outside New York.

7.1 GENERAL DISCUSSIONS

3887 Adam, H.-T. **Les organismes internationaux spécialisés: Contribution à la théorie générale des établissements publics internationaux.** Paris, Pinchon et Durand-Auzias, 1965. 2 vols.

3888 Asher, Robert E.; Kotschnig, Walter M.; Brown, William Adams, Jr.; Green, James Frederick; Sady, Emil J.; *et al.* **The United Nations and Economic and Social Cooperation.** Washington, Brookings, 1957. xi + 561 p.

   Excerpts from the authors' *The United Nations and the Promotion of the General Welfare.*

3889 — —. **The United Nations and the Promotion of the General Welfare.** Washington, Brookings, 1957. xvi + 1,216 p.

   Very detailed treatment.

3890 Ball, M. Margaret and Killough, Hugh B. **International Relations.** New York, Ronald, 1956.

   Chapter XVII.

3891 Beckel, Graham. **Workshops for the World: The Specialized Agencies of the United Nations.** New York, Abelard-Schuman, 1954. 213 p.

Part D. — *United Nations System*

3892 Bolles, Blair. **Pillars of the United Nations — International Economic and Social Agencies,** *Foreign Policy Reports,* XXI (December 1, 1945), 246–55.

3893 Chase, Eugene P. **The United Nations in Action.** New York, McGraw-Hill, 1950.

Chapters XII, XIII.

3894 Cheever, Daniel S. and Haviland, H. Field, Jr. **Organizing for Peace.** Boston, Houghton, Mifflin, 1954.

Chapters VIII, IX.

3895 Courlander, Harold. **Shaping Our Times.** New York, Oceana, 1960.

Chapters IV, V, VII.

3896 Dolivet, Louis. **The United Nations.** New York, Farrar and Straus, 1946.

Chapter V.

3897 Eagleton, Clyde. **International Government.** 3d ed. New York, Ronald, 1957.

Chapter XIII.

3898 Eichelberger, Clark M. **UN: The First Twenty Years.** New York, Harper, 1965.

Chapter VII.

3899 Evans, Luther H. **The United Nations Family of Agencies: Origins and Relationships,** *The Quest for Peace,* Andrew W. Cordier and Wilder Foote (eds.). New York, Columbia University Press, 1965, pp. 355–82.

3900 Finer, Herman. **The United Nations Economic and Social Council.** Boston, World Peace Foundation, 1946. 121 p.

Part D. — United Nations System

3901 Goodrich, Leland M. **The United Nations.** New York, Crowell, 1963.
Chapter XII.

3902 Goodspeed, Stephen S. **The Nature and Function of International Organization.** New York, Oxford University Press, 1963.
Chapters XII—XIV.

3903 Gordenker, Leon. **The USSR, the United Nations, and the General Welfare,** *World Politics,* XVII (April 1965), 495—502.

3904 Gregg, Robert W. **The Economic and Social Council: Politics of Membership,** *Western Political Quarterly,* XVI (March 1963), 109—32.

3905 Haas, Ernst B. **Regionalism, Functionalism, and Universal International Organization,** *World Politics,* VII (January 1956), 238—63.

3906 Hill, Norman L. **International Politics.** New York, Harper and Row, 1963.
Chapter XX.

3907 Hoffman, Paul G. **The Six Imperatives of Economic and Social Progress,** *The United States and the United Nations,* Francis O. Wilcox and H. Field Haviland, Jr. (eds.). Baltimore, Johns Hopkins Press, 1961, pp. 27—48.

3908 Jacob, Philip E. and Atherton, Alexine L. **Dynamics of International Organization.** Homewood, Dorsey, 1964.
Chapters XII, XVII.

3909 Jacobson, Harold Karan. **Economic and Social Matters,** *The United States and the United Nations,* Franz B. Gross (ed.). Norman, University of Oklahoma Press, 1964, pp. 226—62.

3910 Jessup, Philip C., Lande, Adolf, and Lissitzyn, Oliver J. **International Regulation of Economic and Social Questions.** New York, Carnegie, n. d. 173 p.

> The volume also contains an essay by Joseph P. Chamberlain, "International Organization," which is reprinted from *International Conciliation;* the cover title of this book is given as *International Organization*, in contradistinction to the title page.

3911 Kennedy, A. L. **The Non-Political Value of the League,** *Quarterly Review*, CCLXX (January 1938), 146—65.

3912 Labeyrie-Ménahem, C. **Des institutions spécialisées: Problèmes juridiques et diplomatiques de l'adminsitration internationale.** Preface by Pierre Mendès-France. Paris, Pedone, 1953. 168 p.

3913 Loveday, A. **Suggestions for the Reform of the UNESCO and ECOSOC Machinery,** *International Organization*, VII (August 1953), 325—41.

3914 — —. **An Unfortunate Decision,** *International Organization*, I (June 1947), 279—90.

> Deals with the failure to allow persons on ECOSOC to represent their own views, rather than those of their respective governments.

3915 Lubin, Isador and Murden, Forrest. **ECOSOC: Concept Versus Practice,** *Journal of International Affairs*, IX, 2 (1955), 67—78.

3916 Maclaurin, John (pseud.). **The United Nations and Power Politics.** New York, Harper, 1951.

> Chapter VIII.

3917 McNeil, Hector. **Accomplishments in the Economic and Social Field,** *International Conciliation*, CDXLV (November 1948), 633—50.

3918 Malik, Charles. **The Economic and Social Council,** *Peace on Earth*, Trygve Lie, Herbert V. Evatt, Charles Malik, Eleanor Roosevelt, Jaime Torres Bodet, Brock Chisholm, John Boyd-Orr, Ralph Bunche, Benjamin Cohen, Ludwick Rajchman, and Carlos P. Romulo. New York, Hermitage, 1949, pp. 49—64.

Part D. — *United Nations System*

3919 Malinowski, W. R. **Centralization and Decentralization in the United Nations Economic and Social Activities,** *International Organization,* XVI (Summer, 1962), 521—41.

3920 Mander, Linden. **The United Nations and the Specialized Agencies During the Next Generation,** *Western Political Quarterly,* XVI (September 1963), Supplement, 30—32.

3921 Padelford, Norman J. **Politics and the Future of ECOSOC,** *International Organization,* XV (Autumn, 1961), 564—80.

3922 Pollaczek, Gustav. **The United Nations and Specialized Agencies,** *American Journal of International Law,* XL (July 1946), 592—618.

3923 Raju, G. S. and Rao, P. Chandrasekhara. **The Specialised Agencies and Their Interpretive Mechanism,** *Indian Journal of International Law,* I (July-October 1961), 613—28.

3924 Riefler, Winfield W. **The Work of the Economic and Social Council of the United Nations,** *Academy of Political Science Proceedings,* XXII (January 1947), 182—90.

3925 Rubinstein, Alvin Z. **Soviet Policy Toward Under-Developed Areas in the Economic and Social Council,** *International Organization,* IX (May 1955), 232—43.

3926 Saba, H. **Quasi-Legislative Activities of the Specialised Agencies of the United Nations,** *Recueil des Cours,* CXI (1964), 607—90.

3927 Schleicher, Charles P. **International Relations.** Englewood Cliffs, Prentice-Hall, 1962.
Chapter XVI.

3928 Sharp, Walter R. **The Administration of United Nations Operational Programs,** *International Organization,* XIX (Summer, 1965), 581—602.

3929 — —. **Field Administration in the United Nations System: The Conduct of International Economic and Social Problems.** New York, Praeger, 1961. 570 p.

3930 — —. **The Specialized Agencies and the United Nations,** *International Organization,* I (September 1947), 460–74; II (June 1948), 247–67.

3931 Stinebower, Leroy D. **The Economic and Social Council: An Instrument of International Cooperation.** New York, Commission to Study the Organization of Peace, 1946. 39 p.

3932 Vandenbosch, Amry and Hogan, Willard N. **The United Nations.** New York, McGraw-Hill, 1952.

Chapters X, XVII.

3933 Van Dyke, Vernon. **International Politics.** 2d ed. New York, Appleton-Century-Crofts, 1966.

Chapter XXI.

7.2 ECONOMIC EFFORTS

7.2.1 GENERAL OBSERVATIONS

3934 Asher, Robert E. **Economic Cooperation Under UN Auspices,** *International Organization,* XII (Summer, 1958), 288–302.

3935 Cheever, Daniel S. and Haviland, H. Field, Jr. **Organizing for Peace.** Boston, Houghton, Mifflin, 1954.

Chapter XIX.

3936 Comstock, Alzada. **The UN's Economic Problems,** *Current History,* New Series, XI (September 1946), 195–200.

Part D. — *United Nations System*

3937 Fisher, Allan G. B. **International Economic Collaboration and the ECOSOC,** *International Affairs,* XXI (October 1945), 459–68.

3938 Gross, Ernest A. **The United Nations.** New York, Harper, 1962.

Chapter IV.

3939 Hadsel, Fred L. **Technical Specialized Agencies of the UN — Finance, Transport and Communication, and Trade,** *Foreign Policy Reports,* XXIII (November 15, 1947), 214–23.

3940 Jacob, Philip E. and Atherton, Alexine L. **Dynamics of International Organization.** Homewood, Dorsey, 1964.

Chapter XIV.

3941 Leonard, L. Larry. **International Organization.** New York, McGraw-Hill, 1951.

Chapters XX, XXII.

3942 Rubinstein, Alvin Z. **Soviet and American Policies in International Economic Organizations,** *International Organization,* XVIII (Winter, 1964), 29–52.

3943 Schwarzenberger, Georg. **Power Politics.** 3d ed. London, Stevens, 1964.

Chapter XXV.

3944 Staley, Eugene. **World Organization on the Economic Fronts,** *Peace, Security, and the United Nations,* Hans J. Morgenthau (ed.). Chicago, University of Chicago Press, 1945, pp. 107–29.

3945 Strange, Susan. **The Economic Work of the United Nations,** *Year Book of World Affairs,* VIII (1954), 118–40.

Part D. — United Nations System

3946 Vandenbosch, Amry and Hogan, Willard N. **Toward World Order.** New York, McGraw-Hill, 1963.

Chapter XI.

3947 Viner, Jacob. **Economic Foundations of International Organization,** *Perspectives on a Troubled Decade,* Lyman Bryson, Louis Finkelstein and R. M. MacIver (eds.). New York, Harper, 1950, pp. 816—32.

7.2.2 COMMUNICATIONS AND TRANSPORTATION

7.2.2.1 GENERAL OBSERVATIONS

3948 Mance, Harry Osborne and Wheeler, J. E. **International Road Transport, Postal, Electricity and Miscellaneous Questions.** London, Oxford University Press, 1947. 258 p.

7.2.2.2 COMMUNICATIONS

3949 Alexandrowicz, Charles Henry. **World Economic Agencies.** London, Stevens, 1962.

Chapters I, II.

3950 Bureau International de l'Union Postale Universelle. **L'Union Postale Universelle: Sa fondation et son développement, 1874—1949.** Bern, 1949. 311 p.

3951 Codding, George Arthur, Jr. **The Universal Postal Union.** New York, New York University Press, 1964. 296 p.

3952 Huth, Arno G. **Cooperative Radio Agreements,** *International Organization,* VI (August 1952), 396—406.

3953 Mance, Harry Osborne and Wheeler, J. E. **International Telecommunications.** London, Oxford University Press, 1944. xii + 90 p.

3954 Mander, Linden A. **Foundations of Modern World Society.** 2d ed. Stanford, Stanford University Press, 1947.

Chapter IX.

3955 Menon, M. A. K. **The Universal Postal Union,** *International Conciliation*, DLII (March 1965), 3—64.

3956 Tomlinson, John D. **The International Control of Radio-Communications.** Ann Arbor, Edwards, 1945. 314 p.

3957 Wolf, Francis Colt de. **Telecommunications in the New World,** *Yale Law Journal*, LV (August 1946), 1281—90.

7.2.2.3 TRANSPORTATION

See also E 9.3

3958 Alexandrowicz, Charles Henry. **World Economic Agencies.** London, Stevens, 1962.

Chapter VII.

3959 Bloet-Hamorlijnck, Rita Jong. **The Development of Air Law and European Cooperation,** *International Relations*, II (April 1965), 736—53.

3960 Cooper, John C. **Air Transport and World Organization,** *Yale Law Journal*, LV (August 1946), 1191—1213.

3961 Jennings, R. Y. **Recent Conventions on International Civil Aviation,** *British Yearbook of International Law*, XXIII (1946), 358—63.

3962 Johnson, D. H. N. **IMCO: The First Four Years (1959—1962),** *International and Comparative Law Quarterly*, XII (January 1963), 56—87.

3963 Lepawsky, Albert. **International Development of River Resources,** *International Affairs*, XXXIX (October 1963), 533—50.

3964 Little, Virginia. **Control of International Air Transport,** *International Organization*, III (February 1949), 29—45.

3965 McKim, Anson C. **World Order in Air Transport,** *International Journal*, II (Summer, 1947), 226—36.

3966 Mance, Harry Osborne. **Frontiers, Peace Treaties, and International Organization.** London, Oxford University Press, 1946. x + 196 p.

3967 Mance, Harry Osborne and Wheeler, J. E. **International Air Transport.** London, Oxford University Press, 1944. 117 p.

3968 — —. **International River and Canal Transport.** London, Oxford University Press, 1945. viii + 115 p.

3969 — —. **International Sea Transport.** London, Oxford University Press, 1945. xii + 198 p.

3970 Marx, Daniel, Jr. **International Organization of Shipping,** *Yale Law Journal*, LV (August 1946), 1214—32.

3971 — —. **International Shipping Cartels.** Princeton, Princeton University Press, 1953. 323 p.

3972 Padera, David J. **The Curriculum of IMCO,** *International Organization*, X (Autumn, 1960), 524—47.

3973 Schenkman, Jacob. **International Civil Aviation Association.** Geneva, Droz, 1955. 410 p.

3974 Thomas, Ivor. **Civil Aviation: International Questions Outstanding,** *International Affairs,* XXV (January 1949), 56–65.

3975 Van Zandt, J. Parker. **Civil Aviation and Peace.** Washington, Brookings, 1944. x + 157 p.

3976 Wedgwood, Ralph L. **International Rail Transport.** New York, Oxford University Press, 1946. 162 p.

7.2.3 ECONOMIC DEVELOPMENT AND TECHNICAL ASSISTANCE

3977 Ahmed, Latheef N. **The United Nations Technical Assistance Board (TAB),** *Philippine Journal of Public Administration,* II (January 1958), 20–30.

3978 Ahmed, S. Habib. **Operations of the UN Technical Assistance Program,** *Pakistan Horizon,* XII (September 1959), 191–96.

3979 Ali, Syed Amjad. **United Nations Conference on Trade and Development,** *Pakistan Horizon,* XVII, 3 (1964), 262–71.

3980 Allen, Robert Loring. **United Nations Technical Assistance: Soviet and East European Participation,** *International Organization,* XI (Autumn, 1957), 615–34.

3981 Ascher, Charles S. **Recent Developments in the Technical Assistance Programme of the United Nations,** *Revue International des Sciences Administratives,* XVI (1950), 896–99.

3982 Asher, Robert E. **Multilateral Versus Bilateral Aid: An Old Controversy Revisited,** *International Organization,* XVI (Autumn, 1962), 697—719.

3983 Basu, R. K. **Public Administration Under UN Technical Assistance Programme,** *Indian Journal of Public Administration,* IV (October-December 1958), 420—34.

3984 — —. **Regional Cooperation in Technical Assistance,** *India Quarterly* XIV (October-December 1958), 350—63.

3985 Belshaw, Cyril. **Training and Recruitment: Some Principles of International Aid,** *International Journal,* XVIII (Winter, 1962—63), 43—57.

3986 Blelloch, David. **Bold New Programme: A Review of the United Nations Technical Assistance,** *International Affairs,* XXXIII (January 1957), 36—50.

3987 Bloch, Henry Simon. **The Fiscal Advisory Functions of United Nations Technical Assistance,** *International Organization,* XI (Spring, 1957), 248—60.

3988 Blough, Roy. **The Furtherance of Economic Development,** *International Organization,* XIX (Summer, 1965), 562—80.

3989 Cheever, Daniel S. and Haviland, H. Field, Jr. **Organizing for Peace.** Boston, Houghton, Mifflin, 1954.

Chapter XVIII.

3990 Clapp, Gordon R. **An Approach to Economic Development: A Summary of the Reports of the United Nations Survey Mission for the Middle East,** *International Conciliation,* CDLX (April 1950), 203—17.

3991 Courlander, Harold. **Shaping Our Times.** New York, Oceana, 1960.

Chapter VI.

3992 Dean, Vera Micheles. **The UN Today.** New York, Holt, Rinehart and Winston, 1965.

Chapter VI.

3993 Dickson, A. G. **Technical Assistance and Idealism: Misgivings and Mistakings,** *Year Book of World Affairs,* XII (1958), 198—225.

3994 E., G. **The United Nations and Under-Developed Countries: Technical and Economic Assistance,** *World Today,* **New Series,** VII (November 1951), 489—98.

3995 Espy, W. R. **Bold New Program.** New York, Harper, 1950. x + 273 p.

3996 Flere, Janvid. **UN Conference on Trade and Development,** *Pakistan Horizon,* XVI, 2 (1963), 103—12.

3997 Fortman, W. F. de Gaay. **The United Nations and the Underdeveloped Areas,** *The United Nations: Ten Years, Legal Progress,* Gezina J. H. Van Der Molen, W. P. J. Pompe and J. H. W. Verzijl (eds.). Hague, Nederlandse Studentenvereniging Voor Wereldrechtsorde, 1956, pp. 108—25.

3998 Fox, Annette Baker. **President Truman's Fourth Point and the United Nations,** *International Conciliation,* CDLII (June 1949), 465—85.

3999 Franch, Peter G. and Franck, Dorothea Seelye. **Implementation of Technical Assistance,** *International Conciliation,* CDLXVIII (February 1951), 61—80.

4000 Ganguli, B. N. and Sen, S. R. **The Role of the United Nations in the Development of Less Developed Countries,** *International Studies,* V (April 1964), 353—65.

4001 Gardner, Richard N. **In Pursuit of World Order.** New York, Praeger, 1964.

Chapter V.

4002 Gilchrist, Huntington. **Technical Assistance from the United Nations — As Seen in Pakistan,** *International Organization,* XIII (Autumn, 1959), 505—19.

4003 Glick, Philip M. **The Administration of Technical Assistance: Growth in the Americas.** Chicago, University of Chicago Press, 1957. 390 p.

4004 Goeckingk, Johanna Von. **United Nations Technical Assistance Board: A Case Study in International Administration.** New York, Woodrow Wilson Foundation, 1955. 40 p.

4005 Goodrich, Carter. **Bolivia: Test of Technical Assistance,** *Foreign Affairs,* XXXII (April 1954), 473—81.

4006 — —. **The United Nations Conference on Resources,** *International Organization,* V (February 1951), 48—60.

4007 Gray, A. L., Jr. **The Role of the United Nations in the Financing of Underdeveloped Countries,** *Social Studies,* LIV (February 1963), 59—62.

4008 Haas, Ernst. **Toward Controlling International Change: A Personal Plea,** *World Politics,* XVII (October 1964), 1—12.

4009 Hadwen, John G. and Kaufmann, Johan. **How United Nations Decisions Are Made.** Leyden, Sythoff, 1960.

Chapter IV.

4010 Hagras, Kamal M. **United Nations Conference on Trade and Development: A Case Study in UN Diplomacy.** New York, Praeger, 1965. 184 p.

4011 Hasan, Said. **ECOSOC and the Under-Developed Countries,** *Pakistan Horizon,* V (September 1952), 147—52.

Part D. — *United Nations System*

4012 Henry, Paul-Marc. **The United Nations and the Problem of African Development,** *International Organization,* XVI (Spring, 1962), 362–74.

4013 Hoffmann, Paul G. **Forms and Functions of Development Assistance,** *The Quest for Peace,* Andrew W. Cordier and Wilder Foote (eds.). New York, Columbia University Press, 1965, pp. 227–40.

4014 Huth, Arno. **Communications and Economic Development,** *International Conciliation,* CDLXXVII (January 1952), 3–42.

4015 Jackson, Barbara Ward. **The United Nations and the Decade of Development,** *The Quest for Peace,* Andrew W. Cordier and Wilder Foote (eds.). New York, Columbia University Press, 1965, pp. 201–26.

4016 Johnson, Joseph E. **Helping to Build New States,** *The United States and the United Nations,* Francis O. Wilcox and H. Field Haviland, Jr., (eds.). Baltimore, Johns Hopkins Press, 1961, pp. 3–26.

4017 Jones, Joseph M. **The United Nations at Work: Developing Land, Forests, Oceans, and People.** Oxford, Pergamon, 1965. xiv + 238 p.

4018 Joyce, James Avery. **World of Promise: A Guide to the United Nations Development Decade.** Introduction by David Owen. Dobbs Ferry, Oceana, 1965. xii + 163 p.

4019 Keenleyside, Hugh L. **Administrative Problems of the United Nations Technical Assistance Administration,** *Public Administration* (London), XXXIII (Autumn, 1955), 241–67.

4020 ——. **UN Technical Assistance Program,** *Pakistan Horizon,* V (March 1952), 33–37.

4021 Kirdar, Ü. **The International Administrative Service (OPEX): Provision of Operational, Executive and Administrative Personnel,** *British Yearbook of International Law,* XXXVIII (1962), 407–20.

Part D. — United Nations System

4022 Krishna, Rao K. **The Status of Experts of the Expanded Programme of Technical Assistance of the United Nations,** *Revue de Droit International Pour le Moyen-Orient,* V (June 1956), 42—56.

4023 Kumar, Dharma. **UN Conference on Trade and Development,** *India Quarterly,* XXI (July-September 1965), 311—15.

4024 Leonard, L. Larry. **International Organization.** New York, McGraw-Hill, 1951.

Chapter XXI.

4025 Lepawsky, Albert. **The Bolivian Operation: New Trends in Technical Assistance,** *International Conciliation,* CDLXXIX (March 1952), 103—40.

4026 Lockwood, Agnes Nelms. **Indians of the Andes: Technical Assistance on the Antiplano,** *International Conciliation,* DVIII (May 1956), 355—431.

4027 Louw, Michael H. H. **The United Nations Program in Brazil,** *Annals of the American Academy of Political and Social Science,* CCCXXIII (May 1959), 129—39.

4028 McLaughlin, Kathleen. **The World's War on Want.** Dobbs Ferry, Oceana, 1961. 80 p.

4029 Mikesell, Raymond F. **Barriers to the Expansion of United Nations Economic Functions,** *Annals of the American Academy of Political and Social Science,* CCXCVI (November 1954), 36—45.

4030 Mitrany, David. **The International Technical Assistance Programme,** *Academy of Political Science Proceedings,* XXV (January 1953), 13—23.

Part D. — United Nations System

4031 Myrdal, Gunnar. **Beyond the Welfare State.** New Haven, Yale University Press, 1960. 287 p.

4032 Narasimhan, P. S. **Technical Assistance for Economic Development of Underdeveloped Countries,** *India Quarterly,* VIII (April-June 1952), 142—55.

4033 Neal, Marian. **United Nations Technical Assistance Program in Haiti,** *International Conciliation,* CDLXVIII (February 1951), 81—118.

4034 Owen, David. **International Technical Aid to the Middle East: The United Nations Family,** *Middle Eastern Affairs,* VII (January 1956), 1—10.

4035 — —. **Technical Assistance for Economic Development,** *Journal of International Affairs,* IX, 2 (1955), 39—49.

4036 — —. **The Technical Assistance Programme of the United Nations,** *Political Quarterly,* XXII (October-December 1951), 323—34.

4037 — —. **The United Nations Expanded Program of Technical Co-operation — A Multilateral Approach,** *Annals of the American Academy of Political and Social Science,* CCCXXIII (May 1959), 25—32.

4038 — —. **The United Nations Program of Technical Assistance,** *Annals of the American Academy of Political and Social Science,* CCLXX (July 1950), 109—18.

4039 Papanek, Gustav F. **Framing a Development Program,** *International Conciliation,* DXXVII (March 1960), 307—72.

4040 Patel, H. M. **International Economic Co-operation — A Survey of Foreign Assistance in Post-War Years,** *Indian Year Book of International Affairs,* IV (1955), 70—87.

4041 Penrose, Ernest F. **Economic Planning for the Peace.** Princeton, Princeton University Press, 1953. xiv + 384 p.

4042 Power, Thomas F., Jr. **Development Activities of the United Nations,** *Pakistan Horizon,* XV, 4 (1962), 261–68.

4043 Rao, V. K. R. V. **An International Development Authority,** *India Quarterly,* VIII (July-September 1952), 236–68.

4044 Roosevelt, Eleanor and Witt, William De. **UN: Today and Tomorrow.** New York, Harper, 1953. xiv + 236 p.

4045 Rosenstein-Rodan, P. N. **International Aid for Underdeveloped Countries,** *Review of Economics and Statistics,* XLIII (May 1961), 107–38.

4046 Schaaf, C. Hart. **The Role of Resident Representatives of the UN Technical Assistance Board,** *International Organization,* XIV (Autumn, 1960), 548–62.

4047 Schachter, Oscar. **Private Foreign Investment and International Organization,** *Cornell Law Quarterly,* XLV (Spring, 1960), 415–31.

4048 Sewell, James P. **Functionalism and World Politics: A Study Based on United Nations Programs Financing Economic Development.** Princeton, Princeton University Press, 1965. xii + 359 p.

4049 Sharp, Walter R. **The Institutional Framework for Technical Assistance,** *International Organization,* VII (August 1953), 342–79.

4050 — —. **International Technical Assistance: Programs and Organization.** Ann Arbor, Public Administration Clearing House, 1952. xi + 146 p.

Part D. — *United Nations System*

4051 — —. **The United Nations System in Egypt: A Country Survey of Field Operations,** *International Organization,* X (May 1956), 235–60.

4052 Shippen, Katherine B. **The Pool of Knowledge.** New York, Harper, 1954. 148 p.

4053 Shonfield, Andrew. **The Attack on World Poverty.** New York, Random House, 1960. 269 p.

4054 Stern, Robert M. **Policies for Trade and Development,** *International Conciliation,* DXLVIII (May 1964), 3–63.

4055 Vaizey, John. **International Aid and International Organizations,** *Pakistan Horizon,* XIII, 2 (1960), 144–49.

4056 Wilcox, Francis O. **The United Nations Program for Technical Assistance,** *Annals of the American Academy of Political and Social Science,* CCLXVIII (March 1950), 45–53.

7.2.4 MONETARY AND LENDING AGENCIES

7.2.4.1 GENERAL OBSERVATIONS

4057 Comstock, Alzada. **Bretton Woods and After,** *Current History,* New Series, VII (September 1944), 161–66.

4058 Gardner, Richard N. **In Pursuit of World Order.** New York, Praeger, 1964.
Chapter VII.

4059 Halm, George N. **International Monetary Cooperation.** Chapel Hill, University of North Carolina Press, 1945. vii + 355 p.

4060 Hawtrey, Ralph George. **Bretton Woods: For Better or Worse.** New York, Longmans, Green, 1947. 142 p.

4061 Heilperin, Michael A. **International Monetary Reconstruction: The Bretton Woods Agreements.** New York, American Enterprise Association, 1945. 112 p.

4062 Kindleberger, Charles P. **Bretton Woods Reappraised,** *International Organization,* V (February 1951), 32–47.

4063 Knorr, Klaus. **The Bretton Woods Institutions in Transition,** *International Organization,* II (February 1948), 19–38.

4064 Mander, Linden A. **Foundations of Modern World Society.** 2d ed. Stanford, Stanford University Press, 1947.

Chapter VI.

4065 Mann, F. A. **International Monetary Co-operation,** *British Yearbook of International Law,* XXII (1945), 251–58.

4066 Metzger, Laure. **Bretton Woods: Three Years After,** *American Perspective,* II (December 1948), 378–81.

4067 Metzler, Lloyd A., Triffin, R., and Haberler, G. **International Monetary Policies.** Washington, Board of Governors of the Federal Reserve System, 1947. 102 p.

4068 Morgan, Carlyle. **Bretton Woods: Clues to a Monetary Mystery.** Boston, World Peace Foundation, 1945. 143 p.

Part D. — *United Nations System*

4069 Morgenthau, Henry, Jr. **Bretton Woods and International Cooperation,** *Foreign Affairs,* XXIII (January 1945), 182–94.

4070 Newcomer, Mabel. **Bretton Woods and a Durable Peace,** *Annals of the American Academy of Political and Social Science,* CCXL (July 1945), 37–42.

4071 Dulles, Eleanor Lansing. **Bretton Woods Monetary Conference,** *Foreign Policy Reports,* XX (September 1, 1944), 138–47.

4072 Pehle, John W. **The Bretton Woods Institutions,** *Yale Law Journal,* LV (August 1946), 1127–39.

4073 Tew, Brian. **International Monetary Co-operation.** 6th ed. London, Hutchinson, 1962. 192 p.

4074 Tobin, James. **Economic Progress and the International Monetary System,** *Academy of Political Science Proceedings,* XXVII (May 1963), 271–86.

Comments by Temple, Woolley, Mason and Lary.

4075 Weyl, Nathaniel. **The Role of International Monetary Agencies,** *Twentieth Century Economic Thought,* Glenn Hoover (ed.). New York, Philosophical Library, 1950, pp. 745–87.

4076 Williams, John H. **International Monetary Plans: After Bretton Woods,** *Foreign Affairs,* XXIII (October 1944), 38–56.

4077 — —. **Postwar Monetary Plans and Other Essays.** 2d ed. New York, Knopf, 1945. lxi + 391 p.

7.2.4.2 INTERNATIONAL BANK FOR RECONSTRUCTION AND DEVELOPMENT (Washington)

4078 Baldwin, David A. **The International Bank in Political Perspective,** *World Politics,* XVIII (October 1965), 68–81.

4079 Basch, Antonin. **Financing of Economic Development and the International Bank,** *Academy of Political Science Proceedings,* XXV (January 1953), 157–70.

4080 — —. **International Bank for Reconstruction and Development, 1944–1949: A Review,** *International Conciliation,* CDLV (November 1949), 791–827.

4081 Beyen, J. W. **The International Bank for Reconstruction and Development,** *International Affairs,* XXIV (October 1948), 534–42.

4082 Black, Eugene R. **The World Bank at Work,** *Foreign Affairs,* XXX (April 1952), 401–11.

4083 Comstock, Alzada. **World Bank and World Trade,** *Current History,* New Series, XII (March 1947), 193–98.

4084 Diamond, William. **Activities of the International Bank in the Middle East,** *Middle East Journal,* III (October 1949), 455–60.

4085 Jawed, Tufail. **The World Bank and the Indus Basin Dispute: Background,** *Pakistan Horizon,* XVIII (1965), 226–37.

4086 Kamarck, Andrew M. **The Activities of the World Bank in Africa,** *Africa: A Handbook to the Continent,* Colin Legum (ed.). London, Blond, 1961, pp. 505–7.

Part D. — *United Nations System*

4087 McCloy, John J. **The Lesson of the World Bank,** *Foreign Affairs,* XXVII (July 1949), 551—60.

4088 Meyer, Eugene. **The International Bank for Reconstruction and Development,** *Academy of Political Science Proceedings,* XXII (January 1947), 148—55.

4089 Michaelis, Alfred. **International Bank Activities in the Middle East,** *Middle Eastern Affairs,* VIII (May 1957), 180—85.

4090 Morris, James. **The Road to Huddersfield: A Journey to Five Continents.** New York, Pantheon, 1963. 235 p.

4091 Reid, Escott. **The Future of the World Bank: An Essay.** Washington, International Bank for Reconstruction and Development, 1965. 71 p.

4092 Rucinski, J. **Operations of the International Bank for Reconstruction and Development,** *Pakistan Horizon,* III (June 1950), 69—83.

4093 Siddiqi, Q. S. **World Bank and State Policies for Economic Development,** *Pakistan Horizon,* XV, 4 (1962), 285—95.

4094 Weyl, Nathaniel and Wasserman, M. J. **The International Bank,** *American Economic Review,* XXXVII (March 1947), 92—106.

7.2.4.3 INTERNATIONAL MONETARY FUND (WASHINGTON)

4095 Aufricht, Hans. **The International Monetary Fund: Legal Bases, Structure, Functions.** New York, Praeger, 1964. 126 p.

4096 Beckhart, B. H. **The Bretton Woods Proposal for an International Monetary Fund,** *Political Science Quarterly,* LIV (December 1944), 489—528.

4097 Bernstein, Edward M. **The United States and the International Monetary Fund,** *Public Policy,* XI (1961), 281–93.

4098 Fawcett, J. E. S. **The Place of Law in an International Organization,** *British Yearbook of International Law,* XXXVI (1960), 321–42.

4099 Fleming, J. Marcus. **International Monetary Fund: The Supply of International Liquidity,** *Public Policy,* XI (1961), 294–311.

4100 Gold, Joseph. **The International Monetary Fund and International Law: An Introduction.** Washington, International Monetary Fund, 1965. 26 p.

4101 Gutt, Camille. **The International Monetary Fund and Its Functions,** *Academy of Political Science Proceedings,* XXII (January 1947), 157–64.

4102 Hexner, Ervin P. **The Executive Board of the International Monetary Fund: A Decision-Making Instrument,** *International Organization,* XVIII (Winter, 1964), 74–96.

4103 — —. **Institutional and Practical Limitations on the Activities of the International Monetary Fund,** *Public Policy,* XI (1961), 312–37.

4104 Horie, Shigeo. **The International Monetary Fund: Retrospect and Prospect.** New York, St. Martin's, 1964. 208 p.

4105 Machlup, Fritz. **Plans for Reform of the International Monetary System.** Princeton, Princeton University, Department of Economics, International Finance Section, 1964. 93 p.

4106 Mikesell, Raymond F. **The International Monetary Fund, 1944–1949,** *International Conciliation,* CDLV (November 1949), 828–74.

4107 Rooth, Ivar. **IMF and Under-Developed Countries,** *Pakistan Horizon,* VIII (March 1955), 249–54.

4108 Scammell, W. M. **The International Monetary Fund: An Interim Judgment,** *World Affairs,* New Series, V (October 1951), 467–78.

4109 Schmitt, Hans A. **Political Conditions for International Currency Reform,** *International Organization,* XVIII (Summer, 1964), 543–57.

4110 Sohmen, Egon. **International Monetary Problems and the Foreign Exchanges.** Princeton, Princeton University, Department of Economics, International Finance Section, 1963. 81 p.

4111 White, Harry D. **The International Monetary Fund: The First Year,** *Annals of the American Academy of Political and Social Science,* CCLII (July 1947), 21–29.

4112 — —. **The Monetary Fund: Some Criticisms Examined,** *Foreign Affairs,* XXIII (January 1945), 195–210.

4113 Zahid, Munawar A. **The International Liquidity Problem and the Under-Developed Countries,** *Pakistan Horizon,* XV, 1 (1962), 30–41.

7.2.4.4 OTHER AGENCIES

4114 Elder, Robert E. and Murden, F. D. **Economic Development: Special UN Fund for Economic Development.** New York, Woodrow Wilson Foundation, 1954. 27 p.

4115 Hadwen, John G. and Kaufmann, Johan. **How United Nations Decisions Are Made.** Leyden, Sythoff, 1960.
Chapters V and VI are about Sunfed.

Part D. — *United Nations System*

4116 Manzer, Ronald A. **The United Nations Special Fund,** *International Organization,* XVIII (Autumn, 1964), 766—89.

4117 Matecki, B. E. **Establishment of the International Finance Corporation: A Case Study,** *International Organization,* X (May 1956), 261 75.

4118 — —. **Establishment of the International Finance Corporation and United States Policy.** New York, Praeger, 1957. 194 p.

4119 Rozental, Alec A. **International Finance Corporation and Private Foreign Investments,** *Economic Development and Cultural Change,* V (April 1957), 277—85.

4120 Weaver, James H. **The International Development Association: A New Approach to Foreign Aid.** New York, Praeger, 1965. ix + 268 p.

7.2.5 REGIONAL ECONOMIC COMMISSIONS

7.2.5.1 GENERAL OBSERVATIONS

4121 H., D. K. R. **The Regional Economic Commissions of the United Nations,** *World Today,* New Series, V (May 1949), 218—30.

7.2.5.2 ECONOMIC COMMISSION FOR AFRICA
(Addis Ababa)

4122 Evans, Gordon. **The United Nations Economic Commission for Africa: The Tangier Meeting,** *World Today,* New Series, XVI (April 1960), 176—80.

4123 Legum, Colin. **Economic Commission for Africa: Progress Report,** *World Today,* New Series, XVII (July 1961), 299—307.

7.2.5.3 ECONOMIC COMMISSION FOR ASIA AND THE FAR EAST (Bangkok)

4124 Gordon, Bernard K. **Regional Cooperation in Southeast Asia,** *Current History*, XLVIII (February 1965), 103—8 ff.
ECAFE and the Association of Southeast Asia.

4125 Hasan, Mohammad. **Economic Commission for Asia and the Far East,** *Pakistan Horizon*, II (September 1949), 152—55.

4126 Lokanathan, P. S. **Regional Economic Co-operation in Asia,** *India Quarterly*, VII (January-March 1951), 3—9.

4127 — —. **The Task Before the Economic Commission for Asia and the Far East,** *India Quarterly*, III (October-December 1947), 333—40.

4128 Purcell, V. W. W. S. **The Economic Commission for Asia and the Far East,** *International Affairs*, XXIV (April 1948), 181—95.

4129 Rubinstein, Alvin Z. **Soviet Policy in ECAFE: A Case Study of Soviet Behavior in International Economic Organization,** *International Organization*, XII (Autumn, 1958), 459—72.

4130 Schaaf, C. Hart. **Economic Cooperation in Asia,** *International Conciliation*, CDLX (April 1950), 218—48.

4131 — —. **The United Nations Economic Commission for Asia and the Far East,** *International Organization*, VII (November 1953), 463—81.

4132 Wightman, David. **Efforts for Economic Cooperation in Asia and the Far East: The Experience of ECAFE,** *World Today*, New Series, XVIII (January 1962), 30—42.

Part D. — United Nations System

4133 — —. **Toward Economic Cooperation in Asia: The United Nations Economic Commission for Asia and the Far East.** New Haven, Yale University Press, 1963. 400 p.

7.2.5.4 ECONOMIC COMMISSION FOR EUROPE
(Brussels)

4134 Alexandrowicz, C. **The Economic Commission for Europe,** *World Affairs*, New Series, III (January 1949), 43–54.

4135 Hoffman, Michael L. **Problems of East-West Trade,** *International Conciliation*, DXI (January 1957), 259–308.

4136 Myrdal, Gunnar. **The Economic Commission for Europe,** *United Nations Review*, IV (July 1957), 24–25 ff.

4137 Pinto, Roger. **Les organisations européennes.** 2d ed. Paris, Payot, 1965.

Chapter XI.

4138 Rostow, Walt W. **The Economic Commission for Europe,** *International Organization*, III (May 1949), 254–68.

4139 Siotis, Jean. **The Secretariat of the United Nations Commission for Europe and European Economic Integration: The First Ten Years,** *International Organization*, XIX (Spring, 1965), 177–202.

4140 Wightman, David. **East-West Cooperation and the United Nations Economic Commission for Europe,** *International Organization*, XI (Winter, 1957), 1–12.

4141 — —. **Economic Co-operation in Europe.** New York, Praeger, 1956. 288 p.

7.2.5.5 ECONOMIC COMMISSION FOR LATIN AMERICA
(Santiago)

4142 Cohen, Alvin. **ECLA and the Economic Development of Peru,** *Inter-American Economic Affairs*, XVII (Summer, 1963), 3–28.

4143 Plaza, Galo. **For a Regional Market in Latin America,** *Foreign Affairs*, XXXVII (July 1959), 607–16.

7.2.6 TRADE ORGANIZATIONS

7.2.6.1 GENERAL OBSERVATIONS

4144 Brown, William A. **The United States and the Restoration of World Trade: An Analysis and Appraisal of the ITO Charter and the General Agreement on Tariffs and Trade.** Washington, Brookings, 1950. xiii + 572 p.

4145 Condliffe, J. B. **International Trade and Economic Nationalism,** *International Conciliation*, CDLXXVI (December 1951), 549–81.

4146 Frank, Isaiah. **Issues Before the UN Conference,** *Foreign Affairs*, XLII (January 1964), 210–26.

4147 Gardner, Richard N. **In Pursuit of World Order.** New York, Praeger, 1964.

Chapter VI.

4148 Kravis, Irving B. **Domestic Interests and International Trade Organizations.** Philadelphia, University of Pennsylvania Press, 1964. 448 p. 448 p.

4149 Mander, Linden A. **Foundations of Modern World Society.** 2d ed. Stanford, Stanford University Press, 1947.

Chapter VIII.

4150 Weintraub, Sidney. **After the UN Trade Conference: Lessons and Portents,** *Foreign Affairs,* XLIII (October 1964), 37–50.

7.2.6.2 PROPOSED INTERNATIONAL TRADE ORGANIZATION

4151 Alexandrowicz, C. **The Havana Charter,** *World Affairs,* New Series, II (October 1948), 398–409.

4152 Armstrong, Willis C. **The Soviet Approach to International Trade,** *Political Science Quarterly,* LXIII (September 1948), 368–82.

4153 Bronz, George. **An International Trade Organization: The Second Attempt,** *Harvard Law Review,* LXIX (January 1956), 440–82.

4154 Brown, William A., Jr. **The United States and the Restoration of World Trade.** Washington, Brookings, 1950. xiv + 572 p.

4155 Diebold, William, Jr. and Bidwell, Percey, W. **The United States and the International Trade Organization,** *International Conciliation,* CDXLIX (March 1949), 187–239.

4156 Fawcett, J. E. S. **The International Trade Organization,** *British Yearbook of International Law,* XXIV (1947), 376–82.

4157 Feis, Herbert. **The Geneva Proposals for an International Trade Charter,** *International Organization,* II (February 1948), 39–52.

4158 Killheffer, Elvin H. **ITO — Illusion or Reality?** *Annals of the American Academy of Political and Social Science*, CCLXIV (July 1949), 75—86.

4159 Knorr, K. E. **The Functions of an International Trade Organization: Possibilities and Limitations,** *American Economic Review*, XXXVII, Supplement (May 1947), 542—53.

4160 McClellan, Grant S. **International Trade Organization — Proposals for World Economic Recovery,** *Foreign Policy Reports*, XXII (March 15, 1946), 2—11.

4161 Mallery, Otto Tod. **The Coming World Trade Conference,** *International Conciliation*, CDVI (December 1944), 749—56.

4162 Mikesell, Raymond F. **International Trade Practices Under the ITO Charter,** *Annals of the American Academy of Political and Social Science*, CCLII (July 1947), 30—34.

4163 Murkland, Harry B. **Latin America at Havana,** *Current History*, New Series, XIV (June 1948), 332—35.

4164 Pardasani, N. S. **International Trade Organization,** *India Quarterly*, II (July-September 1946), 259—68.

4165 Thomas, Brinley. **Britain and the International Trade Organization,** *World Affairs*, New Series, II (January 1948), 23—29.

4166 Viner, Jacob. **Conflicts of Principle in Drafting a Trade Charter,** *Foreign Affairs*, XXV (July 1947), 612—28.

4167 Wilcox, Clair. **A Charter for World Trade.** New York, Macmillan, 1949. xvii + 333 p.

4168 — —. **Organization to Liberate World Trade,** *Annals of the American Academy of Political and Social Science*, CCXLVI (July 1946), 95—100.

4169 — —. **The Promise of the World Trade Charter,** *Foreign Affairs,* XXVII (April 1949), 486—96.

4170 — —. **Why the International Trade Organization?** *Annals of the American Academy of Political and Social Science,* CCLXIV (July 1949), 67—74.

4171 Wilgress, Edward D. **A New Attempt at Internationalism: The International Trade Conference and the Charter, a Study of Ends and Means.** Paris, Société d'Edition d'Enseignement Supérieur, 1949. 172 p.

4172 Williams, John H. **International Trade with Planned Economies: The ITO Charter,** *Academy of Political Science Proceedings,* XXII (May 1947), 288—302.

4173 Wilson, Kenneth R. **Geneva and the ITO,** *International Journal,* II (Summer, 1947), 242—49.

7.2.6.3 GENERAL AGREEMENT ON TARIFFS AND TRADE
(Geneva)

4174 Alexandrowicz, Charles Henry. **World Economic Agencies.** London, Stevens, 1962.

Chapter IX.

4175 Allen, James Jay. **The European Common Market and the GATT.** Washington, University Press, 1960. xii + 244 p.

4176 — —. **The European Common Market and the General Agreement on Tariffs and Trade: A Study in Comparability,** *Law and Contemporary Problems,* XXVI (Summer, 1961), 559—71.

4177 Barkway, Michael. **GATT Revised,** *International Journal,* X (Summer, 1955), 192—97.

4178 Canadian Institute of International Affairs. **Japan and the GATT,** *International Journal,* IX (Summer, 1954), 216—19.

4179 Clayton, William L. **GATT, the Marshall Plan, and OECD,** *Political Science Quarterly,* LXXVIII (December 1963), 493—503.

4180 Fisher, M. H. **What Chance of Lower Tariffs? GATT and the Kennedy Round,** *World Today,* New Series, XIX (May 1963), 208—12.

4181 Galbraith, Virginia. **The General Agreement on Tariffs and Trade,** *Current History,* New Series, XLIII (July 1962), 23—28.

4182 Gardner, Richard N. **GATT and the United Nations Conference on Trade and Development,** *International Organization,* XVIII (Autumn, 1964), 685—704.

4183 General Agreement on Tariffs and Trade. **GATT Bibliography.** Geneva, Palais des Nations, 1954. 40 p. Supplements.

4184 Gorter, Wytze. **GATT After Six Years: An Appraisal,** *International Organization,* VIII (February 1954), 1—18.

4185 Jacobson, Harold Karan. **The Soviet Union, the UN and World Trade,** *Western Political Quarterly,* XI (September 1958), 673—88.

4186 Kass, Stephen L. **Obligatory Negotiations in International Organizations,** *Canadian Yearbook of International Law,* III (1965), 36—72.

4187 Kravis, Irving B. **Domestic Interests and International Obligations: Safeguards in International Trade Organizations.** Philadelphia, University of Pennsylvania Press, 1963. 448 p.

4188 Schonfield, Andrew. **Trade As a Tool of Development: The Issues at Geneva,** *International Affairs,* XL (April 1964), 219–31.

4189 Vernon, Raymond. **Organizing for World Trade,** *International Conciliation,* DV (November 1955), 163–222.

7.3 SOCIAL QUESTIONS

7.3.1 GENERAL DISCUSSIONS

4190 Branscombe, Martha. **Intergovernmental Channels: Activities in the Social Field,** *Annals of the American Academy of Political and Social Science,* CCCXXIX (May 1960), 32–43.

4191 Cheever, Daniel S. and Haviland, H. Field, Jr. **Organizing for Peace.** Boston, Houghton, Mifflin, 1954.

Chapters VII, XXI.

4192 Davidson, George F. **International Horizons for Health and Welfare,** *Social Services Review,* XXII (September 1948), 279–85.

4193 Eagleton, Clyde. **International Government.** 3d ed. New York, Ronald, 1957.

Chapter XIV.

4194 Hadsel, Fred L. **Human Welfare Specialized Agencies of the UN — Labor, Food, Education, Health, and Refugees,** *Foreign Policy Reports,* XXIII (February 1, 1948), 274–83.

4195 Leonard, L. Larry. **International Organization.** New York, McGraw-Hill, 1951.

Chapters XXIII, XXIV.

Part D. — United Nations System

4196 Myrdal, Alva. **World Action Against Social Ills,** *Annals of the American Academy of Political and Social Science,* CCLXIV (July 1949), 98—105.

4197 Vandenbosch, Amry and Hogan, Willard N. **Toward World Order.** New York, McGraw-Hill, 1963.
Chapter XII.

7.3.2 HEALTH ORGANIZATIONS

7.3.2.1 GENERAL OBSERVATIONS

4198 **American Journal of Public Health.** New York, American Public Health Association, Monthly, 1941—.

4199 Boudreau, Frank G. **The United Nations and the World's Health,** *Academy of Political Science Proceedings,* XXV (January 1953), 134—44.

4200 Chisholm, Brock. **Barriers to World Health,** *International Conciliation,* CDXCI (May 1953), 260—66.

4201 Goodman, Neville M. **International Health Organizations and Their Work.** London, Churchill, 1952. 327 p.

4202 Rusk, Howard A. and Wilson, Donald V. **New Resources for Rehabilitation and Health,** *Annals of the American Academy of Political and Social Science,* CCCXXIX (May 1960), 97—106.

7.3.2.2 COMMISSION ON NARCOTIC DRUGS
(Geneva)

4203 Carnegie Endowment for International Peace. **Narcotic Drug Control,** *International Conciliation,* CDLXXXV (November 1952), 491—536.

4204 Goodrich, Leland M. **New Trends in Narcotics Control,** *International Conciliation*, DXXX (November 1960), 181–242.

4205 Gregg, Robert W. **The United Nations and the Opium Problem,** *International and Comparative Law Quarterly*, XIII (January 1964), 96–115.

4206 Lande, Adolf. **The Single Convention on Narcotic Drugs,** *International Organization* XVI (Autumn, 1962), 776–97.

4207 May, Herbert L. **The International Control of Narcotic Drugs: Introduction,** *International Conciliation*, CDXLI (May 1948), 303–6.

Issue contains a report on UN activities and various documents.

4208 Renborg, B. A. **International Control of Narcotics,** *Law and Contemporary Problems*, XXII (Winter, 1957), 86–112.

7.3.2.3 FOOD AND AGRICULTURE ORGANIZATION
(Rome)

4209 Alexandrowicz, Charles Henry. **World Economic Agencies.** London, Stevens, 1962.

Chapter IV.

4210 Anon. **Four Years of the FAO,** *India Quarterly*, V (April-June 1949), 163–75.

4211 Belshaw, H. **The Food and Agriculture Organization of the United Nations,** *International Organization*, I (June 1947), 291–306.

4212 Black, John D. **The International Food Movement,** *American Economic Review*, XXXIII (December 1943), 791–811.

Part D. — United Nations System

4213   Bolles, Blair. **World Nutrition and Agrarian Stability — Proposals for a Food Board,** *Foreign Policy Reports,* XXII (December 1, 1946), 218 —27.

4214   D., M. **Planning the World's Food,** *World Today,* New Series, III (March 1947), 142—50.

4215   Dodd, Norris E. **FAO Work and Aims in Asia,** *United Asia,* III, 2 (1950), 103—18.

4216   — —. **A Summary of the Food and Agricultural Organization in the Middle East,** *Middle East Journal,* IV (July 1950), 352—55.

4217   Flexner, Jean Atherton. **Good Policies of the United Nations,** *American Economic Review,* XXXIII (December 1943), 812—24.

4218   Hambridge, Gove. **The Food and Agriculture Organization at Work,** *International Conciliation,* CDXXXII (June 1947), 347—64.

4219   — —. **The Story of FAO.** New York, Van Nostrand, 1955. xii + 303 p.

4220   Jones, Joseph M. **The United Nations at Work: Developing Land, Forests, Oceans, and People.** Oxford, Pergamon, 1965. xiv + 238 p.

4221   Orr, John Boyd. **Freedom from Want,** *Peace on Earth,* Trygve Lie, Herbert V. Evatt, Charles Malik, Eleanor Roosevelt, Jaime Torres Bodet, Brock Chisholm, John Boyd-Orr, Ralph Bunche, Benjamin Cohen, Ludwick Rajchman, and Carlos P. Romulo. New York, Hermitage, 1949, pp. 101—12.

4222   Piquet, Howard S. **Functional International Organization,** *Annals of the American Academy of Political and Social Science,* CCXL (July 1945), 43—50.

Part D. — United Nations System

4223 — —. **Text of the Constitution of the Food and Agriculture Organization of the United Nations,** *International Conciliation,* CDXII (June 1945), 412–33.

4224 Schultz, Theodore W. (ed.). **Food for the World.** Chicago, University of Chicago Press, 1945. 353 p.

4225 Tolley, Howard. **Raising the Food: World Needs and the Role of the Food and Agriculture Organization,** *Academy of Political Science Proceedings,* XXI (May 1945), 313–81.

4226 UNESCO, Youth Institute. **Food for Life — Food for Thought.** Dobbs Ferry, Oceana, 1962.

Part II.

4227 Vajda, Andrew de. **FAO's Role in River Basin Development,** *Institute of World Affairs Proceedings,* XXXIII (1957), 211–17.

4228 Vallarché, Jean. **L'Organisation pour l'Alimentation et l'Agriculture ou FAO,** *Les institutions internationales et transnationales,* Fernand L'Huillier (ed.). Paris, Presses Universitaires, 1961, pp. 219–27.

4229 Yates, P. Lamartine. **Food Resources and Human Needs,** *Yale Law Journal,* LV (August 1946), 1233–41.

4230 — —. **So Bold an Aim: Ten Years of International Co-operation Toward Freedom from Want.** Rome, Food and Agriculture Organization, 1955, 174 p.

7.3.2.4 WORLD HEALTH ORGANIZATION
(Geneva)

4231 Alexandrowicz, Charles Henry. **World Economic Agencies.** London, Stevens, 1962.

Chapter V, VI.

Part D. — *United Nations System*

4232   Allen, Charles E. **World Health and World Politics,** *International Organization,* IV (February 1950), 27–43.

4233   Ascher, Charles S. **Current Problems in the World Health Organization's Program,** *International Organization,* VI (February 1952), 27–50.

4234   Berkov, Robert. **The World Health Organization: A Study in Decentralized International Administration.** Geneva, Droz, 1957. 173 p.

4235   Brockington, Colin F. **World Health.** Harmondsworth, Eng., Penguin, 1958. 405 p.

4236   Chisholm, Brock. **The World Health Organization,** *World Today,* New Series, VI (September 1950), 386–94.

4237   ———. **The World Health Organization: Introduction,** *International Conciliation,* CDXXXIX (March 1948). 111–15.

4238   ———. **World Health,** *Peace on Earth,* Trygve Lie, Herbert V. Evatt, Charles Malik, Eleanor Roosevelt, Jaime Torres Bodet, Brock Chisholm, John Boyd-Orr, Ralph Bunche, Benjamin Cohen, Ludwick Rajchman, and Carlos P. Romulo. New York, Hermitage, 1949, pp. 89–101.

4239   Clements, F. W. **The World Health Organization in Southern Asia and the Western Pacific,** *Pacific Affairs,* XXV (December 1952), 334–48.

4240   Deutsch, Albert. **The World Health Organization: Its Global Battle Against Disease.** New York, Public Affairs Committee, 1958. 24 p.

4241   Grant, Madeleine P. **Biology and World Health.** New York, Abelard-Schuman, 1955. 202 p.

473

4242 Jacob, Philip E. and Atherton, Alexine L. **Dynamics of International Organization.** Homewood, Dorsey, 1964.

Chapter XVI.

4243 Mackenzie, Melville. **International Collaboration in Health,** *International Affairs,* XXVI (October 1950), 515–21.

4244 Mudalier, Arcot. **World Health Problems,** *International Conciliation,* CDXCI (May 1953), 229–59.

4245 Sharp, Walter R. **The New World Health Organization,** *American Journal of International Law,* XLI (July 1947), 509–30.

4246 UNESCO, Youth Institute. **Toward Mankind's Better Health.** Dobbs Ferry, Oceana, 1963. 104 p.

4247 Winslow, C. E. A. **The World Health Organization: Its Program and Accomplishments,** *International Conciliation,* CDXXXIX (March 1948), 116–45.

7.3.2.5 UNITED NATIONS CHILDREN'S FUND

4248 Calder, Ritchie. **Growing Up with UNICEF.** New York, Public Affairs Committee, 1962. 24 p.

4249 Heilbroner, Robert L. **Mankind's Children: The Story of UNICEF.** New York, Public Affairs Committee, 1959. 20 p.

4250 Hoskins, Lewis. **Voluntary Agencies and Foundations in International Aid,** *Annals of the American Academy of Political and Social Science,* CCCXXIX (May 1960), 57–68.

4251 Keeny, S. M. **Half the World's Children: A Diary of UNICEF at Work in Asia.** New York, Association Press, 1957. 243 p.

Part D. — United Nations System

4252 Ording, Aake. **The United Nations and the World's Children,** *Annals of the American Academy of Political and Social Science*, CCLII (July 1947), 63—65.

4253 Rajchman, Ludwick, **What is UNICEF?** *Peace on Earth*, Trygve Lie, Herbert V. Evatt, Charles Malik, Eleanor Roosevelt, Jaime Torres Bodet, Brock Chisholm, John Boyd-Orr, Ralph Bunche, Benjamin Cohen, Ludwick Rajchman, and Carlos P. Romulo. New York, Hermitage, 1949, pp. 141—48.

4254 Shaffer, Alice C. **UNICEF in Central America,** *Annals of the American Academy of Political and Social Science*, CCCXXIX (May 1960), 69—77.

7.3.3 HUMAN RIGHTS AND MINORITIES

See also E 8.4.4.

4255 Ahmed, Begum Aziz. **UN and the Status of Women,** *Pakistan Horizon*, XI (June 1958), 64—69.

4256 — —. **Women and the United Nations,** *Pakistan Horizon*, XVI, 4 (1963), 318—23.

4257 Bagley, Tennent H. **General Principles and Problems in the International Protection of Minorities.** Geneva, Imprimeries Populaires. 222 p.

4258 Ball, M. Margaret and Killough, Hugh B. **International Relations.** New York, Ronald, 1956.

Chapter XV.

4259 Beckett, W. Eric. **Human Rights,** *Transactions* (Grotius Society), XXXIV (1948), 69—72.

Comments by Bentwich, Bienenfeld, Green, Zaslawski, Loewenfeld, Lauterpacht, and Hurst.

4260 Blaustein, Jacob. **Human Rights: A Challenge to the United Nations and to Our Generation,** *The Quest for Peace,* Andrew W. Cordier and Wilder Foote (eds.). New York, Columbia University Press, 1965, pp. 315–30.

4261 Bogardus, Emory S. **Cooperation in Human Relations,** *World Affairs Quarterly,* XXV (July 1954), 182–91.

4262 Brohi, A. K. **ECOSOC and Forced Labour,** *Pakistan Horizon,* IV (June 1951), 67–80.

4263 Buergenthal, Thomas. **The United Nations and the Development of Rules Relating to Human Rights,** *American Society of International Law Proceedings,* LIX (1965), 132–36.

4264 Cassin, R. **The Universal Declaration of Human Rights and Its Implementation,** *Recueil des Cours,* LXXIX (1951), 241–365.

4265 Chakravart, Raghubir. **Human Rights and the United Nations.** Foreword by G. D. H. Cole. Calcutta, Progressive, 1958. xvi + 218 p.

4266 Claude, Inis L., Jr. **The Nature and Status of the Sub-Commission on Prevention of Discrimination and Protection of Minorities,** *International Organization,* V (May 1951), 300–12.

4267 Coyle, David Cushman. **The United Nations and How It Works.** New York, Columbia University Press, 1966.
Chapter V.

4268 Das, Kamleshwar. **Human Rights and the United Nations,** *Indian Year Book of International Affairs,* VII (1958), 52–88.

4269 Das, Taraknath. **The United Nations and Human Rights,** *Annals of the American Academy of Political and Social Science,* CCLII (July 1947), 53–62.

Part D. — *United Nations System*

4270 Eichelberger, Clark M. **UN: The First Twenty Years.** New York, Harper, 1965.
Chapter V.

4271 Ganji, Manouchehr. **International Protection of Human Rights.** Geneva, Droz, 1962. 317 p.

4272 Gardner, Richard N. **In Pursuit of World Order.** New York, Praeger, 1964.
Chapter X.

4273 Goodrich, Leland M. **The United Nations.** New York, Crowell, 1963.
Chapter XI.

4274 Green, James F. **The United Nations and Human Rights.** Washington, Brookings, 1956. 194 p.

4275 Henkin, Louis. **The United Nations and Human Rights,** *International Organization,* XIX (Summer, 1965), 504–17.

4276 Higgins, Rosalyn. **Technical Assistance for Human Rights: A New Approach to an Old Problem,** *World Today,* New Series, XIX (April 1963), 174–80.

4277 — —. **Technical Assistance for Human Rights: The Programme in Action,** *World Today,* New Series, XIX (May 1963), 219–24.

4278 Hiscocks, C. R. **The United Nations and Anti-Semitism,** *International Journal,* XV (Spring, 1960), 143–46.

4279 Holcombe, Arthur N. **Human Rights in the Modern World.** New York, New York University Press, 1948. 162 p.

4280 Humphrey, John P. **The Universal Declaration of Human Rights,** *International Journal,* IV (Autumn, 1949), 351–61.

4281 Ikramullah, Shaista S. **United Nations Discussions on Human Rights and Genocide,** *Pakistan Horizon,* I (December 1948), 228–35.

4282 Jacob, Philip E. and Atherton, Alexine L. **Dynamics of International Organization.** Homewood, Dorsey, 1964.

Chapters XVIII, XIX.

4283 Lauterpacht. H. **An International Bill of the Rights of Man.** New York, Columbia University Press, 1946. 234 p.

4284 — —. **The International Protection of Human Rights,** *Recueil des Cours,* LXX (1947), 5–107.

4285 — —. **The Universal Declaration of Human Rights,** *British Yearbook of International Law,* XXV (1948), 354–81.

4286 Loewenstein, Karl. **An International Bill of Human Rights,** *Current History,* New Series, IX (October 1945), 273–83.

4287 McDougal, Myres S. and Bebr, Gerhard. **Human Rights in the United Nations,** *American Journal of International Law,* LVIII (July 1964), 603–41.

4288 Malik, Charles. **Human Rights in the United Nations,** *International Journal,* VI (Autumn, 1951), 275–80.

4289 Mander, Linden A. **Foundations of Modern World Society.** 2d ed. Stanford, Stanford University Press, 1947.

Chapter XIII.

Part D. — United Nations System

4290 Mitrany, David. **Human Rights and International Organizations,** *India Quarterly,* III (April-June 1947), 115—26.

4291 Moskowitz, Moses. **Human Rights and World Order: The Struggle for Human Rights in the United Nations.** New York, Oceana, 1958. 239 p.

4292 — —. **Human Rights and World Politics.** New York, Oceana, 1958. 160 p.

4293 Mousheng, Lin. **United Nations Seminars on Human Rights,** *India Quarterly,* XVII (July-September 1961), 227—41.

4294 Neal, Marian. **The United States and Human Rights,** *International Conciliation,* CDLXXXIX (March 1953), 113—74.

4295 Nolde, O. Frederick. **Human Rights and the United Nations,** *Academy of Political Science Proceedings,* XXV (January 1953), 171—80.

4296 Robinson, Nehemiah. **The Universal Declaration of Human Rights.** New York, Institute of Jewish Affairs, 1958. 173 p.

4297 Roosevelt, Eleanor. **Human Rights,** *Peace on Earth,* Trygve Lie, Herbert V. Evatt, Charles Malik, Eleanor Roosevelt, Jaime Torres Bodet, Brock Chisholm, John Boyd-Orr, Ralph Bunche, Benjamin Cohen, Ludwick Rajchman, and Carlos P. Romulo. New York, Hermitage, 1949, pp. 65—74.

4298 Sandifer, Durward V. **The International Protection of Human Rights: The United Nations System,** *American Society of International Law Proceedings,* XLIII (1949), 59—65.

4299 Schechtman, Joseph B. **Decline of the International Protection of Minority Rights,** *Western Political Quarterly,* IV (March 1951), 1—11.

4300 Schwarzenberger, Georg. **Power Politics.** 3d ed. London, Stevens, 1964.

Chapter XXVI.

4301 Schwelb, Egon. **Human Rights and the International Community: The Roots and Growth of the Universal Declaration of Human Rights, 1948–1963.** Chicago, Quadrangle, 1964. 96 p.

4302 — —. **International Conventions on Human Rights,** *International and Comparative Law Quarterly,* IX (October 1960), 654–75.

4303 Shotwell, James T. **The Idea of Human Rights,** *Survey Graphic,* XXXV (December 1946), 489–91.

4304 Simsarian, James. **United Nations Work on Human Rights,** *World Affairs Quarterly,* XX (October 1949), 256–63.

4305 Sorensen, Max. **The Quest for Equality,** *International Conciliation,* DVII (March 1956), 291–346.

4306 Swygard, Kline. **The Problem of Human Rights,** *Institute of World Affairs Proceedings,* XXI (1945), 75–84.

4307 Tiwari, S. C. **Forms of International Organization Action for the Protection of Human Rights,** *Indian Year Book of International Affairs,* XIII, 1 (1964), 28–58.

4308 Trinker, Frederick W. **The Anatomy of World Order.** Mexico City, Costa-Amic, 1946.

Chapter VII.

4309 UNESCO (ed.). **Human Rights: Comments and Interpretations.** Introduction by Jacques Maritain. London, Wingate, 1949. 288 p.

4310 UNESCO, Youth Institute. **For Peace and the Dignity of Life.** Dobbs Ferry, Oceana, 1964. 117 p.

4311 Vandenbosch, Amry and Hogan, Willard N. **The United Nations.** New York, McGraw-Hill, 1952.
Chapter XIX.

4312 Wortley, B. A. **Human Rights,** *Political Quarterly*, XX (April-June 1949), 135–45.

4313 Wright, Quincy. **Human Rights and Charter Revision,** *Annals of the American Academy of Political and Social Science*, CCXCVI (November 1954), 46–55.

7.3.4 INTELLECTUAL COOPERATION

See also F 4.

7.3.4.1 UNITED NATIONS EDUCATIONAL, SCIENTIFIC AND CULTURAL ORGANIZATION (PARIS)

4314 Anon. **The First UNESCO Conference,** *World Today*, New Series, III (January 1947), 41–50.

4315 Armstrong, John A. **The Soviet Attitude Toward UNESCO,** *International Organization*, VIII (May 1954), 217–33.

4316 Ascher, Charles S. **The Development of UNESCO's Program,** *International Organization*, IV (February 1950), 12–26.

4317 — —. **Program-Making in UNESCO, 1946–1951.** Chicago, Public Administration Service, 1951. ix + 84 p.

4318 Ashley-Montagu, Montague F. **Statement on Race: An Extended Discussion in Plain Language of the UNESCO Statement by Experts on Race Problems.** New York, Schuman, 1951. xi + 182 p.

4319 Behrman, Daniel. **98 Nations Chart a Two-Year Plan for World Action,** *Problems in International Relations,* Andrew Gyorgy and Hubert S. Gibbs (eds.). Englewood Cliffs, Prentice-Hall, 1962, pp. 361–67.

4320 — —. **Web of Progress: UNESCO at Work in Science and Technology.** Paris, UNESCO, 1964. 106 p.

4321 Besterman, Theodore. **UNESCO: Peace in the Minds of Men.** London, Methuen, 1951. 132 p.

4322 Blagg, Mary Evelyn. **UNESCO: Product of Contradictions,** *Southwestern Social Science Quarterly,* XXXII (September 1951), 79–85.

4323 Bonnet, Henri. **The Path to Intellectual Co-operation,** *Perspectives on Peace,* Carnegie Endowment for International Peace (ed.). New York, Praeger, 1960, pp. 163–75.

4324 Calder, Ritchie. **UNESCO's Task,** *Political Quarterly,* XVIII (April-June 1947), 123–36.

4325 Cantril, Hadley. **The Human Sciences and World Peace: A Report on the UNESCO Project: "Tensions Affecting International Understanding."** *Public Opinion Quarterly,* XII (Summer, 1948), 236–42.

4326 Carr, William G. **Only by Understanding: Education and International Organization.** New York, Foreign Policy Association, 1945. 96 p.

4327 Constable, W. G. **The Arts, UNESCO, and International Understanding,** *Learning and World Peace,* Lyman Bryson, Louis Finkelstein, and R. M. MacIver (eds.). New York, Harper, 1948, pp. 592–600.

4328 Coyle, David Cushman. **The United Nations and How It Works.** New York, Columbia University Press, 1966.
Chapter II.

4329 Craemer, Alice R. **Intellectual Solidarity,** *Current History*, New Series, XII (March 1947), 230–35.

4330 D., C. H. **UNESCO: Achievements in 1947,** *World Today*, New Series, III (December 1947), 545–53.

4331 — —. **UNESCO: Background to the May Conference,** *World Today*, New Series, VI (May 1950), 205–13.

4332 — —. **UNESCO in 1948: An Impartial Assessment,** *World Today*, New Series, V (March 1949), 115–23.

4333 D., H. D. **Co-operation in Education, Science, and Culture: The Work of UNESCO,** *World Today*, New Series, II (July 1946), 339–48.

4334 Dexter, Byron. **UNESCO Faces Two Worlds,** *Foreign Affairs*, XXV (April 1947), 388–407.

4335 — —. **Yardstick for UNESCO,** *Foreign Affairs*, XXVIII (October 1949), 56–67.

4336 Evans, Luther H. **Some Management Problems of UNESCO,** *International Organization*, XVIII (Winter, 1963), 76–90.

4337 — —. **UNESCO in Africa,** *American Behavioral Scientist*, V (April 1962), 25–27.

4338 Garcia, Antonio. **United States Commitments to UNESCO and Federal Control of Education,** *Southwestern Social Science Quarterly*, XXIX (September 1948), 119–24.

Part D. — United Nations System

4339 Harley, J. Eugene. **UNESCO — United Nations Educational, Scientific, and Cultural Organization,** *World Affairs Quarterly,* XVII (April 1946), 53—72.

4340 Haruki, Takeshi. **UNESCO Activities in Japan,** *World Affairs Quarterly,* XXII (April 1951), 76—87.

4341 Havet, Jacques. **Is There a Philosophy of UNESCO?** *Learning and World Peace,* Lyman Bryson, Louis Finkelstein, and R. M. MacIver (eds.). New York, Harper, 1948, pp. 601—7.

4342 Henderson, J. L. **UNESCO in Focus.** New York, Anti-Defamation League of B'nai B'rith, 1949. 55 p.

4343 Huxley, Julian Sorell. **UNESCO: Its Purpose and Its Philosophy.** Washington, Public Affairs Press, 1947. 62 p.

4344 Johnson, Charles S. **UNESCO and the Social Sciences,** *Learning and World Peace,* Lyman Bryson, Louis Finkelstein, and R. M. MacIver (eds.). New York, Harper, 1948, pp. 608—13.

4345 Johnson, Richard A. **The Origin of the United Nations Educational, Scientific and Cultural Organization,** *International Conciliation,* CDXXIV (October 1946), 441—48.

4346 Khanna, R. S. **UNESCO,** *Indian Journal of Political Science,* XIII (April 1952), 33—42.

4347 Klineberg, Otto **UNESCO and the Cultural Basis for Peace,** *Academy of Political Science Proceedings,* XXV (January 1953), 55—65.

4348 Kolasa, Jan. **International Intellectual Cooperation (The League Experience and the Beginnings of UNESCO).** Warsaw, Nauk, 1962. 208 p.

Part D. — *United Nations System*

4349 Kugimoto, H. **UNESCO's Activities in Japan, 1951—1954,** *Contemporary Japan*, XXIII (1955), 279—95.

4350 Laves, Walter H. C. **UNESCO and the Achievement of Peace,** *Political Quarterly*, XXII (April-June 1951), 163—74.

4351 Laves, Walter H. C. and Thomson, Charles A. **UNESCO: Purpose, Progress, Prospects.** Bloomington, University of Indiana Press, 1957. 469 p.

4352 Lucharrière, Guy de. **L'UNESCO,** *Les institutions internationales et transnationales*, Fernand L'Huillier (ed.). Paris, Presses Universitaires, 1961, pp. 159—74.

4353 McKeon, Richard P. **Knowledge and World Organization,** *Foundations of World Organization*, Lyman Bryson, Louis Finkelstein, Harold D. Lasswell, and R. M. MacIver (eds.). New York, Harper, 1950, pp. 289—329.

UNESCO's assumptions. Comment by H. Slochower.

4354 —— ——. **The Program of UNESCO for 1947 and 1948,** *Learning and World Peace*, Lyman Bryson, Louis Finkelstein, and R. M. MacIver (eds.). New York, Harper, 1948, pp. 577—91.

4355 Maller, Sandor. **Hungary and UNESCO,** *New Hungarian Quarterly*, V (Spring, 1964), 128—33.

4356 Mander, Linden A. **Foundations of Modern World Society.** 2d ed. Stanford, Stanford University Press, 1947.

Chapter XV.

4357 Marshall, James. **UNESCO in an Anxious World,** *Learning and World Peace*, Lyman Bryson, Louis Finkelstein, and R. M. MacIver (eds.). New York, Harper, 1948, pp. 619—28.

Comments by G. H. Stevenson, H. B. Friedgood, S. G. Cole, R. McKeon.

4358 Martin, P. W. **UNESCO and Psychology,** *Journal of Social Issues*, III (Winter, 1947), 10—20.

4359 Niebuhr, Reinhold. **The Theory and Practice of UNESCO,** *International Organization*, IV (February 1950), 3—11.

4360 Parker, Harrison. **UNESCO and the Student of International Affairs,** *Journal of International Affairs*, I (Spring, 1947), 43—53.

4361 Pillsbury, Kent. **UNESCO Education in Action: A Field Study of the UNESCO Department of Education.** Columbus, Ohio State University Press, 1963. 106 p.

4362 Sathyamurthy, T. V. **The Politics of International Cooperation: Contrasting Conceptions of UNESCO.** Geneva, Droz, 1964. 314 p.

4363 Sharan, P. **UNESCO,** *Indian Journal of Political Science*, XIII (April 1952), 26—32.

4364 Sharp, Walter R. **The Role of UNESCO: A Critical Evaluation,** *Academy of Political Science Proceedings*, XXIV (January 1951), 249—62.

4365 Shuster, George N. **UNESCO: Assessment and Promise.** New York, Harper and Row, 1963. 130 p.

4366 Thomas, Jean. **UNESCO.** Paris, Gallimard, 1962. 266 p.

4367 Thompson, C. Mildred. **The Educational, Scientific and Cultural Organization of the United Nations — With Text of Constitution,** *Foreign Policy Reports*, XXI (February 15, 1946), 310—16.

4368 — —. **United Nations Plans for Post-War Education,** *Foreign Policy Reports*, XX (March 1, 1945), 310—19.

Part D. — United Nations System

4369 Torres Bodet, Jaime. **UNESCO,** *Peace on Earth,* Trygve Lie, Herbert V. Evatt, Charles Malik, Eleanor Roosevelt, Jaime Torres Bodet, Brock Chisholm, John Boyd-Orr, Ralph Bunche, Benjamin Cohen, Ludwick Rajchman, and Carlos P. Romulo. New York, Hermitage, 1949, pp. 75—88.

4370 Tripp, Brenda M. H. **UNESCO in Perspective,** *International Conciliation,* CDXCVII (March 1954), 323—83.

4371 Turcotte, Edmond. **The World of UNESCO,** *International Journal,* I (October 1946), 365—69.

4372 UNESCO, Youth Institute. **Food for Life — Food for Thought.** Dobbs Ferry, Oceana, 1962.

Part I.

4373 — —. **International Social Science Journal.** Paris, Quarterly, 1949—.

Each issue reports on research and lists documents pertaining to the social sciences.

4374 Wallace, R. C. **UNESCO,** *International Journal,* I (January 1946), 68—70.

4375 Wilson, Howard E. **The Development of UNESCO,** *International Conciliation,* CDXXXI (May 1947), 295—16.

4376 — —. **International Cultural Cooperation,** *International Conciliation,* CDXV (November 1945), 707—21.

4377 — —. **Problems of UNESCO,** *Learning and World Peace,* Lyman Bryson, Louis Finkelstein, and R. M. MacIver (eds.). New York, Harper, 1948, pp. 629—36.

Comments by Starr, McKeon.

7.3.4.2 SCIENTIFIC COOPERATION

4378 Aaronson, Michael. **Towards the Peaceful Uses of Outer Space,** *International Relations,* I (October 1959), 611—19.

4379 Bathurst, M. E. **Legal Aspects of the International Control of Atomic Energy,** *British Yearbook of International Law,* XXIV (1947), 1—32.

4380 Bechhoefer, Bernhard. **Negotiating the Statute of the International Atomic Energy Agency,** *International Organization,* XIII (Winter, 1959), 38—59.

4381 Beckhoefer, Bernard G. and Stein, Eric. **Atoms for Peace: The New International Atomic Energy Agency,** *Michigan Law Review,* LV (April 1957), 747—98.

4382 Bloomfield, Lincoln P. **Outer Space and International Cooperation,** *International Organization,* XIX (Summer, 1965), 603—21.

4383 Caver, D. F. **International Cooperation in the Peaceful Uses of Atomic Energy,** *Vanderbilt Law Review,* XII (December 1958), 17—49.

4384 Cheng, Bin. **United Nations Resolutions on Outer Space: "Instant" International Customary Law?** *Indian Journal of International Law,* V (January 1965), 23—48.

4385 Cockcroft, John. **The United Nations and Atomic Energy,** *The Quest for Peace,* Andrew W. Cordier and Wilder Foote (eds.). New York, Columbia University Press, 1965, pp. 343—54.

4386 Fischer, G. **Le système de controle au sein de l'Agence Internationale de L'Energie Atomique,** *Indian Year Book of International Affairs,* VI (1957), 112—25.

Part D. — United Nations System

4387 Frutkin, Arnold W. **Space Cooperation: International?** *Bulletin of the Atomic Scientists,* XIX (October 1963), 33—35.

4388 Gardner, Richard N. **In Pursuit of World Order.** New York, Praeger, 1964.
Chapter IX. Outer space.

4389 Gorrve, Stephen. **Humanizing the Atom: Establishment of the International Atomic Energy Agency,** *New York Law Forum,* III (July 1957), 245—79.

4390 Hydeman, Lee M. and Berman, William H. **International Control of Nuclear Maritime Activities.** Ann Arbor, University of Michigan Law School, 1960, 384 p.

4391 Jenks, C. Wilfred. **An International Régime for Antartica?** *International Affairs,* XXXII (October 1956), 414—26.

4392 Jessup, Philip C. and Taubenfeld, Howard J. **Outer Space, Antartica, and the United Nations,** *International Organization,* XIII (Summer, 1959), 363—79.

4393 Kaplan, Joseph. **The Impacts of the International Geophysical Year,** *Institute of World Affairs Proceedings,* XXXV (1959), 238—47.

4394 King, A. **International Scientific Cooperation — Its Possibilities and Limitations,** *Impact of Science on Society,* IV (Winter, 1953), 189—220.

4395 McNaughton, A. G. L. **National and International Control of Atomic Energy,** *International Journal,* III (Winter, 1947—48), 11—23.

4396 Meeker, Leonard C. **The International Atomic Energy Agency,** *American Society of International Law Proceedings,* LI (1957), 155—58.

4397 Mehren, Robert B. von. **The International Atomic Energy Agency in World Politics,** *Journal of International Affairs,* XIII, 1 (1959), 57—69.

4398 Odishaw, Hugh. **The International Geophysical Year and World Politics,** *Journal of International Affairs,* XIII, 1 (1959), 47—56.

4399 Patterson, Morehead. **Atoms for Peace and the International Community,** *American Society of International Law Proceedings,* XLIX (1955), 125—31.

4400 Rodgers, Raymond Spencer. **The Headquarters Agreement of the International Atomic Energy Agency of 1 March 1958 at Vienna,** *British Yearbook of International Law,* XXXIV (1958), 391—95.

4401 Rubinstein, Alvin Z. **The United States, the Soviet Union, and Atoms-for-Peace: Background to the establishment of the United Nations International Atomic Energy Agency,** *World Affairs Quarterly,* XXX (April 1959), 46—62.

4402 Rudd, F. A. **Atomic Energy and World Government,** *International Journal,* II (Summer, 1947), 237—41.

4403 Schwartz, Leonard E. **When Is International Space Cooperation International?** *Bulletin of the Atomic Scientists,* XIX (June 1963), 12—17.

4404 Shotwell, James T. **The United Nations Atomic Energy Commission: Introduction,** *International Conciliation,* CDXXIII (September 1946), 309—32.

4405 Simsarian, James. **Outer-Space Co-operation in the United Nations,** *American Journal of International Law,* LVII (October 1963), 854—67.

4406 Smith, Thomas V. **Atomic Power and Moral Faith.** Foreword by Robert J. Bernard. Claremont, Calif., Claremont College, 1946. vii + 56 p.

4407 Stein, Eric. **The New International Atomic Energy Agency,** *American Society of International Law Proceedings,* LI (1957), 158–64.

4408 Stoessinger, John G. **Atoms for Peace: The International Atomic Energy Agency,** *Organizing Peace in the Nuclear Age,* Commission to Study the Organization of Peace (ed.). New York, New York University Press, 1959, pp. 117–233.

4409 — —. **The International Atomic Energy Agency: The First Phase,** *International Organization,* XIII (Summer, 1959), 394–411.

4410 Sullivan, Walter. **The International Geophysical Year,** *International Conciliation,* DXXI (January 1959), 259–336.

4411 Taubenfeld, Howard J. (ed.). **Space and Society: Studies for the Seminar on Problems of Outer Space.** Dobbs Ferry, Oceana, 1964. xviii + 172 p.

4412 — —. **A Treaty for Antarctica,** *International Conciliation,* DXXXI (January 1961), 245–322.

4413 Urey, Harold C. **Atomic Energy in International Politics,** *Foreign Policy Reports,* XXII (June 15, 1946), 82–91.

4414 Vandenbosch, Amry and Hogan, Willard N. *Toward World Order.* New York, McGraw-Hill, 1963.
Chapter XIII. Atomic energy.

4415 Yemelyanov, V. S. **Atomic Energy for Peace: The USSR and International Cooperation,** *Foreign Affairs,* XXXVIII (April 1960), 465–75.

Part D. — *United Nations System*

7.3.4.3 INFORMATION POLICIES

4416 Binder, Carroll. **Freedom of Information and the United Nations,** *International Organization,* VI (May 1952), 210–26.

4417 Cohen, Benjamin V. **The UN's Department of Public Information,** *Public Opinion Quarterly,* X (Summer, 1946), 145–55.

4418 Cory, Robert H., Jr. **Forging an Information Policy for the United Nations,** *International Organization,* VII (May 1953), 229–42.

4419 Das, Kamleshwar. **United Nations Convention on the International Right of Correction,** *Indian Year Book of International Affairs,* XII (1963), 68–107.

4420 Eek, Hilding. **Freedom of Information As a Project of International Legislation.** Uppsala, Sweden, Lundequistska Bokhandeln, 1953. 176 p.

4421 Gordenker, Leon. **Policy-Making and Secretariat Influence in the UN General Assembly: The Case of Public Information,** *American Political Science Review,* LIV (June 1960), 359–73.

4422 Kaufman, Herbert. **The UN Publications Board.** University, Ala., University of Alabama Press, 1952. iii + 33 p.

4423 Mercey, Arch A. **The UN Information Program: Some Recommendations of the Advisory Committee,** *Public Opinion Quarterly,* XII (Fall, 1948), 481–87.

4424 Siegmann, Charles A. **Propaganda and Information in International Affairs,** *Yale Law Journal,* LV (August 1946), 1258–80.

Part D. — *United Nations System*

4425 Stoner, Frank E. **United Nations Information Requirements,** *Charter Review Conference: Ninth Report and Papers Presented to the Commission,* Commission to Study the Organization of Peace (ed.). New York, Commission to Study the Organization of Peace, 1955, pp. 212–26.

4426 Swift, Richard N. **The United Nations and Its Public,** *International Organization,* XIV (Winter, 1960), 60–91.
Concerns the Office of Public Information.

4427 Whitton, John B. **The United Nations Conference of Freedom of Information and the Movement Against International Propaganda,** *American Journal of International Law,* XLIII (January 1949), 73–87.

4428 Xydis, Stephen G. **The Press in World Politics and in the Conduct of Foreign Policy,** *Journal of International Affairs,* X, 2 (1956), 201–10.

7.3.5 INTERNATIONAL LABOR ORGANIZATION
(Geneva)

4429 Alexandrowicz, Charles Henry. **World Economic Agencies.** London, Stevens, 1962.
Chapter III.

4430 Anon. **Report of the Board of Directors of the Academy for 1956,** *Annals of the American Academy of Political and Social Science,* CCCX (March 1957), 182–95.

4431 Beguin, Bernard. **ILO and the Tripartite System,** *International Conciliation,* DXXIII (May 1959), 405–48.

4432 Brand, G. **International Labour Organization in Transition,** *World Affairs,* XII (April 1946), 81–89.

4433 Cook, A. H. **The International Labor Organization and Japanese Politics,** *Industrial and Labor Relations Review*, XIX (October 1965), 41–57.

4434 Fernbach, Alfred. **Soviet Coexistence Strategy: A Case Study of Experience in the International Labor Organization.** Washington, Public Affairs Press, 1960. 63 p.

4435 Fried, John H. E. **Relations Between the United Nations and the International Labor Organization,** *American Political Science Review*, XLI (October 1947), 963–77.

4436 Goodrich, Carter. **The ILO: A Going Concern,** *Annals of the American Academy of Political and Social Science*, CCXLVI (July 1946), 110–16.

4437 Green, L. C. **The International Labour Organisation Under Pressure,** *Current Legal Problems*, X (1957), 57–84.

4438 Haas, Ernst B. **Beyond the Nation-State: Functionalism and International Organization.** Stanford, Stanford University Press, 1964. 595 p.

The International Labor Organization as a case study of the functional approach to international organization.

4439 — —. **System and Process in the International Labor Organization: A Statistical Afterthought,** *World Politics*, XIV (January 1962), 322–52.

4440 Hediger, Ernest S. **The International Labor Organization and the United Nations,** *Foreign Policy Reports*, XXII (June 1, 1946), 70–79.

4441 International Labour Office. **The International Labour Organisation Since the War,** *International Labour Review*, LXVII, 2 (1953), 109–55.

4442   Jacobson, Harold Karan. **Labor, the UN and the Cold War,** *International Organization,* XI (Winter, 1957), 55–67.

4443   — —. **The USSR and ILO,** *International Organization,* XIV (Summer, 1960), 402–28.

4444   Jenks, C. Wilfred. **Constitutional Changes in the ILO,** *British Yearbook of International Law,* XXIII (1946), 303–17.

4445   — —. **Human Rights and International Labor Standards.** New York, Praeger, 1960. 159 p.

4446   Lodge, George C. **Spearheads of Democracy: Labor in the Developing Countries.** New York, Harper and Row, 1962. 249 p.

4447   Malik, A. M. **Pakistan and ILO,** *Pakistan Horizon,* VII (June 1954), 47–55.

4448   Mander, Linden A. **Foundations of Modern World Society.** 2d ed. Stanford, Stanford University Press, 1947.

Chapter VII.

4449   Morse, David A. **The International Labor Organization in a Changing World,** *Annals of the American Academy of Political and Social Science,* CCCX (March 1957), 31–38.

4450   Nordskog, John Eric. **International Labor and the Peace Plan,** *World Affairs Quarterly,* XVI (July 1945), 194–204.

4451   Phelan, V. C. **Human Welfare and the ILO,** *International Journal,* IX (Winter, 1954), 24–33.

4452 Pillai, P. P. **The ILO and Asia,** *Indian Year Book of International Affairs,* I (1953), 78—87.

4453 Price, John. **The International Labour Organisation,** *International Affairs,* XXI (January 1945), 30—39.

4454 Raeburn, Walter. **Features and Development of the International Labour Organisation,** *Transactions* (Grotius Society), XXXV (1949), 57—71.

4455 Riegelman, Carol. **Labor's Bridgehead: The ILO,** *Political Science Quarterly,* LV (June 1945), 205—21.

4456 Sulkowski, Joseph. **Competence of the International Labor Organization Under the United Nations System,** *American Journal of International Law,* XLV (April 1951), 286—313.

4457 Tayler, William Lonsdale. **The International Labor Organization,** *Contemporary World Politics,* Francis J. Brown, Charles Hodges and Joseph S. Roucek (eds.). New York, Wiley, 1939, pp. 471—86.

4458 Tessier, Jacques. **L'Organisation Internationale du Travail (O. I. T.),** *Les institutions internationales et transnationales,* Fernand L'Huillier (ed.). Paris, Presses Universitaires, 1961, pp. 266—78.

4459 Thomas, Elbert D. **Report on the Paris Conference of the International Labor Organization,** *Institute of World Affairs Proceedings,* XXI (1945), 118—22.

4460 Tipton, John B. **Participation of the United States in the International Labor Organization.** Urbana, University of Illinois, Institute of Labor and Industrial Relations, 1959. 150 p.

4461 UNESCO, Youth Institute. **Energy and Skills for Human Progress.** Dobbs Ferry, Oceana, 1963. 103 p.

7.3.6 REFUGEES AND MIGRATION

7.3.6.1 GENERAL OBSERVATIONS

4462 Bailey, Sydney D. **The United Nations.** New York, Praeger, 1963.
Chapter VII.

4463 Balogh, E. **La paix mondiale et le problème des réfugiés,** *Recueil des Cours,* LXXV (1949), 305–507.

4464 Caldwell, M. J. **Refugees and the United Nations,** *International Journal,* II (Spring, 1947), 102–105.

4465 Chamberlain, Joseph P. **The Fate of Refugees and Displaced Persons,** *Academy of Political Science Proceedings,* XXII (January 1947), 192–202.

4466 Chandler, Edgar H. S. **The High Tower of Refuge.** New York, Praeger, 1959. 264 p.

4467 Fertig, Norman R. and Peters, Donald W. **A Survey of the International Refugee Organization,** *World Affairs Quarterly,* XVIII (October 1947), 305–13.

4468 G., H. **Progress in Refugee Settlement,** *World Today,* New Series, IX (October 1953), 449–59.

4469 Goedhart, G. J. Van Heuven. **People Adrift,** *Journal of International Affairs,* VII, 1 (1953), 7–29.

4470 — —. **Le problème des réfugiés,** *Recueil des Cours,* LXXXII (1953), 265–371.

4471 — —. **Refugees: An Unsolved Problem,** *World Today,* New Series, VIII (August 1952), 324–32.

4472 Holborn, Louise W. **International Organizations for Migration of European Nationals and Refugees,** *International Journal,* XX (Summer, 1965), 331–49.

4473 — —. **The International Refugee Organization: A Specialized Agency of the United Nations; Its History and Work, 1946–1952.** London, Oxford University Press, 1956. 805 p.

4474 — —. **The Problem of Refugees,** *Current History,* XXXVIII (June 1960), 342–46.

4475 Hosain, H. Tafazzul. **International Migration and International Organizations,** *Pakistan Economic Journal,* XIII (March 1963), 50–60.

4476 Lorimer, Frank; Lenroot, Katharine F.; and Coil, E. J. **Problems Relating to Migration and Settlement in the Postwar Period,** *The Transitional Period: Second Report and Papers Presented to the Commission,* Commission to Study the Organization of Peace (ed.). New York, Commission to Study the Organization of Peace, 1942, pp. 184–94.

4477 Malin, Patrick M. **The Refugee: A Problem for International Organization,** *International Organization,* I (September 1947), 443–59.

4478 Read, James M. **The United Nations and Refugees — Changing Concepts,** *International Conciliation,* DXXXVII (March 1962), 5–58.

4479 Rees, Elfan. **Century of the Homeless Man,** *International Conciliation,* DXV (November 1957), 193–254.

4480 — —. **The Refugee and the United Nations,** *International Conciliation,* CDXCII (June 1953), 269–314.

4481 — —. **The Refugee Problem: Joint Responsibility,** *Annals of the American Academy of Political and Social Science,* CCCXXIX (May 1960), 15–22.

4482 Reut-Nicolussi, E. **Displaced Persons and International Law,** *Recueil des Cours,* LXXIII (1948), 5–67.

4483 Richardson, Channing B. **The Refugee Problem,** *Academy of Political Science Proceedings,* XXIV (1952), 483–90.

4484 Riggs, Fred W. **The World's Refugee Problem,** *Foreign Policy Reports,* XXVI (January 15, 1951), 190–99.

4485 Ristelhueber, René. **The International Refugee Organization,** *International Conciliation,* CDLXX (April 1951), 167–228.

4486 Rucker, Arthur. **The Work of the International Refugee Organization,** *International Affairs,* XXV (January 1949), 66–73.

4487 Schechtman, Joseph B. **The Refugee in the World: Displacement and Integration.** New York, Barnes, 1964. 424 p.

4488 Stoessinger, John G. **The Refugee and the World Community.** Minneapolis, University of Minnesota Press, 1956. 239 p.

4489 UNESCO, Youth Institute. **World Peace and the United Nations.** Dobbs Ferry, Oceana, 1962.

Part III.

7.3.6.2 PALESTINE REFUGEE PROBLEM

4490 Baldwin, Roger N. **The Palestine Refugees,** *Current History,* New Series, XXXIII (November 1957), 295—98.

4491 Coate, Winifred A. **The Condition of Arab Refugees in Jordan,** *International Affairs,* XXIX (October 1953), 449—56.

4492 Harvey, Mary Frances. **The Palestine Refugee Problem: Elements of a Solution,** *Orbis,* III (Summer, 1959), 193—208.

4493 Peretz, Don. **The Arab Refugee Dilemma,** *Foreign Affairs,* XXXIII (October 1954), 134—48.

4494 — —. **The Arab Refugees: A Changing Problem,** *Foreign Affairs,* XLI (April 1963), 558—70.

4495 — —. **Problems of Arab Refugee Compensation,** *Middle East Journal,* VIII (Autumn, 1954), 403—16.

4496 Richardson, Channing B. **880,000 Arab Refugees,** *Journal of International Affairs,* VI (Winter, 1952), 21—24.

4497 — —. **The United Nations Relief for Palestine Refugees,** *International Organization,* IV (February 1950), 44—58.

4498 St. Aubin, W. de. **Peace and Refugees in the Middle East,** *Middle East Journal,* III (July 1949), 249—59.

4499 Tweedy, Owen. **The Arab Refugees: Report on a Middle East Journey,** *International Affairs,* XXVIII (July 1952), 338—43.

4500 W., D. **Hope for the Arab Refugees: The Yarmuk Project,** *World Today,* New Series, VIII (December 1952), 512—21.

7.3.7 RELIEF AND REHABILITATION

4501 Alexandrowicz, Charles Henry. **World Economic Agencies.** London, Stevens, 1962.

Chapter VIII. UNRRA.

4502 Arnold-Forster, W. **UNRRA's Prospects,** *Political Quarterly,* XV (January-March 1944), 57—65.

4503 — —. **UNRRA's Work for Displaced Persons in Germany,** *International Affairs,* XXII (January 1946), 1—12.

Discussion by Rathbone, Philips, Turner.

4504 Brand, George. **International Relief Machinery,** *World Affairs,* IX (April 1944), 144—48.

4505 Brodsky, Nathan. **Some Aspects of International Relief,** *Quarterly Journal of Economics,* LXII (August 1948), 596—609.

4506 Comstock, Alzada. **Reconstruction and World Exchange,** *Current History,* New Series, VII (August 1944), 81—88.

4507 Dean, Vera Micheles. **UNRRA — A Step Toward Reconstruction,** *Foreign Policy Reports,* XIX (January 1, 1944), 266—70.

4508 Fay, Sidney B. **UNRRA,** *Current History,* New Series, VII (July 1944), 8—12.

4509 Fisher, Allan G. B. **The Constitution and Work of UNRRA,** *International Affairs,* XX (July 1944), 317—29.

Comments by Price, Byrt.

Part D. — United Nations System

4510 Fox, Grace. **The Origins of UNRRA,** *Political Science Quarterly,* LXV (December 1950), 561–85.

4511 Friedmann, W. **UNRRA and National Sovereignty.** *Fortnightly,* New Series, CLV (January 1944), 17–25.

4512 Goodman, G. G. **UNRRA in Perspective,** *Year Book of World Affairs,* II (1948), 197–224.

4513 Guins, George C. **Basic Principles of UNRRA's Policy,** *Southwestern Social Science Quarterly,* XXVI (September 1945), 127–34.

4514 Harris, Joseph P. **The Development of an International Civil Service for the Administration of Relief and Rehabilitation of War Devastated Areas.** Washington, UNRRA, 1944. 12 p.

4515 — —. **Some Problems of International Administration, Illustrated by UNRRA,** *Institute of World Affairs Proceedings,* XXI (1945), 85–86.

4516 Hoehler, Fred K. **What Is UNRRA Doing?** *Survey Midmonthly,* LXXXI (April 1945), 99–102.

4517 Hutcheson, Harold H. **International Agencies for European Reconstruction,** *Foreign Policy Reports,* XXIII (July 15, 1947), 110–16.

4518 Jessup, Philip C. **UNRRA: Sample of World Government,** *Foreign Affairs,* XXII (April 1944), 362–73.

4519 Johnson, Robert H. **International Politics and the Structure of International Organization: The Case of UNRRA,** *World Politics,* III (July 1951), 520–38.

Part D. — United Nations System

4520 Keyser, John A. and Marsh, Leonard C. **UNRRA and Its Task,** *World Affairs,* XI (January 1946), 325–35.

4521 Klemme, Marvin. **The Inside Story of UNRRA.** New York, Lifetime Editions, 1949. 307 p.

4522 Kraus, Hertha. **International Relief in Action, 1914–43: Selected Records with Notes.** Scottdale, Pa., Herald, 1944. 248 p.

4523 Lehman, Herbert H. **Relief and Rehabilitation,** *Foreign Policy Reports,* XIX (July 15, 1943), 101–105.

4524 — —. **Some Problems in International Administration,** *Public Administration Review,* V (Spring, 1945), 93–101.

UNRRA.

4525 — —. **UNRRA on the March,** *Survey Graphic,* XXXIII (November 1944), 437–40 ff.

4526 Leonard, L. Larry. **UNRRA and the Concept of Regional International Organization,** *Iowa Law Review,* XXXI (May 1945), 489–514.

4527 Martin, Paul. **Food Relief Discussions at the UN Assembly,** *International Journal,* II (Summer, 1947), 96–101.

UNRRA.

4528 O., E. R. **International Mutual Aid: The Task of UNRRA,** *World Today,* New Series, II (January 1946), 35–44.

4529 R., J. **UNRRA 1945–1947: The End of a Chapter,** *World Today,* New Series, III (August 1947), 370–74.

Part D. — United Nations System

4530 Robertson, A. H. **Some Legal Problems of the UNRRA,** *British Yearbook of International Law*, XXIII (1946), 142–67.

4531 Solovehtchik, George. **After the Armies — UNRRA,** *Survey Graphic*, XXXIII (July 1944), 311–12 ff.

4532 Staley, Eugene. **Economic Aspects of Relief and Rehabilitation,** *Vital Speeches*, IX (September 15, 1943), 730–34.

4533 — —. **Relief and Rehabilitation in China,** *Far Eastern Survey*, XIII (October 4, 1944), 183–85.

4534 Sumberg, Theodore A. **The Financial Experience of UNRRA,** *American Journal of International Law*, XXXIX (October 1945), 698–712.

4535 Weintraub, Philipp. **UNRRA: An Experiment in International Welfare Planning,** *Journal of Politics*, VII (February 1945), 1–24.

4536 Wilson, Francesca. **Aftermath: France, Germany, Yugoslavia; 1945 and 1946.** Baltimore, Penguin, 1947. 253 p.
Work of UNRRA.

4537 Woodbridge, George (comp.). **UNRRA: The History of the United Nations Relief and Rehabilitation Administration.** New York, Columbia University Press, 1950. 3 vols.

8. TRUSTEESHIP SYSTEM AND NON-SELF-GOVERNING TERRITORIES

Perhaps the most successful organ in achieving its purposes, the Trusteeship Council has observed the independence of nearly all Asian and African colonies. By refusing to place her League mandate, Southwest Africa, under the trusteeship system, the Republic of South Africa has been able to avoid the more stringent regulations imposed elsewhere by the Trusteeship Council. Unlike the League, however, the UN did not receive even nominal authority in supervising such areas as Germany and Japan during their postwar occupation.

8.1 GENERAL DISCUSSIONS

4538 Anon. **International Responsibility for Colonial Peoples: The United Nations and Chapter XI of the Charter,** *International Conciliation*, CDLVIII (February 1950), 51—112.

Contains commentary, documents, reading list.

4539 Armstrong, Elizabeth. **The United States and Non-Self-Governing Territories,** *International Journal*, III (Autumn, 1948), 327—33.

4540 Bailey, Sydney D. **The Future Composition of the Trusteeship Council,** *International Organization*, XIII (Summer, 1959), 412—21.

4541 — —. **The United Nations.** New York, Praeger, 1963.

Chapter VI.

4542 Ball, M. Margaret and Killough, Hugh B. **International Relations.** New York, Ronald, 1956.

Chapter XVI.

4543 Bentwich, Norman. **Colonial Mandates and Trusteeships,** *Transactions* (Grotius Society), XXXII (1946), 121—34.

4544 — —. **Colonies and International Accountability,** *Political Quarterly*, XVI (July-September 1945), 253—60.

4545 Bunche, Ralph. **The International Trusteeship System,** *Peace on Earth*, Trygve Lie, Herbert V. Evatt, Charles Malik, Eleanor Roosevelt, Jaime Torres Bodet, Brock Chisholm, John Boyd-Orr, Ralph Bunche, Benjamin Cohen, Ludwick Rajchman, and Carlos P. Romulo. New York, Hermitage, 1949, pp. 113—28.

4546 Chase, Eugene P. **Dependent Areas and the Trusteeship System of the United Nations,** *World Affairs Quarterly*, XVII (October 1946),. 293—305.

4547 — —. **The United Nations in Action.** New York, McGraw-Hill, 1950.
Chapters XIV, XV.

4548 Chieh, Liu. **International Trusteeship System,** *International Conciliation*, CDXLVIII (February 1949), 99—105.
Issue contains a discussion on, and two reports of, visiting missions.

4549 Chowdhuri, R. N. **International Mandate and Trusteeship Systems: A Comparative Study.** Hague, Nijhoff, 1955. 328 p.

4550 Comstock, Alzada. **The Trusteeship Plan,** *Current History*, New Series, VIII (June 1945), 511—16.

4551 Conover, Helen F. (comp.). **Non-Self-Governing Areas with Special Emphasis on Mandates and Trusteeships: A Selected List of References.** Washington, Library of Congress, 1947. 2 vols.

Part D. — *United Nations System*

4552 Coyle, David Cushman. **The United Nations and How It Works.** New York, Columbia University Press, 1966.

Chapter VI.

4553 Dean, Vera Micheles. **The UN Today.** New York, Holt, Rinehart and Winston, 1965.

Chapter V.

4554 Dolivet, Louis. **The United Nations.** New York, Farrar and Straus, 1946.

Chapter VI.

4555 Easton, Stewart C. **The Twilight of European Colonialism.** New York, Holt, Rinehart and Winston, 1960. 571 p.

4556 Eichelberger, Clark M. **UN: The First Twenty Years.** New York, Harper, 1965.

Chapter VI.

4557 Emerson, Rupert. **Colonialism, Political Development, and the UN,** *International Organization,* XIX (Summer, 1965), 484–503.

4558 Fox, Annette Baker. **International Organization for Colonial Development,** *World Politics,* III (April 1951), 340–68.

4559 — —. **The United Nations and Colonial Development,** *International Organization,* IV (May 1950), 199–218.

4560 Fraser, Peter. **The Work of the Trusteeship Council,** *International Conciliation,* CDXLV (November 1948), 651–66.

4561 Frazao, Sergio Armando. **International Responsibility for Non-Self-Governing Peoples,** *Annals of the American Academy of Political and Social Science,* CCXCVI (November 1954), 56–67.

4562 Gerig, Benjamin, *et al.* **Colonial Aspects of the Postwar Period,** *The Transitional Period: Second Report and Papers Presented to the Commission,* Commission to Study the Organization of Peace (ed.). New York, Commission to Study the Organization of Peace, 1942, pp. 218—35.

4563 — —. **Significance of the Trusteeship System,** *Annals of the American Academy of Political and Social Science,* CCLV (January 1948), 39—47.

4564 Gilchrist, Huntington. **Trusteeship and the Colonial System,** *Academy of Political Science Proceedings,* XXII (January 1947), 203—17.

4565 Goodrich, Leland M. **The United Nations.** New York, Crowell, 1963.
Chapter XIII.

4566 Goodspeed, Stephen S. **The Nature and Function of International Organization.** New York, Oxford University Press, 1963.
Chapter XV.

4567 Gross, Leo. **United Nations Trusteeship and the League of Nations Mandate Systems,** *India Quarterly,* IV (July-September 1948), 224—39.

4568 Haas, Ernst B. **The Attempt to Terminate Colonialism: Acceptance of the United Nations Trusteeship System,** *International Organization,* VII (February 1953), 1—21.

4569 Hall, Hessel Duncan. **The British Commonwealth and Trusteeship,** *International Affairs,* XXII (April 1946), 199—213.
Discusses similarities between the two arrangements.

4570 — —. **Mandates, Dependencies and Trusteeship.** Washington, Carnegie, 1948. 429 p.

4571 — —. **The Trusteeship System,** *British Yearbook of International Law,* XXIV (1947), 33—73.

4572 Hayden, Sherman S. **The Trusteeship Council: Its First Three Years,** *Political Science Quarterly,* LXVI (June 1951), 226—47.

4573 Hayden, Sherman S. and Rivlin, Benjamin. **Non Self-Governing Territories: Status of Puerto Rico.** New York, Woodrow Wilson Foundation, 1954. 23 p.

4574 Holcombe, Arthur N. **Dependent Areas in the Post-War World.** Boston, World Peace Foundation, 1941. 108 p.

4575 — —. **The International Trusteeship System,** *Annals of the American Academy of Political and Social Science,* CCXLVI (July 1946), 101—9.

4576 Jacob, Philip E. and Atherton, Alexine L. **Dynamics of International Organization.** Homewood, Dorsey, 1964.

Chapter XX.

4577 Jacobson, Harold K. **The United Nations and Colonialism: A Tentative Appraisal,** *International Organization,* XVI (Winter, 1962), 37—56.

4578 Kelsen, Hans. **The Law of the United Nations.** New York, Praeger, 1951.

Chapter XVI.

4579 Khan, Begum Liaquat Ali. **United Nations and the Self-Determination of Peoples,** *Pakistan Horizon,* VI (March 1953), 10—16.

4580 Kohn, Hans. **The United Nations and Self-Determination,** *Review of Politics,* XX (October 1958), 526

4581 Lakshminarayan, C. V. **Analysis of the Principles and System of International Trusteeship in the Charter.** Geneva, Impr. Populaires, 1951. 206 p.

4582 Lawson, Ruth C. **Trusteeship — 1945—50,** *Current History,* New Series, XIX (November 1950), 261—66.

4583 Leonard, L. Larry. **International Organization.** New York, McGraw-Hill, 1951.

Chapters XXV—XXVII.

4584 McHenry, Dean E. **The United Nations Trusteeship System,** *World Affairs Quarterly,* XIX (July 1948), 149—58.

4585 McKay, Vernon. **International Trusteeship — Role of United Nations in the Colonial World,** *Foreign Policy Reports,* XXII (May 15, 1946), 54—67.

4586 Maclaurin, John (pseud.). **The United Nations and Power Politics.** New York, Harper, 1951.

Chapter IX.

4587 Mander, Linden A. **Foundations of Modern World Society.** 2d ed. Stanford, Stanford University Press, 1947.

Chapter XIV.

4588 Meron, T. **The Question of the Composition of the Trusteeship Council,** *British Yearbook of International Law,* XXXVI (1960), 250—78.

4589 Mortimer, Molly. **Trusteeship in Practice.** London, Fabian, 1951. 52 p.

4590 Murray, James N., Jr. **The United Nations Trusteeship System.** Urbana, University of Illinois Press, 1957. 283 p.

4591 Nawaz, M. K. **Colonies, Self-Government and the United Nations,** *Indian Year Book of International Affairs,* XI (1962), 3—47.

4592 Parry, C. **The Legal Nature of the Trusteeship Agreements,** *British Yearbook of International Law,* XXVI (1949), 164—85.

4593 Rao, B. Shiva. **The United Nations and Non-Self-Governing Territories,** *India Quarterly,* VI (July-September 1950), 227—33.

4594 Rappard, William E. **The Mandates and the International Trusteeship System,** *Political Science Quarterly,* LXI (September 1946), 408—19.

4595 — —. **Mandates and Trusteeships: With Particular Reference to Palestine,** *Journal of Politics,* VIII (November 1946), 520—30.

4596 Riggs, Fred W. **Wards of the UN: Trust and Dependent Areas,** *Foreign Policy Reports,* XXVI (June 1, 1950), 54—63.

4597 Rivlin, Benjamin. **Self-Determination and Dependent Areas,** *International Conciliation,* DI (January 1955), 195—271.

4598 Robinson, Kenneth. **World Opinion and Colonial Status,** *International Organization,* VIII (November 1953), 468—83.

4599 Romulo, Carlos P. **Whither, Submerged Milions?** *Journal of International Affairs,* IX, 2 (1955), 21—30.

4600 Rowe, Edward T. **The Emerging Anti-Colonial Consensus in the United Nations,** *Journal of Conflict Resolution,* VIII (September 1964), 209—30.

4601 Rowley, C. D. **The United Nations, Colonialism, and Australia,** *Australian Outlook,* II (June 1953), 120–28.

4602 Sady, Emil J. **The United Nations and Dependent Peoples.** Washington, Brookings, 1956. viii + 205 p.

4603 Sayre, Francis Bowes. **The Advancement of Dependent Peoples,** *International Conciliation,* CDXXXV (November 1947), 693–99.

4604 — —. **Dependent Peoples and World Order,** *Foundations for World Order,* University of Denver, Social Science Foundation (ed.). Denver, University of Denver Press, 1949, pp. 117–36.

4605 — —. **Legal Problems Arising from the United Nations Trusteeship System,** *American Journal of International Law,* XLII (April 1948), 263–98.

4606 Schwarzenberger, Georg. **Power Politics.** 3d ed. London, Stevens, 1964.

Chapter XXVII.

4607 Singh, L. P. **The Goal of Trusteeship — Self-Government or Independence,** *Australian Outlook,* XV (December 1961), 295–306.

4608 — —. **Notes and Memoranda: The Commonwealth and the United Nations Trusteeship of Non-Self-Governing Peoples,** *International Studies,* V (January 1964), 296–303.

4609 Soward, F. H. **Canada, the Eleventh General Assembly and Trusteeship,** *International Journal,* XII (Summer, 1957), 167–81.

4610 Stone, Julius. **Colonial Trusteeship in Transition.** Sydney, Australian Institute of International Affairs, 1944. 31 p.

4611 Thompson, David. **How International Is Colonial Trusteeship?** *Political Quarterly* XVIII (October-December 1948), 341—50.

4612 Thuller, George. **Problems of the Trusteeship System: A Study of Political Behavior in the United Nations.** Geneva, Droz, 1964. 217 p.

4613 Toussaint, Charmian Edwards. **The Trusteeship System of the United Nations.** New York, Praeger, 1956. 288 p.

4614 — —. **The United Nations and Dependent Peoples,** *Year Book of World Affairs,* VIII (1954), 141—69.

4615 Vandenbosch, Amry and Hogan, Willard N. **Toward World Order.** New York, McGraw-Hill, 1963.

Chapter XIV.

4616 — —. **The United Nations.** New York, McGraw-Hill, 1952.

Chapters XI, XVIII.

4617 Wainhouse, David W. **Remnants of Empire: The United Nations and the End of Colonialism.** New York, Harper and Row, 1964. 156 p.

4618 Welensky, Roy. **The United Nations and Colonialism in Africa,** *Annals of the American Academy of Political and Social Science,* CCCLIV (July 1964), 145—52.

8.2 PARTICULAR TERRITORIES

8.2.1 AFRICAN TRUSTEESHIPS

4619 Abneton, Barid. **Eritrea: United Nations Problem and Solution,** *Middle Eastern Affairs,* II (February 1951), 35—51.

4620 Bates, Margaret L. **Tanganyika: The Development of a Trust Territory,** *International Organization,* IX (February 1955), 32–51.

4621 Becker, George H. **The Disposition of the Italian Colonies, 1941–1951.** Annemasse, France, Granchamp, 1952. 270 p.

4622 Castagno, Alphonso A., Jr. **Somalia,** *International Conciliation,* DXXII (March 1959), 339–400.

4623 Chidzero, B. T. G. **Tanganyika and International Trusteeship.** New York, Oxford University Press, 1961. x + 286 p.

4624 Coleman, James S. **Togoland,** *International Conciliation,* DIX (September 1956), 3–91.

4625 Cumming, Duncan Cameron. **The Disposal of Eritrea,** *Middle East Journal,* VII (Winter, 1953), 18–32.

4626 Dearden, Ann. **Independence of Libya: The Political Problems,** *Middle East Journal,* IV (October 1950), 395–410.

4627 Finkelstein, Lawrence S. **Somaliland Under Italian Administration: A Case Study in United Nations Trusteeship.** New York, Woodrow Wilson Foundation, 1955. 40 p.

4628 Gardiner, David E. **Cameroon: United Nations Challenge to French Policy.** New York, Oxford University Press, 1963. 142 p.

4629 Haines, C. Grove. **The Problem of the Italian Colonies,** *Middle East Journal,* I (October 1947), 417–31.

4630 Harrison-Church, R. J. **The Problem of the Italian Colonies,** *World Affairs,* New Series, III (January 1949), 77–86.

Part D. — *United Nations System*

4631 Karp, Mark. **The Economics of Trusteeship in Somalia.** Boston, Boston Univesity Press, 1960. x + 190 p.

4632 McKay, Vernon. **Too Slow or Too Fast? Political Change in African Trust Territories,** *Foreign Affairs,* XXXV (January 1957), 295—310.

4633 Petrović, N. **Zapadnoevropski Radnički Pokret i Integracija,** *Medunarodni problemi,* XIII (October-December 1961), 99—140.

4634 Rivlin, Benjamin. **The Italian Colonies and the General Assembly,** *International Organization,* III (August 1949), 459—70.

4635 — —. **The United Nations and the Italian Colonies.** New York, Carnegie, 1950. iv + 114 p.

4636 Stafford, F. E. **The Ex-Italian Colonies,** *International Affairs,* XXV (January 1949), 47—55.

8.2.2 SOUTHWEST AFRICAN "MANDATE"

4637 A., H. **The High Commission Territories and the Union of South Africa,** *World Today,* New Series, VI (February 1950), 83—94.

4638 Ballinger, Ronald. **The Territory of South West Africa,** *Current History,* New Series XLV (December 1963), 361—65.

4639 D., G. V. **Recent Developments in the High Commission Territories,** *World Today,* New Series, XVIII (January 1962), 17—23.

4640 FitzGerald, Richard C. **South Africa and the High Commission Territories,** *World Affairs,* IV (July 1950), 306—20.

4641 Goldblatt, Israel. **The Conflict Between the United Nations and the Union of South Africa in Regard to South West Africa.** Windhoek, South West Africa, Goldblatt, 1961. 30 p.

4642 — —. **The Mandated Territory of South West Africa in Relation to the United Nations.** Capetown, Struik, 1961. 67 p.

4643 Hailey, Lord. **The Republic of South Africa and the High Commission Territories.** New York, Oxford University Press, 1963. 136 p.

4644 Hall, H. Duncan. **The Trusteeship System and the Case of South-West Africa,** *British Yearbook of International Law,* XXIV (1947), 385—89.

4645 Jennings, R. Y. **The International Court's Advisory Opinion on Voting Procedure on Questions Concerning Southwest Africa,** *Transactions* (Grotius Society), XLII (1956), 85—97.

4646 Keppel-Jones, **South Africa and the High Commission Territories,** *International Journal,* VI (Spring, 1951), 85—93.

4647 Nayak, Sanjeeva. **South-West Africa in the United Nations,** *Africa Quarterly,* III (January 1964), 255—41.

4648 R., M. **South West Africa Before the United Nations,** *World Today,* New Series, XVI (August 1960), 334—45.

4649 Scott, Michael. **The International Status of South West Africa,** *International Affairs,* XXXIV (July 1958), 318—29.

4650 W., M. **South-West Africa and the Union.** *World Today,* New Series, VI (November 1950), 459—69.

Part D. — *United Nations System*

8.2.3 PACIFIC TRUSTEESHIPS

4651 Bailey, K. H. **Dependent Areas of the Pacific: An Australian View,** *Foreign Affairs,* XXIV (April 1946), 494—512.

4652 Codding, George A., Jr. **The United States Trusteeship in the Pacific,** *Current History,* New Series, XXIX (December 1955), 358—64.

4653 Coulter, John Wesley. **The Pacific Dependencies of the United States.** New York, Macmillan, 1957. 388 p.

4654 Crosby, Josiah. **The Future of Western Samoa,** *International Affairs,* XXIV (January 1948), 89—94.

4655 Finkelstein, Lawrence S. **Trusteeship in Action: The United Nations Mission to Western Samoa,** *International Organization,* II (June 1947), 268—82.

4656 Fletcher-Cooke, John. **Some Reflections on the International Trusteeship System, with Particular Reference to Its Impact on the Governments and Peoples of the Trust Territories,** *International Organization,* XIII (Summer, 1959), 422—30.

4657 Keesing, Felix M. **Administration in Pacific Islands,** *Far Eastern Survey,* XVI (March 26, 1947), 61—65.

4658 Leifer, Michael. **Australia, Trusteeship and New Guinea,** *Pacific Affairs,* XXXVI (Fall, 1963), 250—64.

4659 McDonald, Alexander Hugh (ed.). **Trusteeship in the Pacific.** Sydney, Angus and Robertson, 1949. x + 171 p.

Part D. — United Nations System

4660 Mair, L. P. **Australia in New Guinea.** London, Christophers, 1949. 238 p.

4661 Maki, John M. **U.S. Strategic Area or UN Trusteeship,** *Far Eastern Survey,* XVI (August 13, 1947), 175—78.

4662 Mander, Linden A. **The UN Mission's 1956 Survey of the Pacific Trust Territory,** *Pacific Affairs,* XXIX (December 1956), 367—74.

4663 Pelzer, Karl J. **Micronesia — A Changing Frontier,** *World Politics,* II (January 1950), 251—66.

4664 Trumbell, Robert. **Paradise in Trust: A Report on Americans in Micronesia, 1946—1958.** New York, Sloane, 1959. 204 p.

4665 W., F. **American Trusteeship in the Pacific Islands,** *World Today,* New Series, III (July 1947), 317—22.

8.3 ADMINISTRATION OF SPECIAL AREAS

See also D 2.5.

4666 Kelsen, H. **The Free Territory of Trieste Under the United Nations,** *Year Book of World Affairs,* IV (1950), 174—90.

4667 Obieta, Joseph A. **The International Status of the Suez Canal.** Foreword by Richard R. Baxter. Hague, Nijhoff, 1960. ix + 137 p.

4668 Roegele, O. **Aspects of the Saar Problem,** *Review of Politics,* XIV (October 1952), 484—500.

4669 Schonfield, Hugh J. **The Suez Canal in World Affairs.** New York, Philosophical Library, 1953. x + 174 p.

Part D. — *United Nations System*

9. INTERNATIONAL COURT OF JUSTICE (Hague)

The world court has witnessed in the postwar era the rise to prominence of many states with legal systems that tend to regard existing International law as "bourgeois" or "Western" in orientation. This view has resulted in attempts to de-Westernize international law and to rely on advisory opinions and resolutions rather than judgments in cases as vehicles for developing a worldwide legal system.

9.1 GENERAL DISCUSSIONS

4670 **American Journal of International Law.** Washington, American Society of International Law, Quarterly, 1955–.

> Notes on legal questions concerning the United Nations are included in each issue, written by Yuen-li Liang, Secretary of the International Law Commission.

4671 Anand, R. P. **The International Court of Justice and Impartiality Between Nations.** Durham, World Rule of Law Center, Duke University, 1965. 45 p.

> Reprinted from *Indian Year Book of International Affairs*, 1963.

4672 Bastid, S. **The "Jurisprudence" of the International Court of Justice,** *Recueil des Cours*, LXXVIII (1951), 579–686.

4673 Bradley, Rolland. **Statement on the International Court of Justice,** *World Affairs Quarterly*, XVII (July 1946), 149–59.

4674 Brooks, E. A. S. **Subsidiary Judicial Authorities of the United Nations Organization to Hear and Decide Claims by Individuals and Corporations Against States,** *International Law Quarterly*, III (October 1950), 523–29.

Part D. — *United Nations System*

4675 Chase, Eugene P. **The United Nations in Action.** New York, McGraw-Hill, 1950.

Chapter XVII.

4676 Cheever, Daniel S. and Haviland, H. Field, Jr. **Organizing for Peace.** Boston, Houghton, Mifflin, 1954.

4677 Cordoba, R. **The Development and Codification of International Law,** *The United Nations: Ten Years, Legal Progress,* Gezina J. H. Van Der Molen, W. P. J. Pompe and J. H. W. Verzijl (eds.). Hague, Nederlandse Studentenvereniging Voor Wereldrechtsorde, 1956, pp. 43—60.

4678 Courlander, Harold. **Shaping Our Times.** New York, Oceana, 1960.

Chapters III, X.

4679 Dixit, R. K. **Access to the International Court,** *Indian Journal of International Law,* I (1960—61), 67—74.

4680 Dolivet, Louis. **The United Nations.** New York, Farrar and Straus, 1946.

Chapter VII.

4681 Doub, George Cochran. **The Unused Potential of the World Court,** *Foreign Affairs,* XL (April 1962), 463—70.

4682 Fitzmaurice, Gerald. **The Law and Procedure of the International Court of Justice: International Organizations and Tribunals,** *British Yearbook of International Law,* XXIX (1952), 1—62.

4683 — —. **The Law and Procedure of the International Court of Justice, 1954—9: General Principles and Sources of International Law,** *British Yearbook of International Law,* XXV (1959), 183—231.

4684 — —. **The Law and Procedure of the International Court of Justice 1951—4: Treaty Interpretation and Other Treaty Points,** *British Yearbook of International Law,* XXXIII (1957), 203—93.

4685 Gilmore, Grant. **The International Court of Justice,** *Yale Law Journal,* LV (August 1946), 1049—66.

4686 Goodspeed, Stephen S. **The Nature and Function of International Organization.** New York, Oxford University Press, 1963.

Chapter X.

4687 Gross, Ernest A. **The United Nations.** New York, Harper, 1962.

Chapter VII.

4688 Gross, Leo. **The Jurisprudence of the World Court: Thirty-Eighth Year (1959),** *American Journal of International Law,* LVII (October 1963), 751—80.

4689 — —. **Some Observations on the International Court of Justice,** *American Journal of International Law,* LVI (January 1962), 33—62.

4690 Hambro, Edward. **Function of the International Court of Justice in the Framework of the International Legal Order,** *The United Nations: Ten Years' Legal Progress,* eds. Gezina J. H. Van Der Molen, W. P. J. Pompe and J. H. W. Verzijl, Hague, Nederlandse Studentenvereniging Voor Wereldrechtsorde, 1956, pp. 92—107.

4691 — —. **The International Court of Justice,** *International Affairs,* XXX (January 1954), 31—39.

4692 — —. **The International Court of Justice,** *Year Book of World Affairs,* III (1949), 188—204.

4693 — —. **The Reasons Behind the Decisions of the International Court of Justice,** *Current Legal Problems,* VII (1954), 212—27.

4694 — —. **The Relations Between the International Court of Justice and International Organization,** *Western Political Quarterly,* III (June 1950), 326—34.

4695 Head, Ivan L. **The Contribution of the International Court of Justice to the Development of International Organization,** *American Society of International Law Proceedings,* LIX (1965), 177—81.

4696 Hill, Norman L. **International Organization.** New York, Harper, 1952.
Chapter VII.

4697 Honig, F. **The Diminishing Role of the World Court,** *International Affairs,* XXXIV (April 1958), 184—94.

4698 — —. **Progress in the Codification of International Law,** *International Affairs,* XXXVI (January 1960), 62—72.

4699 Hudson, Manley O. **The New Bench of the World Court,** *American Bar Association Journal,* XXXII (March 1946), 140—44, 163.

4700 — —. **The New World Court,** *Foreign Affairs,* XIV (October 1945), 75—84.

4701 — —. **Succession of the International Court of Justice to the Permanent Court of International Justice,** *American Journal of International Law,* LI (July 1957), 569—73.

4702 — —. **The Twenty-Fourth Year of the World Court,** *American Journal of International Law,* XL (January 1946), 1—52.
Professor Hudson continued these articles in subsequent years with each January issue, his last in 1959, "The Thirty-Seventh Year of the World Court."

4703 Jenks, C. Wilfred. **The Status of International Organizations in Relation to the International Court of Justice,** *Transactions* (Grotius Society), XXXII (1946), 1—41.

4704 Jessup, Philip C. **The Court As an Organ of the United Nations,** *Foreign Affairs,* XXIII (January 1945), 233—46.

4705 — —. **Diversity and Uniformity in the Law of Nations,** *The Quest for Peace,* Andrew W. Cordier and Wilder Foote (eds.). New York, Columbia University Press, 1965, pp. 293—314.

4706 — —. **The International Court of Justice of the United Nations — With Text of Statute,** *Foreign Policy Reports,* XXI (August 15, 1945), 154—72.

4707 Kerno, I. S. **The Organisation of the United Nations and of the International Court of Justice,** *Recueil des Cours,* LXXVIII (1951), 511—74.

4708 Khan, M. Zafrullah. **The International Court and the Maintenance of World Peace,** *Pakistan Horizon,* X (December 1957), 189—96.

4709 Lauterpacht, Hersch. **The Development of International Law by the International Court.** 2d ed. New York, Praeger, 1958. 408 p.

4710 Lawson, Ruth C. **The World Court — 1946,** *Current History,* New Series, XI (July 1946), 1—7.

4711 Leonard, L. Larry. **International Organization.** New York, McGraw-Hill, 1951.

Chapter XV.

4712 Lissitzyn, Oliver J. **The International Court of Justice: Its Role in the Maintenance of International Peace and Security.** New York, Carnegie, 1951. ix + 118 p.

4713 Maclaurin, John (pseud.). **The United Nations and Power Politics.** New York, Harper, 1951.

Chapter X.

4714 O'Brien, William V. **The Role of Force in the International Judicial Order,** *Catholic Lawyer,* VI (Winter, 1960), 22—32.

4715 Padelford, Norman J. **Fourth Commission: The Judicial Organization,** *International Conciliation,* CDXIII (September 1945), 469—79.

4716 Pella, Vespasian V. **Towards an International Criminal Court,** *American Journal of International Law,* XLIV (January 1950), 37—68.

4717 Pollock, Frederick. **The Permanent Court of International Justice,** *British Yearbook of International Law,* VII (1926), 135—40.

4718 Rao, K. Krishna. **The Advisory Jurisdiction of the International Court of Justice,** *Indian Journal of International Law,* I (1960—61), 53—66.

4719 Read, John E. **The World Court and the Years to Come,** *Canadian Yearbook of International Law,* II (1964), 164—71.

4720 Rosenne, Shabtai. **The Court and the Judicial Process,** *International Organization,* XIX (Summer, 1965), 518—36.

4721 — —. **The International Court and United Nations: Reflections on the Period 1946—1954,** *International Organization,* IX (May 1955), 244—56.

4722 — —. **The International Court of Justice: An Essay in Political and Legal Theory.** Leyden, Sythoff, 1961. 592 p.

4723 — —. **The World Court: What It Is and How It Works.** Dobbs Ferry, Oceana, 1962. 230 p.

4724 Samore, W. **The World Court Statute and Impartiality of the Judges,** *Nebraska Law Review,* XXXIV (May 1955), 618—29.

4725 Schwartz, William. **The International Court's Role As an Advisor to the United Nations,** *Boston University Law Review,* XXXVII (Fall, 1957), 404—29.

4726 Schwarzenberger, G. **Problems of International Criminal Law Before the International Court of Justice,** *Indian Year Book of International Affairs,* V (1957), 63—80.

4727 Simpson, J. L. **The 1960 Elections to the International Court of Justice,** *British Yearbook of International Law,* XXXVII (1961), 527—35.

4728 Sorensen, Max. **The International Court of Justice: Its Role in Contemporary International Relations,** *International Organization,* XIV (Spring, 1960), 261—76.

4729 Stone, Julius. **The International Court and World Crisis,** *International Conciliation,* DXXVI (January 1962), 3—60.

4730 UNESCO, Youth Institute. **World Peace and the United Nations.** Dobbs Ferry, Oceana, 1962.

Part II.

4731 Vandenbosch, Amry and Hogan, Willard N. **Toward World Order.** New York, McGraw-Hill, 1963.

Chapter VIII.

4732 — —. **The United Nations.** New York, McGraw-Hill, 1952.

Chapter XIII.

4733 White, Gilliam N. **The Use of Experts by International Tribunals.** Syracuse, Syracuse University Press, 1965. xv + 259 p.

4734 Wright, Quincy. **Proposal for an International Criminal Court,** *American Journal of International Law,* XLVI (January 1952), 60—72.

9.2 JURISDICTIONAL PROBLEMS

4735 Anand, R. P. **Compulsory Jurisdiction of the International Court of Justice.** London, Asia Publishing House, 1961. 342 p.

4736 Bains, J. S. **Domestic Jurisdiction and the World Court,** *Indian Journal of International Law,* V (October 1965), 464–92.

4737 Briggs, H. W. **Reservations to the Acceptance of Compulsory Jurisdiction of the International Court of Justice,** *Recueil des Cours,* XCIII (1958), 223–367.

4738 Farmanfarma, Ali N. **The Declaration of the Members Accepting the Compulsory Jurisdiction of the International Court of Justice.** Montreux, Ganguin and Laubscher, 1952. 192 p.

4739 Fitzmaurice, Gerald. **The Law and Procedure of the International Court of Justice, 1951–4: Questions of Jurisdiction, Competence and Procedure,** *British Yearbook of International Law,* XXXIV (1958), 1–161.

4740 Hambro, E. **La compétence de la Cour Internationale de Justice,** *Recueil des Cours,* LXXVI (1950), 125–215.

4741 — —. **The Jurisdiction of the International Court of Justice,** *Transactions* (Grotius Society), XXXIV (1948), 127–40.

4742 — —. **Some Observations on the Compulsory Jurisdiction of the International Court of Justice,** *British Yearbook of International Law,* XXV (1948), 133–57.

4743 Hudson, Manley O. **Compulsory Jurisdiction of the International Court of Justice,** *American Society of International Law Proceedings,* XL (1946), 12–21.

4744 Jennings, R. Y. **The International Court's Advisory Opinion on Voting Procedure on Questions Concerning Southwest Africa,** *Transactions* (Grotius Society), XLII (1956), 85—97.

4745 Lawson, Ruth C. **The Problem of the Compulsory Jurisdiction of the World Court,** *American Journal of International Law*, XLVI (April 1952), 219—38.

4746 McDonald, E. J. **"Automatic Reservations" and the World Court,** *Georgetown Law Journal*, XLVII (Fall, 1958), 106—23.

4747 Rolin, Henri. **The International Court of Justice and Domestic Jurisdiction,** *International Organization*, VIII (February 1954), 36—44.

4748 Shihata, Ibrahim F. I. **The Power of the International Court to Determine Its Own Jurisdiction: compétence de la compétence.** Hague, Nijhoff, 1965. 400 p.

4749 Verzijl, J. H. W. **The Competence of the International Court of Justice,** *International Relations*, I (October 1954), 39—49.

4750 — —. **The System of the Optional Clause,** *International Relations*, I (October 1959), 585—610.

4751 Waldock, C. H. M. **Decline of the Optional Clause,** *British Yearbook of International Law*, XXXII (1955—56), 244—87.

4752 — —. **Forum Prorogatum or Acceptance of a Unilateral Summons to Appear Before the International Court,** *International Law Quarterly*, II (Autumn, 1948), 377—91.

9.3 ROLE OF THE UNDERDEVELOPED COUNTRIES

4753 Anand, R. P. **Notes and Memoranda: India and the World Court,** *International Studies*, II (July 1960), 80—96.

4754 — —. **Survey of Recent Research — International Law: Attitude of the "New" Asian-African Countries Toward the International Court of Justice,** *International Studies,* IV (July 1962), 119—32.

4755 Castaneda, Jorge. **The Underdeveloped Nations and the Development of International Law,** *International Organization,* XV (Winter, 1961), 38—48.

4756 Shihata, Ibrahim F. I. **The Attitude of New States Toward the International Court of Justice,** *International Organization,* XIX (Spring, 1965), 203—21.

9.4 ROLE OF THE UNITED STATES

4757 Anand, R. P. **The United States and the World Court,** *International Studies,* VI (January 1965) 254—84.

4758 Briggs, Herbert W. **The United States and the International Court of Justice,** *American Journal of International Law,* LIII (April 1959), 301—18.

4759 Gambrell, E. Smythe. **The UN, the World Court and the Connally Reservation,** *American Bar Association Journal,* XLVII (January 1961), 57—62.

4760 Preuss, Lawrence. **The International Court of Justice, the Senate, and Matters of Domestic Jurisdiction,** *American Journal of International Law,* XL (October 1946), 720—36.

4761 Wilcox, Francis O. **The United States Accepts Compulsory Jurisdiction,** *American Journal of International Law,* XL (October 1946), 699—719.

9.5 PERMANENT COURT OF ARBITRATION
(Hague)

See B 6.3.

Part D. — *United Nations System*

10. POLITICAL ACTIVITIES: GENERAL ISSUES

The success of the United Nations is associated with the use of several tools of statecraft that were absent in the League of Nations. Collective security in Korea, international peacekeeping forces on the Israeli borders, and the use of observers in such trouble spots as Laos and Cyprus have paid large dividends insofar as peace has resulted. Conditions under which such techniques operate successfully have been a subject for intensive analysis.

10.1 COLLECTIVE SECURITY AND SANCTIONS

See also 11.3.

4762 Anderson, Totton. **A Progress Report of the International Police Force of the United Nations,** *World Affairs Quarterly,* XVIII (January 1948), 404—22.

4763 Arechaga, M. E. J. de. **Co-ordination of the Systems of the United Nations and the Organization of American States for the Pacific Settlement of Disputes, and Collective Security,** *Recueil des Cours,* CXI (1964), 423—526.

4764 Ball, M. Margaret and Killough, Hugh B. **International Relations.** New York, Ronald, 1956.

Chapter XXI.

4765 Bancroft, Harding F. **Collective Security Under the United Nations,** *American Society of International Law Proceedings,* XLV (1951), 159—65.

4766 Bebler, Aleš. **The Yardstick of Collective Interest,** *Annals of the American Academy of Political and Social Science,* CCXCVI (November 1954), 85—92.

Part D. — United Nations System

4767 Bloomfield, Lincoln P. **The UN and National Security,** *Foreign Affairs,* XXXVI (July 1958), 597–610.

4768 Bonnet, Henri. **Security Through the United Nations,** *Annals of the American Academy of Political and Social Science,* CCXLVI (July 1946), 13–18.

4769 Calvocoressi, Peter. **World Order and New States: Problems of Keeping the Peace.** Foreword by Donald Tyerman. New York, Praeger, 1964. viii + 113 p.

4770 Claude, Inis L., Jr. **Power and International Relations.** New York, Random House, 1962. viii + 310 p.

4771 – –. **Swords Into Plowshares.** 3d ed. New York, Random House, 1964.

Chapter XII.

4772 Cockram, B. **The United Nations and Resistance to Aggression,** *South African Law Journal,* LXXX (November 1963), 490–504.

4773 Cohen, Benjamin V. **Principles Governing the Imposition of Sanctions Under the United Nations Charter,** *American Journal of International Law Proceedings,* XLV (1951), 153–59.

4774 Commission to Study the Organization of Peace. **Collective Security Under the United Nations.** New York, Commission to Study the Organization of Peace, 1951. 41 p.

Contains the Commission's seventh report.

4775 Current, Richard N. **The United States and "Collective Security": Notes on the History of an Idea,** *Isolation and Security,* Alexander DeConde (ed.). Durham, Duke University Press, 1957, pp. 33–35.

Part D. — United Nations System

4776 Eggleston, Frederic. **The United Nations As an Instrument for Preserving Peace,** *Paths to Peace*, Victor H. Wallace (ed.). Melbourne, Melbourne University Press, 1957, pp. 317—35.

4777 Eichelberger, Clark M. **Collective Security,** *Charter Review Conference: Ninth Report and Papers Presented to the Commission*, Commission to Study the Organization of Peace (ed.). New York, Commission to Study the Organization of Peace, 1955, pp. 167—75.

4778 Fenwick, Charles G. **The Development of Collective Security 1914—1954,** *American Society of International Law Proceedings*, XLVIII (1954), 2—13.

Comments by Woolsey, Hornbeck, Morris, Flanders.

4779 Fleming, D. F. **The Soviet Union and Collective Security,** *Journal of Politics*, X (February 1948), 117—30.

4780 — —. **Woodrow Wilson and Collective Security Today,** *Journal of Politics*, XVIII (November 1956), 611—24.

4781 Fox, William T. R. **Collective Enforcement of Peace and Security,** *American Political Science Review*, XXXIX (October 1945), 970—81.

4782 Fulljames, R. **Security Under the United Nations,** *World Affairs*, New Series, I (October 1947), 402—8.

4783 Goodrich, Leland M. **The United Nations.** New York, Crowell, 1963.

Chapter VIII.

4784 Goodrich, Leland M. and Simons, Anne P. **The United Nations and the Maintenance of International Peace and Security.** Washington, Brookings, 1955.

Chapter IV.

4785 Goodspeed, Stephen S. **The Nature and Function of International Organization.** New York, Oxford University Press, 1963.

Chapter VIII.

4786 Haas, Ernst B. and Whiting, Allen S. **Dynamics of International Relations.** New York, McGraw-Hill, 1956.

Chapter XX.

4787 Higgins, Rosalyn. **The Legal Limits to the Use of Force by Sovereign States: United Nations Practice,** *British Yearbook of International Law,* XXXVII (1961), 269–319.

Definitions of force and illegal force according to UN practice.

4788 Hill, Norman L. **International Organization.** New York, Harper, 1952.

Chapter X.

4789 Hogan, Willard N. **International Conflict and Collective Security: The Principle of Concern in International Organization.** Lexington, University of Kentucky Press, 1955. 202 p.

4790 Holland, Robert. **Under the United Nations Flag,** *International Journal,* VI (Spring, 1951), 136–45.

4791 Holt, W. Stull. **The Functions of the Military Staff Committee, United Nations Organization,** *Institute of World Affairs Proceedings,* XXI (1945), 32–37.

4792 Hula, Erich. **The Evolution of Collective Security Under the United Nations Charter,** *Alliance Policy in the Cold War,* Arnold Wolfers (ed.). Baltimore, Johns Hopkins Press, 1959, pp. 75–102.

4793 Jacob, Philip E. and Atherton, Alexine L. **Dynamics of International Organization.** Homewood, Dorsey, 1964.

Chapters III, IV.

Part D. — *United Nations System*

4794 Jebb, Gladwyn. **The Role of the United Nations,** *International Organization*, VI (November 1952), 509–20.

Conditions under which collective security operates.

4795 Johnson, Howard C. and Niemeyer, Gerhart. **Collective Security: The Validity of an Ideal,** *International Organization*, VIII (February 1954), 19–35.

4796 Kelsen, Hans. **Collective Security and Collective Self-Defense Under the Charter of the United Nations,** *American Journal of International Law*, XLII (October 1948), 783–96.

4797 ———. **Sanctions in International Law Under the Charter of the United Nations,** *Iowa Law Review*, XXXI (May 1946), 499–543.

4798 Khan, Rahmatulla. **Collective Security Versus Preventive Diplomacy: The Role of the United Nations in the Maintenance of World Peace and Security,** *Indian Journal of International Law*, IV, 3 (1964), 408–27.

4799 Kirk, Grayson. **The Enforcement of Security,** *Yale Law Journal*, LV (August 1946), 1081–96.

4800 Kunz, Joseph L. **The Idea of "Collective Security" in Pan-American Developments,** *Western Political Quarterly*, VI (December 1953), 658–79.

4801 Lalive, J. F. **International Organization and Neutrality,** *British Yearbook of International Law*, XXIV (1947), 72–89.

4802 Mander, Linden A. **Foundations of Modern World Society.** 2d ed. Stanford, Stanford University Press, 1947.

Chapter II.

4803 Martin, Andrew. **Collective Security: A Progress Report.** Paris, UNESCO, 1952. 243 p.

4804 Milhaud, Edgard. **La France avait raison, sécurité collective.** Neuchâtel, Baconnière, 1945. 351 p.

4805 Mills, Lennox A. and McLaughlin, Charles H. **Word Politics in Transition.** New York, Holt, 1957.

Chapter XVI.

4806 Nawaz, Mohammad. **Regulating the Use of Force in International Relations,** *Pakistan Horizon*, XIV, 2 (1961), 121–27.

4807 Osgood, Robert E. **Woodrow Wilson, Collective Security, and the Lessons of History,** *Confluence*, VI (Winter, 1957), 341–54.

4808 Ross, Lawrence F. J. **Total War and the United Nations,** *Pakistan Horizon*, XVII, 3 (1964), 253–61.

4809 Schick, Franz B. **Peace on Trial: A Study of Defense in International Organization,** *Western Political Quarterly*, II (March 1949), 1–44.

Historical survey of collective security from League of Nations and Kellogg Pact to NATO.

4810 Schwarzenberger, Georg. **Power Politics.** 3d ed. London, Stevens, 1964.

Chapter XXIII.

4811 Slater, Jerome. **A Revaluation of Collective Security: The Organization of American States in Action.** Columbus, Ohio State University Press, 1965. 56 p.

4812 Sohn, Louis B. **The Definition of Aggression,** *Virginia Law Review*, XLV (June 1959), 697–701.

Part D. — United Nations System

4813 Stromberg, Roland N. **The Idea of Collective Security,** *Journal of the History of Ideas,* XVII (April 1956), 250–63.

4814 — —. **The Riddle of Collective Security,** *Issues and Conflicts: Studies in 20th Century American Diplomacy,* G. L. Anderson (ed.). Lawrence, University of Kansas Press, 1959, pp. 147–67.

4815 Taubenfeld, Howard J. **The "Economic Weapon": The League and the United Nations,** *American Society of International Law Proceedings,* LVIII (1964), 183–204.

Concerns economic sanctions.

4816 Thompson, Kenneth W. **Isolationism and Collective Security: The Uses and Limits of Two Theories of International Relations,** *Isolation and Security,* Alexander DeConde (ed.). Durham, Duke University Press, 1957, pp. 159–83.

4817 UNESCO, Youth Institute. **World Peace and the United Nations.** Dobbs Ferry, Oceana. 1962.

Part I.

4818 Vandenbosch, Amry and Hogan, Willard N. **Toward World Order.** New York, McGraw-Hill, 1963.

Chapter IX.

4819 Van Langenhove, Fernand. **La crise du système de sécurité collective des Nations Unies, 1946–1957.** Hague, Nijhoff, 1958. 272 p.

4820 Watkins, James T., IV. **United States Leadership and Collective Security: The Meaning of Korea,** *Institute of World Affairs Proceedings,* XXIX (1953), 191–99.

4821 Wolfers, Arnold. **Collective Security and the War in Korea,** *Discord and Collaboration.* Baltimore, Johns Hopkins Press, 1962, pp. 167–80.

Reprinted, with minor changes, from *Yale Review,* June 1954.

4822 Wright, Quincy. **Collective Security in the Light of the Korean Experience,** *American Society of International Law Proceedings,* XLV (1951), 165—82.

4823 — —. **Problems of Stability and Progress in International Relations.** Berkeley, University of California Press, 1954.
Chapter VI.

10.2 COLONIALISM

See D 8.1.

10.3 DISARMAMENT

4824 Arneson, R. Gordon. **The Role of the United Nations in Disarmament,** *Journal of International Affairs,* IX, 2 (1955), 50—54.

4825 Babovič, B. **Disarmament and International Community,** *Jugoslovenska Revija za Međunarodno Pravo,* VII, 2 (1960), 233—39.

4826 Bailey, Sydney D. **The United Nations.** New York, Praeger, 1963.
Chapter V.

4827 Barker, Charles A. (ed.). **Problems of World Disarmament.** Boston, Houghton, Mifflin, 1963. 170 p.

4828 Barnet, Richard J. **Who Wants Disarmament?** Introduction by Chester Bowles. Boston, Beacon, 1960. xviii + 141 p.

4829 — —. and Falk, Richard A. **Security in Disarmament.** Princeton, Princeton University Press, 1965. ix + 441 p.

Part D. — *United Nations System*

4830   Bechhoefer, Bernhard G. **The Disarmament Deadlock: 1946—1955,** *Current History*, New Series, XLII (May 1962), 257—66.

4831   — —. **Postwar Negotiations for Arms Control.** Washington, Brookings, 1961. xiv + 641 p.

4832   — —. **United Nations Procedures in Case of Violations of Disarmament Agreements,** *Journal of Arms Control*, I (July 1963), 191—202.

4833   Blackett, P. M. S. **Steps Toward Disarmament,** *Scientific American*, CCVI (April 1962), 3—11.

4834   Bloomfield, Lincoln P. **The United Nations and Arms Control,** *Arms Control: A Symposium*, Ernest Lefever (ed.). New York, Praeger, 1962, pp. 169—78.

4835   Bodnar, James S. **Report on the Debate in the United Nations Disarmament Commission, April 21-June 16, 1965.** Washington, United States Arms Control and Disarmament Agency, 1965. iv + 128 p.

4836   Bolté, Charles G. **The Price of Peace: A Plan for Disarmament.** Boston, Beacon, 1956. 108 p.

4837   Bose, C. **The Problem of Disarmament,** *Indian Journal of Political Science*, XVII (July 1957), 210—16.

4838   Burton, John W. **Peace Theory: Preconditions of Disarmament.** New York, Knopf, 1962. 200 p.

4839   Cadogan, Alexander. **Disarmament and Security,** *Annals of the American Academy of Political and Social Science*, CCLII (July 1947), 84—92.

Part D. — United Nations System

4840 Cavers, David F. **Disarmament and the Charter,** *Charter Review Conference: Ninth Report and Papers Presented to the Commission*, Commission to Study the Organization of Peace (ed.). New York, Commission to Study the Organization of Peace, 1955, pp. 130–52.

4841 — —. **International Control of Armaments: Analysis and Proposition,** *Annals of the American Academy of Political and Social Science*, CCXCVI (November 1954), 117–23.

Comments by Clark, Cohen, Cole, and Spender.

4842 Chamberlain, Waldo. **Arms Control and Limitation,** *The United States and the United Nations*, Franz B. Gross (ed.). Norman, University of Oklahoma Press, 1964, pp. 65–86.

4843 Chase, Eugene P. **The United Nations in Action.** New York, McGraw-Hill, 1950.

Chapter XI.

4844 Cheever, Daniel S. **The UN and Disarmament,** *International Organization*, XIX (Summer, 1965), 463–82.

4845 Claude, Inis L., Jr. **Swords Into Plowshares.** 3d ed. New York, Random House, 1964.

Chapter XIII.

4846 Collart, Yves. **Disarmament: A Study Guide and Bibliography on the Efforts of the United Nations.** Hague, Nijhoff, 1958. 110 p.

4847 Commission to Study the Organization of Peace. **Security and Disarmament Under the United Nations.** New York, Commission to Study the Organization of Peace, 1947. 35 p.

Contains the Commission's fifth report.

4848 Conway, John S. **Disarmament Reconsidered,** *International Journal*, XIII (Spring, 1958), 100–9.

Part D. — United Nations System

4849 Cory, Robert H., Jr. **International Inspection: From Proposals to Realization,** *International Organization*, XIII (Autumn, 1959) 495–504.

4850 Courlander, Harold. **Shaping Our Times.** New York, Oceana, 1960.

Chapter IX.

4851 Cousins, Norman. **In Place of Folly.** New York, Harper, 1961. 224 p.

4852 Coyle, David Cushman. **The United Nations and How It Works.** New York, Columbia University Press, 1966.

Chapter IX.

4853 Dallin, Alexander, *et al.* **The Soviet Union, Arms Control, and Disarmament: Study of Soviet Attitudes.** New York, Columbia University, School of International Affairs, 1964. xi + 282 p.

4854 Deshpande, N. R. **UN and Disarmament,** *Indian Journal of Political Science*, XVIII (January 1957), 55–60.

4855 **Disarmament and Arms Control: An International Journal.** Oxford, Pergamon, Semiannually, 1963–.

4856 Dulles, Allen W. **Disarmament in the Atomic Age,** *Foreign Affairs*, XXV (January 1947), 204–16.

4857 Eichelberger, Clark M. **UN: The First Twenty Years.** New York, Harper, 1965.

Chapter IV.

4858 Falk, Richard A. **Provision for Peaceful Change in a Disarming World,** *Security in Disarmament*, Richard J. Barnet and Richard A. Falk (eds.). Princeton, Princeton University Press, 1965, pp. 347–60.

Part D. — *United Nations System*

4859 Falk, Richard A. and Mendlovitz, Saul H. (eds.). **The Strategy of World Order,** (vol. 4: *Disarmament and Economic Development*). Foreword by J. David Singer. New York, World Law Fund, 1966. xv + 672 p.

4860 Feld, Bernard T. **The Geneva Negotiations on General and Complete Disarmament,** *Disarmament: Its Politics and Economics*, Seymour Melman (ed.). Boston, American Academy of Arts and Sciences, 1962, pp. 7–17.

4861 Finkelstein, Lawrence S. **Arms Inspection,** *International Conciliation*, DXL (November 1962), 5–87.

4862 — —. **The United Nations and Organizations for the Control of Armaments,** *International Organization*, XVI (Winter, 1962), 1–19.

4863 Fisher, Roger. **International Police: A Sequential Approach to Effectiveness and Control,** *Security in Disarmament*, Richard J. Barnet and Richard A. Falk (eds.). Princeton, Princeton University Press, 1965, pp. 240–85.

4864 Forbes, Henry W. **The Strategy of Disarmament.** Introduction by Quincy Wright. Washington, Public Affairs Press, 1962. 158 p.

4865 Fradkin, Elvira K. **A World Airlift: The United Nations Air Police Patrol.** New York, Funk and Wagnalls, 1950. 216 p.

4866 Frisch, David H. (ed.). **Arms Reduction: Programs and Issues.** New York, Twentieth Century Fund, 1961. 162 p.

4867 Frye, William R. **The Quest for Disarmament Since World War II,** *Arms Control*, Louis Henkin (ed.). Englewood Cliffs, Prentice-Hall, 1961, pp. 18–48.

4868 Fuller, J. F. C. **Armament and History.** New York, Scribner, 1945. xvii + 207 p.

The author, a general, sees futility in the prohibition of particular weapons.

Part D. — *United Nations System*

4869 Goodrich, Leland M. **The United Nations.** New York, Crowell, 1963.
Chapter X.

4870 Goodrich, Leland M. and Simons, Anne P. **The United Nations and the Maintenance of International Peace and Security.** Washington, Brookings, 1955.
Chapter V.

4871 Goodspeed, Stephen S. **The Nature and Function of International Organization.** New York, Oxford University Press, 1963.
Chapter IX.

4872 Harrington, Charles W. **The Problem of Disarmament in the United Nations.** Geneva, Impr. Centrale, 1950. 179 p.

4873 Henkin, Louis (ed.). **Arms Control: Issues for the Public.** Englewood Cliffs, Prentice-Hall, 1961. ix + 207 p.

4874 Jack, Homer A. **Nonalignment and a Test Ban Agreement: The Role of the Nonaligned States,** *Journal of Conflict Resolution*, VII (September 1963), 542–52.

4875 Jacob, Philip E. **The Disarmament Consensus,** *International Organization*, XIV (Spring, 1960), 233–60.

4876 — —. and Atherton, Alexine L. **Dynamics of International Organization.** Homewood, Dorsey, 1964.
Chapters VIII, IX.

4877 Jensen, Lloyd. **Postwar Disarmament Negotiations,** *Current History*, New Series, XLVI (June 1964), 336–40 ff.

4878 Kelman, Herbert C. **Internationalizing Military Force,** *Preventing World War III: Some Proposals,* Quincy Wright, William M. Evan, and Morton Deutsch, (eds.). New York, Simon and Schuster, 1962, pp. 106–22.

4879 Knorr, Klaus. **Supranational Versus International Models for General and Complete Disarmament,** *Security in Disarmament,* Richard J. Barnet and Richard A. Falk (eds.). Princeton, Princeton University Press, 1965, pp. 15–36.

4880 Lawson, Ruth C. **The United Nations: Disarmament and Propaganda,** *Current History,* New Series, XXII (April 1952), 216–20.

4881 Leonard, L. Larry. **International Organization.** New York, McGraw-Hill, 1951.

Chapter XVI.

4882 Linde, Hans A. **Organization of a "Mixed" National and International Inspectorate,** *Security in Disarmament,* Richard J. Barnet and Richard A. Falk (eds.). Princeton, Princeton University Press, 1965, pp. 80–106.

4883 McCloy, John. **Balance Sheet on Disarmament,** *Foreign Affairs,* XL (April 1962), 339–59.

4884 McVitty, Marion H. **A Comparison and Evaluation of Current Disarmament Proposals As of March 1, 1964.** New York, World Law Fund, 1965. x + 43 p.

4885 — —. **The Role of the United Nations,** *Current History,* New Series, XLVI (June 1964), 331–35.

4886 Marshall, Charles Burton. **Character and Mission of a United Nations Peace Force, Under Conditions of General and Complete Disarmament,** *American Political Science Review,* LIX (June 1965), 350–64.

Part D. — *United Nations System*

4887 Martin, Andrew. **Legal Aspects of Disarmament.** London, British Institute of International and Comparative Law, *International and Comparative Law Quarterly*, Supplement, 1963. 133 p.

4888 Martin, Paul. **Recent Developments in Disarmament,** *International Journal*, XI (Spring, 1956), 79—84.

4889 Matteson, Robert E. **Disarmament Prospects After Cuba,** *Journal of Conflict Resolution*, VII (September 1963), 338—50.

4890 Melman, Seymour (ed.). **Inspection for Disarmament.** New York, Columbia University Press, 1958. xii + 291 p.

4891 Meyer, Cord, Jr. **Peace or Anarchy.** Boston, Little, Brown, 1947. 233 p.

4892 Moch, Jules. **Towards a Disarmed Peace,** *International Journal*, XI (Spring, 1956), 85—92.

4893 Morgenthau, Hans J. **The Impartiality of the International Police,** *Security in Disarmament*, Richard J. Barnet and Richard A. Falk (eds.). Princeton, Princeton University Press, 1965, pp. 320—40.

4894 Myrdal, Alva. **Disarmament and the United Nations,** *The Quest for Peace*, Andrew W. Cordier and Wilder Foote (eds.). New York, Columbia University Press, 1965, pp. 149—66.

4895 Nanes, Allan S. **Disarmament: The Last Seven Years,** *Current History*, New Series XLII (May 1962), 267—74.

4896 Neidle, Alan F. **Peace-Keeping and Disarmament,** *American Journal of International Law*, LVII (January 1963), 46—72.

4897 Noel-Baker, Philip. **The Arms Race: A Programme for World Disarmament.** Dobbs Ferry, Oceana, 1959. 603 p.

4898 Nogee, Joseph L. **The Diplomacy of Disarmament,** *International Conciliation*, DXXVI (January 1960) 235—303.

4899 — —. **Propaganda and Negotiation: The Case of the Ten-Nation Disarmament Committee,** *Journal of Conflict Resolution*, VII (September 1963), 510—21.

4900 Nutting, Anthony. **Disarmament: An Outline of the Negotiations.** London, Oxford University Press, 1959. 51 p.

4901 Osborn, Frederick. **The USSR and the Atom,** *International Organization*, V (August 1951), 480—98.

4902 Osgood, Robert E. **An International Military Force in a Disarming and Disarmed World.** Washington, Institute for Defense Analyses, 1963. 59 p.

4903 Pitersky, Nikolai A. **A Soviet View of a Disarmed World,** *Toward a Strategy of Peace*, Walter C. Clemens, Jr. (ed.). Chicago, Rand McNally, 1965, pp. 171—90.

4904 Salter, Arthur. **The United Nations and the Atomic Bomb,** *International Conciliation*, CDXVII (January 1946), 40—48.

4905 Salvin, Marina. **Soviet Policy Toward Disarmament,** *International Conciliation*, CDXXVIII (February 1947), 43—111.

Appendix contains documents.

4906 Schwarzenberger, Georg. **Power Politics.** 3d ed. London, Stevens, 1964.

Chapter XXIV.

4907 Singer, J. David. **From Deterrence to Disarmament,** *International Journal*, XVI (Autumn, 1961), 307—26.

Part D. — United Nations System

4908 Sington, Derrick. **How the Press Covers the Geneva Negotiations,** *Disarmament and Arms Control,* II (Autumn, 1964), 422–33.

4909 Slessor, John. **Geneva, Disarmament and Security: A British View,** *International Relations,* I (October 1955), 123–27.

4910 Spanier, John W. and Nogee, Joseph L. **The Politics of Disarmament: A Study in Soviet-American Gamesmanship.** New York, Praeger, 1962. ix + 226 p.

4911 Tait, R. M. **In Defence of the Big Conference,** *Disarmament and Arms Control,* II (Summer, 1964), 331–41.

4912 Tondel, Lyman M., Jr. (ed.). **Disarmament.** Dobbs Ferry, Oceana, 1964. xii + 98 p.

4913 Tozzoli, Gian Puolo. **The Geneva Negotiations As a Constituent Assembly,** *Disarmament and Arms Control,* II (Spring, 1964), 126–35.

4914 Vandenbosch, Amry and Hogan, Willard N. **Toward World Order.** New York, McGraw-Hill, 1963.
Chapter X.

4915 — —. **The United Nations.** New York, McGraw-Hill, 1952.
Chapter XVI.

4916 Van Slyck, Philip. **Peace: The Control of National Power.** Boston, Beacon, 1963. 126 p.

4917 Wadsworth, James J. **The Price of Peace.** New York, Praeger, 1962. 127 p.

4918 Warburg, James P. **Disarmament: The Challenge of the Nineteen Sixties.** Garden City, Doubleday, 1961. 288 p.

4919 Waskow, Arthur I. **The Worried Man's Guide to World Peace.** Garden City, Doubleday, 1963. xix + 219 p.

4920 Wimperis, H. C. **Atomic Energy Control: The Present Position,** *International Affairs,* XXIV (October 1948), 515–23.

4921 Wolfers, Arnold. **Disarmament, Peacekeeping, and the National Interest,** *The Peacekeeping Proposals of the U. S.: Outline of Basic Provisions of a Treaty of General and Complete Disarmament in a Peaceful World,* Johns Hopkins University, School of Advanced International Studies (ed.). Baltimore, SAIS, 1964, pp. 11–26.

4922 — —. **International Arms Control,** *An American Foreign Policy Reader,* Harry Howe Ransom (ed.). New York, Crowell, 1965, pp. 242–47.

Reprinted from U. S. Senate Committee on Foreign Relations Study No. 8.

4923 Wright, Quincy. **Conditions for Successful Disarmament,** *Journal of Conflict Resolution,* VII (September 1963), 286–92.

4924 X. Y. Z. **Disarmament: Proposals and Negotiations, 1946–1955,** *World Today.* New Series, XI (August 1955), 334–46.

Appendix contains a comparative tabulation of USA and USSR proposals.

10.4 PACIFIC SETTLEMENT

4925 Arangio-Ruiz, Gaetano. **Development of Peaceful Settlement and Peaceful Change in the United Nations System,** *American Society of International Law Proceedings,* LIX (1965), 124–31.

4926 Arechaga, M. E. J. de. **Co-ordination of the Systems of the United Nations and the Organisation of American States for the Pacific Settlement of Disputes, and Collective Security,** *Recueil des Cours,* CXI (1964), 423–526.

Part D. — *United Nations System*

4927 Bloomfield, Lincoln P. **Evolution or Revolution? The United Nations and the Problem of Peaceful Territorial Change.** Cambridge, Harvard University Press, 1957. 220 p.

4928 Claude, Inis L., Jr. **Swords Into Plowshares.** 3d ed. New York, Random House, 1964.

Chapters XI, XV.

4929 Cory, Robert H., Jr. **Conflict Resolution in the United Nations: A Review of Three Studies by the Brookings Institution,** *Journal of Conflict Resolution*, II (June 1958), 184—87.

4930 Eagleton, Clyde. **International Government.** 3d ed. New York, Ronald, 1957.

Chapters IX, XVII.

4931 — —. **The Pacific Settlement of Disputes Under the Charter,** *Annals of the American Academy of Political and Social Science*, CCXLVI (July 1946), 24—29.

4932 Fenwick, Charles G. **Inter-American Regional Procedures for the Settlement of Disputes,** *International Organization*, X (February 1956), 12—21.

4933 Goodrich, Leland M. **Pacific Settlement of Disputes,** *American Political Science Review*, XXXIX (October 1945), 956—70.

4934 — —. **The Peaceful Settlement of Disputes,** *Journal of International Affairs*, IX, 2 (1955), 12—20.

4935 — —. **The United Nations.** New York, Crowell, 1963.

Chapter IX.

4936 Goodrich, Leland M. and Simons, Anne P. **The United Nations and the Maintenance of International Peace and Security.** Washington, Brookings, 1955.

Chapter III.

4937 Goodspeed, Stephen S. **The Nature and Function of International Organization.** New York, Oxford University Press, 1963.

Chapter VII.

4938 Hamzeh, F. S. **International Conciliation (With Special Reference to the Work of the United Nations Conciliation Commission for Palestine).** Hague, Pasmans, 1963. x + 177 p.

4939 Henderson, William. **Pacific Settlement of Disputes: The Indonesia Question, 1946–1949.** New York, Woodrow Wilson Foundation, 1954. 89 p.

4940 Hovet, Thomas, Jr. **United Nations Diplomacy,** *Journal of International Affairs,* XVII, 1 (1963), 29–41.

4941 Hurewitz, J. C. **The United Nations Conciliation Commission for Palestine,** *International Organization,* VII (November 1953), 482–97.

4942 Hyde, James Nevins. **The Development of Procedures for the Peaceful Adjustment of Disputes,** *Charter Review Conference: Ninth Report and Papers Presented to the Commission,* Commission to Study the Organization of Peace (ed.). New York, Commission to Study the Organization of Peace, 1955, pp. 153–66.

4943 — —. **Peaceful Settlement Studies in the Interim Committee,** *International Conciliation,* CDXLIV (October 1948), 531–59.

Issue contains selected documents.

4944 — —. **The United Nations and the Peaceful Adjustment of Disputes,** *Academy of Political Science Proceedings,* XXV (January 1953), 212–21.

4945 Jackson, Elmore. **Developing the Peaceful Settlement Functions of the United Nations,** *Annals of the American Academy of Political and Social Science,* CCXCVI (November 1954), 27–35.

4946 Jacob, Philip E. and Atherton, Alexine L. **Dynamics of International Organization.** Homewood, Dorsey, 1964.

Chapters X, XI.

4947 Lerche, Charles O., Jr. **Principles of International Politics.** New York, Oxford University Press, 1956.

Chapter VIII.

4948 Martin, Laurence W. **Peaceful Settlement and Peaceful Change,** *The Peacekeeping Proposals of the U. S.: Outline of Basic Provisions of a Treaty of General and Complete Disarmament in a Peaceful World,* Johns Hopkins University, School of Advanced International Studies (ed.). Baltimore, SAIS, 1964, pp. 55–63.

4949 Morse, O. **Methods of Pacific Settlement of International Disputes: Difficulties and Revision,** *Brooklyn Law Review,* XXV (December 1958), 20–32.

4950 Parodi, Alexandre. **Peaceful Settlement of Disputes,** *International Conciliation,* CDXLV (November 1948), 616–32.

4951 Schleicher, Charles P. **International Relations.** Englewood Cliffs, Prentice-Hall, 1962.

Chapter X.

4952 Schwarzenberger, Georg. **Power Politics.** 3d ed. London, Stevens, 1964.

Chapter XXII.

4953 Stone, Julius. **Aggression and World Order: A Critique of United Nations Theories of Aggression.** Berkeley, University of California Press, 1958. 226 p.

4954 — —. **Legal Controls of International Conflict.** Rev. ed. New York, Rinehart, 1959. IV + 903 p.

4955 Vandenbosch, Amry and Hogan, Willard N. **Toward World Order.** New York, McGraw-Hill, 1963.

Chapter VII.

4956 — —. **The United Nations.** New York, McGraw-Hill, 1952.

Chapter XIV.

10.5 PEACEKEEPING WITH INTERNATIONAL FORCES

See also D 11.5 and D 11.6.

4957 Bailey, Sydney D. **The United Nations.** New York, Praeger, 1963.

Chapter IV.

4958 Bishop, Peter V. **Peace-Keeping Operations,** *International Journal,* XVIII (Autumn, 1963), 525—31.

4959 Bloomfield, Lincoln P., with Bowman, Edward H.; Dicks, Henry V.; Fanning, James E.; Hoffmann, Stanley; Morgenthau, Hans J.; Nicholas, Herbert; Schelling, Thomas C.; and Urquhart, Brian E. **International Military Forces: The Question of Peacekeeping in an Armed and Disarming World.** Boston, Little, Brown, 1964. 256 p.

4960 Borchard, Edwin. **The Impracticability of "Enforcing" Peace,** *Yale Law Journal,* LV (August 1946), 966—73.

4961 Bowett, D. W. **United Nations Forces: A Legal Study of United Nations Practice.** New York, Praeger, 1964. xxiv + 579 p.

Part D. — *United Nations System*

4962 Bowitz, Gustav C. **Central Administration of UN Security Forces,** *Peace-Keeping: Experience and Evaluation; The Oslo Papers,* Per Frydenberg (ed.). Oslo, Norwegian Institute of International Affairs, 1964, pp. 103–15.

4963 Bowman, Edward H. and Fanning, James E. **The Logistics Problems of a UN Military Force,** *International Organization,* XVII (Spring, 1963), 355–76.

4964 Buchan, A. **Arms and Security, II: Preserving the Peace; The Role of the UN,** *Australian Outlook,* XVI (August 1962), 131–45.

4965 Burns, Arthur L. and Heathcote, Nina. **Peace-Keeping by UN Forces.** New York, Praeger, 1963. 256 p.

4966 — —. **The United Nations As a Peace-Preserving Force,** *International Stability,* Dale J. Hekhuis, Charles G. McClintock, and Arthur L. Burns (eds.).New York, Wiley, 1964, pp. 261–89.

Condensation and revision from their *Peace-Keeping by UN Forces.*

4967 Carter, W. H. **Thoughts on International Policing,** *Contemporary Review,* CXCIV (December 1958), 313–15.

The international police force concept is traced in theory and in practice.

4968 Citrin, Jack. **United Nations Peacekeeping Activities: A Case Study in Organizational Task Expansion.** Denver, University of Denver, Social Science Foundation, 1965. 85 p.

4969 Claude, Inis L., Jr. **The United Nations and the Use of Force,** *International Conciliation,* DXXXII (March 1961), 325–84.

4970 — —. **United Nations Use of Military Force,** *Journal of Conflict Resolution,* VII (June 1963), 117–29.

Part D. — United Nations System

4971 Eastman, S. Mack. **A United Nations Guard: Historical Background,** *International Journal,* IV (Spring, 1949), 137–46.

4972 Egge, Bjørn. **Regional Command of UN Security Forces,** *Peace-Keeping: Experience and Evaluation; The Oslo Papers,* Per Frydenberg (ed.). Oslo, Norwegian Institute of International Affairs, 1964, pp. 135–39.

4973 Eide, Abbjørn. **UN Forces in Domestic Conflicts,** *Peace-Keeping: Experience and Evaluation; The Oslo Papers,* Per Frydenberg (ed.). Oslo, Norwegian Institute of International Affairs, 1964, pp. 247–75.

4974 Evensen, Jens. **Problems of International Law Relating to the Establishment of UN Security Forces,** *Peace-Keeping: Experience and Evaluation; The Oslo Papers,* Per Frydenberg (ed.). Oslo, Norwegian Institute of International Affairs, 1964, pp. 213–45.

4975 Frydenberg, Per (ed.). **Peace-Keeping: Experience and Evaluation; The Oslo Papers.** Oslo, Norwegian Institute of International Affairs, 1964. 339 p.

4976 Frye, William R. **A United Nations Peace Force.** New York, Oceana, 1957. 216 p.

4977 Gardner, Richard N. **The Development of the Peace-Keeping Capacity of the United Nations,** *American Society of International Law Proceedings,* LVII (1963), 224–34.

Comments by J. N. Hyde.

4978 — —. **In Pursuit of World Order.** New York, Praeger, 1964.

Chapter IV.

4979 Goodrich, Leland M. **The Maintenance of International Peace and Security,** *International Organization,* XIX (Summer 1965), 429–43.

Part D. — *United Nations System*

4980 Grønning, Jacob. **Recruitment and Training,** *Peace-Keeping: Experience and Evaluation; The Oslo Papers,* Per Frydenberg (ed.). Oslo, Norwegian Institute of International Affairs, 1964, pp. 173–77.

4981 Haekkerup, Per. **Scandinavia's Peace-Keeping Forces for UN,** *Foreign Affairs,* XLII (July 1964), 675–81.

4982 Halderman, John W. **Legal Basis for United Nations Armed Forces,** *American Journal of International Law,* LVI (October 1962), 971–96.

4983 Holmes, John W. **The Political and Philosophical Aspects of UN Security Forces,** *International Journal,* XIX (Summer, 1964), 292–307.

4984 Jacob, Philip E. and Atherton, Alexine L. **Dynamics of International Organization.** Homewood, Dorsey, 1964.

Chapter VII.

4985 James, Alan. **UN Action for Peace: I, Barrier Forces,** *World Today,* New Series, XVIII (November 1962), 478–96.

4986 — —. **UN Action for Peace: II, Law and Order Forces,** *World Today,* New Series, XVIII (December 1962), 503–14.

4987 Johnsen, Julia E. (comp.). **International Police Force.** New York, Wilson, 1944. 253 p.

Excellent bibliography.

4988 Lerche, Charles O., Jr. **Development of Rules Relating to Peace-Keeping by the Organization of American States,** *American Society of International Law Proceedings,* LIX (1965), 60–66.

4989 MacEoin, Sean. **Establishment of a Staff Element in the UN Secretariat,** *Peace-Keeping: Experience and Evaluation; The Oslo Papers,* Per Frydenberg (ed.). Oslo, Norwegian Institute of International Affairs, 1964, pp. 117—22.

4990 McVitty, Marion H. **Wanted: Rules to Guide UN Peace-Making Operations of the Future,** *New Federalist Papers,* I (1965), 1—50.

4991 Malicky, Neal. **To Keep the Peace: A Churchman's Proposal for a Stronger United Nations.** Washington, General Board of Christian Social Concerns of the Methodist Church, 1965. 64 p.

4992 Marshall, Charles Burton. **A United Nations Peace Force I: Character and Mission,** *The Peacekeeping Proposals of the U. S.: Outline of Basic Provisions of a Treaty of General and Complete Disarmament in a Peaceful World,* **Johns Hopkins University, School of Advanced International** Studies (ed.), Baltimore, SAIS, 1964, pp. 92—122.

4993 Martin, Paul. **Peace-Keeping and the United Nations — The Broader View,** *International Affairs,* XL (April 1964), 191—204.

4994 Merchant, Livingston T. **A United Nations Peace Force II: Control and Accountability,** *The Peacekeeping Proposals of the U. S.: Outline of Basic Provisions of a Treaty of General and Complete Disarmament in a Peaceful World,* Johns Hopkins University, School of Advanced International Studies (ed.).

4995 Midgaard, Knut. **Preparation for Future Contingencies,** *Peace-Keeping: Experience and Evaluation; The Oslo Papers,* Per Frydenberg (ed.). Oslo, Norwegian Institute of International Affairs, 1964, pp. 69—79.

4996 Munro, Leslie. **Can the United Nations Enforce Peace?** *Foreign Affairs,* XXXVIII (January 1960), 209—18.

4997 Murray, G. S. **United Nations Peace-Keeping and Problems of Political Control,** *International Journal*, XVIII (Autumn, 1963), 442—57.

4998 Neidle, Alan F. **Peace-Keeping and Disarmament,** *American Journal of International Law*, LVII (January 1963), 46—72.

4999 Nicholas, Herbert. **UN Peace Forces and the Changing Globe: The Lessons of Suez and Congo,** *International Organization*, XVII (Spring, 1963), 321—36.

5000 Ninčić, Đ. **The Question of a United Nations Force,** *Jugoslovenska Revija za Mezhdunarodno Pravo*, VII, 2 (1960), 227—33.

5001 Pearson, Lester B. **Force for UN,** *Foreign Affairs*, XXXV (April 1957), 395—404.

5002 Pierson, Sherleigh G. **What Does a UN Soldier Do?** New York, Dodd, Mead, 1965. 64 p.

5003 Reith, Charles. **International Authority and the Enforcement of Law,** *Transactions* (Grotius Society), XXXVIII (1952), 109—24.

5004 Rikhye, Indarjit, **Preparation and Training of UN Peacekeeping Forces,** *Peace-Keeping: Experience and Evaluation; The Oslo Papers*, Per Frydenberg (ed.). Oslo, Norwegian Institute of International Affairs, 1964, pp. 179—96.

5005 Roshwald, Mordecai. **An International Force,** *Bulletin of the Atomic Scientists*, XIX (April 1963), 24—27.

5006 Russell, Ruth B. **Development by the United Nations of Rules Relating to Peace-Keeping,** *American Society of International Law Proceedings,* LIX (1965), 53–59.

5007 — —. **United Nations Experience with Military Forces: Political and Legal Aspects.** Washington, Brookings, 1964. xiii + 174 p.

5008 Seyersted, Finn. **United Nations Forces: Some Legal Problems,** *British Yearbook of International Law,* XXXVII (1961), 351–475.

5009 Sohn, Louis. **The Role of the United Nations in Civil Wars,** *American Society of International Law Proceedings,* LVII (1963), 208–15.

5010 Solum, Ingebrigt. **Armed UN Action,** *Peace-Keeping: Experience and Evaluation; The Oslo Papers,* Per Frydenberg (ed.). Oslo, Norwegian Institute of International Affairs, 1964, pp. 141–45.

5011 Stokke, Olav. **United Nations Security Forces: Some Political Problems,** *Peace-Keeping: Experience and Evaluation; The Oslo Papers,* Per Frydenberg (ed.). Oslo, Norwegian Institute of International Affairs, 1964, pp. 27–67.

5012 Stone, Julius. **Legal Bases for the Establishment of Forces Performing United Nations Security Functions,** *Peace-Keeping: Experience and Evaluation; The Oslo Papers,* Per Frydenberg (ed.). Oslo, Norwegian Institute of International Affairs, 1964, pp. 277–302.

5013 Urquhart, Brian E. **United Nations Peace Forces and the Changing United Nations: An Institutional Perspective,** *International Organization,* XVII (Spring, 1963), 337–54.

5014 Young, Oran R. **Trends in International Peace Keeping.** Princeton, Center of International Studies, 1966. 45 p.

Part D. — *United Nations System*

10.6 PREVENTIVE DIPLOMACY

5015 Claude, Inis L., Jr. **Swords Into Plowshares.** 3d ed. New York, Random House, 1964.

Chapter XIV.

5016 Curtis, Gerald L. **The United Nations Observation Group in Lebanon,** *International Organization,* XVIII (Autumn, 1964), 738—65.

5017 Freymond, Jacques. **Supervising Agreements: The Korean Experience,** *Foreign Affairs,* XXXVII (April 1959), 496—503.

5018 Lourie, Sylvan. **The UN Military Observer Group in India and Pakistan,** *International Organization,* IX (February 1955), 19—31.

5019 Lund, Erling. **Observation Service,** *Peace-Keeping: Experience and Evaluation; The Oslo Papers,* Per Frydenberg (ed.). Oslo, Norwegian Institute of International Affairs, 1964, pp. 147—61.

5020 Mohn, Paul. **Problems of Truce Supervision,** *International Conciliation,* CDLXXVIII (February 1952), 51—99.

5021 Pyman, T. A. **The Significance of the United Nations "Presence" for International Security,** *Australian Outlook,* XIV (December 1960), 229—45.

5022 Stanton, Edwin F. **A "Presence" in Laos,** *Current History,* XXXVIII (June 1960), 337—41.

11. POLITICAL ACTIVITIES: PARTICULAR DISPUTES

11.1 INDO-PAKISTANI CONFLICT (1946–)

5023 Ahmad, Mushtaq. **Kashmir in the United Nations,** *Pakistan Horizon,* IV (December 1951), 217–31.

5024 Alexandrowicz, C. H. **The Kashmir Deadlock,** *Political Quarterly,* XXV (July-September 1954), 236–45.

5025 Barton, William. **Pakistan's Claim to Kashmir,** *Foreign Affairs,* XXVIII (January 1959), 299–308.

5026 Birdwood, Christopher B. B. **Kashmir,** *International Affairs,* XXVIII (July 1952), 299–309.

5027 — —. **Two Nations and Kashmir.** London, Hale, 1956. 237 p.

5028 Brecher, Michael. **Kashmir: A Case Study in United Nations Mediation,** *Pacific Affairs,* XXVI (September 1953), 195–207.

5029 — —. **Kashmir in Transition: Social Reform and the Political Future,** *International Journal,* VIII (Spring, 1953), 104–12.

5030 — —. **The Struggle for Kashmir.** New York, Oxford University Press, 1953. xii + 211 p.

5031 Burns, Eedson L. M. **Between Arab and Israeli.** Toronto, Clarke, Irwin, 1962. 336 p.

Part D. — *United Nations System*

5032 Chaudhri, Mohammed Ahsen. **Kashmir: The Latest Phase,** *Pakistan Horizon,* VII (June 1954), 79—87.

5033 Das, Taraknath. **The Kashmir Issue and the United Nations,** *Political Science Quarterly,* LXV (June 1950), 264—82.

5034 Das Gupta, Jyoti B. **Indo-Pakistan Relations, 1947—1955.** Amsterdam, Djambatan, 1958. xi + 254 p.

5035 Glick, Edward B. **Latin America and the Palestine Problem.** New York, Herzl, 1958. viii + 199 p.

5036 Gupta, Sisir. **The Kashmir Question Today,** *International Studies,* VI (January 1965), 217—53.

5037 Hasan, K. Sarwar. **Kashmir Before the Security Council,** *Pakistan Horizon,* X (March 1957), 26—33.

5038 Hutchinson, Elmo H. **Violent Truce: A Military Observer Looks at the Arab-Israeli Conflict, 1951—1955.** Forewords by Vagn Bennike, W. T. McAninch and John R. De Barr. New York, Devin-Adair, 1956. xxvi + 199 p.

5039 Ibrahim, Sardar Mohammad. **Kashmir in the Security Council,** *Pakistan Horizon,* III (June 1950), 59—68.

5040 Korbel, Josef. **Danger in Kashmir,** *Foreign Affairs,* XXXII (April 1954), 482—90.

5041 — —. **Danger in Kashmir.** Foreword by C. W. Nimitz. Princeton, Princeton University Press, 1954. 851 p.

5042 — —. **The Kashmir Dispute After Six Years,** *International Organization,* VII (November 1953), 498—510.

5043 — —. **The Kashmir Dispute After Ten Years,** *World Today,* New Series, XIV (February 1958), 61—70.

5044 — —. **The Kashmir Dispute and the United Nations,** *International Organization,* III (May 1949), 278—87.

5045 Lal, Mukut Behari. **The Kashmir Issue,** *India Quarterly,* XXI (October-December 1965), 345—74.

5046 Lourie, Sylvan. **The UN Military Observer Group in India and Pakistan,** *International Organization,* IX (February 1955), 19—31.

5047 McLeish, Alexander. **The Kashmir Dispute,** *World Affairs,* IV (January 1950), 60—71.

5048 Madhok, Bal Raj. **Kashmir: Centre for New Alignments.** New Delhi, Prakashan, 1964. 196 p.

5049 Millar, T. B. **Kashmir, the Commonwealth and the United Nations,** *Australian Outlook,* XVII (April 1963), 54—73.

5050 O., S. **The Kashmir Problem: End of a Stalemate?** *World Today,* New Series, IX (September 1953), 393—99.

5051 Shwadran, Benjamin. **The Seventh United Nations Assembly and the Palestine Question,** *Middle Eastern Affairs,* IV (April 1953), 113—26.

5052 Talbot, Phillips. **Kashmir and Hyderabad,** *World Politics,* I (October 1948 — July 1949), 321—32.

5053 Thorner, Alice. **The Kashmir Conflict,** *Middle East Journal,* III (January 1949), 17—30.

11.2 ARAB-ISRAELI CONFLICT (1947—)

See also D 7.3.6.2 and D 11.5.

5054 Alami, Musa. **The Lesson of Palestine,** *Middle East Journal,* III (October 1949), 373—405.

5055 Allan, Yigal. **The Arab-Israeli Conflict: Some Suggested Solutions,** *International Affairs,* XL (April 1964), 205—18.

5056 Armstrong, Hamilton Fish. **The UN Experience in Gaza,** *Foreign Affairs,* XXXV (July 1957), 600—19.

5057 Benton, Wilbourn E. **United Nations Action in the Suez Crisis,** *Tulane Studies in Political Science,* IV (1957), 5—23.

5058 Bonne, Alfred. **The Return to Israel,** *International Journal,* VI (Spring, 1951), 127—35.

5059 Brook, David. **Preface to Peace: The United Nations and the Arab-Israeli Armistice System.** Washington, Public Affairs Press, 1964. 151 p.

5060 Burns, E. L. M. **Between Arab and Israeli.** Toronto, Clark, Irwin, 1962. 336 p.

5061 Chase, Eugene P. **The United Nations in Action.** New York, McGraw-Hill, 1950.
Chapter IX.

5062 Cohen, Maxwell. **The United Nations Emergency Force: A Preliminary View,** *International Journal,* XII (Spring, 1957), 109—27.

5063 Corbett, Percy E. **Power and Law at Suez,** *International Journal*, XII (Winter, 1956—57), 1—12.

5064 Doherty, Katheryn B. **Jordan Waters Conflict,** *International Conciliation*, DLIII (May 1965), 3—66.

5065 Eagleton, Clyde. **The United Nations and the Suez Crisis,** *Tensions in the Middle East*, Philip W. Thayer (ed.). Baltimore, Johns Hopkins Press, 1958, pp. 273—84.
Comments by Francis O. Wilcox.

5066 Eayrs, James. **Canadian Policy and Opinion During the Suez Crisis,** *International Journal*, XII (Spring, 1957), 97—108.

5067 Eban, A. S. **The United Nations and the Palestine Question,** *World Affairs*, New Series, II (April 1948), 124—35.

5068 Gabbay, Rony. **A Political Study of the Arab-Jewish Conflict.** Geneva, Droz, 1959. 611 p.

5069 Glubb, J. B. **Violence on the Jordan-Israel Border: A Jordanian View,** *Foreign Affairs*, XXXII (July 1954), 552—62.

5070 Goodhart, A. L. **Some Legal Aspects of the Suez Situation,** *Tensions in the Middle East*, Philip W. Thayer (ed.). Baltimore, Johns Hopkins Press, 1958, pp. 243—60.
Comments by Quincy Wright.

5071 Goodrich, Leland M. and Rosner, Gabriella E. **The United Nations Emergency Force,** *International Organization*, XI (Summer, 1957), 413—30.

Part D. — *United Nations System*

5072 Hamilton, Thomas J. **Partition of Palestine,** *Foreign Policy Reports,* XXIII (February 15, 1948), 286—95.

5073 Hamzeh, F. S. **International Conciliation (With Special Reference to the Work of the United Nations Conciliation Commission for Palestine).** Hague, Pasmans, 1963. x + 177 p.

5074 Hoffmann, Stanley. **Sisyphus, and the Avalanche: The United Nations, Egypt, and Hungary,** *International Organization,* XI (Summer, 1957), 446—69.

5075 Holm-Johsen, Arne and Øyen, Odd. **Experiences Relating to Logistics in Gaza and the Congo,** *Peace-Keeping: Experience and Evaluation; The Oslo Papers,* Per Frydenberg (ed.). Oslo, Norwegian Institute of International Affairs, 1964, pp. 163—71.

5076 Hudson, G. F. **The United Nations Emergency Force: A Notable Precedent,** *Current History,* XXXVIII (June 1960), 326—31.

5077 Hurewitz, Jacob C. **The Israeli-Syrian Crisis in the Light of the Arab-Israel Armistice System,** *International Organization,* V (August 1951), 459—79.

5078 — —. **The United Nations Conciliation Commission for Palestine,** *International Organization,* VII (November 1953), 482—97.

5079 Hutchinson, E. H. **Violent Truce: A Military Observer Looks at the Arab-Israeli Conflict 1051—1955.** New York, Devin-Adair, 1956. 150 p.

5080 Lauterpacht, Elihu (ed.). **The United Nations Emergency Force.** New York, Praeger, 1960. 49 p.
A collection of documents.

5081 Lawson, Ruth C. **United Nations: III, Heir to the Palestine Problem,** *Current History,* New Series, XIV (March 1948), 159–63.

5082 Leonard, L. Larry. **The United Nations and Palestine,** *International Conciliation,* CDLIV (October 1949), 607–786.
Appendices contain various documents.

5083 L., H. G. **The Palestine Problem,** *World Today,* New Series, III (October 1947), 453–62.

5084 Liveran, Arthur C. A. **Israel in the Middle East,** *Current History,* New Series, XXXIII (November 1957), 289–94.

5085 McGeachy, J. B. **Is It Peace in Palestine?** *International Journal,* III (Summer, 1948), 239–48.

5086 Mahmood, Khalid. **Britain and the Suez Crisis,** *Pakistan Horizon,* XV, 2 (1962), 111–28.

5087 Mason, Henry L. **The United Nations Emergency Force,** *Tulane Studies in Political Science,* IV (1957), 25–48.

5088 Mohan, Jitrendra. **South Africa and the Suez Crisis,** *International Journal,* XVI (Autumn, 1961), 327–57.

5089 Mohn, Paul. **Jerusalem and the United Nations,** *International Conciliation,* CDLXIV (October 1950), 425–71.

5090 — —. **Problems of Truce Supervision,** *International Conciliation,* CDLXXVIII (February 1952), 51–99.

Part D. — United Nations System

5091 Nathan, Robert R.; Gass, Oscar; and Creamer, Daniel. **Palestine: Promise and Problem.** Washington, American Council on Public Affairs, 1946. x + 675 p.

5092 Peretz, Don. **Israel and the Arab Nations,** *Journal of International Affairs,* XIX, 1 (1965), 100–10.

5093 ——. **Jerusalem — A Divided City,** *Journal of International Affairs,* XVIII, 2 (1964), 211–20.

5094 Poirier, Pierre. **La Force Internationale d'Urgence.** Preface by Charles Rousseau. Paris, Pinchon et Durand-Auzias, 1962. 385 p.

5095 Price, David B. **The Charter of the United Nations and the Suez War,** *International Relations,* I (October 1958), 494–511.

5096 Prince, A. E. **The Palestine Impasse,** *International Journal,* I (April 1946), 122–33.

5097 Roosevelt, K. **The Partition of Palestine,** *Middle East Journal,* II (January 1948), 1–6.

5098 Rosner, Gabriella. **The United Nations Emergency Force.** New York, Columbia University Press, 1963. xiv + 294 p.

5099 Schmidt, Dana Adams. **Prospects for a Solution of the Jordan River Dispute,** *Middle Eastern Affairs,* VI (January 1955), 1–12.

5100 Schneider, Carl J. **The Suez Crisis of 1956 and Its Aftermath,** *Problems in International Relations,* eds. Andrew Gyorgy and Hubert S. Gibbs (eds.). 2d ed. Englewood Cliffs, Prentice-Hall, 1962, pp. 277–94.

Part D. — United Nations System

5101 Sherf, Zeev. **Three Days,** Julian L. Meltzer (trans.). Garden City, Doubleday, 1962. 298 p.

5102 Shwadran, Benjamin. **Israel-Jordan Border Tension,** *Middle Eastern Affairs,* IV (December 1953), 385—401.

5103 — —. **The Palestine Conciliation Commission,** *Middle Eastern Affairs,* I (October 1950), 271—85.

5104 Spry, Graham. **Canada, the United Nations Emergency Force, and the Commonwealth,** *International Affairs,* XXXIII (July 1957), 289—300.

5105 Stanley, George F. G. **Failure at Suez,** *International Journal,* XII (Spring, 1957), 90—96.

5106 Stevens, Georgiana. **The Jordan River Valley,** *International Conciliation,* DVI (January 1956), 227—83.

5107 Strange, Susan. **Palestine and the United Nations,** *Year Book of World Affairs,* III (1949), 151—68.

5108 Thompson, Carol L. **Palestine: The Promised Land,** *Current History,* New Series, XII (April 1947), 345—53.

5109 Van Alstyne, Richard W. **Whither Palestine?** *Current History,* New Series, XIV (February 1948), 76—83; (March 1948), 153—58.

5110 Voss, Carl Hermann. **Palestine: Acid Test of the United Nations,** *Annals of the American Academy of Political and Social Science,* CCLVIII (July 1948), 14—21.

5111 Welles, Sumner. **We Need Not Fail.** Boston, Houghton, Mifflin, 1948. xiv + 143 p.

5112 Wright, Quincy. **Intervention, 1956,** *American Journal of International Law*, LI (April 1957), 257—76.

5113 Zasloff, Joseph J. **Great Britain and Palestine: A Study of the Problem Before the United Nations.** Munich, Verlagshaus der Americanischen Hechkommission, 1952. xi + 187 p.

11.3 KOREAN WAR (1950—1953)

5114 Altstedter, Norman. **Problems of Coalition Diplomacy: The Korean Experience,** *International Journal*, VIII (Autumn, 1953), 256—65.

5115 Bell, Coral. **Korea and the Balance of Power,** *Political Quarterly*, XXV (January-March 1954), 17—29.

5116 Cottrell, Alvin J. and Dougherty, James E. **The Lessons of Korea: War and the Power of Man,** *Orbis*, II (Spring, 1958), 39—65.

5117 Dayal, Shiv. **India's Role in the Korean Question: A Study in the Settlement of International Disputes Under the United Nations.** Delhi, Chand, 1959. 360 p.

5118 Freymond, Jacques. **Supervising Agreements: The Korean Experience,** *Foreign Affairs*, XXXVII (April 1959), 496—503.

5119 Goodrich, Leland M. **Collective Action in Korea,** *Current History*, XXXVIII (June 1960), 332—36.

5120 — —. **Korea: A Study of U. S. Policy in the United Nations.** New York, Council on Foreign Relations, 1956. 235 p.

5121 — —. **Korea: Collective Measures Against Aggression,** *International Conciliation,* CDXCIV (October 1953), 131–92.

5122 — —. **The United Nations and Korea,** *India Quarterly,* VII (July-September 1951), 255–68.

5123 — —. **The United Nations and Korea,** *Journal of International Affairs,* VI (Spring 1952), 115–28.

5124 — —. **The United Nations and the Korean War: A Case Study,** *Academy of Political Science Proceedings,* XXV (January 1953), 222–36.

5125 Gordenker, Leon. **The United Nations and the Peaceful Unification of Korea.** Hague, Nijhoff, 1959. 306 p.

5126 — —. **The United Nations, the United States Occupation and the Election in Korea,** *Political Science Quarterly,* LXXIII (September 1958), 426–50.

5127 — —. **United Nations Use of Mass Communications in Korea, 1950–1951,** *International Organization,* VIII (August 1954), 331–45.

5128 Green, L. C. **Korea and the United Nations,** *World Affairs,* (October 1950), 414–37.

5129 Gross, Ernest A. **The Testing of the United Nations,** *Academy of Political Science Proceedings,* XXV (January 1953), 247–55.

5130 Guelzo, Carl M. **Korea: The Divided Peace,** *Yale Review,* LI (Spring, 1962), 428–37.

5131 Harley, J. Eugene. **United Nations International Police Action in Korea,** *World Affairs Quarterly,* XXII (April 1951), 88–96.

Part D. — *United Nations System*

5132 Hartmann, Frederick H. **The Relations of Nations.** 3d ed. New York, Macmillan, 1967.

Chapter XXI.

5133 Hitchcock, Wilbur W. **North Korea Jumps the Gun,** *Current History,* New Series, XX (March 1951), 136–44.

5134 Kahn, Ely Jacques, Jr. **The Peculiar War.** New York, Random House, 1952. 211 p.

5135 Lawson, Ruth C. **The United Nations Faces War,** *Current History,* New Series, XX (March 1951), 158–62.

5136 Lee, Chong-Sik. **Korean Partition and Unification,** *Journal of International Affairs,* XVIII, 2 (1964), 221–33.

5137 Lyons, Gene M. **American Policy and the United Nations Program for Korean Reconstruction,** *International Organization,* XII (Spring, 1958), 180–92.

5138 — —. **Military Policy and Economic Aid: The Korean Case, 1950–1953.** Columbus, Ohio State University Press, 1961. xiii + 298 p.

5139 Mukerjee, S. **The UN Action in Korea,** *Indian Journal of Political Science,* XIII (January 1952), 69–77.

5140 Oliver, Robert T. **Why War Came in Korea,** *Current History,* New Series, XIX (September 1950), 139–43.

5141 Padelford, Norman J. **The United Nations and Korea,** *International Organization,* V (November 1951), 685–708.

Part D. — United Nations System

5142 Parr, E. Joan. **Korea — Its Place in History,** *Political Quarterly,* XXIII (October-December 1952), 352—67.

5143 Poplair, S. L. **The Korea Crisis: Some International Aspects,** *India Quarterly,* VI (October-December 1950), 315—25.

5144 Power, Terry. **New Zealand and the Korean War,** *Political Science,* XVI (September 1964), 52—70.

5145 Rao, B. Shiva and Kondapi, C. **India and the Korean Crisis,** *India Quarterly,* VII (October-December 1951), 295—314.

5146 Rucker, Arthur. **Korea — The Next Stage,** *International Affairs,* XXX (July 1954), 313—19.

5147 Schick, Franz B. **Videant Consules,** *Western Political Quarterly,* III (June 1950), 311—25.

5148 Soward, F. H. **The Korean Crisis and the Commonwealth,** *Pacific Affairs,* XXIV (June 1951), 115—30.

5149 Stanley, G. F. G. **The Korean Dilemma,** *International Journal,* VII (Autumn, 1952), 278—82.

5150 Vandenbosch, Amry and Hogan, Willard N. **The United Nations.** New York, McGraw-Hill, 1952.

Chapter XV.

5151 Vatcher, William H., Jr. **Panmunjom: The Story of the Korean Military Armistice Negotiations.** Foreword by C. Turner Joy. New York, Praeger, 1958. 322 p.

5152 Watkins, James T., IV. **United States Leadership and Collective Security: The Meaning of Korea,** *Institute of World Affairs Proceedings,* XXIX (1953), 191—99.

5153 Wolfers, Arnold. **Collective Security and the War in Korea,** *Discord and Collaboration.* Baltimore, Johns Hopkins Press, 1962, pp. 167—80.

Reprinted, with minor changes, from *Yale Review,* June 1954.

5154 Woodman, Dorothy. **Korea, Formosa and World Peace,** *Political Quarterly,* XXI (October-December 1950), 364—73.

5155 Wright, Quincy. **Collective Security in the Light of the Korean Experience,** *American Society of International Law Proceedings,* XLV (1951), 165—82.

5156 Yoo, Tae-ho. **The Korean War and the United Nations: A Legal and Diplomatic Historical Study.** Louvain, Desbarax, 1964. 215 p.

11.4 HUNGARIAN REVOLUTION (1956)

5157 Anabtawi, Samir N. **The Afro-Asian States and the Hungarian Question,** *International Organization,* XVII (Autumn, 1963), 872—900.

5158 Grosser, Alfred. **Suez, Hungary and European Integration,** *International Organization,* XI (Summer, 1957), 470—80.

5159 Hoffmann, Stanley. **Sisyphus, and the Avalanche: The United Nations, Egypt, and Hungary,** *International Organization,* XI (Summer, 1957), 446—69.

5160 Organski, A. F. K. **The Hungarian Question,** *Current History,* XXXVIII (June 1960), 347—51.

5161 Wright, Quincy. **Intervention, 1956,** *American Journal of International Law,* LI (April 1957), 257–76.

11.5 SUEZ CONFLICT (1956)

5162 Barker, A. J. **Suez: The Seven Day War.** New York, Praeger, 1965. 223 p.

5163 Bloomfield, Lincoln P. **Headquarters-Field Relations: Some Notes on the Beginning and End of ONUC,** *International Organization,* XVII (Spring, 1963), 377–92.

5164 Grosser, Alfred. **Suez, Hungary and European Integration,** *International Organization,* XI (Summer, 1957), 470–80.

5165 Macdonald, R. St. J. **Hungary, Egypt, and the United Nations,** *Canadian Bar Review,* XXXV (January 1957), 38–71.

5166 Mohan, Jitendra. **India, Pakistan, Suez and the Commonwealth,** *International Journal,* XV (Summer, 1960), 185–99.

5167 Nicholas, Herbert. **UN Peace Forces and the Changing Globe: The Lessons of Suez and Congo,** *International Organization,* XVII (Spring, 1963), 321–36.

5168 Price, David B. **The Charter of the United Nations and the Suez War,** *International Relations,* I (October 1958), 494–511.

5169 Schneider, J. W. **Congo Force and Standing UN Force: Legal Experience with ONUC,** *Indian Journal of International Law,* IV (1964), 269–300.

11.6 CONGO CONFLICT (1960–1964)

5170 Bunche, Ralph J. **The United Operations in the Congo,** *The Quest for Peace,* Andrew W. Cordier and Wilder Foote (eds.). New York, Columbia University Press, 1965, pp. 119–39.

5171 Cheever, Daniel S. **The United Nations and the Congo Incident,** *Problems in International Relations,* Andrew Gyorgy and Hubert S. Gibbs (eds.). 2d ed. Englewood Cliffs, Prentice-Hall, 1962, pp. 342–60.

5172 Cleveland, Harlan. **The United Nations and the Congo: Three Questions,** *Department of State Bulletin,* XLVIII (February 4, 1963), 165–70.

5173 Cruise O'Brien, Conor. **To Katanga and Back: A UN Case History** London, Hutchinson, 1962. 371 p.

5174 Davenport, John. **An Ugly Face in Africa,** *Fortune,* XLVII (February 1963), 84 ff.

A negative view.

5175 Franck, Thomas M. and Carey, John. **The Legal Aspects of the United Nations Action in the Congo: Background Papers and Proceedings of the Second Hammarskjold Forum,** Lyman M. Tondel, Jr. (ed.). Dobbs Ferry, Oceana, 1963. xv + 137 p.

5176 Good, Robert C. **The Congo Crisis: A Study of Postcolonial Politics,** *Neutralism and Nonalignment,* Lawrence W. Martin (ed.). New York, Praeger, 1962, pp. 34–63.

5177 Gordon, King. **The United Nations in the Congo: A Quest for Peace.** New York, Carnegie, 1962. 184 p.

5178 Halpern, Manfred. **The UN in the Congo,** *World View,* VI (October 1963), 4–8.

Part D. — United Nations System

5179 Heathcote, N. **American Policy Towards the UN Operation in the Congo,** *Australian Outlook,* XVIII (April 1964), 77—97.

5180 Hempstone, Smith. **Rebels, Mercenaries, and Dividends: The Katanga Story.** New York, Praeger, 1962, vi + 250 p.

5181 Hoffmann, Stanley. **In Search of a Thread — The UN in the Congo Labyrinth,** *International Organization,* XVI (Spring, 1962), 291—302.

5182 Holmes, John. **The United Nations in the Congo,** *International Journal,* XVI (Winter, 1960—61), 1—16.

5183 Holm-Johsen, Arne and Øyen, Odd. **Experiences Relating to Logistics in Gaza and the Congo,** *Peace-Keeping: Experience and Evaluation; The Oslo Papers,* Per Frydenberg (ed.). Oslo, Norwegian Institute of International Affairs, 1964, pp. 163—71.

5184 Hoskyns, Catherine. **The Congo Since Independence, January 1960-December 1961.** London, Oxford University Press, 1965. xii + 518 p.

5185 Jacobson, Harold Karan. **ONUC's Civilian Operations: State-Preserving and State-Building,** *World Politics,* XVII (October 1964), 75—107.

5186 Karabus, Alan. **United Nations Activities in the Congo,** *American Society of International Law Proceedings,* LV (1961), 30—38.

5187 Lefever, Ernest W. **Crisis in the Congo: A United Nations Force in Action.** Washington, Brookings, 1965. xii + 215 p.

5188 — —. **Power and Purpose in World Politics: The Congo Drama,** *Institute of World Affairs Proceedings,* XL (1964), 7—15.

Part D. — United Nations System

5189 Legum, Colin. **Congo Disaster.** Baltimore, Penguin Books, 1961. 174 p.

5190 Markowitz, Marvin D. and Weiss, Herbert F. **Rebellion in the Congo,** *Current History,* New Series, XLVIII (April 1965), 213–18 ff.

5191 Merrian, Alan P. **Congo: Background of Conflict.** Evanston, Northwestern University Press, 1961. 368 p.

5192 Neff, Charles B. **Conflict, Crisis and the Congo: A Review,** *Journal of Conflict Resolution,* VIII (March 1964), 86–92.

5193 Nicholas, Herbert. **UN Peace Forces and the Changing Globe: The Lessons of Suez and Congo,** *International Organization,* XVII (Spring, 1963), 321–36.

5194 O'Donovan, Patrick. **The Precedent of the Congo,** *International Affairs,* XXXVII (April 1961), 181–88.

5195 Okumu, Washington. **Lumumba's Congo: Roots of Conflict.** New York, Obolensky, 1963. 250 p.

5196 Riad, F. A. M. **United Nations Action in the Congo, and Its Legal Basis,** *Revue Égyptienne de Droit International,* XVII (1961), 1–53.

5197 Rudin, Harry R. **Aftermath in the Congo,** *Current History,* New Series, XLV (December 1963), 341–46.

5198 Schachter, Oscar. **Legal Aspects of the United Nations' Action in the Congo,** *American Journal of International Law,* LV (January 1961), 1–28.

5199 Schuyler, Philippa. **Who Killed the Congo?** Chicago, Regnery, 1961. 240 p.

5200 Tondel, Lyman M., Jr. **The Legal Aspects of the United Nations Action in the Congo: Background Papers and Proceedings of the Second Hammarskjöld Forum.** Dobbs Ferry, Oceana, 1963. 137 p.

5201 Twitchett, Kenneth J. **The Racial Issue at the United Nations: A Study of the African States' Reaction to the American-Belgian Congo Rescue Operation of November 1964,** *International Relations,* II (October 1965), 830—46.

5202 Valahu, Mugur. **The Katanga Circus: A Detailed Account of Three UN Wars.** New York, Speller, 1964. 364 p.

5203 Van Bilsen, A. A. J. **Some Aspects of the Congo Problem,** *International Affairs,* XXXVIII (January 1962), 41—51.

5204 Van Langenhove, Fernand. **La role prominent du Secrétaire Général dans l'opération des Nations Unies au Congo.** Hague, Nijhoff, 1964. 260 p.

5205 Wright, Quincy. **Legal Aspects of the Congo Situation,** *International Studies,* IV (July 1962), 1—23.

11.7 MINOR DISPUTES INVOLVING INDIA

5206 Eagleton, Clyde. **The Case of Hyderabad Before the Security Council,** *American Journal of International Law,* XLIV (April 1950), 277—302.

5207 Jawed, Tufail. **The World Bank and the Indus Basin Dispute: Background,** *Pakistan Horizon,* XVIII (1965), 226—37.

5208 Rabl, Kurt. **Harmony and Disharmony of Basic UN Charter Concepts — Some Notes on the Goa Issue,** *Indian Year Book of International Affairs,* XIII, 1 (1964), 3—27.

5209 Talbot, Phillips. **Kashmir and Hyderabad,** *World Politics,* I (October 1948 — July 1949), 321–32.

11.8 DISPUTES INVOLVING INDONESIA

5210 Albinski, Henry S. **Australia and the Dutch New Guinea Dispute,** *International Journal,* XVI (Autumn, 1961), 358–82.

5211 Collins, J. Foster. **The United Nations and Indonesia,** *International Conciliation,* CDLIX (March 1950), 115–200.

5212 Emerson, Rupert. **Reflections on the Indonesian Case,** *World Politics,* I (October 1948–July 1949), 59–81.

5213 Green, L. C. **Indonesia, the United Nations and Malaysia,** *Journal of Southeast Asian History,* VI (September 1965), 71–86.

5214 Henderson, William. **Pacific Settlement of Disputes: The Indonesia Question, 1946–1949.** New York, Woodrow Wilson Foundation, 1954. 89 p.

5215 Perkins, Whitney T. **Sanctions for Political Change — The Indonesian Case,** *International Organization,* XII (Winter, 1958), 26–42.

5216 Taylor, Alastair M. **Indonesian Independence and the United Nations.** London, Stevens, 1960. xxix + 503 p.

5217 Van Der Kroef, Justus M. **The West New Guinea Dispute.** New York, Institute of Pacific Relations, 1958. 43 p.

5218 — —. **The West New Guinea Settlement: Its Origins and Implications,** *Orbis,* VII (Spring, 1963), 120—49.

5219 Van der Veur, Paul W. **The United Nations in West Irian: A Critique,** *International Organization,* XVIII (Winter, 1964), 53—73.

5220 Wehl, David. **The Birth of Indonesia.** London, Allen and Unwin, 1949. 216 p.

11.9 MINOR DISPUTES IN THE LEVANT AND NORTH AFRICA

5221 Adams, T. W. and Cottrell, Alvin J. **The Cyprus Conflict,** *Orbis,* VIII (Spring, 1964), 66—83.

5222 Alwan, Mohamed. **Algeria Before the United Nations.** Foreword by W. Wendell Cleland. New York, Speller, 1959. 121 p.

5223 Atyeo, Henry C. **Morocco, Tunisia and Algeria Before the United Nations,** *Middle Eastern Affairs,* VI (August 1955), 229—48.

5224 Curtis, Gerald L. **The United Nations Observation Group in Lebanon,** *International Organization,* XVIII (Autumn, 1964), 738—65.

5225 Dejany, Aouney W. **Competence of the United Nations General Assembly in the Tunisian-Moroccan Questions,** *American Society of International Law Proceedings,* XLVII (1953), 53—59.

5226 E., W. G. **France, Syria, and the Lebanon,** *World Today,* New Series, II (March 1946), 112—22.

5227 Gordon, J. King. **The UN in Cyprus,** *International Journal,* XIX (Summer, 1964), 326—47.

5228 McBrayer, James D., Jr. **The United Nations and the Lebanon Incident,** *Problems in International Relations,* Andrew Gyorgy and Hubert S. Gibbs (eds.). 2d ed. Englewood Cliffs, Prentice-Hall, 1962, pp. 294—309.

5229 Royal Institution of International Affairs. **Cyprus: The Dispute and the Settlement.** Rev. ed. London, Royal Institute of International Affairs, 1959. xi + 62 p.

5230 Woodhouse, C. M. **Cyprus and the Middle Eastern Crisis,** *International Journal,* XI (Winter, 1955—56), 1—15.

11.10 DISPUTES IN SOUTHERN AFRICA

5231 Bains, J. S. **Angola, the UN and International Law,** *Indian Journal of International Law,* III (1963), 63—71.

5232 Leiss, Amelia C. (ed.). **Apartheid and United Nations Collective Measures: An Analysis.** New York, Carnegie, 1965. viii + 170 p.

5233 Malhotra, Ram C. **Apartheid and the United Nations,** *Annals of the American Academy of Political and Social Science,* CCCLIV (July 1964), 135—44.

5234 Nogueira, Franco. **The United Nations and Portugal: A Study of Anti-Colonialism.** London, Sidgwick and Jackson, 1963. 188 p.

5235 Okuma, Thomas M. **Angola in Ferment: The Background and Prospects of Angolan Nationalism.** Boston, Beacon, 1962. 137 p.

5236 Parsons, Clifford J. **Background to the Angola Crisis,** *World Today,* New Series, XVII (July 1961), 278–88.

5237 United Nations Special Committee. **Apartheid in South Africa: Defiance of the United Nations,** *Tension Areas in World Affairs,* Arthur C. Turner and Leonard Freedman (eds.). Belmont, Calif., Wadsworth, 1964, pp. 165–75.

From the Report of the UN Special Committee on the Policies of Apartheid of the Government of the Republic of South Africa, September 1963, issued as Document A/5497.

5238 Venkatavaradan, T. **The Question of Southern Rhodesia,** *Indian Year Book of International Affairs,* XIII, 1 (1964), 112–50.

5239 Wohlgemuth, Patricia. **The Portuguese Territories and the United Nations,** *International Conciliation,* CDXLV (November 1963), 3–68.

11.11 OTHER DISPUTES

5240 Henkin, Louis (ed.). **The Berlin Crisis and the United Nations.** New York, Carnegie, 1959. 30 p.

5241 Khan, Rahmatulla. **Cuban Quarantine and the Charter of the UN,** *Indian Journal of International Law,* IV (1964), 107–23.

5242 Stanton, Edwin F. **A "Presence" in Laos,** *Current History,* XXXVIII (June 1960), 337–41.

12. NATIONAL ACTORS AND THE UNITED NATIONS SYSTEM

See also A 6.2.1, D 7.2.5, D 8.2, D 9.4, D 11.

12.1 GENERAL DISCUSSIONS

5243 Akzin, Benjamin. **New States and International Organization.** Paris International Political Science Association, 1955. 200 p.

5244 Anabtawi, Samir N. **The Afro-Asian States and the Hungarian Question,** *International Organization,* XVII (Autumn, 1963), 872–900.

5245 Aspaturian, Vernon V. **The Metamorphosis of the United Nations,** *Yale Review,* XLVI (Summer, 1957), 551–65.

5246 Bebler, Ales. **Developing Countries and the United Nations,** *Pakistan Horizon,* XVIII, 2 (1965), 124–30.

5247 Dixit, R. K. **Non-Member States and the Settlement of Disputes in the Security Council,** *University of Toronto Law Journal,* XII, 2 (1958), 246–81.

5248 Faraj Allah, S. B. **Le groupe afro-asiatique dans le cadre des Nations Unies.** Geneva, Droz, 1963. 511 p.

5249 Fawcett, J. E. S. **The New States and the United Nations,** *Yearbook of World Polity,* III (1965), 229–52 ff.

5250 Finkelstein, Lawrence S. **National Policies and Attitudes Toward the United Nations,** *World Politics,* V (October 1952), 129–32.

5251 Friedmann, W. G. **The United Nations and National Loyalties,** *International Journal,* VIII (Winter, 1952–53), 17–26.

5252 Glazebrook, George De T. **The Middle Powers in the United Nations,** *International Organization,* I (June 1947), 307–15.

5253 Gregoire, Roger. **National Administration and International Organization: The Administrative Problems Arising in Newly-Independent Countries As a Result of Their Participation in the United Nations and Specialized Agencies.** Paris, UNESCO, n. d. 84 p.

5254 Gross, Ernest A. **The New United Nations.** New York, Foreign Policy Association, 1957. 62 p.

5255 Gross, Leo. **Immunities and Privileges of Delegations to the United Nations,** *International Organization,* XVI (Summer, 1962), 483–520.

5256 Haas, Ernst B. **The Comparative Study of the United Nations,** *World Politics,* XII (January 1960), 298–322.

5257 ——. **Regionalism, Functionalism, and Universal International Organization,** *World Politics,* VIII (January 1956), 238–63.

5258 Hadow, Robert Henry. **Ideological Conflicts Within UN,** *Annals of the American Academy of Political and Social Science,* CCLII (July 1947), 16–20.

5259 Hadwen, John G. and Kaufmann, Johan. **How United Nations Decisions Are Made.** Foreword by Paul G. Hoffmann. Leyden, Sythoff, 1960. 144 p.

5260 Hoffmann, Stanley. **National Attitudes and International Order: The National Studies on International Organization,** *International Organization*, XIII (Spring, 1959), 189—204.

5261 Howard, Harry N. **The Arab-Asian States in the United Nations,** *Middle East Journal*, VII (Summer, 1953), 279—92.

5262 International Institute of Administrative Sciences. **National Administration and International Organization: A Comparative Study of Fourteen Countries.** Brussels, International Institute of Administrative Sciences, 1951. 78 p.

5263 Kaeckenbeeck, Georges. **The Function of Great and Small Powers in the International Organization,** *International Affairs*, XXI (July 1945), 306—12.

5264 Keynes, Mary Knatchbull. **The Arab-Asian Bloc,** *International Relations*, I (October 1956), 238—50.

5265 Kohn, Hans. **Nationalism in the United Nations,** *The United States and the United Nations*, Franz B. Gross (ed.). Norman, University of Oklahoma Press, 1964, pp. 42—64.

5266 Little, Tom. **Mr. Khrushchev and the Neutrals at the United Nations,** *World Today*, New Series, XVI (December 1960), 510—19.

5267 MacIver, Robert Morrison. **The Nations and the United Nations.** New York, Manhattan, 1959. 186 p.

5268 Maslow, Will. **The Afro-Asian Bloc in the United Nations,** *Middle Eastern Affairs*, VIII (November 1957), 372—77.

5269 Nawaz, Mohammed. **Afro-Asians and the United Nations,** *Pakistan Horizon*, XV, 1 (1962), 42—48.

Part D. — United Nations System

5270 Nicholas, Herbert George. **The United Nations As a Political Institution.** 2d ed. London, Oxford University Press, 1962.

Chapter VIII.

5271 Palmer, Norman D. **The Afro-Asians in the United Nations,** *The United States and the United Nations,* Franz B. Gross (ed.). Norman, University of Oklahoma Press, 1964, pp. 125–69.

5272 Pedersen, Richard F. **National Representation in the United Nations,** *International Organization,* XV (Spring, 1961), 256–66.

5273 Smithies, Arthur. **The U. S., the U. N. and the Underdeveloped World,** *Orbis,* II (Fall, 1958), 337–55.

5274 Sohn, Louis B. **Neutralism and the United Nations,** *Preventing World War III: Some Proposals,* Quincy Wright, William M. Evan, and Morton Deutsch (eds.). New York, Simon and Schuster, 1962, pp. 355–68.

5275 Sørensen, Max. **Nyere udvikslinglinier i international organization,** *Statsvetenskaplig Tidskrift,* LIV, 2 (1951), 113–29.

Discusses trend to extend representation in international organizations to subnational groups.

5276 Stein, Eric. **Some Implications of Expanding United Nations Membership.** New York, Carnegie, 1956. 77 p.

5277 Stone, Julius. **Aggression and World Order: A Critique of United Nations Theories of Aggression.** London, Stevens, 1958. xiv + 226 p.

5278 Triska, Jan and Koch, Howard E., Jr. **The Asian-African Nations and International Organization: Third Force or Collective Impotence?** *Review of Politics,* XXI (April 1959), 416–55.

5279 Vandenbosch, Amry. **Small States in International Politics and Organization,** *Journal of Politics,* XXVI (May 1964), 293–312.

Surveys the role of small states from the Congress of Vienna to the United Nations.

5280 Vincent, Jack Ernest. **The Caucusing Groups of the United Nations: An Examination of Their Attitudes Toward the Organization.** Stillwater, Oklahoma State University, 1964. 152 p.

5281 Wilcox, Francis O. **The Nonaligned States and the United Nations,** *Neutralism and Nonalignment,* Lawrence W. Martin (ed.). New York, Praeger, 1962, pp. 121–51.

5282 — —. **UN and the Nonaligned Nations.** New York, Foreign Policy Association, 1962. 55 p.

12.2 PARTICULAR COUNTRIES

12.2.1 AFRICAN COUNTRIES

5283 Cohen, Andrew. **The New Africa and the United Nations,** *Africa: A Handbook to the Continent,* Colin Legum (ed.). London, Blond, 1961, pp. 491–99.

5284 — —. **The New Africa and the United Nations,** *International Affairs,* XXXVI (October 1960), 476–88.

5285 Cottrell, W. F. **The United Nations and Africa,** *Annals of the American Academy of Political and Social Science,* CCCVI (July 1956), 55–61.

5286 Governor's Conference on the United Nations. **The United Nations and the Emerging African Nations.** Milwaukee, University of Wisconsin, Institute for World Affairs Education, 1961. 40 p.

5287 Henry, Paul-Marc. **The United Nations and the Problem of African Development,** *International Organization,* XVI (Spring, 1962), 362–74.

5288 Hoskyns, Catherine. **The African States and the United Nations,** *International Affairs,* XI (July 1964), 466–80.

5289 Hovet, Thomas, Jr. **Africa in the United Nations.** Evanston, Northwestern University Press, 1963. 336 p.

5290 — —. **African Policies in the United Nations,** *American Behavioral Scientist,* V (April 1962), 28–30.

5291 — —. **The Role of Africa in the United Nations,** *Annals of the American Academy of Political and Social Science,* CCCLIV (July 1964), 122–34.

5292 Irvine, Keith. **African Nationalism and the United Nations,** *Current History,* XXXVIII (June 1960), 352–57.

5293 Johnson, Carol A. and Russell, Sara A. **Selected Bibliography: Africa and International Organization,** *International Organization,* XVI (Spring, 1962), 449–64.

5294 Kamarck, Andrew M. **The Activities of the World Bank in Africa,** *Africa: A Handbook to the Continent,* Colin Legum (ed.). London, Blond, 1961. pp. 505–7.

5295 Karefa-Smart, John. **Africa and the United Nations,** *International Organization,* XIX (Summer, 1965), 764–73.

5296 Kelfa-Caulker, Richard E. **The Role of the African States in the United Nations,** *Institute of World Affairs Proceedings,* XXXIX (1963), 290–97.

5297 McKay, Vernon. **Africa in World Politics.** New York, Harper and Row, 1963.
Chapters II–IV.

5298 Maxrui, Ali A. **The United Nations and Some African Political Attitudes,** *International Organization,* XVIII (Summer, 1964), 499—520.

5299 Neal, Marian. **The United Nations and the Union of South Africa,** *Journal of International Affairs,* VII, 2 (1953), 151—54.

5300 Spencer, John H. **Africa at the UN: Some Observations,** *International Organization,* XVI (Spring, 1962), 375—86.

5301 Spense, J. E. **The African States and the UN,** *Optima,* XIV (June 1964), 77—87.

5302 Twitchett, Kenneth J. **The Racial Issue at the United Nations: A Study of the African States' Reaction to the American-Belgian Congo Rescue Operation of November 1964,** *International Relations,* II (October 1965), 830—46.

5303 Wilcox, Francis O. **The New Africa and the United Nations.** Washington, U. S. Government Printing Office, 1960. 21 p.

12.2.2 ASIAN COUNTRIES

See also D 5.4.2.

5304 Ahmad, Mushtaq. **Pakistan and the United Nations,** *Karachi, Pakistan Horizon,* IV (September 1951), 130—50.

5305 — —. **The United Nations and Pakistan.** Pakistan Institute of International Affairs, 1955. III + 162 p.

5306 Appadorai, A. **India's Participation in International Organizations,** *India Quarterly,* VI (July-September 1950), 247—61.

Part D. — *United Nations System*

5307 Asirvathan, Eddy. **The United Nations and India,** *Annals of the American Academy of Political and Social Science,* CCXLVI (July 1946), 55–63.

5308 Berkes, Ross N. and Bedi, Mohinder S. **The Diplomacy of India: Indian Foreign Policy in the United Nations.** Stanford, Stanford University Press, 1958. 221 p.

5309 Brohi, A. K. **Five Lectures on Asia and the United Nations,** *Recueil des Cours,* CII (1961), 122–212.

5310 Canadian Institute of International Affairs. **Japan and the GATT,** *International Journal,* IX (Summer, 1954), 216–19.

5311 China Institute of International Affairs. **China and the United Nations.** New York, Manhattan, 1959. 285 p.

5312 Clements, F. W. **The World Health Organization in Southern Asia and the Western Pacific,** *Pacific Affairs,* XXV (December 1952), 334–48.

5313 Cook, A. H. **The International Labor Organization and Japanese Politics,** *Industrial and Labor Relations Review,* XIX (October 1965), 41–57.

5314 Coreo, C. **Ceylon at the United Nations,** *Ceylon Today,* VIII (March 1959), 7–15.

5315 Dayal, Shiv. **India's Role in the Korean Question: A Study in the Settlement of International Disputes Under the United Nations.** Delhi, Chand, 1959. 360 p.

5316 Dodd, Norris E. **FAO Work and Aims in Asia,** *United Asia,* III, 2 (1950), 103–18.

Part D. — United Nations System

5317 Finkelstein, Lawrence S. **Indonesia's Record in the United Nations,** *International Conciliation,* CDLXXV (November 1951), 513—46.

5318 Gilchrist, Huntington. **Technical Assistance from the United Nations — As Seen in Pakistan,** *International Organization,* XIII (Autumn, 1959), 505—19.

5319 Haruki, Takeshi. **UNESCO Activities in Japan,** *World Affairs Quarterly,* XXII (April 1951), 76—87.

5320 Hasan, K. Sarwar. **Pakistan and the United Nations.** New York, Manhattan, 1960. vii + 328 p.

5321 Hovet, Thomas, Jr. **Southeast Asia and the United Nations,** *American Behavioral Scientist,* V (June 1962), 23—24.

5322 Indian Council of World Affairs. **India and the United Nations.** New York, Manhattan, 1957. xi + 229 p.

5323 Japanese Association of International Law. **Japan and the United Nations.** New York, Manhattan, 1958. 246 p.

5324 Kondapi, C. **Indian Opinion of the United Nations,** *International Organization,* V (November 1951), 709—21.

5325 Kugimoto, H. **UNESCO's Activities in Japan 1951—1954,** *Contemporary Japan,* XXIII (1955), 279—95.

5326 Lall, Arthur. **The Asian Nations and the United Nations,** *International Organization,* XIX (Summer, 1965), 728—48.

5327 Levi, Werner. **China and the United Nations,** *Current History,* XLVII (September 1964), 149—55.

5328 Malik, A. M. **Pakistan and ILO,** *Pakistan Horizon,* VII (June 1954), 47–55.

5329 Misra, K. P. **Succession of States: Pakistan's Membership in the United Nations,** *Canadian Yearbook of International Law,* III (1965), 281–88.

5330 Mohan, Jitendra. **India, Pakistan, Suez and the Commonwealth,** *International Journal,* XV (Summer, 1960), 185–99.

5331 Mudaliar, A. L. **United Nations, Its Specialised Agencies and India's Part Therein,** *Indian Year Book of International Affairs,* I (1953), 35–45.

5332 Nihon, Kokusaiho K. **Japan and the United Nations.** New York, Manhattan, 1958. xv + 246 p.

5333 Nishida, Seiya. **Japan's Activities in the United Nations in 1959,** *Japanese Annual of International Law,* IV (1960), 79–90.

5334 Pillai, P. P. **The ILO and Asia,** *Indian Year Book of International Affairs,* I (1953), 78–87.

5335 Rao, B. Shiva and Kondapi, C. **India and the Korean Crisis,** *India Quarterly,* VII (October-December 1951), 295–314.

5336 Rao, T. S. Rama. **India and the United Nations,** *Indian Year Book of International Affairs,* I (1953), 246–57.

5337 Sato, N. **The United Nations and Japan,** *Contemporary Japan,* XXIII (1955), 605–10.

5338 Setalvad, M. C. **India and the United Nations,** *India Quarterly,* VI (April-June 1951), 107–29.

5339 Trager, Frank N., Wohlgemuth, Patricia, and Kiang, Lu-Yu. **Burma's Role in the United Nations.** New York, Institute of Pacific Relations, 1956. 100 p.

5340 Unni, A. C. C. **Indonesia's Withdrawal from the United Nations,** *Indian Journal of International Law,* V (April 1965), 128—46.

5341 Woodman, Dorothy. **Korea, Formosa and World Peace,** *Political Quarterly,* XXI (October-December 1950), 364—73.

12.2.3 ENGLISH-SPEAKING COMMONWEALTH COUNTRIES

5342 Yokota, Kisaburo and Otaka, Tomoo. **Japan and the United Nations: A Study of the National Policy and Public Attitudes of Japan Towards the United Nations,** *India Quarterly,* XI (January-March 1955), 3—14.

5343 Beloff, Max. **New Dimensions in Foreign Policy: A Study in British Administrative Experience, 1947—59.** New York, Macmillan, 1961. 208 p.

5344 Bishop, Peter V. **Canada's Policy on the Financing of UN Peace-Keeping Operations,** *International Journal,* XX (Autumn, 1965), 463—83.

5345 Carnegie Endowment for International Peace. **Canada and the United Nations.** New York, Manhattan, 1956. 262 p.

5346 Carter, Gwendolen. **The Commonwealth in the United Nations,** *International Organization,* IV (May 1950), 247—60.

5347 Cunningham, J. K. **New Zealand As a Small Power in the United Nations,** *Political Science,* IX (September 1957), 33—47.

5348 Eayrs, James. **Canadian Policy and Opinion During the Suez Crisis,** *International Journal,* XII (Spring, 1957), 97—108.

5349 Fawcett, J. E. S. **The Commonwealth in the United Nations,** *Journal of Commonwealth Political Studies,* I (May 1962), 123—35.

5350 Goodwin, Geoffrey L. **Britain and the United Nations.** New York, Manhattan, 1957. 478 p.

5351 — —. **The Commonwealth and the United Nations,** *International Organization,* XIX (Summer, 1965), 678—94.

5352 Goswami, B. N. **The Commonwealth and the "Uniting For Peace" Resolution: A Study of the Legal Stand of Some Commonwealth Countries,** *International Studies,* III (April 1962), 451—60.

5353 Great Britain, Central Office of Information. **Britain and the United Nations.** London, Curwen, n. d. 92 p.

5354 Groot, E. H. U. de. **Great Britain and the United Nations,** *Year Book of World Affairs,* VIII (1954), 21—45.

5355 Hanning, Hugh. **Britain and the United Nations: Proposals for Peacekeeping Including a Commonwealth Force.** London, Bow, 1964. 8 p.

5356 Harper, Norman and Sissons, David. **Australia and the United Nations.** New York, Manhattan, 1959. xiii + 423 p.

5357 Howell, John M. **The French and South African Walkouts and Domestic Jurisdiction,** *Journal of Politics,* XVIII (February 1956), 95—104.

5358 Institute of Public Administration (London). **United Kingdom Administration and International Organizations.** London, Oxford University Press, 1951. 55 p.

5359 Leifer, Michael. **Australia, Trusteeship and New Guinea,** *Pacific Affairs*, XXXVI (Fall, 1963), 250—64.

5360 McNaught, Kenneth. **Ottawa and Washington Look at the UN,** *Foreign Affairs*, XXXIII (July 1955), 663—78.

5361 Mahmood, Khalid. **Britain and the Suez Crisis,** *Pakistan Horizon*, XV, 2 (1962), 111—28.

5362 Millar, Thomas B. **The Commonwealth and the United Nations,** *International Organization*, XVI (Autumn, 1962), 736—57.

5363 Power, Terry. **New Zealand and the Korean War,** *Political Science*, XVI (September 1964), 52—70.

5364 Rowley, C. D. **The United Nations, Colonialism, and Australia,** *Australian Outlook*, VII (June 1953), 120—28.

5365 Royal Institute of International Affairs. **United Kingdom Administration and International Organizations.** London, Royal Institute of International Affairs, 1951. 55 p.

5366 Sabourin, Louis. **La participation des provinces canadiennes aux organisations internationales,** *Canadian Yearbook of International Law* III (1965), 73—99.

5367 Singh, L. P. **Notes and Memoranda: The Commonwealth and the United Nations Trusteeship of Non-Self-Governing Peoples,** *International Studies*, V (January 1964), 296—303.

5368 Smith, I. Norman. **Security Council Membership — A Challenge to Canada,** *International Journal*, III (Spring, 1948), 111—19.

5369 Soward, F. H. **Canada, The Eleventh General Assembly and Trusteeship,** *International Journal*, XII (Summer, 1957), 167—81.

5370 — —. **The Korean Crisis and the Commonwealth,** *Pacific Affairs*, XXIV (June 1951), 115—30.

5371 Soward, F. H. and McInnis, Edgar, with the assistance of O'Hearn, Walter. **Canada and the United Nations.** New York, Manhattan, 1957. 285 p.

5372 Spry, Graham. **Canada, The United Nations Emergency Force, and the Commonwealth,** *International Affairs*, XXXIII (July 1957) 289—300.

5373 Thomas, Brinley. **Britain and the International Trade Organisation,** *World Affairs*, New Series, II (January 1948), 23—29.

5374 Tomalin, Beth. **Canada at the Opening Sessions of UNO,** *International Journal*, I (July 1946), 243—65.

5375 Western, Maurice. **Canada's Role in the Second Assembly,** *International Journal*, III (Spring, 1948), 120—31.

5376 Wolfsohn, H. **The Evolution of Australia in World Affairs,** *Australian Outlook*, VII (March 1953), 5—21.

12.2.4 LATIN AMERICAN COUNTRIES

5377 Castañeda, Jorge. **Mexico and the United Nations.** New York, Manhattan, 1958. 232 p.

5378 Cohen, Alvin. **ECLA and the Economic Development of Peru,** *Inter-American Economic Affairs*, XVII (Summer, 1963), 3—28.

Part D. — United Nations System

5379 Faust, John R. and Stansifer, Charles L. **Mexican Foreign Policy in the United Nations: The Advocacy of Moderation,** *Southwestern Social Science Quarterly,* XLIV (September 1963), 121–29.

5380 Glick, Edward B. **Cuba and the Fifteenth General Assembly: A Case Study in Regional Disassociation,** *Journal of Inter-American Studies,* VI (April 1964), 235–48.

5381 — —. **Latin America and the Palestine Problem.** New York, Herzl, 1958. viii + 199 p.

5382 — —. **The Vatican, Latin America, and Jerusalem,** *International Organization,* XI (Spring, 1957), 213–19.

5383 Goodrich, Carter. **Bolivia: Test of Technical Assistance,** *Foreign Affairs,* XXXII (April 1954), 473–81.

5384 Harley, J. Eugene. **Latin America and the United Nations,** *World Affairs Quarterly,* XVIII (July 1947), 137–47.

5385 Holte-Castello, Edmundo de. **Colombia in the United Nations,** *Annals of the American Academy of Political and Social Science,* CCLII (July 1947), 66–70.

5386 Hoskins, Alice C. **UNICEF in Central America,** *Annals of the American Academy of Political and Social Science,* CCCXXIX (May 1960), 69–77.

5387 Houston, John A. **Latin America in the United Nations.** New York, Carnegie, 1956. 345 p.

5388 Lepawsky, Albert. **The Bolivian Operation: New Trends in Technical Assistance,** *International Conciliation,* CDLXXIX (March 1952), 103 –40.

5389 Lockwood, Agnes Nelms. **Indians of the Andes: Technical Assistance on the Antiplano,** *International Conciliation,* DVIII (May 1956), 355–431.
Bolivia, Chile, Ecuador, Peru.

5390 Louw, Michael H. H. **The United Nations Program in Brazil,** *Annals of the American Academy of Political and Social Science,* CCCXXIII (May 1959), 129–39.

5391 Neal, Marian. **United Nations Technical Assistance Program in Haiti,** *International Conciliation,* CDLXVII (February 1951), 81–118.

5392 Shaffer, Alice C. **UNICEF in Central America,** *Annals of the American Academy of Political and Social Science,* CCCXXIX (May 1960), 69–77.

5393 Uruguayan Institute of International Law. **Uruguay and the United nations.** New York, Manhattan, 1958. xi + 129 p.

5394 Whitaker, Arthur P. **The Latin-American Bloc,** *The United States and the United Nations,* Franz B. Gross (ed.). Norman, University of Oklahoma Press, 1964, pp. 170–96.

5395 Wood, Bruce and Morales, Minerva M. **Latin America and the United Nations,** *International Organization,* XIX (Summer, 1965), 714–27.

12.2.5 MIDDLE EASTERN COUNTRIES

See also D 7.3.6.2.

5396 Afifi, Mohammed. **The Arabs and the United Nations.** London, Longmans, Green, 1964. xiii + 212 p.

5397 Ataöv, Türkkaya and Gönlübol, Mehmet. **Turkey in the United Nations: A Legal and Political Appraisal.** Ankara, Ajans, 1960. 46 p.

5398 Bentwich, Norman. **The Middle East and the United Nations,** *Middle Eastern Affairs,* II (November 1951), 351—60.

5399 Clapp, Gordon R. **An Approach to Economic Development: A Summary of the Reports of the United Nations Survey Mission for the Middle East,** *International Conciliation,* CDLX (April 1950), 203—17.

5400 Diamond, William. **Activities of the International Bank in the Middle East,** *Middle East Journal,* III (October 1949), 455—60.

5401 Dib, George Mousa. **The Arab Bloc in the UN.** Amsterdam, Djambatan, 1956. 128 p.

5402 Dodd, Norris, E. **A Summary of the Food and Agricultural Organization in the Middle East,** *Middle East Journal,* IV (July 1950), 352—55.

5403 Egyptian Society of International Law. **Egypt and the United Nations.** New York, Manhattan, 1957. xiv + 197 p.

5404 El-Hadi Afifi, Mohamed. **The Arabs and the United Nations.** London, Longmans, Green, 1964. 202 p.

5405 Gönlübol, Mehmet. **Turkish Participation in the United Nations, 1945—1954.** Ankara, Ankara Üniversitesi Basimevi, 1963. vii + 180 p.

5406 Hurewitz, J. C. **The UN and Disimperialism in the Middle East,** *International Organization,* XIX (Summer, 1965), 749—63.

5407 Jerusalem, Hebrew University. **Israel and the United Nations.** New York, Manhattan, 1956. 322 p.

5408 Michaelis, Alfred. **International Bank Activities in the Middle East,** *Middle Eastern Affairs,* VIII (May 1957), 180—85.

5409 Owen, David. **International Technical Aid to the Middle East: The United Nations Family,** *Middle Eastern Affairs,* VII (January 1956), 1–10.

5410 Sharp, Walter R. **The United Nations System in Egypt: A Country Survey of Field Operations,** *International Organization,* X (May 1956), 235–60

5411 University of Ankara, Institute of International Relations. **Turkey and the United Nations.** New York, Manhattan, 1961. ix + 228 p.

12.2.6 SOVIET BLOC COUNTRIES

5412 Allen, Robert Loring. **United Nations Technical Assistance: Soviet and East European Participation,** *International Organization,* XI (Autumn, 1957), 615–34.

5413 Appleton, Sheldon. **Communist China: New World Power,** *Current History,* New Series, XLI (September 1961), 141–45.

5414 Armstrong, John A. **The Soviet Attitude Toward UNESCO,** *International Organization,* VIII (May 1954), 217–33.

5415 Berkes, Ross N. **The Soviet Union in the United Nations,** *Current History,* New Series, XLI (November 1961), 257–61.

5416 Browne, Louis E. **Will the Soviet Union Co-operate with the United Nations?** *Annals of the American Academy of Political and Social Science,* CCXLVI (July 1946), 42–48.

5417 Dallin, Alexander. **The Soviet Union, Arms Control and Disarmament: A Study of Soviet Attitudes.** New York, Columbia University, School of International Affairs, 1964. vii + 282 p.

5418 — —. **The Soviet Union at the United Nations: An Inquiry into Soviet Motives and Objectives.** New York, Praeger, 1962. viii + 244 p.

5419 — —. **The Soviet View of the United Nations,** *International Organization*, XVI (Winter, 1962), 20—36.

5420 Emerson, Rupert and Claude, Inis L., Jr. **The Soviet Union and the United Nations: An Essay in Interpretation,** *International Organization*, VI (February 1952), 1—26.

5421 Fehimović, Zoran. **Yugoslavia and the United Nations,** Radmila Pavlović and Milorad Vučković (trs.). Belgrade, Međunarodna Politika, 1964. 37 p.

5422 Fleming, D. F. **The Soviet Union and Collective Security,** *Journal of Politics*, X (February 1948), 117—30.

5423 Frankel, J. **The Soviet Union and the United Nations,** *Year Book of World Affairs*, VIII (1954), 69—94.

5424 Fuller, C. Dale. **Soviet Policy in the United Nations,** *Annals of the American Academy of Political and Social Science*, CCLXIII (May 1949), 141—51.

5425 Gardner, Richard N. **In Pursuit of World Order.** New York, Praeger, 1964.

Chapter II. USSR.

5426 — —. **The Soviet Union and the United Nations,** *Law and Contemporary Problems*, XXIX (Autumn, 1964), 845—57.

5427 Glick, Edward B. **Cuba and the Fifteenth UN General Assembly: A Case Study in Regional Disassociation,** *Journal of Inter-American Studies*, VI (April 1964), 235—48.

5428 Goodman, Elliot R. **The Cry of National Liberation: Recent Soviet Attitudes Toward National Self-Determination,** *International Organization,* XIV (Winter, 1960), 92—106.

5429 Gordenker, Leon. **The USSR, the United Nations, and the General Welfare,** *World Politics,* XVII (April 1965), 495—502.

5430 Gouré Léon. **The Eastern European Bloc and the United Nations Charter,** *Journal of International Affairs,* III (Spring, 1949), 36—46.

5431 Grzybowski, Kazimierz. **International Organizations from the Soviet Point of View,** *Law and Contemporary Problems,* XXIX (Autumn, 1964), 882—95.

5432 Hazard, John N. **The Soviet Union and the United Nations,** *Yale Law Journal,* LV (August 1946), 1016—35.

5433 Jacobson, Harold Karan. **The Soviet Union, the UN and World Trade,** *Western Political Quarterly,* XI (September 1958), 673—88.

5434 — —. **The USSR and ILO,** *International Organization,* XIV (Summer, 1960), 402—28.

5435 — —. **The USSR and the UN's Economic and Social Activities.** Notre Dame, University of Notre Dame Press, 1963. xviii + 309 p.

5436 Johnson, Joseph E. **The Soviet Union, the United States and International Security,** *International Organization,* III (February 1949), 1—13.

5437 Little, Tom. **Mr. Khrushchev and the Neutrals at the United Nations,** *World Today,* New Series, XVI (December 1960), 510—19.

5438 Maller, Sandor. **Hungary and UNESCO,** *New Hungarian Quarterly,* V (Spring, 1964), 128—33.

Part D. — United Nations System

5439 Masters, Roger. **Russia and the United Nations,** *Yale Review*, LII (Winter, 1963), 176—87.

5440 Morozov, P. D. **Soviet Policy Toward Revision,** *Annals of the American Academy of Political and Social Science*, CCXCVI (November 1954), 157—60.

5441 Mosely, Philip E. **Soviet Policy in the United Nations,** *Academy of Political Science Proceedings*, XXII (January 1947), 136—45.

5442 — —. **The Soviet Union and the United Nations,** *International Organization*, XIX (Summer, 1965), 666—77.

5443 O., A. N. **The Soviet Union and the United Nations,** *World Today*, New Series, IV (January 1948), 9—15.

5444 Olynyk, Stephen D. **Membership of the Soviet Ukraine in the United Nations: Background, Status, and Legal Implications.** Washington, 1959. viii + 168 p.

5445 Osborn, Frederick. **The USSR and the Atom,** *International Organization*, V (August 1951), 480—98.

5446 Pethybridge, Roger. **Soviet Nationals at the United Nations,** *International Relations*, II (April 1965), 709—20 f.

5447 Pitersky, Nikolai A. **A Soviet View of a Disarmed World,** *Toward a Strategy of Peace*, Walter C. Clemens, Jr. (ed.). Chicago, Rand McNally, 1965, pp. 171—90.

5448 Rubinstein, Alvin Z. **Soviet and American Policies in International Economic Organizations,** *International Organization*, XVIII (Winter, 1964), 29—52.

5449 — —. **The Soviet Image of the United Nations,** *Proceedings of the American Philosophical Society,* CVII (April 1963), 132—37.

5450 — —. **The Soviets in International Organization.** Princeton, Princeton University Press, 1964. xix +380 p.

5451 — —. **Soviet Policy in ECAFE: A Case Study of Soviet Behavior in International Economic Organization,** *International Organization,* XII (Autumn, 1958), 459—72.

5452 — —. **Soviet Policy Toward Under-Developed Areas in the Economic and Social Council,** *International Organization,* IX (May 1955), 232—43.

5453 — —. **The United States, the Soviet Union, and Atoms-for-Peace: Background to the Establishment of the United Nations International Atomic Energy Agency,** *World Affairs Quarterly,* XXX (April 1959), 46—62.

5454 Rudzinski, Aleksander W. **The Influence of the United Nations on Soviet Policy,** *International Organization,* V (May 1951), 282—99.

5455 Salvin, Marina. **Soviet Policy Toward Disarmament,** *International Conciliation,* CDXXVIII (February 1947), 43—111.

Appendix contains documents.

5456 Schapiro, L. B. **Soviet Participation in International Institutions,** *Year Book of World Affairs,* III (1949), 205—40.

5457 Steiner, H. Arthur. **Communist China in the World Community,** *International Conciliation,* DXXXIII (May 1961), 389—454.

5458 Stoessinger, John George. **The United Nations and the Super Powers: United States-Soviet Interaction at the United Nations.** New York, Random House, 1965. xvii + 206 p.

5459 Yemelyanov, V. S. **Atomic Energy for Peace: The U. S. S. R. and International Cooperation,** *Foreign Affairs,* XXXVIII (April 1960), 465–75.

12.2.7 UNITED STATES

See also D 9.4.

5460 Appleton, Sheldon. **The Eternal Triangle? Communist China, the United States and the United Nations.** East Lansing, Michigan State University Press, 1961, 264 p.

5461 Armstrong, Elizabeth. **The United States and Non-Self-Governing Territories,** *International Journal,* III (Autumn, 1948), 327–33.

5462 Bernstein, Edward M. **The United States and the International Monetary Fund,** *Public Policy,* XI (1961), 281–93.

5463 Blaisdell, Donald C. **Coordination of American Security Policy at the United Nations,** *International Organization,* II (September 1948), 469–77.

5464 — —. **United States Representation at International Organizations, Geneva,** *Public Administration Review,* XIV (Spring, 1954), 119–24.

5465 Bloomfield, Lincoln Palmer. **American Policy Toward the UN – Some Bureaucratic Reflections,** *International Organization,* XII (Winter, 1958), 1–16.

5466 — —. **The Department of State and the United Nations,** *International Organization,* IV (August 1950), 400–11.

5467 — —. **The United Nations and U. S. Foreign Policy,** Boston, Little, Brown. 1960. 276 p.

5468 — —. **The United Nations in Crisis: The Role of the United Nations in United States Foreign Policy,** *Daedalus,* CXI (Fall, 1962), 749–65.

5469 Booth, D. A. **The United Nations, the United States and the International Civil Service,** *Revue Internationale des Sciences Administratives,* XXI, 4 (1955), 703–40.

5470 Boyer, William W. and Akra, Neylan. **The United States and the Admission of Communist China,** *Political Science Quarterly,* LXXVI (September 1961), 332–53.

5471 Brown, Benjamin H. (ed.). **The U. S. Stake in the UN: Problems of United Nations Charter Review.** New York, Columbia University, Graduate School of Business, American Assembly, 1954. 139 p.

5472 Brown, Benjamin and Johnson, Joseph E. **The U. S. and the U. N.** New York, Foreign Policy Association, 1954. 62 p.

5473 Brown, William A. **The United States and the Restoration of World Trade: An Analysis and Appraisal of the ITO Charter and the General Agreement on Tariffs and Trade.** Washington, Brookings, 1950. xiii + 572 p.

5474 Buehrig, Edward H. **The United States, the United Nations and Bi-Polar Politics,** *International Organization,* IV (November 1950), 573–84.

5475 Cohen, Benjamin V. **The Impact of the United Nations on United States Foreign Policy,** *International Organization,* V (May 1951), 274–81.

5476 Cohen, M. **The United States and the United Nations Secretariat: A Preliminary Appraisal,** *McGill Law Journal,* I (Autumn, 1953), 169–98.

Part D. — *United Nations System*

5477 Corbett, P. E. **National Interest, International Organization, and American Foreign Policy,** *World Politics,* V (October 1952), 46—65.

5478 Cory, Robert H., Jr. **Communicating Information and Ideas About the United Nations to the American People.** New York, Carnegie, 1955. 82 p.

5479 — —. **The Role of Public Opinion in United States Policies Towards the United Nations,** *International Organization,* XI (Spring 1957), 220—27.

5480 Courlander, Harold. **Shaping Our Times.** New York, Oceana, 1960.
Chapter XI.

5481 Dangerfield, Royden. **The United States, the United Nations, and the Emerging Nations,** *American Government Annual,* V (1963/64), 131—55.

5482 Diebold, William, Jr. and Bidwell, Percy, W. **The United States and the International Trade Organization,** *International Conciliation,* CDXLIX (March 1949), 187—239.

5483 Donovan, William J. **American Foreign Policy and the United Nations,** *Academy of Political Science Proceedings,* XXV (January 1953), 256—60.

5484 Eichelberger, Clark M. **UN: The First Twenty Years.** New York, Harper, 1965.
Chapter IX.

5485 Elliott, William Y. **Applied Ethics: The United Nations and the United States,** *The United States and the United Nations,* Franz B. Gross (ed.). Norman, University of Oklahoma Press, 1964, pp. 318—40.

5486 Fairchild, Muir S. **America's Military Role in the United Nations,** *Academy of Political Science Proceedings,* XXII (January 1947), 230–35.

5487 Fedder, Edwin H. **United States Loyalty Procedures and the Recruitment of International Personnel,** *Western Political Quarterly,* XV (December 1962), 705–12.

5488 Fleming, D. F. **The United States in the United Nations,** *Annals of the American Academy of Political and Social Science,* CCLXXVIII (September 1951), 73–82.

5489 Garcia, Antonio. **United States Commitments to UNESCO and Federal Control of Education,** *Southwestern Social Science Quarterly,* XXIX (September 1948), 119–24.

5490 Gardner, Richard N. **In Pursuit of World Order.** New York, Praeger, 1964.

Chapter I.

5491 Goodrich, Leland M. **American National Interests and the Responsibilities of United Nations Membership,** *International Organization,* VI (August 1952), 369–80.

5492 Gordenker, Leon. **U. S. and U. N.: Contributions to a "Great Debate"; A Review,** *Journal of Conflict Resolution,* VI (September 1962), 269–76.

5493 Gross, Ernest A. **The United States National Interest and the United Nations,** *The Quest for Peace,* Andrew W. Cordier and Wilder Foote (eds.). New York, Columbia University Press, 1965, pp. 83–98.

5494 Gross, Franz B. (ed.). **The United States and the United Nations.** Norman, University of Oklahoma Press, 1964. x + 356 p.

5495 Gross, Franz B. **The United States National Interest and the United Nations,** *The United States and the United Nations,* Franz B. Gross (ed.). Norman, University of Oklahoma Press, 1964, pp. 22—41.
Reprinted from *Orbis,* Summer, 1963.

5496 Gross, Leo. **Charter of the United Nations and the Lodge Reservations,** *American Journal of International Law,* XLI (July 1947), 531—54.

5497 Haviland, H. Field, Jr. **The United Nations: Effects on American Government,** *Current History,* New Series, XXII (January 1952), 13—18.

5498 — —. **The United States and the United Nations,** *International Organization,* XIX (Summer, 1965), 643—65.

5499 Heathcote, N. **American Policy Towards the UN Operation in the Congo,** *Australian Outlook,* XVIII (April 1964), 77—97.

5500 Higgins, Benjamin. **United Nations and U. S. Foreign Economic Policy.** Homewood, Irwin, 1962. viii + 235 p.

5501 Hiss, Donald. **United States Participation in the United Nations.** New York, Commission to Study the Organization of Peace, 1947. 47 p.

5502 Hoffman, Paul G. **The United Nations and the Bricker Amendment,** *World Affairs Quarterly,* XXIV (January 1954), 348—56.

5503 Holcombe, Arthur N. **The United Nations and American Foreign Policy,** *University of Illinois Bulletin,* LV (October 1957), 3—22.

5504 Hula, Erich. **The United States and the United Nations,** *Beyond the Cold War: Essays on American Foreign Policy in a Changing World Environment,* Robert A. Goldwin (ed.). Chicago, Rand McNally, 1963, pp. 216—35.

5505 Hyde, James N. **United States Participation in the United Nations,** *International Organization,* X (February 1956), 22–34.

5506 Hyde, Louis K., Jr. **The United States and the United Nations: Promoting the Public Welfare; Examples of American Cooperation, 1945–1955.** New York, Manhattan, 1960. xiv + 249 p.

5507 Johnson, Joseph E. **The Soviet Union, the United States and International Security,** *International Organization,* III (February 1949), 1–13.

5508 Key, David McKendree. **United States Planning for Charter Review,** *Annals of the American Academy of Political and Social Science,* CCXCVI (November 1954), 151–55.

5509 Lawson, Ruth C. **The United Nations: Our Policies Succeed,** *Current History,* New Series, XXII (January 1952), 19–25.

5510 — —. **The United States and the United Nations,** *Current History,* New Series, XXVIII (January 1955), 51–56.

5511 Liska, Jiri. **Multiple Equilibrium and the American National Interest in International Organizaton,** *Harvard Studies in International Affairs,* (February 1954), 35–50.

5512 Little, Herbert S. **The United States, the Atlantic Pact, and the United Nations,** *Institute of World Affairs Proceedings,* XXVII (1949), 128–36.

5513 Lyons, Gene M. **American Policy and the United Nations Program for Korean Reconstruction,** *International Organization,* XII (Spring, 1958), 180–92.

5514 McNaught, Kenneth. **Ottawa and Washington Look at the UN,** *Foreign Affairs,* XXXIII (July 1955), 663–78.

Part D. — United Nations System

5515 Mangone, Gerard J. **The United Nations and United States Foreign Policy,** *Texas Quarterly*, VI (Spring, 1963), 11–18.

5516 Marcy, Carl and Wilcox, Francis O. **Congress and the United Nations,** *Foreign Policy Reports*, XXVII (May 15, 1951), 50–60.

5517 Mishler, E. **The Peace Movement and the Foreign Policy Process,** *International Conflict and Behavioral Science*, Roger Fisher (ed.). New York, Basic Books, 1964, pp. 257–65.

5518 Neal, Marian. **United States Attitude Towards Charter Review,** *India Quarterly*, XI (October-December 1955), 354–64.

5519 Popper, David H. **American Security and the United Nations,** *World Affairs Quarterly*, XXV (April 1954), 9–32.

Published also in *Institute of World Affairs Proceedings*, 1953.

5520 Rajan, M. S. **United States Attitude Toward Domestic Jurisdiction in the United Nations,** *International Organization*, XIII (Winter, 1959), 19–37.

5521 Richardson, Channing B. **The United States Mission to the United Nations,** *International Organization*, VII (February 1953), 22–34.

5522 Riggs, Robert E. **Politics in the United Nations: Study of United States Influence in the General Assembly.** Urbana, University of Illinois Press, 1958. 208 p.

5523 Robinson, J. William. **The United Nations: Instrumentality of United States Foreign Policy,** *World Affairs Quarterly*, XXIII (January 1953), 394–403.

Published also in *Institute of Woreld Affairs Proceedings*, 1952.

5524 Rubinstein, Alvin Z. **Soviet and American Policies in International Economic Organizations,** *International Organization*, XVIII (Winter, 1964), 29–52.

5525 — —. **The United States, the Soviet Union, and Atoms-for-Peace: Background to the Establishment of the United Nations International Atomic Energy Agency,** *World Affairs Quarterly,* XXX (April 1959), 46–62.

5526 Scott, William A. and Withey, Stephen B. **The United States and the United Nations: The Public View.** New York, Manhattan, 1958. 314 p.

5527 Sharp, Walter R. **American Foreign Relations Within an Organized World Framework,** *American Political Science Review,* XXXVIII (October 1944), 931–44.

5528 Smithies, Arthur. **The U. S., the U. N. and the Underdeveloped World,** *Orbis,* II (Fall, 1958), 337–55.

5529 Steiner, H. Arthur. **United States' Role in the United Nations,** *Institute of World Affairs Proceedings,* XXIII (1946), 173–76.

5530 Stoessinger, John George. **The United Nations and the Super Powers: United States-Soviet Interaction at the United Nations.** New York, Random House, 1965. xvii + 206 p.

5531 Stromberg, Roland N. **Collective Security and American Foreign Policy: From the League of Nations to NATO.** New York, Praeger, 1963. 301 p.

5532 Summers, Robert E. (ed.). **The United States and International Organizations.** New York, Wilson, 1952. 194 p.

5533 Surr, J. V. **American Taxation of the United Nations,** *Harvard International Law Club Journal,* V (Spring, 1964), 195–208.

5534 Sweetser, Arthur. **The United States, the United Nations and the League of Nations,** *International Conciliation,* CDXVIII (February 1946), 51–59.

5535 Swift, Richard N. **United States Leadership in the United Nations,** *Western Political Quarterly,* XI (June 1958), 183–94.

Part D. — United Nations System

5536 Taylor, George Edward and Cashman, Ben. **The New United Nations: A Reappraisal of United States Policies.** Washington, American Enterprise Institute for Public Policy Research, 1965. vi +117 p.

5537 Thompson, Carol L. **The United Nations: As We Planned It,** *Current History*, New Series, XXII (January 1952), 2—8.

5538 Tipton, John B. **Participation of the United States in the International Labor Organization.** Champaign, University of Illinois, Institute of Labor and Industrial Relations, 1959. iv + 150 p.

5539 Uhl, Alexander. **The U. S. and the UN: Partners for Peace.** Washington, Public Affairs Institute, 1962. iv + 81 p.

5540 United States, Department of State, Bureau of United Nations Affairs. **International Organizations in Which the United States Participates, 1949.** Washington, 1950. viii + 335 p.

5541 Van Alstyne, Richard W. **The United States: One World,** *Current History*, XI (December 1946), 453—58.

5542 Van Wagenen, Richard W. **American Defense Officials' Views on the United Nations,** *Western Political Quarterly*, XIV (March 1961), 104—19.

5543 Watkins, James T., IV. **To What Extent Should America Base Her Security on International Organization and Alliances?** *Institute of World Affairs Proceedings*, XXXIV (1958), 209—17.

5544 ———. **United States Leadership and Collective Security: The Meaning of Korea,** *Institute of World Affairs Proceedings*, XXIX (1953), 191—99.

5545 Wilcox, Francis O. **United States Policy in the United Nations,** *The United States and the United Nations*, Francis O. Wilcox and H. Field Haviland, Jr. (eds.). Baltimore, Johns Hopkins Press, 1961, pp. 151—78.

5546 Wilcox, Francis O. and Haviland, H. Field, Jr. (eds.). **The United States and the United Nations.** Baltimore, Johns Hopkins Press, 1961. 188 p.

5547 Wiley, Alexander. **The Senate and the Review of the United Nations Charter,** *Annals of the American Academy of Political and Social Science,* CCXCVI (November 1954), 156—62.

5548 Winkler, Henry R. **The United States and the United Nations,** *Year Book of World Affairs,* VIII (1954), 46—68.

5549 Wolfers, Arnold. **The United States in Search of a Peace Policy,** *International Affairs,* XXIII (January 1947), 20—26.

Comments by Mander, Peel, Eliot, Keighley-Bell, Raffety, Haig.

5550 Wright, Quincy. **Policies for Strengthening the United Nations,** *The Liberal Papers,* James Roosevelt (ed.). Chicago, Quadrangle, 1962, pp. 313—40.

5551 — —. **Problems of Stability and Progress in International Relations.** Berkeley, University of California Press, 1954.

Chapter III.

12.2.8 WESTERN EUROPEAN COUNTRIES

5552 Belin, Jacqueline, **La Suisse et les Nations Unies.** New York, Manhattan, 1956. 139 p.

5553 Black, C. E. **Greece and the United Nations,** *Political Science Quarterly,* LXIII (December 1948), 551—68.

5554 Calogéropoulos-Stratis, S. In collaboration with Argyropoulo, P. A., Castanos, B. and Sidjanski, D. **La Grèce et les Nations Unies.** New York, Manhattan, 1957. xiii + 190 p.

5555 Chamberlin, Waldo. **The North Atlantic Bloc in the UN General Assembly,** *Orbis,* I (Winter, 1958), 459–73.

5556 Duroselle, Jean-Baptiste. **France and the United Nations,** *International Organization,* XIX (Summer, 1965), 695–713.

5557 Fischer, Georges. **France and the Proposed Revision of the UN Charter,** *India Quarterly,* XI (October-December 1955), 365–75.

5558 Forster, Kent. **Finland's Policy in the United Nations and the Paasikivi Line,** *Journal of Central European Affairs,* XXI (January 1962), 465–76.

5559 Fox, Annette Baker. **The Small States of Western Europe in the United Nations,** *International Organization,* XIX (Summer, 1965), 774–88.

5560 Freymond, Jacques. **Switzerland's Position in the World Peace Structure,** *Political Science Quarterly,* LXVII (December 1952), 521–33.

5561 Glick, Edward B. **The Vatican, Latin America, and Jerusalem,** *International Organization,* XI (Spring, 1957), 213–19.

5562 Gross, Franz B. **Western Europe and the United Nations,** *The United States and the United Nations,* Franz B. Gross (ed.). Norman, University of Oklahoma, 1964, pp. 197–225.

5563 Habicht, Max. **The Special Position of Switzerland in International Affairs,** *International Affairs,* XXIX (October 1953), 457–63.

5564 Haekkerup, Per. **Scandinavia's Peace-Keeping Forces for the UN,** *Foreign Affairs,* XLII (July 1964), 675–81.

5565 Houston, John A. **The United Nations and Spain,** *Journal of Politics,* XIV (November 1952), 683–709.

5566 Howell, John M. **The French and South African Walkouts and Domestic Jurisdiction,** *Journal of Politics,* XVIII (February 1956), 95—104.

5567 L'Institut Royal des Relations Internationales (Brussels). **La Belgique et les Nations Unies.** New York, Manhattan, 1958. xi + 372 p.

5568 Italian Society for International Organization (Rome). **Italy and the United Nations.** New York, Manhattan, 1959. 208 p.

5569 Lerner, Daniel and Kramer, Marguerite N. **French Elite Perspective on the United Nations,** *International Organization,* XVII (Winter, 1963), 54—75.

5570 Loridan, Walter. **Belgium and the United Nations,** *Annals of the American Academy of Political and Social Science,* CCXLVII (September 1946), 165—70.

5571 Martelli, George. **Portugal and the United Nations,** *International Affairs,* XL (July 1964), 453—65.

5572 Rappard, William E. **The United Nations and Switzerland,** *Annals of the American Academy of Political and Social Science,* CCXLVI (July 1946), 64—71.

5573 Sørensen, Max and Haagerup, Niels J. **Denmark and the United Nations.** New York, Manhattan, 1956. xi + 154 p.

5574 Svennevig, T. P. **The Scandinavian Bloc in the UN,** *Social Research,* XXII (Spring, 1955), 39—56.

5575 Swedish Institute of International Affairs. **Sweden and the United Nations.** New York, Manhattan, 1956. 515 p.

5576 Zemanek, Karl. **Neutral Austria in the United Nations,** *International Organization,* XV (Summer, 1961), 408—22.

Part E.
REGIONAL INTERNATIONAL ORGANIZATIONS

Part E. — *Regional International Organization*

However difficult it may be to define analytically the boundaries of a group of states constituting a region, one characteristic is shared by regional international organizations: they do not admit as members states perceived to lie outside a certain geographically, culturally or historically associated group of peoples and countries. The "regions" delineated below are those which have proved in practice most successful in forming such regional associations.

1. GENERAL BIBLIOGRAPHIES AND DOCUMENTS

See A 3.4.1. and A 5.4.

2. GENERAL DISCUSSIONS

See also A 4.4.

5577 Alexandrowicz, Charles Henry. **International Economic Organizations.** London, Stevens, 1952. xii + 263 p.

5578 — —. **World Economic Agencies: Law and Practice.** London, Stevens, 1962. xvi + 310 p.

5579 American Council on Public Affairs (ed.). **Regionalism and World Federation.** Washington, American Council on Public Affairs, 1944. 162 p.

5580 Armstrong, Hamilton Fish. **Regional Pacts: Strong Points or Storm Cellars?** *Foreign Affairs,* XXVII (April 1949), 351–68.

5581 Balassa, Bela. **The Theory of Economic Intergration.** Homewood, Irwin, 1961. 304 p.

5582 Ball, M. Margaret and Killough, Hugh B. **International Relations.** New York, Ronald, 1956.
Chapter XXII.

Part E. — *Regional International Organization*

5583 Brassert J. E. **Power Politics Versus Political Ecology,** *Political Science Quarterly*, LXXI (December 1956), 553–68.

5584 Buell, Raymond Leslie. **International Relations.** New York, Holt, 1929.
Chapter X.

5585 Carr, Edward Hallett. **Nationalism and After.** London, Macmillan, 1945. 76 p.
Foresees a regional nationalism.

5586 Cheever, Daniel S. and Haviland, H. Field, Jr. **Organizing for Peace.** Boston, Houghton, Mifflin, 1954.
Chapter XXVII.

5587 Coolidge, Archibald Cary. **The Grouping of Nations,** *Foreign Affairs*, V (January 1927), 175–88.

5588 Coyle, David Cushman. **The United Nations and How It Works.** New York, Columbia University Press, 1966.
Chapter VIII.

5589 Dell, Sidney S. **Trade Blocs and Common Markets.** New York, Knopf, 1963. 384 p.

5590 Deutsch, Karl W. **Supranational Organizations in the 1960's,** *Journal of Common Market Studies*, I (May 1963), 212–18.

5591 Elliott, Randle. **Regional Dynamics in World Affairs,** *Annals of the American Academy of Political and Social Science*, CCLXIV (July 1949), 31–38.

5592 Friedmann, Wolfgang Gaston. **The Crisis of the National State.** New York, Macmillan, 1943. 197 p.
Argument for supranational regionalism.

Part E. — Regional International Organization

5593 — —. **An Introduction to World Politics.** 2d ed. London, Macmillan, 1952.

Chapter II.

5594 Furniss, Edgar S., Jr. **A Re-Examination of Regional Arrangements,** *Journal of International Affairs,* IX (May 1955), 79—89.

5595 Glynn, John J. **EEC — EFTA — COMECON — CAC — LAFTA,** *International Manual on the European Economic Community,* H. K. Junckerstorff (ed.). St. Louis, Saint Louis University Press, 1963, pp. 21—50.

5596 Goodspeed, Stephen S. **The Nature and Function of International Organization.** New York, Oxford University Press, 1963.

Chapter XVI.

5597 Gordon, Lincoln. **Economic Regionalism Reconsidered,** *World Politics,* XIII (January 1961), 231—53.

5598 Gras, N. S. B. **Regionalism and Nationalism,** *Foreign Affairs,* VII (April 1929), 454—67.

5599 Green, Elizabeth and Handy, Craighill. **Regionalism and the New Political Philosophy,** *Social Forces,* XXIV (March 1946), 267—73.

5600 Griffin, Keith and French-Davis, Ricardo. **Customs Unions and Latin American Integration,** *Journal of Common Market Studies,* IV (October 1965), 1—21.

Presents a theory of economic integration.

5601 Haas, Ernst B. **The Challenge of Regionalism,** *International Organization,* XII (Autumn, 1958), 440—58.

5602 — —. **Regional Integration and National Policy,** *International Conciliation,* DXIII (May 1957), 381—442.

5603 Haas, Ernst B. and Whiting, Allen S. **Dynamics of International Relations.** New York, McGraw-Hill, 1956.

Chapter XXI.

5604 Haberler, Gottfried von. **The Political Economy of Regional or Continental Blocs,** *Postwar Economic Problems,* Seymour E. Harris (ed.). New York, McGraw-Hill, 1943, pp. 325—44.

5605 Hadow, Robert Henry. **A British View of Regionalism,** *International Conciliation,* CDXIX (March 1946), 158—63.

5606 Hartmann, Frederick H. **The Relations of Nations.** 3d ed. New York, Macmillan, 1967.

Chapter XV.

5607 Hill, Norman L. **International Organization.** New York, Harper, 1952.

Chapter IV.

5608 — —. **International Politics.** New York, Harper and Row, 1963.

Chapter XVII.

5609 Hitchner, Dell G. **The Function of Regionalism,** *Institute of World Affairs Proceedings* XXXVI (1960), 177—84.

5610 Jacob, Philip E. and Atherton, Alexine L. **Dynamics of International Organization.** Homewood, Dorsey, 1964.

Chapters V, VI, XV.

5611 Joyce, James Avery. **World in the Making.** New York, Schuman, 1953.

Chapter XI.

5612 van Kleffens, E. N. **Regionalism and Political Pacts,** *American Journal of International Law*, XLIII (October 1949), 666–78.

A definition of regionalism in relation to NATO; antecedents of regionalism.

5613 Lahnman, Werner J. **The Concept of Raum and the Theory of Regionalism,** *American Sociological Review*, IX (October 1944), 445–62.

5614 Leonard, L. Larry. **International Organization.** New York, McGraw-Hill, 1951.

Chapter XVII.

5615 — —. **UNRRA and the Concept of Regional International Organization,** *Iowa Law Review*, XXXI (May 1945), 489–514.

5616 Lester, Sydney. **Structure of World Order in Terms of Regional Functional Organizations,** *Social Forces*, XXIX (October 1950), 52–56.

5617 L'Huillier, Fernand. **Conditions de la coopération économique,** *Les institutions internationales et transnationales*, Fernand L'Huillier (ed.). Paris, Presses Universitaires, 1961, pp. 175–80.

5618 Liang, Yuen-li. **Regional Arrangements and International Security,** *Transactions* (Grotius Society), XXXI (1945), 216–31.

5619 Lleras Camargo, Alberto. **Regionalism and the International Community,** *Perspectives on Peace*, Carnegie Endowment for International Peace (ed.). New York, Praeger, 1960, pp. 107–19.

5620 Lundberg, George A. **Regionalism, Science, and the Peace Settlement,** *Social Forces*, XXI (December 1942), 131–37.

5621 Mackay, Ronald William Gordon. **You Can't Turn the Clock Back.** Chicago, Ziff-Davis, 1948. 367 p.

Part E. — Regional International Organization

5622 Mander, Linden A. **Foundations of Modern World Society.** Rev. ed. Stanford, Stanford University Press, 1947.

Chapter III.

5623 Mangone, Gerard J. **A Short History of International Organization.** New York, McGraw-Hill, 1954.

Chapter VIII.

5624 May, Stacy. **Regional Economic Accords and World Development,** *South Asia Pacific Crisis,* Margaret Grant (ed.). New York, Dodd, Mead, 1964, pp. 201–20.

5625 Moore, Harry Estill. **Regionalism and Permanent Peace,** *Social Forces,* XXIII (October 1944), 15–19.

5626 — —. **What Is Regionalism?** Chapel Hill, University of North Carolina Press, 1937. 16 p.

5627 Morgner, Aurelius. **The Economics of International Integration,** *Institute of World Affairs Proceedings,* XXXIX (1963), 27–37.

5628 Myers, Denys. **Handbook of the League of Nations.** Boston, World Peace Foundation, 1935.

Chapter IX.

5629 Orué y Arregui, José Ramon de. **Le régionalisme dans l'organisation internationale,** *Recueil des Cours,* LIII (1935), 7–94.

5630 Padelford, Norman J. **Recent Developments in Regional Organizations,** *American Society of International Law Proceedings,* XLIX (1955), 23–41.

Comments by J. W. Bishop, Jr., K. Steiner, A. V. Freeman, and R. R. Baxter.

5631 Padelford, Norman J. and Lincoln, George A. **International Politics.** New York, Macmillan, 1954.

Chapter XXI.

5632 Palmer, Norman D. and Perkins, Howard C. **International Relations.** 2d ed. Boston, Houghton, Mifflin, 1957.

Chapter XX.

5633 Panikkar, K. M. **Regionalism and World Security,** *India Quarterly,* II (April-June 1946), 120—23.

5634 Panikkar, K. M.; Krishnamachari, V. T.; Evatt, H. V.; Santhanam, K.; Baqai, I. H.; Johnson, G. A.; Canyes Santacana, Manuel S. **Regionalism and Security.** Bombay, Oxford University Press, 1948. vi + 73 p.

5635 Parmelee, Maurice. **Geo-Economic Regionalism and World Federation.** New York, Exposition Press, 1949. 137 p.

5636 Pope, James R. **Regional Development As a Dynamic Force,** *Journal of Politics,* V (February 1943), 41—47.

5637 Potter, Pitman B. **Universalism vs. Regionalism in International Organization,** *American Political Science Review,* XXXVII (October 1943), 850—62.

5638 Ramani, R. **Regional Legal Institutions As Instruments of Development,** *South Asia Pacific Crisis,* Margaret Grant (ed.). New York, Dodd, Mead, 1964, pp. 189—200.

5639 Rich, S. Grover, Jr. **Power, Regionalism, and Empire,** *Institute of World Affairs Proceedings,* XXVIII (1952), 42—48.

5640 Rienow, Robert. **Contemporary International Politics.** New York, Crowell, 1961.

Chapters XVII, XVIII.

5641 Ropke, Wilheim. **International Order and Economic Integration.** Dordrecht, Holland, Reidel, 1960. viii + 276 p.

5642 Russell, Frank M. **Theories of International Relations.** New York, Appleton-Century, 1936.

Chapter XX.

5643 Schleicher, Charles P. **International Relations.** Englewood Cliffs, Prentice-Hall, 1962.

Chapter IX.

5644 Schuman, Frederick L. **Regionalism and Spheres of Influence,** *Peace, Security, and the United Nations,* Hans J. Morgenthau (ed.). Chicago, University of Chicago Press, 1945, pp. 83—106.

5645 Schwarzenberger, Georg. **Power Politics.** 3d ed. London, Stevens, 1964.

Chapter XXXV.

5646 SEATO. **Collective Security: Shield of Freedom.** 2d ed. Foreword by Pote Sarasin. Bangkok, SEATO, 1963, 164 p.

5647 Spate, O. H. K. **"Region" As a Term of Art,** *Orbis,* I (Fall, 1957), 343—51.

5648 Spraos, J. **The Conditions for a Trade-Creating Customs Union,** *Economic Journal,* LXXIV (March 1964), 101—9.

Part E. — Regional International Organization

5649 Steinberg, Dand J. **New Forces and Old Impulses in a Changing World Economy,** *Atlantic Community Quarterly,* III (Spring, 1965), 76—92.

5650 Stoessinger, John. **The Might of Nations.** New York, Random House, 1962.

Chapter XI.

5651 Strausz-Hupé, Robert. **Regionalism in World Politics,** *International Conciliation,* CDXIX (March 1946), 117—19.

5652 Strausz-Hupé, Robert and Possony, Stefan T. **International Relations in the Age of Conflict Between Democracy and Dictatorship.** New York, McGraw-Hill, 1954.

Chapter XXIX.

5653 Streeten, Paul. **Economic Integration: Aspects and Problems.** Leyden, Sijthoff, 1961. 150 p.

5654 Talbott, E. Guy. **The Need for World Organization,** *World Affairs Quarterly,* XI (October 1940), 287—95.

Contains a listing of historic precedents beginning with the Achaean League through the British Commonwealth, as well as a listing of historic proposals for world organization.

5655 Tornudd, Klaus. **Soviet Attitudes Toward Non-Military Regional Cooperation.** 2d ed. Helsinki, Societas Scientiarum Fennica, 1963. 324 p.

5656 Vandenbosch, Amry and Hogan, Willard N. **Toward World Order.** New York, McGraw-Hill, 1963.

Chapters XV, XVI.

Part E. — Regional International Organization

5657 Vanek, Jaroslav. **General Equilibrium of International Discrimination: The Case of Customs Unions.** Cambridge, Harvard University Press, 1965. ix + 234 p.

5658 Watkins, James T., IV. **Regionalism and Plans for Post-War Reconstruction: The First Three Years,** *Social Forces,* XXI (May 1943), 379–89.

5659 Wright, Quincy. **The History of Regional Arrangements,** *Regional Arrangements for Security and the United Nations,* Commission to Study the Organization of Peace (ed.). New York, Commission to Study the Organization of Peace, 1953, pp. 36–41.

5660 — —. **Regional Arrangements,** *Charter Review Conference: Ninth Report and Papers Presented to the Commission,* Commission to Study the Organization of Peace (ed.). New York, Commission to Study the Organization of Peace, 1955, pp. 176–82.

5661 Wurtele, Allan Ramsey. **Continentalism: For Enduring Peace.** New Orleans, Pelican, 1944. 234 p.

5662 Yalem, Ronald J. **Regionalism and the World Order,** *International Affairs,* XXXVIII (October 1962), 460–71.

5663 — —. **Regionalism and World Order.** Washington, Public Affairs Press, 1965. vi + 160 p.

3. REGIONALISM IN RELATION TO THE UNITED NATIONS SYSTEM

See also E 7.3.2. and E 8.1.2.

5664 Ago, R. **Comunità internazionale universale e comunità internazionale particolari,** *Comunità Internazionale,* II (April 1950), 195—202.

5665 Aranha, Oswaldo. **Regional Systems and the Future of UN,** *Foreign Affairs,* XXVI (April 1948), 415—20.

5666 Ascoli, Max. **The Future of the UN,** *Reporter,* XXV (October 26, 1961), 21—23.

5667 Bebr, Gerhard. **Regional Organization: A United Nations Problem,** *American Journal of International Law,* XLIX (January 1955), 166—84.

Relation of regionalism to the UN Charter; examination of treaties setting up early regional organizations.

5668 Berkes, Ross N. **Do Regional Pacts Violate the Spirit of the United Nations? NATO As Case Study,** *World Affairs Quarterly,* XXIV (July 1953), 151—65.

5669 Bowett, D. W. **Collective Self-Defense Under the Charter of the United Nations,** *British Yearbook of International Law,* XXXII (1955—56), 130—61.

5670 Boyd, Andrew and Metson, William. **Atlantic Pact, Commonwealth and United Nations.** London, Hutchinson, 1949. 100 p.

5671 Burton, J. W. **Regionalism, Functionalism, and the United Nations,** *Australian Outlook,* XV (April 1961), 73—87.

Part E. — *Regional International Organization*

5672 Canyes Santacana, Manuel. **The Inter-American System and the United Nations Organization,** *Regionalism and Security*, K. M. Panikkar, V. T. Krishnamachari, H. V. Evatt, K. Santhanam, I. H. Baqai, G. A. Johnson, Manuel Canyes Santacana. Bombay, Oxford University Press, 1948, pp. 57–73.

5673 Commission to Study the Organization of Peace. **Collective Self-Defense Under the United Nations: Memorandum and Draft Treaty for Implementation of Article 51.** New York, Commission to Study the Organization of Peace, 1948. 18 p.

Contains the Commission's sixth report.

5674 — —. **Regional Arrangements for Security and the United Nations.** New York, Commission to Study the Organization of Peace, 1953. 144 p.

Contains the Commission's eighth report.

5675 Etzioni, Amitai. **The Hard Way to Peace.** New York, Collier, 1962.

Chapter VIII.

5676 Gibson, John S. **Article 51 of the Charter of the United Nations,** *India Quarterly*, XIII (April-June 1957), 121–37.

5677 Goodrich, Leland M. **Regionalism and the United Nations,** *Journal of International Affairs*, III (Spring, 1949), 5–20.

Condensed in *Academy of Political Science Proceedings*, May 1949.

5678 Goodspeed, Stephen S. **The United Nations and Regionalism,** *Problems in International Relations*, Andrew Gyorgy and Hubert S. Gibbs (eds.). 2d ed. Englewood Cliffs, Prentice-Hall, 1962, pp. 309–42.

5679 Haas, Ernst B. **Regionalism, Functionalism, and Universal International Organization,** *World Politics*, VII (January 1956), 238–63.

Part E. — *Regional International Organization*

5680 Haldermaw, J. W. **Regional Enforcement Measures and the United Nations,** *Georgetown Law Journal,* LII (Fall, 1963), 89—118.

5681 Hindaman, Wilbert L. **Regionalism and the United Nations,** *Institute of World Affairs Proceedings,* XXIV (1948), 167—73.

5682 Krezdorn, Franz J. **Les Nations Unies et les accords regionaux.** Speyer am Rhein, Taegersche Buchdruckerei, 1954. 176 p.

5683 Martin, Charles E. **Universalism and Regionalism in International Law and Organization.** Havana, Academia Interamericana de Derecho Comparado e Internacional, 1959. 590 p.

5684 Nyun, U. **Regional Cooperation and the United Nations,** *South Asia Pacific Crisis,* Margaret Grant (ed.). New York, Dodd, Mead, pp. 180—88.

5685 Padelford, Norman J. **Regional Organizations and the United Nations,** *International Organization,* VIII (May 1954), 203—16.

An explanation of the rise of regionalism since 1944.

5686 Reid, Helen Dwight. **Regionalism Under the United Nations Charter,** *International Conciliation,* CDXIX (March 1946), 120—27.

5687 Rockefeller, Nelson. **The Inter-American System and the United Nations,** *Academy of Political Science Proceedings,* XXII (January 1947), 120—270.

5688 Saba, H. **Regional Arrangements in the U. N. O. Charter,** *Recueil des Cours,* LXXX (1952), 635—716.

5689 Wilcox, Francis O. **Regionalism and the United Nations,** *International Organization,* XIX (Summer, 1965), 789—811.

Part E. — Regional International Organization

4. AFRICA

African regionalism has been handicapped in the past by a total absence of the cooperative efforts conducive to the growth of international institutions. Federation has succeeded only in the case of the union of Tanganyika and Zanzibar into Tanzania. With the establishment in 1963 of the Organization of African Unity, however, a common framework has developed.

4.1 BIBLIOGRAPHIES

See A 3.4.2.

4.2 GENERAL DISCUSSIONS ON PAN AFRICANISM

5690 Abraham, Willie E. **The Mind of Africa.** Chicago, University of Chicago Press, 1962. 206 p.

5691 American Society of African Culture (ed.). **Pan-Africanism Reconsidered.** Berkeley and Los Angeles, University of California Press, 1962. xix + 376 p.

5692 Busia, K. **The Challenge of Africa.** New York, Praeger, 1962. vi + 150 p.

5693 Crutcher, John. **Pan Africanism: African Odyssey,** *Current History*, XLIV (January 1963), 1–7.

5694 Décraene, Philippe. **Le panafricanisme.** 3d ed. Paris, Presses Universitaires de France, 1964. 128 p.

5695 Du Bois, W. E. B. **Black Africa Tomorrow,** *Foreign Affairs*, XVII (October 1938), 100–10.

5696 Emerson, Rupert. **Pan-Africanism,** *International Organization*, XVI (Spring, 1962), 275–90.

5697 Henry, Paul-Marc. **Pan-Africanism: A Dream Come True,** *Foreign Affairs*, XXXVII (April 1959), 443–52.

5698 Kraft, Louis. **Pan-Africanism: Political, Economic, Strategic or Scientific?** *International Affairs*, XXIV (April 1948), 218–28.

5699 Legum, Colin. **Pan-Africanism: A Short Political Guide.** New York, Praeger, 1962. 296 p.

5700 ———. **The Roots of Pan-Africanism,** *Africa: A Handbook to the Continent*, Colin Legum (ed.). London, Blond, 1961, pp. 452–62.

5701 Lewis, I. M. **Pan Africanism and Pan-Socialism,** *Journal of Modern African Studies*, I (June 1963), 147–62.

5702 Logan, Rayford W. **Will African Federalism Work?** *Current History*, New Series, XLI (October 1961), 200–4.

5703 McKay, Vernon. **Africa in World Politics.** New York, Harper and Row, 1963.

Chapters VI–IX.

5704 McWilliams, Wilson C. and Polier, Jonathan. **Pan-Africanism and the Dilemmas of National Development,** *Phylon*, XXV (Spring, 1964), 44–64.

5705 Malinowski, Bronislaw. **The Pan-African Problem of Culture Contact,** *American Journal of Sociology*, XLVIII (May 1943), 649–65.

Part E. — *Regional International Organization*

5706 Mazrui, Ali A. **On the Concept of "We Are All Africans,"** *American Political Science Review*, LVII (June 1963), 88—97.

5707 Munger, Edwin S. **Pan Africanism Versus Southern Africa — The Strategic Role of Bechuanaland,** *Institute of World Affairs Proceedings*, XXXIX (1963), 141—56.

5708 Nkrumah, Kwame. **Africa Must Unite.** New York. Praeger, 1963. xvii + 229 p.

5709 Nyerere, J. K. **A United States of Africa,** *Journal of Modern African Studies*, I (March 1963), 1—6.

5710 Okechukwi Mezu, S. (ed.). **The Philosophy of Pan-Africanism: A Collection of Papers on the Theory and Practice of the African Unity Movement.** Washington, Georgetown University Press, 1965. 142 p.

5711 Padmore, George. **Pan-Africanism or Communism? The Coming Struggle for Africa.** London, Dobson, 1956. 463 p.

5712 Rothchild, Donald S. **The Politics of African Separation,** *Journal of International Affairs*, XV, 1 (1961), 18—28.

5713 Selassie, Haile I. **Towards African Unity,** *Journal of Modern African Studies*, I (September 1963), 281—91.

5714 Shepherd, George W. **The Politics of African Nationalism: Challenge to American Policy.** New York, Praeger, 1962. 244 p.

5715 Thiam, Doudou. **The Foreign Policy of African States: Ideological Bases, Present Realities, Future Prospects.** Preface by Roger Decottignies. New York, Praeger, 1965. xv + 134 p.

Part E. — Regional International Organization

4.3 ATTEMPTS AT FEDERATION

4.3.1 CENTRAL AFRICA

5716 Irvine, Keith. **The Central African Federation,** Current History, New Series, XXX (May 1956), 285–92.

5717 L., H. **The Future of the Central African Federation,** World Today, New Series, XI (December 1955), 539–48.

5718 Lemkin, J. A. **Two Views of the Central African Federation: I, Constitutional Realities,** World Today, New Series, XIX (June 1963), 265–70.

5719 Mason, Philip. **Partnership in Central Africa,** International Affairs, XXXVIII (April 1957), 154–64: (July 1965), 310–18.

5720 — —. **Problems and Prospects in the Central African Federation,** World Today, New Series, XVII (August 1961), 325–35.

5721 M., W. M. **The Federation Issue in Central Africa,** World Today, New Series, VIII (November 1952), 450–60.

5722 Oldham, J. H. **Report of the Commission on the Closer Union of the Eastern and Central African Dependencies,** International Affairs, VIII (May 1929), 227–46.

Comments by Buxton, Leggett, Hamilton, Allen, Smith, Meston, Oldham.

5723 Pratt, R. C. **Federation in Central Africa: The 1960 Conference,** World Today, New Series, XVI (January 1960), 7–15.

5724 Rothchild, Donald S. **Toward Unity in Africa: A Study of Federalism in British Africa.** Washington, Public Affairs, 1960. vii + 224 p.

5725 Somerville, J. J. B. **The Central African Federation,** *International Affairs*, XXXIX (July 1963), 386–402.

5726 Welensky, Roy. **Toward Federation in Central Africa,** *Foreign Affairs*, XXXI (October 1952), 142–49.

5727 Wright, Peter and Varna, S. N. **The Central African Federation in Retrospect,** *India Quarterly*, XII (July-September 1956), 250–67.

4.3.2 EAST AFRICA

5728 Banfield, Jane. **Federation in East Africa,** *International Journal*, XVIII (Spring, 1963), 181–93.

5729 Franck, Thomas M. **East African Unity Through Law.** New Haven, Yale University Press, 1964. xi + 184 p.

5730 Johns, David H. **East African Unity — Problems and Prospects,** *World Today*, New Series, XIX (December 1963), 533–40.

5731 Leyum, Colin and Robson, Peter (eds.). **Federation in East Africa: Opportunities and Problems.** New York, Oxford University Press, 1965. 244 p.

Conference papers delivered in Nairobi in 1963 on problems of a common market or federation in the region.

5732 Mazrui, Ali A. **Tanzania Versus East Africa: A Case of Unwitting Federal Sabotage,** *Journal of Commonwealth Political Studies*, III (November 1965), 209–25.

5733 Nye, Joseph S., Jr. **Pan-Africanism and East African Integration.** Cambridge, Harvard University Press, 1965. 307 p.

5734 Oldham, J. H. **Report of the Commission on the Closer Union of the Eastern and Central African Dependencies,** *International Affairs*, VIII (May 1929), 227—46.

Comments by Buxton, Leggett, Allen, Smith, Meston, Oldham.

5735 Rosberg, Carl G., Jr. with Segal, Aaron. **An East African Federation,** *International Conciliation*, DXLIII (May 1963), 5—72.

5736 Rotberg, Robert I. **The Federation Movement in British East and Central Africa, 1889—1953,** *Journal of Commonwealth Political Studies*, II (May 1964), 141—64.

5737 Rothchild, Donald S. **A Hope Deferred: East African Federation, 1963—64,** *Politics in Africa: Seven Cases*, Gwendolen M. Carter (ed.). New York, Harcourt, Brace and World, 1966, pp. 209—44.

5738 — —. **Toward Unity in Africa: A Study of Federalism in British Africa.** Washington, Public Affairs, 1960. vii + 224 p.

4.3.3 WEST AFRICA

5739 Foltz, William J. **An Early Failure of Pan-Africanism: The Mali Federation, 1959—60,** *Politics in Africa: Seven Cases*, Gwendolen M. Carter (ed.). New York, Harcourt, Brace and World, 1966, pp. 33—66.

5740 Hodgkin, Thomas and Schachter, Ruth. **French-Speaking West Africa in Transition,** *International Conciliation*, DXXVIII (May 1960), 375—436.

5741 Khan, Hafeezur Rehman. **The Ghana-Guinea Federation,** *Pakistan Horizon*, XI (December 1958), 257—62.

5742 Newbury, C. W. **The West African Commonwealth.** Durham, Duke University Press, 1964. xiv + 106 p.

5743 Senghor, Leopold Sedar. **West Africa in Evolution,** *Foreign Affairs,* XXXIX (January 1961), 240–46.

4.4 ATTEMPTS TO FORM INTERAFRICAN ORGANIZATIONS BEFORE THE ORGANIZATION OF AFRICAN UNITY

See also E 10.3.

5744 Cox, Richard. **Pan-Africanism in Practice: An East African Study; PAFMESCA 1958–1964.** New York, Oxford University Press, 1964. 95 p.

5745 Gladden, E. N. **The East African Common Services Organization,** *Parliamentary Affairs,* XVI (Autumn, 1963), 428–39.

5746 Kloman, Erasmus H. **New Directions in the Drive Toward African Unity,** *Orbis,* VI (Winter, 1963), 575–92.

5747 L., C. **The Accra Conference of African States,** *World Today,* New Series, XIV (June 1958), 259–66.

5748 Lattre, Jean Michel de. **An African Economic Community,** *International Development Review,* II (January 1961), 22–27.

5749 Liebenow, J. Gus. **Which Road to Pan-African Unity?: The Sanniquellie Conference, 1959,** *Politics in Africa: Seven Cases,* Gwendolen M. Carter (ed.). New York, Harcourt, Brace and World, 1966, pp. 1–32.

5750 Nye, Joseph S., Jr. **East African Economic Integration,** *International Political Communities.* Garden City, Doubleday, 1966, pp. 405–36.

Revision of the author's article in *Journal of Modern African Studies,* December 1963.

Part E. — Regional International Organization

5751 Quigley, Caroll. **The Brazzaville Twelve,** *Current History*, New Series, XLIII (December 1962), 346–53.

5752 Rivkin, Arnold. **An Economic Development Proposal for Africa: A New Multilateral Aid Organization,** *International Organization*, XII (Summer, 1958), 303–19.

5753 Sanger, Clyde. **Toward Unity in Africa,** *Foreign Affairs*, XLII (January 1964), 269–81.

5754 Tevoedjre, Albert. **Pan-Africanism in Action: An Account of the UAM.** Cambridge, Harvard University, Center for International Affairs, 1965. 88 p.

Union Africaine et Malagache.

5755 Williams, David. **How Deep the Split in West Africa?** *Foreign Affairs*, XL (October 1961), 118–27.

5756 Worthington, E. B. **Science in African International Relations,** *International Affairs*, XXIX (January 1953), 52–58.

Formation of the Commission for Technical Cooperation in Africa South of the Sahara.

5757 Zartman, I. William. **The Sahara: Bridge or Barrier,** *International Conciliation*, DXLI (January 1963), 3–32.

4.5 ORGANIZATION OF AFRICAN UNITY
(Addis Ababa)

5758 Boutros-Ghali, Boutros Y. **The Addis Ababa Charter,** *International Conciliation*, DXLVII (January 1964), 5–49.

Part E. — Regional International Organization

5759 Burke, Frederick G. **Africa's Quest for Order.** Englewood Cliffs, Prentice-Hall, 1964. 174 p.

5760 Delanney, L. **L'ONU et son destin,** *Revue Politique et Parliamentaire,* LXVI (May 1964), 38—49.

5761 Elias, T. O. **The Charter of the Organization of African Unity,** *American Journal of International Law,* LIX (April 1965), 243—67.

5762 Nambiar, K. R. **The Charter of the Organisation of African Unity,** *Indian Journal of International Law,* III (1963), 422—31.

5763 Padelford, Norman J. **The Organization of African Unity,** *International Organization,* XVIII (Summer, 1964), 521—42.

5764 Rivkin, Arnold. **The Organization of African Unity,** *Current History,* New Series, XLVIII (January 1965), 193—200 ff.

5765 Sanger, Clyde. **Toward Unity in Africa,** *Foreign Affairs,* XLII (January 1964), 269—81

5766 Wallerstein, Immanuel M. **Africa: The Politics of Independence.** New York, Vintage, 1961.
Chapter VI.

4.6 ARAB AFRICA

See E 6.4.

Part E. — *Regional International Organization*

5. ASIA AND THE PACIFIC

Of all the continents of the world, Asia alone has been unable to develop a common institution that can transcend the intense rivalries of India and Pakistan, of Indonesia and Malaysia, and of the two Chinas, Koreas and Vietnams, or the Australian and New Zealand policies of racial exclusion.

5.1 BIBLIOGRAPHIES

See A 3.4.3.

5.2 GENERAL DISCUSSIONS

See also E 10.3.

5767 Brown, W. Norman. **Religion and Language As Forces Affecting Unity in Asia,** *Annals of the American Academy of Political and Social Science,* CCCXVIII (July 1958), 8–17.

5768 Chow, S. R. **A Permanent Order for the Pacific,** *World Peace Plans,* Julia E. Johnsen (ed.). New York, Wilson, 1943, pp. 168–73.

Paper submitted to the Eighth Conference of the Institute of Pacific Relations.

5769 Gordon, Bernard K. **Problems of Regional Cooperation in Southeast Asia,** *World Politics,* XVI (January 1964), 222–53.

5770 — —. **Regional Cooperation in Southeast Asia,** *Current History,* XLVIII (February 1965), 103–108 f.

ECAFE and the Association of Southeast Asia.

5771 Gungwu, Wang. **Nation Formation and Regionalism in Southeast Asia,** *South Asia Pacific Crisis,* Margaret Grant (ed.). New York, Dodd, Mead, 1964, pp. 125–35.

Part E. — *Regional International Organization*

5772 Gupta, Sisir. **India and Regional Integration in Asia.** New York, Asia Publishing House, 1964. x + 155 p.

5773 Henderson, William. **The Development of Regionalism in Southeast Asia,** *International Organization,* IX (November 1955), 463–76.

5774 ———. **Regionalism in Southeast Asia,** *Journal of International Affairs,* X, 1 (1956), 69–76.

5775 Lakdawala, D. T. **Trends in Regional Cooperation in Asia,** *South Asia Pacific Crisis,* Margaret Grant (ed.). New York, Dodd, Mead, 1964, pp. 77–100.

5776 Levi, Werner. **Political and Military Arrangements in the Far East and Pacific,** *Regional Arrangements for Security and the United Nations,* Commission to Study the Organization of Peace (ed.). New York, Commission to Study the Organization of Peace, 1953. pp. 126–30.

5777 Lobanov-Rostovsky, Andre. **The Problem of Pan-Asianism,** *Institute of World Affairs Proceedings,* XVI (1938), 22–26.

5778 Meyer, Milton W. **Regional Cooperation in Southeast Asia,** *Journal of International Affairs,* III (Spring, 1949), 68–77.

5779 Palmer, Norman D. **Organizing for Peace in Asia,** *Western Political Quarterly,* VIII (March 1955), 1–43.

5780 Roerich, G. N. **Cultural Unity of Asia,** *India Quarterly,* VI (January-March 1950), 38–43.

5781 Romulo, Carlos P. **Asian Unity and the Politics of Fear,** *Pakistan Horizon,* XVIII (1965), 220–25.

Part E. — Regional International Organization

5782 Talbot, Phillips. **South and Southeast Asia,** *Regional Arrangements for Security and the United Nations,* Commission to Study the Organization of Peace (ed.). New York, Commission to Study the Organization of Peace, 1953, pp. 126–30.

5783 Taylor, Alastair M. **Malaysia, Indonesia — and Maphilindo,** *International Journal,* XIX (Spring, 1964), 155–71.

5784 Vandenbosch, Amry and Butwell, Richard. **Southeast Asia Among the World Powers.** Lexington, University of Kentucky Press, 1957.

Chapter VIII.

5785 Venkatasubbiah, H. **Prospects of an Asian Union,** *India Quarterly,* V (July-September 1949), 212–27.

5786 — —. **Prospects of an Asian Union: Lessons from the Organization of American States,** *India Quarterly,* V (April-June 1949), 99–111.

5787 Wang, C. C. **The Pan-Asiatic Doctrine of Japan,** *Foreign Affairs,* XIII (October 1934), 59–67.

5788 Williams, L. **Overseas Chinese Nationalism: The Genesis of the Pan-Chinese Movement in Indonesia.** Glencoe, Free Press, 1960. 235 p.

5789 Wint, Guy. **South Asia: Unity and Disunity,** *International Conciliation,* D (November 1954), 131–91.

5790 Zagday, M. I. **The First Pan-Asiatic Conference,** *World Affairs,* New Series, I (July 1947), 311–19.

5.3 FAR EASTERN COMMISSION (Tokyo)

See D 2.5.

5.4 ANZUS

5791 Bishop, Peter V. **Anzus: Shield or Shroud?** *International Journal*, XVI (Autumn, 1961), 405–9.

5792 McHenry, Dean E. and Rosecrance, Richard N. **The "Exclusion" of the United Kingdom from the ANZUS Pact,** *International Organization*, XII (Summer, 1958), 320–29.

5793 Padelford, Norman J. **Collective Security in the Pacific: Nine Years of the ANZUS Pact,** *United States Naval Institute Proceedings*, LXXXV (September 1960), 38–47.

5794 Sissons, D. C. S. **The Pacific Pact,** *Australian Outlook*, VI (March 1952), 20–26.

5795 Starke, Joseph G. **The ANZUS Treaty Alliance.** Melbourne, Melbourne University Press, 1965. xiv + 315 p.

5796 Stone, Julius. **The Anzac Treaty and United Kingdom — Australian Relations,** *World Affairs*, XI (July 1945), 138–55.

5797 Tapp, E. J. **An Australia-New Zealand Community — An Appraisal,** *Australian Outlook*, XVIII (August 1964), 143–50.

5798 Wood, F. L. W. **The Anzac Dilemma,** *International Affairs*, XXIX (April 1953), 184–92.

5.5 SOUTHEAST ASIAN TREATY ORGANIZATION
(Bangkok)

5799 Ball, M. Margaret. **SEATO and Subversion,** *Political Science*, XI (March 1959), 25–40.

Part E. — Regional International Organization

5800 Ball, W. Macmahon. **A Political Re-examination of SEATO,** *International Organization,* XII (Winter, 1958), 17—25.

5801 Boyd, R. Gavin. **Communist China and SEATO,** *SEATO: Six Studies,* George Modelski (ed.). Melbourne, Cheshire, 1962, pp. 167—201.

5802 Braibanti, Ralph. **The Southeast Asia Collective Defense Treaty,** *Pacific Affairs,* XXX (December 1957), 321—41.

5803 Brissenden, Rosemary. **India, Neutralism, and SEATO,** *SEATO: Six Studies,* George Modelski (ed.). Melbourne, Cheshire, 1962, pp. 205—50.

5804 — —. **Indian Opposition to SEATO: A Case Study in Neutralist Diplomacy,** *Australian Journal of Politics and History,* VI (November 1960), 219—32.

5805 Chaudhri, M. A. **The Southeast Asia Collective Defense Treaty,** *Revue Égyptienne de Droit International,* XX (1964), 81—108.

5806 Dean, Arthur H. **Collective Defence in Southeast Asia,** *Current History,* New Series, XXXI (July 1956), 7—14.

5807 Eayrs, James. **A Pacific Pact: "Step in the Right Direction?"** *International Journal,* VII (Autumn, 1952), 293—302.

5808 Frankel, J. **The Pacific Pact,** *World Affairs,* New Series, V (October 1951), 490—501.

5809 Harper, Norman D. **Australia and Regional Pacts, 1950—57,** *Australian Outlook,* XII (March 1958), 3—22.

5810 — —. **Pacific Security As Seen from Australia,** *International Organization,* VII (May 1953), 312—28.

5811 Hogan, Warren P. **Economic Relationships and the SEATO Powers,** *SEATO: Six Studies*, George Modelski (ed.). Melbourne, Cheshire, 1962, pp. 253—88.

5812 Leifer, Michael. **Cambodia and SEATO,** *International Journal*, XVII (Spring, 1962), 122—32.

5813 Lerche, Charles O., Jr. **The United States, Great Britain, and SEATO: A Case Study in the Fait Accompli,** *Journal of Politics*, XVIII (August 1956), 459—78.

5814 Levi, Werner. **The Chances of an Asian NATO,** *Fortnightly*, MXXXIX (July 1953), 3—8.

5815 Limb, Ben C. **The Pacific Pact: Looking Forward or Backward?** *Foreign Affairs*, XXIX (July 1951), 539—49.

5816 Modelski, George A. **The Asian States' Participation in SEATO,** *SEATO: Six Studies*, George Modelski (ed.). Melbourne, Cheshire, 1962, pp. 87—163.

5817 ———. **Australia and SEATO,** *International Organization*, XIV (Summer, 1960), 429—37.

5818 ———. **SEATO: Its Function and Organization,** *SEATO: Six Studies*, George Modelski (ed.). Melbourne, Cheshire, 1962, pp. 3—45.

5819 ———. (ed.). **SEATO: Six Studies.** Foreword by John Crawford. Melbourne, Cheshire, 1962. xxxiii + 302 p.

5820 ———. **The South-East Asia Treaty Organization,** *Australian Journal of Politics and History*, V (May 1959), 24—40.

5821 Nuechterlein, D. E. **Thailand and SEATO: A Ten-Year Appraisal,** *Asian Survey*, IV (December 1964), 174–81.

5822 Padelford, Norman J. **SEATO and Peace in Southeast Asia,** *Current History*, XXXVIII (February 1960), 95–101.

5823 Peffer, Nathaniel. **Regional Security in Southeast Asia,** *International Organization*, VIII (August 1954), 311–15.

5824 Royal Institute of International Affairs. **Collective Defence in South East Asia.** London, Royal Institute of International Affairs, 1956. 167 p.

5825 Thomas, M. Ladd. **A Critical Appraisal of SEATO,** *Western Political Quarterly*, X (December 1957), 926–36.

5826 Webb, Leicester C. **Australia and SEATO,** *SEATO: Six Studies*, George Modelski (ed.). Melbourne, Cheshire, 1962, pp. 49–83.

5.6 SOUTH PACIFIC COMMISSION
(Noumea)

5827 Andrews, John. **Regionalism in the South Seas,** *Australian Outlook*, I (March 1947), 11–16.

5829 D., H. A. C. **The South Pacific Commission: A New Experiment in Regionalism,** *World Today*, New Series, VI (September 1950), 394–406.

5830 Gilson, Richard P. **The South Pacific Commission,** *World Affairs Quarterly*, XXI (July 1950), 181–90.

Part E. — Regional International Organization

5831 Holland, Robert. **Pacific Pact,** *Dalhousie Review,* XXXIV (January 1955), 341—54.

5832 McHenry, Dean E. **Regionalism in the South Pacific,** *World Affairs Quarterly,* XXVI (January 1956), 378—86.

5833 McKay, C. **The Pacific Islands and the South Pacific Commission.** Wellington, Government Printer, 1956. 31 p.

5834 Obern, Alfred G. **Personnel Administration in the Caribbean and South Pacific Commissions,** *International Review of Administrative Sciences,* XXV, 3 (1959), 263—69.

5835 Padelford, Norman J. **Regional Cooperation in the South Pacific: Twelve Years of the South Pacific Commission,** *International Organization,* XIII (Summer, 1959), 380—93.

5836 Robson, N. **South Pacific Conference,** *Australian Outlook,* VII (September 1953), 164—70.
Regionalism and the creation of the South Pacific Commission.

5837 Ryan, P. L. **The South Pacific Commission: What It Is — What It Does,** *South Pacific Bulletin,* XIII (October 1963), 30—35.

5838 Ward, J. M. **Collaboration for Welfare in the Southwest Pacific,** *Australian Outlook,* I (March 1947), 17—28.

Part E. — *Regional International Organization*

6. MIDDLE EAST AND THE ISLAMIC WORLD

In the Middle East the main source of disunity is the existence of the non-Moslem state of Israel, which neighboring Arab countries are unwilling to accept. This disunity has resulted in bipolarized yet fragmented leadership. The League of Arab States has continued to operate despite revalries between some of its members, such as Egypt, Saudi Arabia, and Iraq. Turkey, Iran, and the non-Arab North African Moslem states, however, have had to turn elsewhere to form regional indentification.

6.1 GENERAL DISCUSSIONS

See also E 10.3.

5839 Antonius, George. **The Arab Awakening: The Story of the Arab National Movement.** Philadelphia, Lippincott, 1939. xi + 471 p.

5840 Badeau, John S. **Islam and the Modern Middle East,** *Foreign Affairs*, XXXVIII (October 1959), 61—74.

5841 Baker, Robert L. **Islam in Quest of Unity,** *Current History*, XXXVIII (July 1933), 418—23.

5842 Baroody, Jamil M. **Middle East — Balance of Power Versus World Government,** *Annals of the American Academy of Political and Social Science*, CCLXIV (July 1949), 46—51.

5843 Beling, Willard A. **Pan-Arabism and Labor.** Cambridge, Harvard University Press, 1960. x + 127 p.

Part E. — Regional International Organization

5844 Berger, Morroe. **The Arab World Today.** Garden City, Doubleday, 1962. 480 p.

5845 Browne, E. G. **Pan-Islamism,** *Lectures on the History of the Nineteenth Century,* F. A. Kirkpatrick (ed.). Cambridge, Cambridge University Press, 1902, pp. 306–30.

5846 Brinton, J. Y. **Aden and the Federation of South Arabia.** Washington, American Society of International Law, 1964. 81 p.

5847 Carmichael, Joel. **Islam and Arab Nationalism: The Role of Religion in Middle Eastern Politics,** *Commentary,* XXIV (July 1957), 20–27.

5848 — —. **Notes on Arab Unity,** *Foreign Affairs,* XXII (October 1943), 148–53.

5849 — —. **Prospects for Arab Unity,** *Dalhousie Review,* XXXIV (January 1956), 448–57.

5850 Chaudhri, Mohammed Ahsen. **Pakistan and the Muslim World,** *Pakistan Horizon,* X (September 1957), 156–65.

5851 Cramer, Frederick H. **The Arab Empire: A Religious Imperialism,** *Current History,* New Series, XXII (June 1952), 340–47.

5852 Duprée, Louis. **A Suggested Pakistan-Afghanistan-Iran Federation,** *Middle East Journal,* XVII (Autumn, 1963), 383–99.

5853 Eban, Aubrey S. **The Near East and World Government,** *Annals of the American Academy of Political and Social Science,* CCLXIV (July 1949), 58–66.

5854 Etzioni, Amitai. **Political Unification.** New York, Holt, Rinehart and Winston, 1965.

Chapter IV.

5855 Foda, Ezzeldin. **The Projected Arab Court of Justice: A Study in Regional Jurisdiction with Specific Reference to the Muslim Law of Nations.** Presentation by A. H. Badawi. Hague, Nijhoff, 1957. xvi + 258 p.

5856 Frye, Richard N. **Islam and the Middle East,** *Current History*, New Series, XXX (June 1956), 327—30.

5857 Garnick, Daniel H. **On the Economic Feasibility of a Middle Eastern Common Market,** *Middle East Journal*, XIV (Summer, 1960), 265—76.

5858 — —. **Regional Integration and Economic Development in the Middle East,** *Middle Eastern Affairs*, XII (December 1961), 294—300.

5859 Gibb, H. A. R. **Toward Arab Unity,** *Foreign Affairs*, XXIV (October 1945), 119—29.

5860 Habib, Mohammed. **Recent Political Trends in the Middle East: From Pan-Islamism to Nationalism,** *India Quarterly*, I (April 1945), 134—38.

5861 Haleem, A. B. A. **The Baghdad World Muslim Conference,** *Pakistan Horizon*, XV, 3 (1962), 169—74.

5862 Hazan, Z. **Iran, Pakistan and Turkey — Regional Cooperation for Development,** *Pakistan Horizon*, XVII, 3 (1964), 276—85.

5863 Hill, John G. **Pan-Arabism and the Jew in Palestine,** *World Affairs Quarterly*, VIII (October 1937), 282—89.

5864 Hitti, Philip K. **The Possibility of Unity Among the Arab States,** *American Historical Review*, XLVIII (April 1943), 722–32.

5865 Hurewitz, J. C. **Unity and Disunity in the Middle East,** *International Conciliation*, CDLXXXI (May 1952), 199–260.

5866 Issawi, Charles. **The Bases of Arab Unity,** *International Affairs*, XXXI (January 1955), 36–47.

5867 Kabir, Mafizollah. **Arab Federalism: Recent Developments,** *Pakistan Horizon*, XI (March 1958), 19–22.

5868 Kedourie, Elie. **Pan-Arabism and British Policy,** *Political Quarterly*, XXVIII (April-June 1957), 137–48.

5869 Kenny, L. M. **The Goal of Arab Unification,** *International Journal*, XIX (Winter, 1963–64), 50–61.

5870 Kent, Raymond K. **Soviet Muslims, the Arab World and the Myth of Synthesis,** *Journal of International Affairs*, XIII, 2 (1959), 141–48.

5871 Khadduri, Majid. **The Islamic System: Its Competition and Co-existence with Western Systems,** *American Society of International Law Proceedings*, LIII (1959), 49–52.

5872 — —. **The Problem of Regional Security in the Middle East: An Appraisal,** *Middle East Journal*, XI (Winter, 1957), 12–22.

5873 — —. **The Scheme of Fertile Crescent Unity,** *The Near East and the Great Powers*, R. Frye (ed.). Cambridge, Harvard University Press, 1951, pp. 137–77.

5874 — —. **Toward an Arab Union,** *American Political Science Review*, XL (February 1946), 90–101.

5875 Khan, Nazid Ahmad. **A Commonwealth of Muslim Nations,** *Pakistan Horizon,* XIV, 2 (1961), 103–11.

5876 Kohn, Hans. **The Unification of Arabia,** *Foreign Affairs,* XIII (October 1934), 91–103.

5877 Little, T. R. **The Meaning of the United Arab Republic,** *World Today,* New Series, XIV (March 1958), 93–101.

5878 Laquer, Walter Z. **Arab Unity vs. Soviet Expansion,** *Problems of Communism,* VIII (May-June 1959), 42–48.

5879 Lee, Dwight E. **The Origins of Pan-Islamism,** *American Historical Review,* XLVII (January 1942), 278–87.

5880 Lybyer, Albert Howe. **Proposed Union of Syria and Iraq,** *Current History,* XXXV (February 1932), 751–53.

5881 — —. **The Quest for Moslem Unity,** *Current History,* XXXV (January 1932), 621–23.

5882 Major, John. **The Search for Arab Unity,** *International Affairs,* XXXIX (October 1963), 551–63.

5883 Marmorstein, Emile. **The Fate of Arabdom: A Study in Comparative Nationalism,** *International Affairs,* XXV (October 1949), 475–91.

5884 Mokarzel, S. A. **Arab Empire — The Near East Stirs to Make a Dream Come True,** *Current History,* XLV (November 1936), 53–58.

5885 Montagne, Robert. **Modern Nations and Islam,** *Foreign Affairs,* XXX (July 1952), 580–92.

5886 Proctor, J. Harris (ed.). **Islam and International Relations.** New York, Praeger, 1965. viii + 221 p.

5887 Rafa'i, Abdul Monem. **The Arab Commonwealth,** *Annals of the American Academy of Political and Social Science,* CCXCIV (July 1954), 147–50.

5888 Rafig, M. **Unification of Islamic World,** *Islamic Literature,* XI (March-April 1959), 21–26.

5889 Ramazani, R. K. **The Shi'i System: Its Conflict and Interaction with Other Systems,** *American Society of International Law Proceedings,* LIII (1959), 53–59.

5890 Reese, Howard C. **Pan-Arab Unity — Is It Possible?** *Military Review,* XLII (July 1962), 87–92.

5891 Rihani, Ameen. **Palestine and the Proposed Arab Federation,** *Annals of the American Academy of Political and Social Science,* CLXIV (November 1932), 62–71.

5892 Roosevelt, Kermit. **The Middle East and the Prospect for World Government,** *Annals of the American Academy of Political and Social Science,* CCLXIV (July 1949), 52–57.

5893 S., G., and S., H. **The First Arab Petroleum Congress,** *World Today,* New Series, XV (June 1959), 246–53.

5894 Saab, H. **The Arab Search for a Federal Union,** *World Justice,* VI (December 1964), 147–71.

5895 Salem, Elie. **Arab Nationalism: A Reappraisal,** *International Journal,* XVII (Summer, 1962), 289–99.

Part E. — Regional International Organization

5896 Sayegh, Fayez A. **Arab Unity: Hope and Fulfillment.** New York, Devin-Adair, 1958. xvii + 272 p.

5897 Scheltema, J. F. **The Moslem World of Today,** *Current History* XIII (December 1920), 507–9.

5898 Seale, Patrick. **The Break-up of the United Arab Republic,** *World Today*, New Series, XVII (November 1961), 471–79.

5899 Shatara, Fuad. **Arab-Jewish Unity in Palestine,** *Annals of the American Academy of Political and Social Science*, CLXIV (November 1932), 178–83.

5900 Siegman, Henry. **Arab Unity and Disunity,** *Middle East Journal*, XVI (Winter, 1962), 48–59.

5901 Stackleberg, G. A. von. **Changing Soviet Views on Arab Unification,** *Russian News Bulletin*, VII (March 1960), 3–12.

5902 Steiner, Morris J. **Inside Pan-Arabia.** Chicago, Packard, 1947. xv + 237 p.

5903 Vaktikiotis, P. J. **Recent Developments in Islam,** *Tensions in the Middle East*, Philip W. Thayer (ed.). Baltimore, Johns Hopkins Press, 1958, pp. 165–80.

Comments by George Makdisi.

5904 Woolbert, Robert Gale. **Pan Arabism and the Palestine Problem,** *Foreign Affairs*, XVI (January 1938), 309–22.

5905 Wright, Esmond. **The "Greater Syria" Project in Arab Politics,** *World Affairs*, New Series, V (July 1951), 318–29.

5906 Young, T. Cuyler. **Pan-Islamism in the Modern World: Solidarity and Conflict Among Muslim Countries,** *Islam and International Relations,* J. Harris Proctor (ed.). New York, Praeger, 1965, pp. 194—221.

5907 Zenkovsky, Serge A. **Pan-Turkism and Islam in Russia.** Cambridge, Harvard University Press, 1960. 345 p.

5908 Zurayk, Costi K. **The Essence of Arab Civilization,** *Middle East Journal,* III (Spring, 1949), 125—32.

6.2 LEAGUE OF ARAB STATES
(Cairo)

5909 Agwani, Mahomed Shafi. **The Arab League: An Experiment in Regional Organization,** *India Quarterly,* IX (October-December 1953), 355—66.

5910 Anderson, Totton J. **The Arab League,** *World Affairs Quarterly,* XXIII (October 1952), 237—58.

5911 Anon. **The Second Arab Cultural Congress,** *Middle Eastern Affairs,* I (November 1950), 320—22.

5912 Atiyah, E. **The Arab League,** *World Affairs,* New Series, I (January 1947), 34—47.

5913 Atyeo, Henry C. **Arab Politics and Pacts,** *Current History,* New Series, XXX (June 1956), 339—46.

5914 Aziz, M. A. **The Origin and Birth of the Arab League,** *Revue Égyptienne de Droit International,* XI (1955), 39—58.

5915 Baqai, I. H. **The Pan-Arab League,** *India Quarterly,* II (April-June 1946), 144—49.

Part E. — Regional International Organization

5916 Bentwich, Norman. **The Palestine Mandate and the League of Arab States,** *World Affairs,* XI (July 1945), 131–37.

5917 Boutros-Ghali, Boutros Y. **The Arab League: 1945–1955,** *International Conciliation,* CDXCVIII (May 1954), 387–448.

5918 Campbell, John C. **Defense of the Middle East.** New York, Harper, 1958.
Chapter XIV.

5919 D., A. **The Arab League: Development and Difficulties,** *World Today* New Series, VII (May 1951), 197–96.

5920 Fay, Sidney B. **Egypt and the Arab League,** *Current History,* New Series, XIII (August 1947), 82–87.

5921 — —. **The New Arab Federation,** *Current History,* New Series, VIII (May 1945), 398–402.

5922 Goren, Asher. **The Arab League, 1945–1954.** Tel Aviv, 'Ayanet, 1954. 104 p.
In Hebrew.

5923 Hall, Harvey P. **The Arab League States,** *Current History,* New Series, XXIX (August 1955), 97–101.

5924 Hassouna, Abdel Khalek. **Arab League: A Step in the Fulfillment of the Ideals of Arab Nationalism,** *Nationalism and International Progress,* Urban G. Whitaker, Jr. (ed.). Rev. ed. San Francisco, Chandler, 1960, pp. 134–44.

5925 Hoskins, Halford L. **The Middle East.** New York, Macmillan, 1954.
Chapter VIII.

5926 Howard, Harry N. **Middle Eastern Regional Organization: Problems and Prospects,** *Academy of Political Science Proceedings,* XXIV (January 1952), 541–51.

Part E. — Regional International Organization

5927 Issawi, Charles. **Joint Defense and Economic Cooperation Between States of the Arab League,** *Middle East Journal*, VI (Spring, 1952), 238—40.

5928 K., G. E. **Cross-Currents Within the Arab League,** *World Today*, New Series, IV (January 1948), 15—25.

5929 — —. **Iraq, Egypt, and the Arab League,** *World Today*, New Series, XI (April 1955), 145—51.

5930 Khadduri, Majid. **The Arab League As a Regional Arrangement,** *American Journal of International Law*, XL (October 1946), 756—77.

5931 — —. **Regional and Collective Defense Arrangements in the Middle East,** *Regional Arrangements for Security and the United Nations*, ed. Commission to Study the Organization of Peace (ed.). New York, Commission to Study the Organization of Peace, 1953, pp. 100—17.

5932 Khalil, Muhammad (ed.). **The Arab States and the Arab League: A Documentary Record.** Beirut, Khayats, 1962. 2 vols.

5933 Kloman, Erasmus H., Jr. **African Unification Movements,** *International Organization*, XVI (Spring, 1962), 387—404.

5934 Lenczowski, George. **The Middle East in World Affairs.** 3d ed. Ithaca, Cornell University Press, 1962.

Chapter XVI.

5935 Little, T. R. **The Arab League: A Reassessment,** *Middle East Journal*, X (Spring, 1956), 138—50.

5936 Macdonald, Robert W. **The League of Arab States: A Study in the Dynamics of Regional Organization.** Princeton, Princeton University Press, 1965. xiii + 407 p.

5937 McKay, Vernon. **The Arab League in World Politics,** *Foreign Policy Reports,* XXII (November 15, 1946), 206—15.

5938 Moyal, M. **Post-Mortem on the Arab League,** *World Affairs,* New Series, III (April 1949), 187—95.

5939 Perlemann, M. **The Turkish-Arab Diplomatic Tangle,** *Middle Eastern Affairs,* VI (January 1955), 13—17.

5940 Raleigh, J. S. **Ten Years of the Arab League,** *Middle Eastern Affairs,* VI (March 1955), 65—77.

5941 Saud, Mahmoud Abu. **The Arab League and the Muslim World,** *Pakistan Horizon,* VII (March 1954), 17—21.

5942 Seabury, Paul. **The League of Arab States: Case Study of a Regional Pact,** *Journal of International Affairs,* III (Spring, 1949), 56—67.

5943 — —. **The League of Arab States: Debacle of a Regional Arrangement,** *International Organization,* III (November 1949), 633—42.

6.3 CENTO (Ankara)

5944 Atyeo, Henry C. **Arab Politics and Pacts,** *Current History,* New Series, XXX (June 1956), 339—46.

5945 Campbell, John C. **Defense of the Middle East.** New York, Harper, 1958.
Chapter V.

5946 Ferris, John P. **Organization for Regional Economic Development Projects: A Middle East Experience,** *Public Administration Review,* XXV (June 1965), 128—34.

5947 Perlemann, M. **Egypt Versus the Bagdad Pact,** *Middle Eastern Affairs,* VII (March 1956), 95—101.

5948 Remba, Oded. **The Bagdad Pact: Economic Aspect,** *Middle Eastern Affairs,* IX (April 1958), 131—40.

6.4 MAGHREB

5949 Aboud, El-Mehdi Ben. **America and the Future of the Maghreb,** *Annals of the American Academy of Political and Social Science,* CCCXXX (July 1960), 29—36.

5950 Akhund, Hameeda. **The Maghreb in Search of a Union,** *Pakistan Horizon,* XI (June 1958), 79—84; XI (September 1958), 165—72.

5951 Diop, Cheikh Anta. **Les fondements culturels, techniques et industriels d'un futur état fédéral d'Afrique Noire.** Paris, Presence Africaine, 1960. 114 p.

5952 Hodgkin, Thomas. **The Battle for the Maghreb,** *Political Quarterly,* XXIX (October-December 1958), 348—55.

5953 — —. **France and the Maghreb,** *Current History,* New Series, XXXIV (February 1958), 75—83.

5954 Institut Africain de Genève. **Repertoire des principales institutions s'intéressant à l'Afrique Noire.** Geneva, Institut Universitaire des Hautes Études Internationales, 1963. n. p.

5955 Liska, George. **The Greater Maghreb: From Independence to Unity?** Washington, Center of Foreign Policy Research, 1963. 75 p.

5956 Rivlin, Benjamin. **Arab Africa in the Emerging African Community,** *Journal of International Affairs,* XV, 1 (1961), 42—51.

Part E. — *Regional International Organization*

7. WESTERN HEMISPHERE

The oldest regional institutions, and at the same time the strongest in terms of political activities, are those in the Western Hemisphere. Only recently have Latin American states begun to form institutions on their own, without the often dominating assistance of the United States. Canada, having been dealt out of regional developments, has turned its attention to membership in the expanding notion of a North Atlantic community.

7.1 BIBLIOGRAPHIES

See A 3.4.4.

7.2 GENERAL DISCUSSIONS

5957 Alvarez, Alejandro. **The Monroe Doctrine: Its Importance in the International Life of the States of the New World.** New York, Oxford University Press, 1924. 582 p.

5958 — —. **Pan-Americanism As a Working Program,** *Academy of Political Science Proceedings,* VII, 2 (1917), 495—501.

5959 Babson, Roger W. **Drawing Together the Americas,** *Academy of Political Science Proceedings,* VII, 2 (1917), 442—51.

5960 Bailey, Thomas A. **A Multilateral Monroe Doctrine,** *Institute of World Affairs Proceedings,* XV (1937), 73—76.

5961 Ball, M. Margaret. **The Problem of Inter-American Organization.** Stanford, Stanford University Press, 1944. 117 p.

5962 Barratt, Arthur. **The Real Monroe Doctrine,** *Transactions* (Grotius Society), XIV (1928), 1–28.

Comments by Bewes.

5963 Barrows, David P. **All America,** *Institute of World Affairs Proceedings,* III (1928), 251–58.

5964 Beals, Carleton. **Latin-American Nations' Failure to Attain Unity,** *Current History,* XXVI (September 1927), 862–70.

5965 — —. **Pan America.** Boston, Houghton, Mifflin, 1940. 545 p.

5966 Briggs, Ellis O. **Pan America: A Postwar Estimate,** *International Conciliation,* CDXIX (March 1946), 144–49.

5967 C. **The Future of the Monroe Doctrine,** *Foreign Affairs,* II (March 15, 1924), 373–89.

5968 Caldera Rodriguez, Rafael. **El bloque latinoamericano.** Prologue by Gonzalo García Bustillos. Santiago, Editorial del Pacifico, 1961. 128 p.

5969 Calderón, Francisco García. **Geneva Protocol As It Affects the Monroe Doctrine,** *Current History,* XXI (December 1924), 506–11.

5970 Castañeda, Jorge. **Pan Americanism and Regionalism: A Mexican View,** *International Organization,* X (August 1956), 373–89.

5971 Castle, William R. **The Monroe Doctrine and Pan-Americanism,** *Annals of the American Academy of Political and Social Science,* CCIV (July 1939), 111–18.

5972 Claude, Inis L., Jr. **Problems of Inter-American Neighborliness: A Review,** *Journal of Conflict Resolution,* VI (December 1962), 355–58.

5973 Comstock, Alzada. **Danger — Pan-American Bloc!** *Current History,* New Series, IX (July 1945), 1—6.

5974 Costillo Najero, Francisco. **Remarks on Pan Americanism,** *World Affairs Quarterly,* VI (October 1935), 273—83.

5975 Dávila, Carlos. **Peace Among Equals,** *Annals of the American Academy of Political and Social Science,* CCX (July 1940), 139—44.

5976 ― ―. **We of the Americas.** Chicago, Ziff-Davis, 1949. viii + 264 p.

5977 Dozer, Donald M. **Economic Aspects of Pan-Americanism,** *World Affairs Quarterly,* XII (October 1941), 284—88.

5978 Duggan, Lawrence. **The Americas.** Foreword by Herschel Brickele. New York, Holt, 1949. ix + 242 p.

5979 Duggan, Stephen. **The New Orientation of the Western Hemisphere,** *Annals of the American Academy of Political and Social Science,* CCX (July 1940), 127—32.

5980 Gil, Enrique. **Evolución del panamericanismo: El credo Wilson y el panamericanismo.** Buenos Aires, Menéndez, 1933. xvi + 490 p.

5981 Goldsmith, Peter H. and Calderón, Ygnacio. **Discussion of Pan-Americanism,** *Academy of Political Science Proceedings,* VII, 2 (1917), 514—23.

5982 Gómez Robledo, Antonio. **Idea y experiencia de América.** Mexico City, Fondo de Cultura Económica, 1958. 250 p.

5983 Goodspeed, S. C. **The Latin American Community: An Exploratory Note,** *Social Science,* XXXIV (June 1959), 144—48.

5984 Green, Philip Leonard. **Pan American Progress.** New York, Hastings, 1942. 214 p.

5985 Griffin, Keith. **The Potential Benefits of Latin American Integration,** *Inter-American Economic Affairs,* XVII (Spring, 1964), 3—20.

5986 Guani, Albert. **La solidarité internationale dans l'Amerique Latine,** *Recueil des Cours,* VIII (1925), 207—337.

5987 **Handbook of Latin American Studies.** Gainesville, University of Florida Press, Annually, 1935—.
Annoted bibliography with a section on international relations.

5988 Hansen, Alvin H. **Hemisphere Solidarity,** *Foreign Affairs,* XIX (October 1940), 12—21.

5989 Holman, Alfred. **Latin-American Cooperation for International Peace,** *Academy of Political Science Proceedings,* XII, 1 (1926), 347—53.

5990 Hull, Cordell. **Foreword,** *Bulletin of the Pan American Union,* LXXIV (April 1940), 189—91.

5991 Inman, Samuel Guy. **Hacia la solaridad americana.** Madrid, Jorro, 1924. 448 p.

5992 ———. **Obstacles to Pan-American Concord,** *Current History,* XVII (February 1922), 789—99.

5993 ———. **Problems in Pan Americanism.** New York, Doran, 1925. xii + 439 p.

5994 Institute of Inter-American Studies. **Inter-American Economic Affairs.** Washington, Quarterly, 1947—.

Part E. — *Regional International Organization*

5995 Kemmerer, E. W. **A Proposal for Pan-American Monetary Unity,** *Political Science Quarterly,* XXXI (March 1916), 66–80.

5996 Kubitschek, Juscelino. **Operation Pan-America,** *The Ideologies of the Developing Nations,* edited and with an introduction by Paul E. Sigmund, Jr. New York, Praeger, 1963, pp. 320–23.

Excerpt from a speech delivered by Kubitschek at Harvard University on March 7, 1962.

5997 Kunz, Joseph L. **The Idea of "Collective Security" in Pan-American Developments,** *Western Political Quarterly,* VI (December 1953), 658–79.

5998 Lenoir, James L. **The Monroe Doctrine and International Law,** *Journal of Politics,* IV (February 1942), 47–67.

5999 Lima, Alceu Amoroso. **Cultural Inter-Americana.** Rio de Janeiro, Agir, 1962. 60 p.

Inter-American Cultural Council.

6000 Lockey, Joseph Byrne. **Essays on Pan-Americanism.** Berkeley, University of California Press, 1939. 174 p.

Essays are revised from articles previously published in various sources.

6001 ——. **The Meaning of Pan-Americanism,** *American Journal of International Law,* XIX (January 1925), 104–17.

6002 Martin, Charles E. **Regionalism and Neutrality As the Bases of Peace in the Americas,** *American Society of International Law Proceedings,* XXXIV (1940), 18–21.

6003 ——. **Regionalism As Illustrated by the Western Hemisphere: Solidarity of the Americas,** *Social Forces,* XXI (March 1943), 272–75.

6004 Mathews, L. K. **Benjamin Franklin's Plans for a Colonial Union, 1750–1775,** *American Political Science Review,* VIII (August 1914), 393–412.

6005 Mayobre, José A. **Regional Cooperation: Latin American Experience,** *South Asia Pacific Crisis,* Margaret Grant (ed.). New York, Dodd, Mead, 1964, pp. 160–79.

6006 Mecham, Lloyd. J. **Conflicting Ideals of Pan-Americanism,** *Current History,* XXXIII (December 1930), 401–4.

6007 Monbeig, Pierre. **Le panaméricanisme,** *Les institutions internationales et transnationales,* Fernand L'Huillier (ed.). Paris, Presses Universitaires, 1961, pp. 72–78.

6008 Oreamuno, J. R. **The Bases of Inter-American Economic Cooperation,** *Social Science,* XXVIII (October 1953), 216–21.

6009 Padilla, Ezequiel. **The Meaning of Pan-Americanism,** *Foreign Affairs,* XXXII (January 1954), 270–81.

6010 Pereyra, Diomedes de. **The Pan-American Illusion,** *Current History,* XXXIII (November 1930), 239–43.

6011 Perkins, Dexter. **Bringing the Monroe Doctrine Up to Date,** *Foreign Affairs,* XX (January 1942), 253–65.

6012 Polyzoides, Admantios T. **Fifty Years of Pan-America,** *World Affairs Quarterly,* X (July 1939), 185–96.

6013 Popper, David H. **Hemisphere Solidarity in the War Crisis,** *Foreign Policy Reports,* XVIII (May 15, 1942), 50–63.

6014 Quintanilla, Luis. **Panamericanism and Democracy.** Boston, Boston University Press, 1952. 53 p.

Part E. — *Regional International Organization*

6015 Rippy, J. Fred. **Pan-Americanism,** *Federation,* Howard O. Eaton (ed.). Norman, University of Oklahoma Press, 1944. 11–24.

6016 Rowe, L. S. **Bringing the Americas Together,** *Academy of Political Science Proceedings,* VII, 2 (1917), 464–70.

6017 Usher, Roland G. **Pan-Americanism: A Forecast of the Inevitable Clash Between the United States and Europe's Victor.** New York, Century, 1915. xix + 466 p.

6018 Van Aken, Mark Jay. **Pan-Hispanism: Its Origin and Development to 1866.** Berkeley, University of California Press, 1959. ix + 166 p.

6019 Wilcox, Francis O. **The Monroe Doctrine and World War II,** *American Political Science Review,* XXXVI (June 1942), 433–53.

6020 Wilgus, A. Curtis (ed.). **Modern Hispanic America.** Washington, George Washington University Press, 1933. ix + 630 p.

6021 Zimmerman, James Fulton. **Social and Cultural Elements of Pan-Americanism,** *Institute of World Affairs Proceedings,* X (December 1932), 69–73.

7.3 PAN AMERICAN CONFERENCES AND THE PAN AMERICAN UNION (Washington) BEFORE 1948

6022 Albes, Edward. **The Pan American Union,** *Southwestern Social Science Quarterly,* I (December 1920), 248–57.

6023 Barrett, John. **Pan American Union: Peace, Friendship, Commerce.** Washington, Pan American Union, 1911. 253 p.

6024 Beals, Carleton. **Pan Americanism: 1937 Style,** *Political Quarterly,* VIII (October-December 1937), 597—607.

6025 Berkes, Ross N. **River Plate Regional Conference,** *World Affairs Quarterly,* XII (April 1941), 87—90.

6026 Blackmer, Henry M. **United States Policy and the Inter-American Peace System, 1889—1952.** Paris, 1952. 221 p.

6027 Brum, Baltasar. **Steps Toward Latin-American Solidarity,** *Current History,* XXVI (September 1927), 893—96.

6028 Buell, Raymond Leslie. **The Montevideo Conference and the Latin American Policy of the United States,** *Foreign Policy Reports,* IX (November 22, 1933), 210—20.

6029 Bustamante, Antonio S. de. **The Results of the Pan-American Peace Conference,** *World Affairs,* III (March 1937), 410—19.

6030 Canyes Santacana, Manuel. **The Inter-American System and the Conference of Chapultepec,** *American Journal of International Law,* XXXIX (July 1945), 504—517.

6031 Carnegie Endowment for International Peace. **Conferencias internationales americanas, 1889—1936.** Preface by Leo S. Rowe; introduction by James Brown Scott. Washington, Carnegie, 1938. lviii + 746 p.

6032 — —. **Conferencias internationales americana: primer suplemento, 1938—1942.** Washington, Carnegie, 1943. 501 p.

6033 Carson, James. **Commercial and Financial Agencies of Pan-American Union,** *Academy of Political Science Proceedings,* VII, 2 (1917), 452—63.

Part E. — *Regional International Organization*

6034 Chapman, Charles E. **The International Relations of Hispanic America,** *Institute of World Affairs Proceedings,* XIII (1935), 61–65.

6035 Cleven, Andrew N. **Pan-American Problems at the Havana Conference,** *Current History,* XXVII (March 1928), 858–67.

6036 Dávila, Carlos. **The Montevideo Conference and Accomplishments,** *International Conciliation,* CCC (May 1934), 119–58.

6037 Doyle, Michael Francis. **Explanatory Introduction,** *International Conciliation,* CCCXXVIII (March 1937), 197–203.

Documents on the Inter-American Conference for the Maintenance of Peace. Addresses by Justo, Roosevelt, Hull and texts of treaties, acts, and resolutions adopted by the conference.

6038 Dozer, Donald M. **Pan America Consults,** *World Affairs Quarterly,* XI (January 1941), 378–85.

6039 Fenwick, Charles G. **The Buenos Aires Conference: 1936,** *Foreign Policy Reports,* XIII (July 1, 1937), 90–100.

6040 — —. **The Inter-American Conference for the Maintenance of Peace,** *American Society of International Law Proceedings,* XXXI (1937), 34–44.

6041 — —. **The Inter-American Regional System,** *American Political Science Review,* XXXIX (June 1945), 490–99.

6042 — —. **The Inter-American Regional System: Fifty Years of Progress,** *American Journal of International Law,* L (January 1956), 18–31.

6043 Finch, George A. **Explanatory Introduction,** *International Conciliation,* CCCXLIX (April 1939), 145–51.

Issue contains documents pertaining to the eighth conference of American States.

6044 Foreign Policy Association. **Pan Americanism and the Pan American Conferences,** *Foreign Policy Reports,* III (November 25, 1927), 272–91.

6045 — —. **The Sixth Pan American Conference,** *Foreign Policy Reports,* IV (April 27, 1928), 50–85; (July 6, 1928), 188–222.

6046 Francis, Michael J. **The United States and the Act of Chapultepec,** *Southwestern Social Science Quarterly,* XLV (December 1964), 249–57.

6047 Gomez Robledo, Antonio. **Idea y experiencia de América.** Mexico City, Fondo de Cultura Económica, 1958. 250 p.

6048 Gruening, Ernest. **Pan-Americanism Reborn,** *Current History,* XXXIX (February 1934), 529–34.

Montevideo conference.

6049 Hackett, Charles W. **How Plans for a Pan-American League of Nations Miscarried,** *Current History,* XXVII (January 1928), 529–34.

6050 Henderson, Hubert. **The Havana Charter,** *American Economic Review,* XXXIX (June 1949), 605–17.

6051 Herrera, Roberto. **Evolution of Equality of States in the Inter-American System,** *Political Science Quarterly,* LXI (March 1946), 90–119.

6052 Holmes, Olive. **The Mexico City Conference and Regional Security,** *Foreign Policy Reports,* XXI (May 1, 1945), 42–49.

6053 Hudson, Manley O. **The Inter-American Treaties of Pacific Settlement,** *Foreign Affairs,* XV (October 1936), 165–78.

6054 Hughes, Charles Evans. **The Outlook for Pan Americanism — Some Observations on the Sixth International Conference of American States,** *American Society of International Law Proceedings,* XXII (1928), 1–18.

Part E. — *Regional International Organization*

6055 — —. **Pan American Peace Plans.** New Haven, Yale University Press, 1929. 68 p.

6056 Hull, Cordell. **The Results and Significance of the Buenos Aires Conference,** *Foreign Affairs*, XV (April 1937), I–X.

6057 Inman. Samuel Guy. **Hacia la solaridad americana.** Madrid, Jorro, 1924. 448 p.

Santiago conference.

6058 — —. (ed.). **The Lima Conference and the Future of Pan-Americanism,** *Annals of the American Academy of Political and Social Science*, CCIV (July 1939), 129–36.

6059 — —. **Pan-American Conferences and Their Results,** *Southwestern Social Science Quarterly*, IV (December 1923), 238–66; (March 1924), 341–68.

6060 — —. **The Pan American System — An Illustration of Regional Organization for Peace,** *World Affairs*, VI (January 1941), 208–21.

6061 — —. **Pan-American Unity in the Making,** *Current History*, XVIII (September 1923), 919–25.

Santiago conference.

6062 — —. **Results of the Pan-American Congress,** *Current History*, XXVIII (April 1928), 97–108.

6063 Johnson, D. D. **The Mexico City Conference,** *World Affairs Quarterly*, XVI (July 1945), 162–72.

6064 Jones, F. Llewellyn. **The Concert of America — The New World's League of Nations,** *Transactions* (Grotius Society), XI (1925), 117–35.

Comments by Manisty, Keen, Bewes, Palliccia, Fraser, Goitein, Omond, and Bellot.

Part E. — Regional International Organization

6065 Kain, Ronald Stuart. **Peace and the Americas: The Aims and Problems of the Pan American Conference,** *Current History,* XLV (December 1936), 57–61.

6066 Kelchner, Warren. **The Pan American Highway,** *Foreign Affairs,* XVI (July 1938), 723–27.

6067 Ladas, Stephen P. **Pan American Conventions on Industrial Property,** *American Journal of International Law,* XXII (October 1928), 803–21.

6068 Laves, Walter H. C. (ed.). **Inter-American Solidarity.** Chicago, University of Chicago Press, 1941. xiii + 227 p.

6069 Lleras, Alberto. **The Inter-American System,** *Federal World Government,* Julia E. Johnsen (ed.). New York, Wilson, 1948, pp. 46–54.

6070 Lockey, Joseph B. **Pan-Americanism: Its Beginnings.** New York, Macmillan, 1920. 503 p.

6071 Loewenstein, Karl. **Pan Americanism in Action,** *Current History,* New Series, V (November 1943), 229–36.

Rio de Janeiro conference.

6072 McAdoo, W. G. **The International High Commission and Pan-American Cooperation,** *American Journal of International Law,* XI (October 1917), 772–89.

6073 McCulloch, John I. B. **Challenge to the Americas.** New York, Foreign Policy Association, 1940. 64 p.

Havana conference.

6074 McKelvey, Raymond G. **Achievements of the Buenos Aires Conference,** *Institute of World Affairs Proceedings,* XV (1937), 69–72.

Part E. — Regional International Organization

6075 Manger, William. **The Pan American Union at the Sixth International Conference of American States,** *American Journal of International Law,* XXII (October 1928), 764–75.

6076 Masters, Ruth D. **International Agencies in the Western Hemisphere,** *American Journal of International Law,* XXXIX (October 1945), 713–35.

6077 Mecham, J. Lloyd. **The United States and Inter-American Security, 1889–1960.** Austin, University of Texas Press, 1961. xii + 514 p.

6078 Moore, John Bassett. **The Pan-American Financial Conferences and the Inter-American High Commission,** *American Journal of International Law,* XIV (July 1920), 343–55.

6079 Mora, José A. **Contributions of the American States to World Peace,** *American Society of International Law Proceedings,* LI (1957), 186–92.

6080 Moreno Quintana, Lucio Manuel. **El sistema internacional americano.** Buenos Aires, Facultad de Derecho y Ciencias Sociales, 1925–26. 2 vols.

6081 Pezet, F. Alfonso. **Pan-American Cooperation in Pan-American Affairs,** *American Political Science Review,* XI (May 1917), 217–30.

6082 Popper, David H. **The Rio de Janeiro Conference of 1942,** *Foreign Policy Reports,* XVIII (April 15, 1942), 26–35.

6083 Potter, Pitman B. **This World of Nations.** New York, Macmillan, 1929. Chapter XVI.

6084 Reid, William A. **Story of the Pan American Union.** Philadelphia, Dorrance, 1924. 86 p.

Part E. — Regional International Organization

6085 Reinsch, Paul S. **The Fourth International Conference of American Republics,** *American Journal of International Law,* IV (October 1910), 777–93.

6086 — —. **The Third International Conference of American States,** *American Political Science Review,* I (February 1907), 187–99.

6087 Reynolds, Thomas H. (ed.). **The Progress of Pan Americanism.** Washington, Public Affairs Press, 1942. 418 p.

6088 Robertson, William Spence. **The Monroe Doctrine Abroad in 1823–24,** *American Political Science Review,* VI (November 1912), 546–63.

6089 Schain, Josephine. **A Peace Audit of the Americas,** *Annals of the American Academy of Political and Social Science,* CCX (July 1940), 133–38.

6090 Scott, James Brown. **International Conferences of American States, 1889–1940.** New York, Oxford University Press, 1931. 551 p.

A supplement for the years 1933–1940 was issued in 1940 by the Carnegie Endowment for International Peace.

6091 — —. **Seventh Annual Conference of American States,** *American Journal of International Law,* XXVIII (April 1934), 219–30.

6092 — —. **The Sixth International Conference of American States: A Survey,** *International Conciliation,* CCXLI (June 1928), 9–58.

Some of the remarks are taken from the author's April 1928 article in the *American Journal of International Law.*

6093 Shotwell, James T. **On the Rim of the Abyss.** New York. Macmillan, 1936.

Chapter V.

6094 Showman, Richard K. and Judson, Lyman S. (comps.). **The Monroe Doctrine and the Growth of Western Hemisphere Solidarity.** New York, Wilson, 1941. 302 p.

6095 Stone, William T. **The Pan-American Arbitration Treaty,** *Foreign Policy Reports,* V (November 13, 1929), 313–26.

6096 Stuart, Graham. **The Eighth International Conference of American States,** *World Affairs Quarterly,* X (April 1939), 9–14.

6097 —— ——. **The Rio Conference,** *World Affairs Quarterly,* XIII (April 1942), 13–21.

6098 Tannenbaum, Frank. **An American Commonwealth of Nations,** *Foreign Affairs,* XXII (July 1944), 577–87.

6099 —— ——. **The Future of the Inter-American System,** *Academy of Political Science Proceedings,* XXI (May 1945), 415–20.

6100 Thomson, Charles A. **Results of the Lima Conference,** *Foreign Policy Reports,* XV (March 15, 1939), 1–8.

6101 —— ——. **The Seventh Pan-American Conference: Montevideo,** *Foreign Policy Reports,* X (June 6, 1934), 86–96.

6102 —— ——. **Toward a New Pan-Americanism,** *Foreign Policy Reports,* XII (November 1, 1936), 202–12.
Buenos Aires conference.

6103 Tomlinson, Edward. **The Meaning of Lima: Secretary Hull's Handling of the Argentina Problem was the Highspot of the Conference,** *Current History,* XLIX (February 1939), 37–40.
Followed by selected documents.

6104 Trueblood, Howard J. **The Havana Conference of 1940,** *Foreign Policy Reports,* XVI (September 15, 1940), 158–64.

6105 —— —— . **Progress of Pan-American Cooperation,** *Foreign Policy Reports,* XV (February 15, 1940), 286–300.

6106 Villasenor, Eduardo. **The Inter-American Bank: Prospects and Dangers,** *Foreign Affairs,* XX (October 1941), 165–74.

6107 Vought, Robert L. **The Administration of an Inter-American Cooperative Health Program,** *Public Administration Review,* VI (Winter, 1946), 42–52.

6108 Warshaw, J. **The Fifth Pan-American Conference,** *Southwestern Social Science Quarterly,* III (March 1923), 323–42.

6109 Welles, Sumner. **Results of the South American Conference,** *Academy of Political Science Proceedings,* XVII, 3 (1936), 297–308.

6110 Whitaker, Arthur P. **Inter-American Intervention,** *Current History,* New Series, X (March 1946), 206–11.

6111 —— —— . **Latin America and Postwar Organization,** *Annals of the American Academy of Political and Social Science,* CCXL (July 1945), 109–15.

6112 —— —— . **The Western Hemisphere Idea: Its Rise and Decline.** Ithaca, Cornell University Press, 1954. x + 194 p.

6113 Williams, John. **The Pan American and League of Nations Treaties of Arbitration and Conciliation,** *British Yearbook of International Law,* X (1929), 14–31.

6114 Wood, Bryce. **Maintaining Peace in the Americas,** *International Conciliation,* CDXIX (March 1946), 134–43.

6115 — —. **The Making of the Good Neighbor Policy.** New York, Columbia University Press, 1961. x + 438 p.

7.4 ORGANIZATION OF AMERICAN STATES
(Washington)

7.4.1 GENERAL OBSERVATIONS

6116 Alexander, R. **Labor and Inter-American Relations,** *Annals of the American Academy of Political and Social Science,* CCCXXXIV (March 1961), 41–53.

6117 Aufricht, Hans. **Principles and Practices of Recognition by International Organizations,** *American Journal of International Law,* XLIII (October 1949), 679–704.

6118 Azicri, Max. **The OAS and the Communist Challenge,** *International Development Review,* VII (July 1964), 8–12.

6119 Ball, M. Margaret. **Issue for the Americas: Non-Intervention v. Human Rights and the Preservation of Democratic Institutions,** *International Organization,* XV (Winter, 1961), 21–37.

6120 — —. **The Organization of American States and the Council of Europe,** *British Yearbook of International Law,* XXVI (1949), 150–76.

6121 Cline, Howard F. **The Inter-American System,** *Current History,* New Series, XXVIII (March 1955), 177–84.

Part E. — Regional International Organization

6122 Conde, Alexander de. **The Organization of American States — Peace and Power Politics,** *World Affairs Quarterly*, XXII (January 1952), 402–14.

6123 Cornell-Smith, Gordon. **The Future of the Organization of American States: Significance of the Punta del Este Conference,** *World Today*, New Series, XVIII (March 1962), 112–20.

6124 — —. **The Organization of American States,** *World Today*, New Series, XVI (October 1960), 447–56.

6125 Cuevas, Francisco. **The Bogotá Conference and Recent Developments in Pan-American Relations: A Mexican View,** *International Affairs*, XXIV (October 1948), 524–33.

6126 Davis, Harold E. **The Charter of the Organization of American States,** *Western Political Quarterly*, I (December 1948), 439–48.

6127 Dozer, Donald M. (ed.). **The Monroe Doctrine: Its Modern Significance.** New York, Knopf, 1965. xiv + 208 p.

6128 Dreier, John C. **The Organization of American States and the Hemisphere Crisis.** New York, Harper and Row, 1962. xii + 147 p.

6129 — —. **The Organization of American States and United States Policy,** *International Organization*, XVII (Winter, 1963), 36–53.

6130 Duggan, Laurence. **The Americas: The Search For Hemisphere Security.** Foreword by Herschel Brickell. New York, Holt, 1949. ix + 242 p.

6131 Fenwick, Charles G. **Inter-American Regional Procedures for the Settlement of Disputes,** *International Organization*, X (February 1956), 12–21.

Part E. — Regional International Organization

6132 — —. **The Inter-American Regional System.** New York, McMullen, 1949. 96 p.

6133 — —. **The Inter-American Regional System,** *Journal of International Affairs,* IX, 1 (1955), 93–100.

6134 — —. **The Inter-American Regional System,** *Regional Arrangements for Security and the United Nations,* Commission to Study the Organization of Peace (ed.). New York, Commission to Study the Organization of Peace, 1953, pp. 42–48.

6135 — —. **The Organization of American States: The Inter-American Regional System.** Washington, Kaufman, 1963. xxxiii + 601 p.

6136 Fitzgibbon, Russell H. **The Organization of American States: Time of Ordeal,** *Orbis,* V (Spring, 1961), 74–86.

6137 Francis, Michael J. **The United States and the Act of Chapultepec,** *Southwestern Social Science Quarterly,* XLV (December 1964), 249–57.

6138 Furniss, Edgar S., Jr. **The Inter-American System and Recent Caribbean Disputes,** *International Organization,* IV (November 1950), 585–97.

6139 — —. **Recent Changes in the Inter-American System,** *International Organization,* II (September 1948), 455–68.

6140 Goodspeed, Stephen S. **Political and Military Teeth for the Organization of American States,** *World Affairs Quarterly,* XXII (April 1951), 12–20.

6141 Guerrant, Edward O. **The Council of the Organization of American States: Watchdog of the Hemisphere,** *World Affairs Quarterly,* XXVI (January 1956), 387–97.

6142 Hadley, Paul E. **The Caracas Conference,** *World Affairs Quarterly,* XXV (July 1954), 123–39.

6143 — —. **The Case of Operation Pan America,** *Institute of World Affairs Proceedings,* XXXV (1959), 195–203.

6144 — —. **Ninth International Conference of American States at Bogotá, Colombia, March 30–May 2, 1948,** *World Affairs Quarterly,* XIX (July 1948), 181–93.

6145 Hall, Rufus G., Jr. **Actions of the Council of the Organization of American States Under the Rio Pact,** *Southwestern Social Science Quarterly,* XXXII (September 1951), 69–78.

6146 Inman, Samuel Guy. **Failure at Bogotá,** *World Affairs,* New Series, II (October 1948), 429–33.

6147 Kass, Stephen L. **Obligatory Negotiations in International Organizations,** *Canadian Yearbook of International Law,* III (1965), 36–72.

6148 Kisler, Margaret. **Organization of American States.** 4th ed. Washington, U. S. Government Printing Office, 1955. 74 p.

6149 Kunz, Josef L. **The Bogotá Charter of the Organization of American States,** *American Journal of International Law,* XLII (July 1948), 568–89.

6150 Lacarte, Julio A. **The Latin American System,** *American Society of International Law Proceedings,* LIII (1959), 62–68.

6151 Lerche, Charles O., Jr. **Development of Rules Relating to Peace-Keeping by the Organization of American States,** *American Society of International Law Proceedings,* LIX (1965), 60–66.

6152 Lleras, Alberto. **The Inter-American System Today,** *Annals of the American Academy of Political and Social Science,* CCLXXXII (July 1952), 97–103.

6153 — —. **The Organization of American States.** Lewisburg, Pa., Bucknell University Press, 1954. 16 p.

6154 Ogden, Georgine L. **The Organization of American States,** *Journal of International Affairs,* III (Spring, 1949), 47–55.

6155 Onody, Oliver. **The Rio de Janeiro Treaty (Inter-American Treaty of Reciprocal Assistance),** *India Quarterly,* IX (April-June 1953), 136––59.

6156 Plank, John N. **The Alliance for Progress: Problems and Prospects,** *Daedalus,* XCI (Fall, 1962), 800–11.

6157 — —. **The American Committee on Dependent Territories,** *Public Policy,* VII (1956), 25–61.

6158 MacQuarrie, H. N. **Pan Americanism: Pattern of Regional Cooperation,** *Dalhousie Review,* XXXII (Autumn, 1954), 223–34.

6159 Manger, William. **The Organization of American States: Present Problems and Future Prospects,** *World Justice,* IV (September 1962), 5–13.

6160 — —. **Pan America in Crisis: The Future of the OAS.** Washington, Public Affairs Press, 1961. 104 p.

6161 — —. **Regional Collective Security in the Americas,** *Social Science,* XXVIII (October 1953), 199–204.

6162 Mayobre, José A. **Regional Cooperation: Latin American Experience,** *South Asia Pacific Crisis*, Margaret Grant (ed.). New York, Dodd, Mead, 1964, pp. 160–79.

6163 Miller, Edward G., Jr. **A Fresh Look at the Inter-American Community,** *Foreign Affairs*, XXXIII (July 1955), 634–47.

6164 Mora, José A. **The Organization of American States,** *International Organization*, XIV (Autumn, 1960), 514–23.

6165 Morgan, G. G. **The Organization of American States: A Problem of Administrative Reorganization,** *Revue Internationale des Sciences Administratives*, XVIII, 3 (1952), 501–29.

6166 Ronning, C. Neale. **Punta del Este: The Limits of Collective Security in a Troubled Hemisphere.** New York, Carnegie, 1963. 31 p.

6167 Sanders, William. **The OAS – The New Diplomacy,** *Institute of World Affairs Proceedings*, XXXVI (1960), 224–37.

6168 — —. **The Organization of American States: Summary of the Conclusion of the Ninth International Conference of American States, Bogotá, Colombia, March 30-May 2, 1948,** *International Conciliation*, CDXLII (June 1948), 383–433.

6169 Slater, Jerome. **A Revaluation of Collective Security: The Organization of American States in Action.** Columbus, Ohio State University Press, 1965. 56 p.

6170 — —. **The United States, the Organization of American States, and the Dominican Republic, 1961–1963,** *International Organization*, XVIII (Spring, 1964), 268–91.

Part E. — Regional International Organization

6171 Stoetzer, O. Carlos. **The Organization of American States.** New York, Praeger, 1965. 213 p.

6172 Thomas, A. J., Jr. **The Organization of American States and Subversive Intervention,** *American Society of International Law Proceedings,* LV (1961), 19—24.
Comments by H. H. Godoy.

6173 Thomas, Ann (Van Wynen) and Thomas, A. J., Jr. **The Organization of American States.** Dallas, Southern Methodist University Press, 1963. 530 p.

6174 Travis, Martin B., Jr. **Collective Intervention by the Organization of American States,** *American Society of International Law Proceedings,* LI (1957), 100—10.

6175 — —. **The Organization of American States: A Guide to the Future,** *Western Political Quarterly,* X (September 1957), 491—511.

6176 Venkatasubbiah, H. **Prospects of an Asian Union: Lessons from the Organization of American States,** *India Quarterly,* V (April-June 1949), 99—111.

6177 Wells, Henry. **The OAS and the Dominican Elections,** *Orbis,* VII (Spring, 1963), 150—63.

6178 Whitaker, Arthur P. **Cuba's Intervention in Venezuela: A Test of the OAS,** *Orbis,* VIII (Fall, 1964), 511—36.

6179 — —. **Development of American Regionalism: The Organization of American States,** *International Conciliation,* CDLXIX (March 1951), 123—64.

6180 Willauer, Whiting. **The Practical Workings of the OAS Conference,** *Institute of World Affairs Proceedings,* XXXVI (1960), 219–23.

7.4.2 RELATION TO OTHER INTERNATIONAL ORGANIZATIONS

6181 Arechaga, M. E. J. de. **Co-ordination of the Systems of the United Nations and the Organisation of American States for the Pacific Settlement of Disputes, and Collective Security,** *Recueil des Cours,* CXI (1964), 423–526.

6182 Ball, M. Margaret. **Inter-American and World Organization,** *Current History,* New Series, X (January 1946), 1–7.

6183 — —. **The Inter-American System and the United Nations,** *World Affairs,* XII (April 1946), 48–61.

6184 Canyes Santacana, Manuel. **The Inter-American System and the United Nations Organization,** *Regionalism and Security,* K. M. Panikkar, V. T. Krishnamachari, H. V. Evatt, K. Santhanam, I. H. Baqai, G. A. Johnson, Manuel Canyes Santacana. Bombay, Oxford University Press, 1948, pp. 57–73.

6185 — —. **The Organization of American States and the United Nations.** 4th ed. Washington, Pan American Union 1958. 37 p.

6186 Furniss, Edgar S., Jr. **The United States, the Inter-American System and the United Nations,** *Political Science Quarterly,* LXV (September 1950), 415–30.

6187 Hadley, Paul E. **Organization of American States: A Regional System Within the United Nations,** *World Affairs Quarterly,* XXII (April 1951), 31–43.

Part E. — Regional International Organization

6188 Hayton, Robert D. **The Inter-American Regional Group in the Community of Nations,** *American Society of International Law Proceedings,* XLVIII (1954), 60–67.

6189 Humphreys, Robin. **The Pan American System and the United Nations,** *International Affairs,* XXII (January 1946), 75–84.

6190 Macdonald, R. St. J. **The Developing Relationship Between Superior and Subordinate Political Bodies at the International Level: A Note on the Experience of the United Nations and the Organization of American States,** *Canadian Yearbook of International Law,* II (1964), 21–54.

6191 Mecham, J. Lloyd. **The Integration of the Inter-American Security System into the United Nations,** *Journal of Politics,* IX (May 1947), 178–96.

6192 Organization of American States, Pan American Union, Department of Legal Affairs. **The Organization of American States and the United Nations.** Washington, Annually, 1949–.

6193 Padilla, Ezequiel. **The American System and the World Organization,** *Foreign Affairs,* XXIV (October 1945), 99–107.

6194 Sharp, Walter R. **The Inter-American System and the United Nations,** *Foreign Affairs,* XXIII (April 1945), 450–64.

6195 Whitaker, Arthur P. **The Role of Latin America in Relation to Current Trends in International Organization,** *American Political Science Review,* XXXIX (June 1945), 500–10.

7.4.3 ROLE OF CANADA

6196 Anglin, Douglas G. **U. S. Opposition of Canadian Membership in the Pan American Union: A Canadian View,** *International Organization,* XV (Winter, 1961), 1–20.

6197 Harbron, John D. **Canada and the Organization of American States.** Washington, Canadian American Committee, 1963. vii + 31 p.

6198 Massey, Vincent. **Canada and the Inter-American System,** *Foreign Affairs,* XXVI (July 1948), 693—700.

6199 Miller, Eugene H. **Canada and the Pan American Union,** *International Journal,* III (Winter, 1947—48), 24—38.

6200 — —. **Canada, the United States and Latin America,** *Essays in History and International Relations in Honor of George Hubbard Blakeslee,* Dwight E. Lee and George E. McReynolds (eds.). Worcester, Mass., Clark University Press, 1949, pp. 83—103.

6201 Nicholson, Norman L. **Canada in the American Community.** Princeton, Van Nostrand, 1963. 128 p.

6202 Podea, Iris S. **Pan American Sentiment in French Canada,** *International Journal,* III (Autumn, 1948), 334—48.

6203 Roussin, Marcel. **Le Canada et le système interaméricain.** Ottawa, Editions de l'Université d'Ottawa, 1959. ix + 285 p.

7.5 CARIBBEAN REGIONALISM

7.5.1 CARIBBEAN COMMISSION
(Hato Rey)

6204 Anon. **Caribbean Laboratory: Study of New Mechanisms for International Collaboration; Their Workings and Postwar Promise,** *Fortune,* XXIX (February 1944), 124—27 ff.

Part E. — Regional International Organization

6205 Bough, James A. **The Caribbean Commission,** *International Organization,* III (November 1949), 643–55.

6206 Bunche, Ralph J. **The Anglo-American Caribbean Commission: An Experiment in Regional Cooperation.** New York, Institute of Pacific Relations, 1945. 29 p.

6207 Fox, Annette Baker. **Freedom and Welfare in the Caribbean.** New York, Harcourt, Brace, 1949. 272 p.

6208 Jordan, Henry P. **Regional Experiment in the Caribbean,** *Current History,* New Series, VI (May 1944), 389–404.

6209 Obern, Alfred G. **Personnel Administration in the Caribbean and South Pacific Commissions,** *International Review of Administrative Sciences,* XXV, 3 (1959), 263–69.

6210 Poole, Bernard L. **The Caribbean Commission: Background of Cooperation in the West Indies.** Columbia, University of South Carolina Press, 1960. xix + 303 p.

6211 Stockdale, Frank. **The Work of the Caribbean Commission,** *International Affairs,* XXIII (April 1947), 213–20.

6212 Strange, Susan. **The Four-Power Caribbean Commission,** *World Affairs,* New Series, I (April 1947), 171–80.

6213 Taussig, Charles W. **A Four-Power Program in the Caribbean,** *Foreign Affairs,* XXIV (July 1946), 699–710.

6214 Wilgres, A. C. **The Caribbean: Contemporary Trends.** Gainesville, University of Florida Press, 1953. 292 p.

7.5.2 WEST INDIES FEDERATION EFFORTS

6215 Archibald, Charles H. **The Failure of the West Indies Federation,** *World Today*, New Series, XVIII (June 1962), 233–42.

6216 Burns, Alan. **Towards a Caribbean Federation,** *Foreign Affairs*, XXXIV (October 1955), 128–40.

6217 Campbell, Jock. **The West Indies: Can They Stand Alone?** *International Affairs*, XXXIX (July 1963), 335–44.

6218 Etzioni, Amitai. **Political Unification.** New York, Holt, Rinehart and Winston, 1965.

Chapter V.

6219 Hewitt-Myring, Philip. **British Caribbean Federation,** *Parliamentary Affairs*, VIII (Autumn, 1955), 436–44.

6220 Lewis, Gordon. **The British Caribbean Federation: The West Indian Background,** *Political Quarterly*, XXVII (January-March 1957), 49–65.

6221 Lowenthal, David (ed.). **The West Indies Federation: Perspectives on a New Nation.** New York, Columbia University Press, 1961. 142 p.

6222 MacColl, E. Kimbark. **Poverty and Politics in the Caribbean,** *International Journal*, VII (Winter, 1951–52), 12–22.

6223 Mahabir, Dennis J. **The Caribbean Federation,** *India Quarterly*, XIII (January-March 1957), 32–39.

6224 P., H. **Background to West Indian Federation,** *World Today*, New Series, VI (June 1950), 255–64.

6225 P., M. **Federation in the British West Indies: Problems and Prospects,** *World Today,* New Series, XIII (March 1957), 109—17.

6226 Proctor, Jesse Harris, Jr. **The Functional Approach to Political Union: Lessons from the Effort to Federate the British Caribbean Territories,** *International Organization,* X (February 1956), 35—48.

6227 Springer, Hugh W. **Federation in the Caribbean: An Attempt That Failed,** *International Organization,* XVI (Autumn, 1962), 758—75.

6228 — —. **Reflections on the Failure of the First West Indian Federation.** Cambridge, Harvard University, Center for International Affairs, 1962. 66 p.

6229 Wallace, Elisabeth. **The West Indies Federation: Decline and Fall,** *International Journal,* XVII (Summer, 1962), 269—88.

6230 Washington, S. Walter. **Crisis in the British West Indies,** *Foreign Affairs,* XXXVIII (July 1960), 646—55.

7.6 CENTRAL AMERICAN REGIONALISM

6231 Anderson, Luis. **The Peace Conference of Central America,** *American Journal of International Law,* II (January 1908), 144—51.

History of Central American integration efforts.

6232 Anon. **The Central American Convention Compared,** *Journal of the International Commission of Jurists,* VI (Summer, 1965), 136—87.

A comparison with the Inter-American Draft Convention on Human Right and the European Convention for the Protection of Human Rights and Fundamental Freedoms.

6233 Barnes, Robert. **Bibliografía preliminar sobre la integración económica centroamericana.** Washington, Pan American Union, 1961. 5 p.

Part E. — Regional International Organization

6234 Buell, Raymond Leslie. **Union or Disunion in Central America?** *Foreign Affairs*, XI (April 1933), 478–89.

6235 Busey, James L. **Central American Union: The Latest Attempt,** *Western Political Quarterly*, XIV (March 1961), 49–63.

6236 Chamorro, Pedro J. **Historia de la federación de la America Central 1823–1840.** Madrid, Ediciones Culturas Hispánicas, 1951. 644 p.

6237 Dawley, Thomas R., Jr. **How the Central American Union Was Born,** *Current History*, XV (January 1922), 616–26.

6238 Gray, Beryl. **The Central American Union and the United States,** *Current History*, XIV (May 1921), 294–97.

6239 Hudson, Manley O. **Central American Court of Justice,** *American Journal of International Law*, XXVI (October 1932), 759–86.

6240 Huelin, David. **Economic Integration in Latin America: Progress and Problems,** *International Affairs*, XL, (July 1964) 430–39.
LAFTA.

6241 International Commission of Jurists. **The Central American Draft Convention on Human Rights and the Central American Court,** *Journal of the International Commission of Jurists*, VI (Summer, 1965), 129–35.

6242 Karnes, Thomas L. **The Failure of Union: Central America, 1924–1960.** Chapel Hill, University of North Carolina Press, 1961. xii + 277 p.

6243 A Latin-American Observer. **Failure of the Central American Union,** *Current History*, XVI (May 1922), 285–87.

6244 Martz, John D. **Justo Rufino Barrios and Central American Union.** Gainesville, University of Florida Press, 1963. 51 p.

6245 Myers, Denys P. **A New Era in Central America,** *Current History,* XVIII (June 1923), 407–9.

6246 Padelford, Norman J. **Cooperation in the Central American Region: The Organization of Central American States,** *International Organization,* XI (Winter, 1957), 41–54.

6247 Puig, Amaro. **Integración y fomento económico centroamericano,** *Humanismo* (Mexico City), IV (January-February 1954), 88–90.

6248 Roberts, W. Adolphe. **Can Central America Unite?** *Current History,* XL (September 1934), 669–75.

6249 Scott, James Brown. **The Central American Peace Conference of 1907,** *American Journal of International Law,* II (January 1908), 121–43.

6250 Sol Castellanos, Jorge. **La integración económica de Centroamérica,** *Economía Salvadoreña,* IV (April-June 1958), 11–22.

7.7 SOUTH AMERICAN REGIONALISM AND THE LATIN AMERICAN FREE TRADE ASSOCIATION
(Montevideo)

6251 Aguiar, Pinto de. **Fundamentos, objectivos e bases do Mercado Regional Latinoamericano.** Salvador, Progresso, 1959. 238 p.

6252 Campbell, John C. **Nationalism and Regionalism in South America,** *Foreign Affairs,* XXI (October 1942), 132—48.

6253 Farag, Attiat A. **The Latin American Free Trade Area,** *Inter-American Economic Affairs,* XVII (Summer, 1963), 73—84.

6254 Griffin, Keith and Ffrench-Davis, Ricardo. **Customs Unions and Latin American Integration,** *Journal of Common Market Studies,* IV (October 1965), 1—21.

6255 Haas, Ernst B. and Schmitter, Phillipe C. **Economics and Differential Patterns of Political Integration: Projections About Unity in Latin America,** *International Organization,* XVIII (Autumn, 1964), 705—37.

6256 Huelin, David. **A Free Trade Area in South America,** *World Today,* New Series, XVI (February 1960), 79—88.

6257 Maschko, Arturo. **Mercado común para os países du continente americano (discurso),** *Revista du Conselho Nacional de Economia* (Rio de Janeiro), V (November-December 1956), 48—53.

6258 Morales, Cecilio. **Trade and Economic Integration in Latin America,** *Social Science,* XXXV (October 1960), 231—37.

6259 Sammons, Robert L. **Proposals for a Common Market in Latin America,** *Public Policy,* X (1960), 268—96.

6260 Schmitter, Philippe C. and Haas, Ernst B. **Mexico and Latin American Economic Regionalism.** Berkeley, University of California, Institute of International Studies, 1964. 43 p.

6261 — —. **The Politics of Economics in Latin American Regionalism: The Latin American Free Trade Association After Four Years of Operation.** Denver, University of Denver, Social Science Foundation and Graduate School of International Studies, 1965. 78 p.

6262 Sedwitz, Walter J. **A Common Market for Latin America?** *Current History*, New Series, XLIII (July 1962), 1—10.

6263 Wionczek, Miguel S. **Latin American Free Trade Association,** *International Conciliation*, DLI (January 1965), 3—79.

7.8 INTER-AMERICAN DEVELOPMENT BANK
(Washington)

6264 Adam, H.-T. **Les organismes internationaux spécialisés.** Paris, Pinchon et Durand-Auzias, 1965.

Volume II, Chapter VII.

6265 Herrera, Felipe. **The Inter-American Development Bank,** *Social Science*, XXX (October 1960), 216—21.

8. WESTERN EUROPE AND THE NORTH ATLANTIC

Of all the regional organizations reviewed so far, only those of Europe deserve to be called supranational. The growth of economic institutions with a capability of overruling domestic actions has been a much heralded development.

8.1 BIBLIOGRAPHY

See A 3.4.5.

8.2 GENERAL DISCUSSIONS

8.2.1 EUROPE VERSUS ATLANTICA AS INTEGRATING COMMUNITIES

6266 Acheson, Dean. **The Dilemmas of Our Times,** *Atlantic Community Quarterly,* I (Winter, 1963—64), 570—85.

6267 Albonetti, Achille. **The New Europe and the West,** *Daedalus,* XCIII (Winter, 1964), 6—42.

6268 Allais, Maurice. **Toward an Integrated Atlantic Community,** *NATO in Quest of Cohesion,* Karl H. Cerny and Henry W. Briefs (eds.). New York, Praeger, 1965, pp. 359—86.

6269 Allen, H. C. **The Anglo-American Predicament: The British Commonwealth, the United States and European Unity.** New York, St. Martin's, 1960. 241 p.

6270 Amery, L. S. **The British Empire and the Pan-European Idea,** *International Affairs,* IX (January 1930), 1—12.

Comments by Goad, Hobson, Reade, Deverell, Malcolm.

6271 Aris, R. **Nationalism and Europe,** *Contemporary Review,* CLVII (November 1940), 537—43.

6272 Aron, Raymond. **Old Nations, New Europe,** *Daedalus,* XCIII (Winter, 1964), 43—66.

6273 **Atlantic Community Quarterly.** Baltimore, Atlantic Council of the United States, Quarterly, 1963—.

Each issue contains a section of documents entitled "Source Material."

6274 Bell, Coral. **The Diplomatic Meaning of "Europe,"** *Europe Without Britain,* Coral Bell (ed.). Melbourne, Cheshire, 1963, pp. 1—26.

6275 Beloff, Max. **The United States and the Unity of Europe.** Washington, Brookings, 1963. xii + 124 p.

6276 Bieri, Ernst. **An Atlantic Dialogue in Bruges,** *Orbis,* I (Winter, 1958), 397—407.

6277 Birrenbach, Kurt. **Europe and America: Partners in Atlantic Community,** *Atlantic Community Quarterly,* I (Summer, 1963), 213—18.

6278 — —. **The Future of the Atlantic Community: Toward European-American Partnership.** Preface by Christian A. Herter. New York, Praeger, 1963. xii + 94 p.

6279 Boel, René. **European Community — Atlantic Community,** *Atlantic Community Quarterly,* I (March 1963), 72—78.

Reprinted from *Revue Politique* (Brussels), May 1962.

6280 Bowie, Robert R. **Prospects for Atlantic Community,** *Harvard Review,* I (Fall, 1962), 7—15.

6281 Braden, Thomas W. **The Possibilities for Organization in Europe,** *Foundations of World Organization,* Lyman Bryson, Louis Finkelstein, and R. W. MacIver (eds.). New York, Harper, 1950, pp. 113—18.

6282 Brierly, Caroline. **The Making of European Policy.** London, Oxford University Press, 1963. 53 p.

6283 Brown, Seyom. **An Alternative to the Grand Design,** *World Politics,* XVII (January 1965), 232—42.

6284 Brugmans, Henri. **The Dynamics of European Integration,** *European Integration,* C. Grove Haines (ed.). Baltimore, Johns Hopkins Press, 1959, pp. 161—76.

6285 Burgess, W. Randolph. **Reply to Lord Gladwyn,** *Atlantic Community Quarterly,* II (Summer, 1964), 192—97.

Comment on Gladwyn Jebb's article in *Encounter,* December 1963.

6286 Cabot, Thomas D. **Common Market: Economic Federation for U. S. of Europe?** New York, Committee for Economic Development, 1959. 28 p.

6287 Carey, Jane Perry Clark. **Western European Union and the Atlantic Community,** *Foreign Policy Reports,* XXVI (June 15, 1950), 66—80.

6288 Carter, W. Horsfall. **The European Commonwealth,** *International Relations,* I (October 1954), 50—57.

6289 Catlin, George E. G. **The Atlantic Community.** London, Coram, 1959. 146 p.

6290 Christol, Carl Q. **Europe 1950,** *World Affairs Quarterly,* XXI (January 1951), 417—27.

6291 Collier, David S. and Glaser, Kurt (eds.). **Western Integration and the Future of Eastern Europe.** Chicago, Regnery, 1964. 207 p.

6292 Coser, Lewis A. **Europe's Neurotic Nationalism: Tribalism Replaces Freedom and the Rights of Man,** *Commentary,* I (June 1946), 58—63.

6293 Coudenhove-Kalergi, Richard N. **The Pan-European Movement,** *International Federation of Democracies (Proposed),* Julia E. Johnsen (ed.). New York, Wilson, 1941, pp. 193—98.

Reprinted from *Labour,* February 1939.

6294 Cox, R. W. **The Study of European Institutions: Some Problems of Economic and Political Organization,** *Journal of Common Market Studies,* III (February 1965), 102—17.

6295 Dennett, Raymond. **The International Organization of the Free World,** *Academy of Political Science Proceedings,* XXIV (January 1951), 181 —90.

6296 Deutsch, Karl W. **Towards Western European Integration: An Interim Assessment,** *Journal of International Affairs,* XVI, 1 (1962), 89—101.

6297 Dorpalen, A. **New Nationalism in Europe,** *Virginia Quarterly Review,* XX (July 1944), 335—49.

6298 Elliott, William Y. **Proposal for a North Atlantic Round Table for Freedom,** *Orbis,* II (Summer, 1958), 221—35.

6299 Englemann, Hugo O. **The European Empire from Charlemagne to the Common Market,** *Social Forces,* XLI (May 1962), 297—301.

Part E. — Regional International Organization

6300 **European Yearbook.** Hague, Nijhoff, Annually, 1955—.

6301 Fay, Sidney B. **Co-operative Policies in Europe,** *Current History,* New Series, XXVI (January 1954), 18—24.

6302 Forthomme, Pierre-A. **Some Complexities of European Integration,** *Journal of International Affairs,* XVI, 1 (1962), 47—57.

6303 Fulbright, J. William. **A Community of Free Nations,** *Atlantic Community Quarterly,* I (Summer, 1963), 113—30.

6304 — —. **The Concert of Free Nations,** *International Organization,* XVII (Summer, 1963), 787—803.

6305 Goormaghtigh, John. **European Integration,** *International Conciliation,* CDLXXXVIII (February 1953), 50—109.

6306 Gordon, Lincoln. **Myth and Reality in European Integration,** *Yale Review,* XLV (September 1955), 80—103.

6307 — —. **NATO and European Integration,** *World Politics,* X (January 1958), 219—31.

6308 — —. **Political Integration in the Free World Community,** *The United States and the Western Community,* H. Field Haviland (ed.). Haverford, Pa., Haverford College Press, 1957, pp. 65—79.

6309 Graubard, Stephen R. **A New Europe?** *Daedalus,* XCIII (Winter, 1964), 543—66.

6310 Grosser, Alfred. **France and Germany in the Atlantic Community,** *International Organization,* XVII (Summer, 1963), 550—73.

Part E. — Regional International Organization

6311 — —. **Suez, Hungary and European Integration,** *International Organization,* XI (Summer, 1957), 470—80.

6312 Haas, Ernst B. **International Integration: The European and the Universal Process,** *International Organization,* XV (Summer, 1961), 366—92.

6313 — —. **Persistent Themes in Atlantic and European Unity,** *World Politics,* X (July 1958), 614—28.

6314 Haekkerup, Per. **Europe: Basic Problems and Perspectives,** *International Affairs,* XLI (January 1965), 1—10.

6315 Haesaert, J. **Obstacles à la cohésion de l'Europe,** *Bulletin de la Classe des Lettres et des Sciences Morales et Politiques,* Series 5, XXXVI, 3, (1951), 68—103.

6316 Hahn, Hugo J. **Constitutional Limitations in the Law of the European Organisations,** *Recueil des Cours,* CVIII (1963), 195—306.

6317 Haines, C. Grove (ed.). **European Integration.** Baltimore, Johns Hopkins Press, 1957. 310 p.

6318 Halle, Louis J. **The Western Alliance: Its Cultural Foundation,** *Journal of International Affairs,* XII, 1 (1958), 9—16.

6319 — —. **Where Is Europe Heading?** *Atlantic Community Quarterly,* I (Fall, 1963), 405—12.

Reprinted from the *New York Times,* June 2, 1963.

6320 Hallstein, Walter. **The European Community and Atlantic Partnership,** *International Organization,* XVII (Summer, 1963), 771—86.

6321　Hartley, Livingston. **An Atlantic Commission,** *Orbis*, VII (Summer, 1963), 300—7.

6322　— —. **Atlantic Partnership — How?** *Orbis*, VIII (Spring, 1964), 141—52.

6323　Hay, Denys. **Europe: The Emergence of an Idea.** Edinburgh, Edinburgh University Press, 1957. 132 p.

6324　Heilbroner, Robert L. **Forging a United Europe: The Story of the European Community.** New York, Public Affairs Committee, 1961. 32 p.

6325　Heldring, J. L. **Atlantic Partnership: European Unity,** *Survival*, VII (January-February 1965), 30—37.

6326　Herriot, Édouard. **Pan-Europe?** *Foreign Affairs*, VIII (January 1930), 237—47.

6327　Hill, Russell. **The Organization of Europe,** *Foundations of World Organization*, Lyman Bryson, Louis Finkelstein, and R. W. MacIver (eds.). New York, Harper, 1950, pp. 71—78.

6328　Hitchner, Dell G. **Supranational Organizations and Democracy in Western Europe,** *Parliamentary Affairs*, XI (Summer, 1958), 273—86.

6329　Hoffmann, Stanley H. **Discord in Community: The North Atlantic Area As a Partial International System,** *International Organization*, XVII (Summer, 1963), 521—49.

6330　— —. **European Process at Atlantic Cross Purposes,** *Journal of Common Market Studies*, III (February 1965), 85—101.

6331 — —. **Problems of Atlantic Partnership,** *Harvard Review*, I (Fall, 1962), 16—25.

6332 Jebb, Gladwyn. **Atlantic Dreams and Realities,** *Encounter*, XXI (December 1963), 57—63.
Critiqued by W. Randolph Burgess in *Atlantic Community Quarterly*, Summer, 1964.

6333 Johnson, G. A. **European Regionalism,** *India Quarterly*, II (April-June 1946), 136—43.

6334 Kaiser, Karl. **L'Europe des Savants: European Integration and the Social Sciences,** *Journal of Common Market Studies*, IV (October 1965), 36—46.

6335 Kaltefleiter, Werner. **Funktion und Verantwortung in den Europäischen Organisationen.** Frankfurt, Verlag, 1964. xii + 176 p.

6336 Kennedy, Sinclair. **The Pan-Angles: A Consideration of the Federation of the Seven English-Speaking Nations.** New York, Longmans, Green, 1915. ix + 244 p.

6337 Klausner, Leopold C. **What Hope for Europe?** *World Affairs Quarterly*, XXV (April 1954), 33—41.

6338 Kleiman, Robert. **Atlantic Crisis: American Diplomacy Confronts a Resurgent Europe.** New York, Norton, 1964. 158 p.

6339 — —. **Background for Atlantic Partnership,** *NATO in Quest of Cohesion*, Karl H. Cerny and Henry W. Briefs (eds.). New York, Praeger, 1965, pp. 431—60.

6340 Kohn, Hans, **The Atlantic Community and the World,** *Orbis*, I (Winter, 1958), 418—27.

6341 — —. **Nationalism and the Integration of Europe,** *European Integration,* C. Grove Haines (ed.). Baltimore, Johns Hopkins Press, 1959, pp. 21—36.

6342 — —. **Nationalism in the Atlantic Community,** *Atlantic Community Quarterly,* III (Fall, 1965), 293—313.

6343 — —. **Western Europe and Atlantic Unity,** *Current History,* XXXIX (September 1960), 153—57.

6344 Kohnstamm, Max. **The European Tide,** *Daedalus,* XCIII (Winter, 1964), 83—108.

6345 Köver, J. F. **The Integration of Western Europe,** *Political Science Quarterly,* LXIX (September 1954), 354—73.

6346 Kraft, Joseph. **The Grand Design: From Common Market to Atlantic Partnership.** New York, Harper, 1962. 122 p.

6347 Lawson, Ruth C. **Concerting Policies in the North Atlantic Community,** *International Organization,* XII (Spring, 1958), 163—79.

6348 — —. **The North Atlantic Community: Steps Toward Union,** *Current History,* New Series, XXIV (February 1953), 72—79.

6349 Lerner, Daniel. **Britain Faces the Continent,** *Virginia Quarterly Review,* XXXIX (Winter, 1963), 12—25.

6350 Letiche, John M. **Is There a Dichotomy of the Atlantic and European Communities?** *Institute of World Affairs Proceedings,* XXXIX (1963), 73—84.

6351 L'Huillier, Fernand. **La communanté occidentale,** *Les institutions internationales et transnationales,* Fernand L'Huillier (ed.). Paris, Presses Universitaires, 1961, pp. 28—36.

Part E. — Regional International Organization

6352 — —. **L'Europe,** *Les institutions internationales et transnationales*, Fernand L'Huillier (ed.). Paris, Presses Universitaires, 1961, pp. 79—90.

6353 Lichtheim, George. **The New Europe: Today — and Tomorrow.** New York, Praeger, 1963. xv + 232 p.

6354 Lindberry, Leon H. **Decision Making and Integration in the European Community,** *International Organization,* XIX (Winter, 1965), 56—80.

6355 Lippmann, Walter. **Western Unity and the Common Market.** Boston, Little, Brown, 1962. 51 p.

6356 Liska, George. **Europe Ascendant: The International Politics of Unification.** Baltimore, Johns Hopkins Press, 1964. x + 182 p.

6357 Liska, Jiri. **The Pattern of Integration: Western Europe and the Atlantic Community,** *Public Policy,* VI (1955), 85—114.

6358 Loftus, John A. **An Inquiry into Feasible Forms of European Intergration,** *European Integration,* C. Grove Haines (ed.). Baltimore, Johns Hopkins Press, 1959, pp. 97—113.

6359 Lohman, Phillip Hans. **The Fourth Paneuropean Conference at Vienna,** *World Affairs Quarterly,* VI (October 1935), 242—49.

6360 Loveday, A. **The European Movement,** *International Organization,* III (November 1949), 620—32.

6361 Lowenstein, Hubertus zu. **Modern United Europe and the Holy Roman Empire,** *Pakistan Horizon,* XVIII (1965), 238—46.

6362 McWhinney, Edward. **"Classical" Federalism and Supra-National Integration or Treaty-Based Association: The European Community Movement As a Case-Study,** *American Society of International Law Proceedings,* LVII (1963), 241—48.

6363 Mally, Gerhard. **A "Forward Strategy" for Atlantica,** *Atlantic Community Quarterly,* III (Fall, 1965), 318–25.

6364 — —. **Proposals for Integrating the Atlantic Community,** *Orbis,* IX (Summer, 1965), 378–92.

6365 Mendershausen, Horst. **Europe in Flux,** *Atlantic Community Quarterly,* III (Summer, 1965), 206–16.

6366 Middleton, Drew. **The Atlantic Community: A Study in Unity and Disunity.** New York, McKay, 1965. x + 303 p.

6367 — —. **The Supreme Choice: Britain and Europe.** New York, Knopf, 1963. ix + 292 p.

6368 Munk, Frank. **Atlantic Dilemma: Partnership or Community?** Foreword by Henry Cabot Lodge. Dobbs Ferry, Oceana, 1964. xii + 177 p.

6369 Nord, Hans. **In Search of a Political Framework for an Integrated Europe,** *European Integration,* C. Grove Haines (ed.). Baltimore, Johns Hopkins Press, 1959, pp. 215–30.

6370 Norstad, Lauris. **The Future of the Atlantic Community,** *International Organization,* XVII (Summer, 1963), 804–12.

6371 Overstreet, Alan Burr. **The Nature and Prospects of European Institutions,** *Journal of Common Market Studies,* III (February 1965), 124–68.

6372 Padelford, Norman J. **Political Cooperation in the North Atlantic Community,** *International Organization,* IX (August 1955), 353–65.

6373 Perroux, François. **L'Europe sans rivages.** Paris, Presses Universitaires de France, 1954. vii + 668 p.

Part E. — Regional International Organization

6374 Philip, André. **L'Europe et le monde d'aujourd'hui.** Neuchâtel. Editions de la Baconnière, 1958. 346 p.

6375 ———. **L'Europe unie et sa place dans l'économie internationale.** Paris, Presses Universitaires de France, 1953. 364 p.

6376 Pryce, Roy. **The Political Future of the European Community.** London, Marshbank, 1962. 107 p.

6377 Reichenberg, Frederick von. **Balance of Power or Pan-Europa,** *Institute of World Affairs Proceedings*, X (December 1932), 35—39.

6378 Reuter, Paul. **Juridical and Institutional Aspects of the European Regional Communities,** *Law and Contemporary Problems*, XXVI (Summer, 1961), 381—99.

6379 Reynaud, Paul. **The Unifying Force for Europe,** *Foreign Affairs*, XXVIII (January 1950), 255—64.

6380 Richardson, James. **The Concept of Atlantic Community,** *Journal of Common Market Studies*, III (October 1964), 1—22.

6381 Robertson, A. H. **European Institutions: Co-operation, Integration, Unification.** New York, Praeger, 1959. XV + 372 p.

6382 Rohn, Peter H. **How United Is Which Europe? A Review,** *Journal of Conflict Resolution*, VI (March 1962), 82—87.

6383 Roper, Elmo. **The Future of the Atlantic Community,** *Atlantic Community Quarterly*, I (Fall, 1963), 316—23.

6384 Schmidt, Adolph. **The Atlantic Community,** *Atlantic Community Quarterly*, I (Summer, 1963), 219—30.

6385 Schokking, Jan J. and Anderson, Nels. **Observation on the European Integration Process,** *Journal of Conflict Resolution*, IV (December 1960), 385—410.

6386 Schuman, Robert. **The Atlantic Community and Europe,** *Orbis*, I (Winter, 1958), 408—10.

6387 Sidgwick, Henry. **The Development of European Polity.** London, Macmillan, 1903.

Chapter XXIX.

6388 Siotis, Jean. **Some Problems of European Secretariats,** *Journal of Common Market Studies*, II (May 1964), 222—50.

6389 Spaak, Paul-Henri. **Europe in a Western Community,** *Annals of the American Academy of Political and Social Science*, CCLXXXII (July 1952), 45—52.

6390 — —. **The Integration of Europe: Dreams and Realities,** *Foreign Affairs*, XXIX (October 1950), 94—100.

6391 Spinelli, Altiero. **Atlantic Pact or European Unity,** *Foreign Affairs*, XL (July 1962), 542—52.

6392 — —. **The Growth of the European Movement Since World War II,** *European Integration*, C. Grove Haines (ed.). Baltimore, Johns Hopkins Press, 1959, pp. 37—63.

6393 Syed, Anwar. **Walter Lippmann on Europe and the Atlantic Community,** *Orbis*, VII (Summer, 1963), 308—35.

6394 Tsatsos, Constantine. **The Consolidation of the Western World,** *Atlantic Community Quarterly*, I (Fall, 1963), 337—45.

Reprinted from *International Relations* (Athens), May 1963.

Part E. — *Regional International Organization*

6395 Uri, Pierre. **A French View of the Western Community,** *The United States and the Western Community*, H. Field Haviland (ed.). Haverford, Pa., Haverford College Press, 1957, pp. 81—92.

6396 Van Kleffens, E. N. **The Case for European Integration: Political Considerations,** *European Integration*, C. Grove Haines (ed.). Baltimore, Johns Hopkins Press, 1959, pp. 80—96.

6397 van Vredenburch, H. E. Jonkheer. **European Co-operation As Seen from the Hague,** *International Relations*, I (April 1959), 521—28.

6398 Walton, Clarence C. **The Hague "Congress of Europe": A Case Study of Public Opinion,** *Western Political Quarterly*, XII (September 1959), 738—52.

6399 Wandyez, Piotr S. **Regionalism and European Integration,** *World Affairs Quarterly*, XXVIII (October 1957), 229—59.

6400 Wolfers, Arnold (ed.). **Changing East-West Relations and the Unity of the West.** Baltimore, Johns Hopkins Press, 1965. 242 p.

6401 — —. **Integration in the West: The Conflict of Perspectives,** *International Organization*, XVIII (Summer, 1963), 753—70.

6402 Zurcher, Arnold J. **The Struggle to Unite Europe, 1940—1958.** New York, New York University Press, 1958. xix + 254 p.

8.2.2 RELATION TO OTHER INTERNATIONAL ORGANIZATIONS

6403 Allen, James Jay. **The European Common Market and the General Agreement on Tariffs and Trade: A Study in Comparability,** *Law and Contemporary Problems*, XXVI (Summer, 1961), 559—71.

6404 Alting von Gensan, F. A. M. **European Organizations and Foreign Relations of States: A Comparative Analysis of Decision-Making.** Leyden, Sythoff, 1962. xv + 290 p.

6405 Beckett, William Eric. **The North Atlantic Treaty, the Brussels Treaty and the Charter of the United Nations.** London, Stevens, 1950. viii + 75 p.

6406 Berkes, Ross N. **NATO and the United Nations,** *Current History,* XXXIX (September 1960), 158–62.

6407 Carrington, C. E. **Between the Commonwealth and Europe,** *International Affairs,* XXXVIII (October 1962), 449–59.

6408 Cordier, Andrew W. **European Union and the League of Nations, Geneva Studies,** II (June 1931), 1–72.

6409 Deniau, J. F. **The External Policy of the European Common Market,** *Law and Contemporary Problems,* XXVI (Summer, 1961), 364–80.

6410 Etzioni, Amitai. **Atlantic Union, the Southern Continents, and the United Nations,** *International Conflict and Behavioral Science: The Craigville Papers,* Roger Fisher (ed.). New York, Basic Books, 1964, pp. 179–207.

6411 Jenks, C. Wilfred. **The Common Law of Mankind.** New York, Praeger, 1958.

Chapter IV.

6412 Jessup, Philip C. **The Atlantic Community and the United Nations,** *Academy of Political Science Proceedings,* XXIII (May 1949), 312–24.

6413 Kohnstamm, Max. **The European Community and Its Role in the World.** Columbia, University of Missouri Press, 1964. xi + 82 p.

6414 Mackay, R. W. G. **NATO and UN,** *Annals of the American Academy of Political and Social Science,* CCLXXXVIII (July 1953), 119—25.

6415 Munroe, Leslie. **The NATO and the UN,** *Indian Year Book of International Affairs,* XII (1963), 108—15.

6416 Paymann, J. **The United States of Europe and Latin America,** *World Justice,* IV (June 1963), 475—92.

6417 Pescatore, Pierre. **The Foreign Relations of the European Communities,** *Atlantic Community Quarterly,* I (Fall, 1963), 413—25.

Reprinted from *Osterreichische Zeitschrift für Aussenpolitik,* April 1963.

6418 — —. **Les relations extérieures des communautés européennes: contribution à la doctrine de la personalité des organisations internationales,** *Recueil des Cours,* CIII (1961), 1—242.

6419 Rohn, Peter H. **Relations Between the Council of Europe and International Non-Governmental Organizations.** Brussels, Union of International Associations, 1957. 79 p.

6420 Siddiqi, Qamar Saeed. **European Integration and Economic Development in the Commonwealth,** *Pakistan Horizon,* XIII, 4 (1960), 318—23.

6421 Socini, Roberto. **Rapports et conflits entre organisations européenes.** Leyden, Sythoff, 1960. 168 p.

6422 Soto, M. J. de. **Les relations internationales de la commonauté européenne du Charbon et de l'Acier,** *Recueil des Cours,* XC (1956), 29—115.

6423 Uri, Pierre. **Partnership for Progress: A Program for Transatlantic Action.** Preface by Henry Cabot Lodge. New York, Harper and Row, 1963. 126 p.

Part E. — *Regional International Organization*

6424 Vosper, Dennis. **The Commonwealth and the European Economic Community,** *Pakistan Horizon,* XV, 1 (1962), 3—12.

6425 Wilcox, Francis O. **The Atlantic Community and the United Nations,** *International Organization,* XVII (Summer, 1963), 683—708.

8.3 ECONOMIC ORGANIZATIONS

8.3.1 GENERAL OBSERVATIONS

6426 Alexandrowicz, C. **The European Economic Organisations,** *Year Book of World Affairs,* II (1948), 162—96.

6427 Beever, R. Colin. **European Unity and the Trade Union Movement.** Leyden, Sythoff, 1960. 303 p.

6428 Bell, Harold. **Regionalism or World Trade,** *Europe Without Britain,* Coral Bell (ed.). Melbourne, Cheshire, 1963, pp. 107—17.

6429 Cates, William C. **International Economic Organization and European Stability,** *Journal of International Affairs,* IV (Winter, 1950), 56—65.

6430 Cheever, Daniel S. and Haviland, H. Field, Jr. **Organizing for Peace.** Boston, Houghton, Mifflin, 1954.

Chapter XXV.

6431 Compagnie d'Outremer. **Problems of Financial Integration,** *Atlantic Community Quarterly,* I (Fall, 1963), 438—47.

Reprinted from the annual report of the Compagnie d'Outremer pour l'Industrie et la Finance (Brussels), March 1963.

6432 Dean, Vera Micheles. **European Efforts for Economic Collaboration,** *Foreign Policy Reports,* VII (August 19, 1931), 219—40.

6433 Delouvrier, Paul. **Economic Integration: Problems and Possibilities,** *European Integration,* C. Grove Haines (ed.). Baltimore, Johns Hopkins Press, 1959, pp. 114—24.

6434 Demaria, Giovanni. **European Integration and the World Economy,** *European Integration,* C. Grove Haines (ed.). Baltimore, Johns Hopkins Press, 1959, pp. 150—60.

6435 Diebold, William, Jr. **Economic Aspects of an Atlantic Community,** *International Organization,* XVII (Summer, 1963), 663—82.

6436 — —. **The Process of European Integration,** *Current History,* XLII (March 1962), 129—35.

6437 — —. **Theory and Practice of European Integration,** *World Politics,* XI (July 1959), 621—28.

6438 Etzioni, Amitai. **European Unification and Perspectives on Sovereignty,** *Daedalus,* XCII (Summer, 1963), 498—520.

6439 H., R. G. **Western Union, II: Economic Aspects,** *World Today,* New Series, V (April 1949), 178—83.

6440 Haberler, Gottfried, **Economic Aspects of a European Union,** *World Politics,* I (October 1948 — July 1949), 431—41.

6441 Hallstein, Walter. **European Economy and European Policy,** *Atlantic Community Quarterly,* III (Fall, 1965), 364—68.

6442 Heckscher, Eli Filip. **The Continental System: An Economic Interpretation.** Harold Westergaard (ed.). Oxford, Clarendon, 1922. xvi + 420 p.

6443 Heilperin, Michael. **Economic Integration: Commercial and Financial Postulates,** *European Integration,* C. Grove Haines (ed.). Baltimore, Johns Hopkins Press, 1959, pp. 125–36.

6444 Henderson, W. O. **The Zollverein.** Chicago, Quadrangle, 1959. 375 p.

6445 La Malfa, Ugo. **The Case for European Integration: Economic Considerations,** *European Integration,* C. Grove Haines (ed.). Baltimore, Johns Hopkins Press, 1959, pp. 64–79.

6446 Lindberg, Leon N. **The Political Dynamics of European Economic Integration.** Stanford, Stanford University Press, 1963. xiv + 367 p.

6447 Manshott, S. L. **Toward European Integration: Beginnings in Agriculture,** *Foreign Affairs,* XXXI (October 1952), 106–113.

6448 Maury, René. **L'intégration européenne.** Paris, Sirey, 1958. 338 p.

6449 Monnet, Jean. **Economic Integration: New Forms of Partnership,** *Perspectives on Peace,* Carnegie Endowment for International Peace (ed.). New York, Praeger, 1960, pp. 97–106.

6450 Morgan, D. J. **Next Steps in Europe's Economic Integration,** *World Affairs,* New Series, IV (October 1950), 449–59.

6451 Musy, Jean Marie. **Les bases de l'organisation économique de l'Europe,** *Recueil des Cours,* LVI (1936), 535–83.

6452 Nussbaum, Frederick L. **A History of the Economic Institutions of Modern Europe and an Introduction to "Der Moderne Kapitalismus" of Werner Sombart.** New York, Crofts, 1933. xvi + 448 p.

6453 Rueff, Jacques. **The Case for the Free Market,** *Foreign Affairs,* XXVI (April 1948), 528–41.

6454 Sannwald, Rolf and Stohler, Jacques. **Economic Integration: Theoretical Assumptions and Consequences of European Unity,** Herman F. Karreman (trans.). Princeton, Princeton University Press, 1959. 276 p.

6455 Scitovsky, Tibor. **Economic Theory and Western European Integration.** London, Allen and Unwin, 1958. 160 p.

6456 Siotis, Jean. **The Secretariat of the United Nations Commission for Europe and European Economic Integration: The First Ten Years,** *International Organization,* XIX (Spring, 1965), 177–202.

6457 — —. **Some Problems of European Secretariats,** *Journal of Common Market Studies,* II (May 1964), 222–50.

6458 Soldati, Agostino. **Economic Disintegration in Europe,** *Foreign Affairs,* XXXVIII (October 1959), 75–83.

6459 Stikker, Dirk U. **The Functional Approach to European Integration,** *Foreign Affairs,* XXIX (April 1951), 436–44.

6460 Strange, Susan. **A European Agricultural Authority,** *World Affairs,* New Series, V (October 1951), 454–66.

6461 Thorp, Willard L. **Europe's Progress Toward Economic Integration,** *Foreign Affairs,* XXXIII (January 1955), 282–97.

6462 Triffin, Robert. **Economic Integration: Institutions, Theories, and Policies,** *World Politics,* VI (July 1954), 526–37.

6463 Truchy, Henri. **L'union douanière européenne,** *Recueil des Cours,* XLVIII (1934), 575–629.

6464 Verdoorn, P. J. **A Customs Union for Western Europe: Advantages and Feasibility,** *World Politics,* VI (July 1954), 482–500.

6465 Vernon, Raymond. **Economic Aspects of the Atlantic Community,** *The United States and the Western Community,* H. Field Haviland (ed.). Haverford, Pa., Haverford College Press, 1957, pp. 53–64.

6466 Wallich, Henry C. and Loud, Frederick V. **Intra-European Trade and European Integration,** *Journal of International Affairs,* IV (Winter, 1950), 33–45.

6467 Weil, Gordon L. **Europe Moves Toward Unity,** *Current History,* New Series, XLVII (December 1964), 321–25 f.

8.3.2 BENELUX AND ITALO-FRENCH CUSTOMS UNIONS

6468 C., A. **The Franco-Italian Customs Union,** *World Today,* New Series, IV (November 1948), 481–88.

6469 Cammaerts, E. **The Meaning of Benelux,** *World Affairs,* New Series, II (July 1948), 253–60.

6470 Eyck, F. Gunther. **Benelux in the Balance,** *Political Science Quarterly,* LXIX (March 1954), 65–91.

6471 Meade, James E. **Benelux: The Formation of the Common Customs,** *Economica,* XXIII (August 1956), 201–13.

6472 — —. **Negotiations for Benelux: An Annotated Chronicle, 1943–1956.** Princeton, N. J., Princeton Studies in International Finance, 1957. 89 p.

6473 — —. **The Theory of Customs Unions.** Amsterdam, North-Holland, 1955. 121 p.

Benelux.

6474 Robertson, W. **Benelux and Problems of European Integration,** *Oxford Economic Papers,* VII (February 1956), 35–50.

6475 Valentine, A. **Benelux: Pilot Plant of Economic Union,** *Yale Review,* XLIII (Summer, 1954), 23–32.

6476 Van Mensbrugghe, Jean. **Benelux,** *India Quarterly,* V (January-March 1949), 53–59.

6477 Wemelsfelder, J. **Benelux: An Experiment in Economic Integration,** *Economia Internazionale,* VIII (August 1955), 543–60.

8.3.3 EUROPEAN PAYMENTS UNION

6478 B., P. **The European Payments Union: A Step Towards Economic Integration,** *World Today,* New Series, VI (November 1950), 490–98.

6479 Diebold, William, Jr. **Trade and Payments in Western Europe: A Study in Economic Cooperation, 1947–51.** New York, Harper, 1952. 488 p.

6480 Flexner, Kurt. **The Creation of the European Payments Union: An Example in International Compromise,** *Political Science Quarterly,* LXXII (June 1957), 241–60.

6481 H., R. G. **The Future of the European Payments Union,** *World Today,* New Series, X (June 1954), 255–58.

6482 Krivine, J. D. **The Little Marshall Plan,** *World Affairs,* New Series, III (October 1949), 337–45.

6483 L'Huillier, Fernand. **L'organisation de paiements,** *Les institutions internationales et transnationales,* Fernand L'Huillier (ed.). Paris, Presses Universitaires, 1961, pp. 201–18.

6484 Triffin, Robert. **Monetary Reconstruction in Europe,** *International Conciliation,* CDLXXXII (June 1952), 263–308.

6485 Williams, John H. **The Revision of the Intra-European Payments Plan,** *Foreign Affairs,* XXVIII (October 1949), 153–55.

8.3.4 MARSHALL PLAN, OEEC, AND OECD
(Paris)

6486 Alexander, Sidney S. **The Marshall Plan.** Washington, National Planning Association, 1948. 68 p.

6487 Bidwell, Percy W. and Diebold, William, Jr. **New Aid for New Europe,** *Foreign Affairs,* XXVI (October 1947), 169–86.

6488 Blaisdell, Thomas C., Jr. **The European Recovery Program – Phase Two,** *International Organization,* II (September 1948), 443–54.

6489 Bonn, M. J. **The Implications of the Marshall Plan,** *World Affairs,* New Series, II (January 1948), 1–12.

Part E. — Regional International Organization

6490 Clayton, William L. **GATT, the Marshall Plan, and OECD,** *Political Science Quarterly,* LXXVIII (December 1963), 493–503.

6491 Clough, Shepard B. **Toward European Economic Organization,** *Academy of Political Science Proceedings,* XXIII (January 1950), 369–80.

6492 Ellis, Howard S. **The Economics of Freedom: The Progress and Future of Aid to Europe.** New York, Council on Foreign Relations, 1952. xviii + 549 p.

6493 Esman, Milton J. **Europe in the Common Aid Effort,** *Public Policy,* XIV (1965), 3–27.

Discusses OECD's Development Assistance Committee.

6494 Fay, Sidney B. **The Marshall Plan,** *Current History,* New Series, XIII (September 1947), 129–34.

6495 Finletter, Thomas K. **The European Recovery Programme in Operation,** *International Affairs,* XXV (January 1949), 1–7.

6496 Fox, Melvin J. and Winslow, Anne. **European Recovery.** *International Conciliation,* CDXLVII (January 1945), 3–95.

Introduction by James T. Shotwell.

6497 — —. **The European Recovery Program,** *International Conciliation,* CDXXXVI (December 1947) 785–881.

Contains a commentary and various documents.

6498 Gordon, Lincoln. **The Organization for European Economic Cooperation,** *International Organization,* X (February 1956), 1–11.

6499 H., P. I. J. **The Marshall Plan in Operation,** *World Today,* New Series, IV (October 1948), 430–36.

6500 Harris, Seymour E. **The European Recovery Program.** Cambridge. Harvard University Press, 1948. xvii + 309 p.

6501 Henderson, Hubert. **The European Economic Report,** *International Affairs,* XXIV (January 1948), 19—29.

6502 Hickman, Warren L. **Genesis of the European Recovery Program: A Study on the Trend of American Economic Policies.** Geneva, Imprimeries Populaires, 1949. 297 p.

6503 Koefod, Paul. **New Concept in the Quest for Peace: Marshall Plan; Aspect of Power Politics.** Geneva, Imprimeries Populaires, 1950. 235 p.

6504 Krivine, J. D. **The European Recovery Program,** *Year Book of World Affairs,* IV (1950), 234—63.

6505 — —. **The Marshall Plan — Where Does It Lead?** *World Affairs,* New Series, II (October 1948), 387—97.

6506 Lintott, H. J. B. **The Organization for European Economic Cooperation,** *International Organization,* III (May 1949), 269—77.

6507 Moore, Harry H. **The Marshall Plan — An Adventure in Friendliness,** *Survival or Suicide,* Harry H. Moore (ed.). New York, Harper, 1948, pp. 143—48.

6508 Organisation Européenne de Coopération Économique. **Aide américaine a l'Europe 1947—1953: bibliographie sélectionnée.** Paris, Bibliothèque de l'OECE, 1954. 54 p.

6509 Organization for European Economic Cooperation. **History and Structure.** 7th ed. Paris, Château de la Muette, 1958. 59 p.

6510 Price, Harry B. **The Marshall Plan and Its Meaning.** Ithaca, Cornell University Press, 1955. 424 p.

Part E. — *Regional International Organization*

6511 Royal Institute of International Affairs, Information Department. **The Organization for European Economic Co-operation.** New York, Oxford University Press, 1958. 16 p.

6512 Salter, Arthur. **European Recovery: A Look Ahead,** *Foreign Affairs,* XXVII (January 1949), 289–301.

6513 Sidjanski, Dusan. **Federal Aspects of the European Community,** *Public Policy,* XIV (1965), 416–43.

6514 Stone, Donald C. **The Impact of U. S. Assistance Programs on the Political and Economic Integration of Western Europe,** *American Political Science Review,* XLVI (December 1952), 1100–16.

6515 Szuldoynski, Jan. **Legal Aspects of OEEC,** *International and Comparative Law Quarterly,* II (October 1953), 579–95.

6516 Willams, John H. **End of the Marshall Plan,** *Foreign Affairs,* XXX (July 1952), 593–611.

6517 — —. **The Marshall Plan Halfway,** *Foreign Affairs,* XXVIII (April 1950), 463–76.

6518 Winks, Robin W. **The Marshall Plan and the American Economy.** New York, Holt, 1960. 62 p.

8.3.5 THE COMMUNITIES

8.3.5.1 GENERAL OBSERVATIONS

6519 B., G. **The New Institutions for European Integration: Their Structure and Aims,** *World Today,* New Series, XIV (July 1958), 294–304.

Part E. — Regional International Organization

6520 Bebr, Gerhard. **The European Coal and Steel Community: A Political and Legal Innovation,** *Yale Law Journal*, (November 1953), 1—43.

6521 Benoit, Emile. **Europe at Sixes and Sevens: The Common Market, the Free Trade Association, and the United States.** New York, Columbia University Press, 1961. 275 p.

6522 Birrenbach, Kurt. **Europe, the European Economic Community, and the Outer Seven,** *International Journal*, XV (Winter, 1960), 59—65.

6523 Bower, Robert T. **Prospects for Atlantic Community,** *Harvard Review*, I (Fall, 1962), 7—15.

6524 Camps, Miriam. **Division in Europe.** Princeton, Center of International Studies, 1960. 61 p.

6525 — —. **The European Common Market and Free Trade Area.** Princeton, Center of International Studies, 1957. xii + 30 p.

6526 — —. **What Kind of Europe? The Community Since De Gaulle's Veto.** New York, Oxford University Press, 1965. 145 p.

6527 Coppe, Albert. **The Economic and Political Problems of Integration,** *Law and Contemporary Problems*, XXVI (Summer, 1961), 349—63.

6528 Diebold, William, Jr. **European Economic Integration in a New Phase,** *France and the European Community*, Sydney Nettleton Fisher (ed.). Columbus, Ohio State University Press, 1965, pp. 95—116.

6529 — —. **The Schuman Plan: A Study in Economic Cooperation, 1950 —1959.** New York, Praeger, 1959. xviii + 750 p.

Part E. — Regional International Organization

6530 Efron, Ruben and Nanes, Allan S. **The Common Market and Euratom Treaties: Supranationality and the Integration of Europe,** *International and Comparative Law Quarterly,* VI (October 1957), 670–84.

6531 Everett, Robinson O. (ed.). **European Regional Communities: A New Era on the Old Continent.** Dobbs Ferry, Oceana, 1962. 242 p.

6532 Feld, Werner. **The Association Agreements of the European Communities: A Comparative Analysis,** *International Organization,* XIX (Spring, 1965), 223–49.

6533 Flamme, M. A. **The Institutional Structure of European Economic Integration,** *Revue International des Sciences Administratives,* XXIV, 1 (1958), 33–46.

6534 Frey-Wouters, Ellen. **The Progress of European Integration,** *World Politics,* XVII (April 1965), 460–77.

6535 Haas, Ernst B. **The Uniting of Europe.** Stanford, Stanford University Press, 1958. xx + 552 p.

6536 Hallstein, Walter. **United Europe: Challenge and Opportunity.** Cambridge, Harvard University Press, 1962. 109 p.

6537 Heidelberg, Franz C. **Parliamentary Control and Political Groups in the Three European Regional Communities,** Denis M. More (trans.), *Law and Contemporary Problems,* XXVI (Summer, 1961), 431–37.

6538 Henderson, W. O. **The Genesis of the Common Market.** Chicago, Quadrangle, 1962. xv + 202 p.

6539 Hitchner, D. G. **Supranational Organization and Democracy in Western Europe,** *Parliamentary Affairs,* XI (Summer, 1958), 273–86.

6540 Houben, P.-H. J. M. **Les Conseils de Ministres des Communautés Européenes.** Preface by I. Samkalden. Leyden, Sythoff, 1964. 254 p.

6541 Jacobson, Harold K. **Economic and Political Integration: From Schuman Plan to European Common Market and Euratom,** *Problems in International Relations*, Andrew Gyorgy and Hubert S. Gibbs (eds.). 2d ed. Englewood Cliffs, Prentice-Hall, 1962, pp. 156–73.

6542 Kahn-Freund, Otto. **Social Policy and the Common Market,** *Political Quarterly*, XXXII (October-December 1961), 341–52.

6543 Kish, George. **Europe at Sixes and Sevens: A Review,** *Journal of Conflict Resolution*, V (December 1961), 411–12.

6544 Kitzinger, Uwe W. **Europe: The Six and the Seven,** *International Organization*, XIV (Winter, 1960), 20–36.

6545 — —. **Regional and Functional Integration — Some Lessons of Brussels,** *Journal of Common Market Studies*, III (February 1965), 118–23.

6546 Kravis, Irving B. **Domestic Interests and International Obligations: Safeguards in International Trade Organizations.** Philadelphia, University of Pennsylvania Press, 1963. 448 p.

6547 Lambert, J. R. **Enlargement of the Common Market: Denmark, Norway, and Ireland,** *World Today*, New Series, XVIII (August 1962), 350–60.

6548 Lister, Louis. **Europe's Coal and Steel Community: An Experiment in Economic Union.** New York, Twentieth Century Fund, 1960. 495 p.

6549 Meade, J. E., Liesner, H. H., and Wells, S. J. Edited and with an introduction by J. E. Meade. **Case Studies in European Economic Union: The Mechanics of Integration.** New York, Oxford University Press, 1962. vii + 424 p.

6550 Mendershausen, H. **First Tests of the Schuman Plan,** *Review of Economics and Statistics,* XXXV (November 1953), 269–88.

6551 Parker, William N. **The European Coal and Steel Community,** *Southern Economic Journal* XXVII (October 1960), 128–32.

6552 Pryce, Roy. **The Political Future of the European Community.** London, Marshbank, 1962. 107 p.

6553 Schmitt, Hans A. **The Path to European Union: From the Marshall Plan to the Common Market.** Baton Rouge, Louisiana State University Press, 1962. xii + 272 p.

6554 Snoy et d'Oppuerrs, Baron. **Parliamentary Aspects of the Six and Seven Towards a European Solution,** *Parliamentary Affairs,* XIII (Autumn, 1960), 458–76.

6555 — —. **The European Crisis,** *Atlantic Community Quarterly,* I (Summer, 1963), 131–42.

Reprinted from *Revue Générale Belge,* March 1963.

6556 Spinelli, Altiero. **De Gaulle's Plan,** *Atlantic Community Quarterly,* I (Fall, 1963), 391–99.

Reprinted from *Prévues* (Paris), May 1963.

6557 Van der Beugel, E. H. **The Clash in Europe,** *Atlantic Community Quarterly,* III (Spring, 1965), 27–37.

Reprinted from *European Review,* Winter, 1964–65.

6558 Wild, J. E. **The European Common Market and the European Free Trade Association.** London, Library Association, 1962. 64 p.

8.3.5.2 EUROPEAN COAL AND STEEL COMMUNITY
(Luxembourg)

6559   Bebr, G. **Labor and the Schuman Plan,** *Michigan Law Review*, LII (May 1954), 1007–22.

6560   Bok, Derek C. **The First Three Years of the Schuman Plan.** Princeton, Department of Economics and Sociology, International Finance Section, 1955. 79 p.

6561   C., M. **The European Coal and Steel Community: An Experiment in Integration,** *World Today*, New Series, XI (June 1955), 263–70.

6562   Deciry, Jean. **The Schuman Plan,** *Pakistan Horizon*, VI (June 1952), 64–74.

6563   Diebold, William, Jr. **Imponderables of the Schuman Plan,** *Foreign Affairs*, XXIX (October 1950), 114–29.

6564   F., R. **Labour Under the European Coal and Steel Community,** *World Today*, New Series, IX (November 1953), 497–504.

6565   Gelber, Lionel. **The Schuman Plan and German Revival,** *International Journal*, VI (Summer, 1951), 180–88.

6566   Goormaghtigh, John. **European Coal and Steel Community,** *International Conciliation*, DIII (May 1955), 343–408.

6567   H., R. G. **The European Coal and Steel Community: Implications of the Schuman Plan,** *World Today*, New Series, VII (May 1951), 197–203.

6568   Haesele, Kurt W. **Europas Letzler Weg.** Frankfurt, Knapp, 1958. 352 p.

6569 Harley, J. Eugene. **The Schuman Plan: A Big Step Toward European Unity,** *World Affairs Quarterly,* XXIV (July 1953), 180—99.

6570 Institut für Europäische Politik und Wirtschaft. **Bibliographie zum Schumanplan.** Frankfurt, Institut für Europäische Politik und Wirtschaft, 1953. 151 p.

6571 J., C. **The Schuman Plan and the Council of Europe,** *World Today,* New Series, VIII (November 1952), 473—80.

6572 Josephy, F. L. **What the European Coal and Steel Community Has Done,** *L'Europe Naissante,* I (July 1954), 14—21.

6573 Kaeckenbeeck, H. E. Georges. **The International Authority for the Ruhr and the Schuman Plan,** *Transactions* (Grotius Society), XXXVII (1951), 4—13.

Comments by Green, Goitein, Elkin, Jaffé, Loewenfeld, Moore, Adamkiewicz, Zaslawski.

6574 Kapteyn, Paul J. **L'Assemblée Commune de la Communauté Européenne du Charbon et de l'Acier: un essai de parlementarisme européen.** Preface by Jean de Soto. Leyden, Sythoff, 1952. 270 p.

6575 Kohnstamm, Max. **The European Coal and Steel Community,** *Recueil des Cours,* XC (1956), 1—28.

6576 Kriesberg, L. **German Businessmen and Union Leaders and the Schuman Plan,** *Social Science,* XXXV (April 1960), 114—21.

6577 ———. **German Public Opinion and the European Coal and Steel Community,** *Public Opinion Quarterly,* XXIII (Spring, 1959), 28—42.

6578 Lever, Jeremy. **International Legal Aspects of the European Coal and Steel Community,** *Transactions* (Grotius Society), XLIV (1958—59), 205—20.

6579 McKesson, John A. **The Schuman Plan,** *Political Science Quarterly,* LXVII (March 1952), 18—35.

6580 Mason, Henry L. **The European Coal and Steel Community: Experiment in Supranationalism.** Hague, Nijhoff, 1955. xi + 153 p.

6581 Mayne, Richard. **Economic Integration in the New Europe: A Statistical Approach,** *Daedalus,* XCIII (Winter, 1964), 109—33.

6582 Merry, Henry J. **The European Coal and Steel Community: Operations of the High Authority,** *Western Political Quarterly,* VIII (June 1955), 166—85.

6583 Morard, Nicolas. **Fonctionnement et perspectives de la Communauté Européenne du Charbon et de l'Acier.** Fribourg, Éditions Universitaires, 1962. x + 233 p.

6584 Morgenthau, Hans J. **The Schuman Plan and European Federation,** *American Society of International Law Proceedings,* XLVI (1952), 130 —36.

6585 Munzi, Ugo. **The European Social Fund in the Development of the Mediterranean Regions of the EEC,** *Journal of International Affairs,* XIX, 2 (1965), 286—97.

6586 Muynck, Gust de. **The Social Policy of the European Economic Community, Part I,** *International Manual on the European Economic Community,* H. K. Junckerstorff (ed.). St. Louis, St. Louis University Press, 1963, pp. 421—28.

6587 Parker, William N. **The Schuman Plan: Preliminary Prediction,** *International Organization,* VI (August 1952), 381—95.

6588 Pella, Giuseppe. **The Coal and Steel Community As a Case Study in Integration,** *European Integration,* C. Grove Haines (ed.). Baltimore, Johns Hopkins Press, 1959, pp. 137—49.

Part E. — *Regional International Organization*

6589 Philip, André. **The Schuman Plan: Nucleus of a European Community.** Brussels, European Movement, 1951. 46 p.

6590 Pinto, Roger. **Cours d'organisations européennes.** Paris, Cours de Droit, 1961. 283 p.

6591 Reuter, Paul. **La Communauté Européenne du Charbon et de l'Acier.** Preface by Robert Schuman. Paris, Librarie Générale de Droit et de Jurisprudence, 1953. 320 p.

6592 — —. **Le Plan Schuman,** *Recueil des Cours,* LXXXI (1952), 523—628.

6593 Rieben, Henri. **La Communauté Européenne du Charbon et de l'Acier,** *Les institutions internationales et transnationales,* Fernand L'Huillier (ed.). Paris, Presses Universitaires, 1961, pp. 228—61.

6594 — —. **From the Cartelisation of European Heavy Industries to the European Coal and Steel Community,** *Recueil des Cours,* XC (1956), 117—71.

6595 Sanderson, Fred H. **The Five-Year Experience of the European Coal and Steel Community,** *International Organization,* XII (Spring, 1958), 193—200.

6596 Scheingold, Stuart A. **The Rule of Law in European Integration: The Path of the Schuman Plan.** New Haven, Yale University Press, 1965. xii + 331 p.

6597 Schmitt, Hans A. **The European Communities,** *Current History,* New Series, XLV (November 1963), 257—63 f.

6598 Sethur, Frederick. **The Schuman Plan and Ruhr Coal,** *Political Science Quarterly,* LXVII (December 1952), 503—20.

6599 Shenstone, Michael. **The Schuman Plan — "A Leap into the Unknown,"** *International Journal*, VII (Spring, 1952), 116–26.

6600 Sidjanski, D. **Voting Procedures in an Enlarged Community,** *Journal of Common Market Studies*, I (December 1962), 173–79.

6601 Stein, Eric. **The Common Market and the Free Trade Areas As Examples of Economic Regionalism,** *American Society of International Law Proceedings*, LIV (1960), 153–60.

6602 — —. **The European Coal and Steel Community: The Beginning of Its Judicial Process,** *Columbia Law Review*, LV (November 1955), 985–99.

6603 Summers, Robert E. (comp.). **Economic Aid to Europe: The Marshall Plan.** New York, Wilson, 1948. 271 p.

Excerpts on the subject from various sources. Contains an excellent bibliography.

6604 Townsley, W. A. **The Schuman Plan: An Experiment in Union,** *Australian Outlook*, VII (March 1953), 22–35.

6605 Uri, P. **The Schuman Plan and Certain Problems of International Economics,** *International Social Science Journal*, III (Spring, 1951), 22–28.

6606 Van Raalte, E. **The Treaty Constituting the European Coal and Steel Community,** *International and Comparative Law Quarterly*, I, 1 (1952), 73–85.

6607 Weydert, Jean. **The Social Policy of the European Economic Community, Part II,** *International Manual on the European Economic Community*, H. K. Junckerstorff (ed.). St. Louis, St. Louis University Press, 1963, pp. 429–46.

8.3.5.3 EUROPEAN ECONOMIC COMMUNITY
(Luxembourg)

6608   Allen, James Jay. **The European Common Market and the GATT.** Washington, University Press, 1960. 244 p.

6609   Barzanti, Sergio. **The Underdeveloped Areas Within the Common Market.** Princeton, Princeton University Press, 1965. 437 p.

6610   Bertrand, Raymond. **The European Common Market Proposal,** *International Organization,* X (November 1956), 559—74.

6611   Bramsted, Ernest. **The Six: Attitudes and Institutions, 1946—1963,** *Europe Without Britain,* Coral Bell (ed.). Melbourne, Cheshire, 1963, pp. 45—70.

6612   Brierly, Caroline. **The Making of European Policy.** London, Oxford University Press, 1963. 53 p.

6613   Calderwood, James D. **Western Europe and the Common Market.** Minneapolis, Curriculum Resources, 1963. v + 72 p.

6614   Camps, Miriam. **The First Year of the European Economic Community.** Princeton, Princeton University Press, 1958. 28 p.

6615   Deniau, Jean F. **The Common Market,** Graham Heath (trans.). 3d ed. London, Barrie and Rockliff, 1963. v + 167 p.

6616   — —. **The Objectives and Constitutional Structure of the European Economic Community,** *Legal Problems of the European Economic Community and the European Free Trade Area,* British Institute of International and Comparative Law (ed.). London, International and Comparative Law Quarterly, Supplementary Publication, 1961, pp. 1—7.

Part E. — Regional International Organization

6617 Drouin, Pierre. **L'Europe du Marché Commun.** Paris. Julliard, 1963. 350 p.

6618 Ellis, Harry B. **The Common Market.** Cleveland, World, 1965. 204 p.

6619 Etzioni, Amitai. **Political Unification.** New York, Holt, Rinehart and Winston, 1965.
Chapter VII.

6620 Frank, Isaiah. **The European Common Market: An Analysis of Commercial Policy.** New York, Praeger, 1961. 324 p.

6621 Fulda, Carl H. **The Legal Structure of the European Community,** *France and the European Community,* Sydney Nettleton Fisher, (ed.). Columbus, Ohio State University Press, 1965, pp. 21–36.

6622 Haas, Ernst B. **The Challenge of Regionalism,** *International Organization,* XII (Autumn, 1958), 440–58.

6623 Hallstein, Walter, **The EEC Commission: A New Factor in International Life,** *International and Comparative Law Quarterly,* XIV (April 1965), 727–41.

6624 — —. **The European Economic Community,** *Political Science Quarterly,* LXXVIII (June 1963), 161–78.

6625 — —. **NATO and the European Economic Community,** *Orbis,* VI (Winter, 1963), 564–74.

6626 Holmes, John W. **Political Implications of the European Economic Community,** *Atlantic Community Quarterly,* I (March 1963), 28–36.
Reprinted from *Queen's Quarterly* (Kingston, Ontario), Spring, 1962.

6627 Hurtig, Serge. **The European Common Market,** *International Conciliation,* DXVII (March 1958), 321–81.

Part E. — Regional International Organization

6628 Jensen, Finn B. and Walter, Ingo. **The Common Market: Economic Integration in Europe.** Philadelphia, Lippincott, 1965. vii + 278 p.

6629 Krause, Lawrence B. **The Common Market: Progress and Controversy,** *The Common Market: Progress and Controversy,* Lawrence B. Krause (ed.). Englewood Cliffs, Prentice-Hall, 1964, pp. 1—27.

6630 Lambert, J. R. **Breakdown at Brussels,** *World Today,* New Series, XIX (March 1963), 125—34.

6631 Lemass, S. F. **The European Economic Community — I: The Task of Reorganization,** *Administration,* X (Spring, 1962), 3—7.

6632 L'Huillier, Fernand. **Le Marché Commun,** *Les institutions internationales et transnationales,* Fernand L'Huillier (ed.). Paris, Presses Universitaires, 1961, pp. 262—65.

6633 Macdonald, H. I. **The European Common Market.** Toronto, Canadian Institute of International Affairs, 1959. 16 p.

6634 — —. **The European Economic Community: Background and Bibliography.** Toronto, Canadian Institute of International Affairs, 1962. 16 p.

6635 Maher, D. **The European Economic Community — III: Tasks of the Civil Service,** *Administration,* X (Spring, 1962), 24—28.

6636 Marjolin, Robert. **Prospects for the European Common Market,** *Foreign Affairs,* XXXVI (October 1957), 131—42.

6637 Markham, J. W. **The Common Market: Friend or Competitor?** New York, New York University Press, 1964. xi + 123 p.

6638 Mathieu, Gilbert. **The Six After Two Years,** *India Quarterly,* XVI (July-September 1961), 237–48.

6639 Mayne, Richard. **The Community of Europe.** Introduction by Jean Monnet. New York, Norton, 1963. 192 p.

6640 Mendès-France, Pierre. **The European Community,** *India Quarterly,* XX (January-March 1964), 3–16; (April-June 1964), 140–55.

6641 Mozer, Alfred. **The Nature and Prospects of the Common Market,** *Western Integration and the Future of Eastern Europe,* David S. Collier and Kurt Glaser (ed.). Chicago, Regnery, 1964, pp. 19–28.

6642 Nieburg, Hal. L. **Nuclear Exclusion and the Common Market,** *Midwest Journal of Political Science,* VIII (February 1964), 55–74.

6643 Nystrom, John W. and Malof, Peter. **The Common Market: The European Community in Action.** Princeton, Van Nostrand, 1962. 134 p.

6644 P., J. **The Treaty for a European Economic Community: A Critical Analysis,** *World Today,* New Series, XIV (July 1958), 304–15.

6645 Pickles, William. **Political Power in the EEC,** *Journal of Common Market Studies,* II (October 1963), 63–84.

6646 S., H. **The European Common Market,** *World Today,* New Series, XIII (February 1957), 50–73.

6647 Schuschnigg, Kurt Von. **General Provisions,** *International Manual on the European Economic Community,* H. K. Junckerstorff (ed.). St. Louis, St. Louis University Press, 1963, pp. 447–58.

6648 ― ―. **Principles and Objectives of EEC,** *International Manual on the European Economic Community,* H. K. Junsckerstorff (ed.). St. Louis, St. Louis University Press, 1963, pp. 51–80.

6649 Shanks, Michael and Lambert, John. **The Common Market Today — and Tomorrow.** New York, Praeger, 1963. 253 p.

6650 Stein, Eric and Hay, Peter. **Legal Remedies of Enterprises in the European Economic Community,** *American Journal of Comparative Law,* IX (Summer, 1960), 375—424.

6651 Strauss, Erich. **Common Sense About the Common Market.** London, Allen and Unwin, 1958. 168 p.

6652 Thompson, Dennis. **The European Economic Community: Internal Developments Since the Breakdown of the British Negotiations,** *International and Comparative Law Quarterly,* XIII (July 1964), 830—53.

6653 Weil, Gordon L. **A Handbook on the European Economic Community.** New York, Praeger, 1965. xiv + 479 p.

6654 Willmann, Joachim. **The European Economic Community,** *India Quarterly,* XVI (April-June 1961), 120—38.

8.3.5.4 EUROPEAN FREE TRADE ASSOCIATION
(Geneva)

6655 B., D. L. **The Negotiations for a Free Trade Area,** *World Today,* New Series, XIV (June 1958), 236—47.

6656 Barclay, G. St. J. **Background to E. F. T. A.: An Episode in Anglo-Scandinavian Relations,** *Australian Journal of Politics and History,* XI (August 1965), 185—97.

6657 Camps, Miriam. **The Free Trade Area Negotiations.** Princeton, Center of International Studies, 1959. 51 p.

6658 G., M. **The "Outer Seven" Buying Time in the European Trade Dispute,** *World Today,* New Series, XVI (January 1960), 15—23.

6659 Kreinin, Mordechai E. **The "Outer Seven" and European Integration,** *American Economic Review,* L (June 1960), 370—86.

6660 Lambrinidis, John J. **The Structure, Function, and Law of a Free Trade Area: The European Free Trade Association.** New York, Praeger, 1965. xxii + 303 p.

6661 Meyer, Frederick Victor. **The European Free-Trade Association: An Analysis of "The Outer Seven."** New York, Praeger, 1960. 140 p.

6662 Schopflin, George A. **EFTA: The Other Europe,** *International Affairs,* XL (October 1964), 674—84.

8.3.5.5 EUROPEAN ATOMIC ENERGY COMMUNITY
(Brussels)

6663 Adam, H.-T. **Les organismes internationaux spécialisés.** Paris, Pinchon et Durand-Auzias, 1965.

Volume II, Chapter III.

6664 Armand, Louis. **Atomic Energy and the Future of Europe,** *Foreign Affairs,* XXXIV (July 1956), 655—64.

6665 Bremond, Jean. **La coordination énergétique en Europe: idées et réalisations dans l'Europe des Six.** Geneva, Droz, 1961. 123 p.

6666 Dwarkadas, R. **The European Atomic Energy Community — Organization and Administration,** *Indian Journal of Public Administration,* V (April 1959), 186—98.

Part E. — Regional International Organization

6667   Foch, René. **An Example of Atlantic Partnership: Euratom,** *Atlantic Community Quarterly,* II (Spring, 1964), 72—80.

6668   Gorove, Stephen. **Lessons from the Control of the Peaceful Uses of Atomic Energy in Euratom,** *American Society of International Law Proceedings,* LVIII (1964), 136—40.

6669   Hahn, Hugo J. **Euratom: The Conception of an International Personality,** *Harvard Law Review,* LXXI (April 1958), 1001—56.

6670   Hirsch, Etienne. **A Guide to Euratom,** *Bulletin of the Atomic Scientists,* XV (June 1959), 250—52 f.

6671   Hathijsen, Pierre. **Problems Connected with Creation of Euratom,** *Law and Contemporary Problems,* XXVI (Summer, 1961), 438—53.

6672   Moore, Ben T. **Euratom: The American Interest in the European Atomic Energy Community.** New York, Twentieth Century Fund, 1958. 40 p.

6673   Nanes, Allan S. **The Evolution of Euratom,** *International Journal,* XIII (Winter, 1957—58), 12—20.

6674   Nanes, Alfred S. and Efron, Reuben. **Atomic Energy and the European Community,** *World Affairs Quarterly,* XXVII (January 1957), 356—68.

6675   Nieburg, H. L. **Euratom: A Study in Coalition Politics,** *World Politics,* XV (July 1963), 597—622.

6676   Polach, Jaroslav G. **Euratom: Its Background, Issues and Economic Implications.** Preface by Sam H. Schurr. Dobbs Ferry, Oceana, 1964. xxiv + 232 p.

8.3.5.6 COURT OF THE COMMUNITIES
(Luxembourg)

6677 Bebr, Gerhard. **Judicial Control of the European Communities.** New York, Praeger, 1962. 268 p.

6678 Donner, A. M. **The Court of Justice of the European Communities,** *Legal Problems of the European Economic Community and the European Free Trade Area,* British Institute of International and Comparative Law (ed.). London, International and Comparative Law Quarterly, Supplementary Publication, 1961, pp. 66—75.

6679 Feld, Werner. **The Court of the European Communities: New Dimension in International Adjudication.** The Hague, Nijhoff, 1964. 127 p.

6680 Lagrange, Maurice. **The Role of the Court of Justice of the European Communities As Seen Through Its Case Law,** Jean-Aimé Stoll (trans.), *Law and Contemporary Problems,* XXVI (Summer, 1961), 400—17.

6681 McMahon, J. F. **The Court of the European Communities,** *Journal of Common Market Studies,* I (October 1962), 1—21.

6682 — —. **The Court of the European Communities: Judicial Interpretation and International Organization,** *British Yearbook of International Law,* XXXVII (1961), 320—50.

6683 Schwarzenberger, Georg. **The Contribution of the Court of Justice of the European Communities to European Integration,** *Law, State, and International Legal Order,* Salo Engel (ed.). Knoxville, University of Tennessee Press, 1964, pp. 285—96.

6684 Stewart, S. **The Court of the Coal and Steel Community,** *British Journal of Administrative Law,* I (March 1955), 123—28.

6685 Valentine, D. G. **The Court of Justice of the European Coal and Steel Community.** Hague, Nijhoff, 1955. xi + 273 p.

6686 Valentine, D. G. (ed.). **The Court of Justice of the European Communities.** London, Stevens, 1965. 2 vols.

6687 Valentine, D. G. **The Jurisdiction of the Court of Justice of the European Communities to Annual Executive Action,** *British Yearbook of International Law,* XXXVI (1960), 174—222.

8.3.6 EUROPEAN INVESTMENT BANK
(Brussels)

6688 Adam, H.-T. **Les organismes internationaux spécialisés.** Paris, Pinchon et Durand-Auzias, 1965.

Volume II, Chapter VI.

6689 Campolongo, Alberto. **European Investment Bank: Activity and Prospects,** *Journal of International Affairs,* XIX, 2 (1965), 276—85.

8.3.7 BANK FOR INTERNATIONAL SETTLEMENTS
(Basel)

See C 8.2.5.

8.4 POLITICAL ORGANIZATIONS

8.4.1 EUROPEAN UNION: PRO AND CON

6690 A., G. L. **Towards an Atlantic Union,** *World Today,* New Series, X (July 1954), 309—20.

Part E. — Regional International Organization

6691 Albrecht-Carrié, René. **One Europe: The Historical Background of European Unity.** Garden City, Doubleday, 1965. 346 p.

6692 Alting von Geusau, Frans A. M. **European Organizations and Foreign Relations of States: A Comparative Analysis of Decision-Making.** Leyden, Sythoff, 1962. xiii + 290 p.

6693 Ball, M. Margaret. **NATO and the European Union Movement.** New York, Praeger, 1959. xi + 486 p.

6694 Barraclough, Geoffrey. **European Unity in Thought and Action.** Oxford, Blackwell, 1963. 60 p.

6695 Beever, R. Colin. **European Unity and the Trade Union Movement.** Leyden, Sythoff, 1960. 303 p.

6696 Beloff, Max. **Europe and the Europeans: An International Discussion.** Introduction by Denis de Rougemont. London, Chatto and Windus, 1957. xix + 288 p.

6697 Benda, Julien. **Discours à la nation européenne.** Paris, Gallimard, 1933. 237 p.

6698 Bidmead, H. S. **A Design for the Occident,** *World Affairs,* New Series, II (October 1948), 410–19.

6699 Bingham, Alfred M. **The United States of Europe.** New York, Duell, 1940. 336 p.

6700 Bisschop, W. R. **A Commonwealth of European States,** *Transactions* (Grotius Society), XXV (1939), 1–31.

6701 Bolles, Blair. **Residual Nationalism: A Rising Threat to Projected European Union,** *Annals of the American Academy of Political and Social Science*, CCCXLVIII (1963), 102–9.

6702 Bonn, Moritz J. **Whither Europe — Union or Partnership?** New York, Philosophical Library, 1952. 201 p.

6703 Bonnefous, Edouard. **L'Europe en face de son destin.** Paris, Presses Universitaires, 1951. 386 p.

6704 Boyd, Andrew and Boyd, Frances. **Western Union: UNA's Guide to European Recovery.** London, Hutchinson, 1949. 205 p.

6705 Braham, Harry Lewis. **Permanent Peace for Europe.** Boston, Christopher, 1944. 192 p.

6706 Brugmans, H. **Is European Federalism a Factor for World Peace?** *World Justice*, II (September 1960), 24–42.

6707 C., I. **Western Union: I, Political Origins,** *World Today*, New Series, V (April 1949), 170–78.

6708 Carr, Edward Hallett. **Conditions of Peace.** New York, Macmillan, 1942.

Chapter X.

6709 Catlin, George. **One Anglo-American Nation.** New York, Macmillan, 1941. 155 p.

6710 Chamberlin, William Henry. **The European Cockpit.** New York, Macmillan, 1947. 330 p.

Part E. — Regional International Organization

6711 Coudenhove-Kalergi, Richard Nikolas. **Crusade for Pan-Europe: Autobiography of a Man and a Movement.** New York, Putnam, 1943. 318 p.

6712 — —. **Europe Must Unite.** London, Secker and Warburg, 1940. 160 p.

6713 — —. **Pan-Europe.** Introduction by Nicholas Murray Butler. New York, Knopf, 1926. 215 p.

This work, first published in October 1923, stimulated the formation of a Pan-Europa Movement, which held its first Congress in Vienna in October 1926. The movement soon found an official sponsor in the person of the French Premier and Foreign Minister, Aristide Briand, who proposed the formation of a European Union in a speech of September 5, 1929, before the Assembly of the League of Nations.

6714 — —. **The Pan-European Outlook,** *International Affairs,* X (July 1931), 638—44.

Comments by Amery, Stevens, Ali.

6715 Corbett, John P. **Europe and the Social Order.** Leyden, Sythoff, 1959. 188 p.

6716 Curtis, Lionel. **World Revolution in the Cause of Peace.** Oxford, Blackwell, 1949. xv + 167 p.

Plea for a Western Union.

6717 Curtis, Michael. **Western European Integration.** New York, Harper and Row, 1965.

6718 Davies, David. **A Federated Europe.** London, Gollancz, 1940. 141 p.

6719 Dawson, Christopher Henry. **The Modern Dilemma: The Problem of European Unity.** New York, Sheed, 1933. 113 p.

6720 Deák, Francis. **Can Europe Unite?** *Political Science Quarterly*, XLVI (September 1931), 424–33.

6721 Doman, Nicholas. **World Reconstruction and European Regionalism,** *Social Forces*, XXI (March 1943), 265–72.

6722 Dorpalen, Andreas. **The European Polity: Biography of an Idea,** *Journal of Politics*, X (November 1948), 712–33.

6723 Etzioni, Amitai. **European Unification: A Strategy of Change,** *World Politics*, XVI (October 1963), 32–51.

6724 — —. **A Grand Design? A Review,** *Journal of Conflict Resolution*, VII (June 1963), 155–63.

6725 Fay, Sidney B. **Toward European Unity,** *Current History*, New Series, XXII (June 1952), 321–27.

6726 — —. **Union for Western Europe?** *Current History*, New Series, XVI (March 1949), 156–61.

6727 Firsoff, V. A. **The Unity of Europe: Realities and Aspirations.** London, Drummond, 1947. 305 p.

6728 Fleissig, Andreas. **Paneuropa.** Munich, Duncker und Humblot, 1930. 171 p.

6729 Florinsky, Michael T. **Integrated Europe?** New York, Macmillan, 1955. x + 182 p.

6730 Friedrich, Carl J. **European Unity and the European Tradition,** *Confluence*, II, 3 (1953), 43–53.

6731 — —. **The Grassroots Base of the Unification of Europe,** *Public Policy,* XII (1963), 23—40.

6732 Fulbright, J. William. **A United States of Europe,** *Annals of the American Academy of Political and Social Science,* CCLVII (May 1948), 151—56.

6733 Gallin, Alexander. **Europe: Split or United?** *Foreign Affairs,* XXV (April 1947), 408—20.

6734 Gore-Booth, Paul H. **NATO and European Federation,** *American Society of International Law Proceedings,* XLVI (1952), 125—30.

6735 Guérard, Albert L. **Europe Free and United.** Stanford, Stanford University Press, 1945. xi + 206 p.

6736 Haas, Ernst B. **The United States of Europe,** *Political Science Quarterly,* LXIII (December 1948), 528—50.

An examination of four distinct approaches to a federation of Europe.

6737 Haas, Ernst B. and Merkl, Peter H. **Parliamentarians Against Ministers: The Case of Western European Union,** *International Organization,* XIV (Winter, 1960), 37—59.

6738 Hallstein, Walter. **United Europe: Challenge and Opportunity.** Cambridge, Harvard University Press, 1962. 109 p.

6739 Harrison, George and Jordan, P. **Central Union.** London, British-Continental Syndicate, 1943. 48 p.

6740 Hart, Albert Bushnell. **Disunited Europe,** *Current History,* XXXV (October 1931), 91—93.

Part E. — Regional International Organization

6741 — —. **The Disunited States of Europe,** *Current History,* XXXI (November 1929), 317–21.

6742 Hartley, Livingston. **Atlantic Challenge.** Foreword by Elmo Roper. Dobbs Ferry, Oceana, 1965. xii + 111 p.

6743 — —. **On the Political Integration of the Atlantic Community,** *Orbis,* VI (Winter, 1963), 645–55.

6744 Heiser, Hans J. **British Policy with Regard to the Unification Efforts on the European Continent.** Leyden, Sythoff, 1959. 121 p.

6745 Henig, Stanley. **Voting Procedures — A Reply,** *Journal of Common Markt Studies,* I (May 1963), 219–23.

6746 Herrick, Francis H. **The United States of Europe,** *Institute of World Affairs Proceedings,* V (1929), 162–67.

6747 Herriot, Édouard. **The United States of Europe.** New York, Viking, 1930. 330 p.

6748 Holcombe, Arthur N. **An American View of European Union,** *American Political Science Review,* XLVII (June 1953), 417–30.

6749 Hutchinson, Paul. **The United States of Europe.** Chicago, Willett, Clark, and Colby, 1929. 225 p.

6750 Jameson, Storm. **Federalism and a New Europe,** *Federal Union,* M. Chaning-Pearce (ed.). London, Cape, 1940. pp. 249–62.

6751 Jennings, W. Ivor. **A Federation for Western Europe.** Cambridge, Cambridge University Press, 1940. xi + 208 p.

6752 — —. **The Idea of a United States of Europe,** *Institute of World Affairs Proceedings,* XVI (1938), 250–56.

6753 Jordan, Peter and Harrison, George. **Central Union of Europe.** Introduction by Ernest M. Patterson. New York, McBride, 1944. 110 p.

6754 Kalijarvi, Thorsten V. **Obstacles to European Unification,** *Annals of the American Academy of Political and Social Science,* CCCXLVIII (July 1963), 46–53.

6755 Karp, Basil. **The Draft Constitution for a European Political Community,** *International Organization,* VIII (May 1954), 181–202.

6756 Keeton, George W. **Towards a New Europe,** *World Affairs,* VII (October 1941), 143–48.

6757 — —. **Western European Federation,** *International Law Quarterly,* II (Summer 1948), 214–27.

6758 Klausner, Leopold C. **Proposed Constitution for the United States of Europe,** *World Affairs Quarterly,* XX (October 1949), 241–55.

6759 — —. **Thirty Years Fight for a United States of Europe,** *World Affairs Quarterly,* XXI (January 1951), 376–93.

6760 Knapton, E. J. **A German View of European Federation,** *World Affairs,* VII (July 1941), 25–35.

6761 Knorr, Klaus E. **Union of Western Europe: A Third Center of Power?** New Haven, Yale Institute of International Studies, 1948. 118 p.

Part E. — *Regional International Organization*

6762 — —. **What Manner of Union?** *World Politics*, I (October 1948-July 1949), 233–42.

6763 Kohn, Hans. **The Difficult Road to Western Unity,** *Orbis*, III (Fall, 1959), 297–312.

6764 — —. **The Future of Political Unity in Western Europe,** *Annals of the American Academy of Political and Social Science*, CCCXLVIII (July 1963), 95–100.

6765 Lang, R. D. **Central Europe and European Unity,** *Journal of Central European Affairs*, VI (April 1946), 21–29.

6766 Lange, Halvard M. **European Union: False Hopes and Realities,** *Foreign Affairs*, XXVIII (April 1950), 441–50.

6767 Lawson, Ruth C. **European Union or Atlantic Union?** *Current History*, New Series, XIX (December 1950), 328–33.

6768 Lecerf, Jean. **Histoire de l'unité européenne.** Preface by Jean Monnet. Paris, Gallimard, 1965. 382 p.

6769 Lerner, Daniel. **Will European Union Bring About Merged National Goals?** *Annals of the American Academy of Political and Social Science*, CCCXLVIII (July 1963), 34–41.

6770 Lerner, Harold. **Attitudes Toward European Unification,** *Military Review*, XXXIX (October 1959), 12–23.

6771 Loewenstein, Karl. **Unification of Europe: A Balance Sheet,** *Current History*, New Series, XL (January 1961), 1–10.

6772 — —. **The Union of Western Europe: Illusion and Reality; I, An Appraisal of the Methods,** Columbia Law Review, LII (January 1952), 55–99.

6773 — —. **The Union of Western Europe: Illusion and Reality; II, An Appraisal of the Motives,** Columbia Law Review, LII (February 1952), 209–40.

6774 Lutz, Ralph H. **European Political Unity — An Idle Dream or a Reasonable Prospect,** World Affairs Quarterly, XXI (July 1950), 132–38.

Published concurrently in Institute of World Affairs Proceedings.

6775 McCreery, Henry F. **Western Union,** World Affairs Quarterly, XIX (April 1949), 53–61.

6776 Mackay, Ronald William Gordon. **Peace Aims and the New Order.** New York, Dodd, 1941. 306 p.

6777 — —. **Towards a United States of Europe.** London, Hutchinson, 1961. 160 p.

6778 — —. **Western Union in Crisis.** Oxford, Blackwell, 1949. 138 p.

6779 Madariaga, Salvador de. **Toward the United States of Europe,** Orbis, VI (Fall, 1962), 422–34.

6780 Martin, Charles E. **The United States of Europe,** Institute of World Affairs Proceedings, VII (1930), 23–44.

6781 Martin, William. **European Unity,** Problems of Peace, Series 7 (1932), 156–73.

Part E. — Regional International Organization

6782 Mitchell, Thomas Howard. **Proposed United States of Europe,** *World Affairs Quarterly,* VII (July 1936), 180—91.

6783 Mitrany, David. **The Case Against Pan-Europa,** *Current History,* XXXIII (October 1930), 65—69.

6784 — —. **Pan-Europa — A Hope or a Danger?** *Political Quarterly,* I (October-December 1930), 457—478.

6785 Mookerjee, Girija D. **Steps Towards European Unity,** *India Quarterly,* V (July-September 1949), 235—43.

6786 Mosley, Oswald. **Europe: Faith and Plan.** London, Euphorion, 1958. 147 p.

6787 Muralt, Leonhard von. **From Versailles to Potsdam.** Chicago, Regnery, 1948. 93 p.

6788 Novikov, Iakov Aleksandrovich. **La fédération de l'Europe.** Paris, Alcan, 1901. 807 p.

6789 Pettovich, P. **Europe's Evolution Towards Unity,** *World Justice,* IV (June 1963), 443—74.

6790 Philip, Oliver. **Le problème de l'union européene.** Preface by Denis de Rougemont. Neuchâtel, La Baconnière, 1950. 381 p.

6791 Racine, Raymond (ed.). **Demain l'Europe sans frontières.** Paris, Plon, 1958. vi + 231 p.

6792 Rappard, William E. **Uniting Europe: The Trend of International Cooperation Since the War.** New Haven, Yale University Press, 1930. 309 p.

Part E. — Regional International Organization

6793 Renouvin, Pierre. **L'idée de fédération européenne dans la pensée politique du XIXe siècle.** Oxford, Clarendon Press, 1949. 23 p.

6794 Reynaud, Paul. **Unite or Perish: A Dynamic Program for a United Europe.** New York, Simon and Schuster, 1951. xvii + 214 p.

6795 Robertson, A. H. **Different Approaches to European Unity,** *American Journal of Comparative Law,* III (Autumn, 1954), 502—21.

6796 — —. **The European Political Community,** *British Yearbook of International Law,* XXIX (1952), 383—400.

6797 — —. **Five European Conventions,** *International and Comparative Law Quarterly,* III (October 1954), 642—44.

6798 — —. **The Legal Work of the Council of Europe,** *International and Comparative Law Quarterly,* X (January 1961), 143—66.

6799 Ruml, Beardsley. **The United States of Europe,** *Collier's,* CXXIX (June 21, 1952), 22 f.

6800 Salter, J. Arthur. **The United States of Europe, and Other Papers.** Edited with notes by W. Arnold-Forster. London, Allen and Unwin, 1933. 303 p.

6801 Schuman, Frederick L. **The Disunion of Europe,** *Current History,* New Series, XXI (October 1951), 202—7.

6802 Schwarzenberger, G. **Atlantic Union,** *World Affairs,* V (January 1951), 88—102.

Part E. — Regional International Organization

6803 Sennholz, Hans F. **How Can Europe Survive?** New York, Van Nostrand, 1955. 336 p.

6804 Sidjanski, D. **Voting Procedures in an Enlarged Community,** *Journal of Common Market Studies,* I (December 1962), 173–79.

6805 Stein, Eric. **Assimilation of National Laws As a Function of European Integration,** *American Journal of International Law,* LVIII (January 1964), 1–40.

6806 Stern-Rubarth, Edgar (ed.). **Europa: Grossmacht oder Kleinstaaterei.** Bielefeld, Eilers, 1951. 295 p.

6807 Stone, Willam T. **The Briand Project for European Union,** *Foreign Policy Reports,* VI (September 17, 1930), 261–74.

6808 Szent-Miklosy, Istvan. **The Atlantic Union Movement: Its Significance in World Politics.** New York, Fountainhead, 1965. xx + 264 p.

6809 Vansittart, Robert Gilbert. **Events and Shadows.** London, Hutchinson, 1947. 196 p.

6810 Viereck, Peter. **Warning for a Western Union,** *Current History,* New Series, XVII (July 1949), 7–10; (August 1949), 75–78.

6811 Walton, Clarence C. **The Fate of Neo-Federalism in Western Europe,** *Western Political Quarterly,* V (September 1952), 366–90.

6812 Whitton, John B. **The Briand Plan for European Union,** *Current History,* XXXII (September 1930), 1176–81.

The text of Briand's plan is appended.

6813 — —. **The Proposed Federation of European States: II,** *Current History,* XXXII (July 1930), 662—65.

6814 Wright, Quincy. **Western European Union,** *Regional Arrangements for Security and the United Nations,* Commission to Study the Organization of Peace (ed.). New York, Commission to Study the Organization of Peace, 1953, pp. 80—90.

6815 Yalem, Ronald J. **Prospects for European Political Unification,** *Western Political Quarterly,* XII (March 1959), 50—63.

6816 Zimmern, Alfred. **Europe and the World Community,** *Problems of Peace,* Series 6 (1931), 114—33.
Opposes regionalism of Europe.

6817 — —. **How Can Europe Unite?** *Vital Speeches,* XVII (September 1959), 677—80.

8.4.2 EUROPEAN ASSEMBLIES

6818 Borcier, Paul. **The Political Role of the Assembly of WEU.** Strasbourg, n. p., 1963. 50 p.

6819 Lindsay, Kenneth. **European Assemblies: The Experimental Period 1949—1959.** New York, Praeger, 1960. xxi + 267 p.

6820 — —. **Towards a European Parliament.** Introduction by Robert Boothby. Strasbourg, Council of Europe Secretariat, 1958. xvii + 164 p.

6821 Manzanares, Henri. **Le parlement européen.** Preface by P. O. Lapie. Paris, Berger-Levrault, 1965. 321 p.
Extensive bibliography.

6822 Pryce, Roy. **The Future of the European Parliament,** *Parliamentary Affairs,* XV (Autumn, 1962), 450—60.

6823 Stein, Eric. **Integration, Unification, Harmonization, and the Politics of the Possible: The Convention on "European" Elections,** *Twentieth Century Comparative and Conflicts of Laws,* Kurt H. Nadelmann, Arthur T. von Mehren and John N. Hazard (eds.). Leyden, Sythoff, 1961, pp. 509—32.

European parliamentary assembly.

8.4.3 COUNCIL OF EUROPE (Strasbourg)

6824 Ball, M. Margaret. **The Organization of American States and the Council of Europe,** *British Yearbook of International Law,* XXVI (1949), 150—76.

6825 Boothby, Robert. **The Future of the Council of Europe,** *International Affairs,* XXVIII (July 1952), 331—37.

6826 Carleton, William G. **What of the Council of Europe?** *Virginia Quarterly Review,* XXVII (Spring, 1951), 179—95.

6827 Carter, W. Horsfall. **The Council of Europe,** *International Relations,* II (October 1965), 793—802.

6828 Cheever, Daniel S. and Haviland, H. Field, Jr. **Organizing for Peace.** Boston, Houghton, Mifflin, 1954.

Chapter XXVI.

6829 Crosland, Anthony. **Prospects for the Council of Europe,** *Political Quarterly,* XXII (April-June 1951), 142—53.

6830 Duclos, Pierre. **La réforme du Conseil de l'Europe.** Paris, Librairie Générale de Droit et de Jurisprudence, 1958. 527 p.

6831 Edelman, Maurice. **The Council of Europe, 1950,** *International Affairs,* XXVII (January 1951), 25—31.

6832 European Movement. **European Movement and the Council of Europe.** Forewords by Winston S. Churchill and Paul-Henri Spaak. London, Hutchinson, 1949. 203 p.

6833 Gellner, C. R. **The Council of Europe: A Brief Survey of Its Origin and Development.** Washington, Library of Congress, Legislative Reference Service, 1951. 24 p.

6834 Gimenez Caballero, Ernesto. **La Europa de Estrasburgo.** Madrid, Instituto de Estudias Politicos, 1950. 154 p.

6835 Haas, Ernst B. **Consensus Formation in the Council of Europe.** Berkeley and Los Angeles, University of California Press, 1960. 70 p.

6836 Hollis, Christopher. **The Council of Europe,** *World Justice,* I (December 1959), 215—32.

6837 Hurd, Volney D. **The Council of Europe: Design for a United States of Europe.** New York, Manhattan, 1958. 58 p.

6838 J., C. **The Schuman Plan and the Council of Europe,** *World Today,* New Series, VIII (November 1952), 473—80.

6839 Klausner, Leopold C. **On the Eve of the European Constituent Assembly,** *World Affairs Quarterly,* XX (July 1949), 137—46.

Part E. — Regional International Organization

6840 Major, John. **President Kennedy's "Grand Design": The United States and a United Europe,** *World Today,* New Series, XVIII (September 1962), 383–89.

6841 Merkl, Peter H. **European Assembly Parties and National Delegations,** *Journal of Conflict Resolution,* VIII (March 1964), 50–64.

6842 Mower, A. Glenn, Jr. **The Official Pressure Group of the Council of Europe's Consultative Assembly,** *International Organization,* XVIII (Spring, 1964), 292–306.

6843 Pickles, W. **The Strasbourg Illusion,** *Political Quarterly,* XXI (January-March 1950), 56–68.

6844 Pinto, Roger. **Les organisations européennes.** 2d ed. Paris, Payot, 1965.

Chapter II.

6845 Rentier, Jeannie. **L'activité du Conseil de l'Europe dans le domaine social.** Preface by Fernand Dehousse. Liège, Thone, 1954. xiii + 206 p.

6846 Robertson, A. H. **The Council of Europe: Its Structure, Functions and Achievements.** 2d ed. Foreword by Guy Mollet. New York, Praeger, 1961. xv + 288 p.

6847 — —. **The Council of Europe 1949–1953,** *International and Comparative Law Quarterly,* III (April 1954), 235–55; (July 1954), 404–20.

6848 Rohn, Peter H. **Relations Between the Council of Europe and International Non-Governmental Organizations.** Brussels, Union of International Associations, 1957. 79 p.

6849 Salter, Noel. **Western European Union – The Role of the Assembly, 1954–1963,** *International Affairs,* XL, (January 1964) 34–46.

6850 Schuman, Frederick L. **The Council of Europe,** *American Political Science Review,* XLV (September 1951), 724–40.

6851 Sørensen, Max. **Le Conseil de l'Europe,** *Recueil des Cours,* LXXXI (1952), 121–99.

6852 Stein, Eric. **The European Parliamentary Assembly: Techniques of Emerging "Political Control,"** *International Organization,* XIII (Spring, 1959), 233–54.

6853 Strange, Susan. **The Council of Europe,** *World Affairs,* New Series, III (July 1949), 246–58.

6854 — —. **Strasbourg in Retrospect,** *World Affairs,* IV (January 1950), 3–21.

6855 — —. **Strasbourg Revisited,** *World Affairs,* V (January 1951), 70–87.

8.4.4 CONVENTION ON HUMAN RIGHTS

6856 Anon. **The Central American Convention Compared,** *Journal of the International Commission of Jurists,* VI (Summer, 1965), 136–87.

A comparison with the Inter-American Draft Convention on Human Rights and the European Convention for the Protection of Human Rights and Fundamental Freedoms.

6857 British Institute of International and Comparative Law (ed.). **The European Convention on Human Rights.** Foreword by Lord McNair. London, International and Comparative Law Quarterly Supplement, 1965. viii + 106 p.

Part E. — Regional International Organization

6858 Golsong, H. **The Control Machinery of the European Convention on Human Rights,** *The European Convention on Human Rights*, British Institute of International and Comparative Law (ed.). London, International and Comparative Law Quarterly Supplement, 1965, pp. 38—69.

6859 Green, L. C. **The European Convention on Human Right,** *World Affairs*, New Series, V (October 1951), 432—44.

6860 Lauterpacht, H. **The Proposed European Court of Human Rights,** *Transactions* (Grotius Society), XXXV (1949), 25—41.

Comments by Barrington, Moore, Spens, Bentwich.

6861 Leifer, M. **Human Rights in the European Community,** *Australian Outlook*, XV (August 1961), 169—87.

6862 Petrén, Sture. **The Promotion of Human Rights Through the Council of Europe,** *The Quest for Peace*, Andrew W. Cordier and Wilder Foote (eds.). New York, Columbia University Press, 1965, pp. 331—42.

6863 Robertson, Arthur Henry. **Human Rights in Europe.** Dobbs Ferry, Oceana, 1964. 210 p.

6864 — —. **Human Rights in Europe, Being an Account of the European Convention for the Protection of Human Rights and Fundamental Freedoms Signed in Rome on 4 November 1950, of the Protocol Thereto and of the Machinery Created Thereby: The European Commission of Human Rights and the European Court of Human Rights.** New York, Oceana, 1963. ix + 280 p.

6865 — —. **The European Convention on Human Rights,** *British Yearbook of International Law*, XXIX (1952), 452—54.

6866 — —. **The European Convention for the Protection of Human Rights,** *British Yearbook of International Law*, XXVII (1950), 145—63.

6867 — —. **The Political Background and Historical Development of the European Convention on Human Rights,** *The European Convention on Human Rights*, British Institute of International and Comparative Law (ed.). London, International and Comparative Law Quarterly, 1965, pp. 24—37.

6868 Schwelb, Egon. **On the Operation of the European Convention on Human Rights,** *International Organization*, XVIII (Summer, 1964), 558—85.

6869 Triska, J. F. **The Individual and His Rights in the European Community: An Experiment in International Law,** *Tulane Law Review*, XXXI (February 1957), 283—302.

6870 Waldock, C. Humphrey M. **The European Convention for the Protection of Human Rights and Fundamental Freedoms,** *British Yearbook of International Law*, XXXIV (1958), 356—63.

6871 — —. **Human Rights in Contemporary International Law and the Significance of the European Convention,** *The European Convention on Human Rights*, British Institute of International and Comparative Law (ed.). London, International and Comparative Law Quarterly Supplement, 1965, pp. 1—23.

8.5 MILITARY ORGANIZATIONS

8.5.1 ABORTIVE EUROPEAN DEFENSE COMMUNITY

6872 Armstrong, Hamilton Fish. **Postscript to E. D. C.,** *Foreign Affairs*, XXXIII (October 1954), 17—27.

6873 Aron, Raymond and Lerner, Daniel (eds.). **France Defeats EDC.** New York, Praeger, 1957. 225 p.

Part E. — Regional International Organization

6874 Bebr, G. **The European Defense Community and the Western European Union: An Agonizing Dilemma,** *Stanford Law Review,* VII (March 1955), 169—236.

6875 Goormaghtigh, John. **France and the European Defence Community,** *International Journal,* IX (Spring, 1954), 96—106.

6876 J., C. N. **The European Defence Community: Problems of Ratification,** *World Today,* New Series, X (August 1954), 326—37.

Appendix on additional protocols.

6877 L., H. G. **The European Defence Community,** *World Today,* New Series, VIII (June 1952), 236—48.

6878 Rolin, Henri. **The European Defence Community,** *Transactions* (Grotius Society), XXXVIII (1952), 4—17.

Comments by Boeg, Jaffe, Pinna, Picarda, Adamkiewicz, Moore, Spens.

6878a Trempont, Jacques. **La Communauté Européenne de Défense,** *International and Comparative Law Quarterly,* 1, 4 (1952), 519—232.

6879 Walton, Clarence C. **Background for the European Defense Community,** *Political Science Quarterly,* LXVIII (March 1953), 42—69.

8.5.2 NORTH ATLANTIC TREATY ORGANIZATION
(Brussels)

6880 B., U. **NATO and the Sovereign State,** *World Today,* New Series, XIV (January 1958), 11—17.

6881 Ball, M. Margaret. **NATO and the European Union Movement.** New York, Praeger, 1959. xi + 486 p.

6882 Benoit, Emile. **The Economic Aspect of the Western Alliance,** *Journal of International Affairs,* XII, 1 (1958), 27–43.

6883 Bentinck, H. E. A. **The Present Position and Potentialities of the Atlantic Alliance,** *International Relations,* I (April 1957), 277–80 f.

6884 Berkes, Ross N. **Do Regional Pacts Violate the Spirit of the United Nations? NATO As Case Study,** *World Affairs Quarterly,* XXIV (July 1953), 151–65.

6885 Beukema, Herman. **The Military Organization of the Free World,** *Academy of Political Science Proceedings,* XXIV (1951), 150–60.

6886 Birgi, Nuri. **The Unfolding Alliance,** *Atlantic Community Quarterly,* II (Fall, 1964), 408–12.
Reprinted from *NATO Letter,* April 1964.

6887 Birrenbach, Kurt. **European Integration and Atlantic Partnership,** *NATO in Quest of Cohesion,* Karl H. Cerny and Henry W. Briefs (eds.). New York, Praeger, 1965, pp. 271–88.

6888 ——. **Partnership and Consultation in NATO,** *Atlantic Community Quarterly,* II (Spring, 1964), 62–71.

6889 ——. **The Reorganization of NATO,** *Orbis,* VI (Summer, 1962), 244–57.

6890 Bolles, Blair. **NATO — An American View,** *International Journal,* VI (Autumn, 1951), 281–91.

6891 Bowie, Robert R. **Strategy and the Atlantic Alliance,** *International Organization,* XVII (Summer, 1963), 709–32.

Part E. — *Regional International Organization*

6892 Boyd, Andrew. **What Is NATO?** London, Batchworth, 1952. 40 p.

6893 Brandt, Karl. **An Economic Strategy for NATO,** *NATO in Quest of Cohesion*, Karl H. Cerny and Henry W. Briefs (eds.). New York, Praeger, 1965, pp. 327–44.

6894 Brown, George W. **The "Atlantic Alliance" in Perspective,** *International Journal*, XII (Spring, 1957), 79–82.

6895 Buchan, Alastair. **Europe and the Atlantic Alliance: Two Strategies or One?** *Journal of Common Market Studies*, I (May 1963), 224–55.

6896 — —. **The Multilateral Force: A Study in Alliance Politics,** *International Affairs*, XL (October 1964), 619–37.

6897 — —. **NATO in the 1960s: The Implications of Interdependence.** New York, Praeger, 1960. xii + 131 p.

6898 — —. **NATO Today.** Toronto, Canadian Institute of International Affairs, 1959. 16 p.

6899 — —. **The Reform of NATO,** *Foreign Affairs*, XL (January 1962), 165–82.

6900 Burgess, W. Randolf. **NATO — The First Ten Years,** *Academy of Political Science Proceedings*, XXVI (May 1959), 334–38.

6901 Burns, A. L. **NATO and Nuclear Sharing,** *NATO and American Security*, Klaus Knorr (ed.). Princeton, Princeton University Press, 1959, pp. 151–75.

6902 Cerny, Karl H. and Briefs, Henry W. (eds.). **NATO in Quest of Cohesion.** Foreword by Lauris Norstad. New York, Praeger, 1965. xii + 476 p.

Part E. — Regional International Organization

6903 Cheever, Daniel S. and Haviland, H. Field, Jr. **Organizing for Peace.** Boston, Houghton, Mifflin, 1954.

Chapter XXIV.

6904 Coffey, J. I. **A NATO Nuclear Deterrent?** *Orbis*, VIII (Fall, 1964), 584–94.

6905 Collins, J. Lawton. **NATO: Still Vital for Peace,** *Foreign Affairs*, XXXIV (April 1956), 367–79.

6906 Cottrell, Alvin J. and Doughtery, James E. **The Politics of the Atlantic Alliance.** New York, Praeger, 1964. 264 p.

6907 Crathorne, Lord. **NATO and European Unity,** *Atlantic Community Quarterly*, I (Summer, 1963), 157–74.

Selections from a debate in the House of Lords, February 13, 1963.

6908 Daniels, Walter M. (comp.). **Defense of Western Europe.** New York, Wilson, 1950. 242 p.

6909 Dawson, Raymond H. **What Kind of NATO Nuclear Force?** *Annals of the American Academy of Political and Social Science*, CCCLI (January 1964), 30–39.

6910 Dean, Vera Micheles and Bolles, Blair. **North Atlantic Defense Pact — Background and Pros and Cons,** *Foreign Policy Reports*, XXIV (February 15, 1949), 226–32.

6911 Delmas, Claude. **L'alliance atlantique: essai de phénoménologie politique.** Preface by General Valluy. Paris, Payot, 1962. 278 p.

6912 Dexter, Byron. **Locarno Again,** *Foreign Affairs*, XXXII (October 1953), 24–47.

Part E. — Regional International Organization

6913 Duchene, François. **Beyond Alliance.** Boulogne-sur-Seine, Atlantic Institute, 1965. 63 p.

6914 Eagleton, Clyde. **The North Atlantic Defense Pact,** *Journal of International Affairs,* III (Spring, 1949), 21–35.

6915 — —. **The North Atlantic Treaty Organization,** *Regional Arrangements for Security and the United Nations,* Commission to Study the Organization of Peace (ed.). New York, Commission to Study the Organization of Peace, 1953, pp. 91–99.

6916 Eliot, George Fielding. **Military Organization Under the Atlantic Pact,** *Foreign Affairs,* XXVII (July 1949), 640–50.

6917 — —. **Organizing the Atlantic Community: The Strategic Problem,** *Academy of Political Science Proceedings,* XXIII (May 1949), 302–309.

6918 Ellert, Robert B. **NATO "Fair Trial" Safeguards.** Hague, Nijhoff, 1963. vi + 89 p.

6919 Emmet, Christopher. **The U. S. Plan for a NATO Nuclear Deterrent,** *Orbis,* VII (Summer, 1963), 265–77.

6920 Falls, Cyril. **The Progress of NATO,** *International Relations,* I (April 1954), 17–22.

6921 Farran, Charles d'Olivier. **Atlantic Democracy.** New York, Praeger, 1958. 212 p.

6922 Fay, Sidney B. **Toward the Defense of Europe,** *Current History,* New Series, XXII (May 1952), 257–64.

Part E. — Regional International Organization

6923 Fox, William T. R. **NATO and Coalition Diplomacy,** *Annals of the American Academy of Political and Social Science* CCLXXXVIII (July 1953), 114–18.

6924 Freedman, Max. **The Lisbon Conference,** *International Journal,* VII (Spring, 1952), 85–93.

6925 Friedmann, Wolfgang. **New Tasks for NATO?** *International Journal,* XI (Summer, 1956), 157–64.

6926 Furniss, Edgar S., Jr. **A Personal Evaluation of the Western Alliance,** *The Western Alliance,* Edgar S. Furniss, Jr. (ed.). Columbus, Ohio State University Press, 1965, pp. 159–78.

6927 Furniss, Edgar S., Jr. (ed.). **The Western Alliance: Its Status and Prospects.** Columbus, Ohio State University Press, 1965. vii + 182 p.

6928 Gallois, Pierre M. **New Teeth for NATO,** *Foreign Affairs,* XXXIX (October 1960), 67–80.

6929 Giffin, S. F. **Untangling an Alliance,** *Orbis,* VII (Fall, 1963), 465–77.

6930 Goodhart, A. L. **The North Atlantic Treaty,** *Recueil des Cours,* LXXIX (1951), 187–236.

6931 Goodman, Elliott R. **The Dunystee Plan,** *Atlantic Community Quarterly,* III (Fall, 1965), 340–46.

Reprinted from *NATO Letter,* July-August 1965.

6932 — —. **Five Nuclear Options for the West,** *Atlantic Community Quarterly,* XX (Winter, 1964–65), 571–87.

Reprinted from *Forensic Quarterly,* August 1964.

Part E. — Regional International Organization

6933 Goodpaster, Andrew J. **The Development of SHAPE — 1950–1953,** *International Organization,* IX (May 1955), 257–62.

6934 Goold-Adams, Richard. **Political Cooperation in NATO,** *The Western Alliance,* Edgar S. Furniss, Jr. (ed.). Columbus, Ohio State University Press, 1965, pp. 49–70.

6935 Gordon, Bernard K. **NATO's Missing Shield,** *Bulletin of the Atomic Scientists,* XV (June 1959), 229–33.

6936 Gordon, Lincoln. **Economic Aspects of Coalition Diplomacy — The NATO Experience,** *International Organization,* X (November 1956), 529–43.

6937 Guttenberg, Karl Theodore von und zu. **NATO and the Need for a New Policy,** *Western Integration and the Future of Eastern Europe,* David S. Collier and Kurt Glaser (eds.). Chicago, Regnery, 1964, pp. 46–53.

6938 Hallstein, Walter. **NATO and the European Economic Community,** *Orbis,* VI (Winter, 1963), 564–74.

6939 Hassel, Kai-Uwe von. **Organizing Western Defense,** *Foreign Affairs,* XLIII (January 1965), 209–16.

6940 Herod, W. R. **Strength of the Atlantic Community,** *Annals of the American Academy of Political and Social Science,* CCLXXXII (July 1952), 19–29.

6941 Hilsman, Roger. **NATO: The Developing Strategic Context,** *NATO and American Security,* Klaus Knorr (ed.). Princeton, Princeton University Press, 1959, pp. 11–36.

6942 Hinterhoff, Eugene. **Problems Along NATO's Flanks,** *Orbis,* VIII (Fall, 1964), 607–23.

6943 Hoag, Malcolm W. **On NATO Pooling,** *World Politics,* X (April 1958), 475–83.

6944 — —. **Rationalizing NATO Strategy,** *World Politics,* XVII (October 1964), 121–42.

6945 Holmes, John W. **The Advantages of Diversity in NATO,** *NATO in Quest of Cohesion,* Karl H. Cerny and Henry W. Briefs (eds.). New York, Praeger, 1965, pp. 289–302.

6946 Hotz, Alfred J. **NATO: Myth or Reality,** *Annals of the American Academy of Political and Social Science,* CCLXXXVIII (July 1953), 125–33.

6947 Hughes, H. Stuart. **Disengagement and NATO,** *The Liberal Papers,* James Roosevelt (ed.). Chicago, Quadrangle, 1962, pp. 303–12.

6948 Ismay, Lord. **Atlantic Alliance,** *International Journal,* IX (Spring, 1954), 79–86.

6949 — —. **NATO: The First Five Years, 1949–1954.** Utrecht, Bosch, 1955. xi + 280 p.

6950 James, F. Cyril. **The Scope of Strategy,** *Annals of the American Academy of Political and Social Science,* CCLXXXVIII (July 1953), 20–26.

6951 Jebb, Gladwyn. **The Organization of Defense Against Aggression in the Free World,** *Academy of Political Science Proceedings,* XXIV (January 1951), 267–79.

6952 Johnson, Franklyn A. **The British Committee of Imperial Defense: Prototype of U. S. Security Organization,** *Journal of Politics,* XXIII (May 1961), 231–61.

Part E. — *Regional International Organization*

6953 Kaplan, Lawrence S. **NATO and Its Commentators, the First 5 Years,** *International Organization,* VIII (November 1954), 447–67.

6954 King, James E., Jr. **NATO: Genesis, Progress, Problems,** *National Security in the Nuclear Age: Basic Facts and Theories,* Gordon B. Turner and Richard D. Challener (eds.). New York, Praeger, 1960, pp. 143–72.

6955 Kintner, William R. and Possony, Stefan T. **NATO's Nuclear Crisis,** *Orbis,* VI (Summer, 1962), 217–43.

6956 Kirk, Grayson. **The Atlantic Pact and International Security,** *International Organization,* III (May 1949), 239–53.

6957 Kissinger, Henry A. **The Troubled Partnership.** New York, McGraw-Hill, 1965. 266 p.

6958 Knorr, Klaus (ed.). **NATO and American Security.** Princeton, Princeton University Press, 1959. 342 p.

6959 Knowlton, William A. **Early Stages in the Organization of SHAPE,** *International Organization,* XIII (Winter, 1959), 1–18.

6960 Kohl, Wilfrid L. **Nuclear Sharing in NATO and the Multilateral Force,** *Political Science Quarterly,* LXXX (March 1965), 88–109.

6961 Krause, Lawrence B. **Economic Problems of the Alliance,** *NATO in Quest of Cohesion,* Karl H. Cerny and Henry W. Briefs (eds.). New York, Praeger, 1965, pp. 303–20.

6962 Kulski, W. W. **The Soviet System of Collective Security Compared with the Western System,** *American Journal of International Law,* XLIV (July 1950), 453–76.

6963 Lawson, Ruth C. **Some Contributions of the North Atlantic Community Towards Improving Organization for Security,** *American Society of International Law Proceedings,* LI (1957), 117–27.

6964 Lindsay, Richard C. **The Military Potential of NATO,** *Annals of the American Academy of Political and Social Science,* CCCXII (July 1957), 89–93.

6965 Löwenstein, Hubertus zu and Zühlsdorff, Volkmar. **NATO and the Defense of the West,** Edward Fitzgerald (trans.). New York, Praeger, 1962. viii + 383 p.

6966 McClintock, Charles G. and Hekhuis, Dale J. **European Community Deterrence: Its Organization, Utility, and Political Feasibility,** *Journal of Conflict Resolution,* V (September 1961), 230–53.

6967 McInnis, Edgar. **The Atlantic Triangle and the Cold War.** Toronto, University of Toronto Press, 1959. 163 p.

6968 Mackintosh, W. A. **The Fissure in NATO: North American and Sterling Area Trade,** *Foreign Affairs,* XXXI (January 1953), 268–79.

6969 McQuade, Lawrence C. **NATO's Non-Nuclear Needs,** *International Affairs,* XL (January 1964), 11–21.

6970 Martin, Kingsley, **NATO — A British View,** *International Journal,* VI (Autumn, 1951), 292–99.

6971 Middleton, Drew. **NATO Changes Direction,** *Foreign Affairs,* XXXI (April 1953), 427–40.

6972 Moore, Ben T. **NATO and the Future of Europe.** Foreword by William C. Foster. New York, Harper, 1958. 263 p.

Part E. — *Regional International Organization*

6973 Morgenstierne, Wilhelm Muntle. **The Atlantic Pact: A Norwegian Point of View,** *Academy of Political Science Proceedings*, XXIII (May 1949), 325–42.

6974 Morgenthau, Hans J. **The Crisis of the Alliance,** *NATO in Quest of Cohesion*, Karl H. Cerny and Henry W. Briefs (eds.). New York, Praeger, 1965, pp. 125–34.

6975 Mulley, Frederick William. **NATO's Nuclear Problems: Control or Consultation,** *Orbis*, VIII (Spring, 1964), 21–35.

6976 — —. **The Politics of Western Defense.** New York, Praeger, 1962. 282 p.

6977 Murville, Couve de. **NATO: A French View,** *International Journal*, XIV (Spring, 1959), 85–86.

6978 Niemeyer, Gerhart. **NATO's Strength and Weakness,** *Orbis*, II (Spring, 1958), 83–95.

6979 Nitze, Paul H. **Alternatives to NATO,** *NATO and American Security*, Klaus Knorr (ed.). Princeton, Princeton University Press, 1959, pp. 260–78.

6980 — —. **Collective Defense and the Atlantic Community,** *Harvard Review*, I (Fall, 1962), 26–30.

6981 Nolting, Frederick E. **Status and Prospects of the Western Alliance,** *The Western Alliance*, Edgar S. Furniss, Jr. (ed.). Columbus, Ohio State University Press, 1965, pp. 145–58.

6982 Norstad, Lauris. **NATO, Its Problems and Its Promise,** *Academy of Political Science Proceedings*, XXVII (May 1963), 102–14.

6983 — —. **NATO — A Review,** *Institute of World Affairs Proceedings,* XXXIX (1963), 112—19.

6984 — —. **NATO: Strength and Spirit,** *Institute of World Affairs Proceedings,* XXXV (1959), 13—19.

6985 North Atlantic Treaty Organization. **Bibliography.** Paris, Place Maréchal de Lattre de Tassigny, 1964. 205 p.

6986 — —. **NATO: Facts About the North Atlantic Treaty Organization.** Paris, 1965. ix + 319 p.

6987 Osgood, Robert Endicott. **NATO: The Entangling Alliance.** Chicago, University of Chicago Press, 1962. 416 p.

6988 — —. **NATO: The Entangling Alliance,** *Power and Order: Six Cases in World Politics,* John G. Stoessinger and Alan F. Westin (eds.). New York, Harcourt, Brace and World, 1964, pp. 66—101.

6989 — —. **NATO: Problems of Security and Collaboration,** *American Political Science Review,* LIV (March 1960), 106—29.

6990 Patterson, Gardner and Furniss, Edgar S., Jr. **NATO: A Critical Appraisal.** Princeton, Princeton University Press, 1957. 107 p.

6991 Pearson, Lester B. **After Geneva: A Greater Task for NATO:** *Foreign Affairs,* XXXIV (October 1955), 14—23.

6992 — —. **A Measured Defense for the West,** *Orbis,* I (Winter, 1958), 428—34.

6993 — —. **NATO: Retrospect and Prospects,** *International Journal,* XIV (Spring, 1959), 79—84.

Part E. — Regional International Organization

6994 — —. **Western European Union: Implications for Canada and NATO,** *International Journal,* X (Winter, 1954—55), 1—11.

6995 Pfaltzgraff, Robert L., Jr. **Alternative Designs for the Atlantic Alliance,** *Orbis,* IX (Summer, 1965), 358—77.

6996 Pinto, Roger. **Les organisations européennes** 2d ed. Paris, Payot, 1965.
Chapter III.

6997 Ransom, Harry Howe. **NATO Military Strategy in Transition,** *Journal of International Affairs,* XII, 1 (1958), 44—58.

6998 Ries, John C. **NATO Reorganization: A Critique and Analysis,** *Western Political Quarterly,* XVIII (March 1965), 64—72.

6999 Ritchie, Ronald S. **NATO: The Economics of an Alliance.** Toronto, Ryerson, 1956. 147 p.

7000 Roberts, Owen J. **What Should Follow From NATO?** *Annals of the American Academy of Political and Social Science,* CCLXXXVIII (July 1953), 134—39.

7001 Rosecrance, Richard N. **Shape in Things to Come,** *Institute of World Affairs Proceedings,* XXXIX (1963), 68—72.

7002 Rostow, Eugene V. **Prospects for the Alliance,** *Atlantic Community Quarterly,* III (Spring, 1965), 34—42.

7003 Rotvand, Georges. **NATO — A French View,** *International Journal,* VII (Spring, 1952), 107—15.

7004 Royal Institute of International Affairs. **Atlantic Alliance: NATO's Role in the Free World.** London, Royal Institute of International Affairs, 1952. ix + 172 p.

Part E. — Regional International Organization

7005 Ruge, Friedrich. **The Need for a Common Nuclear Strategy,** *NATO in Quest of Cohesion,* Karl H. Cerny and Henry W. Briefs (eds.). New York, Praeger, 1965, pp. 199–214.

7006 Salvadori, Massimo. **NATO: A Twentieth-Century Community of Nations.** Princeton, Van Nostrand, 1957. 192 p.

7007 — —. **The North Atlantic Treaty Organization: A Western View,** *India Quarterly,* IX (January-March 1953), 59–77.

7008 Salvin, Marina. **The North Atlantic Pact,** *International Conciliation,* CDLI (May 1949), 375–456.

7009 Sandwell, B. K. **North Atlantic — Community or Treaty?** *International Journal,* VII (Summer, 1952), 169–72.

7010 Schaetzel, J. Robert. **The Nuclear Problem and Atlantic Interdependence,** *Atlantic Community Quarterly,* I (Winter, 1963–64), 561–69.

7011 Schmidt, Helmut. **Defense or Retaliation: A German View,** Edward Thomas (trans.). New York, Praeger, 1962. 264 p.

7012 Schwarzenberger, Georg. **The North Atlantic Pact,** *Western Political Quarterly,* II (September 1949), 309–16.

7013 ——. **The North Atlantic Pact,** *World Affairs,* New Series, III (July 1949), 236–45.

7014 Shaw, A. G. L. **Some Principles of International Relations: The Views of Lord Castlereagh,** *Australian Outlook,* VI (September 1952), 137–44.

Relates Castlereagh's theory of alliance functions to NATO and UN Charter.

7015 Slessor, John Cotesworth. **Atlantic Nuclear Policy,** *Atlantic Community Quarterly,* III (Spring, 1965), 56—63.

7016 — —. **The Case for a Multinational Nuclear Striking Force,** *NATO in Quest of Cohesion,* Karl H. Cerny and Henry W. Briefs (eds.). New York, Praeger, 1965, pp. 239—56.

7017 — —. **What Price Coexistence? A Policy for the Western Alliance.** New York, Praeger, 1961. 153 p.

7018 Smith, Sydney E. **NATO and the Challenge of the Missile Age,** *International Journal,* XIII (Summer, 1958), 165—74.

7019 Sohn, Louis B. **European Security — Interrelation of Political, Military and Economic Factors,** *Bulletin of the Atomic Scientists,* X (December 1964), 16—18.

7020 Spaak, Paul-Henri C. **The Atlantic Community and NATO,** *Orbis,* I (Winter, 1958), 411—17.

7021 — —. **NATO and the Communist Challenge,** *International Journal,* XIII (Autumn, 1958), 243—50.

7022 — —. **New Tests for NATO,** *Foreign Affairs,* XXVII (April 1959), 357—65.

7023 — —. **Why NATO?** Hammondsworth, Eng., Penguin, 1959. 62 p.

7024 Spender, Percy C. **NATO and Pacific Security,** *Annals of the American Academy of Political and Social Science,* CCLXXXII (July 1952), 114—18.

7025 Spofford, Charles M. **NATO's Growing Pains,** *Foreign Affairs,* XXXI (October 1952), 95–105.

7026 – –. **Toward Atlantic Security,** *International Affairs,* XXXVII (October 1951), 434–39.

7027 Stanley, Timothy W. **Decentralizing Nuclear Control in NATO,** *Orbis,* VII (Spring, 1963), 41–48.

7028 – –. **NATO in Transition: The Future of the Atlantic Alliance.** New York, Praeger, 1965. xii + 417 p.

7029 Stehlin, Paul. **Some French Reflections on the Alliance,** *The Western Alliance,* Edgar S. Furniss, Jr. (ed.). Columbus, Ohio State University Press, 1965, pp. 71–88.

7030 Stikker, Dirk U. **NATO – The Shifting Western Alliance,** *Atlantic Community Quarterly,* III (Spring, 1965), 7–17.

7031 – –. **The Role of the Secretary General of NATO,** *The Western Alliance,* Edgar S. Furniss, Jr. (ed.). Columbus, Ohio State University Press, 1965, pp. 3–28.

7032 Strauss, Franz Josef. **An Alliance of Continents,** *International Affairs,* XVI (April 1965), 191–203.

7033 Strausz-Hupé, Robert, Dougherty, James E., and Kintner, William R. **Building the Atlantic World.** New York, Harper, 1963. xiv + 400 p.

7034 Streit, Clarence K. **The Diplomatic Potential of NATO,** *Annals of the American Academy of Political and Social Science,* CCCXII (July 1957), 116–26.

7055 — —. **Europe and the NATO Shield,** *International Organization,* XXI (Autumn, 1958), 425—39.

7056 Wood, Robert J. **The First Year of SHAPE,** *International Organization,* VI (May 1952), 175—91.

8.6 INTELLECTUAL AND CULTURAL ORGANIZATIONS

7057 Adam, H.-T. **Les organismes internationaux spécialisés: Contribution à la théorie générale des établissements publics internationaux.** Paris, Pinchon et Durand-Auzias, 1965. Volume II. 325 p.

7058 Berlin, Isaiah. **L'unité européene et ses vicissitudes: Allocution prononcée à l'occasion du Troisième Congrès de la Fondation Européenne de la Culture au Palais Hoflurg à Vienne, le 21 novembre 1959.** Amsterdam, Fondation Européenne de la Culture, 1959. 133 p.

7059 Brugmans, Hendrick. **The College of Europe,** *World Affairs,* New Series, V (October 1951), 445—53.

7060 Holborn, Louise W. **Canada and the ICEM,** *International Journal,* XVIII (Spring, 1963), 211—14.

Canadian withdrawal from the Intergovernmental Committee for European Migration.

7061 Lambert, J. R. **The European University: A European Communities Project,** *World Today,* New Series, XVIII (February 1962), 77—88.

7062 McN., D. **The European Cultural Centre and Its Activities,** *World Today,* New Series, IX (August 1953), 360—67.

7063 Ripley, Josephine. **Peoples on the Move.** Geneva, Intergovernmental Committee for European Migration, 1955. 46 p.

7082 Lambert, J. R. **The European Economic Community and the Associated African States: Partnership in the Making,** *World Today,* New Series, XVII (August 1961), 344–55.

7083 Mazrui, Ali A. **African Attitudes to the European Common Market,** *International Affairs,* XXXIX (January 1963), 24–36.

7084 Partharasarathy, N. **E. E. C. and the Associated Overseas States,** *India Quarterly,* XX (January-March 1964), 51–62.

7085 Rivkin, Arnold. **Africa and the European Common Market: A Perspective.** Denver, University of Denver, Social Science Foundation and Department of International Relations, 1964. iii + 61 p.

7086 Salmon, Jean Charles. **Developing Countries, Common Market and World Trade,** *Pakistan Horizon,* XVI, 4 (1963), 306–17.

7087 van der Lee, Jacob J. **Community Economic Relations with Associated African States and Other Countries,** *Annals of the American Academy of Political and Social Science,* CCCXLVIII (July 1963), 15–24.

7088 — —. **The European Common Market and Africa,** *World Today,* New Series, XVI (September 1960), 370–76.

8.8.2 BRITISH COMMONWEALTH COUNTRIES

7089 Altrincham, Lord. **The British Commonwealth and Western Union,** *Foreign Affairs,* XXVII, (July 1949), 601–17.

7090 Bareau, Paul. **Britain and European Free Trade,** *International Journal,* XII (Spring, 1957), 128–37.

Part E. — Regional International Organization

7091 Barkway, Michael. **Canada's Changing Role in NATO Defence,** *International Journal,* XIV (Spring, 1959), 99—110.

7092 Baumann, Carol Edler. **Britain Faces Europe,** *Political Science Quarterly,* LXXIV (September 1959), 351—71.

Britain's desire for "close association" with EEC and its establishment of the Free Trade Area.

7093 Bell, Coral (ed.). **Europe Without Britain: Six Studies of Britain's Application to Join the Common Market and Its Breakdown.** London, Angus and Robertson, 1963. 120 p.

7094 Beloff, Max. **Britain, Europe, and the Atlantic Community,** *International Organization,* XVII (Summer, 1963), 574—91.

7095 Bilgrami, Ashgar H. **Britain, the Commonwealth, and the European Union Issue.** Amgilly-Annemarse, Les Presses de Savoie, 1961. xv + 147 p.

7096 Burns, A. L. **Australia, Britain, and the Common Market: Some Australian Views,** *World Today,* New Series, XVIII (April 1962), 152—63.

7097 Caine, Sydney. **The Consequences for the Commonwealth and the Underdeveloped World,** *Political Quarterly,* XXXIV (January-March 1963), 55—66.

Concerns British entry into EEC.

7098 Camps, Miriam. **Britain and the European Community 1955—1963.** Princeton, Princeton University Press, 1964. x + 547 p.

7099 — —. **Britain, the Six and American Policy,** *Foreign Affairs,* XXXIX (October 1960), 112—22.

Part E. — Regional International Organization

7100 Carrington, C. E. **The Commonwealth and European Integration,** *Western Integration and the Future of Eastern Europe*, David S. Collier and Kurt Glaser (eds.). Chicago, Regnery, 1964, pp. 29—45.

7101 Clark, Colin, in collaboration with Henryk Frankel and assistance of Lynden Moore. **British Trade in the Common Market: Plain Facts About the Common Market.** London, Stevens, 1962. viii + 149 p.

7102 Clokie, H. M.; Queen-Hughes, R. W.; Bernard, Jaques; Morton, W. L.; Palk, W. L.; Waines, W. J., and Witmore, B. G. **Canada and the North Atlantic Treaty,** *International Journal*, IV (Summer, 1949), 244—49.

7103 Comstock, Alzada. **British Economic Policy, IV: The Schuman Plan,** *Current History*, New Series, XIX (December 1950), 348—51.

7104 — —. **Great Britain,** *Current History*, New Series, XX (January 1951), 7—10.

7105 — —. **Great Britain: An Island View,** *Current History*, New Series, (February 1953), 80—84.

7106 Cunningham, W. B. (ed.). **Canada, the Commonwealth and the Common Market: Report.** Montreal, McGill University Press, 1962. 142 p.

7107 Diebold, William, Jr. **Britain, the Six and the World Economy,** *Foreign Affairs*, XL (April 1962), 407—18.

7108 Elkan, Peter. **Britain and the Common Market: The Test Case of New Zealand,** *World Today*, **New Series,** XVIII (June 1962), 226—33.

7109 Ferguson, George. **Canada and the "Atlantic Alliance,"** *International Journal*, XII (Spring, 1957), 83—89.

7110 Fletcher, B. H. **Australian Opinion on the Common Market,** *Europe Without Britain,* Coral Bell (ed.). Melbourne, Cheshire, 1963, pp. 70–87.

7111 Franks, Oliver. **Britain and Europe,** *Daedalus,* XCIII (Winter, 1964), 67–82.

7112 Harrod, Roy. **Britain and the Common Market,** *Foreign Affairs,* XXXV (January 1957), 225–37.

7113 Hasan, Zubeida. **Britain, the European Common Market and Pakistan,** *Pakistan Horizon,* XV, 4 (1962), 296–309.

7114 Hawtrey, R. G. **Western European Union: Implications for the United Kingdom.** London, Royal Institute of International Affairs, 1949. 126 p.

7115 Healey, Denis. **Britain and NATO,** *NATO and American Security,* Klaus Knorr (ed.). Princeton, Princeton University Press, 1959, pp. 209–35.

7116 — —. **Britain's Attitude Towards European Integration,** *The United States and the Western Community,* H. Field Haviland (ed.). Haverford, Haverford College Press, 1957, pp. 31–52.

7117 Heiser, Hans Joachin. **British Policy with Regard to the Unification Efforts on the European Continent.** Leyden, Sythoff, 1959. 121 p.

7118 Holborn, Louise W. **Canada and the ICEM,** *International Journal,* XVIII (Spring, 1963), 211–14.
Canadian withdrawal from the Intergovernmental Committee for European Migration.

7119 Holmes, Frank. **The Commonwealth and a Free-Trade Area in Europe,** *International Affairs,* XXXIV (January 1958), 38–48.

7120 Hovey, Allan, Jr. **Britain and the Unification of Europe,** *International Organization,* IX (August 1955), 323–37.

7121 Hughes, William. **Canada and the European Common Market.** Vancouver, Best, 1962. 35 p.

7122 Hunt, James C. **Britain and the Common Market,** *Political Quarterly,* XXX (July-September 1959), 293–303.

7123 Kitzinger, Uwe. **Britain and the Common Market: The State of the Debate,** *World Today,* New Series, XVII (June 1961), 233–54.

7124 ——. **The Challenge of the Common Market: In or Out?** 4th ed. Oxford, Blackwell, 1962. viii + 240 p.

7125 ——. **French Thoughts on Britain and the Common Market,** *World Today,* New Series, XVII (September 1961), 388–92.

7126 ——. **The Politics and Economics of European Integration: Britain, Europe, and the United States.** New York, Praeger, 1963. 246 p.

7127 Lamfalussy, A. **The United Kingdom and the Six: An Essay on Economic Growth in Western Europe.** Homewood, Irwin, 1963. xvii + 147 p.

7128 Layton, Lord. **Little Europe and Britain,** *International Affairs,* XXIX (July 1953), 292–301.

7129 McClellan, Grant S. **Britain and Western European Union,** *Foreign Policy Reports,* XXIV (October 15, 1948), 122–32.

7130 McIver, R. Craig. **Canadian Foreign Trade and the European Common Market,** *International Journal,* XIII (Winter, 1957–58), 1–11.

Part E. — Regional International Organization

7131 Mansergh, Nicholas. **Britain, the Commonwealth, and Western Union,** *International Affairs,* XXIV (October 1948), 491–504.

7132 Matthews, Roy A. **Canada, Britain, and the Common Market: A Canadian View,** *World Today,* New Series, XVIII (February 1962), 48–57.

7133 Miller, J. D. B. **Britain Without Europe,** *Europe Without Britain,* Coral Bell (ed.). Melbourne, Cheshire, 1963, pp. 27–45.

7134 — —. **The Commonwealth After De Gaulle,** *International Journal,* XIX (Winter, 1963–64), 30–40.

7135 Mookerjee, Subimal. **India and the Common Market,** *India Quarterly,* XV (October-December 1959), 382–92.

7136 Monroe, Ann D. **Britain and the European Community,** *Current History,* New Series, XLV (November 1963), 271–75 ff.

7137 — —. **The British Dilemma: Commonwealth or Common Market?** *Current History,* New Series, XLIII (July 1962), 11–15.

7138 Pearson, Lester B. **Canada and the North Atlantic Alliance,** *Foreign Affairs,* XXVII (April 1949), 369–78.

7139 — —. **Western European Union: Implications for Canada and NATO,** *International Journal,* X (Winter, 1954–55), 1–11.

7140 Pfaltzgraff, Robert L., Jr. **The Common Market Debate in Britain,** *Orbis,* VII (Summer, 1963), 278–99.

7141 Pickles, William. **The Choice and the Facts,** *Journal of Common Market Studies,* IV (October 1965), 22–35.

Part E. — Regional International Organization

7142 Pinder, John H. M. **Britain and the Common Market.** London, Cresset, 1961. 134 p.

7143 Rangnekar, D. K. **India, Britain and European Common Market.** New Delhi, R and K, 1963. 236 p.

7144 Ray, Jahar. **The European Free Trade Association and Its Impact on India's Trade,** *International Studies,* III (July 1961), 25—44.

7145 Rothchild, D. S. **British Labour and European Union,** *Social Research,* XXIII (Spring, 1956), 89—105.

7146 Royal Institute of International Affairs. **Britain in Western Europe: WEU and the Atlantic Alliance.** London, Royal Institute of International Affairs, 1956. 121 p.

7147 Schonfield, Andrew. **The Commonwealth and the Common Market,** *World Today,* New Series, XVII (December 1961), 532—37.
An appendix lists Associated Overseas Territories of the EEC.

7148 Schuckburgh, Evelyn. **Great Britain and the Western Alliance,** *The Western Alliance,* Edgar S. Furniss, Jr. (ed.). Columbus, Ohio State University Press, 1965, pp. 123—44.

7149 — —. **The Influence of Commonwealth Ties on the Relations of Great Britain and Europe,** *British Affairs,* V (Spring, 1961), 15—23.

7150 Siddiqi, Qamar Saeed. **European Integration and Economic Development in the Commonwealth,** *Pakistan Horizon,* XIII, 4 (1960), 318—23.

7151 Spencer, Robert. **Triangle into Treaty: Canada and the Origins of NATO,** *International Journal,* XIV (Spring, 1959), 87—98.

Part E. — Regional International Organization

7152 Strauss, Erich. **European Reckoning: The Six and Britain's Future.** London, Allen and Unwin, 1962. 177 p.

7153 Thompson, R. W. **Canada, a United Europe and NATO,** *International Journal,* XII (Summer, 1957), 220—26.

7154 Tucker, William R. **The Attitude of the British Labor Party Towards European and Collective Security Problems.** Geneva, Imprimerie du *Journal de Genève,* 1950. 222 p.

7155 Turner, Arthur C. **The British Quandary,** *Institute of World Affairs Proceedings,* XXXIX (1963), 38 —45.

7156 Vosper, Dennis. **The Commonwealth and the European Economic Community,** *Pakistan Horizon,* XV, 1 (1962), 3—12.

7157 Watson, George. **The British Constitution and Europe.** Leyden, Sythoff, 1959. 79 p.

7158 Willoughby, William R. **Canada and the North Atlantic Pact,** *Virginia Quarterly Review,* XXV (Summer, 1949), 429—42.

7159 Woodruff, William. **Britain and European Union,** *Current History,* XLII (March 1962), 136—41.

7160 Worswick, G. D. N. **Britain, the Common Market and the Free Trade Area,** *Year Book of World Affairs,* XII (1958), 181—98.

7161 Younger, Kenneth. **The Consequences for External Policy,** *Political Quarterly,* XXXIV (January-March 1963), 6—17.
Of British entry into EEC.

7162 Zebel, Sydney H. **Britain and West European Integration,** *Current History,* New Series, XL (January 1961), 40—46.

8.8.3 FRANCE

7163 Alphand, Herve. **The "European Policy" of France,** *International Affairs,* XXIX (April 1953), 141—48.

7164 Aron, Raymond. **French Public Opinion and the Atlantic Treaty,** *International Affairs,* XXVIII (January 1952), 1—8.

7165 Barclay, G. St. J. **The Europe of Realities: The Gaullist Impact on European Integration,** *Australian Journal of Politics and History,* X (December 1964), 341—54.

7166 Berkes, Ross N. **France and NATO,** *Current History,* New Series, XXVIII (May 1955), 299—303.

7167 Brzezinski, Zbigniew K. **The Soviet Bloc, the Common Market, and France,** *France and the European Community,* Sydney Nettleton Fisher (ed.). Columbus, Ohio State University Press, 1965, pp. 139—68.

7168 Courtin, René. **French Views on European Unity,** Anthea Mills (tr.), *International Affairs,* XXV (January 1949), 8—22.

7169 Demorest, Jean Jacques. **French Culture and the European Community: The Complexity of Survival,** *France and the European Community,* Sydney Nettleton Fisher (ed.). Columbus, Ohio State University Press, 1965, pp. 3—20.

7170 Ehrmann, Henry W. **The French Trade Associations and the Ratification of the Schuman Plan,** *World Politics,* VI (July 1954), 453—81.

Part E. — *Regional International Organization*

7171 Fisher, Sydney Nettleton (ed.). **France and the European Community.** Columbus, Ohio State University Press, 1965. 176 p.

7172 Fox, Edward W. **France After NATO,** *Current History,* New Series, XXXI (November 1956), 262—67.

7173 Furniss, Edgar S., Jr. **De Gaulle's France and NATO: An Interpretation,** *International Organization,* XV (Summer, 1961), 349—65.

7174 — —. **France, NATO and European Security,** *International Organization,* X (November 1956), 544—58.

7175 — —. **French Attitudes Toward Western European Unity,** *International Organization,* VII (May 1953), 199—212.

7176 Hoffmann, Stanley. **De Gaulle, Europe, and the Atlantic Alliance,** *International Organization,* XVIII (Winter, 1964), 1—28.

7177 Knorr, Klaus. **France and European Security,** *France and the European Community,* Sydney Nettleton Fisher (ed.). Columbus, Ohio State University Press, 1965, pp. 37—58.

7178 Lagarde, Jean de. **The Meaning of NATO for France and Europe,** *Annals of the American Academy of Political and Social Science,* CCLXXXVIII (July 1953), 63—66.

7179 Lerner, Daniel. **French Business Leaders Look at EDC: A Preliminary Report,** *Public Opinion Quarterly,* XX (Spring, 1956), 212—20.

7180 Pleven, René. **France in the Atlantic Community,** *Foreign Affairs,* XXXVIII (October 1959), 19—30.

7181 Schmitt, Hans A. **French Politicians and the European Communities: The Record of the 1950's,** *France and the European Community,* Sydney Nettleton Fisher (ed.). Columbus, Ohio State University Press, 1965, pp. 59—82.

7182 Stikker, Dirk U. **France and Its Diminishing Will to Cooperate,** *Atlantic Community Quarterly,* III (Summer, 1965), 197—205.

Reprinted from *International Spectator,* April 1965.

7183 Willis, Frank R. **France, Germany, and the New Europe.** Stanford, Stanford University Press, 1965. xiv + 397 p.

8.8.4 GERMANY

7184 Bathurst, Maurice E. and Simpson, J. L. **Germany and the North Atlantic Community.** New York, Praeger, 1956. 217 p.

7185 Bechtoldt, Heinrich. **Germany and the Common Market,** *India Quarterly,* XVI (July-September 1961), 249—58.

7186 Blomeyer, Horst. **Germany in NATO,** *The Western Alliance,* Edgar S. Furniss, Jr. (ed.). Columbus, Ohio State University Press, 1965, pp. 89—106.

7187 Craig, Gordon A. **NATO and the New German Army.** Princeton, Center of International Studies, 1955. 30 p.

7188 H., W. **Motives and Methods of European Integration: A German Government View,** *World Today,* New Series, IX (April 1953), 145—53.

7189 Kaplan, Lawrence S. **NATO and Adenauer's Germany: Uneasy Partnership,** *International Organization,* XV (Autumn, 1961), 618—29.

7190 Knappstein, K. Heinrich. **The Projected European Union and the Question of German Unity,** Annals of the American Academy of Political and Social Science, CCCXLVIII (July 1963), 73–81.

7191 Paul, Robert A. **Russia, Germany and the Atlantic Community,** Harvard Review, I (Fall, 1962), 43–48.

7192 Schmokel, Wolfe W. **Germany and the Common Market,** Current History, New Series, XLV (November 1963), 283–88.

7193 Tauber, Kurt P. **German Nationalists and European Union,** Political Science Quarterly, LXXIV (December 1959), 564–89.

7194 Willis, Frank R. **France, Germany, and the New Europe.** Stanford, Stanford University Press, 1965. xiv + 397 p.

8.8.5 MEDITERRANEAN COUNTRIES

7195 C., A. **Italy, the Common Market, and the Free Trade Area,** World Today, New Series, XIV (April 1958), 152–62.

7196 Foa, Bruno. **Italy's Stake in the Common Market,** Current History, New Series, XLV (November 1963), 28–94 ff.

7197 K., D. J. **Greece, Turkey, and NATO,** World Today, New Series, VIII (April 1952), 162–69.

7198 Lambert, J. R. **Greece and the European Economic Community,** World Today, New Series, XVII (April 1961), 142–49.

7199 McGhee, George C. **Turkey Joins the West,** *Foreign Affairs,* XXXII (July 1954), 617—30.

7200 Ramazami, R. **The Middle East and the European Common Market.** Charlottesville, University of Virginia Press, 1964. xxii + 152 p.

7201 Rey, Jean. **The European Community's Role in Mediterranean Europe,** *Journal of International Affairs,* XIX, 2 (1965), 163—69.

7202 Rodo, Laureano Lopez. **Spain and the EEC,** *Foreign Affairs,* XLIV (October 1965), 126—33.

7203 Sforza, Carlo. **Italy, the Marshall Plan and the "Third Force,"** *Foreign Affairs,* XXVI (April 1948), 450—56.

8.8.6 SCANDINAVIAN COUNTRIES

7204 Burbank, Lyman B. **Scandinavia and NATO,** *Current History,* New Series, XXIII (July 1952), 20—22.

7205 — —. **Scandinavian Integration and Western Defense,** *Foreign Affairs,* XXXV (October 1956), 144—50.

7206 Kerry, Richard L. **Norway and the Collective Defense Organization,** *International Organization,* XVII (Autumn, 1963), 960—71.

7207 Krosby, H. Peter. **Norway in NATO: A Partial Commitment?** *International Journal,* XX (Winter, 1964—65), 68—78.

7208 Löchen, Einar. **Norway in European and Atlantic Co-operation.** Oslo, Scandia, 1964. 88 p.

7209 W., A. **Norway and the Atlantic Pact,** *World Today,* New Series, V (April 1949), 154—60.

7210 Wigforss, Harold. **Sweden and the Atlantic Pact,** *International Organization,* III (August 1949), 434—43.

7211 Wilkinson, Joe R. **Denmark and NATO: The Problem of a Small Country in a Collective Security System,** *International Organization,* X (August 1956), 390—401.

7212 Wuorinen, John H. **Scandinavia Looks at European Unity,** *Current History,* XLII (March 1962), 160—65.

8.8.7 SOVIET BLOC COUNTRIES

7213 Black, Cyril E. and Yeager, Frederick J. **The USSR and NATO,** *NATO and American Security,* Klaus Knorr (ed.). Princeton, Princeton University Press, 1959, pp. 37—64.

7214 Brzezinski, Zbigniew K. **The Soviet Bloc, the Common Market, and France,** *France and the European Community,* Sydney Nettleton Fisher (ed.). Columbus, Ohio State University Press, 1965, pp. 139—68.

7215 Fisher, Harold H. **NATO, Russia and the Cold War,** *Current History,* XXXIX (September 1960), 147—52.

7216 Owen, Launcelot A. **Soviet Attitudes to West European Integration and the Common Market,** *Europe Without Britain,* Coral Bell (ed.). Melbourne, Cheshire, 1963, pp. 88—106.

7217 Nagorski, Zygmunt, Jr. **NATO and the Captive Countries,** *Annals of the American Academy of Political and Social Science,* CCLXXXVIII (July 1953), 74—81.

7218 Paul, Robert A. **Russia, Germany and the Atlantic Community,** *Harvard Review*, I (Fall, 1962), 43—48.

7219 Shulman, Marshall D. **The Communist States and Western Integration,** *International Organization*, XVII (Summer, 1963), 649—62.

7220 Zauberman, Alfred. **The Soviet Bloc and the Common Market,** *World Today*, New Series, XIX (January 1963), 30—36.

8.8.8 UNITED STATES

7221 B., J. **The North Atlantic Pact, I: Congress and the Military Commitment,** *World Today*, New Series, V (July 1949), 296—310.

7222 Benoit, Emile. **The United States and a United Europe,** *Current History*, XLII (March 1962), 172—79.

7223 Bowie, Robert R. **European Community and United States,** *India Quarterly*, XVIII (July-September 1962), 219—29.

7224 Cerami, Charles A. **Alliance Born of Danger: America, the Common Market, and the Atlantic Partnership.** New York, Harcourt, Brace and World, 1963. 181 p.

7225 Clayton, William L. **U. S. Trade and the Common Market.** New York, Foreign Policy Association, 1962. 62 p.

7226 Committee for Economic Development. **The European Common Market and Its Meaning to the United States.** New York, Committee for Economic Development, 1959. 152 p.

Part E. — Regional International Organization

7227 Dean, Vera M. **Europe and the United States.** New York, Knopf, 1950. ix + 349 p.

7228 Diebold, William, Jr. **The Changed Economic Position of Western Europe: Some Implications for United States Policy and International Organization,** *International Organization,* XIV (Winter, 1960), 1—19.

7229 Donohue, Thomas C. **American Appraisals of the European Common Market,** *International Manual on the European Economic Community,* H. K. Junckerstorff (ed.). St. Louis, Saint Louis University Press, 1963, pp. 1—20.

7230 Dowd, D. F. **America and the World Economy: Second Thoughts on the Common Market,** *Yale Review,* LIII (Winter, 1964), 643—72.

7231 Fox, Annette Baker. **NATO and Congress,** *Political Science Quarterly,* LXXX (September 1965), 395—414.

7232 Grant, Roderick N. **The European Common Market and U. S. Trade,** *Public Policy,* XI (1961), 233—61.

7233 Haviland, H. Field, Jr. (ed.). **The United States and the Western Community.** Haverford, Pa., Haverford College Press, 1957. v + 161 p.

Papers and an excerpt of proceedings of a conference at Haverford College in 1956.

7234 Hinshaw, Randall. **The European Community and American Trade: A Study in Atlantic Economics and Policy.** New York, Praeger, 1965. xv + 188 p.

7235 Holborn, Hajo. **American Foreign Policy and European Integration,** *World Politics,* VI (October 1953), 1—30.

7236 Humphrey, Don D. **The United States and the Common Market: A Background Study.** New York, Praeger, 1962. 176 p.

7237 Katz, Milton. **The Community of Europe and American Policy,** *The United States and the Western Community*, H. Field Haviland (ed.). Haverford, Pa., Haverford College Press, 1957, pp. 3—16.

7238 Kintner, William R. **The Projected European Union and American Military Responsibilities,** *Annals of the American Academy of Political and Social Science*, CCCXLVIII (July 1963), 121—30.

7239 Little, Herbert S. **The United States, the Atlantic Pact, and the United Nations,** *Institute of World Affairs Proceedings*, XXVII (1949), 128—36.

7240 Merchant, Livingston T. **Evolving United States Relations with the Atlantic Community,** *International Organization*, XVII (Summer, 1963), 610—27.

7241 Nanes, Allan S. **The United States and a United Europe,** *Current History*, New Series, XL (January 1961), 11—16.

7242 Northrop, F. S. C. **European Union and United States Foreign Policy: A Study in Sociological Jurisprudence.** New York, Macmillan, 1954. viii + 230 p.

7243 Polyzoides, A. T. **America and the North Atlantic Treaty,** *World Affairs Quarterly*, XIX (April 1949), 24—33.

7244 Renne, Roland R. **American Agriculture Looks at the Atlantic Community,** *Atlantic Community Quarterly*, I (Summer, 1963), 243—50.

7245 Simmons, Andre. **The European Economic Community and the United States,** *L'Egypte Contemporaine*, LV (October 1964), 5—25.

7246 Stewart, Maxwell S. **The European Common Market and the United States.** New York, Public Affairs Pamphlets, 1960. 20 p.

7247 Tennyson, Leonard B. **The United States in the Atlantic Community,** *Current History,* New Series, XLV (November 1963), 264—70 ff.

7248 Van Sickle, J. V. **The European Common Market and the Experience of the USA,** *Il Politico,* XXV (March 1960), 42—51.

7249 Wright, Quincy. **The Projected European Union and American Institutional Prestige,** *Annals of the American Academy of Political and Social Science,* CCCXLVIII (July 1963), 132—40.

7250 Zeckhauser, Richard J. **Trade and the Atlantic Community,** *Harvard Review,* I (Fall, 1962), 36—42.

8.8.9 OTHER COUNTRIES

7251 Bonesteel, Charles H., III. **NATO and the Underdeveloped Areas,** *Annals of the American Academy of Political and Social Science,* CCLXXXVIII (July 1953), 67—73.

7252 Boyesen, Jens. **Contributions of Small Powers to the Alliance,** *The Western Alliance,* Edgar S. Furniss, Jr. (ed.). Columbus, Ohio State University Press, 1965, pp. 107—22.

7253 Broekmeijer, M. W. J. M. **Developing Countries and NATO: Strategic Importance of the Developing Countries for NATO.** Leyden, Sythoff, 1963. 208 p.

Part E. — Regional International Organization

7254 Clark, William. **New Europe and the New Nations,** *Daedalus,* XCIII (Winter, 1964), 134–52.

7255 Crankshaw, Edward. **Tito and the Cominform,** *International Affairs,* XXVI (April 1950), 208–13.

7256 Emerson, Rupert. **The Atlantic Community and the Emerging Countries,** *International Organization,* XVII (Summer, 1963), 628–48.

7257 Eyck, F. Gunther. **Benelux in the Common Market,** *Current History,* New Series, XLV (November 1963), 295–301.

7258 Fay, Sidney B. **The Cominform,** *Current History,* New Series, XIV (January 1948), 1–5.

7259 Freymond, Jacques. **The European Neutrals and the Atlantic Community,** *International Organization,* XVII (Summer, 1963), 592–609.

7260 Healey, Denis. **The Cominform and World Communism,** *International Affairs,* XXIV (July 1948), 339–49.

7261 Hopper, Bruce C. **Narkomindel and Comintern: Instruments of World Revolution,** *Foreign Affairs,* (July 1941), 737–50.

7262 I., G. **The Evolution of the Cominform 1947–1950: The First Phase (October 1947 – January 1948),** *World Today,* New Series, VI (May 1950), 213–28.

7263 Iriye, Akira. **Japan and the Atlantic Community,** *Harvard Review,* I (Fall, 1962), 31–35.

Part E. — *Regional International Organization*

7264 Kanamori, Hisao. **The European Common Market and Japan's Trade,** *Japan Annual of International Affairs,* II (1962), 117—27.

7265 Khan, Mir Mostofa Ali. **Schemes for Western European Integration — Likely Effects on the Under-developed Regions,** *Pakistan Horizon,* XIII, 1 (1960), 65—77.

7266 Lambert, J. R. **The Neutrals and the Common Market,** *World Today,* New Series, XVIII (October 1962), 444—52.

7267 Lawson, Ruth C. **The Problem of the Compulsory Jurisdiction of the World Court,** *American Journal of International Law,* XLVI (April 1952), 219—38.

7268 Mookerjee, Subimal. **European Economic Integration and Asia's Trade,** *International Studies,* I (July 1959), 1—27.

7269 Morris, Bernard S. **The Cominform: A Five-Year Perspective,** *World Politics,* V (April 1953), 368—76.

7270 Reidy, Joseph W. **Latin America and the Atlantic Triangle,** *Orbis,* VIII (Spring, 1964), 52—65.

7271 Rosegger, Gerhard. **Austrian Neutrality and European Integration,** *Orbis,* VII (Winter, 1964), 849—60.

7272 Wilkinson, Joe R. **Latin America and the European Economic Community: An Appraisal.** Denver, University of Denver Press, 1965. 65 p.

Part E. — *Regional International Organization*

9. EASTERN AND CENTRAL EUROPE

The organs of Communist Eastern European regionalism could be called supranational in character, though the pervasive influence of Soviet policy and the world wide Communist Party organization does much to limit the voluntary nature of separate government actions in the region.

9.1 GENERAL OBSERVATIONS

7273 Dean, Vera Micheles. **European Agreements for Post-War Reconstruction,** *Foreign Policy Reports*, XVIII (March 15, 1942), 2—12.

7274 Deutsch, Karl W. **Problems and Prospects of Federation,** *Challenge in Eastern Europe*, Cyril E. Black (ed.). New Brunswick, N. J., Rutgers University Press, 1954, pp. 219—44.

7275 Doman, Nicholas. **World Reconstruction and European Regionalism,** *Social Forces*, XXI (March 1943), 265—72.

7276 Duchacek, Ivo. **Bonapartist Unity of Eastern Europe,** *Annals of the American Academy of Political and Social Science*, CCLXXI (September 1950), 165—74.

7277 Eisner, Kurt. **The Pan-German Society,** *Current History*, III (January 1916), 674—78.

Reprinted from *Neue Zeit*.

7278 Gross, Feliks. **Crossroads of Two Continents: A Democratic Federation of East-Central Europe.** New York, Columbia University Press, 1945. viii + 162 p.

Part E. — *Regional International Organization*

7279 Grossman, Gregory. **Value and Plan: Economic Calculation and Organization in Eastern Europe.** Berkeley, University of California Press, 1960. 370 p.

7280 Halecki, Oskar. **East Central Europe in Postwar Organization,** *Annals of the American Academy of Political and Social Science,* CCXXVIII (July 1943), 52—59.

7281 Kybal, Vlastimil. **The New Central Europe,** *Institute of World Affairs Proceedings,* XVII (1939), 135—42.

7282 Liszt, Franz von. **The Union of Central Europe: An Argument in Favor of a Union of the States Now Allied with Germany,** *Current History,* I (April 1915), 140—43.

7283 Meyer, Henry C. **Mitteleuropa in German Thought and Action, 1815 —1945.** Hague, Nijhoff, 1955. xv + 378 p.

Pan-Germanism.

7284 Naumann, Friedrich. **Central Europe,** Christabel M. Meredith (tr.). New York, Knopf, 1917. 351 p.

Pan-Germanism.

7285 New York Times. **The Mid-European Union: Declaration Signed in Independence Hall, Philadelphia, Aims at Union of Liberated Nations,** *Current History,* IX (December 1918), 500—1.

7286 Ogg, Frederick A. **Central European Union Again,** *Current History,* XXXVIII (August 1933), 623—25.

7287 Reisky-Dubnic, Vladimir. **The Idea of a Central and Eastern European Regional Federation,** *Regional Arrangements for Security and the United Nations,* Commission to Study the Organization of Peace (ed.). New York, Commission to Study the Organization of Peace, 1953, pp. 131 —44.

7288 Ropes, E. C. **Regionalism in Eastern Europe,** *International Conciliation,* CDXIX (March 1946), 128–33.

7289 Roucek, Joseph S. **The Sociological Weaknesses of Federation Plans for Central-Eastern Europe,** *Journal of Legal and Political Sociology,* II (October 1943), 94–116.

7290 Slosson, Preston. **The Problem of Austro-German Union,** *International Conciliation,* CCL (May 1929), 221–54.

Pan-Germanism.

7291 Stanczyk, Jan. **Social War: Federation of Central Europe,** *Free World,* I (January 1942), 359–61.

7292 Taylor, A. J. P. **National Independence and the "Austrian Idea": Difficulty of Securing National Amalgamation in the New National States,** *Political Quarterly,* XVI (July 1945), 234–46.

7293 Ward, B. **Ignaz Seipel and the Anschluss,** *Dublin Review,* CCIII (July 1938), 33–50.

9.2 BALKAN REGIONALISM

7294 Berard, Victor. **The Russian Empire and Czarism,** G. Fox-Davies and G. O. Pope (trs.); introduction by Frederick Greenwood. London, Nutt, 1905. xxiv + 299 p.

Pan-Slavism.

7295 Braun, Charlotte E. **Balkan Federation — or Chaos,** *Current History,* New Series, VI (February 1944), 144–48.

Part E. — Regional International Organization

7296 Caloyanni, M. A. **The Balkan Union, the Balkan Conferences and the Balkan Pact,** *Transactions* (Grotius Society), XVIII (1932), 97—108; XIX (1933), 89—101.

7297 Galitzi, Christine. **The Third Balkan Conference in Bucharest,** *Institute of World Affairs Proceedings*, X (December 1932), 40—48.

7298 Geshkoff, Theodore I. **Balkan Union: A Road to Peace in Southeastern Europe.** New York, Columbia University Press, 1940. xvi + 345 p.

7299 Hostler, Charles W. **Turkism and the Soviets: The Turns of the World and Their Political Objectives.** London, Allen and Unwin, 1957. xiv + 244 p.

Pan-Turanianism.

7300 Kerner, Robert J. and Howard, Harry N. **The Balkan Conferences and the Balkan Entente, 1930—1935.** Berkeley, University of California Press, 1936. x + 271 p.

7301 Kohn, Hans. **Pan-Slavism and World War II,** *American Political Science Review*, XLVI (September 1952), 699—722.

7302 Levine, Louis. **Pan-Slavism and European Politics,** *Political Science Quarterly*, XXIX (December 1914), 664—86.

7303 Machray, Robert. **The Little Entente and Its Policies,** *Fortnightly Review*, New Series, CXIX (June 1, 1926), 767—74.

7304 Mukerji, K. P. **Green International,** *Indian Journal of Political Science*, XIII (January 1952), 58—68.

Concerns the international peasant union which originated in the Balkans.

Part E. — Regional International Organization

7305 Ogg, Frederick A. **The Quest for Balkan Unity,** *Current History,* XXXIX (March 1934), 750—55.

7306 Padelford, Norman J. **Peace in the Balkans: The Movement Towards International Organization in the Balkans.** New York, Oxford University Press, 1935. ix + 209 p.

7307 Polyzoides, Adamantios T. **The Coming Federation of the Balkan States,** *Institute of World Affairs Proceedings,* VIII (1931), 25—33.

7308 Seton-Watson, R. W. **The Little Entente,** *Contemporary Review,* CXXXII (December 1927), 695—707.

7309 Scammell, J. M. **A Projected Federation of the Balkans,** *Current History,* XXXIII (February 1931), 712—15.

7310 Stavrianos, L. S. **Balkan Federation: A History of the Movement Towards Balkan Unity in Modern Times,** *Smith College Studies in History,* XXVII (October 1941 — July 1942), 1—338.

7311 — —. **The Balkan Federation Movement,** *American Historical Review,* XLVIII (October 1942), 30—51.

7312 Stoddard, T. Lothrop. **Pan-Turanism,** *American Political Science Review,* XI (February 1917), 12—23.

7313 Vucinich, Wayne S. **Growing Unity in Yugoslavia, Greece and Turkey,** *Current History,* New Series, XXIV (February 1953), 103—108.

7314 Wuorinen, John H. **The Efforts to Form a Union of Baltic States,** *Current History,* XX (July 1924), 609—14.

7315 Zenkovsky, Serge A. **Pan-Turkism and Islam in Russia.** Cambridge, Harvard University Press, 1960. 345 p.

9.3 DANUBIAN REGIONALISM

7316 Adam, H.-T. **Les organismes internationaux spécialisés.** Paris, Pinchon et Durand-Auzias, 1965.

Volume II, Chapter X. Danube Commission.

7317 Chamberlain, Joseph P. **The Regime of the International Rivers: Danube and Rhine.** New York, Columbia University Press, 1923. 317 p.

7318 Commission Européenne du Danube. **La Commission Européenne du Danube et son oeuvre de 1856 à 1931.** Paris, Imprimerie Nationale, 1931. viii + 526 p.

7319 Gyorgy, Andrew. **Danubian Federation,** *Thought,* XXIII (March 1948), 36—58.

7320 Hertz, Friedrich O. **Austria and a Danubian Union,** *World Affairs,* VII (October 1941), 100—15.

7321 — —. **Danubian Union,** *Contemporary Review,* CLVII (March 1940), 284—90.

7322 Jászi, Oskar. **Danubia, Old and New,** *Proceedings of the American Philosophical Society for Promoting Useful Knowledge,* XCIII (April 1949), 1—31.

7323 — —. **Future of Danubia,** *Journal of Central European Affairs,* I (July 1941), 127—47.

Part E. — Regional International Organization

7324 Kolnai, Aurel. **Danubia: A Survey of Plans of Solution,** *Journal of Central European Affairs,* III (January 1944), 441–62.

7325 Lehman, John. **Down River: A Danubian Study.** London, Cresset, 1939. 291 p.

7326 M., C. A. **The Regime of the Danube,** *World Today,* New Series, IV (September 1948), 368–75.

7327 Machray, Robert. **The Struggle for the Danube and the Little Entente, 1929–38.** London, Allen and Unwin, 1938. 344 p.

7328 Popper, Otto. **The International Regime of the Danube,** *Geographical Journal,* CII (November-December 1943), 240–52.

Danubian River Commission.

7329 Rasmussen, Charlotte B. **Freedom of the Danube,** *Current History,* New Series, XII (January 1947), 27–31.

7330 Roucek, Joseph S. **The Geopolitics of Danubia,** *World Affairs,* XVII (October 1946), 316–22.

7331 Savic, V. R. **A Danubian Confederation of the Future,** *Annals of the American Academy of Political and Social Science,* LXXXIV (July 1919), 70–80.

7332 Sinclair, I. M. **The Danube Conference of 1948,** *British Yearbook of International Law,* XXV (1948), 398–404.

7333 Traisner, K. **Key Position of Europe; Need of a Danubian Confederation,** *Catholic World,* CLIV (October 1941), 37–45.

7334 Váli, Ferenc A. **The Austro-German Customs Regime Before the Permanent Court, Considered with Reference to the Proposed Federation of Danubian States,** *Transactions* (Grotius Society), XVIII (1932), 79–94.

Comments by Bewes, Alexander, Cairns, Latey, Smith, and Jaffé.

9.4 COMMUNIST EASTERN EUROPEAN REGIONALISM

9.4.1 GENERAL OBSERVATIONS

See also E 10.2.

7335 Howard, Harry N. **The Soviet Alliance System and the Charter of the United Nations,** *Regional Arrangements for Security and the United Nations,* Commission to Study the Organization of Peace (ed.). New York Commission to Study the Organization of Peace, 1953, pp. 65–79.

9.4.2 COMECON (Moscow)

7336 Ágoston, István. **Le marché commun communiste: Principes et practique du COMECON.** Geneva, Droz, 1964. 353 p.

7337 Alexandrowicz, C. **COMECON: The Soviet Retort to the Marshall Plan,** *World Affairs,* IV (January 1950), 35–47.

7338 Caesar, A. A. L. **On the Economic Organization of Eastern Europe,** *Geographical Journal,* CXXI (December 1955), 451–69.

7339 Cattell, David T. **Multilateral Co-operation and Integration in Eastern Europe,** *Western Political Quarterly,* XIII (March 1960), 64—69.
CEMA.

7340 Gamarnikow, Michael. **COMECON Today,** *East Europe,* XIII (March 1964), 3—9.

7341 H., A. **Economic Integration in the Communist World: Recent Developments Assessed,** *World Today,* New Series, XIV (November 1958), 495—506.

7342 Hoffmann, Emil. **COMECON: Der gemeinsamt Markt in Osteuropa.** Poladen, Leske, 1961. 174 p.

7343 Jaksch, Wenzel. **Neo-Imperialism Versus European Partnership,** *Western Integration and the Future of Eastern Europe,* David S. Collier and Kurt Glaser (eds.). Chicago, Regnery, 1964, pp. 54—74.

7344 Jaster, Robert S. **CEMA's Influence on Soviet Policies in Eastern Europe,** *World Politics,* XIV (April 1962), 505—18.

7345 — —. **The Defeat of Khrushchev's Plan to Integrate Eastern Europe,** *World Today,* New Series, XIX (December 1963), 514—22.

7346 Kaser, Michael. **COMECON: Integration Problems of Planned Economies.** London, Oxford University Press, 1965. vi + 215 p.

7347 Korbonski, Andrzej. **COMECON,** *International Conciliation,* DXLIX (September 1964), 3—62.

7348 Kulski, W. W. **The Soviet System of Collective Security Compared with the Western System,** *American Journal of International Law,* XLIV (July 1950), 453—76.

7349 Pinto, Roger. **Les organisations européennes.** 2d ed. Paris, Payot, 1965.

Chapters IX, X.

7350 Stolte, Stefan C. **Recent Progress Toward Communist-Bloc Economic Integration,** *Bulletin* (Institute for the Study of the USSR), VI (July 1959), 32—35.

7351 Wilczynski, J. **COMECON: Success or Failure?** *Australian Outlook*, XIX (April 1965), 47—61.

7352 Zsoldos, Laszlo. **The Economic Integration of Hungary into the Soviet Bloc: Foreign Trade Experience.** Columbus, Ohio State University, Bureau of Business Research, 1963. 149 p.

9.4.3 WARSAW PACT
(Moscow)

7353 Ginsburgs, George. **Soviet Atomic Energy Agreements,** *International Organization*, XV (Winter, 1961), 49—65.

7354 Unterberger, Betty M. **The Russian Alliance System: Its Strengths and Weaknesses,** *Institute of World Affairs Proceedings*, XXXIV (1958), 123—30.

Part E. — Regional International Organization

10. TRANSCONTINENTAL NONUNIVERSAL INTERNATIONAL ORGANIZATIONS

The following set of international organizations, if not strictly regional, at least are not intended to be of universal scope. The Commonwealth of Nations is an outgrowth of the slow devolution of sovereignty within the British dominions and imperial possessions. Worldwide communist party meetings continue the tradition of socialist internationals in furthering a universalistic mission. In practice, the congress of communist parties is a policy-making and accordinating device which brings together representatives of quasigovernmental organs. Delegations from states where communist regimes are in power play a dominant role at these meetings. The French Community, essentially a copy of the British Commonwealth model, is a union of former colonies with the erstwhile mother country. The so-called "third world" of underdeveloped countries, finally, has held a number of conferences but so far has failed to agree on a common institutional framework.

10.1 BRITISH COMMONWEALTH OF NATIONS

10.1.1 BRITISH IMPERIAL ORGANIZATION

7355 Boggs, Theodore H. **The British Empire and Closer Union,** *American Political Science Review,* X (November 1916), 635–53.

7356 Comstock, Alzada. **Britain's Harassed Empire,** *Current History,* New Series, II (March 1942), 33–38.

7357 — —. **Commonwealth and Empire,** *Current History,* New Series, XVI (March 1949), 162–66.

7358 — —. **Tests for British Imperial Unity,** *Current History,* New Series, I (February 1942), 512–16.

7359 Cramer, Frederick H. **The Empire in Transition,** *Current History,* New Series, XXIII (December 1952), 351–66.

7360 Curtis, Lionel (ed.). **The Commonwealth of Nations: An Inquiry into the Nature of Citizenship in the British Empire, and into the Mutual Relations of the Several Communities Thereof.** London, Macmillan, 1916. xix + 722 p.

7361 Jebb, Richard. **The Imperial Conference: A History and a Study.** New York, Longmans, Green, 1911. 2 vols.

7362 Phelan, E. J. **The British Empire and the World Community,** *Problems of Peace,* Series 6 (1931), 253–84.

7363 Robinson, Howard. **The Development of the British Empire,** James T. Shotwell (ed.). Boston, Houghten, Mifflin, 1922. 475 p.

7364 Rowell, Newton Wesley. **The British Empire and World Peace.** New York, Oxford University Press, 1922. 307 p.

7365 Rowse, A. L. **The Early Empire,** *Current History,* New Series, XXIII (December 1952), 344–49.

7366 Sage, Walter N. **The Three British Empires,** *Institute of World Affairs Proceedings,* III (1928), 103–17.

7367 Smellie, K. B. **The British Imperial Conference,** *American Political Science Review,* XXI (May 1927), 376–81.

7368 Smith, W. R. **British Imperial Federation,** *Political Science Quarterly,* XXXVI (June 1921), 274–97.

7369 Swain, James E. **The Expanding Empire,** *Current History,* New Series, XXIII (December 1952), 350–54.

7370 Williamson, James A. **A Short History of British Expansion.** 5th ed. London, Macmillan, 1965. 2 vols.

10.1.2 DEVELOPMENT OF THE COMMONWEALTH IDEA

7371 Angell, Norman. **The British Commonwealth in the World Order,** *Annals of the American Academy of Political and Social Science,* CCXXVIII (July 1943), 65—70.

7372 Bevin, Ernest. **Impressions of the British Commonwealth Conference, 1938,** *International Affairs,* XVIII (January 1939), 56—66.

Comments by Zimmern, Luke, Lothian, Newbold, Stokes, Latham, Middleton, Pratt, Humphreys, Scovell, Byrt, Stewart.

7373 Burt, Alfred LeRoy. **The Evolution of the British Empire and Commonwealth from the American Revolution.** Boston, Heath, 1956. 950 p.

7374 Carter, Gwendolen M. **The British Commonwealth and International Security: The Role of the Dominions, 1919—1939.** Toronto, Ryerson, 1947. xx + 326 p.

7375 Charteris, A. H. **The British Commonwealth Relations Conference at Toronto, 1933,** *Transactions* (Grotius Society), XIX (1933), 137—53.

7376 Cheng, Seymour Ching Yuan. **Schemes for the Federation of the British Empire.** New York, Columbia University Press, 1931. 313 p.

7377 Chevallier, Jean Jacques. **La Société des Nations Britanniques,** *Recueil des Cours,* LXIV (1938), 237—344.

7378 Dorn, Herbert. **The Early Commonwealth,** *Current History,* New Series, XXIII (December 1952), 367—75.

Part E. — Regional International Organization

7379 Eastwood, Reginald Allen. **The Organization of a Brittannic Partnership.** New York, Longmans, Green, 1922. 148 p.

7380 Elliott, William Yandell. **The New British Empire.** New York, McGraw-Hill, 1932. xv + 519 p.

7381 — —. **The Riddle of the British Commonwealth,** *Foreign Affairs*, VIII (April 1930), 442–64.

7382 — —. **A Written Constitution for the British Commonwealth?** *Political Quarterly*, I (July-September 1930), 386–409.

7383 Elliott, William Yandell and Hall, Hessel Duncan (eds.). **The British Commonwealth at War.** New York, Knopf, 1943. 515 p.

7384 Fisher, Allan G. B. **The Commonwealth's Place in the World Economic Structure,** *International Affairs*, XX (January 1944), 32–41.

Comments by Verschoyle, Myers, Horsfall, Wyndham, Sanders.

7385 Gathorne-Hardy, G. M. **The British Commonwealth Relations Conference, 1933,** *International Affairs*, XII (November 1933), 763–74.

7386 Gordon, Donald C. **The Dominion Partnership in Imperial Defense, 1870–1914.** Baltimore, Johns Hopkins Press, 1965. xiv + 315 p.

7387 Hall, Hessel Duncan. **The Balfour Report and Its Historical Background,** *World Peace Foundation Pamphlets*, X, 6 (1927), 589–620.

7388 — —. **The British Commonwealth and Trusteeship,** *International Affairs*, XXII (April 1946), 199–213.

Similarities between the two arrangements.

7389 — —. **The British Commonwealth As a Great Power,** *Foreign Affairs,* XXIII (July 1945), 594—608.

7390 — —. **The British Commonwealth of Nations.** London, Methuen, 1920. 393 p.

7391 — —. **The Community of the Parliaments of the British Commonwealth,** *American Political Science Review,* XXXVI (December 1942), 1128—35.

7392 — —. **The Genesis of the Balfour Declaration of 1926,** *Journal of Commonwealth Political Studies,* I (November 1962), 169—93.

7393 Hall, Walter Phelps. **Empire to Commonwealth.** New York, Holt, 1928. 536 p.

7394 Hankey, Maurice. **Diplomacy by Conference: Studies in Public Affairs, 1920—1946.** London, Benn, 1946. 179 p.

7395 Hughes, Hector. **National Sovereignty and Judicial Autonomy in the British Commonwealth of Nations.** London, King, 1931. 184 p.

7396 Iwi, Edward F. **The Evolution of the Commonwealth Since the Statute of Westminster,** *Transactions* (Grotius Society), XXXVII (1951), 83—97.

7397 Jennings, W. Ivor. **The Constitution of the British Commonwealth,** *Political Quarterly,* IX (October-December 1938), 465—79.

7398 Joyner, Conrad. **W. M. Hughes and the "Powers" Referendum of 1919: A Master Politician at Work,** *Australian Journal of Politics and History,* V (May 1959), 15—23.

Part E. — Regional International Organization

7399 Lindsay, Harry Alexander (ed.). **British Commonwealth Objectives.** London, Joseph, 1946. 288 p.

7400 Lowell, A. Lawrence. **The Imperial Conference,** *World Peace Foundation Pamphlets*, X, 6 (1927), 573—88.

7401 Macdonald, Malcolm. **The British Commonwealth and Empire Today,** *World Affairs*, XI (January 1946), 284—91.

7402 McHenry, Dean E. **The British Commonwealth and World Organization,** *World Affairs Quarterly*, XXII (January 1952), 386—92.

7403 MacKay, Robert A. **The British Commonwealth of Independent Nations,** *Current History*, XXXIV (September 1931), 845—48.

7404 — —. **Changes in the Legal Structure of the British Commonwealth of Nations,** *International Conciliation*, CCLXXII (September 1931), 9—85.

7405 Mander, Linden A. **The British Commonwealth of Nations,** *Institute of World Affairs Proceedings*, IV (December 1928), 95—121.

7406 Massey, Vincent. **British Commonwealth Relations,** *International Affairs*, XIII (November 1934), 815—25.

7407 Mehrotra, S. R. **On the Use of the Term "Commonwealth",** *Journal of Commonwealth Political Studies*, II (November 1963), 1—16.

7408 O'Connell, D. P. **The British Commonwealth and State Succession After the Second World War,** British Yearbook of International Law, XXVI (1949), 454—63.

7409 Preston, Richard A. **The Military Structure of the Old Commonwealth,** *International Journal,* XVII (Spring, 1962), 98—121.

7410 Reeves, Jesse S. **An American View of the British Commonwealth of Nations,** *Institute of World Affairs Proceedings,* III (1928), 118—23.

7411 Robinson, Howard. **The New Magna Carta of British Imperial Unity,** *Current History,* XXV (January 1927), 493—97.

7412 Soward, Frederick Hubert (ed.). **The Changing Commonwealth.** New York, Oxford University Press, 1950. 268 p.

7413 Stewart, Robert B. **Treaty Relations of the British Commonwealth of Nations.** Foreword by W. Y. Elliott. New York, Macmillan, 1939. xxi + 503 p.

7414 Thomas, Brinley. **The Evolution of the Sterling Area and Its Prospects,** *Commonwealth Perspectives,* Nicholas Mansergh, Robert R. Wilson, Joseph J. Spengler, James L. Godfrey, B. U. Ratchford, Brinley Thomas (eds.). Durham, Duke University Press, 1958, pp. 175—207.

7415 Thorson, J. T. **The British Commonwealth of Nations,** *Institute of World Affairs Proceedings,* III (1928), 89—102.

7416 Williamson, James A. **A Notebook of Commonwealth History.** 2d ed. London, Macmillan, 1960. x + 307 p.

10.1.3 CONTEMPORARY COMMONWEALTH

7417 Ali, Mohammed. **The New Commonwealth,** *Pakistan Horizon,* VII (March 1954), 3—8.

7418 Anstey, Vera. **The Intangible Commonwealth,** *Indian Year Book of International Affairs,* V (1956), 254–72.

7419 Arnold, Guy. **Towards Peace and a Multiracial Commonwealth.** London, Chapman and Hall, 1964. 184 p.

7420 Berkes, Ross N. **The Commonwealth: A United States View,** *Current History,* New Series, XXIII (December 1952), 338–43.

7421 Bradley, Kenneth. **The Living Commonwealth.** London, Hutchinson, 1961. 543 p.

7422 Brady, A. **The Modern Commonwealth,** *Canadian Journal of Economics and Political Science,* XXVI (February 1960), 62–73.

7423 Bull, Hedley. **What Is the Commonwealth?** *World Politics,* XI (July 1959), 577–87.

7424 Carnell, Francis (comp.). **The Politics of the New States: A Select Annotated Bibliography with Special Reference to the Commonwealth.** London, Oxford University Press, 1961. xvi + 171 p.

7425 Carrington, C. E. **A New Theory of the Commonwealth,** *International Affairs,* XXXI (April 1955), 137–48.

7426 — —. **The New Zealand Commonwealth Conference and Its Predecessors,** *International Affairs,* XXXV (July 1959), 332–40.

7427 Carter, Gwendolen M. **The British Commonwealth in the Asian Crisis,** *Foreign Policy Reports,* XXVI (October 1, 1950), 106–16.

7428 — —. **The Evolving Commonwealth,** *International Journal,* IV (Summer, 1949), 261–71.

7429 — —. **The Expanding Commonwealth,** *Foreign Affairs,* XXXV (October 1956), 131–43.

7430 Casey, Richard G. C. **The Future of the Commonwealth.** London, Muller, 1963. 187 p.

7431 Chase, Eugene B. **Government by Consultation in the British Commonwealth,** *Journal of Politics,* IX (May 1947), 198–210.

7432 Coatman, John. **The British Family of Nations.** London, Harrap, 1950. 271 p.

7433 Comstock, Alzada. **The Developing Commonwealth,** *Current History.* New Series, XXIII (December 1952), 381–85.

7434 — —. **The New Commonwealth,** *Current History,* New Series, XVI (January 1949), 7–11.

7435 Conway, John. **The Changing Concept of the Commonwealth,** *International Journal,* XII (Winter, 1956–57), 34–31.

7436 Cowen, Zelman. **The Contemporary Commonwealth: A General View,** *International Organization,* XIII (Spring, 1959), 204–18.

7437 Donelly, M. S. **J. W. Dafoe and Lionel Curtis — Two Concepts of the Commonwealth,** *Political Studies,* VIII (June 1960), 170–82.

7438 Fawcett, James Edmund Sanford. **The British Commonwealth in International Law.** London, Stevens, 1963. xvii + 243 p.

7439 Forsey, Eugene. **"The Expanding Commonwealth": A Personal Impression,** *International Journal,* XIV (Summer, 1959), 213–17.

Part E. — Regional International Organization

7440 Friedmann, Wolfgang G. **An Introduction to World Politics.** 2d ed. London, Macmillan, 1952.

Chapter V.

7441 Frost, Richard Aylmer (ed.). **The British Commonwealth and World Society.** New York, Oxford University Press, 1947. 204 p.

7442 Gelber, Lionel M. **America in Britain's Place.** New York, Praeger, 1961. 356 p.

7443 Greenwood, G. **The Lahore Conference and the Contemporary Commonwealth,** *Australian Outlook,* VIII (September 1954), 157—71.

7444 Gupta, K. **The Structure and Function of the Commonwealth,** *Calcutta Review,* CLXXX (November 1959), 115—30.

7445 Hall, H. Duncan. **The British Commonwealth of Nations,** *American Political Science Review,* XLVII (December 1953), 997—1016.

7446 Harvey, Heather Joan. **The British Commonwealth: A Pattern of Co-operation,** *International Conciliation,* CDLXXXVI (January 1953), 13—48.

7447 — —. **Consultation and Co-operation in the Commonwealth: A Handbook on Methods and Practice.** London, Oxford University Press, 1952. viii + 411 p.

7448 Hasan, K. Sarwar. **The Commonwealth — Whither?** *Pakistan Horizon,* XVIII, 1 (1965), 28—37.

7449 Hodson, H. V. **Problems Before the Commonwealth,** *India Quarterly,* V (July-September 1949), 228—34.

7450 — —. **Race Relations in the Commonwealth,** *International Affairs,* XXVI (July 1950), 305—15.

7451 Hoover, Calvin Bryce (ed.). **Economic Systems of the Commonwealth.** Durham, Duke University Press, 1962. 538 p.

7452 Hudson, G. F. **How Unified Is the Commonwealth?** *Foreign Affairs,* XXXIII (July 1955), 679—88.

7453 Ikramullah, Mohammad. **The Commonwealth Economic Committee and Its Work,** *Pakistan Horizon,* XVI, 1 (1963), 15—21.

7454 Ingram, Derek. **The Commonwealth Challenge.** London, Allen and Unwin, 1962. 291 p.

7455 — —. **Commonwealth for a Colour-Blind World.** London, Allen and Unwin, 1965. 224 p.

7456 Jennings, W. Ivor. **The British Commonwealth of Nations.** London, Hutchinson, 1963. 224 p.

7457 — —. **The Commonwealth Conference, 1949,** *British Yearbook of International Law,* XXV (1948), 414—20.

7458 — —. **Problems of the New Commonwealth.** Durham, Duke University Press, 1958. 109 p.

7459 Kumar, Dharma. **The Commonwealth and Problems of World Trade and Development,** *India Quarterly,* XXI (January-March 1965), 41—57.

7460 Laing, Lionel H. **The Diffusion of Political Ideas and Structures in the Commonwealth,** *Parliamentary Affairs,* XVI (Winter, 1962), 46—54.

Part E. — Regional International Organization

7461 Legate, David M. **The Commonwealth Prime Ministers' Conference (Notes and Comments),** *International Journal,* X (Spring, 1955), 120–22.

7462 Loeber, Dietrich A. **The Legal Structure of the Commonwealth Bloc,** *Social Research,* XXVII (Summer, 1960), 183–202.

7463 McGuire, Paul. **The Three Corners of the World.** London, Heineman, 1948. 299 p.

7464 Maitland, Patrick. **Task for Giants: An Expanding Commonwealth.** London, Longmans, Green, 1957. ix + 327 p.

7465 Mansergh, Nicholas. **The Commonwealth at the Queen's Accession,** *International Affairs,* XXIX (July 1953), 277–91.

7466 — —. **The Commonwealth: Problems of Multi-Racial Membership,** *Political Studies,* III (October 1955), 235–46.

7467 — —. **Postwar Strains on the British Commonwealth,** *Foreign Affairs,* XXVII (October 1948), 129–42.

7468 — —. **Survey of British Commonwealth Affairs.** New York, Oxford University Press, 1952–58. 2 vols.

7469 Menzies, Robert Gordon. **The Commonwealth Problem: Union or Alliance?** *Foreign Affairs,* XXVII (January 1949), 263–73.

7470 Michener, Roland. **Commonwealth Institutions,** *Indian Journal of International Law,* V (April 1965), 186–93.

7471 Miller, J. D. B. **The Commonwealth in the World.** Cambridge, Harvard University Press, 1958. 308 p.

7472 — —. **Le Commonwealth,** *Les institutions internationales et transnationales,* Fernand L'Huillier (ed.). Paris, Presses Universitaires, 1961, pp. 54–71.

7473 — —. **The C. R. O. and Commonwealth Relations,** *International Studies,* II (July 1960), 42–59.
   C. R. O.: Commonwealth Relations Office.

7474 Muir, Ramsay. **A Short History of the British Commonwealth.** 7th ed. London, Philip, 1961. 2 vols.

7475 Mullett, Charles F. **The British Empire-Commonwealth: Its Themes and Character; A Plural Society in Evolution.** Washington, Service Center for Teachers of History, 1961. 37 p.

7476 O'Connell, D. P. **The Crown in the British Commonwealth,** *International and Comparative Law Quarterly,* VI (January 1957), 103–25.

7477 Ogden, Richard. **The Commonwealth Prime Ministers' Conference,** *International Journal,* XIX (Autumn, 1964), 545–50.

7478 Polyzoides, A. T. **The British Commonwealth Under Elizabeth II,** *World Affairs Quarterly,* XXIII (April 1952), 60–71.

7479 Rajan, M. S. **The Post-War Transformation of the Commonwealth: Reflections on the African-Asian Contribution.** Bombay, Asia Publishing House, 1961. 67 p.

7480 Rao, V. K. R. V. **The New Commonwealth — Will It Endure?** *India Quarterly,* VI (January-March 1950), 3–17.

7481 Reid, Patrick. **The Contemporary Commonwealth,** *International Journal,* IX (Summer, 1954), 208–15.

7482 Richardson, B. T. **The Evolving Commonwealth,** *International Journal,* XIV (Spring, 1959), 131–38.

7483 Shiels, Thomas Drummond (ed.). **The British Commonwealth: A Family of Peoples.** London, Odham, 1952. 384 p.

7484 Simnett, William E. **Emergent Commonwealth: The British Colonies.** London, Hutchinson, 1954. 190 p.

7485 Smith, S. A. de. **The New Commonwealth and Its Constitutions.** London, Stevens, 1964. xvi + 312 p.

7486 Somerville, D. C. and Harvey, Heather. **The British Empire and Commonwealth.** London, Chatto and Windus, 1964. 444 p.

7487 Strachey, John. **The End of Empire.** New York, Random House, 1960. 351 p.

7488 Trotter, Reginald G. **Bigwin and the Changing Commonwealth,** *International Journal,* V (Winter, 1949), 22–30.

7489 Turner, Arthur C. **The Commonwealth: Evolution or Dissolution?** *Current History,* New Series, XLVI (May 1964), 257–62.

7490 Underhill, Frank H. **The British Commonwealth: An Experiment in Co-operation Among Nations.** Durham, Duke University Press, 1956. xxiii + 127 p.

7491 Walker, Patrick Gordon. **The Commonwealth.** London, Secker and Warburg, 1962. 408 p.

Part E. — Regional International Organization

7492 — —. **Commonwealth Secretary,** *Journal of Commonwealth Political Studies,* I (November 1961), 17—28.

7493 Wheare, K. C. **The Constitutional Structure of the Commonwealth.** London, Oxford University Press, 1960. 201 p.

7494 — —. **Is the British Commonwealth Withering Away?** *American Political Science Review,* XLIV (September 1950), 545—55.

7495 — —. **The Nature and Structure of the Commonwealth,** *American Political Science Review,* XLVII (December 1953), 1016—28.

7496 Williams, Wilbur Laurent. **The British Commonwealth: A Constitutional Survey,** *Foreign Policy Reports,* IX (April 12, 1933), 26—37.

7497 Wiseman, Herbert Victor. **The Cabinet in the Commonwealth: Post-War Developments in Africa, the West Indies, and Southeast Asia.** New York, Praeger, 1959. 364 p.

10.1.4 RELATION TO OTHER INTERNATIONAL ORGANIZATIONS

7498 Carrington, C. E. **Between the Commonwealth and Europe,** *International Affairs,* XXXVIII (October 1962), 449—59.

7499 Gelber, Lionel. **The Commonwealth and the United Nations,** *Regional Arrangements for Security and the United Nations,* Commission to Study the Organization of Peace (ed.). New York, Commission to Study the Organization of Peace, 1953, pp. 49—64.

7500 Millar, T. B. **Kashmir, the Commonwealth and the United Nations,** *Australian Outlook,* XVII (April 1963), 54—73.

Part E. — Regional International Organization

7501 Price, Peter. **Power and the Law: A Study in Peaceful Change, with Special Reference to the British Commonwealth and the United Nations.** Geneva, Droz, 1954. 155 p.

7502 Siddiqi, Qamar Saeed. **European Integration and Economic Development in the Commonwealth,** *Pakistan Horizon,* XIII, 4 (1960), 318–23.

7503 Vosper, Dennis. **The Commonwealth and the European Economic Community,** *Pakistan Horizon,* XV, 1 (1962), 3–12.

10.1.5 COLOMBO PLAN (Colombo)

7504 Benham, Frederic C. **The Colombo Plan: An Economic Survey,** *The Colombo Plan, and Other Essays.* London, Royal Institute of International Affairs, 1956, pp. 1–26.

7505 Burns, C. **The Colombo Plan and Australian Foreign Policy,** *Australian Outlook,* XII (March 1958), 37–49.

7506 Cavell, Nik. **The Colombo Plan,** *Canadian Geographical Journal,* C (May 1952), 212–13.

7507 Cohen, Jerome B. **The Colombo Plan for Cooperative Economic Development,** *Middle East Journal,* V (Winter, 1951), 94–100.

7508 Harper, N. **Australia and Regional Pacts, 1950–57,** *Australian Outlook,* XII (March 1958), 3–22.

7509 James, C. W. **The Colombo Plan Passes Halfway,** *Australian Outlook,* IX (March 1955), 29–42.

7510 Keyfitz, Nathan. **Canada and the Colombo Plan.** Toronto, Canadian Institute of International Affairs, 1961. 15 p.

7511 Singh, L. P. **The Colombo Plan: Some Political Aspects.** Canberra, Australian National University, Department of International Relations, Research School of Pacific Studies, 1963. iv + 57 p.

7512 Spicer, Keith. **The Administration of Canadian Colombo Plan Aid,** *International Journal,* XVI (Spring, 1961), 169–82.

7513 Symon, A. C. B. **The Colombo Plan,** *Royal Central Asian Society Journal,* XXXIX (July 1952), 188–92.

10.1.6 NATIONAL ACTORS AND THE COMMONWEALTH SYSTEM

10.1.6.1 GENERAL OBSERVATIONS ON MEMBERS

7514 Mansergh, Nicholas. **The Commonwealth and the Nations: Studies in British Commonwealth Relations.** London, Royal Institute of International Affairs, 1948. vii + 228 p.

7515 — —. **Commonwealth Membership,** *Commonwealth Perspectives,* Nicholas Mansergh, Robert R. Wilson, Joseph J. Spengler, James L. Godfrey, B. U. Ratchford, Brinley Thomas (eds.). Durham, Duke University Press, 1958, pp. 3–34.

7516 Rajan, M. S. **The Post-War Transformation of the Commonwealth: Reflections on the Asian-African Contribution.** Bombay, Asia Publishing House, 1960. 67 p.

7517 Shearman, H. **The British Commonwealth and Its Members,** *Year Book of World Affairs,* IV (1950), 105–29.

10.1.6.2 AFRICAN COUNTRIES

7518 Austin, Dennis. **West Africa and the Commonwealth.** London, Penguin, 1957. 124 p.

7519 Carter, Gwendolen. **The Commonwealth in Africa.** Toronto, Canadian Institute of International Affairs, 1958. 16 p.

7520 Emmet, Evelyn. **Africa and the Commonwealth,** *Pakistan Horizon,* XVI, 1 (1963), 33–36.

7521 Holmes, John W. **The Commonwealth and Africa,** *International Journal,* XVII (Spring, 1962), 133–36.

7522 — —. **The Impact on the Commonwealth of the Emergence of Africa,** *International Organization,* XVI (Spring, 1962), 291–302.

7523 Younger, Kenneth. **Reflections on Africa and the Commonwealth,** *World Today,* New Series, XVIII (March 1962), 121–29.

10.1.6.3 ASIAN COUNTRIES

7524 Cowan, C. D. **Indonesia and the Commonwealth in South-East Asia: A Re-appraisal,** *International Affairs,* XXXIV (October 1958), 454–68.

7525 Mehrotra, S. R. **Gandhi and the British Commonwealth,** *India Quarterly,* XVII (January-March 1961), 44–57.

7526 Pavadya, Balram Singh. **Notes and Memoranda: Mr. Nehru, the Indian National Congress and India's Membership in the Commonwealth,** *International Studies,* IV (January 1963), 298–311.

7527 Rajan, M. S. **India and the Commonwealth,** *India Quarterly,* XVI (January-March 1961), 31–50.

7528 Robinson, Roland. **India and the Commonwealth Parliamentary Conference,** *Asian Review,* LVIII (April 1962), 84–92.

10.1.6.4 AUSTRALIA AND NEW ZEALAND

7529 Copland, Douglas. **Australia's Attitude to British Commonwealth Relations,** *International Journal,* III (Winter, 1947–48), 39–48.

7530 Hasan, K. Sarwar. **Looking at the Commonwealth from New Zealand,** *Pakistan Horizon,* XII (June 1959), 87–97.

7531 Kendle, J. E. **Round Table Movement, New Zealand and the Conference,** *Journal of Commonwealth Political Studies,* III (July 1965), 104–17.

7532 Key, L. C. **Australia and the Commonwealth,** *International Affairs,* XXI (January 1945), 60–73.

7533 Wolfsohn, H. **The Evolution of Australia in World Affairs,** *Australian Outlook,* VII (March 1953), 5–21.

10.1.6.5 CANADA

7534 Barkway, Michael. **Canada and the Commonwealth Economic Conference,** *International Journal,* VII (Autumn, 1952), 245–52.

7535 Brady, Alexander. **Canada and the Commonwealth,** *International Journal,* IV (Summer, 1949), 189–211.

7536 Comstock, Alzada. **Canada and the Commonwealth,** *Current History,* New Series, XXIX (July 1955), 7—12.

7537 Cunningham, W. B. (ed.). **Canada, the Commonwealth and the Common Market: Report.** Montreal, McGill University Press, 1962. 142 p.

7538 Dafoe, J. W. **Canada, the Empire and the League,** *Foreign Affairs,* XIV (January 1936), 297—308.

7539 Harnetty, Peter. **Canada, South Africa, and the Commonwealth 1960 —61,** *Journal of Commonwealth Political Studies,* I (November 1963), 33—44.

7540 Keyfitz, Nathan. **Canada and the Colombo Plan.** Toronto, Canadian Institute of International Affairs, 1961. 15 p.

7541 Macadam, Ivison S. **Canada and the Commonwealth,** *International Affairs,* XX (October 1944), 519—26.

7542 McCready, H. W. **Canada, the Commonwealth, and the United States,** *International Journal,* X (Summer, 1955), 179—82.

7543 Scott, F. R. **Canada's Future in the British Commonwealth,** *Foreign Affairs,* XV (April 1937), 429—42.

7544 Spicer, Keith. **The Administration of Canadian Colombo Plan Aid,** *International Journal,* XVI (Spring, 1961), 169—82.

10.1.6.6 EUROPEAN COUNTRIES

7545 Cross, J. A. **Whitehall and the Commonwealth: The Development of British Departmental Organization for Commonwealth Affairs,** *Journal of Commonwealth Political Studies,* II (November 1964), 189—206.

7546 Dobie, Edith. **Malta and Her Place in the Commonwealth,** *Western Political Quarterly,* IX (December 1956), 873—83.

7547 The Economist, Intelligence Unit. **The Commonwealth and Europe.** London, White Friars, 1960. xiii + 606 p.

7548 Franks, Oliver. **Britain and the Commonwealth,** *British Affairs,* V (Summer, 1961), 74—79.

7549 Hodson, H. V. **United Kingdom Opinion on a Multi-Racial Commonwealth,** *International Journal,* V (Winter, 1949), 14—21.

7550 Mansergh, Nicholas. **The Implications of Eire's Relationship with the British Commonwealth of Nations,** *International Affairs,* XXIV (January 1948), 1—18.

7551 — —. **Ireland: The Republic Outside the Commonwealth,** *International Affairs,* XXVIII (April 1952), 277—91.

7552 Tierney, James S. **Britain and the Commonwealth: Attitudes in Parliament and Press in the United Kingdom Since 1951,** *Political Studies,* VI (October 1958), 220—33.

10.1.6.7 SOUTH AFRICA

7553 C., C. E and C., M. C. **South Africa's Withdrawal and What It May Mean,** *World Today,* New Series, XVII (April 1961), 135—42.

7554 Harnetty, Peter. **Canada, South Africa, and the Commonwealth 1960—61,** *Journal of Commonwealth Political Studies,* I (November 1963), 33—44.

7555 Hatch, John. **South African Crisis in the Commonwealth,** *Journal of International Affairs,* XV, 1 (1961), 68—76.

7556 Lovell, Colin Rhys. **South Africa in the Commonwealth,** *Current History,* New Series, XXXIV (June 1958), 334—39.

7557 Miller, J. D. B. **South Africa's Departure,** *Journal of Commonwealth Political Studies,* I (November 1961), 56—71.

10.1.6.8 UNITED STATES

7558 Bangsberg, Harry F. **The United States and the Colombo Plan,** *India Quarterly,* XV (April-June 1959), 130—41.

7559 Basch, Antonin. **The Colombo Plan — A Case of Regional Economic Cooperation,** *International Organization,* IX (February 1955), 1—18.

7560 Carr-Gregg, John R. E. **The Colombo Plan: A Commonwealth Program for Southeast Asia,** *International Conciliation,* CDLXVII (January 1951), 3—55.

7561 Comstock, Alzada. **The United States and the Commonwealth,** *Current History,* New Series, XXV (December 1953), 354—69.

7562 Curtin, P. W. E. **The Effect of the Colombo Plan,** *Pakistan Horizon,* VII (June 1954), 76—78.

7563 Glazebrook, G. de T. **Political and Military Relations of the British Commonwealth and the United States,** *International Journal,* I (October 1946), 337—480.

7564 J., I. **The Colombo Conference in Retrospect,** *World Today,* New Series, VI (April 1950), 149—56.

7565 — —. **The Colombo Conference: Neutrality the Keynote,** *World Today,* New Series, X (July 1954), 293—300.

7566 McCready, H. W. **Canada, the Commonwealth, and the United States,** *International Journal,* X (Summer, 1955), 179—82.

7567 Miller, J. D. B. **Le monde de Colombo,** *Les institutions internationales et transnationales,* Fernand L'Huillier (ed.). Paris, Presses Universitaires, 1961, pp. 106—16.

7568 Prasad, P. S. Narayan. **The Colombo Plan,** *India Quarterly,* VIII (July-September 1952), 158—70.

7569 Rees, Elfan. **Century of the Homeless Man,** *International Conciliation,* DXV (November 1957), 193—254.

7570 Swinnerton, A. R. **The Colombo Plan and Pakistan,** *Pakistan Horizon,* VI (September 1953), 117—22.

10.2 COMMUNIST WORLD AND SOCIALIST INTERNATIONALS

7571 Braunthal, Julius. **The Historical Significance of the Socialist International,** *India Quarterly,* XI (April-June 1955), 125—37.

7572 — —. **The Origins of the Socialist International: On the Occasion of the Ninetieth Anniversary of Its Founding on 28 September 1864,** *Socialist International Information,* IV (1954), 1—38.

7573 Brzezinski, Zbigniew K. **The Organization of the Communist Camp,** *World Politics,* XIII (January 1961), 175—209.

7574 — —. **The Soviet Bloc: Unity and Conflict.** Cambridge, Harvard University Press, 1960. 470 p.

7575 C., J. C. **The Berlin Youth Festival: Its Role in the Peace Campaign,** *World Today,* New Series, VII (July 1951), 306—15.

Part E. — *Regional International Organization*

7576 Degras, Jane. **The Communist Camp Ten Years After Stalin,** *World Today,* New Series, XIX (March 1963), 108—15.

7577 Dutt, Rajani P. **The Internationale.** London, Laurence and Wishart, 1964. 418 p.

7578 — —. **The Two Internationals.** Westminster, Labour Research Department, 1920. iv + 92 p.

7579 Foster, William Z. **History of the Three Internationals.** New York, International, 1955. 580 p.

7580 Grzybowski, Kazimierz. **The Socialist Commonwealth of Nations: Organizations and Institutions.** New Haven, Yale University Press, 1964. xvii + 300 p.

7581 Hopper, Bruce. **Pan-Sovietism: The Issue Before America and the World.** Boston, Houghton, Mifflin, 1931. xii + 287 p.

7582 Howard, Harry N. **The Soviet Alliance System and the Charter of the United Nations,** *Regional Arrangements for Security and the United Nations,* Commission to Study the Organization of Peace (ed.). New York, Commission to Study the Organization of Peace, 1953, pp. 65—79.

7583 Jaksch, Wenzel. **Neo-Imperialism Versus European Partnership,** *Learning and World Peace,* Lyman Bryson, Louis Finkelstein and R. M. MacIver (eds.). New York, Harper, 1948, pp. 54—76.

7584 Joll, James. **The Second International, 1889—1914.** New York, Praeger, 1956. 213 p.

7585 Kecskemeti, Paul. **Diversity and Uniformity in Communist Bloc Politics,** *World Politics,* XIII (January 1961), 313—22.

Part E. — Regional International Organization

7586 Kennan, George F. **Polycentrism and Western Policy,** *Foreign Affairs,* XLII (January 1964), 171—83.

7587 Kertesz, Stephen D. **The USSR and the Communist Bloc,** *Current History,* New Series, XLI (December 1961), 280—85.

7588 L'Huillier, Fernand. **Le bloc soviétique,** *Les institutions internationales et transnationales,* Fernand L'Huillier (ed.). Paris, Presses Universitaires, 1961, pp. 37—53.

7589 London, Kurt L. **The Socialist Commonwealth of Nations; Pattern for Communist World Organization,** *Orbis,* III (Winter, 1960), 424—42.

7590 Lowenthal, Richard. **Disarray in the East,** *Atlantic Community Quarterly,* II (Winter, 1964—65), 646—54.

Reprinted from the *New York Times,* October 25, 1964.

7591 Lyons, Francis S. L. **Internationalism in Europe, 1815—1914.** Leyden, Sythoff, 1963.

Chapter II.

7592 Modelski, George. **The Communist International System.** Princeton, Center of International Studies, 1960. 78 p.

7593 North, Robert C. **Frictions in the Sino-Soviet Alliance,** *Institute of World Affairs Proceedings,* XXXVI (1960), 113—25.

7594 Paige, Glenn D. **Korea and the Comintern, 1919—1935,** *Bulletin of the Korean Research Center,* XIII (December 1960), 1—25.

7595 Puech, J. L. **La Société des Nations et ses précurseurs socialistes,** *Revue Politique et Littéraire, Revue Bleue,* LIX (February 5, 1921), 82—85; (March 5, 1921), 147—51.

7596 Sworakowski, Witold S. **The Communist International and Its Front Organizations: A Research Guide and Checklist of Holdings in American and European Libraries.** Stanford, Hoover Institution, 1965. 493 p.

7597 Tripathi, Krishna Dev. **International Socialist Co-operation — 1848— 1954,** *India Quarterly,* XI (January-March 1955), 63—77.

7598 Triska, Jan F. **Conflict and Integration in the Communist Bloc: A Review,** *Journal of Conflict Resolution,* V (December 1961), 418—25.

7599 — —.**Stanford Studies of the Communist System: The Sino-Soviet Split,** *Background,* VIII (November 1964), 143—60.

7600 Ulam, Adam B. **Titoism and the Cominform.** Cambridge, Harvard University Press, 1952. viii + 243 p.

10.3 FRENCH COMMUNITY

7601 Borella, François. **L'évolution politique et juridique de l'Union Française depuis 1946.** Paris, Librairie Générale de Droit et de Jurisprudence, 1958. 499 p.

7602 Catroux, Georges. **The French Union,** *International Conciliation,* CDXCV (November 1953), 192—256.

7603 Deschamps, Hubert. **L'Union Française: Histoire, institutions, réalités.** Paris, Éditions Berger-Levrault, 1952. 214 p.

7604 Houphouet-Boigny, Felix. **Black Africa and the French Union,** *Foreign Affairs,* XXXV (June 1957), 593—99.

7605 Irvine, Keith. **The Franco-African Community in Transition,** *Current History,* New Series, XLI (October 1961), 205—9.

7606 Julien, C. A. **From the French Empire to the French Union,** *International Affairs,* XXVI (October 1950), 487—502.

7607 L'Huillier, Fernand. **Le Communinauté Franco-Africaine,** *Les institutionis internationales et transnationales,* Fernand L'Huillier (ed.). Paris, Presses Universitaires, 1961, pp. 91—105.

7608 Merle, Marcel. **Federalism and France's Problems with Its Former Colonies (1945—1963),** *Public Policy,* XIV (1965), 403—15.

7609 Moussa, Pierre. **Les chances économiques de la Communauté Franco-Africaine.** Paris, Colin, 1957. 271 p.

7610 Rivlin, Benjamin. **De Gaulle's French Community,** *Current History,* New Series, XXXVI (May 1959), 278—83.

7611 Savary, Alan. **The French Union: Centralism or Federalism?** *International Journal,* VII (Autumn, 1952), 258—64.

7612 Thien, Ton That. **The Influence of Indo-China on the Formation of the French Union,** *India Quarterly,* X (October-December 1954), 295—313.

10.4 THE "THIRD WORLD"

10.4.1 GENERAL DISCUSSIONS

7613 Dvonn, Eugene P. **Afro-Asia in Perspective,** *Institute of World Affairs Proceedings,* XXXVII (1961), 40—49.

7614 El-Farra, Muhammad H. **The Asian-African Group in a Changing World,** *The Dynamics of Neutralism in the Arab World,* Fayez Sayegh (ed.). San Francisco, Chandler, 1964, pp. 227—43.

7615 Fitzgerald, C. P. **Southeast Asia After Bandung,** *Australian Quarterly,* XXVII (September 1955), 9—17.

7616 Hayden, S. S. **The Arab-Asian Bloc,** *Middle Eastern Affairs,* V (May 1954), 149—53.

7617 Karane, Rachid. **The Afro-Asian Group,** *Pakistan Horizon,* XVI, 1 (1963), 3—5.

7618 Liska, George. **The "Third Party": The Rationale of Nonalignment,** *Neutralism and Nonalignment,* Lawrence W. Martin (ed.). New York, Praeger, 1962, pp. 80—92.

7619 — —. **Tripartism: Dilemmas and Strategies,** *Neutralism and Nonalignment,* Lawrence W. Martin (ed.). New York, Praeger, 1962, pp. 211—38.

7620 Logan, Rayford W. **Is There an Afro-Asian Bloc?** *Current History.* New Series, XL (February 1961), 65—69.

7621 Neumann, Robert G. **The Dynamics of Neutralism,** *Institute of World Affairs Proceedings,* XXXVI (1960), 58—67.

7622 Nofal, Sayed. **The Role of the Arab World in the Afro-Asian Conferences from Bandung to Belgrade,** *The Dynamics of Neutralism in the Arab World,* Fayez Sayegh (ed.). San Francisco, Chandler, 1964, pp. 244—57.

7623 Spector, Ivar. **Russia and Afro-Asian Neutralism,** *Current History,* New Series, XXXVII (November 1959), 272—77.

10.4.2 AFRICAN-ASIAN CONFERENCES

7624 Ahmed, Mushtaq. **The Bandung Conference,** *Pakistan Horizon*, VIII (June 1955), 362—65.

7625 Appadorai, A. **The Bandung Conference.** New Delhi, Indian Council of World Affairs, 1956. 32 p.

7626 Jha, C. S. **The Algiers Conference,** *India Quarterly*, XXI (October-December 1965), 375—86.

7627 Kahin, George M. **The Asian-African Conference: Bandung, Indonesia, April 1955.** Ithaca, Cornell University Press, 1956. vii + 88 p.

A brief study of Bandung followed by excerpts from speeches of Soekarno, Chou En-lai, Nehru.

7628 Keynes, Mary Knatchbull. **The Bandung Conference,** *International Relations*, I (October 1957), 362—76.

7629 Mansergh, Nicholas. **The Asian Conference,** *International Affairs*, XXIII (July 1947), 295—306.

7630 Millar, T. B. and Miller, J. D. B. **Afro-Asian Disunity: Algiers, 1965,** *Australian Outlook*, XIX (December 1965), 306—21.

7631 Romulo, Carlos Pena. **The Meaning of Bandung.** Chapel Hill, University of North Carolina Press, 1956. 102 p.

Part F.
NONGOVERNMENTAL ORGANIZATIONS

Part F. — Nongovernmental Organizations

Private international associations, known popularly as "NGOs," have not been chronicled in as much detail as have the intergovernmental organizations. One of the reasons for scholarly neglect of NGOs may be that they have operated not as international pressure groups but as behind-the-scenes coordinators of economic and other policies among leaders concerned chiefly with national politics. But the proliferation of functionally specialized intergovernmental organizations (IGOs) has often led to a more intimate connection between the two types of international institutions.

1. GENERAL DISCUSSIONS

7632 Adam, H.-T. **Les organismes internationaux spécialisés: Contribution à la théorie générale des établissements publics internationaux.** Paris, Pinchon et Durand-Auzias, 1965. 2 vols.

7633 Alexandrowicz-Alexander, C. H. **Vertical and Horizontal Divisions of the International Society,** *Indian Year Book of International Affairs*, I (1953), 88—96.

7634 Brackett, Russell D. **Pathways to Peace.** Minneapolis, Denison. 387 p.

7635 Elias, Julius A. **The Relation Between Voluntary Agencies and International Organizations,** *Journal of International Affairs*, VII, 1 (1953), 30—34.

7636 Evan, William M. **Transnational Forums for Peace,** *Preventing World War III: Some Proposals*, Quincy Wright, William M. Evan and Morton Deutsch (eds.). New York, Simon and Schuster, 1962, pp. 393—409.

7637 Garrigue, Katharine C. **A Directory of Non-Governmental Organizations.** New York, Foreign Policy Association, 1953. iii + 389 p.

7638 Harley, John E. **International Understanding: Agencies Educating For a New World.** Stanford, Stanford University Press, 1931. 604 p.

Part F. — Nongovernmental Organizations

7639 Hero, Alfred. **Voluntary Organizations in World Affairs Communication.** Foreword by Max F. Millikan. Boston, World Peace Foundation, 1960. iv + 153 p.

7640 Knott, James E., Jr. **Freedom of Association: A Study of the Role of International Non-Governmental Organizations in the Development Process of Emerging Countries.** Brussels, Union of International Associations, 1962. 93 p.

7641 Lador-Lederer, J. J. **International Non-Governmental Organizations and Economic Entities: A Study in Autonomous Organization and Ius Gentium.** Leyden, Sythoff, 1963. 403 p.

7642 Mangone, Gerard J. **A Short History of International Organization.** New York, McGraw-Hill, 1954.

Chapter III.

7643 Pickard, Bertram. **The Greater United Nations: An Essay Concerning the Place and Significance of International Non-Governmental Organizations.** New York, Carnegie, 1956. 86 p.

7644 Potter, Pitman B. **An Introduction to the Study of International Organization.** 4th ed. New York, Appleton-Century, 1935.

Chapter II.

7645 — —. **This World of Nations.** New York, Macmillan, 1929.

Chapter IV.

7646 Rodger, Raymond Spencer. **Facilitation Problems of International Associations.** Brussels, Union of International Associations, 1960. 167 p.

7647 Rosenhaupt, Hans W. **How to Wage Peace.** New York, Day, 1949. 248 p.

Part F. — Nongovernmental Organizations

7648 Scott, James Brown. **The Work of Non-Official Organizations,** *Problems of Peace,* Series 1 (1926), 313—25.

7649 Sharp, Walter and Kirk, Grayson. **Contemporary International Politics.** New York, Farrar and Rinehart, 1941.

Chapter VIII.

7650 Stosic, Borko D. **Les organisations non-gouvernementales et les Nations Unies.** Geneva, Droz, 1964. 367 p.

7651 Union of International Associations. **International Associations.** Brussels, Union of International Associations, monthly, 1948—.

7652 — —. **International Initialese: Guide to Initials in Current International Use.** Brussels, Union of International Associations, 1963. 48 p.

7653 — —. **The 1,978 International Organizations Founded Since the Congress of Vienna: Chronological List.** Introduction by G. P. Speeckaert. Brussels, Union of International Associations, 1957. xxviii + 204 p.

7654 — —. **Yearbook of International Organizations.** Brussels, Union of International Associations, annually, 1948—.

The Union of International Associations is an international non-profit organization, founded in Brussels in 1907, to study and facilitate international cooperation with special reference to non-government activities.

7655 United Nations Educational, Scientific, and Cultural Organization. **Directory of International Scientific Organizations.** 2d ed. Paris, UNESCO, 1953. 312 p.

7656 White, Lyman C. **Peace by Pieces: The Role of Non-Governmental Organizations.** New York, United Nations, Department of Public Information, Press and Publications Bureau, 1949. 17 p.

Reprinted from *Annals of the American Academy of Political and Social Science,* July 1949.

7657 — —. **The Structure of Private International Organizations.** Philadelphia, Ferguson, 1933. 326 p.

7658 White, Lyman C. and Zocca, Marie R. **International Non-Governmental Organizations: Their Purposes, Methods, and Accomplishments.** New Brunswick, N. J., Rutgers University Press, 1951. xi + 325 p.

2. NINETEENTH CENTURY EFFORTS

See A 5.2.

3. BUSINESS AND COMMERCIAL ORGANIZATIONS

7659 Domeratzky, Louis. **The Continental Steel Cartel,** *Academy of Political Science Proceedings,* XII, 4 (1928), 894—907.

7660 Drayton, Geoffrey. **The Travails of OPEC,** *World Today,* New Series, XIX (November 1963), 485—90.

Organization of Petroleum Exporting Countries.

7661 Geneva Research Center. **Agriculture As a World Problem,** *Geneva Studies,* II (May 1931), 1—22.

International Institute of Agriculture.

7662 Hobson, Asher. **The International Institute of Agriculture: An Historical and Critical Analysis of Its Organization, Activities and Policies of Administration.** Berkeley, University of California Press, 1931. xi + 356 p.

7663 Institut International d'Agriculture. **Quelques aspects de l'activité de l'Institut International d'Agriculture (1905—1940).** Rome, Institut International d'Agriculture, 1941. 136 p.

Part F. — Nongovernmental Organizations

7664 International Bureau for the Standardization of Man-Made Fibres. **Twenty-Five Years of Activity of BISFA.** Basel, International Bureau for the Standardization of Man-Made Fibres, 1953. 70 p.

7665 International Institute of Agriculture. **The International Institute of Agriculture: Organization, Activity and Results.** Rome, Caso, 1927. 51 p.

7666 Keppel, Fredrick P. **The International Chamber of Commerce,** *International Conciliation*, CLXXIV (May 1922), 189–201.

7667 Phillips, R. W. **The Work of the International Rice Commission: Past and Future,** *News Letter* (International Rice Commission), XI (1954), 1–10.

7668 Ridgeway, George L. **Merchants of Peace.** New York, Columbia University Press, 1938. 419 p.

History of the International Chamber of Commerce.

7669 S., H. M. **Belgium on the Eve of the International Exhibition,** *World Today*, New Series, XIV (April 1958), 144–52.

7670 Wilk, Kurt. **International Organization and the International Chamber of Commerce,** *Political Science Quarterly*, LV (June 1940), 231–48.

7671 Zapf, Lacey C. **The International Chamber of Commerce,** *Current History*, XVIII (September 1923), 1025–27.

4. INTELLECTUAL ORGANIZATIONS

7672 Anderson, N. and Nijkerk, K. **International Seminars: An Analysis and Evaluation,** *Administrative Science Quarterly*, III (September 1958), 229–50.

Part F. — Nongovernmental Organizations

7673 Bradley, Phillips. **Private International Organizations and International Cooperation: The Institute of Pacific Relations,** *Social Forces,* XVII (March 1939), 417—23.

7674 Coudert, Frederic R. **The Inter-American Bar Association,** *International Conciliation,* CCCLXXXVI (February 1943), 130—32.

7675 Egger, Rowland. **The Brussels Public Administration Center,** *Public Management,* XIX (September 1937), 266—69.

7676 Lesoir, Edmond. **The International Institute of Administrative Sciences,** *National Municipal Review,* XXV (September 1936), 487—89.

7677 Murra, Kathrine O. (comp.). **International Scientific Organizations: A Guide to Their Library, Documentation, and Information Services.** Washington, Library of Cngress, 1962. xi + 794 p.

7678 Wright, Quincy. **The International Political Science Association,** *American Political Science Review,* XLIII (December 1949), 1252—55.

5. RELIGIOUS ORGANIZATIONS

7679 Beckelman, M. W.; Jordan, Charles H.; Kahn, Avren; Katzki, Herbert; Solver, Henry; Stein, Herman D. **The American Jewish Joint Distribution Committee As Related to the Experience of Private Cooperation in the Areas of International Cooperation,** *Foundations of World Organization,* Lyman Bryson, Louis Finkelstein, and R. W. MacIver (eds.). New York, Harper, 1950, pp. 153—70.

7680 Best, Ethelwyn and Pike, Bernard. **International Voluntary Service for Peace, 1920—1946.** London, Allen and Unwin, 1948. viii + 155 p.

7681 Bingle, E. J. **The World Council of Churches,** *World Affairs,* New Series, III (January 1949), 87—96.

7682 Gurian, W. and Fitzsimons, M. A. (eds.). **The Catholic Church in World Affairs.** Notre Dame, Notre Dame University Press, 1954. ix + 420 p.

7683 Knapp, Forrest L. **Contributions of the Christian Movement to Foundations of World Organization,** *Foundations of World Organization,* Lyman Bryson, Louis Finkelstein, and R. W. MacIver (eds.). New York, Harper, 1950, pp. 95—102.

7684 Macfarland, Charles S. **International Christian Movements.** New York, Revill, 1924. 223 p.

7685 Parsons, Edward L. **The World Conference on Faith and Order,** *Institute of World Affairs Proceedings,* II (1927), 182—93.

7686 Rice, A. V. **A History of the World Women's Christian Association.** New York, Women's Press, 1947. 299 p.

7687 Vail, James G. **Observations from American Friends Service Committee Experience in Transnational Activity and Organization,** *Foundations of World Organization,* Lyman Bryson, Louis Finkelstein, and R. W. MacIver (eds.). New York, Harper, 1950, pp. 141—52.

Comment by Akhilananda.

7688 Van Kirk, Walter W. **Religion and World Order,** *Annals of the American Academy of Political and Social Science,* CCLXIV (July 1949), 106—14.

6. RED CROSS

7689 Barton, Clara H. **A Story of the Red Cross: Glimpses of Field Work.** New York, Appleton, 1929. viii + 199 p.

7690 Boardman, Mabel T. **Under the Red Cross Flag at Home and Abroad.** Foreword by Woodrow Wilson. Philadelphia, Lippincott, 1915. 341 p.

Part F. — Nongovernmental Organizations

7691 Borel, Eugene. **L'Organisation Internationale de la Croix-Rouge,** *Recueil des Cours* I (1923), 573–607.

7692 Bossy, Sanda. **The International Red Cross,** *International Journal,* VII (Summer, 1952), 204–12.

7693 Breycha-Vauthier, A. C. and Potulicki, M. **The Order of St. John in International Law: A Forerunner of the Red Cross,** *American Journal of International Law,* XLVIII (October 1954), 554–64.

7694 Dulles, Foster R. **The American Red Cross: A History.** New York, Harper, 1950. ix + 554 p.

7695 Hamburger, Kaete. **The Red Cross in the Nineteenth Century,** *Social Forces,* XXI (October 1942), 22–27.

7696 Huber, Max. **The Principles of the Red Cross,** *Foreign Affairs,* XXVI (July 1948), 723–27.

7697 Joyce, James Avery. **Red Cross International and the Strategy of Peace.** London, Hodder and Stoughton, 1959. 270 p.

7698 Pictet, Jean-S. **La Croix-Rouge et les conventions de Genève,** *Recueil des Cours,* LXXVI (1950), 5–119.

7699 Strong, Richard P. **Public Health, the League, and the Red Cross,** *The League of Nations Starts,* Raymond B. Fosdick, George Rublee, J. T. Shotwell, Léon Bourgeois, André Weiss, Lt.-Col. Requin, W. Ormsby-Gore, el Vizconde de Eza, H. B. Butler, Richard P. Strong, J. A. Salter, A. Claveille, Henri La Fontaine, Paul Otlet. London, Macmillan, 1920, pp. 155–69.

7. TRADE UNIONS

7700 Beever, R. Colin. **European Unity and the Trade Union Movement.** Leyden, Sythoff, 1960. 303 p.

7701 Brown, J. W. **The International Trade Union Movement,** *International Affairs,* VII (January 1928), 29—35.

Comments by Pugh, Shaw, Leveson-Gower, Power, Wood, Green, Deverell, O'Connor, Vaughn-Williams.

7702 Carr, E. H. **Two Currents in World Labor,** *Foreign Affairs,* XXV (October 1946), 72—81.

Concerning the Communist World Federation of Trade Unions.

7703 Deakin, Arthur. **The International Trade Union Movement,** *International Affairs,* XXVI (April 1950), 167—71.

7704 Dubinsky, David. **World Labor's New Weapon,** *Foreign Affairs,* XVIII (April 1950), 451—62.

7705 F., R. **The International Confederation of Free Trade Unions,** *World Today,* New Series, IX (January 1953), 38—45.

7706 — —. **The World Federation of Trade Unions and Its Trade Departments,** *World Today,* New Series, VIII (August 1952), 342—52.

7707 Lorwin, Lewis L. **The Structure of International Labor Activities,** *Annals of the American Academy of Political and Social Science,* CCCX (March 1957), 1—11.

ICFTU and WFTU.

7708 Millard, C. H. **Free Trade Unions in the Developing Democracies,** *International Journal,* XIII (Autumn, 1958), 251—57.

7709 Reiser, Pedro. **L'Organisation Regional Interamericaine des Travailleurs (O. R. I. T.) de la Confédération Internationale des Syndicats Libres (C. I. S. L.) 1951—1961.** Geneva, Droz, 1962. 268 p.

7710 Snow, Sinclair. **The Pan-American Federation of Labor.** Durham, Duke University Press, 1964. vii + 159 p.

7711 Starr, Mark. **The Basis of World Organization and Labor's Contribution to International Understanding,** *Foundations of World Organization,* Lyman Bryson, Louis Finkelstein, Harold D. Lasswell, and R. W. MacIver (eds.). New York, Harper, 1950, pp. 127—39.

Comment by Salomon.

7712 Steinbach, Arnold L. **Regional Organizations of International Labor,** *Annals of the American Academy of Political and Social Science,* CCCX (March 1957), 12—20.

7713 Sturmthal, Adolf F. **Foundations for World Organization: The Experience of International Working Class Organizations,** *Foundations of World Organization,* Lyman Bryson, Louis Finkelstein, Harold D. Lasswell, and R. M. MacIver (eds.). New York, Harper, 1950, pp. 119—25.

Comments by A. Salomon, M. Starr.

7714 ——. **International Labor Problems,** *World Politics,* VIII (April 1956), 441—53.

7715 ——. **Russia and World Labor,** *Current History,* New Series, VIII (May 1945), 385—90.

7716 Toth, Charles W. **The Pan American Federation of Labor: Its Political Nature,** *Western Political Quarterly,* XVIII (September 1965), 615—20.

8. OTHER NONGOVERNMENTAL ORGANIZATIONS

See also E 10.2.

7717 Kieran, John and Daley, Arthur. **The Story of the Olympic Games: 776 B. C. to 1964.** Rev. ed. Philadelphia, Lippincott, 1964. 448 p.

7718 Marcy, Carl, in collaboration with Hansen, Morella. **A Note on American Participation in Interparliamentary Meetings,** *International Organization,* XIII (Summer, 1959), 431–38.

7719 Morán, Carol M. **Intermunicipal Cooperation in the Americas,** *Public Management,* XXV (December 1943), 354–56.

7720 Spry, D. C. **One Scouting World,** *International Journal,* III (Spring, 1948), 156–59.

7721 Vinck, Emile. **The International Union of Local Authorities,** *National Municipal Review,* XXV (September 1936), 483–86.

Part G.
PROPOSALS FOR WORLD GOVERNMENT

Part G. — *Proposals for World Government*

One of the ideological biases shared by a large number of students of international organization has been their hope for the establishment of world government. The means for attainment of a level of political rule superordinate to that of the nation state has been the subject of much debate. Some experts believe regional institutions will form the appropriate building blocks; others favor a confederation or federation of states based on the model of the American constitution; a third school advocates the "functional approach" through gradual growth in scope of organizations performing nonpolitical functions.

See also D 4.2.

1. GENERAL DISCUSSIONS

7722 Atwater, Elton; Butz, William; Forster, Kent; and Riemer, Neal. **World Affairs: Problems and Prospects.** New York, Appleton-Century-Crofts, 1958.

Chapter XIV.

7723 Baldwin, Roger N. **What Road to World Government?** *Annals of the American Academy of Political and Social Science*, CCLXIV (July 1949), 14–19.

7724 Barnard, Chester I. **On Planning for World Government,** *Approaches to World Peace*, Lyman Bryson, Louis Finkelstein and Robert W. MacIver (eds.). New York, Harper, 1944. pp. 825–58.

7725 Benoit, Emile. **An American Foreign Policy for Survival,** *Ethics*, LXI (July 1946), 280–90.

7726 Bernstein, George A. **World Government: Progress Report,** *Nation*, CLXVI (June 5, 1948), 628–30; (June 12, 1948), 660–62.

7727 Bogardus, Emory S. **Toward a World Community.** Los Angeles, University of Southern California Press, 1964. iv + 101 p.

7728 Borgese, Guiseppe A. **Foundations of the World Republic.** Chicago, University of Chicago, 1953. xi + 328 p.

7729 Bowen, I. **World Government: A Threat to the Constitution,** *American Bar Association Journal*, XLI (February 1955), 146—49 f.

7730 Bull, Hedley. **World Opinion and International Organisation,** *International Relations*, I (April 1958), 428—39.

7731 Burns, Edward M. N. **The Movement for World Government,** *Social Science*, XXIII (January 1948), 5—13.

7732 Carr, Edward Hallett. **The Moral Foundations for World Order,** *Foundations for World Order*, University of Denver, Social Science Foundation (ed.). Denver, University of Denver Press, 1949, pp. 55—76.

7733 Chamberlin, William Henry. **End of a Fantasy,** *The United Nations: The Continuing Debate*, Charles A. McClelland (ed.). San Francisco, Chandler, 1960, pp. 45—48.

Reprinted from *Wall Street Journal*, July 8, 1957.

7734 Chevalier, Stuart. **A World Community or a World State?** *Vital Speeches*, XIII (March 1, 1947), 309—18.

7735 Claude, Inis L., Jr. **Swords Into Plowshares.** 3d ed. New York, Random House, 1964.

Chapter VI.

7736 Committee to Frame a World Constitution. **Preliminary Draft of a World Constitution.** Chicago, University of Chicago Press, 1948. 91 p.

By Hutchins, Borgese, Adler, Barr, Guérard, Innis, Kahler, Katz, McIlwain, Redfield, Tugwell.

7737 Corbett, Percy E. **Congress and Proposals for International Government,** *International Organization*, IV (August 1950), 383—99.

Part G. — Proposals for World Government

7738 Cornell, Julien. **New World Primer.** New York, New Directions, 1947. 174 p.

7739 Doman, Nicholas. **The Coming Age of World Control.** New York, Harper, 1942. 301 p.

7740 Eagleton, Clyde. **World Government Discussion in the United States,** *World Affairs,* XII (April 1946), 251—58.

7741 Eichelberger, Clark M. **World Government Via the United Nations,** *Annals of the American Academy of Political and Social Science,* CCLXIV (July 1949), 20—25.

7742 Etzioni, Amitai. **The Hard Way to Peace: A New Strategy.** New York, Collier, 1962. 285 p.

7743 Ewing, Alfred C. **The Individual, the State, and World Government.** New York, Macmillan, 1947. 322 p.

7744 Falk, Richard A. and Mendlovitz, Saul H. **Towards a Warless World: One Legal Formula to Achieve Transition,** *Yale Law Journal,* LXXIII (January 1964), 399—424.

7745 Fawcett, Charles Bungay. **The Bases of a World Commonwealth.** London, Watts, 1941. 167 p.

7746 Fox, Byron L. **International Cultural Relations,** *American Sociological Review,* XV (August 1950), 489—95.

7747 Goodman, Elliot R. **Soviet Design for a World State.** Foreword by Philip E. Mosely. New York, Columbia University Press, 1960. 512 p.

7748 — —. **The Soviet Union and World Government,** *Journal of Politics,* XIV (May 1953), 231—53.

Part G. — Proposals for World Government

7749 Hill, Norman L. **International Organization.** New York, Harper, 1952.
Chapter XVIII.

7750 Hocking, William E. **Problems of World Order in the Light of Recent Philosophical Discussions,** *American Political Science Review,* XLVI (December 1952), 1117–29.

7751 Houghton, Neal D. **The Case for World Government As an Outgrowth of the United Nations,** *Western Political Quarterly,* XVIII (September 1965), supplement, 40–41.

7752 Hutchins, Robert Maynard. **The Constitutional Foundations for World Order,** *Foundations for World Order,* University of Denver, Social Science Foundation (ed.). Denver, University of Denver Press, 1949, pp. 97–113.

7753 Jessup, Philip C. **The International Problem of Governing Mankind.** Claremont, Calif., Claremont College Press, 1947. 63 p.

7754 Johnsen, Julia E. (ed.). **United Nations or World Government?** New York, Wilson, 1947. 285 p.
A collection of readings with a comprehensive bibliography.

7755 Keys, Donald F. **The American Peace Movement,** *The Nature of Human Conflict,* Elton B. McNeil (ed.). Englewood Cliffs, Prentice-Hall, 1965, pp. 295–306.

7756 Knoles, Tully C. **The Three Internationalisms,** *Institute of World Affairs Proceedings,* IV (December 1928), 173–78.

7757 Kohn, Hans. **One World?** *International Journal,* II (Autumn 1947), 308–15.

7758 — —. **World Order in Historical Perspective.** Cambridge, Harvard University Press, 1942. 352 p.

Part G. — Proposals for World Government

7759 Kornhauser, Samuel. **World Government Under Law,** *American Bar Association Journal,* XXXIII (June 1947), 563—66.

7760 La Farge, John. **Perspective for World Government,** *America,* LXXIX (May 8, 1948), 105—7.

7761 Lansing, Robert. **Notes on World Sovereignty,** *American Journal of International Law,* XV (January 1921), 13—27.

7762 Levontin, Avigdor Victor. **The Myth of International Security: A Juridical and Critical Analysis.** Jerusalem, Magnes, 1957. 346 p.

7763 Lilienthal, Alfred M. **Which Way to World Government?** New York, Foreign Policy Association, 1950. 62 p.

7764 McClintock, Robert Mills. **The United Nations or World Government,** *Annals of the American Academy of Political and Social Science,* CCLXIV (July 1949), 26—30.

7765 McDougal, Myres and Florentino, Feliciano P. **Law and Minimum World Public Order: The Legal Regulation and International Coercion.** New Haven, Yale University Press, 1961. xxvi + 872 p.

7766 Mackay, Ronald William Gordon. **You Can't Turn the Clock Back.** Chicago, Ziff-Davis, 1948. 367 p.
Argument for a federation of socialist regional states.

7767 Maclaurin, John (pseud.). **The United Nations and Power Politics.** New York, Harper, 1951.
Chapter XII.

7768 Madariaga, Salvador de. **The World's Design.** London, Allen and Unwin, 1938. xx + 291 p.

Part G. — *Proposals for World Government*

7769 Meyer, Cord, Jr. **A Plea for World Government,** *Annals of the American Academy of Political and Social Science,* CCLXIV (July 1949), 6–13.

7770 Morgenthau, Hans J. **Politics Among Nations.** 3d ed. New York, Knopf, 1960.
Chapter XXIX.

7771 Nabuco, Mauricio. **World Government As a Goal,** *Annals of the American Academy of Political and Social Science,* CCLXIV (July 1949), 1–5.

7772 Nash, Philip Curtis. **An Adventure in World Order.** Boston, Beacon, 1944. 139 p.

7773 Nash, Vernon. **The World Must Be Governed.** New York, Harper, 1949. xvi + 206 p.

7774 Nathan, Otto and Heinz, Norden (eds.). **Einstein on Peace.** New York, Simon and Schuster, 1960.
Chapter XIII.

7775 Parmelee, Maurice. **Geo-Economic Regionalism and World Federation.** New York, Exposition Press, 1949. 137 p.

7776 Peaslee, Amos Jenkins. **United Nations Government.** New York, Putnam, 1945. 183 p.

7777 Potter, Pitman B. **The Concept of "International Government,"** *American Political Science Review,* XXV (August 1931), 713–17.

7778 Rhyne, C. S. **World Peace Through Law,** *American Bar Association Journal,* XLIV (October 1958), 937–40; 997–1001.

Part G. — Proposals for World Government

7779 Riddell, Walter A. **World Security by Conference.** Toronto, Ryerson, 1947.

Part II — Chapter V.

7780 Rothwell, Easton. **The United Nations or World Government,** *Institute of World Affairs Proceedings,* XXIV (1948), 146—60.

7781 Royal Institute of International Affairs (ed.). **World Order Papers.** London, Royal Institute of International Affairs, 1940. 176 p.

7782 Schuman, Frederick L. **The Commonwealth of Man: An Inquiry into Power Politics and World Government.** New York, Knopf, 1952. 494 p.

7783 Schwarzenberger, Georg. **Power Politics.** 3d ed. London, Stevens, 1964.

Chapter IV deals with the multinational state.

7784 Sen, B. R. **An Asian Views World Government,** *Annals of the American Academy of Political and Social Science,* CCLXIV (July 1949), 39—45.

7785 Sharp, Walter and Kirk, Grayson. **Contemporary International Politics.** New York, Farrar and Rinehart, 1941.

Chapter XXXII.

7786 Slick, Tom. **Permanent Peace: A Check and Balance Plan.** New York, Prentice-Hall, 1958. 181 p.

7787 Stocks, John L. **Patriotism and the Super-State.** London, Swarthmore, 1920. 105 p.

7788 Thurber, Clarence Howe. **The United Nations As the Nucleus of World Organization,** *Global Politics,* Russell H. Fitzgibbon (ed.). Berkeley, University of California Press, 1944, pp. 31—42.

Part G. — Proposals for World Government

7789 Toynbee, Arnold J. **Civilisation on Trial.** London, Oxford University Press, 1948.

Chapter V.

7790 — —. **The Unification of the World and the Change in Historical Perspective,** *History,* XXXIII (February, June 1948), 1—28.

7791 University of Denver, Social Science Foundation (ed.). **Foundations for World Order.** Denver, University of Denver Press, 1949. 174 p.

7792 Voeglin, Eric. **World Empire and the Unity of Mankind,** *International Affairs,* XXXVIII (April 1962), 170—88.

7793 Warburg, James P. **How to Achieve One World,** *Federal World Government,* Julia E. Johnsen (ed.). New York, Wilson, 1948, pp. 102—8.

7794 Watkins, James T., IV. **Variations upon a Theme,** *Institute of World Affairs Proceedings,* XXXVI (1960), 185—92.

7795 Wells, H. G. **An Apology for a World Utopia,** *The Evolution of World-Peace,* Francis S. Marvin (ed.). London, Oxford University Press, 1921, pp. 159—78.

7796 Willkie, Wendell L. **One World.** New York, Simon and Schuster, 1943. ix + 206 p.

7797 Wilkin, Robert N. **World Order: Law and Justice or Power and Force?** *American Bar Association Journal,* XXXIII (January 1947), 18—21.

7798 Williamson, Hugh. **World Government.** London, Chancery, 1963. 173 p.

Part G. — *Proposals for World Government*

7799 Wirth, Louis. **World Community, World Society, and World Government: An Attempt at a Clarification of Terms,** *The World Community,* Quincy Wright (ed.). Chicago, University of Chicago Press, 1948, pp. 9—20.

Comments by Young, Guérard, Angell, Mead, Wright, Benedict, Warner, Parsons, Bloch, Marschak, McKeon, Schultz, Herring, Morris, Morgenthau, Polanyi.

7800 Woodward, Ernest Llewellyn. **The Historical and Political Foundations for World Order,** *Foundations for World Order,* University of Denver, Social Science Foundation (ed.). Denver, University of Denver Press, 1949, pp. 11—34.

7801 Wright, Quincy. **Empires and World Governments Before 1918,** *Current History,* New Series, XXXIX (August 1960), 65—74.

2. WORLD FEDERALISM

7802 Adam, George B. **The British Empire and a League of Peace, Together with an Analysis of Federal Government, Its Function and Its Method.** New York, Putnam, 1919. iii + 115 p.

7803 Alsberg, Henry Garfield. **Let's Talk About the Peace.** New York, Hastings, 1945. 324 p.

7804 American Council on Public Affairs (ed.). **Regionalism and World Federation.** Washington, American Council on Public Affairs, 1944. 162 p.

7805 Andrews, Paul Shipman. **Blueprint for a Peaceful World,** *Current History,* New Series, XXXIX (August 1960), 65—74.

7806 Benson, George C. S. **Unexplored Problems of Federalism,** *World Affairs,* V (December 1939), 216—29.

Part G. — Proposals for World Government

7807 Benson, Oliver. **Machinery of Federal Government,** *Federation*, Howard O. Eaton (ed.). Norman, University of Oklahoma Press, 1944, 80—92.

7808 Bergman, G. Merle. **A World Legislature,** *Federation*, Howard O. Eaton (ed.). Norman, University of Oklahoma Press, 1944, 133—45.

7809 Beveridge, William. **Peace by Federation?** *World Order Papers*, Royal Institute of International Affairs (ed.). London, Royal Institute of International Affairs, 1940, pp. 65—96.

Followed by comments of J. A. Spender.

7810 Birdwood, Lord. **Reflections on World Government,** *Twentieth Century*, CLVI (October 1953), 269—74.

Outlines history of Federal World Government Movement and associations working on parallel lines up to Copenhagen Conference of 1953.

7811 Bonn, M. J. **Union Now?** *World Affairs*, New Series, II (July 1948), 243—52.

7812 Bourgeois, Nicolas. **Les théories du droit international chez Proudhon: Le fédéralisme et la paix.** Paris, Rivière, 1927. 138 p.

7813 Bowie, Robert R. and Friedrich, Carl J. (eds.). **Studies in Federalism.** Boston, Little, Brown, 1954. xlii + 887 p.

7814 Butler, Nicholas M. **Toward a Federal World,** *International Federation of Democracies (Proposed)*, Julia E. Johnsen (ed.). New York, Wilson, 1941, pp. 36—44.

7815 Center for the Study of Democratic Institutions. **A Constitution for the World.** Santa Barbara, Center for the Study of Democratic Institutions, 1965. 111 p.

7816 Chaning-Pearce, M. (ed.). **Federal Union.** London, Cape, 1940. 336 p.

Part G. — *Proposals for World Government*

7817 — —. **Survey,** and **Conclusion,** *Federal Union*, M. Chaning-Pearce (ed.). London, Cape, 1940. pp. 301–27.

7818 Charteris, A. H. **An Australian Comment on Streit's Union,** *World Affairs*, V (April 1940), 314–21.

7819 Clark, Grenville and Sohn, Louis B. **World Peace Through World Law.** 2d ed. Cambridge, Harvard University Press, 1964. liv + 387 p.

7820 Commission to Study the Organization of Peace. **Federalism,** *Reconstituting the League of Nations*, Julia E. Johnsen (ed.). New York, Wilson, 1943, pp. 251–53.

From *Toward Greater Freedom: Problems of War and Peace.*

7821 — —. **Toward Greater Freedom: Problems of War and Peace.** New York, Commission to Study the Organization of Peace, 1942. 80 p.

7822 Culbertson, Ely. **Summary of the World Federation Plan, an Outline of a Practical and Detailed Plan for World Settlement.** Garden City, Garden City Publishing Company, 1943. 64 p.

7823 Curtis, Lionel. **Faith and Works.** New York, Oxford University Press, 1943. 120 p.

Argument for a federation of democracies.

7824 Dangerfield, Royden J. **Plans of Federation,** *Federation*, Howard O. Eaton (ed.). Norman, University of Oklahoma Press, 1944, 46–57.

7825 Dennett, Raymond. **The International Organization of the Free World,** *Academy of Political Science Proceedings*, XXIV (January 1951), 181–90.

7826 Dexter, Lewis A. **Implications of Supranational Federation,** *American Sociological Review*, VII (June 1942), 400–6.

Part G. — Proposals for World Government

7827 Eagleton, Clyde. **The League of Nations and Federal Union,** *World Affairs,* V (September 1939), 119–30.

7828 Eaton, Howard O. **The Economics of Federation: Money and Credit,** *Federation,* Howard O. Eaton (ed.). Norman, University of Oklahoma Press, 1944, 93–103.

7829 — —. (ed.). **Federation: The Coming Structure of World Government.** Norman, University of Oklahoma Press, 1944. 234 p.

7830 Ewing, Cortez A. M. **The Federal Instrument,** *Federation,* Howard O. Eaton (ed.). Norman, University of Oklahoma Press, 1944. 58–68.

7831 Federal Union. **Freedom and Union.** Washington, monthly, 1946–.

7832 Freedom and Union. **The New Federalist by Publius II.** Foreword by Clarence Streit; introduction by John Foster Dulles. New York, Harper, 1950. xvii + 109 p.

Authors are Justice Owen J. Roberts, John F. Schmidt, and Clarence K. Streit.

7833 Freeman, Harrop A. and Paullin, Theodore. **Coercion of States: The Federal Unions.** Philadelphia, Pacifist Research Bureau, 1943. 68 p.

7834 Fuchs, Laurence H. **The World Federation Resolution: A Case Study in Congressional Decision-Making,** *Midwest Journal of Political Science,* I (August 1957), 151–62.

7835 Garnett, J. C. Maxwell. **Federation and the League of Nations,** *Federal Union,* M. Chaning-Pearce (ed.). London, Cape, 1940, pp. 229–38.

7836 Gill, Charles A. **World Republic.** Philadelphia, Dorrance, 1943. 119 p.

7837 Graham, Malbone W. **The Problem of World Federation,** *Global Politics,* Russell H. Fitzgibbon (ed.). Berkeley, University of California Press, 1944, pp. 17–30.

Part G. — Proposals for World Government

7838 Greaves, Harold R. G. **Federal Union in Practice.** London, Allen and Unwin, 1940. 135 p.

7839 Greene, Roger S. **Asia and Africa and the Union of the Free,** *World Affairs*, V (December 1939), 237—43.

7840 Halecki, Oscar. **Federalism As an Answer,** *Annals of the American Academy of Political and Social Science*, CCLVIII (July 1948), 66—69.

7841 Harris, Errol E. **The Survival of Political Man.** Johannesburg, Witwatersrand University Press, 1950. 225 p.

7842 Hayek, F. A. von. **Economic Conditions of Inter-State Federalism,** *World Affairs*, V (September 1939), 131—49.

7843 Hennessy, Bernard. **A Case Study of Intra-Pressure Group Politics: The United World Federalists,** *Journal of Politics*, XVI (February 1954), 76—95.

7844 Hill, Norman L. **The National State and Federation,** *Federation*, Howard O. Eaton (ed.). Norman, University of Oklahoma Press, 1944, pp. 124—32.

7845 Hutchins, Robert Maynard. **The Constitutional Foundations for World Order,** *Federal World Government*, Julia E. Johnsen (ed.). New York, Wilson, 1948, pp. 108—19.

7846 Jacks, L. P. **Federalism and Peace Policy,** *Federal Union*, M. Chaning-Pearce (ed.). London, Cape, 1940, pp. 281—300.

7847 Johnsen, Julia E. (comp.). **Federal World Government.** New York, Wilson, 1948. 280 p.
Contains a comprehensive bibliography.

Part G. — *Proposals for World Government*

7848 — —. **International Federation of Democracies (Proposed).** New York, Wilson, 1941. 263 p.

7849 Keeton, George W. **Federalism and World Order,** *World Affairs,* V (June 1939), 6–10.

7850 Lent, Ernest S. **The Development of United World Federalist Thought and Policy,** *International Organization,* IX (November 1955), 486–501.

7851 Lippmann, Walter. **On the Unity of Mankind,** *Rotarian,* LXXI (October 1947), 9–12.

7852 Maddox, William P. **The Political Basis of Federation,** *American Political Science Review,* XXXV (December 1941), 1120–27.

7853 Marriott, John Arthur Ransom. **Federalism and the Problem of the Small State.** New York, Norton, 1944. 125 p.

7854 Millard, Everett L. **Freedom in a Federal World: How We Can Learn to Live in Peace and Liberty by Means of World Law.** Dobbs Ferry, Oceana, 1959. 224 p.

7855 Mousley, Edward. **The Meaning of Federalism,** *Federal Union,* M. Chaning-Pearce (ed.). London, Cape, 1940, pp. 21–38.

7856 Muller, Edwin and Urey, Harold C. **Proposals for World Government,** *Survival or Suicide,* Harry H. Moore (ed.). New York, Harper, 1948, pp. 115–26.

7857 Muret, Charlotte. **The Swiss Pattern for a Federated Europe,** *Nationalism and Internationalism,* Edward Mead Earle (ed.). New York, Columbia University Press, 1950, pp. 261–84.

Part G. — Proposals for World Government

7858 Murray, Gilbert. **Federation and the League,** *World Order Papers,* Royal Institute of International Affairs (ed.). London, Royal Institute of International Affairs, 1940, pp. 41–64.

Followed by comments of J. A. Spender.

7859 Newfang, Oscar. **The Road to World Peace: A Federation of Nations.** New York, Putnam, 1924. 372 p.

7860 — —. **The United States of the World: A Comparison Between the League of Nations and the United States of America.** New York, Putnam, 1930. 284 p.

7861 — —. **World Federation,** P. Gault (tr.). New York, Barnes and Noble, 1939.

Chapters XI, XIII.

7862 Nordskog, John Eric. **The Functions of Federalism in National and World Organization,** *World Affairs Quarterly,* XIX (July 1948), 194–207.

7863 Osborne, Henry. **World Federal Government,** *Pakistan Horizon,* II (September 1949), 129–42.

7864 — —. **World Federal Government As a Means of Maintaining Peace,** *Paths to Peace,* Victor H. Wallace (ed.). Melbourne, Melbourne University Press, 1957, pp. 359–81.

7865 Pei, Mario Andrew. **The American Road to Peace: A Constitution for the World.** New York, Vanni, 1945. 168 p.

7866 Potter, Pitman B. **Sanctions Against a Recalcitrant State,** *Federation,* Howard O. Eaton (ed.). Norman, University of Oklahoma Press, 1944, 104–14.

Part G. — Proposals for World Government

7867 — —. **This World of Nations.** New York, Macmillan, 1929.

Chapter XIII.

7868 Sandrasegara, M. **"World Peace Through World Law" (A Comment),** *Indian Year Book of International Affairs,* IX—X (1960—61), 143—48.

7869 Scelle, George. **"Union" Versus "League,"** *World Affairs,* V (December 1939), 204—15.

7870 Schuman, Frederick L. **International Anarchy,** *Current History,* New Series, VI (April 1944), 289—95.

7871 — —. **Toward the World State,** *United Nations or World Government?* Julia E. Johnsen (ed.). New York, Wilson, 1947, pp. 182—87.

7872 Schwarzenberger, Georg. **Power Politics.** 3d ed. London, Stevens, 1964.

Chapter XXXVI.

7873 Scott, James Brown (ed.). **James Madison's Notes of Debates in the Federal Convention of 1787 and Their Relation to a More Perfect Society of Nations.** New York, Oxford University Press, 1918. 149 p.

7874 Steed, H. Wickham. **Federalism and War Policy,** *Federal Union,* M. Chaning-Pearce (ed.). London, Cape, 1940, pp. 263—80.

7875 Steinbecker, Paul G. **The Streit and Catlin Proposals,** *Federation,* Howard O. Eaton (ed.). Norman, University of Oklahoma Press, 1944. 25—45.

7876 Stowe, Leland. **Target: You.** New York, Knopf, 1949. 288 p.

Argues for United World Federalists.

Part G. — Proposals for World Government

7877 Streit, Clarence K. **Atlantic Union — Freedom's Answer to Malenkov,** *Annals of the American Academy of Political and Social Science,* CCLXXXVIII (July 1953), 2–12.

7878 — —. **The Atlantic Union Plan and the Americas,** *Annals of the American Academy of Political and Social Science,* CCIV (July 1939), 93–101.

7879 — —. **Should the United States Unite with the British Empire Now? With Germany, Italy and Japan Allied Against Us, It Is Time to Decide Whether to Join Britain Before It Is Too Late,** *Current History,* LII (October 1940), 14–17.

7880 — —. **Two Ways to Unite Atlantica — The Federal and the Functional,** *Freedom and Union,* XVIII (July-August 1963), 20–23.

7881 — —. **Union Now: A Proposal for a Federal Union of Democracies of the North Atlantic.** New York, Harper, 1939. 315 p.

This book was first distributed in a private edition of 300 copies in September 1938; following Hitler's conquest of Continental Europe it was reissued in 1941 as *Union Now With Britain.* After American entry into the war and the brightening of the prospect for liberating Continental Europe, subsequent editions, starting in 1943, reverted to the original proposals in *Union Now.*

7882 — —. **United States Federal Union As a Model for World Organization,** *World Peace Plans,* Julia E. Johnsen (ed.). New York, Wilson, 1943, pp. 149–51.

Reprinted from *Congresional Record,* May 7, 1943.

7883 — —. **World Organization Through Democracy,** *Problems of Peace,* Series 10 (1935), 216–52.

7884 Van Jamel, Joost A. **Federating As a Motive Power Towards Peace,** *Transactions* (Grotius Society), XXIII (1937), 1–23.

7885 Vinacke, Harold M. **International Organization.** New York, Crofts, 1934.

Chapter IV.

Part G. — *Proposals for World Government*

7886 Warburg, James P. **Federal Principles and Common Concept of Justice,** *International Federation of Democracies (Proposed)*, Julia E. Johnsen (ed.). New York, Wilson, 1941, pp. 53—58.

Reprinted from the *New York Times*, February 2, 1941.

7887 Wheare, K. C. **Federal Government.** 3d ed. New York, Oxford University Press, 1953. 278 p.

7888 White, Elwyn Brooks. **The Wild Flag: Editorials from the New Yorker on Federal World Government and Other Matters.** Boston, Houghton, Mifflin, 1946. 187 p.

7889 Whitelaw, W. Menzies. **The Prospect for a Union of Democracies,** *Annals of the American Academy of Political and Social Science*, CCXVIII (November 1941), 132—40.

7890 Williams, John Fischer. **World Order: An Attempt at an Outline,** *World Order Papers*, Royal Institute of International Affairs (ed.). London, Royal Institute of International Affairs, 1940, pp. 15—40.

7891 Wilson, Duncan. **The History of Federalism,** *Federal Union*, M. Chaning-Pearce (ed.). London, Cape, 1940, pp. 83—91.

7892 Wilson, Duncan and Wilson, Elizabeth. **Federation and World Order.** Preface by C. E. M. Joad. London, 1939 xiv + 184 p.

7893 Wofford, Harris, Jr. **It's Up to Us.** New York, Harcourt, 1946. 146 p.

7894 **World Federalist.** Amsterdam, World Association of World Federalists, bimonthly, 1954—.

7895 **World Federalist.** Hague, World Association of World Federalists, quarterly, 1954—.

7896 Wynner, Edith. **World Federal Government.** Afton, N. Y., Federal Press, 1954. 84 p.

3. FUNCTIONALISM

7897 Claude, Inis L., Jr. **Swords Into Plowshares.** 3d ed. New York, Random House, 1964.

Chapter XVII.

7898 Freeman, Harrop A. and Paullin, Theodore. **Road to Peace: A Study in Functional International Organization.** Philadelphia, Pacifist Research Bureau, 1947. 62 p.

7899 Haas, Ernst B. **Beyond the Nation-State: Functionalism and International Organization.** Stanford, Stanford University Press, 1964. 595 p.

The International Labor Organization as a case study of the functional approach to international organization.

7900 Heymann, Hans. **Plan for a Permanent Peace.** New York, Harper, 1941. 315 p.

7901 Laski, Harold J. **The Theory of an International Society,** *Problems of Peace,* Series 6 (1931), 188—209.

7902 Mitrany, David A. **The Functional Approach to World Organization,** *International Affairs,* XXIV (July 1948), 350—60.

Comments by Osborne, Dangerfield, Hancock, Curtis, Young.

7903 — —. **A Working Peace System.** London, Royal Institute of International Affairs, 1944. 60 p.

7904 Morgenthau, Hans J. **Politics Among Nations.** 3d ed. New York, Knopf, 1960.

Chapter XXX.

7905 Paullin, Theodore. **A New International Order — Functional or Constitutional,** *Peace is the Victory,* Harrop A. Freeman (ed.). New York, Harper, 1944, pp. 120—37.

Part G. — *Proposals for World Government*

7906 Rappard, William E. **The Economic Foundations for World Order,** *Foundations for World Order,* University of Denver, Social Science Foundation (ed.). Denver, University of Denver Press, 1949, pp. 79—93.

7907 Streit, Clarence. **Two Ways to Unite Atlantica — The Federal and the Functional,** *Freedom and Union,* XVIII (July-August 1963), 20—23.

4. CRITICAL DISCUSSIONS

7908 Berns, Walter F. **The Case Against World Government,** *Readings in World Politics,* Robert A. Goldwin (ed.). with Ralph Lerner and Gerald Stourzh. New York, Oxford University Press, 1959, pp. 425—38.

7909 Bigman, Stanley K. **The "New Internationalism" Under Attack,** *Public Opinion Quarterly,* XIV (Summer, 1950), 235—61.

7910 Bloomfield, Lincoln P. **Arms Control and World Government,** *World Politics,* XIV (July 1962), 633—45.

7911 Borchard, Edwin. **The Impracticability of "Enforcing" Peace,** *Yale Law Journal,* LV (August 1946), 966—73.

7912 Bowman, Isaiah. **Is an International Society Possible?** *United Nations or World Government?* Julia E. Johnsen (ed.). New York, Wilson, 1947, pp. 173—78.

7913 Brecht, Arnold. **Distribution of Powers Between an International Government and the Governments of the National States,** *American Political Science Review,* XXXVII (October 1943), 862—72.

7914 ———. **Limited-Purpose Federations,** *Social Research,* X (May 1943), 135—51.

Part G. — Proposals for World Government

7915 Burns, Edward McN. **Myths of World Government,** *Free World,* XI (June 1946), 19–21.

7916 Carleton, William G. **What Our World Federalists Neglect,** *Antioch Review,* VIII (Spring, 1948), 3–16.

7917 Claude, Inis L., Jr. **Power and International Relations.** New York, Random House, 1962. viii + 310 p.

7918 — —. **Swords Into Plowshares.** 3d ed. New York, Random House, 1964.

Chapter XVIII.

7919 Cook, Thomas I. **Concerning a World Government,** *Western Political Quarterly,* I (December 1948), 449–50.

7920 — —. **Theoretical Foundations of World Government,** *Review of Politics,* XII (January 1950), 20–55.

7921 Corbett, Percy E. **World Government — In Whose Time?** *International Affairs,* XXV (October 1949), 426–30.

Comments by Catlin, Corbett, Elliot, Atholl, Usborne, Watts.

7922 Deutsch, Karl W. **Possible Effects of the Movement for World Government Today,** *United Nations or World Government?* Julia E. Johnsen (ed.). New York, Wilson, 1947, pp. 178–82.

7923 Fisher, Roger. **Internal Enforcement of International Rules,** *Disarmament: Its Politics and Economics,* Seymour Melman (ed.). Boston, American Academy of Arts and Sciences, 1962, pp. 99–120.

7924 Keith, A. B. **The Practicability of Working a Federation,** *World Affairs,* VI (July 1940), 3–24.

7925 Mackay, R. J. **Federalism and Sociology,** *Federal Union,* M. Chaning-Pearce (ed.). London, Cape, 1940, pp. 139–54.

Part G. — *Proposals for World Government*

7926 Mangone, Gerard J. **The Fallacy of World Federalism,** *Current History,* XXXIX (September 1960), 163–68.

7927 — —. **The Idea and Practice of World Government.** New York, Columbia University Press, 1951. 278 p.

7928 Murry, J. Middleton. **Pre-Conditions of Federal Union,** *Federal Union,* M. Chaning-Pearce (ed.). London, Cape, 1940, pp. 155–63.

7929 Niebuhr, Reinhold. **The Children of Light and the Children of Darkness.** New York, Scribner, 1944. xiii + 190 p.

7930 — —. **The Illusion of World Government,** *Foreign Affairs,* XXVII (April 1949), 379–88.

7931 — —. **The Illusion of World Government.** Whitestone, N. Y., Graphics, 1949. 31 p.

7932 — —. **The Myth of World Government,** *Nation,* CLXII (March 1946). 312–14.

7933 Politis, H. E. Nicolas. **La souveraineté et la police internationale,** *World Affairs,* I (October-December 1935), 215–22; (March 1936), 321–27.

7934 Reves, Emery. **The Anatomy of Peace.** New York, Harper, 1946. 293 p.

7935 Wirth, Louis. **The Bearing of Recent Social Trends upon Attainable Programs for Peace and World Organization,** *Approaches to World Peace,* Lyman Bryson, Louis Finkelstein and Robert W. MacIver (eds.). New York, Harper, 1944, pp. 110–23.

AUTHOR INDEX

Author Index

Aaronson, Michael. 3336, 4378
Abbott, Alden H. 2416
Abbott, Alice A. 872
Abbott, Grace. 1851
Abneton, Barid. 4619
Aboud, El-Mehdi Ben. 5949
Abraham, G. 2595
Abraham, Willie E. 5690
Abrams, E. W. 560
Abrams, Irwin. 879
Abrams, Mark. 541
Abt, G. 923, 1865
Academy of International Law. 46
Academy of Political Science. 5, 44
Acheson, Dean. 6266
Adam, George B. 2745, 7802
Adam, H. T. 1709, 3887, 6264, 6663, 6688, 7057, 7316, 7632
Adamkiewicz, W. 3110, 3486, 3528, 6573, 6878
Adams, J. L. 419, 492
Adams, James Truslow. 3016
Adams, T. W. 5221
Addams, Jane. 965, 1987
Adler, Felix .1042
Adler, Mortimer J. 2903, 2943, 7736
Adorno Benítez, Felix. 2667
Afifi, Mohammed. 5396
African Institute of Geneva. 5954
Agar, Herbert. 2904
Agar, William. 2905
Ago, R. 3512, 5664
Ágoston, István. 7336
Agronsky, G. 2073
Aguiar, Pinto de. 6251
Agwani, Mahomed Shafi. 5909
Ahluwalia, Kuljit. 3462, 3513
Ahmad, Mushtag. 3589, 5023, 5304, 5305, 7624
Ahmed, Begum A. 4255, 4256
Ahmed, Latheef N. 3822, 3823, 3977
Ahmed, S. Habib. 3978
Aikman, C. C. 3463
Akhelanda, S. 478, 7687

Akhund, Hameeda. 5950
Akra, Neylan. 3615, 5470
Akzin, Benjamin. 1725, 5243
Alami, Musa. 5054
al-Barghuthi, Omar Bey Salih. 2074
Alberoni, Cardinal. 681, 682, 683
Albes, Edward. 6022
Albinski, Henry S. 5210
Albonetti, Achille. 6267
Albrecht-Carrié, René. 1161, 6691
Aldous, Leslie R. 1852
Alexander (of Macedonia). 601
Alexander I (Russia). 775
Alexander, A. V. 1689
Alexander, M. 7334
Alexander, R. 6116
Alexander, Sidney S. 6486
Alexandrowicz, Charles Henry. 3792, 3949, 3958, 4134, 4151, 4174, 4209, 4231, 4429, 4501, 5024, 5577, 5578, 6426, 7337, 7633
Alfaro, Ricardo J. 2799
Alger, Chadwick F. 433, 434, 435, 436, 542, 543
Ali, A. Y. 1565, 2100, 6714
Ali, Mohammed. 7417
Ali, Syed Amjad. 3558, 3979
Alker, Hayward R., Jr. 508, 509, 510
Allais, Maurice. 6268
Allan, Yigal. 5055
Allen, Charles E. 4232
Allen, Devere. 880
Allen, H. C. 6269
Allen, J. S. 5722, 5734
Allen, James Jay. 4175, 4176, 6403, 6608
Allen, Leonard. 2951
Allen, Miss. 2311, 2333
Allen, Robert Loring. 3980, 5412
Allen, Stephen H. 924, 966, 1248
Alphand, Herve. 7163
Alsberg, Henry Garfield. 7803
Alting von Geusau, F. A. M. 6404, 6692

Altrincham, Lord, 7089
Altstedter, Norman. 5114
Alvarez, Alejandro. 1501, 5957, 5958
Alvarez del Vayo. 2668
Alwan, Mohamed. 5222
Aman, L. 1659
Amerasinghe, C. F. 3070, 3559
American Academy of Political and Social Science. 11
American Association for the United Nations. 108
American Council on Public Affairs. 5579, 7804
American Historical Association. 7
American Political Science Association. 9, 59
American Public Health Association. 4198
American Society of African Culture. 5691
American Society of International Law. 8, 10, 58, 4670
Amery, L. S. 1988, 2506, 6270, 6714
Ames, C. B. 1428, 2417
Ames, Herbert Brown. 1249, 1533, 1612, 2637
Ammende, Ewald. 1901
Anabtawi, Samir N. 511, 5157, 5244
Anand, R. P. 2316, 4671, 4735, 4753, 4754, 4757
Anderson, A. 1659
Anderson, C. P. 1224
Anderson, G. L. 4814
Anderson, K. Gosta A. 2726
Anderson, Luis, 6231
Anderson, Nels. 6385, 7672
Anderson, Totton J. 4762, 5910
Anderson, Violet. 3130
Andrassy, Georges. 1513
Andrassy, Juraj. 3395
Andrews, Fannie Fern. 1043, 1502, 2061, 2138
Andrews, John B. 1749, 5827
Andrews, Paul Shipman. 7805
Angell, J. W. 1225, 1226
Angell, Norman. 1044, 1045, 1162, 1203, 1211, 1250, 1251, 2111, 7371

Angell, Robert C. 374, 375, 376, 419, 430, 492, 7799
Anglin, Douglas G. 3793, 6196
Angus, N. C. 3824
Ankers, P. M. 1989
Anslev, Aksel A. 7078
Anstey, Vera. 7418
Antonius, George. 2062, 2075, 5839
Appadorai, A. 3017, 5306, 7625
Appleman, John Alan. 3091
Appleton, Sheldon. 512, 544, 3613, 3614, 5413, 5460
Aquinas, Thomas. 684
Arangio-Ruiz, Gaetano. 4925
Aranha, Oswaldo. 5665
Arcé, José. 3396
Archibald, Charles H. 6215
Arechaga, M. E. J. de. 3729, 4763, 4926, 6181
Argentier, Clement. 1750
Aris, R. 6271
Aristotle. 685
Armand, Louis. 6664
Armstrong, Elizabeth. 4539, 5461
Armstrong, Hamilton Fish. 1163, 1164, 3131, 3132, 3133, 5056, 5580, 6872
Armstrong, John A. 5414
Armstrong, John H. 4315
Armstrong, Willis C. 4152
Arnade, Charles W. 2683
Arne, Sigrid. 268
Arneson, R. Gordon. 4824
Arnold, Guy. 7419
Arnold-Forster, W. 1253, 2343, 2418, 2419, 2420, 2421, 2422, 2423, 2432, 2596, 3018, 3651, 4502, 4503, 6800
Aron, Raymond. 377, 437, 6272, 6873, 7164
Arthur, P. H. 1090
Asamoah, Obed. 3665
Ascher, Charles S. 3981, 4233, 4316, 4317
Ascoli, Max. 5666
Ashbee, Charles Robert. 1046
Asher, Robert E. 3888, 3889, 3934, 3982

Author Index

Ashley-Montagu, Montague F. 4318,
Ashton, E. B. 3226
Asirvathan, Eddy. 5307
Askew, H. Royston. 1680
Aspaturian, Vernon V. 5245
Aspland, W. H. Graham. 1884
Association of Research Libraries. 60
Aston, G. 2432
Astor, Lady. 856
Ataöv, Türkkaya. 5397
Atherton, Alexine L. 181, 3908, 3940, 4242, 4282, 4576, 4793, 4876, 4946, 4984, 5610
Atholl, Duchess of. 1856, 7921
Atiyah, E. 5912
Atkins, D. 1090
Atkinson, Henry A. 831
Atlantic Council of the United States. 12, 140, 6273
The Atlantic Institute. 141
Attlee, C. R. 3134
Atwater, Elton. 2685, 3135, 7722
Atyeo, Henry C. 5223, 5913, 5944
Aubert, Louis. 1667, 2764
Auden, W. H. 3210
Auer, Paul de. 1429, 1471, 2143, 2344
Aufricht, Hans. 61, 103, 1542, 3590, 4095, 6117, 6668
Augustine, Saint. 686
Austin, Dennis. 7518
Avenol, Joseph. 1254
Aydelotte, Frank. 2904
Aymard, André. 567
Azcarte y Flores, Pablo de. 1885, 1902
Azicri, Max. 6118
Aziz, M. A. 5914

Babovič, B. 4825
Babson, Roger W. 5959
Badawi, A. H. 5855
Badeau, John S. 5840
Baff, William E. 1002
Bagley, Tennent H. 4257
Baich, Emily G. 965
Bailey, Cyril. 580
Bailey, H. R. 2333

Bailey, Helen Miller. 1886
Bailey, K. H. 4651
Bailey, Kenneth. 3338
Bailey, S. H. 153, 1684, 1887
Bailey, Sydney D. 269, 3667, 3759, 3794, 3795, 3796, 4462, 4540, 4541, 4826, 4957
Bailey, Thomas A. 2817, 5960
Bain, Read. 2906
Bains, J. S. 4736, 5251
Baker, Alonzo L. 3071
Baker, P. J. 2303
Baker, Ray Stanard. 1165, 1166
Baker, Robert L. 5841
Balassa, Bela A. 378, 5581
Balch, Thomas W. 696, 1003, 1047
Baldwin, David A. 4078
Baldwin, Roger N. 4490, 7723
Baldwin, Simeon E. 777, 967, 1048, 1049
Balfour, Lord. 2506, 3092
Ball, Joseph H. 2345
Ball, M. Margaret. 154, 513, 2505, 3890, 4258, 4542, 4764, 5582, 5799, 5961, 6119, 6120, 6182, 6183, 6693, 6824, 6881
Ball, W. Macmahon. 5800
Ballantine, Joseph W. 3044
Ballinger, Ronald. 4638
Balogh, E. 4463
Bancroft, Harding F. 4765
Banfield, Jane. 5728
Bangsberg, Harry F. 7558
Baqai, I. H. 5634, 5672, 5915, 6184
Barabas, Frank. 3591
Barclay, G. St. J. 6656, 7165
Barclay, J. 2279
Bareau, Paul. 7090
Barker, A. J. 5162
Barker, Charles A. 4827
Barker, Ernest. 1050, 1406
Barker, P. J. 1503
Barkway, Michael. 4177, 7091, 7534
Barnard, Chester I. 438, 7724
Barnes, George Nicoll. 1751, 2358
Barnes, Harry E. 2729
Barnes, Leonard. 1990

Barnes, Robert. 134, 6233
Barnet, Richard J. 4828, 4829, 4858, 4863, 4879, 4882, 4893
Barnett, Sidney N. 109, 110
Baroody, Jamil M. 5842
Barr, E. Joan. 5142
Barr, Stringfellow. 7736
Barraclough, Geoffrey. 6694
Barratt, Arthur. 5962
Barrett, John A. 1261, 1485, 2279, 2828, 6023
Barrington, J. H. 6860
Barron, Bryton. 3136
Barros, James. 2719, 2720
Barrows, David P. 5963
Bartlett, Ruhl Jacob. 1051
Bartok, Béla. 1983
Barton, Clara. 911, 7689
Barton, William. 5025
Barzanti, Sergio. 6609
Basch, Antonin. 4079, 4080, 7559
Bassett, John S. 238, 778, 2160, 2528, 2547, 2765, 2818
Bastid, S. 4672
Bastillos, Gonzalo Garcia. 5968
Basu, R. K. 3825, 3983, 3984
Bates, Margaret L. 111, 4620
Bathurst, Maurice E. 4379, 7184
Batler, H. B. 1752
Batsell, Walter Russell. 2139
Baty, T. 2128, 2576
Bauer, John. 3397
Baumann, Carol Elder. 7092
Baxter, R. R. 5630
Beales, A. C. F. 643
Beals, Carleton. 5964, 5965, 6024
Beazley, C. R. 745
Bebler, Ales. 4766, 5246
Bebr, Gerhard. 4287, 5667, 6520, 6559, 6677, 6874
Bechhoefer, Bernhard G. 4380, 4381, 4830, 4831, 4832
Bechtoldt, Heinrich. 7185
Beck, James M. 1255
Beckel, Graham. 3891
Beckelman, M. W. 7679
Becker, George H. 4621

Beckett, William Eric. 4259, 6405
Beckhart, B. H. 4096
Beddington-Behrens, Edward. 1753, 1754
Bedi, Mohinder S. 5308
Beer, George Louis. 1167
Beer, Max. 1256
Beever, R. Colin. 6427, 6695, 7700
Beguin, Bernard. 4431
Behavan, K. T. 3826
Behrman, Daniel. 4319, 4320
Belin, Jacqueline. 5552
Beling, Willard A. 5843
Bell, Coral. 3137, 5115, 6274, 6611, 7093, 7110, 7133, 7216
Bell, Harold. 1689, 6428
Bellers, John. 687
Bellot, H. Hale. 697, 737, 1261, 1326, 1429, 1480, 1818, 1914, 2143, 2433, 2536, 2828, 2851, 6064
Beloff, Max. 439, 3138, 5343, 6275, 6696, 7094
Belshaw, Cyril. 3985
Belshaw, H. 4211
Benda, Julien. 6697
Benedict, Ruth. 376, 419, 430, 7799
Beneš, Eduard, 1257, 1258, 2346, 2540, 2548, 2549
Benham, Frederic C. 7504
Bennett, A. Leroy. 3730
Bennike, Vagn. 5038
Benns, F. Lee. 1168, 3072
Benoit, Emile. 6521, 6882, 7222, 7725
Benson, George C. S. 7806
Benson, Oliver. 3019, 7807
Bentham, Jeremy. 688, 690
Bentinck, H. E. A. 6883
Benton, Wilbourn E. 5057
Bentwich, Helen. 2080
Bentwich, Norman. 1903, 1940, 1941, 1949, 1991, 1992, 1993, 1994, 1995, 2060, 2064, 2076, 2077, 2078, 2079, 2080, 2890, 3339, 3340, 3486, 3514, 4259, 4543, 4544, 5398, 5916, 6860
Ben-Zwi, Isaac. 2081
Berard, Victor. 7294
Berber, F. J. 611, 2550, 2765

Author Index

Berdahl, Clarence A. 1559, 1586, 2347, 2424, 2819, 2820, 2821, 2907
Berger, Morroe. 5844
Bergman, G. Merle. 7808
Berkes, Ross N. 3139, 3140, 3141, 5308, 5415, 5668, 6025, 6406, 6884, 7166, 7420
Berkov, Robert. 4234
Berle, A. A., Jr. 3142
Berlin, Isaiah. 7058
Berman, William H. 4390
Bernard, Jacques. 7102
Bernard, Robert I. 4406
Bernier, Robert. 3515
Berns, Walter F. 7908
Bernstein, Edward M. 4097, 5462
Bernstein, George A. 7726
Bernstorff, Count von. 2767
Berry, B. 558
Berthoud, F. G. 3857
Bertrand, Raymond. 6610
Best, Ethelwyn. 7680
Besterman, Theodore. 4321
Beukema, Herman. 6885
Beveridge, William H. 1135, 7809
Bevin, Ernest. 1656, 7372
Bewes, Wyndham A. 912, 1035, 1245, 1326, 1429, 1659, 1680, 1856, 1904, 1914, 2027, 2143, 2221, 2358, 2487, 2536, 2551, 2570, 2593, 2801, 2828, 2851, 5962, 6064, 7334
Beyen, J. W. 4081
Bidmead, H. S. 6698
Bidwell, Percy W. 4155, 5482, 6487
Bie, Pierre de. 545
Bienenfeld, F. R. 4259
Bieri, Ernst. 6276
Bigman, Stanley K. 7909
Bilgrami, Ashgar H. 7095
Binder, Carroll. 4416
Bindschedler, R. 3516
Bingham, Alfred M. 6699
Bingle, E. J. 7681
Binkley, Robert C. 1169
Birdsall, Paul. 1170, 3044
Birdwood, Lord. 5026, 5027, 7810
Birgi, Nuri. 6886

Birkett, Justice. 3093
Birrenbach, Kurt. 6277, 6278, 6522, 6887, 6888, 6889
Bishop, J. W., Jr. 5630
Bishop, Peter V. 3560, 4958, 5344, 5791
Bismarck, Otto von. 807
Bisschop, W. R. 1052, 1818, 2128, 2536, 2551, 2570, 2828, 6700
Black, Cyril E. 5553, 7213, 7274
Black, Eugene R. 4082
Black, J. E. 3398
Black, John D. 4212
Blackburn, Glen A. 1733
Blackett, P. M. S. 4833
Blackmer, Henry M. 6026
Blagg, Mary Evelyn. 4322
Blaisdell, Donald C. 5463, 5464
Blaisdell, Thomas C., Jr. 6488
Blakeslee, George H. 2117, 3094
Bland, J. O. P. 2642
Blaustein, Jacob. 4260
Blelloch, David H. 1755, 3986
Bliokh, Ivan S. 832
Bliss, Tasker H. 1136, 1152, 1171, 2425
Blix, H. 2193
Bloch, Henry Simon. 380, 417, 419, 430, 492, 3987, 7799
Block, Roger. 3827
Bloet-Hamorlijck, Rita Jong. 3959
Blomeyer, Horst. 7186
Bloomfield, Lincoln P. 379, 440, 441, 3143, 3464, 4382, 4767, 4834, 4927, 4959, 5163, 5465, 5466, 5467, 5468, 7910
Blough, Roy. 3988
Blumenson, M. 3061
Bluntschli, Johann Kaspar. 833
Boak, A. E. R. 568
Boardman, Mabel T. 7690
Boasson, Charles. 3144
Bock, Edwin A. 3790
Bodet, Jaime Torres. 3248, 3290, 3373, 3676, 3918, 4221, 4238, 4253, 4297, 4369, 4545
Bodnar, James S. 4835

Boeg, N. V. 6878
Boel, René. 6279
Boer, C. H. de. 1004
Bogardus, Emory S. 3145, 4261, 7727
Boggs, Theodore H. 7355
Bok, Derek C. 6560
Bok, Edward W. 1090
Bokhari, Ahmed S. 3146
Bolles, Blair. 3892, 4213, 6701, 6890, 6910
Bolte, Charles G. 4836
Bonesteel, Charles H. III. 7251
Bonn, Moritz J. 1996, 2686, 2908, 2909, 6489, 6702, 7811
Bonne, Alfred. 5058
Bonnefous, Edouard. 6703
Bonnet, Henri. 1960, 1961, 2910, 2911, 2912, 4323, 4768
Bonsal, Stephen. 1172, 1173
Bonsdorff, Goran von. 7064
Booth, D. A. 3828, 5469
Boothby, Robert. 6820, 6825
Borah, William E. 2521
Borchard, Edwin M. 1090, 1997, 2200, 2304, 2333, 2579, 4960, 7911
Borcier, Paul. 6818
Bordwell, Percy. 2913
Borel, Eugène. 2317, 2529, 7691
Borella, François. 7601
Borg, Dorothy. 1822
Borg, N. V. 3399, 3528
Borgese, Guiseppe A. 2904, 7728, 7736
Borglum, G. 1090
Borton, Hugh. 3095
Bose, C. 4837
Bossy, Sanda. 7692
Bouché, Henri. 2348
Boudreau, Frank G. 1613, 1866, 1867, 1868, 1869, 1870, 2891, 4199
Bough, James A. 6205
Bougle, C. 104
Boulding, Kenneth. 419
Bourdillon, Mr. 2128
Bourgeois, Léon V. A. 242, 928, 933, 1053, 1054, 1259, 1284, 1385, 1635, 1663, 1716, 1757, 1881, 2014, 2142, 2201, 2441, 2737, 7699

Bourgeois, Nicolas. 7812
Bourne, Randolph S. 1005, 1055
Bourquin, Maurice. 764, 765, 1260, 1514, 1726, 2349, 2597
Boutros-Ghali, Boutros Y. 5758, 5917
Bowen, I. 7729
Bower, Graham. 1261, 1480, 2279, 2779
Bower, Robert T. 6523
Bowett, Derek William. 3341, 3465, 4961, 5669
Bowie, Robert R. 6280, 6891, 7223, 7813
Bowitz, Gustav C. 4962
Bowles, Chester. 4828
Bowman, Edward H. 4959, 4963
Bowman, Isaiah. 7912
Boyce, Myrna M. 779
Boyd, Andrew K. H. 270, 3147, 3148, 3149, 5670, 6704, 6892
Boyd, Frances. 6704
Boyd, R. Gavin. 5801
Boyden, R. W. 1227, 1228, 1229
Boyd-Orr, John. *See* Orr, John
Boyer, William W. 3615, 5470
Boyesen, Jens. 7252
Bozeman, Adda B. 569
Brackett, Russell D. 3150, 7634
Braden, Thomas W. 6281
Bradley, Kenneth. 7421
Bradley, Phillips. 1430, 2202, 2687, 2823, 7673
Bradley, Rolland. 3400, 3401, 4673
Brady, Alexander. 7421, 7535
Braham, Harry Lewis. 6705
Braibanti, Ralph. 120, 3121, 5802
Brailsford, Henry Noel. 1056, 1668
Bramsted, Ernest. 6611
Brand, George. 4432, 4504
Brandon, Michael. 3342, 3517
Brandt, Karl. 6893
Brandt, Walther I. 695, 696
Branscombe, Martha. 4190
Brassert, J. E. 5583
Braun, Charlotte E. 7295
Braunthal, Julius. 7571, 7572
Brecher, Michael. 5028, 5029, 5030

Brecht, Arnold. 7913, 7914
Bregman, Alexander. 3020
Bremond, Jean. 6665
Brent, C. H. 1090
Brentano, Heinrich von. 3313
Bresch, M. 3514
Bresler, Harvey J. 685
Brett, Oliver. 1560, 1564
Breycha-Vauthier, A. C. von. 313, 7693
Brickele, Herschel. 5978, 6130
Bridgman, Raymond L. 834
Briefs, Henry W. 6268, 6339, 6887, 6893, 6902, 6945, 6961, 6974, 7005, 7016, 7043, 7051
Brierly, Caroline. 6282, 6612
Brierly, James Leslie. 1431, 1515, 1561, 2203, 3343
Briggs, A. 3089
Briggs, Ellis O. 5966
Briggs, Herbert W. 442, 3344, 3466, 3616, 4737, 4758
Brimmer, Brenda. 332
Brines, Russell. 3118
Brinton, Crane. 381, 570, 612
Brinton, Howard Haines. 881
Brinton, J. Y. 5846
Brissenden, Rosemary. 5803, 5804
British and Foreign Anti-Slavery Society. 913
British Institute of International and Comparative Law. 27, 6857, 6858, 6867, 6871
Broch, Hermann. 2904
Brockelbank, W. J. 2721
Brockington, Colin F. 4235
Brodsky, Nathan. 4505
Broekmeijer, M. W. J. M. 7253
Brohi, A. K. 3151, 4262, 5309
Bronz, George. 4153
Brook, David. 3617, 5059
Brooke, Eileen E. 1885
Brooklyn Daily Eagle. 330
Brooks, E. A. S. 4674
Brooks, Robert C. 2768
Brooks, Van Wyck. 2904
Brouckère, Louis de. 2426, 2769

Brown, Benjamin. H. 3402, 3618, 5471, 5472
Brown, Francis J. 666, 1291, 2202, 4457
Brown, George W. 6894
Brown, J. W. 7701
Brown, Philip Marshall. 1262, 2567, 2824
Brown, Seyom. 6283
Brown, W. Norman. 5767
Brown, William Adams, Jr. 3888, 3889, 4144, 4154, 5473
Browne, E. G. 5845
Browne, Louis E. 5416
Brugmans, Henri. 6284, 6706, 7059
Brum, Baltasar. 6027
Brunaer, Esther Caukin. 2914
Bruncken, E. 1090
Bruner, Jerome. 376, 417, 492
Bruning, H. 1231
Bryan, William Jennings. 1057
Bryant, Stewart F. 1263, 2118
Bryce, James. 443, 1058
Bryson, Lyman. 386, 418, 438, 453, 476, 478, 551, 577, 653, 3152, 3222, 3832, 3880, 3947, 4327, 4341, 4344, 4353, 4354, 4357, 4377, 6281, 6327, 7583, 7679, 7683, 7687, 7711, 7713, 7724, 7935
Brzezinski, Zbigniew K. 382, 7167, 7214, 7573, 7574
Buchan, Alastair. 4964, 6895, 6896, 6897, 6898, 6899
Buchanan, G. S. 1871
Buchanan, R. M. K. 2161
Buchanan, W. H. 3561
Buchanan, William. 546
Buckland, Jesse H. 712
Buehrig, Edward H. 444, 1059, 1060, 5414
Buell, Raymond Leslie. 1264, 1888, 1998, 1999, 2188, 2204, 2205, 2350, 2351, 2352, 2427, 2825, 2826, 5584, 6028, 6234
Buergenthal, Thomas. 4263
Bull, Hedley. 7423, 7730

Bullard, Arthur. 2827
Bullard, Robert Lee. 2428
Bunche, Ralph J. 3248, 3290, 3373, 3676, 3918, 4221, 4238, 4253, 4297, 4369, 4545, 5170, 6206
Bunge, Alejandro E. 2915
Burbank, Lyman B. 7204, 7205
Burge, M. R. K. 1756
Burgess, W. Randolph. 6285, 6332, 6900
Burke, Frederick G. 5759
Burks, David D. 2530
Burnett, Edmund Cody. 571
Burnett, Phillip M. 1230
Burnham, James. 3153
Burns, Alan. 6216
Burns, Arthur L. 4965, 4966, 6901, 7096
Burns, C. 7505
Burns, C. Delisle. 445, 914, 1614, 2746
Burns, Edward McN. 7731, 7915
Burns, Eedson L. M. 5031, 5060
Burns, Josephine J. 1543
Burns, Viktor. 2206
Burrell, Sidney A. 390
Burritt, Elihu. 885
Burt, Alfred Le R. 7373
Burton, John W. 155, 4838, 5671
Burton, Margaret E. 1562
Burton, Wilbur. 2622
Busey, James L. 6235
Bush, Bernard. 851
Busia, K. 5692
Buss, Claude A. 2353, 2623
Bustamante y Sirvén, Antonio Sanchez de. 2207, 2293, 6029
Butler, Geoffrey. 239, 1516, 2429
Butler, Harold B. 242, 928, 933, 1265, 1284, 1385, 1615, 1635, 1663, 1716, 1757, 1881, 2014, 2142, 2201, 2441, 2737, 7699
Butler, Nicholas Murray. 713, 882, 1061, 1062, 1266, 1469, 2568, 2916, 6713, 7814
Butwell, Richard. 5784

Butz, William. 3135, 7722
Buxton, C. 5722, 5734
Buxton, Charles R. 1063, 1068, 2575
Byng, Edward J. 2917
Byrt, A. H. 4509, 7372

Cabot, Thomas D. 6286
Cadogan, Alexander. 4839
Caesar, A. A. L. 7338
Caine, Sydney. 7097
Cairns, A. 7334
Calder, Ritchie. 4248, 4324
Caldera Rodriguez, Rafael. 5968
Calderón, Francisco García. 2531, 5969
Calderón, Ygnacio. 5981
Calderwood, Howard B. 1563, 1905, 1906, 1907
Calderwood, James D. 6613
Caldis, Calliope. 1174
Caldwell, M. J. 4464
Caldwell, Wallace E. 572
Calhoun, Harold. 2318
Callis, Melmut G. 383
Calogéropoulos-Stratis, S. 5554
Caloyanni, Mégalos A. 2208, 2209, 2598, 7296
Calvocoressi, Peter. 4769
Cammaerts, E. 6469
Campbell, Jock. 6217
Campbell, John C. 5918, 5945, 6252
Campbell, R. M. 1656
Campolongo, Alberto. 6689
Camps, Miriam. 6524, 6525, 6526, 6614, 6657, 7098, 7099
Canadian Institute of International Affairs. 27, 4178, 5310
Canning, George. 822, 823
Cantril, Hadley. 4325
Canyes Santacana, Manuel. 5634, 5672, 6030, 6184, 6185
Capper, Arthur. 2569
Cardahi, Choucri. 2063
Carey, Jane Perry Clark. 6287
Carey, John. 5175
Carleton, William G. 6826, 7916

Carlston, Kenneth S. 446, 1006
Carmichael, Joel. 5847, 5848, 5849
Carnegie, Andrew. 835, 836, 844, 851
Carnegie, D. 2358
Carnegie Endowment for International Peace. 26, 78, 156, 337, 882, 893, 968, 1064, 3154, 4203, 4323, 5345, 5619, 6031, 6032, 6090, 6449
Carnell, Francis. 126, 7424
Carpenter, Francis W. 3155
Carpenter, William S. 780
Carr, Edward Hallett. 883, 1267, 2918, 5585, 6708, 7702, 7732
Carr, William G. 271, 3156, 4326
Carr-Gregg, John R. E. 7560
Carrington, C. E. 6407, 7100, 7425, 7426, 7498, 7553
Carroll, Marie J. 314
Carson, James. 6033
Carter, Gwendolen M. 5346, 5737, 5739, 5749, 7374, 7427, 7428, 7429, 7519
Carter, W. Horsfall. 2487, 4967, 6288, 6827,
Cartwright, John K. 644
Casadio, Franco Alberto. 83
Case, S. J. 577
Casey, Richard G. C. 7430
Cashman, Ben. 5536
Cassel, Gustav. 2919
Cassin, R. 4264
Castagno, Alphonso A., Jr. 4622
Castañeda, Jorge. 4755, 5377, 5970
Castanos, P. A. 5554
Castendyck, Elsa. 1853, 1854
Castle, William R. 5971
Castlereagh, Lord. 802, 825, 7014
Castren, Erik. 3157
Cates, William C. 6429
Catlin, George. E. G. 6289, 6709, 7921
Catroux, Georges. 7602
Cattell, David T. 7339
Cavell, Nik. 7506
Caver, David F. 3345, 4383, 4840, 4841
Cecil, Robert A. 240, 771, 1268, 1269, 1290, 1564, 1565, 1578, 2430, 2506, 2920
Center for the Study of Democratic Institutions. 7815
Central Organization for a Durable Peace (The Hague). 1065
Cerami, Charles A. 7224
Cerny, Karl H. 6268, 6339, 6887, 6893, 6902, 6945, 6961, 6974, 7005, 7016, 7043, 7051
Chaffee, Zechariah. 2921
Chakravart, Raghubir. 4265
Chakste, Mintauts. 3346
Challener, Richard D. 6954
Chamberlain, A. 2559
Chamberlain, Joseph P. 1734, 1735, 1745, 1959, 2579, 2669, 2922, 3910, 4465, 7317
Chamberlain, Lawrence. 3081
Chamberlin, Waldo. 112, 332, 333, 338, 368, 3760, 4842, 5555
Chamberlin, William Henry. 2624, 6710, 7733
Chamorro, Pedro J. 6236
Chandler, Edgar H. S. 4466
Chaning-Pearce, M. 6750, 7816, 7817, 7835, 7846, 7855, 7874, 7891, 7925, 7928
Channing, William Ellery. 837
Chapman, Charles E. 6034
Chapman, J. M. 217
Chaput, R. A. 2354
Charnwood, Lord. 2828
Charteris, A. H. 7375, 7818
Charvet, Jean-Felix. 2747
Chase, Eugene P. 272, 1175, 3021, 3073, 3347, 3668, 3731, 3761, 3893, 4546, 4547, 4675, 4843, 5061, 7431
Chatterjee, A. 1535
Chatterjee, Lady. 3486
Chaudhri, Mohammed Ahsen. 5032, 5805, 5850
Chaumont, Charles. 3158
Cheever, Daniel S. 157, 1566, 1587, 1603, 1631, 1645, 1855, 1908, 2000, 2210, 3669, 3762, 3894, 3935, 3989,

4191, 4676, 4844, 5171, 5586, 6430, 6828, 6903
Cheng, Bin. 3467, 4384
Cheng, Seymour Ching Yuan. 7376
Cherwell, Viscount. 3159
Chevalier, Stuart. 3348, 7734
Chevallier, Jean Jacques. 7377
Cheyney, Alice Squires. 1758, 1759
Chidzero, B. T. G. 4623
Chieh, Liu. 4548
Childs, S. Lawford. 1942
China Institute of International Affairs. 5311
Chisholm, Brock. 3248, 3290, 3373, 3676, 3918, 4200, 4221, 4237, 4238, 4253, 4297, 4369, 4545
Choate, Joseph H. 969
Chou En-lai. 3375, 7627
Chow, S. R. 5768
Chowdhuri, R. N. 2001, 4549
Christol, Carl Q. 3160, 6298
Churchill, Winston S. 6832
Citrin, Jack. 4968
Clapp, Gordon R. 3990, 5399
Clark, Colin. 7101
Clark, Evans. 2355.
Clark, G. N. 699
Clark, George Norman. 1715
Clark, Grenville. 4841, 7819
Clark, Hartley. 112, 1565
Clark, John B. 1007, 1988
Clark, Keith. 2829
Clark, William. 3161, 7254
Clarke, John H. 2319, 2532, 2533, 2830
Clarke, R. Floyd. 970
Claude, Inis L., Jr. 158, 447, 448, 449, 450, 3162, 3163, 3164, 3468, 3562, 3585, 3592, 3619, 3629, 3652, 3670, 3829, 4266, 4770, 4771, 4845, 4928, 4968, 4970, 5015, 5420, 5972, 7735, 7897, 7917, 7918
Clave, Viscount. 2828
Claveille, M. A. 242, 928, 933, 1284, 1385, 1635, 1663, 1716, 1757, 1881, 2014, 2142, 2201, 2441, 2737, 7699
Clayton, William L. 4179, 6490, 7225

Cleland, W. Wendell. 5222
Clemens, Walter C., Jr. 4903, 5447
Clements, F. W. 4239, 5312
Cleveland, Harlan. 281, 451, 3165, 3166, 3167, 4272, 5172
Cleven, Andrew N. 6035
Clive, Howard F. 6121
Clokie, H. M. 7102
Clough, Shepard B. 6491
Clyde, Paul Hibbert. 2119
Coate, Winifred A. 4491
Coatman, John. 7432
Cochrane, C. N. 577
Cockcroft, John. 4385
Cocke, Erle, Jr. 3671
Cockram, B. 4772
Codding, George Arthur, Jr. 1727, 1728, 3951, 4652
Coffey, J. I. 6904
Cohen, Alvin. 4142, 5378
Cohen, Andrew. 1270, 5283, 5284
Cohen, Benjamin A. 3168
Cohen, Benjamin V. 3248, 3290, 3349, 3373, 3469, 3676, 3918, 4221, 4238, 4253, 4297, 4369, 4417, 4545, 4773, 4841, 5475
Cohen, I. 1578, 1949
Cohen, Jerome B. 7507
Cohen, Maxwell. 3620, 3763, 3830, 5062, 5476
Cohen, W. 1659
Coil, E. J. 4476
Cole, G. H. D. 4265
Cole, S D. 1818
Cole, S. G. 4357
Cole, W. Sterling. 4841
Colegrove, Kenneth W. 1730
Coleman, James S. 4624
Collart, Yves. 113, 4846
Colliard, Claude-Albert. 159
Collier, David S. 6291, 6641, 6937, 7100, 7343
Collier, W. M. 1039
Collinet, Paul. 737
Collingwood, F. W. 1565
Collins, J. Foster. 5211
Collins, J. Lawton. 6905

Colombos, C. John. 688, 2027, 2570, 2923, 3350

Columbia University, School of International Affairs. 38, 4853

Comay, Joan. 3169

Commission to Study the Organization of Peace. 2891, 2924, 2925, 3170, 3171, 3218, 3345, 3472, 3511, 3556, 3599, 3642, 3783, 3797, 3931, 4408, 4425, 4476, 4562, 4774, 4777, 4840, 4847, 4942, 5659, 5660, 5673, 5674, 5776, 5782, 5931, 6134, 6814, 6915, 7287, 7335, 7499, 7582, 7820, 7821

Committee for Economic Development. 7226

Committee to Frame a World Constitution. 7736

Compagnie d'Outremer. 6431

Comstock, Ada L. 2904

Comstock, Alzada. 3022, 3023, 3936, 4057, 4083, 4506, 4550, 5973, 7103, 7104, 7105, 7356, 7357, 7358, 7433, 7434, 7536, 7561

Conde, Alexander de. 4775, 4816, 6122

Condliffe, John B. 1656, 2599, 2926, 4145

Conference on the Atlantic Community (Bruges). 142

Congalton, A. A. 547

Conover, Helen F. 64, 2002, 4551

Constable, W. G. 4327

Conway, John S. 4848, 7435

Conwell-Evans, Thomas P. 1588

Cook, A. H. 4433, 5313

Cook, Thomas I. 7919, 7920

Coolidge, Archibald Cary. 5587

Cooper, John C. 3024, 3960

Cooper, Russell M. 2670, 2831

Copland, Douglas. 7529

Coplin, William D. 452

Coppe, Albert. 6527

Corbett, John P. 6715

Corbett, Percy E. 160, 1271, 2927, 3555, 5063, 5477, 7737, 7921

Cordier, Andrew W. 3172, 3578, 3899, 4013, 4015, 4260, 4385, 4705, 4894, 5170, 5493, 6408, 6862

Cording, Auke. 4252

Cordoba, R. 4677

Coreo, C. 5314

Cornell, Julien. 7738

Cornell-Smith, Gordon. 6123, 6124

Corwin, Edward S. 3518

Cory, Robert H., Jr. 4418, 4849, 4929, 5478, 5479

Coser, Lewis A. 6292

Coster, Douglas W. 3672

Costillo Najero, Francisco. 5974

Cot, Pierre. 2431

Cotton, Joseph P. 1137

Cottrell, Alvin J. 5116, 5221, 6906

Cottrell, W. F. 5285

Coudenhove-Kalergi, Richard N. 6293, 6711, 6712, 6713, 6714

Coudert, Frederic R. 7674

Coulter, John Wesley. 4653

Coulton, G. G. 2593

Council of Europe. 143, 144

Council on Foreign Relations. 18, 19, 69, 77, 1011, 1911, 2007, 2008, 2067, 2322, 2442, 2443, 2509, 2555, 2839, 6044, 6045, 7637

Coupland, Reginald. 1954, 2112

Courlander, Harold. 273, 3895, 3991, 4678, 4850, 5480

Courtin, Rene. 7168

Courtney, Kathleen D. 3173

Cousins, Norman. 560, 2928, 4851

Cowan, C. D. 7524

Cowen, Zelman. 7436

Cowie, Donald. 2356

Cox, Lucy. 1680

Cox, P. 2064

Cox, R. W. 6294

Cox, Richard H. 719, 5744

Coyle, David Cushman. 274, 4267, 4328, 4552, 4852, 5588

Craemer, Alice R. 4329

Craig, Gordon A. 7187

Cramer, Frederick H. 633, 746, 5851, 7359

Crankshaw, Edward. 7255

Cranston, Alan MacGregor. 1272, 3403
Crathorne, Lord. 6907
Crawford, John. 5819
Creamer, Daniel. 5091
Creighton, J. E. 716
Cremer, Randal. 946
Cresson, William P. 766
Crocker, W. R. 3630, 3764
Crosby, Josiah. 4654
Crosby, Oscar T. 1066, 1273
Crosland, Anthony. 6829
Cross, J. A. 7545
Crosswell, Carol McCormick. 3831
Crowdy, Rachel. 1856, 1889
Crucé, Emeric. 691
Cruickshank, Earl F. 2507
Cruise O'Brien, Conor. 5173
Crutcher, John. 5693
Cruttwell, C. R. M. F. 2600
Cuevas, Francisco. 6125
Culbertson, Ely. 7822
Culbertson, W. S. 1090, 3528
Cumming, Duncan Cameron. 4625
Cunliffe-Owen, F. 1951
Cunningham, Alan. 2082
Cunningham, J. K. 5347
Cunningham, W. B. 7106, 7537
Current, Richard N. 2625, 4775
Currey, M. 1856
Curry, George. 1176
Curti, Merle Eugene. 838, 884, 885, 886
Curtin, P. W. E. 7562
Curtis, Gerald L. 5016, 5224
Curtis, Lionel. 6716, 7360, 7437, 7823, 7902
Curtis, Michael. 6717
Cushendun, Lord. 2432
Cust, A. 2112
Custos. 1760
Czartoryski. 784
Czernin, Ferdinand. 1177

Daenell, Ernst. 634
Dafoe, J. W. 2741, 7437, 7538
Daley, Arthur. 7717

Dallin, Alexander. 4853, 5417, 5418, 5419
Dalton, Hugh. 1567
D'Amato, A. A. 6668
Dangerfield, Royden J. 5481, 7824, 7902
Daniels, Josephus. 2091
Daniels, Walter M. 6908
Dante, Alighieri. 692, 693, 694
Danube Commision. 1737, 7318
Darby, William Evans. 645, 682, 945, 1008, 1261
Darling, Arthur B. 2832
Das, Kamleshwar. 4268, 4419
Das, Taraknath. 4269, 5033
Das Gupta, Jyoti B. 5034
Datta, Ansu Kuman. 2055
Davansati, Forges. 1162, 1203, 1211
Davenport, John. 5174
Davenport, W. S. 527, 3563
David Davies Institute of International Studies. 30
Davidson, George F. 4192
Davidson, Nigel. 2064
Davies, Clement. 3313
Davies, David. 1429, 2143, 2357, 2358, 2359, 2368, 2433, 2434, 2688, 6718
Dávila, Carlos. 5975, 5976, 6036
Davis, Calvin Armond de. 971
Davis, Edward P. 335, 369
Davis, George B. 839, 867
Davis, H. W. E. 613
Davis, Harold E. 6126
Davis, Harriet Eager. 1274, 1392, 1613, 1616, 1769, 1853, 1869, 1893, 1946, 2012, 2146, 2252, 2468
Davis, Kathryn W. 2810, 2811
Davis, Malcolm M. 2435, 2601, 2602, 2658, 3351
Davis, Norman H. 2436, 2552
Dawes, Charles G. 1138, 1231, 2558
Dawley, Thomas R., Jr. 6237
Dawson, Christopher Henry. 6719
Dawson, Kenneth H. 3174
Dawson, Raymond H. 6909
Day, Clive. 1178

Dayal, Rajeshwar. 3313
Dayal, Shiv. 5117, 5315
Deak, Francis. 1469, 1589, 2722, 6720
Deakin, Arthur. 7703
Dean, Arthur H. 5806
Dean, Vera Micheles. 275, 2211, 2689, 2690, 2691, 2929, 2930, 3025, 3074, 3175, 3765, 3992, 4507, 4553, 6432, 6910, 7227, 7273
Dearden, Ann. 4626
DeBarr, John R. 5038
Deciry, Jean. 6562
Decottignies, Roger. 5715
Décraene, Philippe. 5694
Deener, D. R. 434
DeGaulle, Charles. 6556, 7610
Degras, Jane. 7576
Dehn, C. G. 2923
Dehousse, Fernand. 6845
Dejany, Aouney W. 3673, 5225
Delanney, L. 5760
Delbos, B. Victor. 706
Dell, Robert Edward. 2437
Dell, Sidney S. 5589
Delmas, Claude. 6911
Delouvrier, Paul. 6433
Del Rio, F. Nieto. 2671
Demaria, Giovanni. 6434
Demorest, Jean Jacques. 7169
Dendias, Michel. 1632
Deniau, Jean F. 6409, 6615, 6616
Dennett, Raymond. 3732, 6295, 7825
Dennis, William C. 1067
Dent, D. 2551
Dent, F. 2221
Derocque, Gilberte. 735, 1432
Deschamps, Hubert. 7603
Deshpande, N. R. 4854
Dessauer, F. E. 161
Detter, Ingrid. 3470, 3471
Deutsch, Albert. 4240
Deutsch, Karl W. 127, 384, 385, 386, 387, 388, 389, 390, 526, 5590, 6296, 7274, 7922
Deutsch, Morton. 487, 4878, 5274, 7636
Deverell, F. 1988, 6270, 7701

Dewar, A. 2487
Dewar, K. G. B. 1567
Dexter, Byron. 2553, 4334, 4335, 6912
Dexter, Lewis A. 7826
Dexter, Robert C. 1857
Dhadwal, N. S. 3176
Diamond, William. 1124, 4084, 5400
Dib, George Moussa. 5401
Dickinson, Edwin D. 2833
Dickinson, Goldsworthy Lowes. 733, 1046, 1068, 1069, 1070, 1585
Dickinson, Thomas H. 2834
Dicks, Henry V. 391, 4959
Dickson, A. G. 3993
Diebold, William, Jr. 4155, 5482, 6435, 6436, 6437, 6479, 6487, 6528, 6529, 6563, 7107, 7228
Diena, Giulio. 2003
Dillon, Conley H. 1761
Dillon, Emile J. 1179
Diop, Cheikh Anta. 5951
Dixit, R. K. 3733, 4679, 5247
Dixon, Pierson. 3177
Dobie, Edith. 2360, 7546
Dobrée, Bonamy. 720
Dodd, Norris E. 4215, 4216, 5316, 5402
Doherty, Katheryn B. 5064
Dolan, Paul. 7065
Dolivet, Louis. 276, 2931, 3178, 3674, 3734, 3766, 3896, 4554, 4680
Doman, Nicholas. 3096, 6721, 7275, 7739
Domeratzky, Louis. 7659
Donelly, M. S. 7437
Donner, A. M. 6678
Donohue, Thomas C. 7229
Donovan, William J. 5483
Dore, Robert. 68
Dorn, Herbert. 7378
Dorpalen A. 6297, 6722
Dorsey, Gray L. 453, 478
Doub, George Cochran. 4681
Dougherty, James E. 5116, 6906, 7033
Douglas, Emily Taft. 2932
Douglas, Helen Gahagan. 3179
Douglas, Paul H. 1686

Doumia, J. 105, 336
Dowd, D. F. 7230
Dowdall, H. C. 2300
Dowling, Evaline. 1962
Doyle, Michael Francis. 6037
Dozer, Donald M. 5977, 6038, 6127
Dravis, Irving B. 527, 3563
Drayton, Geoffrey. 7660
Dreier, John C. 6128, 6129
Drouin, Pierre. 6617
Drucker, Alfred. 3514, 3519
Drummond, Eric. 253, 1604
Drury, Allen. 3180
Drury-Lowe, S. R. 1254, 1285, 1565, 1567, 1573, 1578, 1680, 2358, 2464, 2506, 2559, 2593
Dubinsky, David. 7704
Dubois, Pierre. 696, 695, 696
Du Bois, W. E. Burghardt. 2808, 2835, 5695
Dubs, Homer H. 608
Duchacek, Ivo. 7276
Duchene, François. 6913
Duchosal, J. M. E. 1009
Duclos, Pierre. 6830
Dugdale, E. 2110
Duggan, Lawrence. 5978, 6130
Duggan, Stephen Pierce. 169, 1137, 1275, 1276, 1323, 1331, 1519, 1628, 1646, 1734, 1749, 1997, 2474, 2514, 2738, 2872, 5979
Dull, Paul. 3097
Dulles, Allen W. 2361, 2438, 2439, 3181, 4856
Dulles, Eleanor Lansing. 1710, 4071
Dulles, Foster R. 7694
Dulles, John Foster. 1232, 3182, 3675, 7832
Dunant, Jean Henri. 915
Dunbabin, T. 2760
Dunn, Frederick S. 392, 781, 782, 1504, 2603
Duplissix, E. 840
Duprée, Louis. 5852
Dupuis, Charles. 646, 767, 768, 783
du Puy, William Atherton. 2212
Durant, E. Dana. 1616

Duroselle, Jean Baptiste. 5556
Dutt, Rajani P. 7577, 7578
Dutton, Samuel T. 1071
Dvonn, Eugene P. 7613
Dwarkadas, R. 6666
  2508, 2933, 2934, 2935, 3026, 3183,
Dziewanowski, M. K. 747, 784

Eagleton, Clyde. 162, 1433, 1472, 3184, 3185, 3186, 3352, 3353, 3354, 3404, 3472, 3473, 3520, 3593, 3735, 3897, 4193, 4930, 4931, 5065, 5206, 6914, 6915, 7740, 7827
Earle, Edward Mead. 841, 842, 1674, 7857
Eastman, Samuel Mack. 2749, 4971
Easton, Stewart C. 4555
Eastwood, Reginald Allen. 7379
Eaton, Howard O. 6015, 7807, 7808, 7824, 7828, 7829, 7830, 7844, 7866, 7875
Eayrs, James. 5066, 5348, 5807
Eban, Aubrey S. 5067, 5853
Eddy, Sherwood. 2626, 2812
Edelman, Maurice. 6831
Eden, Anthony. 1398
Edinger, G. 1565
Edwards, Agustin. 2800, 2801
Edwards, John B. S. 3405, 3427
Eeckman, Paul. 3521
Eek, Hilding. 4420
Efimenco, N. Marbury. 393
Efron, Reuben. 6530, 6674
Egge, Bjorn. 4972
Egger, Rowland. 1617, 3585, 7675
Eggleston, Frederic. 2120, 3187, 4776
Egyptian Society of International Law. 5403
Ehrenfeld, Alice. 3522
Ehrmann, Henry W. 7170
Eichelberger, Clark M. 277, 2616, 3355, 3406, 3898, 4270, 4556, 4777, 4857, 5484, 7741
Eide, Abbjørn. 4973
Einaudi, Luigi. 2936
Einzig, Paul. 1711
Eisenlohr, Louise E. S. 1890

Eisner, Kurt. 7277
Elder, Robert E. 4114
El-Farra, Muhammed H. 7614
El-Hadi Afifi, Mohamed. 5404
Elias, Julius A. 7635
Elias, T. O. 5761
Eliot, Charles William. 1072, 1090
Eliot, E. C. 1074
Eliot, George Fielding. 1139, 1674, 2992, 3007, 3014, 3227, 6916, 6917
Elizabeth II. 7478
Elkan, Peter. 7108
Elkin, A. B. 3110, 3486, 6573
Ellert, Robert B. 6918
Elliot, E. J. 7921
Elliot, W. E. 1585, 2565
Elliott, William Yandell. 1699, 2904, 3188, 5485, 6298, 7380, 7381, 7382, 7383, 7413
Elliott, Randle. 5591
Ellis, A. D. 2750
Ellis, Charles Howard. *See* C. Howard-Ellis
Ellis, Ellen D. 3027
Ellis, Harry B. 6618
Ellis, Howard S. 6492
Ellis, John Tracy. 627
Ellis, William W. 528
Ellison, W. J. 1762
Ely, R. B. 3407
Emmerich, H. 376, 492
Emerson, Rupert. 2065, 4557, 5212, 5420, 5696, 7256
Emmet, Christopher. 6919
Emmet, Evelyn. 7520
Engel, Salo. 1473, 1474, 3385, 3408, 3482, 6683
England, G. A. 887
Englemann, Hugo O. 6299
Eppstein, John. 240, 1763, 1801, 1852, 1909, 1943, 2004, 2049, 2216
Erzberger, Matthias. 241, 785, 925, 1010, 1073, 2440
Esman, Milton J. 6493
Espy, W. R. 3995
d'Estournelles de Constant, Baron. 972

Etzioni, Amitai. 394, 395, 396, 397, 398, 399, 5675, 5854, 6218, 6410, 6438, 6619, 6723, 6724, 7066, 7742
Evan, William M. 487, 4878, 5274, 7636
Evans, Archibald A. 1618, 2937
Evans, Gordon. 4122
Evans, Howard. 946
Evans, Luther Harris. 2005, 2066, 2121, 2122, 3832, 3899, 4336, 4337
Evatt, Herbert V. 3189, 3190, 3248, 3290, 3373, 3676, 3918, 4221, 4238, 4253, 4297, 4369, 4545, 5634, 5672, 6184
Evensen, Jens. 4974
Everett, R. H. 1955
Everett, Robinson O. 6531
Ewing, Alfred C. 1277, 7743
Ewing, Cortez A. M. 7830
Eyck, F. Gunther. 6470, 7257
Eza, el Vizconde de. 242, 928, 933, 1284, 1385, 1635, 1663, 1716, 1757, 1881, 2014, 2142, 2201, 2441, 2737, 7699

Fabre-Luce, Alfred. 2554
Fachiri, Alexander P. 2213, 2214, 2221, 2305, 2320
Fairchild, Muir S. 5486
Fakher, Hossein. 3474
Falk, Richard A. 278, 454, 3523, 3612, 3650, 4829, 4858, 4859, 4863, 4879, 4882, 4893, 7744
Falls, Cyril. 6920
Fanning, James E. 4959, 4963
Fanshawe, Maurice. 1278, 2215, 2299, 3356
Farag, Attiat A. 6253
Faraj Allah, S. B. 5248
Faries, John C. 888
Farmanfarma, Ali N. 4738
Farnham, John D. 1891
Farran, Charles d'Olivier. 3409, 6921
Fatouros, Arghyrios A. 3834
Faust, John R. 5379
Fawcett, Charles Bungay. 7745

Fawcett, James Edmund Sanford. 3475, 3524, 4098, 4156, 5249, 5349, 7438
Fawcett, M. 1856
Fay, H. Van V. 1666
Fay, Sidney B. 2162, 3028, 3029, 3030, 4508, 5920, 5921, 6301, 6494, 6725, 6726, 6922, 7258
Fayle, Charles Ernest. 1140
Fedder, Edwin H. 3833, 5487
Fehimović, Zoran. 5421
Feinberg, Nathan. 1434, 1544, 1910, 2006, 3357, 3594
Feis, Herbert. 1764, 1963, 2363, 2692, 4157
Feist, H. J. 3514
Feld, Bernard T. 4860, 6532
Feld, Werner. 6679
Feller, Abraham H. 2306, 3191, 3192
Fenichell, Stephen S. 3193
Fenwick, Charles G. 1074, 1180, 1469, 2216, 2306, 2579, 4778, 4932, 6039, 6040, 6041, 6042, 6131, 6132, 6133, 6134, 6135
Ferguson, George. 7109
Ferguson, W. S. 573, 577
Fernbach, Alfred. 4434
Ferrero, Guglielmo. 769
Ferris, John P. 5946
Fertig, Norman R. 400, 4467
Fess, Simeon D. 2217
Ffrench-Davis, Ricardo. 403, 5600, 6254
Fiedorowicz, George de. 2362
Fifield, Russell H. 2123
Fike, Linus R. 2938
Filene, Edward A. 1075
Finch, George A. 1181, 1233, 1234, 1235, 2306, 6043
Finer, Herman. 2939, 3900
Finkelstein, Lawrence S. 401, 3194, 3410, 3411, 3684, 4627, 4655, 4861, 4862, 5250, 5317
Finkelstein, Louis. 386, 418, 438, 453, 476, 478, 551, 577, 653, 3152, 3222, 3832, 3880, 3947, 4327, 4341, 4344, 4353, 4354, 4357, 4377, 6281, 6327, 7583, 7679, 7683, 7687, 7711, 7713, 7724, 7935
Finletter, Thomas K. 560, 6495
Firsoff, V. A. 6727
Fischer, Georges. 3412, 4386, 5557
Fischer-Galati, Stephen A. 770
Fischer-Williams, John. *See* Williams, John Fischer
Fisher, Allan G. B. 3031, 3937, 4509, 7384
Fisher, Dorothy Canfield. 2904
Fisher, H. A. L. 2523
Fisher, Harold H. 7215
Fisher, Hilda. 786
Fisher, Irving. 1279, 2836
Fisher, M. H. 4180
Fisher, Roger. 394, 455, 4863, 5517, 6410, 6668, 7923
Fisher, Sydney Nettleton. 6528, 6621, 7167, 7169, 7171, 7177, 7181, 7214
Fitzgerald, C. P. 7615
Fitzgerald, Edward. 6965
Fitzgerald, Richard C. 4640
Fitzgibbon, Russell H. 6136, 7788, 7837
Fitzmaurice, Gerald G. 3476, 4682, 4683, 4684, 4739
Fitzsimons, M. A. 7682
Flack, Horace E. 1120
Flamme, M. A. 6533
Flanders, R. E. 4778
Fleissig, Andreas. 6728
Fleming, Denna Frank. 2321, 2837, 2838, 2940, 4779, 4780, 5422, 5488
Fleming, J. Marcus. 4099
Flere, Janvid. 3996
Fletcher, B. H. 7110
Fletcher-Cooke, John. 4656
Flexner, Jean Atherton. 4217
Flexner, Kurt. 6480
Fling, Fred Morrow. 574
Florentino, Feliciano P. 7765
Florinsky, Michael T. 2163, 6729
Florio, Francesco. 3477
Foa, Bruno. 7196
Foch, Rene. 6667
Foda, Ezzeldin. 5855

Foley, Hamilton. 1280
Follows, John W. 1765
Foltz, William J. 5739
Foote, Wilder. 3172, 3578, 3798, 3899, 4013, 4015, 4260, 4385, 4705, 4894, 5170, 5493, 6862
Forbes, Henry W. 4864
Ford, Thomas King. 973
Foreign Policy Association. *See* Council on Foreign Relations
Forges-Davanzati, Roberto. 2693
Forsey, Eugene. 7439
Forster, Kent. 3135, 5558, 7722
Forsyth, W. D. 3195
Forthomme, Pierre-A. 6302
Fortman, W. F. de Gaay. 3997
Fosdick, Raymond B. 242, 928, 933, 1281, 1282, 1283, 1284, 1385, 1635, 1663, 1716, 1757, 1881, 2014, 2142, 2201, 2218, 2441, 2737, 7699
Foster, Homer P. 2364
Foster, John W. 1012
Foster, William C. 6972
Foster, William Z. 7579
Fouques-Duparc, Jacques. 3196
Fox, Annette Baker. 3998, 4558, 4559, 5559, 6207, 7231
Fox, Byron L. 7746
Fox, Edward W. 7172
Fox, George. 881
Fox, Grace. 4510
Fox, Hazel. 961
Fox, Melvin. J. 6496, 6497
Fox, William T. R. 456, 3076, 3197, 4781, 6923
Fox-Davies, G. 7294
Fradkin, Elvira K. 4865
France, Joseph Irwin. 2840
Franch, Peter G. 3999
Francis, Michael J. 6046, 6137
Franck, Dorothea Seelye. 3999
Franck, Thomas M. 5175, 5729
François, J. P. A. 1013, 1944
Francqueville, Bernard de. 2219
Frank, Glenn. 1646
Frank, Isaiah. 4146, 6620
Frankel, Henryk. 7101

Frankel, Joseph. 163, 5423, 5808
Frankel, W. 2892
Frankfurter, Felix. 2083
Franklin, Benjamin. 860
Franks, Oliver. 7111, 7548
Frascona, J. L. 2923
Fraser, E. 2570
Fraser, Henry L. 947
Fraser, Leon. 1236, 1669
Fraser, Peter. 4560
Fraser, R. 1914, 6064
Frazao, Sergio Armando. 4561
Freedman, Leonard, 5237
Freedman, Max. 3677, 6924
Freeman, A. V. 5630
Freeman, Edward A. 575
Freeman, Harrop A. 457, 2941, 3032, 3478, 7833, 7898, 7905
Fremantle, S. 2368, 2487
Frey-Wouters, 6534
Freymond, Jacques. 3098, 5017, 5118, 5560, 7259
Freytagh-Loringhoven, Axel von. 2556
Fried, John H. E. 279, 4435
Friedensburg, Ferdinand. 2604
Friedgood, H. B. 4357
Friedlander, Lilian M. 1545
Friedmann, Wolfgang G. 3099, 3525, 3526, 3760, 3834, 4511, 5251, 5592, 5593, 6925, 7440
Friedrich, Carl J. 402, 707, 708, 709, 3358, 6730, 6731, 7813
Frisch, David H. 4866
Friters, G. M. 3100
Frost, Richard Aylemer 7441
Frutkin, Arnold W. 4387
Fry, A. Ruth. 687
Frydenberg, Per. 4962, 4972, 4973, 4974, 4975, 4980, 4989, 4995, 5004, 5010, 5011, 5012, 5019, 5075, 5183
Frye, Richard N. 5856, 5873
Frye, William R. 3198, 4867, 4976
Fuchs, Laurence H. 3199, 7834
Fujii, Shin'ichi. 2790
Fulbright, J. William. 6303, 6304, 6732

Fulda, Carl H. 6621
Fuller, Dale C. 1076, 5424
Fuller, J. F. C. 2444, 4868
Fulljames, R. 4782
Furniss, Edgar S., Jr. 5594, 6138, 6139, 6186, 6926, 6927, 6932, 6981, 6990, 7029, 7031, 7148, 7173, 7174, 7175, 7186, 7252
Furse, K. 1856

Gabbay, Rony. 5068
Gahan, F. 2128
Galabert, Henri. 1964
Galbraith, Virginia. 4181
Galitzi, Christine. 7297
Gallin, Alexander. 6733
Gallois, Pierre M. 6928
Gallup International. 548
Galt, T. F. 280
Gamarnikow, Michael. 7340
Gambrell, E. Smythe. 4759
Gamio, Manuel. 2942
Gandhi, Mahatma. 7525
Ganguli, B. N. 4000
Ganji, Manouchehr. 4271
García, Antonio. 4338, 5489
García Bustillos, Gonzalo, 5968
Gardiner, David E. 4628
Gardner, Richard N. 281, 3564, 4001, 4147, 4182, 4272, 4388, 4977, 4978, 5425, 5426, 5490
Gargaz, Pierre A. 698
Garner, James W. 1469, 2841
Garnett, J. C. Maxwell. 1254, 1285, 1573, 1585, 1951, 1965, 1988, 2368, 2487, 2559, 2593, 2760, 7835
Garnick, Daniel H. 5857, 5858
Garratt, G. T. 2084
Garrigue, Katharine C. 7637
Garvin, James L. 1647, 2842
Gascon y Marin, José. 1619
Gasiorowski, Zygmunt T. 2557
Gass, Oscar. 5091
Gathings, James A. 1841
Gathorne-Hardy, Geoffrey N. 1285, 1435, 7385
Gaudemet, Paul Marie. 3835

Gault, P. 1341, 1489, 7861
Gauss, Christian. 2904
Gavit, John P. 1892
Gelber, Lionel. 6565, 7442, 7499
Gelber, Marvin B. 2085
Gellner, C. R. 6833
General Agreement on Tariffs and Trade. 114, 4183
Geneva Research Center. 20, 1436, 1505, 1568, 1687, 1738, 1842, 1843, 1844, 1956, 1966, 2086, 2087, 2323, 2571, 2627, 2628, 2629, 2630, 2631, 2843, 2844, 2845, 7661
Geneva Research Committee. 2632
Gentz, Friedrich von. 787, 805
Géraud, André. 2445
Gerber, Norman. 282
Gerbet, Pierre. 164
Gerig, Benjamin. 2009, 2010, 4562, 4563
Gerould, James Thayer. 2770
Geshkoff, Theodore I. 7298
Ghory, Emile. 2088
Ghoshal, A. K. 3413
Gibb, H. A. R. 2110, 5859
Gibberd, Kathleen. 1286
Gibbons, Herbert Adams. 2011
Gibbs, Hubert S. 4319, 5100, 5171, 5228, 5678, 6541
Gibson, Hugh. 2952
Gibson, John S. 3359, 5676
Gidel, Gilbert. 2747
Giffin, S. F. 6929
Gil, Enrique. 5980
Gilbert, S. P. 1237
Gilchrist, Huntington. 1287, 2012, 2013, 3062, 3077, 3678, 4002, 4564, 5318
Gill, Charles A. 7836
Gilliard, Edward M. 1766
Gilmore, Grant. 4685
Gilson, Richard P. 5830
Gimenez Caballero, Ernesto. 6834
Ginn, Edwin. 848, 889, 890
Ginsburgs, George. 7353
Giraud, Emile. 3414, 3767
Gladden, E. N. 5745

Author Index

Gladstone, William. 807
Glaser, Kurt. 6291, 6641, 6937, 7100, 7343
Glasgow, George. 2558
Glazebrook, George De T. 5252, 7563
Gleason, J. A. 3514
Glick, Edward B. 5035, 5380, 5381, 5382, 5427, 5561
Glick, Philip M. 4003
Glubb, J. B. 5069
Glueck, Sheldon. 3102
Glynn, John J. 5595
Goad, Mr. 6270
Godfrey, James L. 7414, 7515
Godoy, H. H. 6172
Goeckingk, Johanna Von. 4004
Goedhart, G. J. Van Heuven. 4469, 4470, 4471
Göppert, Otto. 243
Goitein, H. 1914, 2570, 3110, 6064, 6573
Gold, Joseph. 4100
Goldblatt, Israel. 4641, 4642
Goldsmith, Peter H. 5981
Goldsmith, Robert. 1077
Goldstein, Walter. 3200
Goldwin, Robert A. 5504, 7908
Golsong, H. 6858
Gomez Robledo, Antonio. 5982, 6047
Gompers, Samuel. 1182, 1767
Gönlübol, Mehmet. 5397, 5405
Gonsiorowski, Miroslas. 1288, 2014, 2572
Gooch, G. P. 748, 2365, 2366
Good, Robert C. 5176
Goode, W. 1659, 1689, 2780
Goodhart, A. L. 2923, 3514, 5070, 6930
Goodman, Elliot R. 5428, 6931, 6932, 7747, 7748
Goodman, G. G. 4512
Goodman, Neville M. 4201
Goodpaster, Andrew. 6933
Goodrich, Carter. 1768, 1769, 4005, 4006, 4436, 5383
Goodrich, Leland M. 283, 284, 458, 529, 1437, 2220, 3078, 3201, 3202, 3270, 3360, 3361, 3462, 3513, 3527, 3595, 3679, 3680, 3736, 3739, 3768, 3799, 3836, 3901, 4204, 4273, 4565, 4783, 4784, 4869, 4870, 4933, 4934, 4935, 4936, 4979, 5071, 5119, 5120, 5121, 5122, 5123, 5124, 5491, 5677
Goodspeed, S. C. 5983
Goodspeed, Stephen S. 165, 3079, 3415, 3416, 3769, 3902, 4566, 4686, 4785, 4871, 4937, 5596, 5678, 6140
Goodwin, Geoffrey L. 514, 3203, 3204, 3205, 5350, 5351
Goold-Adams, Richard. 6934
Goormaghtigh, John. 3098, 6305, 6566, 6875
Gordenker, Leon. 3206, 3681, 3903, 4421, 5125, 5126, 5127, 5429, 5492
Gordon, Bernard K. 4124, 5769, 5770, 6935
Gordon, Donald C. 7386
Gordon, J. King. 5177, 5227
Gordon, Lincoln. 5597, 6306, 6307, 6308, 6498, 6936
Gordon Walker, Patrick C. *See* Walker, P. C. G.
Gore, W. Ormsby. *See* Ormsby-Gore, W.
Gore-Booth, Paul H. 6734
Goren, Asher. 5922
Goriainov, Serge. 788
Gorove, Stephen. 4389, 6668
Gorter, Wytze. 4184
Goswami, B. N. 3417, 5352
Gottschalk, Louis. 376, 419, 492
Goudy, Mr. 1818
Gouré, Léon. 3362, 5430
Govindaraj, V. C. 3479
Grady, Eleanor H. 576
Grady, Henry F. 1688
Graecen, Robert. 3149
Graham, Malbone W. 1289, 1546, 1912, 7837
Grandin, Thomas. 1729
Grant, Arthur James. 771, 1290
Grant, Margaret. 5624, 5638, 5684, 5771, 5775, 6005, 6162
Grant, Roderick N. 7232

893

Grant, Ulysses S. 1141
Gras, N. S. B. 5598
Graubard, Stephen R. 6309
Gray, A. L., Jr. 4007
Gray, Beryl. 6238
Grazia, Alfred de. 70
Great Britain. 2144, 5353
Greaves, Harold R. 1633, 3631, 7838
Green, David. 599
Green, Elizabeth. 5599
Green, Frederick C. 728
Green, James Frederick. 3888, 3889, 4274
Green, L. C. 3103, 3110, 3207, 3682, 3738, 3739, 3837, 4259, 4437, 5128, 5213, 6573, 6859, 7701
Green, O. M. 2642
Green, Philip Leonard. 5984
Greene, Fred. 166, 789, 3618
Greene, Roger S. 7839
Greenwood, Frederick. 7294
Greenwood, G. 7443
Gregg, Robert W. 515, 3904, 4205
Gregoire, Roger. 5253
Gregory, Charles Noble. 1770
Gregory, Winifred. 790
Grey, Edward. 791, 1078, 2575
Griffin, Keith. 403, 5600, 5985, 6254
Grigg, Edward. 2032, 2559, 2760
Grinshaw, H. A. 2015, 2016
Gronning, Jacob. 4980
Groot, E. H. U. de. 5354
Gros, André. 3528
Gross, Ernest A. 285, 3208, 3209, 3418, 3565, 3683, 3740, 3800, 3938, 4687, 5129, 5254, 5493
Gross, Feliks. 7278
Gross, Franz B. 3235, 3304, 3909, 4842, 5265, 5271, 5394, 5485, 5494, 5495, 5562
Gross, Leo. 1547, 2017, 3363, 3480, 3566, 3596, 3597, 4567, 4688, 4689, 5255, 5496
Grosser, Alfred. 5158, 5164, 6310, 6311
Grossman, Gregory. 7279

Grotius, Hugo. 699, 700, 701, 702, 703, 704
Grotius Society. 47
Gruber, John. 614
Gruber, Richard G. 792
Gruening, Ernest. 6048
Grun, George A. 2560
Grzybowski, Kazimierz. 5431, 7580
Guani, Albert. 5986
Guelzo, Carl M. 5130
Guérard, Albert. 430, 6735, 7736, 7799
Guerrant, Edward. 6141
Guerry, Emile M. 647
Guetzkow, Harold. 404, 405, 549
Guggenheim, Paul. 244, 3857,
Guins, George C. 4513
Gung-wu, Wang. 5771
Gupta, K. 7444
Gupta, Sisir. 5036, 5772
Gurian, Waldemar. 2943, 7682
Gutt, Camille. 4101
Guttenberg, Karl Theodore von und zu. 6937
Gutteridge, J. A. C. 2194
Gyorgy, Andrew. 4319, 5100, 5171, 5228, 5678, 6541, 7319

Haagerup, Niels J. 5573
Haas, Ernst B. 167, 406, 407, 408, 459, 516, 530, 2018, 3905, 4008, 4438, 4439, 4568, 4786, 5256, 5257, 5601, 5602, 5603, 5679, 6255, 6260, 6261, 6312, 6313, 6535, 6622, 6736, 6737, 6835, 7899
Haas, Michael. 460
Haas, R. 1717
Haberler, Gottfried von. 4067, 5604, 6440
Habib, Mohammed. 5860
Habicht, Max. 5563
Hackett, Charles W. 6049
Hadas, Moses. 577
Hadi, Aouni Bey Abdul. 2090
Hadley, Paul E. 6142, 6143, 6144, 6187
Hadow, Robert Henry. 5258, 5605

Hadsel, Fred L. 3939, 4194
Hadwen, John G. 4009, 4115, 5259
Haekkerup, Per. 4981, 5564, 6314
Haensch, Günther. 305
Haesaert, J. 6315
Haesele, Kurt W. 6568
Hagras, Kamal M. 4010
Hahn, Hugo J. 6316, 6669
Haider, S. M. 6668
Haig, Harry. 5549
Haile, Pennington. 1291
Hailey, Lord. 4643
Haines, C. Grove. 4266, 4629, 6284, 6317, 6341, 6358, 6369, 6376, 6433, 6434, 6443, 6445, 6588
Halasz, Nicholas. 843
Halderman, John W. 4982, 5680
Hale, Edward Everett. 743
Hale, George Ellery. 1967
Halecki, Oscar. 7280, 7840
Haleem, A. B. A. 5861
Hales, James C. 2019, 2020, 2021
Hall, H. Duncan. 2605, 2893, 3063, 4644, 7447
Hall, Harvey P. 5923
Hall, Hessel Duncan. 4569, 4570, 4571, 7383, 7387, 7388, 7389, 7390, 7391, 7392
Hall, Rufus G., Jr. 6145
Hall, Stephen King. *See* King-Hall, Stephen
Hall, Walter Phelps. 7393
Hallberg, Charles W. 2189
Hallé, Louis J. 6318, 6319
Hallstein, Walter. 6320, 6441, 6536, 6623, 6624, 6625, 6738, 6938
Halm, George N. 4059
Halpern, A. M. 3621
Halpern, Manfred. 5178
Hambridge, Gove. 4218, 4219
Hambro, Carl J. 1306, 2730, 2944, 2945
Hambro, Edvard I. 336, 2946, 3361, 4690, 4691, 4692, 4693, 4694, 4740, 4741, 4742, 7067
Hamburger, Kaete. 7695
Hamilton, Alexander. 578, 1478

Hamilton, Alice. 965
Hamilton, Mary. 1567
Hamilton, R. 5722, 5734
Hamilton, Thomas J. 3801, 5072
Hammarskjöld, Åke. 2221, 2222, 2223
Hammarskjöld, Dag. 3210, 3211, 3212, 3481, 3798, 3802, 3809, 3810, 3814, 3815, 3819, 3838, 3839, 5175, 5200
Hammond, John Hays. 2224
Hammond, L. 2112
Hamori, Laszlo. 128
Hamzeh, F. S. 4938, 5073
Hancock, C. G. 1585, 1856, 7902
Hancock, J. 7902
Handy, Craighill. 5599
Hankey, Maurice P. A. 1142, 1143, 1183, 7394
Hanna, Paul. 2091
Hanning, Hugh. 5355
Hanotaux, Gabriel. 2803.
Hansen, Alvin H. 5988
Hansen, Morella. 7718
Harbron, John D. 6197
Hard, William. 2846
Hardin, C. 380, 417
Hardy, M. J. L. 3840
Harley, J. H. 1565
Harley, John Eugene. 71, 245, 286, 648, 1475, 1771, 2367, 2446, 2633, 2771, 2847, 2947, 2948, 3033, 3213, 3529, 4339, 5131, 5384, 6569, 7638
Harmon, Robert B. 72
Harnetty, Peter. 7539, 7554
Harper, Norman. 3419, 5356, 5809, 5810, 7508
Harriman, Edward A. 1292, 1506
Harrington, Charles W. 4872
Harris, Charles R. S. 3105
Harris, Errol E. 7841
Harris, H. Wilson. 246, 1567, 1659, 1772, 1856, 1858, 1872, 1913, 2022, 2145, 2225, 2447, 2561, 2801
Harris, Joseph P. 3841, 4514, 4515
Harris, Robert E. G. 3214
Harris, Seymour E. 6500

Harris, Walter B. 1565, 2124, 2195, 2221
Harrison, Austin. 710
Harrison, George. 6739, 6753
Harrison-Church, R. J. 4630
Harrod, Roy. 7112
Hart, Albert Bushnell. 579, 615, 635, 6740, 6741
Hart, B. H. Liddell. 2368, 2369
Hart, C. 380, 417
Hartley, Livingston. 6321, 6322, 6742, 6743
Hartmann, Frederick H. 168, 2370, 5132, 5606
Hartog, P. 2079, 2111
Haruki, Takeshi. 4340, 5319
Harvey, Heather Joan. 7446, 7447, 7486
Harvey, Mary Frances. 4492
Harvey, Paul. 1293
Hasan, K. Sarwar. 5037, 5320, 7448, 7530
Hasan, Mohammed. 4125
Hasan, Said. 4011
Hasan, Zubeida. 7113
Haskins, Charles H. 2164
Hasluck, Paul. 3741
Hassel, Kai-Uwe von. 6939
Hassouna, Abdel Khalek. 5924
Hatch, John. 7555
Hatvany, Antonia. 184, 1017, 1441, 1789, 2129, 2261, 2453, 2512
Havet, Jacques. 4341
Havighurst, H. C. 2579
Haviland, Henry Field, Jr. 157, 409, 1566, 1587, 1603, 1631, 1645, 1855, 2000, 2210, 3143, 3163, 3165, 3208, 3669, 3684, 3685, 3762, 3894, 3907, 3935, 3989, 4016, 4191, 4676, 5497, 5498, 5545, 5586, 6308, 6375, 6430, 6465, 6828, 6903, 7116, 7233, 7237
Hawtrey, Ralph George. 4060, 7114
Hay, Denys. 6323
Hay, Peter. 6650
Hayden, Sherman S. 4572, 4573, 7616
Hayek, F. A. von. 7842
Hayes, Carlton J. H. 169, 616

Hays, A. G. 1074
Hayton, Robert D. 6188
Hazan, Z. 5862
Hazard, John N. 5432, 6823
Hazen, Charles D. 749, 793
Head, Ivan L. 4695
Healey, Dennis. 7115, 7116, 7260
Hearnshaw, Fossey J. C. 794
Heathcote, Nina. 4965, 4966, 5179, 5499
Heckscher, Eli Filip. 6442
Hedges, Robert Yorke. 170, 2606
Hediger, Ernest S. 2894, 4440
Hedtoft, Hans. 7068
Heidelberg, Franz C. 6537
Heilbroner, Robert L. 4249, 6324
Heilperin, Michael A. 1648, 4061, 6443
Heinz, Norden. 7774
Heiser, Hans Joachin. 6744, 7117
Hekhuis, Dale J. 559, 4966, 6966
Heldring, J. L. 6325
Hemleben, Sylvester John. 649, 739
Hempstone, Smith. 5180
Henderson, Arthur. 2406
Henderson, Gavin B. 795
Henderson, Hubert. 6050, 6501
Henderson, J. L. 4342
Henderson, W. O. 6444, 6538
Henderson, William. 4939, 5214, 5773, 5774
Hendrick, Burton J. 844
Heneman, Harlow J. 2125
Henig, Stanley. 3632, 6745
Henkin, Louis. 3215, 4275, 4867, 4873, 5240
Hennessy, Bernard. 7843
Henriques, H. S. Q. 1326, 2279, 2300, 2779, 2851
Henry IV (France). 739
Henry, Paul-Marc. 4012, 5287, 5697
Henty, Mr. 2487
Herberichs, Gerard. 550
Herbert, Sydney. 265, 1126, 1217, 1551, 1584, 1611, 1682, 1724, 1833, 1864, 1938, 1984, 2297, 2497
Herford, R. H. 1856

Hero, Alfred, Jr. 7639
Herod, W. R. 6940
Herrera, Felipe. 6265
Herrera, Roberto. 6051
Herrick, Francis H. 6746
Herring, Pendleton. 380, 419, 430, 7799
Herriot, Édouard. 6326, 6747
Hershey, Amos Shartle. 171, 796, 1238
Hershey, Burnet. 2183
Herter, Christian A. 1090, 6278
Hertz, Friedrich O. 7320, 7321
Herz, John H. 172, 2772, 2949
Hevesy, P. De. 3420
Hewes, Amy. 1773
Hewitt, A. R. 73
Hewitt, E. P. 2551
Hewitt-Myring, Philip. 6219
Hexner, Ervin. 1700, 3482, 3530, 4102, 4103
Heyking, Baron. 1914
Heyman, Curt L. 1476
Heymann, Hans. 7900
Heyting, W. J. 2950
Hickman, Warren L. 6502
Hicks, Frederick Charles. 74, 75, 173, 650, 974, 1294, 2448
Hiett, Helen. 2694
Higgins, Alexander Pearce. 845, 975, 2526, 2565
Higgins, Benjamin. 5500
Higgins, Rosalyn. 3483, 4276, 4277, 4787
Higgins, Terence. 3567
High, Stanley. 1670
Higham, J. 115
Highley, Albert E. 2371, 2372, 2695, 2696
Hiitonen, E. 1774
Hill, Chesney. 194, 1469, 1636, 1723, 2269, 2373, 2386
Hill, David Jayne. 174, 976, 977, 1074, 2226, 2306, 2333, 2848, 2849, 2850
Hill, John G. 2092, 5863
Hill, Martin. 1517, 1649

Hill, Norman L. 175, 176, 177, 287, 797, 891, 948, 1295, 1518, 1553, 1569, 2023, 2227, 2607, 3568, 3598, 3770, 3803, 3842, 3906, 4696, 4788, 5607, 5608, 7749, 7844
Hill, Russell. 6327
Hillson, Norman. 1296
Hilsman, Roger. 6941
Hinckley, Frank E. 2228
Hindaman, Wilbert L. 5681
Hindmarsh, Albert E. 2374
Hinshaw, Randall. 7234
Hinsley, Francis H. 178, 651, 689, 711, 729, 798, 846, 1297, 3216
Hinterhoff, Eugene. 6942
Hirsch, Etienne. 6670
Hirsch, Joseph. 2951, 3106
Hirst, Margaret E. 847
Hiscocks, C. R. 4278
Hishida, Seiji G. 2634
Hiss, Donald. 5501
Hitchcock, Gilbert M. 1298
Hitchcock, Wilbur W. 5133
Hitchner, Dell G. 461, 1299, 5609, 6328, 6539
Hitti, Philip K. 5864
Hoag, Charles L. 2448
Hoag, Malcolm W. 6943, 6944
Hobbes, Thomas. 599
Hobman, J. B. 1949
Hobson, Asher. 6270, 7662
Hobson, John A. 1079
Hocking, William E. 2992, 3007, 3014, 3227, 7750
Hodé, Jacques. 652, 772, 799
Hoden, Marcel. 1300
Hodges, Charles. 179, 666, 800, 1291, 1968, 2202, 4457
Hodgkin, Thomas. 5740, 5952, 5953
Hodson, H. V. 7449, 7450, 7549
Hoehler, Fred. K. 4516
Hoffman, Emil. 7342
Hoffman, Michael L. 4135
Hoffman, Paul G. 560, 3531, 3907, 4013, 5259, 5502
Hoffmann, Stanley. 410, 462, 463, 464, 730, 3217, 3532, 3585, 4959,

5074, 5159, 5181, 5260, 6329, 6330, 6331, 7176
Hogan, Warren P. 531, 5811
Hogan, Willard N. 231, 1400, 3090, 3389, 3649, 3661, 3786, 3932, 3946, 4197, 4311, 4414, 4615, 4731, 4789, 4818, 4914, 4955, 5150, 5656
Hohman, Elmo P. 1775
Holborn, Hajo. 3107, 7235
Holborn, Louise W. 3034, 4472, 4473, 4474, 7060, 7118
Holcombe, Arthur N. 848, 2375, 3218, 3599, 4279, 4574, 4575, 5503, 6748
Holland, Robert. 4790, 5831
Holland, Thomas E. 801
Holland, William L. 1701
Hollingsworth, L. 1285
Hollis, Christopher. 6836
Hollond, Tappan. 1162, 1203, 1211
Holls, Frederick William. 978
Holm Johsen, Arne. 5075, 5183
Holman, Alfred. 5989
Holmes, Frank. 7119
Holmes, John W. 4983, 5182, 6626, 6945, 7521, 7522
Holmes, Olive. 6052
Holt, Hamilton. 1080, 1081, 1301, 1302
Holt, W. Stull. 4791
Holte-Castello, Edmundo de. 5385
Honig, F. 3843, 4697, 4698
Hoover, Calvin Bryce. 7451
Hoover, Glen. 4075
Hoover, Herbert Clark. 1144, 2952, 2953
Hopkins, Harry. 3050
Hopkinson, Sir Alfred. 697, 1261, 2279, 2433, 2851
Hopper, Bruce C. 7261, 7581
Horie, Shigeo. 4104
Hornbeck, S. K. 4778
Horsfall, Major A. H. 1565, 7384
Hosain, H. Tafazzul. 4475
Hosch, Louis E. 3844
Hoskins, Alice C. 4250, 5386
Hoskins, Halford L. 5925

Hoskins, Lewis. 4250
Hoskyns, Catherine. 5184, 5288
Hosono, Gunji. 2450
Hostie, Jan. 1477, 1718, 2229, 3421
Hostler, Charles W. 7299
Hotz, Alfred J. 6946
Houben, P. — H. J. M. 6540
Houghton, Neal D. 1303, 7751
Houphouet-Boigny, Felix. 7604
House, Edward M. 1144, 1171, 1182, 1184, 1185, 1187, 1196, 1221, 1670, 1767, 1916, 2024
Houston, John A. 5387, 5565
Hovet, Thomas A., Jr. 332, 333, 517, 518, 4940, 5289, 5290, 5291, 5321
Hovey, Allan, Jr. 3646, 3686, 7120
Howard, Harry N. 5261, 5926, 7300, 7335, 7582
Howard, Lord. 2593
Howard-Ellis, C. 247, 1186, 1438, 1534, 1605, 1776, 2230
Howe, E. J. 1090
Howe, Frederic C. 1650
Howe, John M. 3845
Howell, John M. 3533, 3534, 5357, 5566
Hsia, Chi-feng. 2791
Hsü, Shu-hsi. 2635
Hubbard, Ursula P. 1845, 2852
Huber, Max. 7696
Hudson, Cyril E. 617
Hudson, G. F. 5076, 7452
Hudson, M. P. 2608
Hudson, Manley O. 248, 326, 1014, 1187, 1304, 1439, 1446, 1507, 1548, 1739, 1777, 1846, 1915, 1916, 2024, 2179, 2231, 2232, 2233, 2234, 2235, 2236, 2237, 2238, 2239, 2240, 2241, 2242, 2243, 2244, 2245, 2246, 2247, 2248, 2249, 2250, 2251, 2252, 2253, 2254, 2306, 2307, 2324, 2325, 2326, 2327, 2328, 2333, 2534, 2573, 2672, 2723, 2731, 2853, 2854, 2855, 2856, 2857, 2858, 2859, 2954, 2955, 4202, 4699, 4700, 4701, 4743, 6053, 6239
Huelin, David. 6240, 6256

Hughan, Jessie W. 180, 1440, 2025, 2956
Hughes, Charles Evans. 2255, 2256, 6054, 6055
Hughes, E. 419
Hughes, H. Stuart. 492, 6947
Hughes, Hector. 565, 7395
Hughes, W. M. 7398
Hughes, William. 7121
Hula, Eric. 3219, 3220, 4792, 5504
Hull, Cordell. 3035, 5990, 6037, 6056
Hull, William Isaac. 721, 892, 979, 980, 981, 1015, 1082, 1083, 2329, 2579, 2860
Humber, P. O. 3600
Humphrey, Don D. 7236
Humphrey, John P. 4280
Humphreys, J. H. 7372
Humphreys, Robin. 6189
Hunt, James C. 7122
Huntington, Henry Strong. 1778
Hurd, Volney D. 6837
Hurewitz, Jacob C. 4941, 5077, 5078, 5406, 5865
Hurst, Cecil. 3514, 4259
Hurtig, Serge. 6627
Husseini, Jamaal Bey. 2093
Huston, Howard. 1305
Huszar, George B. de. 2957, 3221
Hutcheson, Austin E. 2257
Hutcheson, Harold H. 4517
Hutchins, Robert Maynard. 560, 684, 3282, 7736, 7752, 7845
Hutchinson, Elme H. 5038, 5079
Hutchinson, Paul. 6749
Huth, Arno G. 3222, 3952, 4014
Hutton, D. G. 1254
Hutton-Ashkenny, A. 2923
Huxley, Julian Sorell. 2958, 4343
Hyamson, Albert M. 2094
Hyde, Charles Cheney. 2258
Hyde, James Nevins. 4942, 4943, 4944, 5505
Hyde, Louis K., Jr. 5506
Hydeman, Lee M. 4390
Hyder, Khurshid. 3223

Ibrahim, A. Rashid. 3224
Ibrahim, Sardar Mohammad. 5039
Ichihashi, Yamato. 2451
Ieveking, L. M. 2155
Ikramullah, Mohammed. 7453
Ikramullah, Shaista S. 4281
Ilsley, Lucretia L. 2056, 2126
Indian Council of International Affairs. 21
Indian Council of World Affairs. 5322
Indian School of International Studies. 32
Indian Society of International Law. 22
Indian Study Group of International Affairs. 23
Ingram, Derek. 7454, 7455
Inman, Samuel Guy. 5991, 5992, 5993, 6057, 6058, 6059, 6060, 6061, 6062, 6146
Innis, Harold A. 7736
Innocent III. 613
Institute for European Politics and Economics. 146, 6570
Institute for World Affairs Education, University of Wisconsin. 5286
Institute of Commonwealth Studies. 36
Institute of Inter-American Studies. 5994
Institute of International Affairs (Toronto). 29
Institute of International Relations (Geneva). 45
Institute of Labor and Industrial Relations, University of Illinois. 4460
Institute of Pacific Relations. 1671
Institute of Public Administration (London). 5358
Institute of World Affairs (London). 57
Institute of World Affairs (Pasadena). 24
Institute on World Organization. 1306, 1351, 1356, 1395, 1477, 1481, 1648, 1718, 1755, 1814, 1854, 1867,

1898, 1930, 1960, 2009, 2156, 2176, 2302, 2467, 2799
International Air Traffic Association. 1740
International Bureau for the Standardization of Man-Made Fibres. 7664
International Commission of Jurists. 6241
International Court of Justice (Hague). 122, 350
International Institute of Administrative Science. 5262
International Institute of Agriculture. 7663, 7665
International Institute of Intellectual Cooperation. 1969, 1970
International Labor Office. 116, 306, 307, 1779, 1780, 2895, 4441
International Labour Review. 307, 1780
International Law Association, Canadian Branch. 14
International Law Association, Japanese Branch. 34
International Political Science Association. 80, 81
International Relations Committee (Nanking). 2636
International Studies Association. 13
Interparliamentary Union. 921
Ion, T. P. 1039, 1074
Ireland, Phillip W. 2068
Iriye, Akira. 7263
Irvine, Keith. 5292, 5716, 7605
Irvine, William. 849
Irving, Clifford. 3771
Isaacs, Leo. 2697
Isaacs, N. 1090
Ismay, Lord. 6948, 6949
Issawi, Charles. 5866, 5927
Italian Society for International Organization (Rome). 5568
Ito, Masanori. 2451a
Ivrakis, Solon Cleanthe. 3535, 3846
Iwi, Edward F. 7396

Jack, Homer A. 519, 4874
Jäckh, Ernest. 2452, 2773
Jacklin, Seymour. 1535
Jacks, Lawrence P. 1307, 1478, 2376, 2377, 7846
Jackson, Barbara Ward. 4015, 7081. 7293
Jackson, Elmore. 3225, 3804, 3805, 4945
Jackson, Judith. 315
Jackson, Robert H. 2959, 3108
Jackson, William Eldred. 3109
Jacob, Philip E. 181, 411, 3908, 3940, 4242, 4282, 4576, 4793, 4875, 4876, 4946, 4984, 5610
Jacobs, A. J. 699, 2551, 2570, 2851
Jacobson, Harold Karan. 3909, 4185, 4442, 4443, 4577, 5185, 5433, 5434, 5435, 6541
Jacoby, Sidney B. 2308
Jaffé, A. 1035, 2851, 3110, 6573, 6878, 7334
Jaksch, Wenzel. 7343, 7583
James, A. M. 3806
James, Alan. 4985, 4986
James, C. W. 7509
James, F. Cyril. 6950
James, William. 850
Jameson, Storm. 6750
Japan Association of International Law. 5323
Jaspers, Karl. 3226
Jaster, Robert S. 7344, 7345
Jászi, Oscar. 653, 2904, 2992, 3007, 3014, 3227, 7322, 7323
Jawed, Tufail. 4085, 5207
Jay, John. 578
Jeanneret-Gris, Charles Edouard. 3772
Jebb, Gladwyn. 2378, 3228, 4794, 6285, 6332, 6951
Jebb, Richard. 7361
Jefferson, Thomas. 860
Jeffries, J. M. N. 2110
Jelf, E. 1914, 2279, 2536, 2551, 2570, 2779, 2851

Author Index

Jenks, Clarence Wilfred. 1016, 1536, 1781, 1782, 1783, 1784, 1785, 1786, 2609, 2610, 3484, 3485, 3486, 3487, 3488, 3536, 3847, 3848, 3849, 3850, 4391, 4444, 4445, 4703, 6411
Jennings, R. Y. 3961, 4645, 4744
Jennings, W. Ivor. 1914, 6751, 6752, 7397, 7456, 7457, 7458
Jensen, Finn B. 6628
Jensen, Lloyd. 4877
Jerrold, Douglas. 1308
Jerusalem, Hebrew University. 5407
Jessup, John K. 3282
Jessup, Philip C. 1971, 2259, 2306, 2330, 2331, 2332, 2333, 2334, 2510, 2511, 2861, 3489, 3687, 3851, 3910, 4392, 4518, 4704, 4705, 4706, 6412, 7753
Jha, C. S. 7626
Jiménez de Aréchaga, Eduardo. 3653
Joad, C. E. M. 7892
Johns, David H. 5730
Johns Hopkins University, School of Advanced International Studies. 4948, 4992, 4994
Johnsen, Julia E. 1309, 2256, 2260, 2914, 2917, 2960, 2961, 2962, 2984, 3036, 3178, 3258, 4987, 5768, 6069, 6293, 7754, 7793, 7814, 7845, 7847, 7848, 7871, 7882, 7886, 7912, 7932
Johnson, Alvin. 2904
Johnson, Bascom. 1957
Johnson, Carol A. 130, 5293
Johnson, Charles S. 4344
Johnson, D. D. 6063
Johnson, D. H. N. 3688, 3962
Johnson, Franklyn A. 6952
Johnson, Grace Allen. 2637, 5634, 5672, 6184, 6333
Johnson, Howard C. 4795
Johnson, Joseph E. 851, 4016, 5436, 5472, 5507
Johnson, Richard A. 4345
Johnson, Robert H. 4519
Johnston, George A. 1570, 1787, 1788, 1859
Johnston, W. H. 1256

Johnstone, William C. 2127
Joll, James. 7584
Jones, Amy Heninway. 893
Jones, F. Llewellyn. 2128, 6064
Jones, Goronwy J. 3229
Jones, H. Stuart. 580
Jones, Joseph M. 4017, 4220
Jones, Rufus M. 847
Jones, Samuel S. 2774
Jordan, Charles H. 7679
Jordan, D. S. 1090
Jordan, Henry P. 6208
Jordan, Peter. 6739, 6753
Jordan, William M. 3230
Joseph, Bernard. 2095
Joseph, R. E. W. 1680
Josephy, F. L. 6572
Jouvenel, Bertrand de. 599
Joy, C. Turner. 5151
Joy, William. 1084
Joyce, James Avery. 182, 183, 581, 582, 618, 619, 654, 655, 1085, 1310, 1311, 3231, 3537, 3807, 4018, 5611, 7697
Joyner, Conrad. 7398
Judson, Lyman S. 6094
Julien, C. A. 7606
Junckerstorff, H. K. 5595, 6586, 6607, 6647, 6648, 7229
Juntke, Fritz. 249
Justo, A. D. 6037

Kabir, Mafizollah. 5867
Kaeckenbeeck, Georges. 926, 2184, 3110, 3364, 5263, 6573
Kahin, George M. 7627
Kahler, Erich. 7736
Kahn, Avren. 7679
Kahn, Ely Jacques, Jr. 5134
Kahn-Freund, Otto. 6542
Kahng, Tae Jin. 3742
Kain, Ronald Stuart. 2673, 2674, 6065
Kaiser, Karl. 147, 6334
Kaliharvi, Thorsten V. 1188, 6754
Kallen, Horace M. 1086
Kaltefleiter, Werner. 6335
Kamarck, Andrew M. 4086, 5294

Kamarguski, L. Alekseivich. 852
Kanamori, Hisao. 7264
Kane, R. Keith. 3743
K'ang Yu-Wei. 705
Kann, Robert A. 390
Kant, Immanuel. 706, 707, 709, 710, 712, 713, 714, 715, 716, 717, 718, 3358
Kantor, Harry. 136
Kantorowicz, Ernst H. 620
Kaplan, Joseph. 4393
Kaplan, Lawrence S. 6953, 7189
Kaplan, Morton A. 465, 466, 467, 468, 504
Kaplan, Robert. 3852
Kapp, Karl W. 1702
Kapteyn, Paul J. 6574
Karabus, Alan. 5186
Karane, Rachid. 7617
Karefa-Smart, John. 5295
Karnes, Thomas L. 6242
Karp, Basil. 6755
Karp, Mark. 4631
Karreman, Herman F. 6454
Kaser, Michael. 7346
Kasme, Badr. 3490
Kass, Stephen L. 3538, 4186, 6147
Kastl, L. 2026
Katz, Milton. 7237
Katz, Wilber G. 7736
Katzenbach, Nicholas de B. 467, 468, 504
Katzki, Herbert. 7679
Katz-Suchy, Juliusz. 3232
Kaufman, Herbert. 4422
Kaufmann, Johan. 4009, 4115, 5259
Kaufmann, Wilhelm. 1651
Kawakami, K. K. 2638, 2792
Kayser, Jacques. 2775
Kecskemeti, Paul. 7585
Kedourie, Elie. 5868
Keen, Frank Noel. 1326, 1479, 1480, 1573, 1578, 1585, 2358, 2526, 2574, 2576, 2760, 2851, 2923, 3486, 6064
Keenleyside, Hugh L. 4019, 4020
Keeny, S. M. 4251
Keesing, Felix M. 4657

Keeton, George W. 3539, 6756, 6757, 7849
Keighley-Bell, G. H. 5549
Keith, A. B. 7924
Kelchner, Warren H. 2802, 6066
Kelfa-Caulker, Richard E. 5296
Kellogg, F. B. 2309
Kellor, Frances A. 184, 1017, 1441, 1789, 2129, 2261, 2453, 2512
Kelman, Herbert C. 542, 4878
Kelsen, Hans. 469, 1442, 1443, 1481, 2310, 2963, 2964, 3037, 3365, 3366, 3367, 3422, 3491, 3492, 3493, 3540, 3541, 3601, 3602, 3689, 3744, 3745, 3746, 3808, 4578, 4666, 4796, 4797
Kemmerer, E. W. 5995
Kendle, J. E. 7531
Kendrick, B. B. 1312
Kennan, George F. 7586
Kennedy, A. L. 2432, 2464, 2565, 3911
Kennedy, Donald B. 3853
Kennedy, Sinclair. 6336
Kenny, L. M. 5869
Kent, Raymond K. 5870
Kenwarthy, J. M. 2110
Kenworthy, L. S. 3233
Kepi. 1189
Keppel, Frederick P. 7666
Keppel-Jones. 4646
Kerley, Ernest L. 3647, 3747
Kerner, Robert J. 7300
Kerno, I. S. 3368, 4707
Kerr, Philip. 2575, 2590
Kerry, Richard L. 7206
Kershaw, Raymond N. 1917
Kertesz, Stephen D. 1313, 3234, 7587
Key, David McKendree. 3423, 5508
Key, L. C. 7532
Keyfitz, Nathan. 7510, 7540
Keynes, John Maynard. 1314
Keynes, Mary Knatchbull. 5264, 7628
Keys, Donald F. 7755
Keyser, John A. 4520
Khadduri, Majid. 5871, 5872, 5873, 5874, 5930, 5931
Khalidi, Awni. 3760

Khalil, Mohammed. 5932
Khan, Begum Liaquat Ali. 4579
Khan, Hafeezur Rehman. 5741
Khan, Mir Mostofa Ali. 7265
Khan, Mohamed Samih. 3622
Khan, Muhammed Zafrullah. 3690, 4708
Khan, Nazid Ahmad. 5875
Khan, Rahmatulla. 3369, 4798, 5241
Khanna, R. S. 4346
Khrushchev, Nikita. 5437
Kiang, Lu-Yu. 5339
Kidd, George. 1482
Kidder, Frederick E. 137
Kieran, John. 7717
Killheffer, Elvin H. 4158
Killough, Hugh B. 154, 3890, 4258, 4542, 4764, 5581
Kimball, Everett. 1519
Kindleberger, Charles P. 3854, 4062
King, A. 4394
King, James E., Jr. 6954
King, John K. 3542, 3855
King-Hall, Stephen. 315, 2575
Kingsbury, H. T. 2333, 2579
Kintner, William R. 3235, 6955, 7033, 7238
Kirdar, U. 4021
Kirk, Grayson. 224, 1206, 1383, 2401, 2516, 3081, 3236, 3748, 4799, 6956, 7649
Kirkpatrick, F. A. 5845
Kirkpatrick, Helen Paull. 1571, 2675
Kisch, C. 1535
Kisch, F. H. 2100
Kish, George. 6543
Kisler, Margaret. 6148
Kissinger, Henry A. 750, 751, 802, 6957
Kitton, M. J. 547
Kitzinger, Uwe. 6544, 6545, 7123, 7124, 7125, 7126
Klausner, Leopold C. 6337, 6758, 6759, 6839
Kleffens, Eelco N. van. 3237, 5612
Kleiman, Robert. 6338, 6339
Klemme, Marvin. 4521

Klineberg, Otto. 551, 4347
Klingberg, Frank J. 1958
Kloman, Erasmus H., Jr. 5746, 5933
Klooz, Marie S. 3603, 3691
Kluyver, Mrs. C. A. 316
Knapp, Forrest L. 7683
Knappstein, K. Heinrich. 7190
Knapton, Ernest J. 773, 6760
Knight, W. S. M. 697, 700, 1261, 1480
Knoles, Tully C. 7756
Knorr, Klaus. 493, 1703, 4063, 4159, 4879, 6761, 6762, 6901, 6941, 6958, 6979, 7115, 7177, 7213
Knott, James E., Jr. 7640
Knowles, G. W. 656
Knowlton, William A. 6959
Knudson, John I. 250, 1087, 1444, 1520, 1634, 1719, 1790, 1972, 2262, 2454, 2611, 2730, 2862
Koch, Howard E., Jr. 525, 5278
Kocourek, Albert. 1088
Koefod, Paul. 6503
Kohl, Wilfrid L. 6960
Kohn, Hans. 2904, 4580, 5265, 5876, 6340, 6341, 6342, 6343, 6763, 6764, 7301, 7757, 7758
Kohn, W. S. G. 3424
Kohnstamm, Max. 6344, 6413, 6575
Kolasa, Jan. 1973, 4348
Kolnai, Aurel. 7324
Komarnicki, T. 3370
Kondapi, C. 5145, 5324, 5335
Koo, Wellington, Jr. 3238, 3633
Kopal, V. 3425
Kopelmanas, L. 2379
Korbel, Josef. 5040, 5041, 5042, 5043, 5044
Korbonski, Andrzej. 7347
Koren, William, Jr. 2698, 2699, 2809, 2863
Kornhauser, Samuel. 7759
Korovine, E. 2513
Kotenev, Anatol M. 2180, 2181
Kotschnig, Walter M. 3888, 3889
Köver, J. F. 6345
Kraft, Joseph. 6346
Kraft, Louis. 5698

Kramer, Marguerite N. 557, 5569
Krappe, A. H. 869
Kraus, Hertha. 4522
Krause, Lawrence B. 6629
Kravis, Irving B. 4148, 4187, 6546
Krehbiel, Edward. 927
Kreinin, Mordechai. 6659
Kreslins, Janis A.
Krey, August C. 621
Krezdorn, Franz J. 5682
Kriesberg, L. 552, 553, 6576, 6577
Krishna, Rao K. 4022
Krishnamachari, V. T. 5634, 5672, 6184
Krivine, J. D. 6482, 6504, 6505
Krock, Arthur. 1172
Krosby, H. Peter. 7207
Krudener, Julie de. 773
Krugman, Herbert E. 546
Krylov, Sergei Borisovich. 288
Ku, Yu-Chang Wellington, Jr. *See* Koo, Wellington, Jr.
Kubitschek, Juscelino. 5996
Kuczynski, R. R. 1239
Kuehl, Warren F. 82, 894
Kugimoto, H. 4349, 5325
Kuhl, Herman von. 1145
Kuhn, A. K. 2579
Kulski, Wladyslaw Wszebor. 185, 6962, 7348
Kumar, Dharma. 4023, 7459
Kunz, Joseph L. 1445, 1446, 1483, 3543, 4800, 5997, 6149
Kybal, Vlastimil. 7281

Labeyrie-Ménahem, C. 3912
Lacarte, Julio A. 6150
Lachs, Manfred. 3494
Ladame, Paul A. 3692
Ladas, Stephen P. 1918, 6067
Ladd, William. 853, 868
Lador-Lederer, J. J. 7641
La Farge, John. 7760
La Fontaine, Henri. 242, 928, 933, 1018, 1074, 1089, 1284, 1385, 1635, 1663, 1716, 1757, 1881, 2014, 2142, 2201, 2441, 2737, 7699

La Foy, Margaret. 2676
La Garde, August. 752
Lagarde, Jean de. 7178
Lagrange, Maurice. 6680
Lahnman, Werner J. 5613
Laidlaw, William Allison. 583
Laing, Lionel H. 7460
Lakdawala, D. R. 5775
Lake Mohonk Conference on International Arbitration. 949, 1019
Lakshminarayan, C. V. 3371, 4581
Lal, Mukut Behari. 5045
Lalive, J. F. 4801
Lall, Arthur. 5326
Lall, S. 3856
Lalovel, H. 1315
La Malfa, Ugo. 6445
Lamb, Beatrice P. 3181
Lambert, John R. 6547, 6630, 6649, 7061, 7082, 7198, 7266
Lambrinidis, John J. 6660
Lamfalussy, A. 7127
Lamington, Lord. 2110
Lammasch, Heinrich. 982, 1020
Lamont, T. W. 1240
Lande, Adolf. 4206
Lande, Gabriella Rosner. 3585, 3693
Landecker, Werner S. 412, 413, 414, 415, 416
Lang, R. D. 6765
Lange, Christian L. 584, 622, 657, 854, 895, 916, 950, 1128, 2776, 7069
Lange, Halvard M. 6766, 7070
Langer, William L. 803
Langerman, F. E. 2523
Langrod, Georges. 3857
Langrod, Jerzy Stefan. *See* Langrod, Georges
Lansing, Robert. 1021, 1190, 1191, 1521, 7761
Lanux, Pierre de. 2965
La Palombara, Joseph. 3874a
Lape, Esther Everett. 1090
Lapie, P. O. 6821
Laquer, Walter Z. 5878
Larson, Arthur. 3239
Larus, Joel. 289

Lary, H. B. 4074
Lash, Joseph P. 3809, 3810
Laski, H. J. 1522, 1752, 7901
Lasswell, Harold D. 453, 478, 492, 551, 653, 3152, 3222, 3240, 3832, 3880, 4353, 7713
Latané, John H. 858, 1091, 2579
Latey, L. J. 2828
Latey, W. 2570, 7334
Latham, R. T. E. 7372
Latheef, N. Ahmed. 3858
Latourette, Kenneth S. 623
Lattre, Jean Michel de. 5748
Lauterpacht, Elihu. 5080
Lauterpacht, Hershel. 1316, 1447, 1448, 2263, 2570, 2593, 2639, 3495, 4259, 4283, 4284, 4285, 4709, 6860
Lauterpacht, T. 2576
Lavallaz, Maurice de. 2455
Laves, Walter H. C. 470, 2346, 2549, 3694, 3773, 3774, 4350, 4351, 6068
Lawrence, Thomas J. 983, 1092
Lawson, Ruth C. 302, 3241, 3242, 3243, 3244, 3695, 3696, 3697, 3698, 3699, 3700, 4582, 4710, 4745, 4880, 5081, 5135, 5509, 5510, 6347, 6348, 6767, 6963, 7267
Layton, Lord. 1659, 1689, 7129
League of Nations. 106, 251, 252, 253, 254, 255, 256, 308, 317, 318, 319, 320, 321, 1317, 1421, 1449, 1537, 1606, 1612, 1620, 1652, 1653, 1654, 1688, 1720, 1721, 1851, 1860, 1866, 1873, 1874, 1875, 1894, 1919, 1920, 1921, 1974, 1975, 1982, 2027, 2028, 2029, 2130, 2150, 2165, 2248, 2264, 2265, 2456, 2457, 2458
League of Nations Union. 1484
League to Enforce Peace, American Branch. 1093, 1094, 1095, 1096
Lecerf, Jean. 6768
Ledermann, Laszlo. 658
Lee, Chong-Sik. 5136
Lee, Duncan Campbell. 2030
Lee, Dwight E. 1168, 2654, 3066, 3072, 3654, 5879, 6200
Lee, Marc J. 3245
Lee, Maurice, Jr. 390
Lee, R. W. 1035, 2570
Leebrick, Karl C. 2577
Lefever, Albert. 716
Lefever, Ernest W. 4834, 5187, 5188
Lefrevre, Jacqueline. 3827
LeFur, Louis. 2724
Legate, Daniel M. 7461
Léger, Paul Émile. 647
Leggett, H. 5722, 5734
Legum, Colin. 4086, 4123, 5189, 5283, 5294, 5699, 5700, 5731
Lehman, Herbert H. 4523, 4524, 4525
Lehman, John. 7325
Leifer, Michael. 4658, 5359, 5812, 6861
Leighton, Richard M. 3064
Leiserson, Avery. 417
Leiss, Amelia C. 5232
Leland, Waldo G. 1976
Lemass, S. F. 6631
Lemkin, J. A. 5718
Lenczowski, George. 5934
Lengyel, Peter. 3859
Lenoir, James L. 5998
Lenroot, Irvine L. 1318
Lenroot, Katharine F. 4476
Lent, Ernest S. 7850
Lentner, Howard H. 3811, 3812
Lentz, Theodore F. 554
Leonard, L. Larry. 186, 1655, 3038, 3082, 3701, 3749, 3775, 3813, 3941, 4024, 4195, 4526, 4583, 4711, 4881, 5082, 5614, 5615
Lepawsky, Albert. 3963, 4025, 5388
Lerche, Charles O., Jr. 4947, 4988, 5813, 6151
Lerner, Daniel. 555, 556, 557, 5569, 6349, 6769, 6873, 7179
Lerner, Edna. 2966
Lerner, Harold. 6770
Lerner, Max. 2966, 2992, 3007, 3014, 3227
Lerner, Ralph. 7908
Leslie, G. 558
Lesoir, Edmond. 7676
Lesseps, Ferdinand M. de. 2190

Lester, Sean. 2380
Lester, Sydney. 5616
Letiche, John M. 6350
Lever, Jeremy. 6578
Levermore, Charles H. 330, 659, 1319
Leverson-Gower, C. C. 7701
Levi, Werner. 187, 188, 471, 5327, 5776, 5814
Levine, Louis. 7302
Levontin, Avigdor V. 7762
Levy, Albert G. D. 3111
Lewis, Gordon. 3860, 6220
Lewis, I. M. 5701
Lewis, Malcolm M. 2151
Lewis, V. J. 585, 726
Leyden University. 290
Leys, Colin. 5731
Leyser, J. 3623
L'Huillier, Fernand. 189, 3246, 4228, 4352, 4458, 5617, 6007, 6351, 6352, 6483, 6593, 6632, 7472, 7567, 7588, 7607
Liang, Yuen-li. 3557, 3604, 3655, 3902, 4670, 5618
Lias, A. G. 1245, 1656, 2701
Lichterman, Martin. 390
Lichtheim, George. 6353
Lie, Trygve. 276, 3247, 3248, 3290, 3373, 3382, 3676, 3801, 3918, 4221, 4238, 4253, 4297, 4369, 4545
Liebenow, J. Gus. 5749
Lieber, Francis. 839, 855, 865, 867
Liesner, H. H. 6549
Lijphart, Arend. 520
Likert, Rensis. 376, 417, 419, 492
Lilienthal, Alfred M. 7763
Liljestrand, G. 864
Lima, Alceu Amoroso. 5999
Limb, Ben C. 5815
Lincoln, George A. 204, 205, 3684, 5631
Lindberg, Leon N. 6446
Lindberry, Leon H. 6354
Linde, Hans A. 4882
Lindgren, Raymond E. 390, 7071, 7072, 7073
Lindsay, Harry Alexander. 7399

Lindsay, J. W. 2677
Lindsay, Kenneth. 6819, 6820
Lindsay, Richard C. 6964
Lindsay, Samuel McCune. 1830, 1847, 2864
Lindsey, Edward. 2266
Lingelbach, William E. 2865
Linnenberg, Clem C., Jr. 418
Lintott, J. H. B. 6506
Lippmann, Walter. 1320, 2459, 3814, 6355, 7851
Liska, George. 472, 473, 502, 5955, 6356, 7618, 7619
Liska, Jiri. 5511, 6357
Lissitzyn, Oliver J. 4712
Lister, Louis. 6548
Liszt, Franz von. 7282
Little, Herbert S. 5512, 7239
Little, T. R. 5877, 5935
Little, Tom. 5437, 5266
Little, Virginia. 3964
Liveran, Arthur C. A. 5084
Livingstone, F. 3605
Lleras Camargo, Alberto. 5619, 6069, 6152, 6153
Llewellyn-Jones, F. 1485
Lloyd, Edward M. H. 1146
Lloyd, Georgia. 680
Lloyd, P. C. 3486
Lloyd George, David. 1192
Lobanov-Rostovsky, Andre. 5777
Löchen, Einar. 7208
Lochner, Louis P. 896
Locke, John. 719
Lockey, Joseph Byrne. 6000, 6001, 6070
Lockhart, John G. 753
Lockwood, Agnes Nelms. 95, 4026, 5389
Lodge, George C. 4446
Lodge, Henry Cabot. 1097, 2866, 3248, 6368
Loeber, Dietrich A. 7462
Loewenfeld, Erwin H. 3110, 3399, 4259, 6573
Loewenheim, Francis L. 390

Loewenstein, Karl. 3039, 4286, 6071, 6771, 6772, 6773
Loftus, John A. 6358
Logan, Rayford W. 2057, 2140, 5702, 7620
Lohman, Philipp H. 2640, 6359
Lokanathan, P. S. 4126, 4127
London, Kurt L. 7589
Long, R. C. 832
Longrigg, S. H. 2069
Lord, Eleanor L. 951
Lord, O. B. 560
Lord, Robert H. 749, 793
Loridan, Walter. 5570
Lorimer, Frank. 4476
Lorimer, James. 845, 856, 857
Lorwin, Lewis L. 1791, 2967, 7707
Lothian, Lady. 7372
Lothian, Lord. 1321
Loud, Frederick V. 6466
Louis, Wm. Roger. 2031
Lourie, Sylvan. 5018, 5046
Louw, Michael H. H. 4027, 5390
Loveday, Alexander. 1656, 3861, 3862, 3913, 3914, 6360
Lovell, Colin Rhys. 7556
Lowe, Boutelle E. 1792, 1793
Lowell, A. Lawrence. 1322, 1323, 1450, 2381, 2535, 2641, 2725, 2867, 7400
Lowenstein, Hubertus zu. 6361, 6965
Lowenthal, David. 6221
Lowenthal, Richard. 7590
Lozier, Marion E. 3112
Luard, David E. T. 474, 475
Lubin, Isador. 3915
Lucharrière, Guy de. 4352
Luckau, Alma M. 1193
Luke, C. H. 7372
Lund, Erling. 5019
Lundberg, George A. 5620
Luns, J .M. A. H. 3250
Lutz, Ralph H. 6774
Lybyer, Albert Howe. 5880, 5881
Lyon, Peter. 685
Lyons, Francis S. L. 897, 917, 929, 1098, 7591

Lyons, Gene M. 5137, 5138, 5513
Lyttelton, E. 1573, 1856, 2730
Lytton, Victor A. G. R. 1324, 1572, 1573, 1585, 2382, 2642, 2730

McAdoo, W. G. 6072
McAninch, W. T. 5038
MacArthur, Douglas. 3118
McBrayer, James D., Jr. 5228
McCallum, Ronald B. 1325
McClellan, Grant S. 4160, 7129
McClelland, Charles A. 291, 3159, 3209, 3321, 7733
McClintock, Charles G. 559, 4966, 6966
McClintock, Robert Lills. 7764
McCloy, John J .4087, 4883
McClure, Wallace M. 1657, 3496
MacColl, E. Kimbark. 6222
MacCracken, John H. 1099
McCready, H. W. 7542, 7566
McCreery, Henry F. 6775
McCulloch, John I. B. 6073
McCurdy, C. A. 1326
McDonald, Alexander Hugh. 4659
McDonald, E. J. 4746
McDonald, James G. 1946, 2141
MacDonald, Malcolm. 7401
MacDonald, William. 2562, 2563
McDougal, Myres S. 4287, 7765
McDougall, F. L. 1876
MacEoin, Sean. 4989
McFadyear, A. 2079, 2100
McFaydean, Andrew. 1245, 1692
McGeachy, J. B. 5085
McGhee, George C. 7199
McGuire, Paul. 3251, 7463
McHenry, Dean E. 3252, 4584, 5792, 5832, 7402
McIlwain, Charles H. 7736
McInnis, Edgar. 3426, 5371, 6967
McIntyre, Elizabeth. 3635
McIver, R. Craig. 7130
MacIver, Robert Morrison. 386, 418, 438, 453, 476, 478, 551, 577, 653, 1690, 3152, 3222, 3832, 3880, 3947, 4327, 4341, 4344, 4353, 4354, 4357,

4377, 5267, 6281, 6327, 7583, 7679, 7683, 7687, 7711, 7713, 7724, 7935
McIvor, Carlisle C. 1673
McKay, C. 5823
McKay, Vernon. 4585, 4632, 5297, 5703, 5937
McKelvey, Raymond G. 3040, 6074
McKenney, F. D. 2579
McKenzie, Vernon. 2968
McKeon, Richard. 376, 417, 419, 430, 476, 492, 4353, 4354, 4357, 7799
McKesson, John A. 6579
McKim, Anson C. 3965
MacKinney, Loren C. 624
MacKintosh, W. A. 6968
McLaughlin, Charles H. 195, 4805
MacLaughlin, Kathleen. 4028
McLeish, Alexander. 5047
McMahon, J. F. 6681, 6682
MacMurray, John V. A. 2643
MacNair, Arnold D. 2267, 2383, 2551
MacNair, H. 419
McNair, Lord. 6857
McNaught, Kenneth. 5360, 5514
McNaughton, A. G. L. 4395
McNeil, Elton B. 7755
McNeil, Hector. 3917
McQuade, Lawrence C. 6969
MacQuarrie, H. N. 3704, 6158
McQueen, Elizabeth L. 2096
McReynolds, George E. 1168, 2654, 3066, 3072, 6200
McVitty, Marion H. 4884, 4885, 4990
McWhinney, Edward. 6362
McWilliams, Wilson. 5704
Maanen-Helmer, Elizabeth van. 2131
Macadam, Ivison S. 7541
Macartney, C. A. 1254, 1278, 1285, 1922, 1945
Macaulay, Neil. 2032
Macdonald, H. I. 6633, 6634
Macdonald, R. St. J. 5165, 6190
Macdonald, Robert W. 5936
Macdonnell, John. 1429, 1794, 2143, 2779
Macedo Soares, José Carlos de. 2803
Macfarland, Charles S. 7684

Machlup, Fritz. 4105
Machray, Robert. 7303, 7327
Mack, Gerstle. 2191
Mackay, R. J. 7925
Mackay, Robert A. 7403, 7404
Mackay, Ronald William Gordon. 3253, 3313, 5621, 6414, 6776, 6777, 6778, 7766
Mackenzie, Melville D. 1877, 4243
Mackinder, Halford F. 1674, 2969
Maclaurin, John (pseud.). 292, 3636, 3703, 3750, 3776, 3916, 4586, 4713, 7767
Macready, Gordon N. 2970
Madalier, Ramaswami. 3266
Madariaga, Salvador de. 1327, 1451, 1471, 1523, 2460, 2461, 2462, 2463, 2918, 6779, 7768
Maddox, William P. 7852
Madhok, Bal Ray. 5048
Madison, James. 578
Magruder, Frank Abbott. 1452
Mah, N. Wing. 2644, 2645
Mahabir, Dennis J. 6223
Mahaim, Ernest, 1795, 1796
Maher, D. 6635
Mahmood, Khalid. 5086, 5361
Maine, Henry Sumner. 586
Mair, John. 3092
Mair, Laan P. 1923, 1924, 1925, 4660,
Maitland, Patrick. 7464
Major, John. 5882, 6840
Makdisi, George. 5903
Maki, John M. 4661
Makin, Norman J. O. 3751
Malcolm, D. O. 1988, 6270
Malcolm, N. 1949, 2499, 2565
Malcolm, Roy. 2971
Malenbaum, Wilfred. 3569
Malhotra, Ram C. 5233
Malicky, Neal. 4991
Malik, A. M. 4447, 5328
Malik, Charles. 1328, 3248, 3254, 3290, 3373, 3676, 3918, 4221, 4238, 4253, 4288, 4297, 4369, 4545
Malin, James C. 2868
Malin, Patrick M. 4477

Malinowski, Bronislaw. 5705
Malinowski, W. R. 3919
Maller, Sandor. 4355, 5438
Mallery, Otto Tod. 2972, 4161
Mallory, L. 2368
Mallory, Walter H. 2646
Mally, Gerhard. 6363, 6364
Malmstrom, Vincent H. 7074
Malof, Peter. 6643
Mance, Harry Osborne. 1951, 3948, 3953, 3966, 3967, 3968, 3969
Mandelstam, Andre Nicolayevitch. 1453, 1590
Mander, Geoffrey. 1254, 1567, 2780, 5549
Mander, Linden A. 190, 1329, 1722, 1878, 1926, 1977, 2132, 2384, 3255, 3920, 3954, 4064, 4149, 4289, 4356, 4448, 4587, 4662, 4802, 5622, 7405
Mandere, Henri C. G. J. van der. 701, 2268
Manger, William. 6075, 6159, 6160, 6161
Mangone, Gerard J. 191, 804, 984, 3570, 3777, 5515, 5623, 7642, 7926, 7927
Manisty, Herbert F. 1429, 2027, 2143, 2433, 2536, 2551, 2779, 2851, 6064
Manly, Chesly. 3256
Mann, F. A. 4065
Mann, Golo. 805
Mann, Thomas. 2904
Manning, Charles A. W. 192, 1486, 1680, 2385, 2612, 2618, 2620, 2751
Manning, E. 2801
Manno, Catherine Serf. 3606
Mansergh, Nicholas. 7131, 7405, 7406, 7414, 7465, 7466, 7467, 7468, 7514, 7515, 7550, 7551, 7629
Manshott, S. L. 6447
Mantoux, Paul. 170, 1591, 1592, 1593
Manzanares, Henri. 6821
Manzer, Ronald A. 4116
Marburg, Theodore. 245, 831, 858, 898, 1022, 1091, 1100, 1101, 1120, 1469
Marcus, Ernst. 2097

Marcy, Carl M. 5516, 7718
Margalith, Aaron M. 2033
Marjolin, Robert. 6636
Markham, J. W. 6637
Markowitz, Marvin D. 5190
Marley, Lord. 949
Marmorstein, Emile. 5883
Marriott, John A. 660, 722, 740, 7853
Marschak, Jacob. 380, 419, 430, 492, 7799
Marsh, Leonard C. 4520
Marshall, Charles Burton. 4886, 4992
Marshall, James. 4357
Marshall, Thomas R. 2869
Marston, Frank Swain. 601, 1147, 1194
Martelli, George. 2700, 5571
Martin, Andrew. 3340, 3405, 3427, 4803, 4887
Martin, Charles E. 1330, 1469, 1675, 5683, 6002, 6003, 6780
Martin, Clarence E. 2335
Martin, Edwin M. 3113
Martin, Kingsley. 6970
Martin, Laurence W. 4948, 5176, 5281, 7618, 7619
Martin, Paul. 4888, 4993
Martin, Percy Alvin. 2804
Martin, P. W. 1691, 4358
Martin, William. 1797, 6781
Martz, John D. 6244
Marvin, Francis S. 601, 602, 613, 699, 745, 748, 806, 1411, 7795
Marx, Daniel, Jr. 3970, 3971
Maschko, Arturo. 6257
Masland, John W. 3778
Maslow, Will. 5268
Mason, Edward S. 3041, 4074
Mason, Henry L. 5087, 6580
Mason, John Brown. 2150, 2153
Mason, Philip. 5719
Massey, Vincent. 6198, 7406
Masters, Roger. 477, 5439
Masters, Ruth D. 138, 1742, 6076
Matecki, B. E. 4117, 4118
Mather, Jeanette E. 3048
Mathews, L. K. 6004

Miller, Richard I. 3815
Miller, Spencer, Jr. 1800
Millikan, Max F. 7639
Mills, D. Handel 1801
Mills, Lennox A. 195, 4805
Mills, Mark Carter. 2035
Mills, Ogden. 2337
Millspaugh, Arthur C. 2973
Mathieu, Gilbert. 6638
Mathieu, Marie Henry Jean. 661
Mathijsen, Pierre. 6671
Matos, José. 2805
Matsushita, Masatoshi. 2793
Matteson, Robert E. 4889
Matthael, Louise E. 952
Matthews, Mary Alice. 662
Matthews, Roy A. 7132
Mattison, Mary. 2670, 2678
Maughan, Viscount. 3114
Maurice, Frederick B. 1148, 1149, 2464, 2506, 3065
Maury, René. 6448
Maxrui, Ali A. 5298
Maxwell, Bertram W. 193
May, Elizabeth S. 1699
May, Herbert L. 1893, 1894, 4207
May, Stacey. 5624
Mayne, Richard. 532, 6581, 6639
Mayobre, José A. 6005, 6162
Mazrui, Ali A. 5706, 5732, 7083
Mead, Edwin Doak. 676, 714, 743, 832, 837, 859, 860, 899, 1023
Mead, Lucia T. Ames. 861, 985
Mead, Margaret. 376, 380, 417, 430, 492, 7799
Mead, Nelson P. 2465, 2537, 2564
Meade, James E. 6471, 6472, 6473, 6549
Meaney, N. K. 2870
Mecham, Lloyd J. 6006, 6077, 6191
Medlicott, William N. 807
Meeker, Leonard C. 4396
Meeker, Royal, 1798
Mehren, Arthur T. von. 6823
Mehren, Robert B. von. 4397
Mehrotra, S. R. 7407, 7525
Meigs, Cornelia. 3257

Melley, John M. 2701
Melman, Seymour. 4860, 4890, 4891, 7923
Meltzer, Julian L. 5101
Mendershausen, Horst. 6365, 6550
Mendès-France, Pierre. 3912, 6640
Mendlovitz, Saul H. 278, 3612, 3650, 4859, 7744
Menon, M. A. K. 3955
Mentschikoff, S. 6668
Menzies, Robert Gordon. 7469
Merchant, Livingston T. 4994, 7240
Mercy, Arch A. 4423
Merkl, Peter H. 516, 521, 6737, 6841
Merle, Marcel. 7608
Meron, T. 4588
Merrian, Alan P. 5191
Merrill, Frederick T. 1879
Merry, Henry J. 6582
Meston, Lord. 5722, 5734
Metson, William. 5670
Metternich. 802, 825
Metz, John. 107, 1102
Metzger, Laure. 4066
Metzler, Lloyd A. 380, 4067
Meulen, Jacob ter. 663, 754, 862, 863
Meyer, Carl L. W. 2336
Meyer, Cord. Jr. 3258, 4891, 7769
Meyer, Eugene. 3089, 4088
Meyer, Frederick Victor. 6661
Meyer, Henry C. 7283
Meyer, Milton W. 5778
Mezeris, A. G. 3624
Miall, Bernard. 241
Michaelis, Alfred. 4089, 5408
Michener, Roland. 7470
Middlebush, Frederick A. 194, 1636, 1723, 2269, 2386, 2647
Middleton, Drew. 6366, 6367, 6971
Middleton, L. 7372
Midgaard, Knut. 4995
Mikesell, Raymond F. 4029, 4106, 4162
Milhaud, Edgard. 4804
Millar, Thomas B. 5049, 5362, 7500, 7630
Millard, C. H. 7708

Millard, Everett L. 3428, 7854
Miller, David Hunter. 986, 1195, 1196, 1197, 1743, 1799, 2034, 2270, 2538, 2578
Miller, Edward G., Jr. 6163
Miller, Eugene H. 6199, 6200
Miller, J. D. B. 1988, 7133, 7134, 7471, 7472, 7473, 7557, 7567, 7630
Millward, Alex. 2387
Minor, Raleigh Colston. 1103, 1104
Mishler, E. 5517
Misra, K. P. 5329
Mitchell, Nicholas Pendleton. 2058
Mitchell, Thomas Howard. 6782
Mitrany, David A. 196, 1471, 1621, 2388, 2974, 4030, 4290, 6783, 6784, 7902, 7903
Miyaoka, Tsunejiro. 2794
Moch, Gaston. 953
Moch, Jules. 4892
Modelski, George. 531, 5801, 5803, 5811, 5816, 5817, 5818, 5819, 5820, 5826, 7592
Mogannam, Mogannam E. 2098
Mogi, Sobi. 2648
Mohan, Jitendra. 5088, 5166, 5330
Mohn, Paul. 5020, 5089, 5090
Mokarzel, S. A. 5884
Moldaver, Arlette, 3657
Molen, Gezina J. H. Van Der. 3491, 3551, 3739, 3997, 4677, 4690
Mollet, Guy. 6846
Monaco, Riccardo. 83, 197
Monbeig, Pierre. 6007
Mondell, Frank W. 2466
Money, Leo George Chiozza. 1150
Monnet, Jean. 6449, 6639, 6768
Monroe, Ann D. 7136, 7137
Montagne, Robert. 5885
Montmorency, J. E. G. 2300
Mookerjee, Girija D. 6785
Mookerjee, Subimal. 7135, 7268
Moon, Parker T. 84, 1198
Moor, Carol Carter. 338
Moore, Arthur. 3429
Moore, Ben T. 6672, 6972
Moore, Bernard. 293, 3259, 3705

Moore, Harry H. 3260, 6507, 7856
Moore, Harry Estill. 1585, 5625, 5626
Moore, John Bassett. 954, 955, 1024, 1025, 1331, 2271, 2634, 6078
Moore, Lynden. 7101
Moore, O. 4949
Moore, Raymond A., Jr. 3261, 3262
Moore, W. Harvey. 3110, 6573, 6860, 6878
Moore, William Harrison. 2752, 2923
Moorhead, Helen Howell. 1891, 1897, 2896
Mora, José A. 6079, 6164
Morales, Cecilio. 6258
Morales, Minerva M. 5395
Morán, Carol M. 7719
Morard, Nicolas. 6583
Moreno Quintana, Lucio Manuel. 6080
Moresco, Emanuel. 2036
Morgan, Carlyle. 4068
Morgan, D. J. 6450
Morgan, G. G. 6165
Morgan, Laura Puffer. 1896, 2467, 2468
Morgan, Shepard. 1241, 1676
Morgenstierne, Wilhelm Muntle. 6973
Morgenthau, Hans J. 198, 376, 380, 417, 419, 430, 478, 479, 492, 3083, 3263, 3264, 3265, 3430, 3944, 4893, 4959, 5644, 6584, 6974, 7770, 7799, 7904
Morgenthau, Henry. 2871
Morgenthau, Henry, Jr. 4069
Morgner, Aurelius. 5627
Moritzen, Julius. 863, 900
Morley, Felix. 901, 1199, 1332, 1574, 1594, 1607, 1637, 2649, 3374
Morley, John. 731
Morozov, P. D. 3431, 5440
Morris, Bernard. 7269
Morris, Charles. 376, 419, 430, 7799
Morris, G. M. 4778
Morris, James. 4090
Morris, Joe Alex. 3005
Morris, Robert C. 956
Morris, Roland S. 2579, 2827

Morrison, Herbert S. 1333
Morrow, Dwight W. 199, 664, 808, 930, 987, 1105, 1137, 1151
Morrow, Ian F. D. 2154, 2155
Morse, David A. 4449
Mortimer, Molley. 4589
Mortished, R. J. P. 1861
Morton, W. L. 7102
Mosely, Philip E. 3084, 5441, 5442, 7747
Moskowitz, Moses. 4291, 4292
Mosley, Oswald. 6786
Moulton, Harold S. 1242
Moulton, Mildred A. 1575
Mousheng, Lin. 4293
Moussa, Pierre. 7609
Mowat, J. 1368
Mowat, Robert B. 200, 732, 809, 810, 1334, 1487
Mower, A. Glenn, Jr. 3706, 6842
Mower, Edmund. 201, 1595, 1638, 1802, 1862, 1880, 1927, 1978, 2037, 2133, 2272, 2469, 2702
Mowrer, Edgar A. 480
Moyal, M. 5938
Moynier, G. 931
Mozer, Alfred. 6641
Mrozek, I. 3425
Mudalier, Arcot. 4244, 5331
Muhlen, N. 3115
Muir, Ramsay. 202, 7474
Mukerjee, S. 3375, 5139
Mukerji, K. P. 7304
Muller, Edwin. 7856
Mullett, Charles F. 7475
Mulley, Frederick William. 6975, 6976
Mumford, Lewis. 2904
Mumford, P. S. 2064
Munch, Peter. 1335, 2777
Munger, Edwin S. 5707
Munk, Frank. 6368
Munro, Henry F. 2872
Munro, Leslie. 3267, 3707, 3752, 4996, 6415
Munzi, Ugo. 6585
Muralt, Leonhard von. 6787

Murden, F. D. 3915, 4114
Muret, Charlotte. 7857
Murkland, Harry B. 4163
Murra, Kathrine O. 7677
Murray, Gilbert. 240, 1254, 1336, 1337, 1338, 1928, 1979, 2923, 4997, 7858
Murray, James N., Jr. 4590
Murry, J. Middleton. 7928
Murville, Couve de. 6977
Mussolini, Benito. 2719
Musy, Jean Marie. 6451
Muther, Jeannette E. 3044
Muynck, Gust. de. 6586
Myers, B. 7384
Myers, Denys P. 257, 258, 330, 481, 932, 957, 988, 1039, 1074, 1106, 1107, 1212, 1243, 1339, 1340, 1488, 1538, 1539, 1576, 1577, 1596, 1639, 2038, 2273, 2306, 2338, 2470, 2471, 2472, 2580, 2613, 2732, 2897, 5628, 6245
Myers, Margaret G. 1677
Myers, S. D., Jr. 503, 2039, 2099
Myers, William Starr. 2581
Myrdal, Alva. 4196, 4894
Myrdal, Gunnar. 420, 482, 4031, 4136

Nabuco, Mauricio. 7771
Nadelmann, Kurt H. 6823
Nagórski, Zygmunt. 2923, 7217
Najan, E. W. 727
Najera, Francesca Castillo, 2975
Nakazawa, Ken. 2650, 2651
Nambiar, K. R. 5762
Nanes, Allan S. 4895, 6530, 6673, 6674, 7241
Narasimhan, P. S. 4032
Narayan, C. V. L. 1026
Nash, E. Gee. 636
Nash, Philip C. 3042, 7722
Nash, Vernon. 7773
Nathan, Manfred. 697
Nathan, Otto. 2389, 7774
Nathan, Robert R. 5091

Panikkar, K. M. 5633, 5634, 5672, 6184
Papanek, Gustav F. 4039
Paparao, A. 3271
Papi, Giuseppe Ugo. 1712
Paradisi, Bruno. 626
Pardasani, N. S. 4164
Pargellis, Stanley. 608, 620, 669, 1209
Parker, Edwin B. 2339
Parker, Harrison. 4360
Parker, John J. 2980
Parker, W. R. 1535
Parker, William N. 6551, 6587
Parkes, Henry B. 2981
Parmelee, Maurice. 5635, 7775
Parodi, Alexandre. 4950
Parry, Clive. 3497, 3780, 4592
Parsons, Clifford J. 5236
Parsons, Edward L. 7685
Parsons, Talcott. 376, 417, 419, 430, 486, 487, 488, 492, 7799
Partharasarathy, N. 7084
Pascal-Bonetti. 1980
Passy, Frederic. 903
Pastuhov, Vladimir D. 1640
Pasvolsky, Leo. 1692, 2777a, 3045
Patch, William H. 339
Patel, H. M. 4040
Paton, H. J. 2186
Patterson, Caleb Perry. 2778
Patterson, Ernest M. 6753
Patterson, Gardner. 6990
Patterson, George B. 2982
Patterson, Morehead. 4399
Paul, Robert A. 7191, 7218
Paullin, Theodore. 665, 7833, 7898, 7905
Paulsen, Friedrich. 716
Pauwels, Peter C. 2134
Pavadya, Balram Singh. 7526
Pavlovic, Radmila. 5421
Paymann, J. 6416
Peace Research Institute (Oslo). 39
Peake, Cyrus H. 2653
Pearson, Lester B. 3272, 3313, 5001, 6991, 6992, 6993, 6994, 7138, 7139

Peaslee, Amos J. 207, 2311, 2333, 2983, 2984, 7776
Pedersen, Richard F. 5272
Peel, V. N. 2100, 5549
Peffer, Nathaniel. 5823
Pehle, John W. 4072
Pehrsson, Hjalmar. 151
Pei, Mario Andrew. 7865
Pella, Giuseppe. 6588
Pella, Vespasian V. 4716
Pelt, Adrian. 3865
Pelzer, Karl J. 4663
Penfield, William L. 958
Penn, William. 717, 720, 721, 723, 724
Penrose, Ernest F. 4041
Pepper, George W. 2276, 2874
Peretz, Don. 4493, 4494, 4495, 5092, 5093
Pereyra, Diomedes de. 6010
Périgord, Paul. 1804
Perkins, Dexter. 6011
Perkins, E. R. 2654
Perkins, Howard C. 206, 5632
Perkins, Merle L. 736
Perkins, Whitney T. 5215
Perlemann, M. 5939, 5947
Permanent Court of Arbitration. 1027
Permanent Court of International Justice (Hague). 324, 325, 326, 2277
Perris, G. H. 208, 589, 812
Perroux, François. 6373
Perry, Ralph B. 2985
Pescatore, Pierre. 6417, 6418
Peters, Donald W. 4467
Petersen, Keith S. 533, 3273, 3434, 3710, 3755
Peterson, Genevieve. 756
Petersson, Hans F. 1111
Pethybridge, Roger. 5446
Petrén, Sture. 6862
Petrovic, N. 4633
Pettovich, P. 6789
Pezet, F. Alfonso. 6081
Pfaltzgraff, Robert L., Jr. 6995, 7140
Pfister, Christian. 741
Pham-Thi-Tu. 1981

Pharand, A. Donat. 3575
Phelan, Edward J. 1346, 1622, 1623, 1693, 1805, 1806, 1807, 1808, 1809, 1810, 1811, 1812, 1813, 1848, 7362
Phelan, V. C. 4451
Phelps, Edith M. 1110, 1347
Philby, H. 2100
Phillimore, Walter G. F. 813, 866, 1429, 2143, 2278, 2279
Philip, André. 6374, 6375, 6589
Philip, Oliver. 6790
Philipps, T. 1988
Philips, J. 4503
Phillips, R. W. 7667
Phillips, Walter Alison. 814
Picarda, P. A. 6878
Pickard, Bertram. 7643
Pickles, William. 6645, 7141
Pictet, Jean-S. 7698
Piercy, A. 3486, 3514
Pierre-Tixier, Andrien. 1814
Pierson, Sherleigh G. 5002
Piip, A. 2779
Pike, Bernard. 7680
Pilkington, R. 2112
Pillai, P. P. 4452, 5334
Pillsbury, Kent. 4361
Pilotti, Massimo. 489
Pinder, John H. M. 7142
Pink, Gerhard P. 1222
Pink, Louis H. 2986
Pinna, L. A. de. 6878
Pinto, Roger. 303, 4137, 6590, 6844, 6996, 7349
Pipkin, Charles W. 1348
Piquet, Howard S. 4222, 4223
Pitersky, Nikolai A. 4903, 5447
Plank, Edward G., Jr. 6163
Plaza, Galo. 3085, 3435, 4143
Pleven, René. 7180
Plimsoll, James. 3436
Podea, Iris S. 6202
Podebrad, George. 726
Pogue, Forrest C. 3066
Poirier, Pierre. 5094
Polach, J. G. 6676
Polanyi, K. 419, 430, 492, 7799

Polier, Jonathan. 5704
Political and Economic Planning (London). 304, 1704
Politis, Nicholas S. 1471, 2280, 2475, 2540, 7933
Pollaczek, Gustav. 3922
Pollard, Albert F. 1112
Pollard, R. S. W. 3486
Pollis, Admantia. 3585
Pollock, Frederick. 259, 815, 989, 1349, 2279, 4717
Pollock, James K. 2167
Pollux. 3378
Polybius. 590
Polyzoides, Adamantios Th. 2703, 3086, 3087, 3274, 3275, 3276, 6012, 7243, 7307, 7478
Pompe, W. P. J. 3439, 3491, 3551, 3997, 4677, 4690
Poole, Bernard L. 6210
Pope, G. O. 7294
Pope, James R. 5636
Poplair, S. L. 5143
Popper, David H. 2102, 5519, 6013, 6082
Popper, Otto. 7328
Possony, Stefan T. 209, 228, 3379, 5652, 6955
Potter, Pitman B. 210, 211, 212, 213, 214, 260, 376, 380, 417, 419, 490, 491, 591, 816, 919, 934, 935, 990, 1350, 1351, 1352, 1353, 1354, 1454, 1455, 1471, 1490, 1579, 1597, 1608, 1641, 1817, 1863, 2041, 2042, 2237, 2281, 2306, 2391, 2392, 2515, 2579, 2614, 2704, 2705, 2733, 2734, 2735, 2753, 2987, 3277, 3866, 5637, 6083, 7644, 7645, 7777, 7866, 7867
Potulicki, M. 7693
Power, J. 1254, 1659, 2432, 7701
Power, Terry. 5144, 5362
Power, Thomas F., Jr. 4042
Prasad, P. S. Narayan. 7568
Pratt, H. M. 1035, 2128, 2570
Pratt, J. 7372
Pratt, R. C. 5723
Pratt, Sereno S. 920

Author Index

Prelot, Marcel. 189
Preston, Richard A. 7409
Preuss, Lawrence, 3544, 3545, 3867, 4760
Pribram, Karl. 1815
Price, Clair. 2071
Price, David B. 3380, 5095, 5168
Price, Harry B. 4509, 6510
Price, John. 1816, 4453
Price, Peter. 7501
Prince, A. E. 5096
Prince, Charles. 2814
Proctor, J. Harris. 5886, 5906, 6226
Projansky, Sonia. 3868
Pryce, Roy. 6376, 6552, 6822
Puech, J. L. 7595
Pugh, A. 7701
Puig, Amaro. 6247
Pullias, E. V. 717, 724
Purcell, Royal. 3278, 3711
Purcell, V. W. W. S. 4128
Purves, Chester. 1624, 1625, 3869
Pyman, T. A. 3816, 5021

Quan, Lau-king, 2797
Queen-Hughes, R. W. 7102
Quigley, Caroll. 5751
Quigley, Harold S. 1355, 2182
Quintanilla, Luis. 6014

Rabe, Olive. 3279
Rabl, Kurt. 5208
Racine, Raymond. 6791
Radin, Max. 3116
Raeburn, Walter. 4454
Rafa'i, Abdul Monem. 5887
Raffety, F. W. 5549
Rafig, M. 5888
Ragg, Lonsdale. 694
Ragonette, Marie. 3712
Rahman, Hafiz H. 215
Rajan, M. S. 3546, 3547, 5520, 7479, 7516, 7527
Rajchman, Ludwick. 3248, 3290, 3373, 3676, 3918, 4221, 4238, 4253, 4297, 4369, 4545
Raju, G. S. 3576, 3923

Raleigh, J. S. 3940
Ralston, Jackson H. 959, 1028, 1029, 1030, 2579, 2988
Ram, Vangala S. 2754
Ramani, R. 5638
Ramazani, R. K. 5889, 7200
Randolph, B. C. 2333
Rangnekar, D. K. 7143
Ranshofen-Wertheimer, Egon F. 1356, 1626, 1627, 2989, 2990, 3781
Ransom, Harry Howe. 4922, 6997
Rao, B. Shiva. 4593, 5145, 5335
Rao, K. Krishna. 3437, 4718
Rao, P. Chandrasekhara. 3923
Rao, T. S. Rama. 3577, 5336
Rao, V. K. R. V. 4043, 7480
Rapisardi-Mirabelli, A. 1642
Rappaport, Armin. 2655
Rappard, William E. 1357, 1358, 1359, 1360, 1361, 1362, 1363, 1364, 1365, 1366, 1367, 1368, 1369, 1471, 2010, 2043, 2044, 2103, 2393, 2736, 2781, 2782, 3280, 3281, 4594, 4595, 5572 ,6792, 7906
Rasmussen, Charlotte B. 7329
Ratchford, B. U. 7414, 7515
Rathbone, E. 2079, 4503
Rauchberg, H. 1456
Ray, Jahar. 7144
Ray, Jean. 1457, 1491, 1508
Read, Elizabeth F. 216, 936, 2207
Read, James M. 4478
Read, John E. 4719
Reade, A. A. E. 6270
Reade, W. A. V. 692
Reading, Marquess of. 1162, 1203, 1211
Reddell, George. 1162, 1203, 1211
Redfield, Robert. 7736
Redlich, Marcellus D. A. R. von. 904
Redmond, D. G. 3046
Redslob, Robert. 1370, 1371
Reed, Edward. 3282
Reed, S. 1565
Rees, Elfan. 4479, 4480, 4481, 7569
Reeves, Jesse S. 1113, 7410
Reid, Douglas. 1680

917

Reid, Escott. 1535, 1585, 1659, 2358, 2701, 4091
Reid, Helen Dwight. 117, 2156, 5686, 5890
Reid, Patrick. 7481
Reid, William A. 6084
Reidy, Joseph W. 7270
Reiff, Henry. 937, 2875, 3283
Reinsch, Paul S. 938, 939, 991, 6085, 6086
Reis, John C. 6998
Reiser, Pedro. 7709
Reisky-Dubnic, Vladimir. 7287
Reith, Charles. 5003
Remba, Oded. 5948
Renborg, Bertl A. 1897, 1898, 4208
Renne, Roland R. 7244
Renouvin, Pierre. 6793
Rentier, Jeannie. 6845
Requin, Lt.-Col. 242, 928, 933, 1284, 1385, 1635, 1663, 1716, 1757, 1881, 2014, 2142, 2201, 2441, 2737, 7699
Research Center for International Social Justice. 51
Research Center on the Social Implications of Industrialization in South Asia. 131
Reston, James B. 3659
Reuter, Paul. 217, 6378, 6591, 6592
Reut-Necolussi, E. 2282, 4482
Reverell, F. 2432
Reves, Emery. 7934
Rey, Jean. 7201
Reynaud, Paul. 6379, 6794
Reynolds, Ernest Edwin. 1372, 1947
Reynolds, Thomas H. 6087
Rheinbaben, Werner von. 1162, 1203, 1211
Rhyne, C. S. 7778
Riad, F. A. M. 5196
Rice, A. V. 7686
Rich, S. Grover, Jr. 5639
Richardson, J. Henry. 1849
Richelieu, duc de. 727
Riches, Cromwell A. 1373, 1554, 1555, 1597, 3637
Richardson, B. T. 7482

Richardson, Channing B. 4483, 4496, 4497, 5521
Richmond, Admiral. 2464
Riddell, Walter A. 218, 2476, 2656, 2706, 3047, 7779
Riddle, J. H. 2991
Rider, Fremont. 3284
Ridgeway, George L. 7668
Rie, Robert. 757
Rieben, Henri. 6593, 6594
Riefler, Winfield W. 419, 3924
Riegelman, Carol. 4455
Riemer, Neal. 3135, 7722
Rienow, Robert. 3285, 5640
Rieselbach, Leroy N. 523
Riesman, David. 419, 430, 492
Riggs, Fred W. 493, 4484, 4596
Riggs, Robert E. 3286, 3381, 5522
Rihani, Ameen. 5891
Rikhye, Indarjit. 5004
Riou, Gaston. 1374
Ripley, Josephine. 7063
Rippy, J. Fred. 376, 380, 419, 492, 6015
Ristelheuber, René. 4485
Ritchie, Hugh. 1153
Ritchie, Ronald S. 6999
Rivero, J. 422
Rivkin, Arnold. 5752, 5764, 7085
Rivlin, Benjamin. 3713, 4573, 4597, 4634, 4635, 5956, 7610
Robbins, Lionel. 1694
Roberts, Henry L. 85
Roberts, Justice Owen J. 560, 7000
Roberts, W. Adolphe. 6248
Robertson, Arthur H. 4530, 6381, 6795, 6796, 6797, 6798, 6846, 6847, 6863, 6864, 6865, 6866, 6867
Robertson, J. M. 638
Robertson, William Spence. 6088, 6474
Robins, Dorothy B. 3287
Robinson, Henry M. 1658
Robinson, Howard. 2992, 3007, 3014, 3227, 7363, 7411
Robinson, J. William. 311, 1081, 3288, 5523

Author Index

Robinson, Jacob. 1929, 1930, 3289, 3438, 3439, 3760
Robinson, Kenneth. 4598
Robinson, Nehemiah. 4296
Robinson, Roland. 7528
Robinson, V. 2760
Robson, N. 5836
Robson, Peter. 5731
Rockefeller, Nelson. 5687
Rodgers, Raymond Spencer. 4400, 7646
Rodo, Laureano Lopez. 7202
Roemer, William F. 627
Roerich, G. N. 5780
Roettger, Gregory J. 647
Rogers, Edith Nourse. 2582
Rogers, John Jacob. 2477
Rogers, Lindsay. 1678, 2478, 2738
Rogers, William C. 86
Rohn, Peter H. 423, 534, 6382, 6419, 6848
Rolin, Henri A. 2045, 2479, 2480, 2615, 2783, 2784, 4747, 6878
Roling, B. V. A. 3440
Romulo, Carlos P. 3248, 3290, 3291, 3373, 3676, 3918, 4221, 4238, 4253, 4297, 4369, 4545, 4599, 5781, 7631
Ronning, C. Neale. 6166
Rooker, J. K. 2575
Roosevelt, Eleanor. 3248, 3290, 3292, 3373, 3676, 3918, 4044, 4221, 4238, 4253, 4297, 4369, 4545
Roosevelt, Franklin D. 3050, 6037
Roosevelt, James. 6947
Roosevelt, K. 5097, 5892
Roosevelt, Theodore. 1109
Root, Elihu. 867, 2283
Rooth, Ivar. 4107
Roper, Elmo. 560, 561, 6383, 6742
Ropes, E. C. 7288
Röpke, Wilheim. 5641
Rosberg, Carl G., Jr. 5735
Rose, William J. 2187
Rosecrance, Richard N. 494, 817, 5792, 7001
Rosegger, Gerhard. 7271
Rosen, S. McKee. 3067
Rosenau, James. 486
Rosenfeld, Marcia. 3585
Rosenhaupt, Hans W. 7647
Rosenne, Shabtai. 535, 3498, 3607, 4720, 4721, 4722, 4723
Rosenstein-Rodan, P. N. 4045
Rosenthal, Abraham Michael. 3293
Roshwald, Mordecai. 5005
Rosner, Gabriella. 5071, 5098
Ross, Alf. 2730, 3382
Ross, Lawrence F. J. 4808
Rössel, Agda. 3578
Rosteng, Helmer. 1931
Rostovtseff, Michael. 592, 593
Rostow, Eugene V. 7002
Rostow, Walt W. 4138
Rotary International. 3383
Rotberg, Robert I. 5736
Rothchild, Donald S. 5712, 5724, 5737, 5738, 7145
Rothstein, Andrew. 2815
Rothwell, Charles Easton. 495, 7780
Rotvand, Georges. 7003
Rouček, Joseph S. 666, 1291, 1932, 1933, 2202, 4457, 7289, 7330
Rougemont, Denis de. 6696, 6790
Rousseau, Charles. 5094
Rousseau, Jean-Jacques. 728, 730, 731, 732, 733, 734
Roussier, Michel. 372
Roussin, Marcel. 6203
Rouyer-Hameray, Bernard. 3499, 3548
Rowan-Robinson, Major General. 1285
Rowe, Edward T. 524, 4600
Rowe, J. W. F. 1699
Rowe, L. S. 6016, 6030
Rowell, Chester G. 2395, 2657, 2707
Rowell, Newton Wesley. 2755, 7364,
Rowley, C. D. 4601, 5364
Rowse, A. L. 7365
Royal Institute of International Affairs (London). 13, 25, 56, 87, 340, 373, 1609, 2104, 2396, 2708, 5229, 5365, 5824, 6511, 7004, 7146, 7781, 7809, 7858, 7890

Royal Institute of International Relations (Brussels). 5567
Rozental, Alec A. 4119
Rubin, Ronald. 3294
Rubinow, Edward S. 2658
Rubinstein, Alvin Z. 118, 3925, 3942, 4129, 4401, 5448, 5449, 5450, 5451, 5452, 5453, 5524, 5525
Rubinstein, J. L. 1948
Rublee, George. 242, 928, 929, 933, 1154, 1284, 1385, 1635, 1663, 1716, 1757, 1881, 2014, 2142, 2201, 2441, 2737, 7699
Rucenski, J. 4092
Ruchenberg, Frederich von. 6377
Rucker, Arthur. 4486, 5146
Rudd, F. A. 4402
Rudin, Harry R. 5197
Rudzinski, Aleksander Witold. 88, 1549, 3549, 3608, 3638, 3639, 3660, 5454
Rueff, Jacques. 6453
Ruge, Friedrich. 7005
Rugg, Harold Ordway. 2993
Ruml, Beardsley. 6799
Rundestein, Simon. 2284
Rusett, Alan W. de. 3295, 3441, 3640, 3641
Rusk, Howard A. 4202
Russell, Frank M. 219, 496, 594, 609, 628, 666, 667, 905, 1375, 1376, 1377, 2168, 2169, 2170, 2397, 2481, 5642
Russell, Justice. 1074
Russell, Ruth B. 497, 3048, 3442, 5006, 5007
Russell, Sara A. 130, 5293
Russett, Bruce M. 498, 499, 536
Rustow, Dankwart A. 424
Rutgers, V. H. 1458, 2583
Ryan, P. L. 5837

Sá, H. T. de. 297
Saba, H. 3926, 5688, 5894
Sabourin, Louis. 5366
Sacks. Benjamin. 668
Sady, Emil John. 3888, 3889, 4602

Sage, Walter N. 7366
St. Aubin, W. de. 4498
Saint-Pierre, C. I. Castel de, Abbé de. 735, 736, 737, 738
Sainte-Aulaire, Auguste Felix Charles de Beaufoil. 1378
Sait, Edward M. 2398
Saito, Hiroshi. 2659
Salem, Elie. 5895
Salmon, Jean Charles. 7086
Salomon, A. 7711, 7713
Salter, James Arthur. 242, 928, 933, 1155, 1284, 1385, 1471, 1492, 1635, 1659, 1660, 1661, 1662, 1663, 1679, 1689, 1716, 1757, 1881, 2014, 2142, 2201, 2441, 2737, 4904, 6512, 6800, 7699
Salter, Noel. 6849
Salvadori, Massimo. 7006, 7007
Salvemini, Gaetano. 2904, 3384
Salvin, Marina. 2402, 2486, 2711, 4905, 5455, 7008
Salvioli, Gabriele. 2285
Salzberg, John. 528
Sammons, Robert L. 6259
Samore, W. 4724
Samuel, Herbert. 2105, 2106, 2107
Samuels, Nathaniel. 3068
Sanders, N. 1245, 7384
Sanders, William. 6167, 6168
Sanderson, Fred. H. 6595
Sanderson, J. 2565
Sandford, D. A. 2709
Sandhaus, Edith. 2046
Sandifer, Durward V. 4298
Sandler, Åke, 3296
Sandrasegara, M. 7868
Sandwell, B. K. 7009
Sanger, Clyde. 5753, 5765
Sanger, Sophy. 1818
Sannwald, Rolf. 6454
Santhanam, K. 5634, 5672, 6184
Sarasin, Pote. 5646
Sarola, Charles. 738
Sathyamurthy, T. V. 4362
Sato, N. 5337
Satow, Ernest M. 818

Saud, Mahmoud Abu. 5941
Saurat, Denis. 1162, 1203, 1211
Savary, Alan. 7611
Savic, V. R. 7331
Sayegh, Fayez A. 5896, 7614, 7622
Sayre, Frances Bowes. 940, 1628, 4603, 4604, 4605
Sayre, Wallace S. 3760
Sbarounis, Athanase J. 3870
Scammell, J. M. 7309
Scammell, W. M. 4108
Scanlon, Helen L. 89, 90
Scarmon, L. G. 1988
Scelle, George. *See* Schelle, Georges
Scerni, Mario. 2286
Schaaf, C. Hart. 4046, 4130, 4131
Schachter, Oscar. 278, 2287, 3385, 3501, 3782, 3804, 4047, 5198
Schachter, Ruth. 5740
Schaetzel, J. Robert. 7010
Shaffer, Alice. 4254
Schain, Josephine. 6089
Schapiro, L. B. 1524, 3550, 5456
Schechtman, Joseph B. 4299, 4487
Scheingold, Stuart A. 6596
Schelle, Georges. 1379, 1819, 2617, 3500, 7869
Schellenberg, T. R. 1380
Schelling, Thomas C. 500, 4959
Scheltema, J. F. 5897
Schenk, Hans G. A. V. 819
Schenkman, Jacob. 3973
Scheuner, U. 3551
Schick, Franz B. 2399, 3443, 3627, 4809, 5147
Schiff, Victor. 1204
Schiffer, Walter. 327, 1459, 3502
Schindler, D. 2312
Schleicher. Charles P. 220, 3927, 4951, 5643
Schlochauer, Hans-Jurgen. 3444
Schloss, H. H. 1713
Schmeckebier, Laurence F. 2876
Schmidt, Adolph. 6384
Schmidt, Dana Adams. 5099
Schmidt, Helmut. 7011
Schmidt, John F. 7832

Schmitt, Hans A. 4109, 6553, 6597, 7181
Schmitter, Philippe C. 408, 6255, 6260, 6261
Schmokel, Wolfe W. 7192
Schnapper, Morris B. 341
Schneider, Carl J. 5100
Schneider, H. W. 693
Schneider, J. W. 3503, 5169
Schokking, Jan J. 6385
Scholefield, Guy H. 2400
Schonfield, Andrew. 4188, 7147
Schonfield, Hugh J. 4669
Schopflin, George A. 6662
Schou, A. 864
Schrader, Charles S. 669
Schück, H. 864
Schuckburgh, Evelyn. 7148, 7149
Schücking, Walter M. A. 261, 992, 1460, 1493
Schultz, Theodore W. 419, 430, 4224, 7799
Schuman, Frederick L. 221, 595, 670, 2994, 5644, 6801, 6850, 7782, 7870, 7871
Schuman, Robert. 6591, 6386
Schurr, Sam H. 6676
Schurz, William L. 2679
Schuschnigg, Kurt von. 6647, 6648
Schuster, E. 2851
Schuyler, Philippa. 5199
Schvan, August. 1114
Schwadran, Benjamin. 3756, 5051
Schwartz, Leonard E. 4403
Schwartz, William. 4725
Schwarz, Wolfgang. 2785
Schwarzenberger, Georg. 222, 562, 868, 1205, 1381, 1494, 1550, 2710, 3049, 3117, 3386, 3445, 3446, 3447, 3504, 3943, 4300, 4606, 4726, 4810, 4906, 4952, 5645, 6683, 6802, 7012, 7013, 7783, 7872
Schwebel, Stephen M. 3783, 3804, 3817, 3871
Schwelb, Egon. 3448, 3449, 3450, 3451, 4301, 4302, 6868
Schwendemann, Karl von. 2786

Scialoja, Vittorio. 2482
Scitovsky, Tibor. 6455
Scott, F. R. 3872, 7543
Scott, James Brown. 425, 703, 868, 960, 993, 994, 995, 996, 1027, 1031, 1032, 1033, 1074, 1115, 1116, 1461, 2288, 2289, 2290, 2291, 2483, 6030, 6090, 6091, 6092, 6249, 7648, 7873
Scott, Michael. 4649
Scott, R. F. 3452
Scott, William A. 563, 564, 5526
Scovell, Miss. 7372
Seabury, Paul. 5942, 5943
Seale, Patrick. 5898
Sebald, William J. 3118
Secretan, Jacques. 1525
Sedwitz, Walter J. 6262
Seidenfaden, Erik. 7076
Seignobos, M. 1386
Selassie, Haile I. 5713
Sen, B. R. 4000, 7784
Senf, Catherine. 3642
Senghor, Leopold Sedar. 5743
Sennholz, Hans F. 6803
Sensenig, Barton, III. 537
Sereni, Angelo Piero. 223
Setalvad, M. C. 5338
Sethur, Frederick. 6598
Seton-Watson, R. W. 2780, 7308
Sewell, James P. 4048
Seyersted, Finn. 3552, 3553, 5008
Seymour, Charles. 1144, 1171, 1182, 1184, 1185, 1187, 1196, 1767, 1916, 2024
Sforza, Carlo. 7203
Shaffer, Alice C. 5392
Shafquat, C. M. 3873
Shanks, Michael. 6649
Sharan, P. 4363
Sharp, Walter R. 224, 820, 1206, 1383, 2401, 2516, 3505, 3585, 3874, 3879, 3928, 3929, 3930, 4049, 4050, 4051, 4245, 4364, 5410, 5527, 6194, 7649, 7785
Shatara, Fuad. 5899
Shaw, A. G. L. 7014
Shaw, F. J. 1689

Shaw, George Bernard. 849, 1132, 1384
Shaw, T. 7701
Shaznicky, Milorad. 2172
Shearman, H. 7517
Shelly, K. E. 3528
Shenton, Herbert N. 1509
Shepard, M. 119
Shepherd, George W. 5714
Sherf, Zeev. 5101
Sherman, Gordon E. 1744
Sherwood, Robert E. 2027, 3050, 3248
Shiels, Thomas Drummond. 7483
Shihata, Ibrahim F. I. 4748, 4756
Shillock, John C., Jr. 2484
Shippen, Katherine B. 4052
Shonfield, Andrew. 4053
Shotwell, James T. 242, 262, 313, 928, 933, 1207, 1284, 1385, 1386, 1635, 1663, 1716, 1757, 1805, 1820, 1821, 1822, 1847, 1881, 1982, 2014, 2142, 2201, 2402, 2441, 2485, 2486, 2517, 2518, 2519, 2541, 2584, 2585, 2586, 2587, 2711, 2737, 2831, 2864, 2877, 2995, 2996, 3297, 3453, 4303, 4404, 6093, 6496, 7363, 7699
Showman, Richard K. 6094
Shulman, Marshall D. 7219
Shuster, George N. 4365
Shwadran, Benjamin. 3714, 5102, 5103
Siddiqi, Qamar Saeed. 4093, 6420, 7150, 7502
Sidebotham, Herbert. 2108
Sidgwick, Henry. 596, 6387
Sidjanski, D. 5554, 6513, 6600, 6804
Siegbahn, M. 864
Siegfried, André. 2192
Siegman, Henry. 5900
Siegmann, Charles A. 4424
Sigmund, Paul E., Jr. 5996
Silberner, Edmund. 869
Sillac, M. Jarousse de. 1034
Simmonds, K. R. 3579
Simmons, André. 7245
Simnett, William E. 7484
Simons, Anne P. 284, 4784, 4870, 4936
Simpson, John Hope. 1949, 1950, 1951

Simpson, John L. 961, 4727,
Simpson, Smith. 1823, 1824, 1825, 1826, 2898, 2899,
Simsarian, James. 4304, 4405
Sinclair, I. M. 7332
Singer, J. David. 426, 1540, 3580, 3581, 3875, 4859, 4907
Singer, Marshall R. 537
Singh, Jitendra. 3818
Singh, L. P. 4607, 4608, 5367, 7511
Singh, Nagendra. 3609
Singh, Sushil Chandra. 3299
Sington, Derrick. 4908
Siotis, Jean. 3582, 3784, 3876, 4139, 6388, 6456, 6457
Sissons, David. 5356, 5794
Sjobert, Leif. 3210
Skelton, Alex. 1699
Skubiszewski, Krzysztof. 3387, 3506, 3715
Slater, Jerome. 4811, 6169, 6170
Slessor, John. 4909, 7015, 7016, 7017
Slick, Tom. 7786
Sloan, F. Blaine. 3716
Slochower, H. 4353
Slocombe, George E. 1387
Slosson, Preston. 1208, 1209, 7290
Sly, John F. 941
Smellie, K. B. 7367
Smend, S. 415
Smiley, Albert K. 949
Smith, E. W. 5722, 5734
Smith, Herbert A. 1035, 1550, 2313, 2358, 2368, 2487, 3717, 7334
Smith, I. Norman 5368
Smith, J. Russell 1664
Smith, R. S. 1714, 1949, 2111, 2780
Smith, S. A. de. 7485
Smith, Sara Rector. 2660
Smith, Sydney E. 7018
Smith, Thomas V. 4406
Smith, W. R. 7368
Smithies, Arthur. 5273, 5528
Smuts, Jan. 1117, 1176
Snell, Lord. 2079
Snow, Alpheus H. 2878
Snow, Sinclair. 7710

Snoy et d'Oppuerrs, Baron. 6554, 6555
Society of Friends. 870
Socini, Roberto. 6421
Soekarno, 7627
Sohmen, Egon. 4110
Sohn, Louis B. 342, 343, 344, 1739, 3454, 3610, 3611, 3643, 3684, 3804, 4812, 5009, 5274, 7019, 7819
Sol Castellanos, Jorge. 6250
Solano, E. John. 1827
Soldati, Agostino. 6458
Solovehtchik, George. 4531
Solum, Ingibrigt. 5010
Solver, Henry. 7679
Somervell, D. C. 7486
Somerville, J. C. 1856
Somerville, J. J. B. 5725
Sørensen, Max. 4305, 4728, 5275, 5573, 6851
Soto, M. J. de. 6422, 6574
Soule, George. 3300
Souleyman, Elizabeth V. 671
South Pacific Commission. 132
Southeast Asia Treaty Organization. 5646
Southern Political Science Association. 40
Soward, F. H. 1598, 2756, 2757, 3301, 3718, 4609, 5148, 5369, 5370, 5371, 7412
Spaak, Paul Henri C. 3719, 6389, 6390, 6832, 7020, 7021, 7022, 7023
Spaight, James M. 1462
Spanier, John W. 4910
Sparkman, John J. 3302
Spate, O. H. K. 5647
Spates, Thomas G. 1694, 1695, 1696
Spector, Ivar. 7623
Speeckaert, G. P. 92, 93, 7653
Spencer, Arthur W. 501
Spencer, John H. 1111, 1526, 2712, 5300
Spencer, Robert. 7151
Spender, Harold. 821
Spender, J. A. 2575, 7809, 7858
Spender, Percy C. 4841, 7024
Spengler, Joseph J. 7414, 7515

Spens, P. 6860, 6878
Spense, J. E. 5301
Spicer, Keith. 7544
Spinelli, Altiero. 6391, 6392, 6556
Spofford, Charles M. 7025, 7026
Spraos, J. 5648
Springer, Hugh W. 6227, 6228
Sprout, Harold H. 225
Sprout, Margaret. 225
Spry, D. C. 7720
Spry, Graham. 5104, 5372
Sreistrup, Hans. 249
Srivastava, Anand K. 3570, 3877, 3878
Stackleberg, G. A. von. 5901
Stafford, F. E. 4636
Stahle, N. K. 864
Staley, Eugene. 3944, 4532, 4533
Stalin, Joseph. 7576
Stallybrass, William T. S. 1118, 1527
Stamp, J. 1689
Stamp, Lord. 1231
Stanczyk, Jan. 7291
Stanfield, T. 1090
Stanley, George F. G. 5105, 5149
Stanley, Timothy W. 7027, 7028
Stansifer, Charles L. 5379
Stanton, Edwin F. 5022
Stanton, Ruth E. 94, 95, 5242
Star, S. 565
Stark, B. 3486
Stark, F. 2112
Stark, W. 427
Starke, J. G. 1510, 5795
Starr, Mark. 3088, 7711
Stavrianos, L. S. 7310, 7311
Stavridi, J. 1565
Stawell, Florence M. 672
Stead, William Thomas. 832, 871, 878
Steed, H. W. 1254, 1285, 2111, 2432, 7874
Steed, Wickham. 2487, 2559, 2567, 2575, 2642, 2701, 2785
Steel-Maitland, A. 1580
Stehlin, Paul. 7029
Stein, Eric. 3819, 3879, 4381, 4407, 5276, 6601, 6602, 6650, 6805, 6823, 6852

Stein, Herman D. 7679
Stein, L. 2110, 2112
Steinbach, Arnold L. 7712
Steinbecker, Paul G. 7875
Steinberg, Dund J. 5649
Steiner, H. Arthur. 226, 2292, 5457, 5529
Steiner, K. 5630
Steiner, Morris J. 5902
Stephan, Mary Vonne. 372
Stephens, Waldo E. 1495
Stern, Robert M. 4054
Stern, W. B. 2713
Stern-Rubarth, Edgar. 6806
Stettinius, Edward R., Jr. 3181
Stevens, Colonel. 6714
Stevens, Georgiana. 5106
Stevenson, Adlai. 3303, 3720
Stevenson, G. H. 4357
Stevenson, J. R. 6668
Stewart, Bryce M. 1828, 2758
Stewart, Irvin. 1730
Stewart, Lady. 1949, 7372
Stewart, Maxwell S. 7246
Stewart, Robert B. 7413
Stewart, S. 6684
Stikker, Dirk U. 6459, 7030, 7031, 7182
Stimson, Henry L. 2588, 2655, 2661, 3118
Stinebower, Leroy D. 3931
Stinson, J. W. 1090
Stockdale, Frank. 6211
Stocks, John L. 7787
Stoddard, T. Lothrop. 7312
Stoessinger, John George. 227, 751, 3582, 3583, 3584, 3585, 4408, 4409, 4488, 5458, 5530, 5650, 6988
Stoetzer, O. Carlos. 6171
Stohler, Jacques. 6454
Stokes, R. 7372
Stokke, Olav. 5011
Stoll, Jean-Aimé. 6680
Stolte, Stefan C. 7350
Stone, Donald C. 3774, 3785, 3880, 3881, 6514
Stone, Julius. 1556, 1934, 1935, 1936,

2171, 4610, 4729, 4953, 4954, 5012, 5277, 5796, 6668
Stone, William T. 2488, 2489, 2490, 2491, 2492, 2616, 6095, 6807
Stoner, Frank E. 4425
Storrs, R. 2100, 2101
Stosic, Borko D. 7650
Stourzh, Gerald. 7908
Stowe, Leland. 7876
Stowell, E. C. 1469
Stoyanovsky, J. 2109
Strachey, John. 7487
Straight, Michael W. 2997, 2998
Strakosch, Henry. 758, 1680
Strange, Susan. 3945, 5107, 6212, 6460, 6853, 6854, 6855
Stratton, George M. 538
Stratton, Samuel S. 3120
Strauss, Erich. 6651, 7152
Strauss, Franz Joseph. 7032
Strausz-Hupé, Robert. 228, 3304, 5651, 5652, 7033
Strayer, Joseph R. 629
Straznicky, Milorad. 2172
Streeten, Paul. 5653
Streit, Clarence K. 1388, 1496, 1581, 7034, 7832, 7877, 7878, 7879, 7880, 7881, 7882, 7883, 7907
Stromberg, Roland N. 4813, 4814, 5531
Strong, Richard P. 242, 928, 933, 1284, 1385, 1635, 1663, 1716, 1757, 1881, 2014, 2142, 2201, 2441, 2737, 7699
Strunsky. 1090
Strupp, Karl. 2617
Stuart, Graham H. 2196, 2197, 2403, 6096, 6097
Stucki, Curtis W. 133
Sturmthal, Adolf F. 7713, 7714, 7715
Sturzo, Luigi. 2999
Suit, Edward M. 906
Sulkowski, Joseph. 4456
Sullivan, Walter. 4410
Sully, Maximilien de Bethune, duc de. 741, 742, 743, 744
Sumberg, Theodore A. 4534
Summers, Robert E. 3051, 5532, 6603

Sundford, D. A. 2709
Surr, J. V. 3554, 5533
Surrey, Walter S. 7035
Suttner, Bertha F. S. von. 872, 873, 874
Svennevig, T. P. 5574
Swain, James E. 7369
Swanwick, Helena Maria. 1856, 2404, 2506, 2565, 2575
Swedish Institute of International Affairs. 5575
Sweetser, Arthur. 1389, 1390, 1391, 1392, 1393, 1394, 1395, 1396, 1643, 1829, 1850, 2340, 2680, 2879, 2880, 2900, 3305, 3306, 3882, 5534
Swerling, Boris C. 1705
Swift, Richard N. 3883, 4426, 5535
Swinnerton, A. R. 7570
Sworakowski, Witold S. 7596
Swygard, Kline. 4306
Syatauw, J. J. G. 345
Syed, Anwar. 6393
Symon, A. C. B. 7513
Synnestvedt, Sig. 539
Szapiro, Jerzy. 296
Szawlowski, Richard. 3586
Sze, Sao-ke Alfred. 2662
Szent-Miklosy, István. 6808
Szinai, Miklos. 1983
Szuldoynski, Jan. 6515

Tabata, Shigejiro. 3628
Taft, D. 380
Taft, Henry W. 1397, 2341, 2881
Taft, William Howard. 1119, 1120, 1463
Tait, R. M. 4911
Talbot, Phillips. 5052, 5209, 5782
Talbott, E. Guy. 229, 673, 3000, 5654
Talmadge, I. D. W. 3721
Tammes, A. J. P. 3507
Tannenbaum, Frank. 6098, 6099
Tansill, Charles S. 674
Tapp, E. J. 5797
Tarazi, Salah el dine. 3455
Tarbell, Ida Minerva. 2493
Tarn, William W. 597

Tate, Merze. 2494
Taubenfeld, Howard J. 2405, 2882, 3585, 3587, 4392, 4411, 4412, 4815
Taubenfeld, Rita Falk. 3587
Tauber, Kurt P. 7193
Taussig, Charles W. 6213
Tayler, William L. 1830, 4457
Taylor, A. J. P. 7292
Taylor, Alastair M. 5216, 5783
Taylor, George Edward. 5536
Taylor, Phillip H. 120, 3121
Taylor, Rear Admiral. 1285, 1565
Tchernoff, J. 2739
Tead, Ordway. 1831
Telfer, Vera. 675
Temperley, Arthur Cecil. 1398
Temperley, Harold W. V. 822, 823, 1210, 1216, 1471
Temple, A. H. 4074
Temple, William. 3001
Ténékidès, George. 598
Tenney, A. A. 1121
Tennyson, Leonard. 7247
Tessier, Jacques 4458
Teune, Henry. 539
Tevoedjre, Albert. 5754
Tew, Brian. 4073
Thant, U. 182, 3818
Thayer, Philip W. 5065, 5070, 5903
Thayer, William R. 749, 793
Theobald, Robert. 3307
Thiam, Doudou. 5715
Thien, Ton That. 7612
Thomas, A. J., Jr. 6172, 6173
Thomas, Albert. 1779, 1813, 2739
Thomas, Ann (Van Wynen). 6173
Thomas, Brinley. 4165, 5373, 7414, 7515
Thomas, Bryn. W. 2406
Thomas, Edward. 7011
Thomas, Elbert D. 286, 4459
Thomas, Ivor. 3974
Thomas, Jean. 4366
Thomas, M. C. 1090
Thomas, M. Ladd. 5825
Thomas, Norman. 3002
Thompson, C. Mildred. 4367, 4368

Thompson, Carol L. 5108, 5537
Thompson, Charles. 4351
Thompson, David. 1399, 3052, 4611
Thompson, Dennis. 6652
Thompson, Dorothy. 1952
Thompson, Elizabeth M. 121
Thompson, Francis Willard. 3308
Thompson, H. K. 2333
Thompson, Kenneth W. 478, 502, 3309, 4816
Thompson, L. G. 705
Thompson, R. W. 7153
Thomson, Charles A. 6100, 6101, 6102
Thomson, David. 3089
Thorner, Alice. 5053
Thorp, Willard L. 6461
Thorson, J. T. 7414
Thucydides. 599
Thurber, Clarence H. 3044, 7788
Tierney, James S. 7552
Tilling, Martha von. 873
Timm, Charles A. 503
Tiner, Hugh. 3310
Tipton, John B. 4460, 5538
Tiwari, S. C. 3003, 4307
Tobin, Harold. 1469, 2740, 2758a
Tobin, James 4074
Tod, Marcus N. 600
Todd, A. J. K. 2112
Toller, Ernst. 1953
Tolley, Howard. 4225
Tomalin, Beth. 5374
Tombs, Laurence C. 1745
Tomlinson, Edward. 6103
Tomlinson, John D. 3956
Tondel, Lyman M., Jr. 4912, 5175, 5200
Tornudd, Klaus. 5655
Torre, Mottram. 566, 3884
Torres-Bodet, Jaime. *See* Bodet, Jaime Torres
Torriente, Cosme de la. 2293, 2806, 2807
Toscano, James V. 411
Toth, Charles W. 7716
Toulmin, G. E. 1746
Toussaint, Charmian E. 4613, 4614

Author Index

Townsley, W. A. 6604
Toye, D. B. 2551
Toynbee, Arnold J. 601, 1162, 1203, 1211, 2110, 2618, 7789, 7790
Tozzoli, Gian Puolo. 4913
Trager, Frank N. 5339
Traisner, K. 7333
Trask, David T. 1156, 2883
Travis, Martin B., Jr. 6174, 6175, 7037
Traynor, Elizabeth. 3053
Trempont, Jacques. 6878a
Triffin, Robert. 4067, 6462, 6484
Trinker, Frederick W. 230, 3644, 4308
Tripathi, Krishna Dev. 7597
Tripp, Brenda M. H. 4370
Triska, Jan F. 525, 5278, 6869, 7598, 7599
Trotter, Reginald G. 7488
Truchy, Henri 6463
Trueblood, Benjamin F. 676, 725, 870, 875, 876, 907, 962, 963, 997, 998, 1021, 1122, 1123, 1157
Trueblood, Howard J. 6104, 6105
Truman, Harry S. 3054, 3998
Trumbell, Robert. 4664
Truyol y Serra, Antonio. 824
Tryon, James L. 900, 1036
Tsatsos, Constantine. 6394
Tucker, Robert W. 504
Tucker, William R. 7154
Tugwell, Rexford G. 7736
Turcotte, Edmond. 4371
Turkel, Harry R. 1731
Turner, Arthur Campbell, 5237, 7039, 7040, 7155, 7489
Turner, Frederick Jackson. 1124
Turner, Gordon B. 6954
Turner, Robert K. 7041
Turner, W. H. 4503
Tweedy, Owen. 4499
Twitchett, Kenneth J. 5201, 5302
Tyerman, Donald. 4769
Tyler, J. E. 3069
Tyler, Royall. 1681
Tyler, William R. 7042

Uhl, Alexander. 3311, 5539
Ulam, Adam B. 7600
Umemura, Michael T. 3097
Underhill, Frank H. 7490
Union of International Associations. 25a, 56, 96, 309, 922, 7646, 7651, 7652, 7653, 7654
United Nations. 97, 98, 123, 124, 297, 298, 299, 346, 347, 348, 349, 352, 353, 354, 355, 356, 357, 3312, 3388, 4226, 4246, 4309, 4310, 4372, 4373, 4461, 4489, 4730, 4817, 5237, 7655, 7656
United States. 18, 99, 125, 310, 328, 359, 360, 361, 362, 363, 364, 365, 366, 1212, 3004, 4835, 5540
Universal Peace Congress. 908
Universal Postal Union. 942, 3950
University of Ankara, Institution of International Relations. 5411
University of California, International Relations Committee. 538, 1289
University of Denver, Social Science Foundation. 4604, 4968, 7085, 7732, 7752, 7791, 7800, 7906
Unni, A. C. C. 5340
Unterberger, Betty M. 7354
Urey, Harold C. 4413, 7856
Uri, Pierre. 6395, 6423, 6605, 7043
Urquhart, Brian E. 4959, 5013
Uruguayan Institute of International Law. 5393
Usborne, C. V. 7921
Usher, Roland G. 6017

Vail, James G. 7687
Vaizey, John. 4055
Vajda, Andrew de. 4227
Vaktikiotis, P. J. 5903
Valahu, Mugur. 5202
Valentine, A. 6475
Valentine, D. G. 6685, 6686, 6687
Váli, Ferenc A. 7334
Vallarché, Jean. 4228
Vallat, F. A. 3648, 3722, 3723, 3757
Valluy, Général. 6911
Van Aken, Mark Jay. 6018

Westermann, W. L. 964
Western, Maurice. 3725, 5375
Westgren, A. 864
Westin, Alan F. 751, 3583, 6988
Wetheimer, Mildred S. 2522
Weydert, Jean. 6607
Weyl, Nathaniel. 4075, 4094
Wheare, K. C. 7493, 7494, 7495, 7887
Wheeler-Bennett, John W. 2298, 2299, 2499, 2500, 2523, 2590
Wheeler, Everett P. 1128
Wheeler, J. E. 3948, 3953, 3967, 3968, 3969
Whelen, F. 1411
Whitaker, Arthur P. 5394, 6110, 6111, 6112, 6178, 6179, 6195
Whitaker, Urban G. 3619, 5924
White, Andrew D. 999
White, Elwyn Brooks. 7888
White, Freda. 1565, 1578, 1585, 2049, 2050, 2110, 2701, 2730, 2780, 3726
White, Gilliam N. 4733
White, Harry D. 4111, 4112
White, Henry. 1039
White, John W. 2681
White, Leonard D. 1627
White, Lyman P. 7656, 7657, 7658
White, Norman. 1882
White, Thomas Raeburn. 1498, 2333
Whitelaw, W. Menzies. 7889
Whiting, Allen S. 167, 4786
Whitney, Edson L. 910
Whittlesey, D. 419
Whitton, John B. 1985, 2591, 2977, 3009, 3010, 4427, 6812, 6813
Whittuck, B. C. L. 2300
Whittuck, E. A. 1326, 1429, 1480, 2143, 2828, 2851
Whyte, Frederic. 878
Wickersham, George W. 1589, 2301, 2314, 2592, 2722
Wickizer, V. D. 1706
Wigforss, Harold. 7210
Wight, Martin. 3320
Wightman, David. 4132, 4133, 4140, 4141
Wilcox, Clair. 4167, 4168, 4169, 4170

Wilcox, Francis O. 1499, 1529, 2727, 3124, 3143, 3163, 3165, 3208, 3321, 3322, 3323, 3324, 3325, 3456, 3457, 3612, 3650, 3662, 3694, 3907, 4016, 4056, 4761, 5065, 5281, 5282, 5303, 5516, 5545, 5546, 5689, 6019, 6425
Wilczynski, J. 7351
Wild, Payson S. 2410
Wilde, John C. de. 1939, 2177, 2411, 2664, 2682
Wilenkin, M. 2923
Wiley, Alexander. 3458, 5547
Wilgres, A. C. 6214
Wilgress, Edward D. 4171
Wilgus, A. Curtis. 6020
Wilk, Kurt. 1707, 1708, 7670
Wilkin, Robert N. 7797
Wilkinson, Joe R. 7211, 7272
Willauer, Whiting. 6180
Williams, Benjamin H. 2501, 2886
Williams, Bruce S. 266, 1412, 1466, 1601, 2524
Williams, David. 5755
Williams, E. S. 1659
Williams, H. 1949
Williams, John Fischer. 1245, 1246, 1467, 1512, 1530, 1557, 1567, 1680, 2358, 2412, 2525, 2526, 2544, 2545, 2593, 2621, 2760, 6113, 7890
Williams, John H. 4076, 4077, 4172, 6485, 6516, 6517
Williams, L. 5788
Williams, Marie V. 605
Williams, Roth (pseud.). *See* Zilliacus, Konni
Williams, Stillman P. 101
Williams, Talcott. 1129, 1413
Williams, Wayne D. 3727
Williams, Wilbur Laurent. 7496
Williams, Wythe. 1665
Williamson, F. H. 1732
Williamson, Hugh. 7798
Williamson, James A. 7370, 7416
Willis, Frank R. 7183, 7194
Willkie, Wendell L. 7796
Willman, Joachim. 6654

Willoughby, Westel W. 1218, 1602, 1899, 2665
Willoughby, William R. 7158
Wilmot, Chester. 7052
Wilson, A. 2801
Wilson, Donald V. 4202
Wilson, Duncan. 1414, 7891, 7892
Wilson, Elizabeth. 1414, 7892
Wilson, Florence. 1219, 1468
Wilson, Francesca. 4536
Wilson, Francis Graham. 1834, 1835, 1836, 1837, 1838
Wilson, George G. 704, 1469
Wilson, Howard E. 4375, 4376, 4377
Wilson, Hugh R. 2502
Wilson, J. V. 3788
Wilson, Kenneth R. 4173
Wilson, Robert R. 2315, 7414, 7515
Wilson, S. P. 1090
Wilson, Woodrow. 1059, 1060, 1106, 1166, 1173, 1176, 1202, 1280, 2817, 2887, 3046, 4780, 4807, 7690
Winant, John G. 1800, 2901
Winchmore, Charles. 3789
Windass, Stanley. 3326
Winkler, Henry R. 1130, 5548
Winkler, Max. 1683
Winks, Robin W. 6518
Winslow, Anne. 6496, 6497
Winslow, C. E. A. 1883, 4297
Winslow, Earle M. 1698
Wint, Guy. 5789
Winter, William L. 641
Winwar, Frances. 734
Wionczek, Miguel S. 6263
Wirth, Louis. 419, 7799, 7935
Wise, E. F. 1245, 1578
Wiseman, Herbert V. 7497
Wishart, Andrew. 877
Wiskemann, Elizabeth. 2178
Withey, Stephen B. 564, 5526
Witmer, John D., III. 3886
Witmore, B. G. 7102
Witt, William De. 3292, 4044
Woetzel, Robert K. 3125, 3126
Wofford, Harris, Jr. 7893
Woglom, W. W. 805

Wohlgemuth, Patricia. 5239, 5339
Woolley, H. 4074
Wohlstetter, Albert. 7053
Wolf, Francis Colt de. 3957
Wolf, L. 1914
Wolfe, George V. 3391
Wolfers, Arnold. 2788, 4792, 4821, 4921, 4922, 5153, 5549, 6400, 6401, 7054, 7055
Wolfsohn, H. 2762, 5376, 7533
Woll, Matthew. 1839
Wood, Bryce. 3327, 5395, 6114, 6115
Wood, E. M. 7701
Wood, F. L. W. 5798
Wood, Hugh McKinnon. 1531, 2302, 2902
Wood, Robert J. 7056
Woodbridge, George. 4537
Woodhead, John. 2112
Woodhouse, C. M. 5230
Woodman, Dorothy. 5154, 5341
Woodruff, William. 7159
Woods, William Seaver, 1415
Woodside, Wilson. 3328
Woodward, David. 2503, 2504
Woodward, Ernest L. 828, 7800
Woody, Thomas. 3011
Woolbert, Robert Gale. 2113, 5904
Woolf, Leonard S. 829, 943, 1131, 1132, 1133, 1416, 1417, 1418, 1419, 1420, 2715, 3012, 3058
Woolf, Lucien. 1261
Woolley, H. 4074
Woolsey, Lester H. 1220, 3459, 4778
Wooster, Harvey Alden. 2992, 3007, 3014, 3227
Work, Ernest. 2716
World Association of World Federalists. 7894, 7895
World Peace Foundation. 29, 53, 79, 312, 329, 330, 1158, 1900, 2543, 3900, 7639
Worsfeld, William Basil. 2114
Worswick, G. D. N. 7160
Worthington, E. B. 5756
Wortley, Ben Atkinson. 3329, 3392, 3664, 4312

Wriggins, Howard. 3790
Wright, Esmond. 5905
Wright, H. 2306, 2333
Wright, Hamilton. 1040
Wright, Herbert F. 686
Wright, Peter E. 1159, 5727
Wright, Quincy. 237, 376, 417, 380, 386, 419, 430, 431, 432, 481, 492, 506, 507, 679, 1221, 1421, 1422, 1469, 1470, 1500, 1532, 1552, 1840, 1959, 2051, 2052, 2053, 2054, 2072, 2115, 2306, 2311, 2333, 2342, 2413, 2527, 2594, 2717, 2728, 2887, 2992, 3007, 3013, 3014, 3015, 3127, 3227, 3330, 3331, 3332, 3333, 3393, 3510, 3511, 3556, 4313, 4724, 4822, 4823, 4864, 4878, 4923, 5070, 5112, 5155, 5161, 5205, 5274, 5550, 5551, 5659, 5660, 6814, 7249, 7636, 7678, 7799, 7801
Wright, Robert F. 630
Wulf, Hanna. 151
Wulf, Maurice de. 631
Wuorinen, John H. 7079, 7080, 7212, 7314
Wurtele, Allan Ramsey. 5661
Wyndham, H. A. 7384
Wynner, Edith. 680, 3460, 7896

Xenophon. 2116
Xydis, Stephen G. 4428

Yalem, Roland J. 3334, 5662, 5663, 6815
Yanaihara, Tadao. 2137
Yang, You Chan. 3313
Yarnell, H. E. 2448
Yates, P. Lamartine. 4229, 4230
Ydit, Méir. 2149, 3128
Yeager, Frederick J. 7213
Yearley, C. K., Jr. 3335
Yemelyanov, V. S. 4415, 5459
Ynsfran, Pablo Max. 2683
Yokota, Kisaburo. 5342
Yoo, Tae-ho. 5156
York, Elizabeth. 606, 776

Young, Allyn A. 1247, 1666
Young, Hilton. 1585
Young, K. 376, 417, 419, 430, 7799
Young, Mrs. 7902
Young, Oran P. 5014
Young, Tien Cheng. 3791
Young, T. Cuyler. 5906
Younger, Kenneth. 3461, 3684, 7161, 7523

Zagayko, Florence F. 102
Zagday, M. I. 5790
Zahid, Munawar A. 4113
Zahler, Walter R. 2789
Zaidi, Manzor. 3728
Zapf, Lacey C. 7671
Zartman, I. William. 5757
Zaslawski, Emil. 3486, 3514, 3528, 4259, 6573
Zaslawski, G. 3110
Zasloff, Joseph J. 5113
Zauberman, Alfred. 7220
Zawodny, J. K.
Zebel, Sydney H. 7162
Zeckhauser, Richard J. 7250
Zemanek, Karl. 5576
Zenkowsky, Serge A. 5907, 7315
Zeydel, Walter H. 368
Zilliacus, Konni. 1423, 1424, 2546, 2761
Zimmerman, James Fulton. 6021
Zimmerman, Michel. 632
Zimmern, Alfred E. 267, 607, 830, 944, 1000, 1041, 1134, 1160, 1285, 1425, 1426, 1427, 1567, 1986, 2414, 2415, 2506, 2666, 2718, 2730, 2744, 2763, 2888, 3059, 3394, 6816, 6817, 7372
Zimmern, Helen. 642
Zocca, Louis. 301
Zocca, Marie R. 301, 7658
Zook, David H. 2683
Zsoldos, Laszlo. 7352
Zuhlsdorff, Volkmar. 6965
Zurayk, Costi K. 5908
Zurcher, Arnold J. 6402
Zvegintzov, M. 2760

SUBJECT INDEX

Subject Index

Africa. 4122—23, 4337, 4618, 4619—4632, 4636, 5283—5303, 5690—5766, 7081—83, 7085, 7087, 7088, 7518—23, 7604, 7605, 7607, 7609
African-Asian conferences. 7624—31
African-Asian countries. 511, 525, 528, 1167, 2055—59, 2796, 4122—33, 4754, 5157, 5244, 5261, 5264, 5268, 5269, 5271, 5278, 7613—23
African regionalism. 130, 5690—5766
Aggression, definition. 2508, 2527, 4812, 5277
Algeria. 5222, 5223
Allied powers. 1135, 1140, 1142, 1144, 1146, 1147, 1149—55, 1157, 1160, 3061, 3064—67, 3069, 3092, 3099, 3100, 3101, 3104, 3105, 3107, 3110, 3113, 3115, 3118, 3120—22
American Council of Learned Societies. 1976
American Friends Service Committee. 7687
American Jewish Joint Distribution Committee. 7679
American regionalism. 5957—6265
Angola. 5231, 5234—36, 5239
Antarctica. 4391—93, 4398, 4410, 4412
Anzus. 5791—98
Arab Africa. *See* Mahgreb
Arab-Israeli conflict (1947—). 4490—4500, 5031, 5035, 5038, 5051, 5054—5113
Arab League. 5909—43
Arbitration. 945—964, 979, 1001—3, 1005—7, 1011, 1012, 1016—22, 1024—26, 1028—35, 1038, 1040, 1041
Asia. 4124—33, 4251, 4452, 5304—42, 5767—90, 7084, 7268, 7615
Asian regionalism. 131—33, 5767—90, 5799—5825
Assembly (League). 1558—85
Association of Southeast Asia. 4124, 5770
Atlantic Charter. 3016, 3018, 3026

Atlantica. 140—42, 394, 410, 6266—6402, 7256, 7259, 7263, 7270
Atomic Energy. 4379—81, 4383, 4385, 4386, 4389, 4390, 4395—98, 4400—2, 4404, 4406—9, 4413—15, 5525
Australia. 2120, 2122, 2750, 2762, 3419, 4601, 4651, 4658, 4660, 5210, 5356, 5359, 5364, 5376, 5791—98, 5809, 5810, 5817, 5826, 7096, 7110, 7271, 7505, 7508, 7529, 7532, 7533
Austria. 5576

Balkan regionalism. 7294—7315
Bank for International Settlements. 1709—14
Behavioralist approaches. 374—566
Belgium. 2769, 2783, 3521, 5567, 5570
Benelux. 545, 2784, 6469—77, 7257
Berlin. 793, 828, 3103, 3122, 3128, 5240, 5388
Bibliographies. 58—152
Bloc voting. 513—15, 517, 518, 520
Bogotá conference (1948). 6125, 6144, 6146, 6149
Bolivia. 2667—83, 5383, 5389
Brazil. 2803, 5390
Bretton Woods conference (1943). 3022, 4057, 4060—63, 4066, 4068—72, 4076, 4096
British and Foreign Anti-Slavery Society. 913
British Commonwealth of Nations. 36, 73, 126, 2058, 2745, 2746, 2748, 2751, 2752, 2755, 2763, 5049, 5104, 5148, 5346, 5349, 5351, 5352, 5362, 5367, 5370, 5372, 6269, 6407, 6420, 6424, 7089, 7095, 7097, 7100, 7101, 7106, 7119, 7131, 7134, 7137, 7147—49, 7156, 7371—7570
British Empire. 2046, 2056, 2058, 2755, 2870, 3420, 6270, 7355—70, 7802
Brussels Public Administration Center. 7675

935

Buenos Aires conference (1936). 6039, 6056, 6074
Bulgaria. 1918, 2720, 2753
Burma. 5339
Business and commercial non-governmental organizations. 7659–71

Cairo conference (1943). 3030
Cambodia. 5812
Cameroons. 4628
Canada. 1598, 1828, 2748, 2749, 2756–58, 3426, 3560, 3718, 3725, 4609, 5104, 5344, 5345, 5348, 5360, 5366, 5368, 5369, 5371, 5372, 5374, 5375, 6196–6203, 7091, 7102, 7106, 7109, 7118, 7121, 7130, 7132, 7138, 7139, 7151, 7153, 7158, 7510, 7512, 7534–44
Caracas conference (1954). 6142
Caribbean Commission. 6204–14
Catholic church. 611–32, 644, 647, 675, 2978, 7682
Central Africa. 5716—27
Central American Common Market. 6233, 6240, 6247, 6250
Central American Court of Justice. 6239, 6241
Central American regionalism. 6231–50
Central American Union. 6235–38, 6242–44
Central Countries' Treaty Organization 5944–48
Central powers. 1145
Ceylon. 5314
Chaco. 2667–83
Charter. 3336–94
Chile. 2671, 5389
China. 512, 544, 608–10, 1218, 1602, 1884, 2622–66, 2791, 2797, 2798, 3613–28, 5311, 5327, 5413, 5457, 5460, 5470, 5801
Classical civilizations. 567–743
Collective security. 1402, 2344–46, 2348, 2349, 2351–61, 2363, 2365–71, 2374–86, 2388–90, 2393–95, 2397–2404, 2406–9, 2413–15, 2825, 4762–72, 4774–96, 4798–4823, 5532, 5544
College of Europe. 7059, 7061
Colombia. 5385
Colombo Plan. 7504–13
Colonialism. 524, 3077, 3337, 4538, 4543, 4544, 4557–59, 4562, 4564, 4568, 4577, 4585, 4591, 4598, 4600, 4601, 4610, 4611, 4618, 5231, 5232, 5364
Combined Raw Materials Board. 3063
Cominform. 7255, 7258, 7260–62, 7269
Commission on Narcotic Drugs. 4206–8
Commonwealth countries *See* British Commonwealth of Nations
Communications and transportation. 1715–48, 3948–76
Communist countries. 7214, 7217, 7219, 7220, 7255
Communist European regionalism. 7335–54
Communist world. 7214, 7219, 7220, 7255, 7573–76, 7580–83, 7585–90, 7593, 7598–7600
Concert of Europe. 777, 786, 788, 790, 792–94, 801, 802, 807, 809, 811, 814, 817, 819, 822, 823, 826
Conference of Ambassadors. 1222
Congo (Leopoldville). 3558, 5075, 5167, 5169, 5170–5205
Congolese Civil War. 5170–5205
Constitutional problems. 1501–57, 3462–3664
Corfu. 2719, 2723, 2725
Council (League). 1586–1602
Council of Europe. 6120, 6419, 6818–28, 6829–33, 6835–38, 6842, 6845,–48, 6850, 6851, 6853
Council of Four. 1174, 1183, 1190
Council of Mutual Economic Assistance (COMECON). 7336–52
Court of the European Coal and Steel Community. 6684, 6685
Court of Justice of the European Community. 6677–83, 6686, 6687
Covenant. 1428–72, 1477, 1480, 1481,

936

Subject Index

1483, 1485, 1486, 1488, 1494, 1498, 3343, 3353, 3357
Cracow. 3128
Cuba. 2806, 2807, 5241, 5380, 5427, 6178
Customs unions. 6468–85, 6521, 6522, 6525, 6558, 6608–54, 7074, 7077, 7624–31
Cyprus. 5221, 5227, 5229, 5230

Danubia. 7319–27, 7330–34
Danubian River Commission. 927, 1733, 1735, 1737, 1744, 7316–18, 7328, 7329
Danzig. 2150–59
Denmark. 2777, 5573, 7211
Depression of the 1930's. 1684–98
Disarmament. 71, 113, 2416–2504, 2886, 4824–4924, 4998
Documents. 305–73
Domestic jurisdiction. 1513–32, 2303–15, 3512–57, 4735–52, 2303–15, 3512–57, 4735–52
Dumbarton Oaks Conference. 1287, 1408, 3017, 3020, 3028, 3032, 3033, 3037, 3039, 3042, 3045, 3051, 3052, 3056, 3062

East Africa. 5728—38
Eastern European countries. 3362, 5412, 5430
Eastern European regionalism. 7273–7323, 7336–52
Economic activities. 1645–98, 3934–4189
Economic Commission for Africa. 4122, 4123
Economic Commission for Asia and the Far East. 4124–33, 5451, 5770
Economic Commission for Europe. 4134–41
Economic Commission for Latin America. 4142, 4143, 5378

Economic development. 3979, 3982, 3985, 3988–92, 3995–98, 4000, 4001, 4006–18, 4021, 4023, 4024, 4027–29, 4031, 4039–45, 4047, 4048, 4051–55
Ecuador. 5389
Egypt. 464, 1167, 3756, 5056, 5074, 5075, 5159, 5162–69, 5403, 5410, 5920, 5929, 5947
Eritrea. 4619, 4625
Ethiopia. 2684–2718
Europe. 143, 145, 150, 151, 532, 1300, 2553, 2871, 4134–41, 5562, 7547
European Atomic Energy Community. 6530, 6541, 6663–76
European Coal and Steel Community. 146, 552, 553, 3110, 6520, 6529, 6541, 6548, 6550, 6551, 6559–6607, 6838, 7103, 7170
European Coal Organization. 3060, 3068
European communities. 389, 548, 6266–6402, 6413, 6519–6654, 6663–76
European Convention on Human Rights. 6856–71
European Cultural Foundation. 7058, 7062
European Defense Community. 556, 6872–79, 7179
European Economic Community. 152, 541, 4175, 4176, 6286, 6299, 6346, 6403, 6405, 6409, 6424, 6521, 6522, 6525, 6527, 6530, 6538, 6541, 6545, 6547, 6553, 6554, 6558, 6608–54, 7081–86, 7093, 7096, 7099, 7101, 7106–8, 7110, 7112, 7113, 7121–25, 7127, 7130, 7132, 7135, 7137, 7140, 7142, 7143, 7147, 7152, 7156, 7160, 7161, 7167, 7185, 7192, 7195, 7196, 7198, 7200, 7202, 7214, 7216, 7220, 7224–26, 7229, 7230, 7232, 7236, 7246, 7248, 7257, 7264, 7266, 7268, 7272, 7503
European economic organizations. 144, 149, 303, 304, 372, 6404, 6421, 6426–6689

937

Subject Index

European Free Trade Association. 152, 6521, 6522, 6525, 6543, 6544, 6554, 6558, 6655—62, 7090, 7144, 7160, 7195

European Investment Bank. 6688, 6689

European Parliament. 6287, 6839, 6841, 6842, 6849, 6852, 7129, 7139, 7146

European Payments Union. 6478—85

European political assemblies. 516, 521, 6824—55

European political unification. 397, 407, 6690—6817

European regionalism. 143, 147, 6266—72, 7089, 7092, 7094, 7095, 7097, 7098, 7100, 7104, 7105, 7111, 7114, 7116, 7117, 7119, 7120, 7126, 7128, 7133, 7136, 7141, 7150, 7155, 7161, 7163—65, 7168, 7169, 7171, 7175—78, 7180—84, 7188, 7190, 7191, 7193, 7194, 7199, 7201, 7208, 7209, 7212, 7216, 7218, 7219, 7221—23, 7227, 7228, 7233—35, 7237—42, 7244, 7245, 7247, 7249, 7250, 7254, 7265, 7271, 7498

European system. 777—830

Far East Commission. 3094, 3095, 3120

Federalism. 5716—43, 6125—6230

Financing. 1533—41, 3558—88

Finland. 2726, 5558

Food and Agriculture Organization. 4210, 4211, 4215, 4216, 4218, 4219, 4223, 4225, 4227, 4228, 5316, 5402

Foodstuffs. 1705, 1706, 1708

France. 556, 557, 748, 2062, 2063, 2067, 2069, 2070, 2072, 2719, 2723, 2764, 2775, 2965, 3158, 3412, 3534, 4536, 4628, 5226, 5357, 5556, 5557, 5567, 5569, 5953, 6872, 6873, 6875—79, 7125, 7163—83, 7194, 7214

French Community. 7601—12

Functional approach to peace. 7897—7907

General Agreement on Tariffs and Trade. 114, 4144, 4174—89, 5310, 6403, 6490, 6608

General Assembly. 508, 510, 513, 520, 522, 523, 533, 3646—50, 3665—3728

Geneva conventions. 1009

Geneva Disarmament Conference (1932). 2436, 2463

Geneva Protocol. 2506, 2528—46

Germany. 552, 553, 1193, 1204, 1223—47, 1903, 1992, 2185, 2724, 2726, 2765—67, 2769—73, 2776, 2778, 2781, 2782, 2785, 2786, 2788, 4503, 4536, 7184—94, 7218

Ghana. 5739—43

Goa. 5208

Great powers. 2744, 3640, 3641, 5263

Greece. 567, 568, 571—78, 583, 585, 587, 592, 597—601, 603—5, 607, 648, 959, 1918, 1951, 2719, 2720, 2723, 2725, 5553, 5554, 7197, 7198

Guinea. 5739—43

Hague conferences (1899 and 1907). 965—1000, 1008, 1015, 1023, 1033, 1039, 1180

Haiti. 5391

Hanseatic League. 633—43

Havana conferences (1928, 1940). 6035, 6050, 6104

Health. 106, 1865—75, 1877, 1878, 1880—83, 4231—54

Holy Alliance. 764—76, 1290

Human rights. 4255—4313, 6856—71

Hungarian revolution (1956). 5157—61

Hungary. 464, 511, 1589, 2722, 4355, 5074, 5157—61, 5164, 5165, 5244, 5438, 7352

Hyderabad. 5052, 5206, 5209

India. 22—24, 2754, 4753, 5018, 5023—53, 5117, 5145, 5166, 5206—9, 5306—8, 5315, 5322, 5324, 5330, 5331, 5335, 5336, 5338, 5772, 5803, 5804, 7135, 7143, 7144, 7525—28

Indochina. 7612
Indonesia. 3605, 5210−20, 5317, 5340, 5783, 5788, 7524
Indus basin. 5207
Information policy. 4416−28
Institute of Pacific Relations. 7673
Integration theory. 374−432
Intellectual cooperation. 1960−86, 4314−4415, 7057, 7672−78
Inter-African organizations. 5744−66
Inter-American Bar Association. 7674
Inter-American Development Bank. 6106, 6264, 6265
Intergovernmental Committee on European Migration. 7060, 7063, 7118
International administration. 86, 119, 120, 156, 175, 1612−30, 2142−49, 5469, 3822−86
International Air Traffic Association. 1740
International Atomic Energy Agency. 4380, 4381, 4386, 4389, 4396, 4397, 4400, 4401, 4407−9, 4415
International Bank for Reconstruction and Development. 4078−94, 5294, 5400, 5408
International Bureau for the Standardization of Man-Made Fibres. 7664
International Chamber of Commerce. 7666, 7668, 7670, 7671
International Civil Aviation Association. 3973
International Confederation of Free Trade Unions. 7705
International Court of Justice. 122, 336, 345, 350, 535, 4670−4761
International Development Association. 4120
International Finance Corporation. 4117−19
International forces. 440, 450, 4959, 4987, 5005, 5167, 5169, 5193
International Institute of Administrative Sciences. 7676
International Institute of Agriculture. 7662, 7663, 7665

International Institute of Intellectual Cooperation. 1961, 1969, 1970, 1982
International Labor Organization. 62, 63, 116, 306, 307, 530, 1749−1850, 2323, 2889, 2895, 2898, 2899, 2901, 4429−61, 5313, 5334, 5434, 5538
International Law Association. 912
International Monetary Fund. 4095−4113, 5462
International Office of Public Hygiene. 923, 1865
International Opium Conference. 1888, 1890, 1894, 1895, 1897, 1898, 1900
International organization (items of general scope only). 59, 61, 68, 74, 79, 83, 87, 88, 92, 93, 96, 100, 102, 153−68, 170−74, 176−237, 305, 310, 311, 369, 374, 442, 457, 460, 463, 478, 484, 490, 491, 495, 549, 551, 835, 840, 1260, 1289, 1294, 1318, 1329, 1350
International Political Science Association. 7678
International Refugee Organization. 4467, 4473, 4485, 4486
International Rice Commission. 7667
International Telecommunications Union. 1726, 1727
International Telegraph Conference of Brussels (1928). 1730
International trade. 1664, 1685, 1688, 4144−89
International Trade Organization. 4144, 4148, 4151−73, 5373, 5473, 5482
International unions (general references only; specific agencies and topics are filed separately). 914, 917, 919, 920, 922, 924−26, 928−30, 932−40, 943, 944
International Voluntary Service for Peace. 7680
Interparliamentary Union. 916, 921

Iraq. 588, 1167, 2064–66, 2068, 2728, 5929
Ireland. 7550, 7551
Israel. 5054–5113, 5162–69
Italo-Ethiopian War (1934–36). 1270, 2684–2718
Italo-French Customs Union. 6468
Italy. 575, 1161, 2684–2719, 2723, 2725, 4621, 4627, 4629, 4630, 4634–36, 5568, 7195, 7196, 7203

Japan. 34, 1602, 2118, 2119, 2121, 2124, 2125, 2127, 2134, 2137, 2622–66, 2790, 2792–95, 4178, 4340, 4349, 4433, 5310, 5313, 5319, 5323, 5325, 5332, 5333, 5337, 5342, 5787, 7263, 7264
Jordan. 4491, 5069, 5102
Jordan River. 5064, 5099, 5106

Kashmir. 5023–33, 5036, 5037, 5039–45, 5047–50, 5052, 5053, 5209
Kellogg-Briand Pact. 2565–94
Korean war. 5017, 5114–56, 5335, 5341, 5370, 5544

Lake Mohonk Conferences on International Arbitration. 949, 1019
Laos. 5022, 5242
Latin America. 134–39, 408, 515, 981, 2799–2802, 2804, 2805, 3085, 4142, 4143, 4163, 5377–95, 5964, 5968, 5983, 5985–87, 5989, 6005, 6416, 7270, 7272
Latin American Free Trade Association. 6251–63
League of Nations (general references only; specific agencies and topics are filed separately). 97, 103–7, 169, 238–67, 308, 313–23, 327–30, 540, 769, 771, 785, 815, 827, 830, 989, 1000, 1010, 1248–1427, 1902–4, 1912, 1915, 1917, 1919–21, 1923, 1931, 1941, 1945, 2323, 2890, 2891, 2894, 2896, 2897, 2900, 2902, 3360, 7827
League of Nations Health Organization. 1866, 1873, 1874
League of Nations Society. 2422
Lebanon. 2063, 2069, 2070, 5016, 5224, 5226, 5228
Leticia. 2682
Liberia. 2808, 2809, 2835, 2863
Library of the Palace of Peace. 1
Libya. 4626
Lima conference (1938). 6058, 6100, 6103
Locarno agreements. 959, 2465, 2499, 2537, 2547–66
London Naval Conference (1930). 2445, 2459, 2490
Lytton report. 2632

Mahgreb. 5949–56
Malaysia. 5213, 5783
Mali 5739–43
Malta. 7546
Manchuria. 2622–66, 2867
Mandates. 64, 1987–2141, 2890, 2893
Marshall Plan. 4179, 6486–6518, 6553, 7203
Membership. 1542–52, 2731–35, 2737–40, 2742, 2743, 3589–3628, 5243–82
Metals. 1699, 1700, 1703
Mexico. 5377, 5379, 5970
Mexico City conference (1945). 6030, 6046, 6052, 6063, 6137
Middle Eastern countries. 5396–5411, 7200
Middle Eastern Countries' Treaty Organization. See Central Countries' Treaty Organization.
Middle Eastern regionalism. 5839–5956
Middle powers. 5252
Military judicial tribunals. 3091, 3093, 3096, 3097, 3102, 3106, 3108, 3109, 3111, 3112, 3116, 3117, 3119, 3123, 3125–27

Minorities. 1901–39, 4255–57, 4278
Monetary and lending agencies. 4057–4120, 6688
Montevideo conference (1933). 6028, 6036
Morocco. 5223, 5225
Moscow conference (1943). 3029, 3030, 3041, 3043

Narcotic drugs. 1884–1900, 4203–8
Netherlands. 571, 641
Neutralism. 5266, 5274, 5281, 5282, 7259, 7266
Neutralist countries. 7613–23
New Zealand. 5144, 5347, 5363, 5791–98, 7108, 7530, 7531
Nongovernmental organizations. 7632–7721
Nonpolitical activities. 1631–44, 3887–3933
Norden. 7074, 7077
Nordic Union. 7064–73, 7075, 7076, 7078–80
North Atlantic Treaty Organization. 148, 3253, 6307, 6405, 6406, 6414, 6415, 6625, 6693, 6880–7056, 7091, 7102, 7115, 7138, 7139, 7151, 7153, 7158, 7166, 7172–74, 7178, 7186, 7187, 7189, 7197, 7204–7, 7210, 7211, 7213, 7215, 7217, 7221, 7231, 7243, 7251–53
North Korea. 5114–56, 7594
Norway. 2776, 2946, 7206–9
Nuremberg. 3091, 3093, 3096, 3102, 3106, 3108, 3109, 3112, 3116, 3117, 3119, 3123, 3125–27
Nutrition. 1867, 1876, 1879, 4209–30
Nyasaland. 5716–27

Observational techniques. 545, 566
Office of Public Information (United Nations). 4417, 4421–24
Opération des Nations Unies au Congo (ONUC). 5170–75, 5177–83, 5185–88, 5193, 5196, 5198, 5200–2, 5204
Organization for Economic Cooperation and Development. *See* Organization for European Economic Cooperation.
Organization for European Economic Cooperation. 4179, 6486–6518
Organization of African Unity. 5758–66
Organization of American States. 370, 371, 6116–6203
Organization of Central American States. 6246
Oslo group. 2784
Outer space. 4378, 4382, 4384, 4387, 4388, 4392, 4403, 4405, 4411
Outlawry of war. 2505–94

PAFMESCA. 5744
Pacific mandates. 2059, 2117–37
Pacific regionalism. 5791–98, 5827–38
Pacific settlement. 2595, 2596, 2601, 2605, 2607, 2608, 2611, 2613–15, 2621, 4925–56
Pacific trusteeships. 4651–65
Pakistan. 42, 4447, 5018, 5023—53, 5166, 5304, 5305, 5318, 5320, 5328–30, 7113
Palestine mandate. 2061, 2073–2116
Pan Africanism. 5690–5715
Pan American conferences. 6024–32, 6034–74, 6076–83, 6085–6115
Pan American Federation of Labor. 7710, 7716
Pan American Railway Congress Association. 918
Pan American Union. 137, 139, 6022, 6023, 6033, 6075, 6084
Pan Americanism. 134, 369, 5957
Pan Arabism. 5843, 5848, 5849, 5852, 5854, 5859, 5867, 5874, 5882, 5890, 5896, 5902
Pan Germanism. 7277, 7280–93
Pan Islamism. 5839–42, 5844
Panama. 2191, 2192
Paraguay. 2667–83
Paris, congress (1856). 793

Subject Index

Peace movement. 66, 649, 651, 656, 660, 662, 665, 671, 674, 676, 879–910, 5517

Peaceful change. 66, 2597–2600, 2602–4, 2606, 2609, 2610, 2612, 2616, 2617–20, 4948

Peacekeeping. 4957–5014

Periodicals. 5–57

Permanent Court of Arbitration. 970, 1013–14, 1027, 1030, 1037

Permanent Court of International Justice. 105, 324–26, 957, 988, 1004, 1012, 1036, 1037, 1558, 1829, 2199–2342, 2806, 2892, 3368

Permanent Mandates Commission. 2008

Peru. 2671, 4142, 5378, 5389

Poland. 3387

Portugal. 5231, 5234–36, 5239, 5571

Preventive diplomacy. 5015–22

Proposals. 644–744, 831–78, 1042–1134, 2903–3015

Punta del Este conference (1962). 6123, 6166

Raw materials. 1699–1788

Reconstruction, Europe. 61, 1667–83

Red Cross. 911, 915, 1881, 7689–99

Reform of the League of Nations. 1471–1500

Reform of the United Nations. 3396–3414, 3416, 3418–33, 3435–58, 3460, 3461

Refugees. 1940–53, 4462–4500

Regional economic commissions. 4121–43

Regionalism (general references only; specific agencies and topics are filed separately). 127–29, 302, 373, 5577–5689

Religious non-governmental organizations. 7679–88

Reparations. 1223–47, 1714

Rhodesia. 5238, 5716–27

Rio de Janeiro conference (1942). 6071, 6082, 6097, 6145, 6155

Roll call analysis. 508–12, 514, 519, 522–25

Rome. 580, 590, 602

Rumania. 1589, 2722

Saar. 2150, 2160–78, 3098, 4668

San Francisco conference (1945). 359, 361, 3070–90

Sanctions. 2343, 2347, 2350, 2362, 2364, 2372, 2373, 2387, 2391, 2392, 2396, 2405, 2410–12, 2684, 2686, 2687, 2695, 2696, 2823, 3349, 3367, 4773, 4797

Scandinavian states. 2774, 4981, 5564, 5574, 7204, 7205, 7212

Schuman Plan. *See* European Coal and Steel Community.

Secretariat (League). 251–56, 1583, 1603–30

Secretariat (United Nations). 355–57, 3759–91, 5476

Secretary General (League). 1603–11

Secretary General (United Nations). 3792–3821

Security Council. 529, 3651–64, 3729–58

Shanghai Mixed Court. 2179–82

Silesia. 1936, 2171, 2183–87

Sino-Japanese War (1937–45). 1602, 2622–66

Slavery. 1954, 1956, 1958, 1959

Small powers. 2729, 2730, 2736, 2741, 2779, 2780, 2787, 2946, 3640, 3641, 5263, 5279, 5559, 7252

Social and humanitarian activities. 1851–64, 4190–4202

Socialist internationals. 7571, 7572, 7577–79, 7584, 7591, 7592, 7594–97

Somalia. 4622, 4627, 4631

South Africa. 3534, 4637, 4640, 4641, 4643, 4646, 5088, 5232, 5233, 5237, 5279, 5357, 7553—57

South Korea. 5114–56, 5513, 7594

South Pacific Commission. 5827–38

942

Southeast Asian Treaty Organization. 531, 5799–5826
Southern Rhodesia. 5238
Southwest African mandate. 2055, 2056, 4637, 4638–50
Soviet Union. 2652, 2726, 2810–16, 3431, 3903, 3942, 4129, 4152, 4315, 4401, 4415, 4434, 4443, 4853, 4901, 4903, 4905, 4924, 5157–61, 5240, 5241, 5412, 5414–20, 5422–26, 5428, 5429, 5431–37, 5439–56, 5458, 5459, 5507, 5524, 5525, 5530, 6962, 7167, 7191, 7213, 7215, 7216, 7218, 7335, 7747, 7748
Spain. 2727, 5565, 7202
Special UN Fund for Economic Development (SUNFED). 4114–16
Stimson Doctrine. 2625, 2655
Suez canal. 4667, 4669
Suez War. 2188–92, 3380, 5057, 5065, 5066, 5070, 5086, 5088, 5095, 5100, 5158, 5162—69, 5330
Supreme War Council. 1136–39, 1141, 1143, 1145, 1148, 1154, 1156, 1158–60, 1180, 2883
Survey research. 541–44, 546–65
Sweden. 640, 5575, 7210
Switzerland. 571, 2768, 2782, 2789, 5552, 5560, 5563, 5572, 7857
Syria. 2062, 2063, 2067, 2069, 2072, 5077, 5226
System theory. 433–507
Systematic case studies. 526–40

Tanganyika. 4620, 4621, 5728–38
Tangier. 2193–98
Tanzania. *See* Tanganyika.
Technical assistance. 3978, 3980, 3981, 3983, 3984, 3986, 3987, 3993, 3994, 3999, 4002, 4003, 4005, 4019, 4020, 4022, 4025, 4026, 4030, 4032—38, 4049, 4050, 4056, 4276, 4277, 5388, 5389, 7504—13
Technical Assistance Board. 3977, 4004, 4046
Teheran Conference (1943). 3030
Tennessee Valley Authority. 2939

Thailand. 5821
Tin 1703
Togoland. 4624
Trade Unions. 7700–16
Traffic in women and children. 1955, 1957
Trieste. 4666
Trusteeship Council. 4540, 4572, 4588
Trusteeship system. 64, 2017, 3080, 3371, 4538–4618
Tunisia. 5223, 5225

Underdeveloped countries. 4753–56, 5246, 5273, 5528, 7086, 7251, 7253, 7254, 7256, 7265
United Kingdom. 541, 555, 637, 639, 760, 779, 823, 825, 948, 2071, 2076, 2091, 2095, 2098, 2104, 2108, 2126, 2565, 2719, 2723, 2728, 2747, 2759 –61, 3461, 4165, 4909, 5086, 5113, 5238, 5241, 5343, 5350, 5353–55, 5358, 5361, 5365, 5373, 5792, 5796, 5813, 6744, 7090, 7092–96, 7098, 7099, 7101, 7103–5, 7107, 7108, 7111–17, 7120, 7122, 7123, 7125 –29, 7131–33, 7136, 7137, 7140, 7142, 7145–48, 7152, 7154, 7155, 7157, 7159–62, 7355–7570
United Nations (general references only; specific agencies and topics are filed separately). 97, 108–25, 268–301, 331–35, 337–44, 346– 49, 353–68, 379, 394, 428, 436, 437, 448, 450, 464, 506, 508–10, 512–15, 517, 518, 520, 522–24, 528, 533, 535, 537, 543, 544, 547, 557, 558, 564, 565, 1572, 3019, 3021, 3023–25, 3027, 3031, 3034– 36, 3038, 3040, 3044, 3046–50, 3053—55, 3057—59, 3114, 3124, 3129—35, 6181—95, 6405, 6406, 6410, 6412, 6414, 6415, 6425, 7239, 7335, 7499, 7500, 7501, 7741, 7754, 7764, 7767, 7776, 7780
United Nations Children's Fund. 4248 –54, 5386, 5393

Subject Index

United Nations Economic and Social Council. 3900, 3904, 3913, 3915, 3918, 3921, 3924, 3925, 3931, 3937, 4011, 4262

United Nations Educational Scientific and Cultural Organization. 32, 3913, 4314–77, 5319, 5325, 5414, 5452, 5489

United Nations Emergency Force. 5167, 5169, 5193, 5372

United Nations Library. 2, 3, 4, 98, 351, 352

United Nations Relief and Rehabilitation Agency. 3526, 4501–4, 4507–16, 4518–22, 4525–32, 4534, 4535, 4537

United States. 99, 328, 359–66, 379, 425, 512, 527, 544, 546, 560, 561, 564, 780, 955, 971, 981, 1044, 1046, 1047, 1161, 1247, 1559, 1586, 1759, 1829, 1841–50, 2138–41, 2316–42, 2501, 2510, 2511, 2530–32, 2553, 2584, 2625, 2641, 3432, 3458, 3547, 3554, 3557, 3613, 3615, 3763, 3828, 3833, 3942, 4097, 5120, 5126, 5137, 5240, 5360, 5460–5551, 5791–98, 5813, 5949, 6137, 6196, 6200, 6238, 6269, 6521, 7099, 7126, 7143, 7221–50, 7558–70, 7725, 7740, 7755

Uniting for Peace resolution. 3395, 3415, 3417, 3434, 3459, 5352

Universal Postal Union. 941, 942, 1725, 1728, 1731, 1732, 3950, 3951, 3955

Uruguay. 5393

Venezuela. 6178
Versailles conference (1919). 1161–1221, 1230, 1234, 1314
Veto. 3392, 3651–64
Vienna, congress (1814–15). 745–63, 792, 793, 811, 1216
Vilna. 2721
Voting procedure. 1553–57, 3629–64

Warsaw Pact. 7353, 7354
Washington Naval Conference (1922). 2416–18, 2420, 2421, 2427, 2448, 2451
West Africa. 5739–43, 7518
West Indies Federation. 6215–30
World Council of Churches. 7681
World federalism. 203, 1341, 7802–96
World Federation of Trade Unions. 7706
World government. 162, 381, 430, 438, 439, 1277, 1379, 7722–7935
World Health Organization. 106, 4231–47, 5312
World Women's Christian Association. 7686

Yugoslavia. 4536, 5421, 7255

Zanzibar. 5728–38
Zollverein. 6444